THE
Traitor's Homecoming
BENEDICT ARNOLD'S RAID
ON NEW LONDON, CONNECTICUT, SEPTEMBER 4–13, 1781

MATTHEW E. REARDON

SB
Savas Beatie
California

First edition, first printing

ISBN-13: 978-1-61121-698-1 (hardcover)
ISBN-13: 978-1-61121-699-8 (ebook)

Library of Congress Cataloging-in-Publication Data

Names: Reardon, Matthew E., 1983- author.
Title: The traitor's homecoming : Benedict Arnold's Raid on New London,
 Connecticut, September 4-13, 1781 / Matthew E. Reardon.
Other titles: Benedict Arnold's Raid on New London, Connecticut, September
 4-13, 1781
Description: El Dorado Hills, CA: Savas Beatie, [2024] | Includes
 bibliographical references and index. | Summary: "This title utilizes
 dozens of newly discovered British and American primary sources to weave
 together a balanced military study of an often forgotten and
 misunderstood campaign. Indeed, Reardon achieves a major
 reinterpretation of the battle while dismantling its myths"-- Provided
 by publisher.
Identifiers: LCCN 2023059680 | ISBN 9781611216981 (hardcover) | ISBN
 9781611216998 (ebook)
Subjects: LCSH: Groton Heights, Battle of, Conn., 1781. | Arnold, Benedict,
 1741-1801. | New London (Conn.)--History--Revolution, 1775-1783. |
 Fires--Connecticut--New London--History--18th century.
Classification: LCC E241.G8 R437 2024 | DDC 973.3/37--dc23/eng/20240108
LC record available at https://lccn.loc.gov/2023059680

SB

Savas Beatie
989 Governor Drive, Suite 102
El Dorado Hills, CA 95762
916-941-6896 / sales@savasbeatie.com / www.savasbeatie.com

All of our titles are available at special discount rates for bulk purchases in the United States. Contact us for information.

Printed and bound in the United Kingdom

For my parents, Brett and Barbara; and grandparents, Andrew and Eleanor, who taught me the value of hard work and encouraged me to follow my passions.

TABLE OF CONTENTS

TABLE OF CONTENTS (continued)

LIST OF MAPS

Photos have been added throughout the text for the convenience of the reader.

LIST OF ABBREVIATIONS

ADM	Admiralty
AH	Arcinsys Hessen, Marburg, Germany
AO	American Office
CCR	Connecticut Colonial Records
CG	Connecticut Gazette
CHS	Connecticut Historical Society, Hartford, Connecticut
CM	Caledonian Mercury
CO	Colonial Office
CSL	Connecticut State Library, Hartford, Connecticut
CSR	Connecticut State Records
JSC	James Steelman Collection
LOC	Library of Congress, Washington D.C.
MS	G. W. Blunt White Library, Mystic Seaport, Mystic, Connecticut
NARA	National Archives, Washington D.C.
NLCHS	New London County Historical Society, New London, Connecticut
PA	Pension Application
PAC	Public Archives of Canada, Ottawa, Ontario, Canada
QLR	Museum of the Queen's Lancashire Regiment, Preston, Lancashire, United Kingdom
TNA	National Archives, Kew, United Kingdom
TO	Treasury Office
WCL	William Clement Library, University of Michigan, Ann Arbor, Michigan
WO	War Office
YU	Yale University
YUL	Yale University Library, New Haven, Connecticut

Preface

In September 1881, exactly one hundred years after Benedict Arnold's raid on New London, the state of Connecticut organized a gigantic two-day "Centennial Celebration" to commemorate the event. It committed massive resources to the affair, including activating four National Guard regiments, and inviting soldiers from the U.S. Army and vessels from the U.S. Navy to participate in a reenactment. Attended by politicians, Civil War veterans, and over 20,000 spectators, it featured military parades, school children singing patriotic songs, poetry readings, fireworks, and political speeches. But the highlight was the dramatic, bloodless reenactment of the attacks on New London and Fort Griswold.

Missing from the commemoration were the grim realities, horrors, and tragedies of the war. As historian Matthew Warshauer correctly surmised in his book, *Connecticut in the American Civil War*, "The memory of war is a tricky thing. It inevitably changes as time marches on and those who participated in a conflict pass on. A new generation can never fully experience the fear, despondence, and the loss, or the joy, victory, and nationalism of those who came before. Every nation desires to remember and promote the justice of its cause and the sacrifice of those who fought. Even defeat can morph into a living force, a consciousness that honors soldiers and commitment, and expands on positive rationales for fighting." While Warshauer was referring to the memory of the American Civil War, the same could be said of the American Revolution.[1]

---

1 Matthew Warshauer, *Connecticut in the American Civil War: Slavery, Sacrifice, & Survival* (Middletown, CT: 2012), 173.

In a hundred years, the memory of the raid had become greatly distorted. This has complicated the modern historian's ability to study and write about it. Initially this distortion was due to a successful Continental anti-British propaganda campaign launched immediately after the battle. Focusing primarily on Fort Griswold, it embellished and "improved" accounts, such as the supposed surrender and subsequent death of Colonel Ledyard, all meant to encourage further support for the war. But even after the war ended, the distorted interpretation of events remained entrenched for many Americans.

Such distortion can be seen at the Fort Griswold Battlefield State Park. The Groton Battle Monument, erected in 1830 and which stands near the remains of the fort, is inscribed to the "memory of the brave Patriots, who fell in the Massacre at Fort Griswold . . . when the British, under the command of the traitor Benedict Arnold, burnt the towns of New London and Groton, and spread desolation and woe throughout this region."

The misleading narrative was furthered by veterans. Survivors like Stephen Hempstead held strong, bitter grudges against the British for decades. This bias is evident in his narrative of the battle. Falsely presenting himself as a witness to every critical moment, Hempstead never missed an opportunity to portray the British in a bad light. Another veteran, Jonathan Rathbun, published his recollections in 1840. The first to make use of Rufus Avery's narrative, he modified it to further the anti-British narrative. These modifications were not detected until the original narrative was discovered nearly forty years later, by which time highly inaccurate interpretations of the raid had taken root.

It was not until 2000, with the publication of Dr. Walter Powell's *Murder or Mayhem? Benedict Arnold's New London, Connecticut Raid, 1781*, that the trend was broken. Powell presented the first unbiased study, publicly questioning the traditional narrative, especially concerning Colonel Ledyard's death. But despite Powell's efforts and extensive research, the traditional interpretation continues to reign as it has for the last two centuries.[2]

While Arnold's expedition lasted ten days, what is remembered occurred on one day, September 6, 1781. That day saw two separate battles. The first was the attack on New London, referred to by veterans as the Battle of New London. This engagement included house to house fighting, an exceedingly rare occurrence during the Revolutionary War. The second was the Battle of Groton Heights, which included the assault on Fort Griswold and skirmishing along Birch Plain Creek. Though not the largest battle of the war, it was the bloodiest in the sense

---

2 Walter L. Powell, *Murder or Mayhem? Benedict Arnold's New London, Connecticut Raid, 1781* (Gettysburg, PA: 2000).

that the percentage of those engaged who became casualties was greater than in any other battle.

None of the events leading up to the expedition, British planning, or the effects on Connecticut have ever been explored. Its impact on the war has also been glossed over. While it did not directly affect the outcome of the larger war, the consequences of the raid showed how well American intelligence deceived the British and took the strategic initiative away from them. Consequent British mistakes further contributed to the defeat at Yorktown. The attack destroyed New London and cemented Benedict Arnold's reputation for villainy.

This study is a military history covering such things as strategy, tactics, and battlefield movements. Second, it offers a balanced portrayal of both sides, drawing upon dozens of hitherto ignored or unpublished narratives and accounts. Third, it will challenge and seek to debunk myths that have flourished for 243 years, utilizing many newly discovered primary sources. Some may see this study as an attempt to condone British actions, but my aim is rather to explain how and why things happened. Lastly, it is my hope that this effort will increase interest in battlefields such as Groton and New London and promote their preservation and interpretation.

Acknowledgments

What today has become *The Traitor's Homecoming* began over a decade ago. It was originally an interpretive guide to the Fort Griswold Battlefield as part of my master's project at Sacred Heart University. But as I compiled material for the guide, it grew into something much larger than I ever planned.

It is my intention to thank everyone who made this book possible, but if I fail to include your name, please know how much I appreciate your help in making this book a reality.

I would like to collectively thank the staffs at the following institutions: the Connecticut State Library, the Connecticut Museum of Culture and History (formerly the Connecticut Historical Society), the New London County Historical Society, the Clement Library at the University of Michigan, and Fort Griswold State Battlefield Park.

Many historians have assisted me in tracking down and sharing resources, as well as answering my numerous and often random questions. A thank you goes out to Don Hagist, Todd W. Braisted, Kevin Johnson, Bob Brooks, Selden West, Dale Plummer, Richard Malley, and Don Troiani who were all helpful beyond words.

My thanks as well to reenactor and historian of the 40th Regiment of Foot, Niels Hobbs, for providing his insight on the regiment, as well as sharing his

Chapter One

Rhode Island:
A Lost Opportunity

The sizeable Palladian window and cupola atop the Georgian mansion at No. 1 Broadway in lower Manhattan offered impressive panoramic views. One could see for miles. The Kennedy house with its grand staircase, large banquet hall, and parlor room represented the height of elegance in New York City. Its splendor attracted Lt. Gen. Sir Henry Clinton, the commander-in-chief of the British army in America, to choose it as his military headquarters.[1]

The 51-year-old Clinton was the son of Adm. George Clinton, who served as the colonial governor of Newfoundland and later New York. Clinton grew up in New York City and began his military career there as a young militia officer. After his father resigned from the governorship of New York, Clinton returned to England, where he purchased a commission in the prestigious Coldstream Guards. He served with distinction in the Seven Years War ending the war as a colonel. Afterward, he obtained a seat in Parliament and was promoted to major general.

Clinton returned to North America in mid-1775 as part of a contingent of reinforcements for the Boston garrison. At the Battle of Bunker Hill, he urged aggressive action by landing in the American rear and cutting them off but was overruled. He nonetheless played a conspicuous role in the subsequent action. The following year, he led a British expeditionary force against Charleston, South Carolina. Foiled at the Battle of Sullivan's Island, Clinton's force retired and joined the main British army in New York. During the ensuing campaign, he took part in the successful operations around New York City, especially at the

---

1 David McCullough, *1776* (New York, 2005), 121.

Battle of Brooklyn, where he led the British troops that outflanked Washington's army. Subsequently, he commanded the force that captured Newport, Rhode Island, establishing it as a British base of operations. Clinton then returned to England on leave in early 1777 and considered resigning. But under the urgings of Lord Germain, the secretary of state for America, along with a knighthood and promotion to lieutenant general, Clinton returned to New York as the British army under General Sir William Howe campaigned in Pennsylvania in 1777. That fall, he led a relief force up the Hudson River to assist Burgoyne's army, which was then engaged at Saratoga. After Howe's resignation as commander-in-chief in 1778, Clinton succeeded him and as the army evacuated Philadelphia, he commanded it ably at the battle of Monmouth in June 1778.

After the British army returned to New York, the war against the rebellious American colonies, now in its third year, was reduced to a stalemate. This was due to the entry into the war of France in 1778 and Spain in 1779 on the side of the Americans. The situation was further complicated in 1780 when the Netherlands declared war on Great Britain. Under orders from Lord Germain, Clinton detached most of his army to shore up the defenses of other key British colonial possessions, including the West Indies, Florida, and Canada.

The British navy, like its land counterpart, had enjoyed early supremacy over the Americans, both in organization and numbers. However, with the entry of France, Spain, and the Netherlands, the maritime situation changed drastically. Like the army, the navy found itself weakened by having to spread its resources to help protect other British possessions across the globe. The British could no longer concentrate a large naval force in a specific theater of war. This frustrated the high command as it now had difficulty maintaining naval superiority over its enemies, a condition it considered vital to ultimate victory.

Clinton wished to launch a decisive strike against the main Continental Army under George Washington. Instead, with the navy, Clinton was ordered to make quick raids along the extensive rebel coastline, but never to remain long. The overall goal was to disrupt and destroy American shipping, slowing down the rebel economy. This strategy was implemented in neighboring Connecticut. In July 1779, Clinton attempted to draw Washington from his strong position in the Hudson Highlands by sending Maj. Gen. William Tryon with a British force to raid the coastal towns of New Haven, Fairfield, and Norwalk. But these attempts ultimately failed.[2]

---

2 Lord Stirling to Washington, Oct. 14, 1778, Papers of George Washington, Library of Congress [hereafter LOC].

General Sir Henry Clinton, British Commander-in-Chief in America, 1778-1782. *Dr. Walter L. Powell*

In 1780, the British war effort shifted to the southern colonies. In March, a British army under Clinton launched its largest operation in North America since 1778. An expeditionary force under his command returned to Charleston, South Carolina, where a month-long siege ended with its capture. After leaving Maj. Gen. Lord Charles Cornwallis in charge of the British Southern Department, Clinton returned to New York. There, he anticipated an attack on the city, a belief furthered by the news in July that an expeditionary force of 5,000 French soldiers, convoyed by a squadron of thirty-five warships, was approaching the city. Clinton was reassured but still concerned when they instead landed at Newport, Rhode Island, which had been abandoned by the British in 1779, as they shifted forces to other parts of the empire.[3]

Instead of waiting for the French to join with American forces under Washington, then at Morristown, New Jersey, Clinton wanted to take the initiative

---

3 Sir Henry Clinton, *Narrative of Lt. Gen. Sir Henry Clinton, K.B. Relative to His Conduct During Part of His Command of the King's Troops in North America*, 2nd ed. (London, 1783), 26.

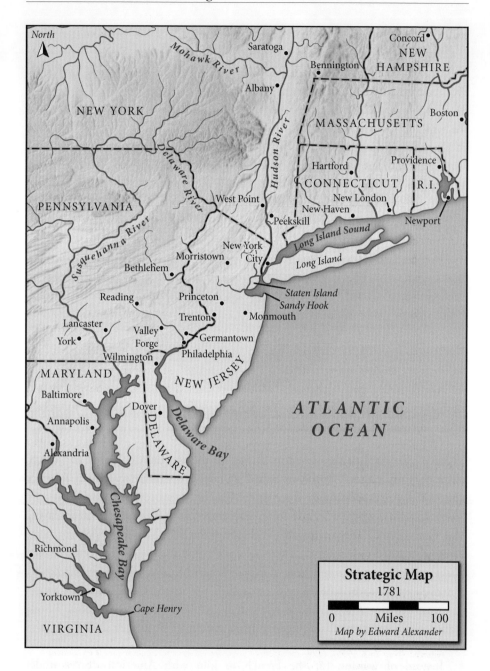

North

NEW YORK

Mohawk River

Saratoga

Concord
NEW
HAMPSHIRE

Bennington

Albany

Boston

MASSACHUSETTS

Hudson River

Delaware River

West Point

Hartford

Providence

R.I.

CONNECTICUT

New London

New Haven

Newport

Peekskill

PENNSYLVANIA

Susquehanna River

Long Island Sound

Morristown

New York
City

Long Island

Bethlehem

Reading

Princeton

Staten Island
Sandy Hook

Lancaster

Valley
Forge

Trenton

Monmouth

York

Germantown

Wilmington

Philadelphia

MARYLAND

NEW JERSEY

Baltimore

Dover

ATLANTIC
OCEAN

Annapolis

DELAWARE

Alexandria

Delaware Bay

Chesapeake Bay

Richmond

Yorktown

Cape Henry

VIRGINIA

Strategic Map
1781

0   Miles   100

Map by Edward Alexander

and launch an attack on the French at Rhode Island. He believed he could eliminate the French army and, more importantly, keep the French navy there from participating in any future operations with the Americans against New York. Moreover, its success could change the direction of the war.

But before Clinton's expedition could proceed, he needed assistance from the navy. Besides needing it to help battle the French navy in Narragansett Bay, he also needed its ships convoy his army. His naval counterpart, Vice-Admiral Marriot Arbuthnot, commander of the North American Station, had convoyed his army to Charleston months earlier. However, the two men did not work well together, their poor relationship becoming visible when Arbuthnot refused to back the Rhode Island operation. The admiral withheld his support and chose to work independently and set up a yearlong blockade of the French at Rhode Island.[4]

The blockade proved embarrassingly ineffective. In mid-June 1781, the French army under Lt. Gen. Jean-Baptiste Donatien de Vimeur, the Comte de Rochambeau, departed Newport on an overland route. Marching westward through Rhode Island and Connecticut, Rochambeau rendezvoused with Washington's army in the Hudson Highlands, some fifty miles north of New York City.[5]

The presence of both armies so close to the city alarmed many British officers and political leaders. As in mid-1780, an attack seemed imminent. An article in the British newspaper *Caledonian Mercury* attests to their uneasiness. It stated that Brig. Gen. Benedict Arnold, the former American general now in British service for almost a year, with the approval of several other army officers, had pressed Clinton to give him 5,000 men to attack the Continental Army of 8,000 in the Hudson Highlands, an area Arnold had once commanded. Notoriously overzealous, Arnold believed most of the Americans were inexperienced and that he could easily defeat them.[6]

Born in Norwich, Connecticut, the 41-year-old Arnold was the oldest of five surviving children of Benedict Arnold Sr. and Hannah (Waterman) King. He lost both parents at a young age and, as his alcoholic father had lost the family fortune, had to struggle to earn a respectable place in society. Through hard work and determination, Arnold established himself as a profitable seafaring merchant

---

4 *George Washington's Generals and Opponents: Their Exploits and Leadership*, 2 vols; George Athan Billias ed. (New York, 1994), 2:266-267; Henry Clinton, *The American Rebellion: Sir Henry Clinton's Narrative of His Campaigns, 1775-1782, with an Appendix of Original Documents*. William B. Willcox, ed. (New Haven, CT, 1954), 444.

5 Clinton, *Narrative* 13, 15.

6 "Extract of a letter from London, Nov 10," *Caledonian Mercury*, Nov. 14, 1781; Thomas Jones, *History of NY During the Revolutionary War and of the Leading Events in the Other Colonies at that Period*, Edward Floyd de Lancey, ed. (New York, 1879), 2:204.

Brigadier General Benedict Arnold. *Clive Arnold Hammond*

and horse trader in New Haven, Connecticut. There, he helped establish the 2nd Company, Governor's Guards, a militia company assigned to protect the governor and General Assembly and became its first captain.[7]

Between 1775 and 1777, Arnold seemed to be everywhere, constantly showcasing his charisma, ingenuity, and courage in leading troops into battle, earning the respect of the men who served under him. In April 1775, and despite orders to the contrary, Arnold led his Governor's Guards to the aid of Massachusetts. In May, he helped capture Fort Ticonderoga. That winter he conducted a legendary march through the wilderness into Canada. In December, he personally led troops at the Battle of Quebec, where he was wounded in the left leg. After his recovery, he organized a fleet of boats on Lake Champlain, which despite losing the Battle of Valcour Island in October 1776, helped delay an expected British invasion from Canada.

In April 1777 Arnold was passed over for promotion to major general. He considered resigning and returned home to New Haven. But the British launched an expedition against the Continental supply depot at Danbury, Connecticut, and Arnold joined in defense of his native state, leading militia and Continentals at the Battles of Ridgefield and Compo Hill. For his actions, he was promoted to major general. In July 1777 he was assigned to the Northern Department, and helped ensure American victories at Fort Stanwix in September, and Saratoga in October. At Saratoga, he was again seriously wounded in the left leg.

Needing time to recuperate from his Saratoga wound, Arnold was appointed military commandant of Philadelphia in 1778. There, he re-entered the merchant trade and made some questionable business decisions. While his actions were legal, his association with suspected loyalists in a highly politically charged city attracted much negative attention. His marriage the following year to Margaret Shippen, the daughter of an alleged loyalist, cultivated more unwanted attention. Citing Arnold's questionable activities and other accusations of misusing his military authority, a group of adversaries persuaded the Continental Congress to appoint a committee to investigate him. Arnold was brought up on eight charges and a court-martial was convened.

Incensed at his treatment, a month before his court-martial Arnold began to correspond secretly with the British in New York. He offered his services to the Crown and gave away American troop strength, positions, and the locations of supply depots, all the while negotiating his compensation. Though the court-

---

7 Today, the unit still exists as the 2nd Company, Governor's Foot Guard.

martial cleared him of all but two charges and allowed him to remain in the army, George Washington was forced to issue a public reprimand against him.[8]

Such public admonishment increased Arnold's resentment, especially toward Washington. He wanted revenge. Instead of returning to field command, Arnold requested a transfer to the command of West Point, along the strategically important Hudson River. He then proffered it to the British, who had desired it for some time, to entice them to raise their compensation. They offered him £20,000 for its successful capture, plus £500 as a life annuity and a commission as brigadier general in the British army; if the plot to hand it over failed they still agreed to pay him £10,000. Arnold accepted, but before the plot could be put into action his contact, John Andre, was unexpectedly captured after meeting with him. Realizing the probable consequences of this development, Arnold fled to the safety of British-occupied New York. He received compensation: a commission as brigadier general and authority to raise his own regiment. What he did not receive, however, was the hero's welcome he felt he deserved, and he was forced to wait months before being given a chance to prove himself.[9]

In December 1780, Clinton dispatched Arnold with 1,500 men to tidewater Virginia, to relieve pressure on Cornwallis and his army, then in North Carolina, and to establish a base at Portsmouth. Arnold achieved great success, especially when conducting raids on Richmond, Chesterfield, and Petersburg, where he destroyed mills, storehouses, a cannon foundry, and numerous military stores.[10]

Arnold was recalled to New York in June 1781. But his relationship with Clinton had soured. While he was gone, Clinton learned Arnold had gone behind his back, writing to Lord Germain, Clinton's superior. Arnold advised Germain how to conduct the war, while offering sharp criticisms of Clinton. So, when Arnold requested to lead an offensive against Philadelphia or against the Americans and the French in the Hudson Highlands, Clinton rebuffed him.[11]

---

8 Willard Sterne Randall, *Benedict Arnold Patriot and Traitor* (New York, 1990), 474; Clare Brandt, *Man in the Mirror: A Life of Benedict Arnold* (New York, 1994), 190; *Proceedings of a general court martial of the line, held in Raritan, in the state of New-Jersey, by order of His Excellency George Washington, Esq. and commander in chief of the Army of the United States of America, for the trial of Major General Arnold, Jun. 1, 1779. Major General Howe, president.: Published by order of Congress* (Philadelphia, 1780), 5.

9 Brandt, *Man in the Mirror*, 206, 220, 223.

10 Randall, *Benedict Arnold*, 581–582; Brandt, *Man in the Mirror*, 242–248; James Robertson, *The Twilight of British Rule in Revolutionary America: The NY Letter Book of General James Robertson 1780-1783*, Milton M. Klein and Ronald W. Howard, eds. (Cooperstown, NY, 1983), 204; Stephen Brumwell, *Turncoat* (New Haven, CT, 2018), 311–313.

11 Brandt, *Man in the Mirror*, 247–248; Randall, *Benedict Arnold*, 581–585.

Clinton spoke little, outside of his inner circle, of his planned Rhode Island expedition. This supposed inaction caused many to criticize his motives openly. Clinton had many detractors in the city, including at times his adviser, Royal Chief Justice William Smith. Smith, a member of a prominent New York family, had served as chief justice of the colony for nearly two decades and remained loyal to Great Britain. Smith noted in his diary as Washington and Rochambeau made their junction: "There seems to be a general Censure of Sir Henry as unprepared for a great Force as he might be and not even for getting behind the Enemy . . . He is incapable of Business. He consults No Body. All about him are Idlers and ignorant."[12]

Arnold continued to sulk was as his resentment towards Clinton grew. He asked Justice Smith, whom he had met shortly after his defection, to use his influence back in England to lobby his ideas. Smith penned in his diary dated August 25: "[V]isited Arnold. He is greatly disconcerted. None of his Propositions of Service are listened to, and he despairs of any Thing great or small from Sir. H. Clinton, who he suspects aims at prolonging the War for his own Interest. He wants me to signify Home his Impatience, his Ideas, and his Overtures."[13]

Clinton was largely able to ignore his detractors, including Arnold, at least for the moment. Though he considered attacking Washington and Rochambeau, he believed the only option that would garner success was against the French navy at Rhode Island. This was based on his belief that he could not adequately defend his post at New York—including Long Island and Staten Island—and at the same time successfully launch an offensive into the Hudson Highlands against an enemy he believed outnumbered him.[14]

In between asking London for reinforcements, Clinton continued to contemplate Rhode Island. Though the bulk of the French army had departed, its siege artillery and stores remained in Providence. In addition, a naval squadron supported by a combined force of some 1,800 French regulars and militia remained at Rhode Island. The isolated French squadron was a tempting target for Clinton. An opportunity presented itself that had the potential, as one British officer believed, "to be a fatal blow to the French." Capturing or destroying the

---

12 William Smith, *Historical Memoirs From 26 August 1778 to 12 November 1783 of William Smith: Historian of the Province of New York; Member of the Governor's Council, and Last Chief Justice of that Province Under the Crown; Chief Justice of Quebec.* William H. W. Sabine, ed. (New York, 1971), 426.

13 Smith, *Historical Memoirs*, 434; Brandt, *Man in the Mirror*, 246–247; *Caledonian Mercury*, Nov. 14, 1781.

14 Clinton, *Narrative*, 11–16. Clinton considered Arnold's option of attacking the allies north of NY City, but also an offensive into the Hudson Highlands, another into New Jersey, and another against Philadelphia, which he overruled due to lack of available troops, sailors, and supplies.

French squadron would eliminate it from future operations against New York. Landing in Rhode Island might even draw Washington and Rochambeau away from New York. It might give Clinton, who planned on leading the expedition, an opportunity to engage the enemy on his own terms on ground he knew well. This could be the decisive battle he had desired ever since taking command.[15]

However, unknown to Clinton, there were problems in his intelligence services. A large portion of the intelligence on which he based his planning and strategy came from intercepted allied correspondence. Clinton placed a great deal of faith in its validity, even sending the captured correspondence back to London. American deserters coming into British lines were also saying similar things. What Clinton did not realize was that Washington deliberately allowed at least some of these letters to be captured. Washington and Rochambeau had met in person earlier that spring in Wethersfield, Connecticut, where they agreed to move south and attack Cornwallis. But they did not want the British to realize their strategy, so they put in place a carefully conceived deception scheme. Each letter the British intercepted contained bits of both factual and false information which led Clinton to believe that Washington preferred a joint Franco-American operation against Cornwallis in Virginia, but had settled for an attack on New York because the French navy was inferior to the British navy and could not hope to contain them. This was in fact the opposite of what they planned to do.[16]

Washington and Rochambeau continued their ploy when the two armies rendezvoused north of New York. To increase the deception's credibility, in early July parts of their armies were detached and sent towards Manhattan on reconnaissance missions to harass the British outposts and alarm the city. Other larger feints were made throughout the month to probe and reconnoiter the British defenses, and siege artillery was brought up to help prop up the ruse. Clinton reacted just as Washington hoped: defensively. Clinton surrendered the initiative

---

15 Clinton, *Narrative*, 11–15; Frederick Mackenzie, *Diary of Frederick Mackenzie: Giving a daily narrative of his military services as an officer in the regiment of Royal Welsh Fusiliers during the years 1775-1781 in MA, RI, and NY*, 2 vols., Allen French, ed. (Cambridge, MA, 1930), 2:598, 600.

16 *London Gazette*, July 10, 1781; Clinton Papers, Volume 165, item 34, University of Michigan, William Clement Library [hereafter WCL]; George Washington to the Marquis de Lafayette, May 31, 1781, Papers of George Washington, LOC. In a captured letter, Washington wrote to the Marquis de Lafayette, who was then in Virginia with a small army, telling him an "Attempt upon NY was deemed preferable to a Southern operation, as we had not the command of the water." One deserter, James Hassard, of the 5th Massachusetts Regiment, told his captors, "The whole talk [within the Continental Army] is about taking NY, this Summer . . ."

General George Washington, Commander-in-Chief of the Continental Army, 1775-1783.

New York Public Library

and went into a defensive siege mode mentality and set about improving the New York fortifications.[17]

By late August, after leaving a small force of Continentals and militia under Maj. Gen. William Heath to defend the Hudson Highlands, Washington and Rochambeau marched their two armies out of Westchester County, crossed the Hudson River, and marched south into northern New Jersey. Covering their movements through Bergen County, they made a feint towards British-held Staten Island. Clinton took the bait because he remembered that prior to capturing New York, in 1776, the British had first taken possession of Staten Island. This ploy was further enhanced when Clinton's intelligence reports warned him of a French naval squadron consisting of 24 ships with 8,000 troops on board. This force was said to have left the West Indies and was now heading up the coast. Its destination was not known, but Clinton believed it to be New York.[18]

Clinton now prepared his southern harbor fortifications to resist a naval attack. He ordered additional heavy cannon to be placed in separate batteries along the heights on Staten Island which commanded the southern entrance into the harbor. Additionally, he continued to build up his defenses in Manhattan, and shifted troops to Denyces Ferry in Brooklyn where they could be moved speedily to wherever a threat was perceived.[19]

Concurrently, Clinton prepared to go on the offensive. Part of his reasoning for bolstering his defenses was the anticipation of taking nearly 5,000 troops on his Rhode Island expedition. The force left behind needed to be able to resist any allied attack in his absence. He informed Frederick Mackenzie, his deputy adjutant general, on August 25 of his intentions, tasking this trusted staff officer with the distribution of troops within his defenses and assembling an expeditionary force.[20]

Recent changes within the British navy bolstered Clinton's resolve. In July, Vice Admiral Arbuthnot had been temporarily replaced by Rear Adm. Thomas Graves. Clinton welcomed the change. Graves was a forty-year veteran of the navy, having served during the War of Austrian Succession, the Seven Years War, and

17 Jones, *History of NY*, 2:204; Robertson, *Twilight*, 214; Clinton planned to attack the allies in Westchester County with 6–7,000 troops from Kingsbridge, but the attack never materialized as the allies crossed the Hudson River before it could be launched. See Mackenzie, Diary, 2:590–592.

18 Mackenzie, *Diary*, 2:590–591.

19 Ibid., 2:590, 597, 599. Two days before Hood's arrival, Mackenzie told Clinton he believed the allies were in New Jersey to block a supposed joint British attack by Clinton and Cornwallis against Philadelphia. Clinton told Mackenzie he "would encourage that Idea as much as possible."

20 Ibid., 2:597–598. Mackenzie had served in Newport during its occupation by the British. He wrote in his diary, "[I] am well acquainted with the works we left there, [Clinton] asked me many questions respecting them."

Rear Admiral Sir Thomas Graves, Commander-in-Chief of the North American Station, 1781.
New York Public Library

the current war. When he arrived, he discussed the Rhode Island operation with Clinton. Graves gave him his support but asked for time to allow naval reinforcements expected daily from Europe.[21]

However, by mid-August, the expedition had moved nowhere, and Clinton's impatience grew. Writing to Graves, he again repeated his desire to pay "a visit to Rhode Island." Graves concurred, but again asked to delay, this time to repair two warships which he deemed essential to success. The expedition was again postponed.[22]

On August 26, Clinton held a meeting with Cmdr. Thomas Wells, a recently exchanged naval officer. Wells brought with him news of a message originally carried aboard the brig *Active* and intended for Graves, which had been captured at sea. Wells rushed to New York to deliver the message personally to Clinton. It revealed that a British fleet under Rear Adm. Samuel Hood was headed to New York from the Caribbean. Wells also told Clinton the French fleet in the Caribbean had left and Hood had attempted to locate it and after being unable to, assumed they were returning to Europe. This helped to further maintain Clinton's belief that the British maintained naval superiority and that he could safely launch a raid against Rhode Island. Hood's squadron also carried two infantry regiments. Clinton was elated.[23]

21 William B. Willcox, "Sir Henry Clinton: Paralysis of Command," in Billias, ed., *Generals and Opponents*, 2:88; William Stewart, *Admirals of the World: A Biographical Dictionary, 1500 to the Present* (Jefferson, NC, 2009), 147–148; Clinton, *Narrative*, 16. Clinton told his superiors that Arbuthnot must be removed, or he would submit his resignation. His request was granted.

22 Extract from Clinton's Letter to Graves, Aug. 16, 1781, in Clinton, *Narrative*, 63.

23 Mackenzie, *Diary*, 2:598; Smith, *Historical Memoirs*, 435. The fleet consisted of the combined squadrons under Hood and Rear Admiral Sir Francis Drake. The news also convinced Clinton that Cornwallis was not in any real danger.

Two days later, on August 28, Hood's twenty warships arrived at Sandy Hook. Mackenzie believed their arrival would "ensure success" on the Rhode Island expedition. It so encouraged Clinton that, "In consequence of his arrival," Mackenzie wrote, "the Commander in Chief has determined to undertake the Expedition to Rhode Island immediately if The Admirals approve of it. He went down early this morning to confer with them upon the matter, and has given orders for all the Military arrangements to be made."[24]

Hood's warships had been sent from the West Indies to pursue a French squadron under Adm. Francois Jean-Paul Comte de Grasse, which Graves expected to unite with the French squadron under Adm. Jacques-Melchoir Saint-Laurent, Comte de Barras, at Newport, in preparation for the allied attack on New York. Hood searched Cape Henry and then Delaware Bay to see if de Grasse intended to interfere with Cornwallis's army, but not finding de Grasse in either location, continued on to Sandy Hook.

Later, while Clinton was away, Mackenzie, also optimistic, closed his diary entry, writing: "If we do not execute something with so powerful a fleet, and a fine Army fit for an undertaking, we shall be deservedly blamed for our supineness. But to let the French Squadron remain quietly and unmolested so near as Newport would be unpardonable. The Navy will no doubt join heartily in this enterprize, wherein they have a fair prospect of signalizing themselves by the Capture or destruction of the Enemy's whole squadron." British success could be achieved.[25]

Clinton met with Graves on Long Island on the same day as Hood's arrival. Hood eventually joined them. In a letter to the secretary of the admiralty, Hood later stated that when he arrived at the meeting, Clinton and Graves were already deliberating the details of the Rhode Island expedition. Hood gave some support to the joint operation but admitted to the secretary that he insisted they actively watch for the French squadrons.[26]

At around 10:00 p.m. someone unexpectedly interrupted the meeting. The disruption came from an unnamed person, presumably a loyalist, who according to Mackenzie had been sent to Montauk Point, at the easternmost tip of Long Island, to monitor de Barras's squadron at Newport and report back any movements. They were told that de Barras had departed three days earlier and was seen to be sailing southward, passing Block Island the following day. The news shocked them.

---

24 Mackenzie, Diary, 2:599, 602. For about a week, Clinton had expected the RI expedition to proceed and had selected the units that would comprise it. The orders to the units were sent out as Clinton left his headquarters to meet with the admirals.

25 Ibid., 2:602.

26 *Letters Written by Sir Samuel Hood In 1781-2-3*, David Hannay, ed. (1895), 24–26.

Justice Smith, who was in attendance, recalled that Hood, upon hearing the news, "looked and behaved like a stiff Yankee colonel."[27]

Angry and disappointed, Clinton wrote, "Thus, to the Admirals great mortification and my own, was lost an opportunity of making the most important attempt that had offered the whole war." An opportunity to divide the allies and destroy an isolated portion of the French navy in America vanished. Clinton's planning, which had spanned over a year, had come to absolute naught. Around midnight, Clinton reluctantly sent out orders countermanding the movements of the troops belonging to the expeditionary force, which was done before any had left their posts.[28]

The capture of the *Active* ultimately led to the end of the Rhode Island expedition. Dispatches aboard which told of Hood's intended movement were not thrown overboard, but instead made their way into the hands of George Washington. Realizing the implications of the British naval movements, Washington wrote to de Barras and warned him about leaving his squadron so isolated, writing, "should [Hood's] squadron actually arrive—form a junction [with Graves] and find the French naval force separated, it might eventually prove fatal."[29]

Mackenzie admitted after the meeting that the "unfortunate Capture of the *Active*, gave the Enemy information of the sailing of The British fleet from the West Indies, and as they knew it might be expected in the course of this Month, they lost no time in removing their fleet from a place in which, in all probability it would have fallen into our hands or have been destroyed." Realizing the implications of the lost opportunity, he sadly admitted, "Thus we have lost the opportunity of giving a capital blow to the French Navy."[30]

Afterwards, Smith blamed it all on the navy, confiding in his diary: "The French Fleet gone from Rhode Island. . .Why was not Graves upon the Look out? Or why did he not send a Detachment the very Night of Hood's arrival?" Despite the lost opportunity, another meeting between Clinton and the admirals was planned for the following day to discuss intelligence reports and future operations.[31]

27 Mackenzie, *Diary*, 2:603; Willcox, "Arbuthnot, Gambier, and Graves: Old Women of the Navy," in Billias, ed., *Generals and Opponents*, 2:279.

28 Clinton, *Narrative*, 17; Mackenzie, *Diary*, 2:603; Smith, *Historical Memoirs*, 435.

29 Washington to de Barras, Aug. 15, 1781, Papers of George Washington, LOC. Washington also utilized Rochambeau's influence to further prod de Barras to move; he wrote, "At the request of the Count de Rochambeau, [it is desired] "that you form a junction, & as soon as possible with the Count de Grasse in Chesapeak bay." The stage was being set for Yorktown.

30 Mackenzie, *Diary*, 2:603.

31 Hood, *Letters*, 26; Smith, *Historical Memoirs*, 435.

Rear Admiral Sir Samuel Hood
New York Public Library

There were now serious concerns about the intentions of the French navy. Where was de Barras headed? And where was de Grasse? Clinton and the admirals could not agree on the objective or destination of either French squadron. Hood believed their target was Cuba, Graves believed they were headed towards East Florida and Georgia, and Clinton feared, again, their target was New York. Even on August 29, as French and American troops marched through New Jersey, Clinton remained convinced New York was their objective and wanted the admirals to assist in its protection. Reports from loyalists in Bergen County warned him that the French were constructing a bakery in Chatham, and that Americans were collecting boats to land on Staten Island—all indicators of a siege.[32]

Hood won the debate. Convinced their combined squadrons "will be superior" to any French naval force opposing them, they would sail for the Chesapeake to locate de Grasse and defeat him, preferably before he was reinforced by de Barras. This would ensure a blow against the French navy. It would also aid Cornwallis's army, now at Yorktown, Virginia, which might otherwise become isolated by the French navy. Even so, Clinton remained stubborn despite some on his staff who, at least privately, believed the British were being purposely deceived. Clinton remained convinced Washington and Rochambeau were not headed to Virginia, and therefore Cornwallis was in no real danger. [33]

Before the admirals departed, Clinton convinced them to let him use a small naval detachment to assist in a diversionary land-naval operation. The commander-in-chief needed to find a quick alternative to Rhode Island. In this new operation, he held the same overall objectives in mind. First, divert attention of the French and Americans away from New York. Second, attack them where he saw a favorable

32 Smith, *Historical Memoirs*, 435; Mackenzie, *Diary*, 2:605–606.

33 Smith, *Historical Memoirs*, 435; Robertson, *Twilight*, 206–208; Mackenzie, *Diary*, 2:606.

opportunity. To accomplish this, he believed it would be necessary to attack the rebel coastline somewhere near the city. He explained, "As I was disappointed of the blow which I intended against Rhode Island, I was unwilling that the preparations for that service should be wholly lost, without some attempt being made to annoy the enemy's coasts and [some] endeavor to cause a diversion somewhere."[34]

Clinton now realized that, except for some American privateers, the British controlled Long Island Sound. Until the French navy was located, there was no longer any large enemy naval presence near him. He discussed this with Justice Smith, who wrote, "Sir Henry has a Choice of Objects. The whole coast is now at the Mercy of the British force, till the French [under de Grasse] appear from the West Indies." A window of opportunity presented itself to Clinton, or so he believed, and he shifted his focus to the Connecticut coastline. What place could he attack that could cause the most attention and not be ignored? One town stood out. This town, Clinton's next target, was New London.[35]

---

34 Clinton, *American Rebellion*, 330–331.

35 Smith, *Historical Memoirs*, 435.

Chapter Two

Protecting New York:
A Diversionary Attack

New London sat about 120 miles east of New York by way of Long Island Sound. Established in 1646 by English settlers headed by John Winthrop Jr., it was originally named "Pequot Plantation," after the native Pequot tribe which inhabited the area. It was later changed to New London and the river renamed the Thames, after the city and river in England. Winthrop chose the spot along the western bank of the Thames River because of its potential as an excellent harbor. Just three miles to the south, the mouth of the river opened into Long Island Sound. With no intricate channel to be navigated, and no extensive shoals or chains of islands, vessels had an unobstructed passage into the harbor, which by the mid-eighteenth century, was "a very compleat one, [holding] a number of shipping [i.e., vessels] , and so deep that the vessels come up and tie to the wharves, where they load and unload with the greatest facility."[1]

New London was an ideal harbor, and the town grew quickly. By the late-eighteenth century, it reached a population of almost 6,000 and its boundaries covered an area of about 100 square miles. It thrived as a commercial center and became the seat of the county government. Many citizens became prosperous from the mercantile trade and shipbuilding industry, others were employed in trades and occupations commonly associated with a port, such as tailors, blacksmiths, coopers, ropemakers, tavern keepers, fishermen, and sailors. By 1774, New London had upwards of 70 sailing vessels, and 3,200 tons of shipping regularly operating within its harbor. Many of these vessels were built in one of the local shipyards:

1 *Norfolk Chronicle*, Nov. 10, 1781.

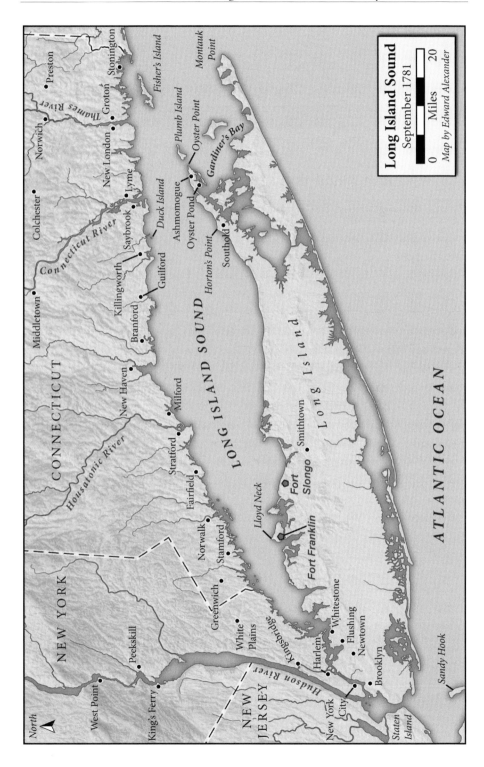

Long Island Sound
September 1781

0   Miles   20

Map by Edward Alexander

Merrill's on Winthrop's Neck, Coit's at the southern end of the Bank near Bream Cove, or across the river in Groton.[2]

Beyond the waterfront, residents engaged in farming, milling, or logging. The most prominent religion was Congregationalism, the established colonial church, though many others were Anglican, or members of non-conformist sects such as the Separatists or a group of Quakers called the Rogerenes.[3]

Built as a port, New London was centered at the waterfront, in an area known as the Parade. The Parade was a large open area that was slightly elevated, near the river's edge, and which bustled with people on any normal day. All roads in town converged on the area. At least four taverns offered lodging, food, and refreshments all within easy walking distance. There stood the county courthouse which remained active throughout the war as judges continued to hear a regular stream of criminal, civil, and probate cases. When goods were taken from illicit traders, the court ruled on those matters. The county maritime court also met there. Legally, any time a privateer brought a captured vessel into the harbor, they had to report it to the maritime court. The judge ruled on the legitimacy of the capture, and then condemned the prize, which allowed it to be sold. County officials also rented out office space for lawyers and for a few small shops. Its cellar was used as an arsenal. The jail stood near the courthouse, holding common criminals and sometimes captured British sailors, soldiers, or imprisoned loyalists.

At the head of Congress Street stood the firehouse, which housed a single fire-engine. Also on the Parade was the Anglican St. James Church and its small burial ground. It had not held a service since late 1775 when, after refusing to stop praying for the king, the minister was barred from holding any services and subsequently forced into exile. Closest to the river's edge stood an earthen river battery, with accompanying powder magazine, constructed at the outset of the French and Indian War to protect the town from French raiders.[4]

---

2 *The Public Records of the Colony of Connecticut*, 15 vols. (Hartford, CT, 1850-1890), 14:487 [hereafter *CCR*]; John Warner Barber, *Connecticut Historical Collections, Containing a General Collection of Interesting Fact, Traditions, Biographical Sketches, Anecdotes, etc. Relating to the History of Antiquities of Every Town in Connecticut with Geographical Descriptions* (New Haven, CT, 1836), 37; Frances Manwaring Caulkins, *History of New London, Connecticut, From the First Survey of the Coast In 1612, to 1852* (Hartford, CT, 1852), 501.

3 Caulkins, *New London*, 201–221, 436; *"General Return of the Number of Inhabitants in the State of Connecticut and also of the Indians and Negroes Feb 1782,"* Governor Trumbull Papers, 24:178, Connecticut State Library [hereafter CSL].

4 Caulkins, *New London*, 258, 263, 444–447, 475–476, 671; James Lawrence Chew, "Facts and Reminiscences," *Records and Papers of the New London County Historical Society* (NLCHS), Vol. II, Pt. 1, (1895): 86–100; *CCR*, 10:350; *Connecticut Gazette* (hereafter *CG*), Jan. 1, 1776, Apr. 24, 1778, Oct. 10, 1780; *Morning News* (New London), Oct. 20, 1845.

The Parade. Present-day view of the Parade area in downtown New London. *Author*

The longest road running to the Parade was Town Street. Running north, it linked with the Norwich Road, the only major overland route to Norwich, about ten miles away, where it terminated. However, the road was crudely constructed and "naturally very rough." The more preferred route between the towns was always the Thames River.[5]

Two other roads, Bradley and Beach Streets, ran parallel to Town Street but only as far as the ferry landing, located near the mouth of Winthrop's Cove. Both roads were linked to Town Street by four smaller side streets. Beach Street, sometimes called Water Street, ran along the waterfront, and contained numerous storehouses, wharves, and docks. Bradley Street, having eight or ten houses, ran in between Town and Beach Streets.

Stretching northwest from the Parade was Congress Street, today's State Street. It ran for about a half-mile where it met Broad Street, which led northward to the Congregational Meetinghouse. The meetinghouse, which stood near the summit, belonged to members of the First Ecclesiastical Society, and gave the hill its name. There on the summit, the road continued westward as the Colchester Road, one of two main routes into the interior of Connecticut.

5 *The Public Records of the State of Connecticut*, 23 vols. (Hartford, CT, 1894–2021), 7:229–230 [hereafter *CSR*].

A booming population over the course of the eighteenth century led many to migrate from the waterfront deeper into the interior. This led to the establishment of the Second Ecclesiastical Society, or North Parish, which grew between the Colchester and Norwich Roads. The North Parish, partly still occupied by members of the Mohegan tribe, later became Montville and parts of Waterford.

One major road ran south from the Parade. Acting as a continuation of Beach Street, this road, called the Bank because of its proximity to the river, ran towards Bream's Cove. Lined with homes, some owned by the town's most prestigious citizens, the road led south to Hog Neck or the Quagonapoxet Highway.

The Quagonapoxet Highway, later called the Town Hill Road, continued southward towards the Quagonapoxet marshes near the coastline, but not before intersecting with the Post Road, the second major route in and out of New London. Built in the mid-seventeenth century, the Post Road was part of a larger route laid out between Boston and New York. It ran westward from the intersection, across the Great Neck, to the Rope Ferry and neighboring town of Lyme.[6]

Beyond the waterfront, to the north, west, and south, farm fields, orchards, and pasturage fields dominated the landscape. Local commodities such as Indian corn, wheat, rye, beef, pork, flax, oats, potatoes, cider, and apples were loaded onto merchant vessels and shipped to markets in New York, Boston, Philadelphia, Virginia, and the Carolinas. Additionally, valuable cargoes of timber, iron, and copper ore were shipped to the West Indies, where they were exchanged for rum, sugar, and molasses, and then brought back to markets throughout the colonies.[7]

The War

Most New Londoners were sympathetic to the American cause. The Sons of Liberty had been there since the mid-1760s and were backed by the local newspaper, the *Connecticut Gazette*. When Parliament closed the port of Boston in 1774, many local merchants and citizens were incensed. A town meeting was held at the Red Lion Tavern on the Parade, where an ordinance was passed supporting their Boston neighbors. The meeting also enacted a boycott of British goods and threw its support behind the First Continental Congress.[8]

But not all supported the ordinances. Those who backed the Crown were termed loyalists and while most loyalists remained quiet until the war broke out,

---

6 The road was also called the Country Road, the Great Neck Road, or the Road to Ropes Ferry.

7 Barber, *Connecticut Historical Collections*, 37.

8 Lawrence H. Gipson, *Jared Ingersoll: A Study of American Loyalism in Relation to British Colonial Government* (New Haven, CT, 1920), 197–198; Caulkins, *New London*, 502–503.

others fled to the protection of the British army either in New York City or on Long Island. Countless others remained in town, albeit secretly, and were often hunted down and harassed by local officials.[9]

It did not take long for New London to mobilize for war. The militia marched to Massachusetts after hearing the news of Lexington and Concord. Days later, merchant Thomas Mumford leveraged   his mercantile company to raise money and gather supplies to support the American mission to take Fort Ticonderoga, a British fortification on Lake Champlain in upstate New York. Other sympathetic merchants sent their vessels to the West Indies, to purchase with their own funds sought-after war supplies, most notably gunpowder. Others went further and repurposed their vessels as either letters of marque or privateers, sanctioned by the colony, and engaged British shipping along the coastline of New England. Their early efforts surprised a seemingly unprepared British Navy.[10]

Privateers were commonly employed by many nations, including Great Britain, throughout the eighteenth century. They came in two forms. The first form was the letter of marque. This is where lightly armed merchant vessels, whose primary purpose was the transportation of cargo, were utilized to serve a dual purpose. They were issued licenses, so that while they transported their cargo, if they came across an exposed enemy ship, they could attack it.

The second form was by commission. Their sole purpose was to attack and capture vulnerable enemy vessels. A Connecticut privateer captain perhaps explained it best: "[I] received a commission to take, burn, sink & destroy the vessels & property of the enemy on the sea." Licenses were granted to individuals or groups who operated privately owned armed vessels. Equipped with light cannon, they were built for speed and maneuverability and were never intended to go up against large warships of an opposing navy, but instead to attack the more vulnerable ones.[11]

9 Christian McBurney, "The Experience of New London Tories and Quakers," *Journal of the American Revolution*, Feb. 14, 2014, https://allthingsliberty.com/2014/02/the-experience-of-new-london-tories-and-quakers/. Caught in between were the pacifist Rogerene Quakers who attempted to remain neutral. They refused to serve in the militia and were often accused of being loyalists and arrested and questioned by local officials.

10 Caulkins, *New London*, 506, 508; Thomas S. Collier, "Revolutionary Privateers of Connecticut," *Records of the NLCHS*, 9, Vol. I, Pt. 4 (1893): 35; D. Hamilton Hurd, *History of New London County, Connecticut: With Biographical Sketches of Many of Its Pioneers and Prominent Men* (Philadelphia, 1882), 424; Captain's Log, HMS *Rose*, ADM 51/804. TNA. On July 31, 1775, the *Rose*, nearing Newport, Rhode Island, reported being "Chac'd by the rebel privateers." "Narrative of Vice Admiral Samuel Graves, Boston, Sep 1, 1775" cited in *Naval Documents of the American Revolution*, 11 vols. (Washington D.C., 1964-2005), 1:1282–1283.

11 PA (Pension Application): Thomas Park (R.7932), National Archives, Washington, D.C. [hereafter NARA].

Privateers went on cruises which sometimes lasted a few weeks or even up to six months, and preyed on enemy merchant ships, supply ships, or dispatch vessels which were not always protected by the larger warships. Often referred to as pirates, the only difference was they were licensed by a government entity and were only to attack and/or capture the shipping of an enemy during war. The license granted them protection insofar as if they were captured they were treated as prisoners of war.

Because of the potential monetary gain, privateers often sought not to destroy enemy ships but to capture them with their cargo. Once a vessel was captured, a "prize crew" sailed it into a friendly port. There the prize vessel was brought before a maritime court, which exercised jurisdiction in maritime affairs, as the captured vessel was subject to condemnation and prize law. Subsequently, the captured ship and its cargo were auctioned. After the governmental fees and the agent's commission had been deducted, half the remaining value went to the owner(s) of the privateer, and the rest was divided between the officers and crew.[12]

It was not until March 1776 that the Continental Congress recognized the worth of using privateers against Great Britain. Congress approved their use and established laws and regulations for the privateer service. Before that, all privateers were sanctioned by individual colonies. The Americans, unlike the British, did not have a navy at the outset of the war. Privateers were used to help level the playing field.

Congress delegated its authority to issue letters of marque and licenses, and to receive and sell prizes to individual state naval agents. In April 1776, it appointed Nathaniel Shaw Jr., of New London, as the naval agent for Connecticut. He also held the same position at the state level. Shaw became responsible for managing naval supplies, which included equipping state vessels, privateers, and Continental naval vessels, as well as taking care of sick seaman in New London. By doing so, Congress ensured that New London became the center of Connecticut's naval wartime activity.[13]

Shaw, 45-years-old, was a prominent, well-respected citizen and one of New London's wealthiest. Two decades earlier, he had partnered with his father and by 1775 owned the family mercantile business. His merchant house employed several vessels and pursued extensive trading relationships in all thirteen colonies and the West Indies. He and his wife, Lucretia, resided in an impressive, two-story stone mansion, built in 1756, on the Bank, which overlooked Bream's Cove.

---

12 *CCR*, 15:280. Connecticut had four maritime courts, one each at New London, New Haven, Norwalk, and Middletown.

13 *CCR*, 15:474.

Shaw, an ardent patriot, labored diligently as the naval agent. He worked long hours out of a small office just outside his house. He had been one of those New London merchants who used their company and ships to obtain badly needed supplies for the Continental army and navy. With his brother, Thomas, he owned, equipped, and sponsored several privateers in between his naval agent duties.[14]

During the war, over 200 privateers were constructed, fitted out, or sponsored from Connecticut, and brought in over 500 prizes. Most originated in or came into New London harbor. These privateers wreaked havoc on the shipping lane between New York and England, on both sides of Long Island, and were exceptionally dangerous when they operated in packs of two or more. The name of New London immediately began to conjure negative feelings among the British.[15]

One British admiral remarked of New London: "The place was a famous receptacle for Privateers and was thought on that account to injure the British trade as much as any harbor in America." A British officer stated, "[it] had been long a nest of pirates and freebooters from every part of America." The loyalist press offered harsher words, calling it "the most detestable nest of pirates on the continent."[16]

Beginning in 1778, privateers operating out of New England, specifically New London, began to take their toll on British shipping. Because of this, British commander Clinton desired to attack the harbor and eliminate the threat. At his headquarters in New York, an attack was discussed and almost initiated at least three times: in 1778, 1779, and again in 1780. Now, in the late summer of 1781,

---

14 Nathaniel Shaw Jr. to Eleazer Pomeroy, Guadeloupe Merchant, New London, Apr. 6, 1775; Nathaniel Shaw Jr. to John Lawrence, Treasurer of Connecticut, New London, May 15, 1775; Nathaniel Shaw Jr. Receipt to William Thompson, Hartford, May 16, 1775; John Foster to Nathaniel Shaw Jr.; Southampton, Virginia, May 18, 1775. All cited in *Naval Documents*, V:169–170, 339, 344, 361; Ernest E. Rogers, *CT's Naval Office at New London During the War, the American Revolution* (New London, CT, 1933), 6–26.

15 Albert E. van Dusen, *Connecticut* (New York, 1961), 158. New London harbor was open to any naval vessel friendly to the American cause. This included Continental and French ships, other privateers, and vessels belonging to other states.

16 Louis F. Middlebrook, *History of Maritime Connecticut During the American Revolution 1775-1783*, 2 vols. (Salem, Mass., 1925), 1: ix; "Extract of a letter from a lieutenant in the 40th regiment, to his friend in London, dated at NY, Sep. 24, 1781," (Letter to friend in London); *Saunders's News-Letter*, Nov. 24, 1781; *Royal Gazette* (NY), Sep. 22, 1781; *Royal Gazette* (NY), Aug. 22, 1781; *NY Gazette and Weekly Mercury*, Aug. 20, 1781. The *NY Gazette and Weekly Gazette* published a list of twenty privateers which operated out of New London. This list suggests the paper had a loyalist contact in the town, because it knew the name of each vessel, the number of guns it carried, the name of its commander, and whether it was in port or out to sea.

Clinton readied another attempt, hoping he could finally eliminate the privateer threat and, at the same time take pressure off New York.[17]

However, by late August, some in Clinton's inner circle, including Major Mackenzie, no longer believed New York was the allies' objective. Mackenzie now thought "that the Scheme of the Enemy has all along . . . been to make their effort against the Army in Virginia under Lord Cornwallis. To this end, they have made all possible shew of attacking New York . . . to induce The Commander." It is unknown if Mackenzie shared his feelings, but Clinton fell for the deception campaign. Nor was he alone: Maj. Gen. James Robertson, the appointed civil governor of New York, also believed it. Robertson wrote at least three letters assuring members of the King's cabinet in London that he expected a major Franco-American attack on New York.[18]

The intercepted American correspondence that had warned of an impending attack on New York also led Clinton to believe that Washington had sent requests to Connecticut's governor, Jonathan Trumbull, for militia reinforcements and supplies. Washington asked Trumbull "to fill up [your] Battalions for the Campaign" and to be sent "ample and regular supplies of Provision."[19]

Trumbull, a native of Lebanon, Connecticut, was 70-years-old but was one of Washington's closest confidants. He had been a profitable merchant before entering politics. He served in a variety of governmental positions, including as delegate and speaker of the house in the General Assembly, as a member of the Governor's Council, Chief Justice of the Superior Court, and lieutenant governor, before being elected governor in 1769. He was the only pre-war colonial governor to take up the American cause.[20]

Clinton reasoned that an attack against Connecticut would cause immediate panic. It would force Trumbull to delay Washington's requests for troops and supplies, possibly postponing or canceling the attack on New York. In addition,

---

17 Clinton, *American Rebellion*, 103, 444. Clinton proposed to attack it in Sep. 1778, in conjunction with the Battle of Rhode Island. He proposed to attack it in July 1780, after learning that the French army had landed at Newport. See also Maj. Patrick Ferguson, Map, May 1779, Sir Henry Clinton Papers, WCL. Ferguson prepared his intelligence report in 1779 for the possible inclusion of New London in Tryon's coastal expedition that summer. By 1781, New London was the only major Connecticut coastal town which had not yet been visited by the British.

18 Mackenzie, *Diary*, 2:606; Robertson, *Twilight*, 206–207, 214–217. Mackenzie noted this entry on Aug. 29, the second time in a week that he believed Clinton was being deceived. Whether he discussed this with Clinton is not known.

19 *London Gazette*, July 10, 1781. The letter was from Washington to the Marquis de Lafayette, dated May 31, 1781.

20 Jonathan Trumbull, *Jonathan Trumbull, Governor of Connecticut*, 1769–1784. (Boston, 1919), 24–25, 30, 34–36, 81–82.

Jonathan Trumbull Sr.
Governor of Connecticut, 1769-1784
New York Public Library

Trumbull would be forced to divert his militia to protect his own coastline, which was over 600 miles long, never knowing if the British intended to attack more than New London. This fear was evident when they raided the Connecticut coast in 1779. For a week in July the British attacked the towns of New Haven, Fairfield, and Norwalk, the latter two set ablaze. After each attack, the governor and militia leaders were uncertain, never knowing where the British would strike next. As a result, almost 4,000 Connecticut militia were mobilized and ordered to various points along the coastline to protect against additional British landings. The threat of Arnold's force on the Connecticut coast might do the same. It might even persuade Trumbull to appeal to Washington to move Continental or French troops to Connecticut, much like he did in 1779, dividing the allied armies and allowing Clinton to attack Washington on better terms.[21]

At the same time, Clinton felt that by attacking New London, he could adhere to his operational orders from Lord Germain. Those were to make quick, destructive attacks along the enemy's coastline. Germain told Clinton in 1778, "I still hope you may find means, in conjunction with the Squadron that will be left in North America, to keep up an alarm on the Sea Coasts of the rebellious Provinces, & perhaps disable them from materially annoying our trade."[22]

---

21 Charles Hervey Townsend, *The British Invasion of New Haven, Connecticut: Together With Some Account of Their Landing and Burning the Towns of Fairfield and Norwalk, July 1779* (New Haven, CT, 1878), 50; *Connecticut Men in the Military and Naval Service During the War of the Revolution, 1775–1783* [hereafter *Connecticut Men*], Henry P. Johnston, ed. (Hartford, CT, 1889), 132. When George Washington learned of the British raid along the Connecticut coastline in 1779, he ordered an entire division from his army to march to the state to assist with its defense.

22 Lord Germain to Sir Henry Clinton, Mar. 21, 1778, CO 5/263/21–23, The National Archives [hereafter NA].

No town annoyed British trade more than New London. Clinton could deal a blow to the American privateers, and he could also strike at the large stores of naval and other military supplies kept there. Several privately-owned storehouses and wharves were filled with stockpiles taken by privateers. Unlike other American supply bases, which were purposely located several miles inland to deter the British from making quick raids, these stores sat right along the waterfront.

The Defenses of New London Harbor

As the war progressed, the increasing military and economic importance of New London harbor required the colonial, then state government, to protect it adequately. It needed to be a permanent post, which required fortifications and a regular garrison. However, it was a slow process. The harbor's only protection was the fort on the Parade, armed with nine cannon which stood in "ruinous condition." It was deemed insufficient to defend the harbor. The Connecticut General Assembly, the state's legislative body, appointed a committee in April 1775 to examine the harbor and to make recommendations for the placement of additional cannon and fortifications. However, when the report was completed, no action was taken due to a lack of available funds. Instead, the local militia were ordered to rehabilitate the old fort.[23]

It took aggressive action by the British to prompt further action by the General Assembly. In July 1775, a small British naval squadron briefly blocked the harbor entrance and then attacked nearby Stonington Point and burned several homes, which caused great alarm.[24]

In response, the Council of Safety dispatched another advisory committee in November to visit New London and neighboring Groton. The Council was a special board authorized by the General Assembly. Since the legislature only met two or three times a year, members realized the governor needed the authority to act more quickly on matters related to the war. So, they established the Council of Safety, headed by the governor, and gave it the authority, when the legislature was not in session, to order and direct the state's militia and naval forces, whether for the defense of Connecticut or of neighboring states.[25]

---

23 Caulkins, *New London*, 517.

24 Ibid., 516. Another small British squadron threatened the harbor in Aug. It turned out to be a foraging expedition against nearby Fisher's Island. This also contributed to the fear of the local citizens.

25 *CCR*, 15:39, 315. The Council met in Lebanon in one of Trumbull's storehouses which had been converted into a small office. Today, "The War Office, owned by the Connecticut Sons of the American Revolution," operates as a museum.

Headed by Jedidiah Elderkin, a member of the Council of Safety, the committee was to make another examination of the places around the harbor recommended by the previous committee. Elderkin, a lawyer from Windham and militia colonel, took his visit seriously. He prepared for it well in advance by writing to several inhabitants who lived along the Thames River or near the harbor, asking them for their advice. When the committee visited, they used many of these contacts as guides.[26]

In New London, the committee toured various locations, but paid particular attention to an island or point known by its Pequot name of Lower Mamacock, just south of the central part of town. Elderkin reported that "on viewing, all were of opinion that [this place] were good for the purpose." The rocky neck of land, owned by Nathaniel Shaw Jr., bounding the harbor on three sides, made it an ideal location for a river battery to impede enemy shipping from approaching the town. The committee recommended if a battery was built here it "would be one hundred and eighty-two rods from the old fort [on the Parade], a little over two miles from the harbour's mouth [meaning that it] would command the harbor in every place northeast and south within reach of their shot."[27]

The General Assembly approved the location, and militia commenced construction during the spring of 1776. Named Fort Trumbull for Connecticut's governor, it was largely completed by late 1777, though intermittent work continued for the next four years. Designed by military engineer Josiah Watrous, it was irregular in shape and resembled the letter "M," with its top pointed towards the river. Mounted atop a single wooden platform, behind its earthen-packed walls were twelve large, garrison-mounted 18-pounders supported by three additional smaller 6-pounders. To save on funding, the fort on the Parade was dismantled in 1777, and its components, including its gun platform, were transported and installed at Fort Trumbull. A large flagstaff and powder magazine were also erected, as well as a barracks building at its southwestern part.[28]

During its November visit, the committee also visited Groton, directly opposite New London on the other side of the Thames River. The committee boarded a ferry in New London, bringing it to the village of Groton Bank. Groton Bank was part of the larger town of Groton, which was incorporated in 1705. Originally part

26 *A Historical Collection from Official Records, Files, &c; of the Part Sustained By Connecticut During the War of the Revolution With an Appendix, Containing Important Letters, Depositions, &c; Written During the War.* Royal R. Hinman, ed. (Hartford, CT, 1842), 551–553.

27 *Historical Collections*, 552. The peninsula was also known as Shaw's Neck.

28 Mackenzie, *Diary*, 2:611. The 6-pounders were mounted on traveling carriages and placed along the rear wall. The Americans planned to use these mobile field pieces to support the militia in defense of the town.

Fort Trumbull. The present-day fort, the third fortification to stand on the site, was built between 1839-1852. The Revolutionary War-era earthen battery stood here closer to the river. *Author*

of New London, Groton encompassed nearly 70 square miles of territory and in 1782 held a population of almost 4,000. Like New London, its population grew extensively throughout the eighteenth century, which led to the establishment of a second ecclesiastical society, known as North Groton or the Second Society.[29]

The citizens of Groton were much like their neighbors across the river. They had two Congregational meetinghouses, one about a mile east of the ferry and another in the Second Society. They enjoyed the many benefits associated with their proximity to the harbor. Two smaller villages grew up along the river, Groton Bank and Gales Ferry. Those that lived or worked in either village were primarily involved in the maritime trade or shipbuilding. Beyond the waterfront, the primary occupation was farming. The Post Road, which passed through New London, was connected to Groton via the ferry across the river. It passed through much of central Groton before it crossed into the neighboring town of Stonington. The road enabled many farmers who resided in the interior, including North Groton, to bring their goods and livestock to market in the harbor.

---

29 *List of Congregational Ecclesiastical Societies Established in Connecticut Before 1818 with Their Changes* (Hartford, CT, 1913), 17. "General Return of the Number of Inhabitants in the State of Connecticut and also of the Indians and Negroes Feb 1782," Governor Trumbull Papers, 24:178, CSL.

While in Groton Bank, the committee was impressed by a hill known as Groton Heights. With an elevation of over a hundred feet, it was devoid of trees and overlooked the village, the harbor, and Long Island Sound. It was ideal for the construction of another battery.[30]

According to Elderkin:

> nearly opposite the old fort, at New-London, a hill or eminence, the summit or top of which is about one hundred and twenty feet above the surface of the water, and within fifty rods of the water's edge, at which place the ship channel is not more than one hundred and sixty rods in width. On the summit of this hill, the harbor, from the entrance to the north part thereof, and some way up this river, is open and in view. On this hill, it seems, nature had prepared a place to plant cannon for the protection of that port or harbor.[31]

The hill was so dominating that it was thought that "no large man-of-war can so elevate her cannon [so] as to annoy a battery at this place; if she could reach thence, they would be random shot." The General Assembly approved the location, and militia began construction on it in 1776, at the same time as Fort Trumbull. It was named Fort Griswold in honor of Deputy Governor Matthew Griswold.[32]

Construction on Fort Griswold took about two years and was largely completed by 1779. It consisted of two parts. One, an earthen river battery of seven heavy garrison-mounted 18-pounders and two additional 12-pounders constructed on the lower summit, faced the harbor. An even more giant enclosed earthen fort built on the upper summit protected the river battery from an assault by land. Additionally, it increased the amount of firepower that could be brought onto the harbor. It also housed the powder magazine and a barracks for the garrison stationed there.[33]

The one-story wooden barracks building stretched the entire length of the east wall, nearly fifty yards, with its roof and chimneys visible over the wall. It consisted of six separate rooms with wooden plank floors, all accessible from each

---

30 When the committee visited the hill, also called Groton Hill, they found some crudely constructed earthworks put up by militia during the British blockade in 1775. These would become part of the river battery.

31 *Historical Collections*, 552.

32 Ibid., 552; "The Plan of New London Harbour," Letters from Carleton and Hutchins, Papers of the Continental Congress, NARA. It is not clear when Fort Griswold received its name. Its original name, according to Samuel Mott, was Fort Washington, though some veterans also referred to it as the "Groton Fort."

33 The current river battery was constructed in the mid-nineteenth century and is much larger than the original one but was built over the original site.

Southeast Corner of Fort Griswold. *Tad Sattler*

adjacent interior room and the parade ground. Each room was furnished with a fireplace for cooking meals and warmth in the winter. Five of the rooms were used as enlisted quarters. These contained three to six bunk-style beds each and possibly a table with bench seating for meals and other leisure activities. Soldiers stored their clothing and other personal belongings in nearby wooden chests. Space along the walls would have been used to store artillery tools and accouterments. The sixth room at the south end was utilized as the officers' quarters, which housed the junior officers, who were responsible for assisting the captain. Officers were entitled to more space than enlisted soldiers. This room probably had beds for one or two officers, a table for meals, leisure activities, and other related work.[34]

An artilleryman who served in New London gave a more detailed description of the upper fort:

34 PA: Gilbert Dennison (S.15805), John Harris (S.10787), NARA; Rufus Avery narrative in William W. Harris, *The Battle of Groton Heights: A collection of narratives, official reports, records, etc. of the storming of Fort Griswold*, Charles Allyn, ed. (New London, CT, 1882), 39; "Account of sales of barracks, powder, & perishable stores at Fort Griswold, 1784," Revolutionary War Records (1763-1789) Series I, XXXII:236, CSL; Robertson, *Twilight*, Robertson to Lord Jeffrey Amherst, Sep. 1781, 216. The setup of the officers and enlisted men's quarters are based on those at Fort Stanwix National Monument. The British claimed the barracks were designed to house 300 soldiers. This seems unlikely. With 6 rooms, 4 beds with 2 bunks each, and 2 or 3 men to a bunk, the barracks could have probably housed between 128-144 enlisted soldiers at most.

Today stone tablets mark the outline of the foundation of the barracks building at the fort. *Author*

The fort was an oblong square, with bastions at opposite angles, its longest side fronting the river in a northwest and southwest direction. Its walls were of stone and were ten or twelve feet high on the lower side and surrounded by a ditch. On the wall were pickets, projecting over twelve feet; above this was a parapet with embrasures, and within a platform for the cannon, and a step to mount upon to shoot over the parapet with small arms. In the southwest bastion was a flag-staff and in the side, in front to which was a triangular breast-work to protect the gate; and to the right of this was a redoubt . . . which was about 120 yards from the gate.[35]

The two parts of the fort were connected by a covered way, a trench-like path that started at the sally port along the south wall of the upper fort and ran down the hill to the river battery.

35 Stephen Hempstead narrative in Harris, *Groton Heights*, 48.

Enlisted Quarters. The interior of the enlisted quarters probably resembled
those reconstructed here at the Fort Stanwix National Monument. *Author*

The total armament of the upper fort in 1781 was over twenty-three pieces of
cannon mounted on both garrison and traveling carriages. Additionally, along its
western wall, a "barbette battery" was constructed overlooking the river battery to
work in conjunction with it.

The fort's heaviest piece, a garrison-mounted 18-pounder, covered the
southeast land approach. There were also fourteen 12-pounders, two 9-pounders,
one 6-pounder, two 4-pounders, and one 3-pounder positioned around the fort,
outer fleche, and outer redoubt to cover other land approaches.[36]

The committee had anticipated the old fort in New London would remain.
It also recommended a third battery be constructed at the northern end of the
harbor near the tip of Winthrop's Neck, a large peninsula named after the founder,
which jutted out into the harbor north of the central part of town. The committee
reasoned that if the enemy navy attempted to enter the harbor, such a battery

---

36 "The Plan of New London Harbour," Letters from Carleton and Hutchins, Papers of the
Continental Congress, NARA. Some of these light field pieces were mounted on field carriages so
they could be used to support the militia outside the fort.

Junior Officer Quarters. The interior of the junior officer quarters may have resembled those reconstructed here at the Fort Stanwix National Monument. *Author*

would be potentially devastating to them. The forts and batteries would be able to create such a destructive interlocking field of fire that they would be able to hit any British naval vessel from multiple sides simultaneously. Elderkin promised "if the batteries were built at all the proposed places, and with a suitable number of proper weight of cannon, the situation and different angles that those places bear one to the other would expose any ship that should come within reach of their shot, within the harbor, to be distressed, annoyed, and raked fore and aft." He assured "that the enemy's fire [would] be drawn to different places" and be very difficult for them to concentrate on any one fortification.[37]

However, due to a lack of funding, by 1779 only a partially finished earthen fort stood on Winthrop's Neck, with no cannon mounted within it. The two fortifications, Fort Trumbull and Fort Griswold, built on opposite sides of the Thames River, almost diagonal from each other, would have to suffice. The forts

---

37 *Historical Collections*, 553. When Samuel Mott prepared a report for the Continental Congress in 1776, he recommended two places closer to the harbor's mouth which would be suitable to place field artillery in the event of a British attack. See "The Plan of New London Harbour."

A present-day view of the remains of the covered way leading down to the river battery at Fort Griswold. The present-day river battery, constructed in the early 1840s, was built over the Revolutionary War-era river battery. *Author*

could act in concert with each other, but with much less effect than the committee had envisaged.[38]

In early 1779, British movements on Long Island suggested an imminent attack on New London. Brigadier General Samuel H. Parsons was ordered by Washington with a detachment of Continental soldiers to help shore up its defenses. During his time there, Parsons toured and examined the defenses. He was impressed with Fort Griswold but was frustrated with Fort Trumbull. He recognized that despite its ideal location and heavy armament, the fort suffered the severe limitation of not being fully enclosed, making it vulnerable to attack from behind. Nowhere was this more noticeable than from the 100-foot-high Town Hill, which stood about a mile directly to the west of the fort. Parsons reported to Governor Trumbull that it would be impossible to hold the fort "in its present state

---

38 "The Plan of New London Harbour." A second reason the old fort was taken down was that it was thought it would draw enemy fire into the town and was therefore not practical. Mott also stated the fort on Winthrop's Neck was to be called Fort Hancock.

for more than one hour after the enemy have possessed themselves [of Town Hill] with artillery." This problem had been noticed before, but due to lack of funding, nothing had been done.[39]

Parsons was concerned with the terrain behind Fort Trumbull, specifically the "ledges and detached highlands," which would conceal a British attack from that direction to "within almost pistol shot" of the fort. Parsons recommended two options to correct it. One, that he be allowed to reconstruct Fort Trumbull so he could raise the walls and the gun platform and enclose the fort with a series of bastions or demi-bastions. But this would be costly. Parsons's second, less expensive option, was to construct a new fortification atop Town Hill. Such a fort would support Fort Trumbull and protect both the south and west land approaches to New London. The governor and Council of Safety consented to the second option and granted permission in March. The site selected was near the summit of Town Hill, atop a plateau, on the farm of Daniel Way Jr.[40]

In comparison to Forts Griswold and Trumbull, the fort on Town Hill was built in record time. This was partly because the Council of Safety mobilized a large number of militia to construct it, promising them that once the fort was built they would be allowed to return home. They finished it in less than four months.[41]

The fort on Town Hill "consist[ed] of an enclosed fort (erected by fascines) large enough to contain three Hundred men, fronting southward [towards Long Island Sound] with one Redoubt on the Right & one on the left." The fort was included in a map drawn by a British officer after the expedition, which matches the above description but does not include the two side redoubts. It was equipped with eight 12-pounders and contained a powder magazine and barracks building. The latter stood along its north wall.[42]

---

39 Hempstead narrative in Harris, *Groton Heights*, 26; "The Plan of New London Harbour," Letters from Carleton and Hutchins, Papers of the Continental Congress, NARA; Samuel H. Parsons, *Life and Letters of Samuel Holden Parsons Major General in the Continental Army and Chief Justice of the Northwestern Territory 1737-1789*, Charles S. Hall, ed. (Binghamton, NY, 1905), 217–220.

40 Parsons, *Life and Letters*, 217–220; "Petition with statements of appraisers, showing his land has been taken for a fort & asking rental," Revolutionary War Records, Series I, XVIII:43-44, CSL. The erection of the fort on the Way farm caused considerable hardship for the family. In Jan. 1780, Way convinced the General Assembly to rent the land from him for £4/year as long as the fort stood there. It stood on the site, along present-day Mahan Street, until probably the War of 1812 and was known in land records, as the "Fort Lot."

41 *CSR*, 2:220, 247, 381. In July a committee appointed by the Council of Safety made a visit to the harbor to inspect the fortifications. Work had almost been completed on Fort Nonsense by that time.

42 *CSR*, 1:262; James Wadsworth to Governor Trumbull, Apr. 6, 1779, Governor Trumbull Papers, 9:162a–b, CSL; Hoadly, *CSR*, 2:385–386; Captain William Horndon's report in Mackenzie, *Diary*, 2:628.

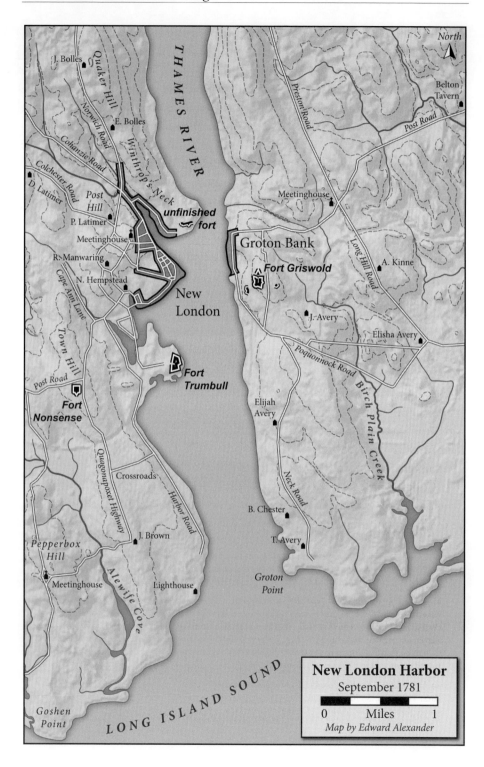

J. Bolles

Quaker Hill

THAMES RIVER

North

Belton
Tavern

E. Bolles

Norwich Road

Winthrop's Neck

Preston Road

Post Road

Cohanzie Road

Colchester Road

D. Latimer

Post
Hill

P. Latimer

**unfinished
fort**

Meetinghouse

Meetinghouse

Groton Bank

R. Manwaring

Long Hill Road

A. Kinne

Fort Griswold

N. Hempstead

New
London

Cape Ann Lane

J. Avery

Elisha Avery

Town Hill

**Fort
Trumbull**

Poquonnock Road

Post Road

Elijah
Avery

**Fort
Nonsense**

Birch Plain Creek

Quagonapoxet Highway

Crossroads

Harbor Road

Neck Road

J. Brown

B. Chester

*Pepperbox
Hill*

T. Avery

Meetinghouse

Lighthouse

Alewife Cove

*Groton
Point*

*Goshen
Point*

LONG ISLAND SOUND

New London Harbor

September 1781

| 0 | Miles | 1 |

Map by Edward Alexander

Unlike the other forts, this one was never given a formal name. In most records, it was called the "Fort on Town Hill," "Town Hill Fort," or "Town Hill Battery." However, the militia who labored on it did not agree with the name. They never understood the fort's strategic location and purpose; it was "considered by them as useless." Because of this, the fort earned its more recognizable, though unofficial, name given to it by the militia themselves: Fort Nonsense.[43]

The New London Expedition

To lead the expedition against New London, Clinton called upon Brig. Gen. Benedict Arnold. Arnold had spent a large portion of his life in the New London area and arguably knew the layout of the town better than any other British general. He was perfect for the assignment. Clinton notified Arnold in writing on August 30 "that he should immediately have 1500 Men for a Descent upon New London." He was "to endeavor to bring off or destroy the prize vessels, traders, or privateers, together with naval and other stores, said to be collected . . . to a very large amount."[44]

When Arnold received his orders, he countered with a more ambitious proposal and asked that if he were given 500 more men, he would strike Providence, or if given 1000 more men, he would attack Boston. These proposals echoed previous proposals that he had made to Clinton. Earlier, Arnold had "offered with but 1500 Men to surprise Philadelphia" and "to attempt Boston, Providence, or New London, and every Harbor of Connecticut, bringing off or destroying whatever is useful to their Army or their Commerce." Clinton rejected Arnold's counterproposals. New London remained his sole target.[45]

Clinton may have chosen Arnold to lead the attack to enhance its effect. Arnold was despised in his home state, and once Trumbull learned of his presence he might commit much of his resources to repulse or capture him. Arnold left no

43 Payne Kenyon Kilbourne, *The History of and Antiquities of the Name and Family of Kilbourn, (In its Varied Orthography* (New Haven, CT, 1856), 137; Kilbourne, *History,* 137; PA: Robert Hungerford (W.19793), NARA. Common throughout pension applications made by militia veterans are statements such as "sent [there] to build a Fort which the men named Fort 'Nonsense'" or "employed in keeping guard . . . upon the Fort called Nonsense." On some maps, the fort is called "Fort Folly," a British synonym for foolishness. Despite this, the fort never had any official name.

44 James Kirby Martin, *Benedict Arnold, Revolutionary Hero: An American Hero Reconsidered* (New York, 1997), 36; Smith, *Historical Memoirs,* 435. Clinton, *American Rebellion,* 331. The expedition was probably planned and/or discussed during the meeting on the previous day between Clinton, Graves, and Hood.

45 Smith, *Historical Memoirs,* 432, 435.

record of his feelings about returning to Connecticut and only admitted privately he accepted the assignment because he feared "a Change of Mind" from Clinton.[46]

On September 1, Clinton ordered the expedition to begin assembling. Arnold was given three veteran British infantry regiments, three provincial or loyalist units, and a small detachment of jaegers and artillery, totaling 1,763 men and officers. The British regiments were the 38th, 40th, and 54th Regiments of Foot. The provincial units were the Loyal American Regiment, the 3rd Battalion, New Jersey Volunteers, and the American Legion.[47]

The 38th Regiment of Foot was led by Capt. Mathew Millet. It had been in America since 1774 and had been quartered in Boston at the outbreak of the war. The veteran regiment had played a conspicuous role in the frontal assault on Breed's Hill, suffering the highest casualty rate of any British unit. Additionally, it had seen action at the Battles of Brooklyn and Fort Washington. In 1778, it garrisoned Newport but was held in reserve during the Battle of Rhode Island. The 38th Foot returned to New York where it participated in the Battles of Connecticut Farms and Springfield, New Jersey in 1780.[48]

The 40th Regiment of Foot under Maj. William Montgomery was selected for the expedition despite having just returned from serving three years in the West Indies and aboard Hood's squadron. Before that, the regiment had distinguished itself at the Battles of Brooklyn, Princeton, Brandywine, Paoli, and Germantown. It disembarked from Hood's fleet on August 31, and moved into barracks in lower Manhattan. Major Mackenzie observed the column and noted they were "weak in point of numbers, but their men look healthy, and in very good order." Their opportunity to get much-needed rest would be short-lived.[49]

Captain John Forbes, of its Grenadier Company, commented in a letter home: "We landed here from Antigua [and] found ourselves in orders for an expedition under the command of Brigadier General Arnold [on an] expedition proved to be against New London . . . a nest of rebel pirates." The entire regiment would be sent on the expedition, including its light and grenadier companies. Realizing the unit

---

46 Ibid., 435.

47 "State of the undermentioned Corps," Frederick Mackenzie Papers, WCL.

48 Ibid. The highest-ranking officer listed present was a captain and Millet is mentioned by name in Arnold's official report.

49 Mackenzie, *Diary*, 2:607–608. When Hood's squadron arrived, Clinton had expected him to be carrying three infantry regiments on board his vessels that could be made available to reinforce his army. But it was learned that Hood only had two regiments with him, the 40th and 69th Regiments of Foot, both serving as marines. Clinton requested both units, but Hood only allowed him the 40th Regiment, explaining, "the fleet will be much short of their complement if they are landed, and has therefore declined it for present."

was "very weak" and numbered "not above 250" men fit for duty, Clinton brought it up to strength before departure. He ordered those recruits who had been drafted into other British regiments in New York should be sent to the regiment, bringing the complement up to around 325 men.[50]

The 54th Regiment of Foot, commanded by Lt. Col. Edmund Eyre, arrived in America in mid-1776 and saw action in the failed attack on Fort Sullivan in an earlier British attempt to capture Charleston, South Carolina. A few months later, it was engaged at the Battle of Brooklyn. Later, it was sent to occupy Newport, Rhode Island where it spent two years of garrison duty, along with the occasional participation in raiding parties. It was present at the Battle of Rhode Island, with the 38th Foot, but did not see action. In 1779, back in New York, the 54th Foot accompanied Tryon's expedition into Connecticut, where it distinguished itself at Norwalk. Tryon noted they led the attack on the town, clashing with "the rebel outposts, and driving the enemy with great alacrity and spirit." It returned to New York where they participated in a small expedition into New Jersey in June 1781.[51]

In March 1777, wealthy New York loyalist Beverly Robinson, a childhood friend of George Washington, raised the Loyal American Regiment. Men from the Hudson River valley, primarily from Westchester and the lower part of Dutchess counties, comprised the regiment. The Loyal Americans had participated in various actions, including the October 1777 assault on Fort Montgomery, in the Hudson Highlands. They also took part in minor excursions, including a raid on Horse Neck in southwestern Connecticut, and were with Arnold during his Virginia expedition. Under the command of the colonel's son, Lt. Col. Beverly Robinson Jr., they had been stationed on Staten Island in anticipation of the expected allied attack.[52]

The 3rd Battalion, New Jersey Volunteers, under Lt. Col. Abraham van Buskirk, was recruited during the fall of 1776. After the British occupation of New York, the battalion became part of the larger brigade of New Jersey loyalists organized and led by Cortland Skinner, the last royal attorney general of New Jersey. Recruited principally in Bergen County, the 3rd Battalion were primarily used as garrison troops but were occasionally dispatched on foraging raids into their native

---

50 CM, Nov. 14, 1781; John Peebles, *American War: The Diary of a Scottish Grenadier, 1776-1782*, Ira D. Gruber, ed. (Stroud, UK, 1998), 469; Muster rolls, 40th Regiment of Foot, WO 12/5318, TNA.

51 *Records of the 54th West Norfolk Regiment* (Roorkee, India, 1881), 4; Townshend, *British Invasion*, 37; Mackenzie, *Diary*, 2:528, 546, 548–549.

52 Mackenzie, *Diary*, 2:599; "State of the undermentioned Corps," Frederick McKenzie Papers, WCL. The return states the highest-ranking officer was a lieutenant colonel. Colonel Beverly Robinson Sr. served at Clinton's headquarters.

county. Some resulted in sporadic skirmishing with their former neighbors in both the militia and the Continental army. They saw their first combat in mid-1777, where they helped repulse an attack on Staten Island made by both militia and Continental troops. The battalion was also present at the Battle of Connecticut Farms in New Jersey in 1780.[53]

The American Legion, formed during late 1780 by Arnold, was a mixed unit of infantry and cavalry. Arnold aspired to recruit his former soldiers from the Continental army to fill its ranks, but despite personal overtures, few responded. A small number were with him in Virginia. But the 120 men placed under Capt. Nathan Frink for the expedition were mostly newer recruits.[54]

At Kingsbridge, along the Harlem River, Col. Ludwig von Wurmb, commander of the Jaegerkorps, provided a detachment to accompany the expedition. The jaegers "were superb soldiers, carefully recruited, often from among woodsmen used to the outdoors and living rough. They were highly trained light troops, armed with short rifles, and known for their marksmanship and skill in open tactics, who could meet patriot militia and light infantry on their own terms." They were frequently tasked with duties like scouting and ambushing, or as advance guards.[55]

A detachment comprised of 112 jaegers, including four officers, from both the Hesse and Ansbach companies, was given to 32-year-old Staff Captain Friedrich Adam Julius von Wangenheim. Born in Sonneborn, near Gotha, in modern-day central Germany, Wangenheim entered the military at a young age in the service of Saxe-Gotha. Wanting to see combat, he resigned and offered his services to the Landgraf of Hesse-Kassel. Accepted in 1777, he arrived in America as a lieutenant and participated in the Philadelphia Campaign, seeing action at Cooch's Bridge and Brandywine. Promoted to staff captain the following year, he was transferred to the Lieutenant Colonel's Company. The previous July he had participated in a sharp

53 Todd W. Braisted, "A History of the 4th Battalion, New Jersey Volunteers," *The On-Line Institute for Advanced Loyalist Studies*, last modified Mar. 1, 2000, www.royalprovincial.com/military/rhist/njv/4njvhist.htm; *Royal Gazette* (NY), Oct. 23, 1780. The battalion was originally designated the 4th Battalion, NJ Volunteers, but when reorganized in 1781 was renumbered the 3rd. Some maps of the expedition list them under either name; "State of the undermentioned Corps," Frederick McKenzie Papers, WCL. The highest-ranking officer present was a lieutenant colonel.

54 Mackenzie, *Diary*, 2:611; Muster rolls, American Legion, British Military and Naval Records (RG 8, I), PAC; Brandt, *Man in the Mirror*, 248; "State of the undermentioned Corps," Frederick McKenzie Papers, WCL. The highest-ranking officers present were two captains, Nathan Frink and Samuel Wogan, both named in Arnold's report. Frink was the senior.

55 Mark Edward Lender and Gary Wheeler Stone, *Fatal Sunday: George Washington, the Monmouth Campaign, and the Politics of Battle* (Norman, OK, 2016), 52; Mackenzie, *Diary*, 2:609, 611; "State of the undermentioned Corps," Frederick McKenzie Papers, WCL.

Staff Captain Friedrich Adam Julius von Wangenheim. *Historic Images*

action against continentals near Valentine Hill, north of Manhattan.[56]

The Expedition Begins

Since the troops involved were spread out over Manhattan, Staten Island, and Long Island, they were given specific times and locations where they needed to be to ensure coordination. Instructed to depart under light marching orders, they were told "to take Blankets, Kettles, Canteens, a few Necessaries, and two days provisions."[57]

Each enlisted soldier also carried a firearm, bayonet, cartridge box, and haversack. Most, except the jaegers, were equipped with the Model 1768 "Short Land" musket. Known more commonly as the "Brown Bess musket," the weapon was a .75 caliber smoothbore, muzzle-loaded firearm. At its end, a thirteen-inch triangular-shaped bayonet could be fixed for close-quarter combat. Inside their leather cartridge boxes, slung over the left shoulder, were up to thirty paper cartridges, each containing a one-ounce lead ball and a set amount of black powder used for priming, loading, and firing muskets. Each redcoat also carried a linen haversack which, slung over their right shoulder, held their issued rations. All their heavy baggage, including tents, regimental colors, and horses were ordered to remain behind.[58]

Movement began before sunrise on September 2, as the expeditionary force was expected to assemble at Newtown, on Long Island, by nightfall. Clinton

---

56 Bruce E. Burgoyne, *Enemy Views: The American Revolutionary War as Recorded by the Hessian Participants* (Berwyn Heights, MD, 2009), 459; Otto Freiherr von Wangenheim, "Biographical Notes of Friedrich Adam Julius Freiherr von Wangenheim," in *Pennsylvania German Society*: VII (1897), trans. Charlotte Grosse: 25–26; Donald M. Londahl-Smidt and Henry J. Retzer, "Letters of Friedrich A.J. von Wangenheim, Lt. and Staff Captain, Hesse Kassel Feldjaeger Corps," *Journal of the Johannes Schwalm Historical Association* 5, Nov. 3, 1995: 1-7; Rangierolle des Hessischene, Nachlass und Familienarchiv Bickell, AH; *Royal Gazette* (NY), July 14, 1781.

57 Mackenzie, *Diary*, 2:611.

58 Ibid.

planned to use the hamlet as a rendezvous point for the expeditionary force to conceal their intended movements. They were to remain in Newtown and not depart for Whitestone, their departure point, until the navy and transport vessels were ready for them.

In northern Manhattan the 38th Foot encamped at McGowan's Pass; the 54th Foot was stationed near the Roger Morris mansion overlooking the Harlem River. The jaegers at Kingsbridge marched at about the same time. Clinton expected them to reach the Horn's Hook Battery, a small fortification on the eastern end of Manhattan overlooking the East River, by 6:00 a.m.[59]

A Hessian officer observed these seemingly abrupt movements and wrote in his diary: "38th English regiment unexpectedly received the order to march immediately. Also, the 54th and 100 Yagers. They were to march to Long Island, but the 38th left their tents standing and all the women and children and disabled remained behind as hut and camp watch." What piqued the officer's curiosity was that they left their tents standing and their women, children, and invalids behind, which implied they were preparing for active service. If it had been just an encampment change everyone, with their tents, would have moved. It became clear to him that something was happening.[60]

Reaching the Horn's Hook Battery, the 38th Foot, 54th Foot, and jaegers were ferried across the East River to Hallet's Cove in Brooklyn. Reaching the opposite bank, they marched for Newtown, about three miles away, and arrived that afternoon, well ahead of the other units.[61]

The 40th Foot departed its barracks at about the same time as the units in northern Manhattan. They crossed the East River just as the sun began to rise and disembarked at the Brooklyn Ferry. From there, the battalion marched through Brooklyn, then Bedford, eventually reaching Newtown.[62]

The 3rd Battalion and the Loyal American Regiment were part of the defenses of Staten Island and had the longest distance to travel. The 3rd Battalion was stationed at the Flagstaff Battery, overlooking the Narrows, and the Loyal American Regiment was further inland at Richmond. Reaching the eastern shore of Staten Island both units, totaling about 400 men, were ferried across to southern

59 Ibid.

60 Johann Carl Philipp von Krafft, *Journal of John Charles Philip Von Krafft: Lt. in the Hessian Regiment von Bose 1776-1784*, Thomas H. Edsall, ed. (New York, 1888), 148.

61 Mackenzie, *Diary*, 2:610.

62 Ibid., 2:555, 566; Muster rolls, 40th Regiment of Foot, WO 12/5318, TNA. Just over three dozen of the regiment's newest members were veterans from the 16th Regiment of Foot. Recently exchanged, these might have joined at Newtown, where they had been encamped since their arrival as parolees from the garrison at Pensacola, Florida, having capitulated to the Spanish four months earlier.

Brooklyn, where they disembarked at Denyces Ferry. From there, they endured a full day's march, roughly 14 miles, which took them through New Utrecht, Flatbush, Bedford, and Newtown.

Three field pieces, two 6-pounders and one 8-inch howitzer, accompanied by four officers and a proportional number of artillerymen, from the Royal Artillery were assigned to Arnold's expedition. After leaving the artillery park in lower Manhattan, they assembled with the quartermaster stores, which consisted of two-hundred hand grenades to be used for combustibles, spare ammunition for 1,500 men, rockets, and twenty-four horses, at the Albany Pier in southern Manhattan. They crossed the East River at around 10:00 a.m. and landed at the Brooklyn Ferry. From there, they followed the path of the 40th Regiment, to the rendezvous point at Newtown.[63]

That same day, the 28-gun frigate *Amphion* and 16-gun sloop *Recovery*, assigned to convoy the expedition, attempted to sail up the East River towards Long Island Sound. This was the second attempt in just as many days, but they were again delayed due to strong winds. Captain John Bazely, of the *Amphion*, in command of the naval convoy, ordered a third attempt at around 8:30 a.m. the following day. This time he succeeded. Born in Dover, England, the 41-year-old veteran naval commander received an "appropriate education" before entering the navy in 1755. He had already served in various posts and had seen action before receiving command of the *Amphion* earlier that year.[64]

As they passed through the Hell Gate, eighteen transport vessels and two horse vessels, all under Capt. Henry Chads, followed. Orders were then sent to Arnold in Newtown, to move to Whitestone where they would meet the navy. Drums rattled as the column marched to Flushing, about three miles away, where they expected to meet the American Legion. The weather was very humid, and an officer remarked, "Thick weather most of the day." When Arnold reached Flushing, he discovered the Legion was not there. Acting against Clinton's orders, they had left early and were already at Whitestone.[65]

---

63 Mackenzie, *Diary*, 2:610–612.

64 Ibid., 2:610; "Biographical Memoir of John Bazely, Esq. Vice Admiral of the Red Squadron," *The Naval Chronicle, for 1805: Containing a General and Biographical History of The Royal Navy of the United Kingdom; With a Variety of Original Papers on Nautical Subjects: Under the Guidance of Several Literary and Professional Men* 14 (July-Dec. 1805): 177–182. His first command was the *Alert*. In Sep. 1777 he led the ship in a three-hour engagement off the coast of France against the American brig *Lexington* and succeeded in capturing it. The victory so impressed the Admiralty he was immediately promoted to Commander.

65 Master's Log, HMS *Amphion*, ADM 52/2133, TNA; Mackenzie, *Diary*, 2:612.

Captain John Bazely

Naval History and Heritage Command

This disobedience might have caused word to get out about the expedition. This had nearly happened twice the day before, once as the troops moved across western Long Island, and then again when an officer stationed in Brooklyn observed "The 40th. 54th. & 38th Regts, Robinson [Loyal Americans] & Buskirks [3rd Battalion, New Jersey Volunteers] Provincial Corps all assemble at Newtown this day & Embark tomorrow at Whitestone." The expedition, he "supposed [was] against Connecticut." The same day they set sail, this officer believed the expedition was "supposed against New London." How he learned this is not known.[66]

Justice Smith was worried about the secrecy of the expedition. He confided to his diary on September 3: "Detachments from Robertson's [Loyal American Regiment] and Skinner's Battalions [3rd Battalion, New Jersey Volunteers] passed thro' Flatbush towards Whitestone but yesterday. Shameful Delays! The Design was known to the whole Town Yesterday." Despite this, Arnold and his force continued. They staggered into Whitestone, near sunset, where they halted for a short rest. At around midnight, they began their embarkation aboard the transport vessels. By then, the weather had cooled considerably. Amidst a fresh southwesterly wind and under the light of a full moon, the embarkation continued into the early hours of the morning.[67]

It took almost three hours to complete, including waiting for the right wind condition, but Captain Bazely, ordered the convoy to weigh anchor at "1/2 past 3 AM." The *Amphion* led the way and, within two hours, came to sail with the sloops *Beaumont* and *Recovery*, the brigs *Lurcher* and *Argo*, the armed galley *Hussar*, and the transport vessels. Sailing "with a fair wind" in a northeastern direction, they crept along the upper shore of Long Island. At about ten in the morning, they reached Oyster Bay, within sight of Lloyd Neck, where they anchored, and waited for another loyalist contingent to join them.[68]

While planning the expedition, Clinton had turned to William Franklin, the former royal governor of New Jersey, for assistance. Unlike his famous father, Benjamin, William was an avowed loyalist. In 1776, while governor, he was arrested by the New Jersey militia, and ordered to be imprisoned by the legislature. He was incarcerated in Connecticut for over two years and when released moved to New York where he was appointed president of the Board of Associated Loyalists in 1780.

---

66 Peebles, *American War*, 469–470.

67 Smith, *Historical Memoirs*, 437. Smith believed Arnold should have set sail the day after he received his orders, but Smith was no military man and did not understand the logistics involved in such an expedition.

68 Master's Log, HMS *Amphion*, ADM 52/2133, TNA; Captain's Log, HMS *Amphion*, 51/39, TNA.

Frustrated by the failure of British efforts to end the war successfully, several prominent loyalist political leaders, led by Franklin, wanted to pursue a more aggressive approach, with the loyalists playing a more central role. Accordingly, they convinced Lord Germain to have the king grant a royal charter in September 1780 to establish the Board of Associated Loyalists. With Franklin as its president, the Board acted independently of the British high command and established its own army and navy. Their goals were to harass the enemy's seacoasts, disrupt enemy trade, and, when the situation warranted it, make diversions in favor of British forces.[69]

Led by their own officers, they were equipped with their own weapons and took no pay or clothing from royal authorities. They chartered their own naval vessels, which they used to transport wood for the British garrison and to forage or plunder rebel coastal towns for subsistence. These vessels also engaged in privateering.

Their main base was on Lloyd Neck on Long Island, over which they assumed control in June 1781. The neck was a peninsula that extended northward into Oyster Bay and Long Island Sound. Once there, they strengthened the fortifications, naming them Fort Franklin. By that summer the fort was garrisoned by some 400 men.[70]

Fort Franklin protected their camps and Oyster Bay, where they kept their armed vessels and smaller boats used to prey along the Connecticut coastline, "distressing the enemy and gaining intelligence necessary for the Commander-in-Chief." Many British general officers knew these loyalists would prove invaluable in the upcoming expedition. One commented, "The Loyal refugees possess a zeal, which with their intimate and minute knowledge of the country will always render them useful in such services."[71]

After the Board accepted Clinton's request, it dispatched its orders with Capt. Abiathar Camp. Camp was a native of New Haven, Connecticut, and a merchant

---

69 Broadside, "Articles of the Associated Loyalists Under the Honourable Board of Directors, 1781," LOC.

70 Jones, *History of NY*, 2:300–301; Mackenzie, *Diary*, 2:637. The post had been manned by provincial forces since 1778 and was abandoned in June 1781 when the garrison was moved to other strategic points around New York for the expected Franco-American siege of the city.

71 Jones, *History of NY*, 2:300; Tryon report cited in Townsend, *British Invasion of New Haven*, 38; Richard F. Welch, "Fort Franklin: Tory Bastion On Long Island Sound," *Journal of the American Revolution*, Mar. 19, 2015, https://allthingsliberty.com/2015/03/fort-franklin-tory-bastion-on-long-island-sound/; Ruma Chopra, *Unnatural Rebellion: Loyalists in New York City during the Revolution* (Charlottesville, VA, 2011), 173, 194; Caleb A. Wall, *Reminiscences of Worcester from the Earliest Period, Historical and Genealogical, With Notices of Early Settlers and Prominent Citizens, and Descriptions of Old Landmarks and Ancient Dwellings, Accompanied By a Map and Numerous Illustrations* (Worcester, MA, 1877), 102-103.

before the war. After refusing to take an oath of allegiance to the state, he was imprisoned and eventually joined the Associated Loyalists. Knowing the coastline well, Camp gathered guides and pilots for the vessels on the expedition.[72]

Camp also delivered the order to Lt. Col. Joshua Upham, the commandant of Fort Franklin. The 40-year-old native of Brookfield, Massachusetts, a small-town west of Worcester, was a Harvard College graduate and practiced law. When the war broke out, he tried to remain neutral, but ended up moving with his family in April 1778 to British-occupied Newport, Rhode Island. Once there, Upham was commissioned as a major in the Loyal Associated Refugees, the precursor to the Associated Loyalists, led by fellow Massachusetts lawyer Edward Winslow. Upham served with them until the unit was disbanded in 1780.[73]

By that time, its remnants, including Upham, were on Long Island. Upham asked Winslow to get authorization from Clinton to organize a new unit and a commission to serve in it. Permission was granted in June 1781; with the support of the Board of Directors, Clinton commissioned Upham as a lieutenant colonel and permitted him to raise a Corps of Associated Loyalists and gave him command of Fort Franklin.[74]

By September, Upham, termed a "brave and good officer," was a seasoned combat leader. In addition to his previous service in the Loyal Associated Refugees, he had participated in several small expeditions along the Connecticut coastline during the last several months. In July, Fort Franklin had been attacked by a combined Franco-American force. A French squadron out of Newport, carrying about 450 French and American troops, landed two miles from the fort, and attempted a night attack. Upham waited until they were in range of his artillery, then opened fire and forced them to make what he termed a "disgraceful retreat to their ships." Afterward, he sent out small reconnoitering parties to exaggerate his

---

72 Franklin B. Dexter, *New Haven Loyalists* (New Haven, CT, 1918), 37; American Loyalist Claims, 1776–1835, AO 12/97/124-140, TNA.

73 Edward Winslow, *Winslow Papers: A.D. 1776–1826*, W.O. Raymond, ed. (St. John, New Brunswick, 1901), 50–51; Esther Clark Wright, *The Loyalists of New Brunswick* (Hantsport, Nova Scotia, 1981), 13–20; *American Journal and General Advertiser* (Providence), Apr. 15, 1779; *Evening Post and General Advertiser* (Boston), Aug. 7, 1779.

74 Joshua Upham to Edward Winslow, Dec. 8, 1780, in Edward Winslow, *Winslow Papers*, 63–64. Upham was also at the time raising a separate provincial unit, the Volunteers of New England. The Corps of Associated Loyalists was organized much like any other militia company of the period. Male refugees who came to the fort and volunteered were organized into companies typically led by a captain, a lieutenant, and an ensign, who were all commissioned by the Board of Directors.

strength and deceive the enemy. No attack was renewed and Upham earned praise from British leadership.[75]

When Upham received his orders, he "made every preparation consistent with the necessary secresy to furnish as many Refugees for the proposed expedition as could be spared from the garrison." After which he claimed, "My first care was to put a supply of provisions on board the vessels." Upham next selected 100 men from the garrison and organized them into two companies and waited for Arnold.[76]

Almost always incorrectly misidentified as "New Jersey loyalists," the Associated Loyalists or Refugees were mainly displaced New England loyalists, with a balance from Connecticut, many former residents of Fairfield or New Haven counties. The expedition was personal for them.

At noon on September 4 the Associated Loyalists joined Arnold's expedition. In addition to providing additional troops, Upham outfitted two armed sloops, the 10-gun *Association* and the 10-gun *Colonel Martin,* plus several small craft. The squadron then sailed throughout the day, continuing uninterrupted along the northern shore of Long Island.[77]

At dawn the next morning, though cloudy, a breeze pushed the squadron to within sight of New Haven, but their presence raised no alarm. According to the logbook of the *Amphion*, the squadron, passing near Setauket "at ½ past 5" that morning, "Recd 3 Batteaux" or small flat-bottomed boats.[78]

Though the logbook does not offer additional details about the bateaux, they were likely a "small party from Vanalstine's Post." The party of 20 men belonged

75 *New York Gazette and the Weekly Mercury*, July 16, 1781; American Loyalist Claims, 1776–1835, AO 13/75/432, 434–436. The attack on Fort Franklin was part of the deception plot organized by Washington, making the British believe an attack on New York was forthcoming. In response to the attack, Maj. Gen. Friedrich Adolf Riedesel, commander of British troops on Long Island, praised Upham, writing, "The presence of Mind, accuracy of Orders & gallant countenance Col. Upham testified in this Engagement does him the greatest honor and must ensure him not only the Admiration but Esteem of every Soldier."

76 *New York Gazette and Weekly Mercury*, Apr. 2, 1781, May 7, 1781; *Royal Gazette* (NY), Apr. 25, 1781; CG, Sep. 7, 1781; Mackenzie, *Diary*, 2:637; American Loyalist Claims, 1776–1835, AO 13/76/209-214, TNA; American Loyalist Claims, 1776–1835, AO 13/80/78, TNA; "A Sketch of New-London & Groton, with Attacks made on Forts Trumbull & Griswold by the British Troops Under the Command of Brig. Gen. Arnold Sep 6th, 1781 by Captain Lyman of ye Prince of Wales American Volunteers," WCL. Based on their overall strength and some limited documentation, including the Daniel Lyman map, the contingent was formed into two companies of 50 men each. Each company would have had a captain, lieutenant, and ensign. One company was led by Capt. Samuel Goldsbury, a Massachusetts loyalist. In his claim after the war, Goldsbury claimed he "was appointed to raise a Company of Associated Loyalists under the Board of Directors in Colonel Uphams Corps, that he completed his Command and did actual duty at Lloyd Neck on Long Island [and] afterwards commanded a Company under General Arnold at the Reduction of New London."

77 Master's Log, HMS *Amphion*, ADM 52/2133, TNA.

78 Ibid.

to the Loyal Refugee Volunteers posted at Fort Slongo in Smithtown, commanded by loyalist Maj. Peter van Alstine, though he was not with them. The party was led by Lt. William Castles, a New York loyalist from Albany County who served with Burgoyne's army. Castles volunteered his party and they temporarily served under Upham.[79]

On September 5, the British squadron continued and "came to a sail running down the Sound" before dropping anchor at around 2:00 p.m. in the waters off Plumb Island. The island was located at the eastern end of Long Island, within sight of New London, about thirty miles to the north. Bazely halted the squadron to wait for the cover of darkness, using the next five hours to make the final arrangements for their descent upon New London harbor.[80]

Bazely wanted to wait for the right wind conditions. He knew that along the southern New England coastline during the summer and early fall months, the wind would blow from the south and the west, gradually increasing for a few hours beginning at around midnight. This pattern happened with great regularity, broken only by an approaching storm. Bazely anticipated this weather pattern to continue and wanted to use it to their advantage. Both he and Arnold expected to move towards the harbor around midnight when the wind changed and then commence landing operations. Under cover of darkness, they planned to surprise and secure the forts and then occupy New London. Unfortunately for them, this night the winds did not cooperate.[81]

79 Upham's report in Harris, *Groton Heights*, 110; American Loyalist Claims, 1776–1835, AO 13/80/77–78, TNA; "Extract From General Orders," *The Norwich Packet and the Weekly Advertiser*, Oct. 18, 1781.

80 Master's Log, HMS *Amphion*, ADM 52/2133, TNA; Arnold report in Mackenzie, *Diary*, 2:623.

81 Harris, *Groton Heights*, 15–16; "Letter to friend in London." The pattern continued when after a short period of time, the wind would again change and begin blowing from the north and the west. This would continue until about noontime and would be followed by a southerly breeze.

Chapter Three

Ledyard's Command

In the late hours of September 5, in a small boat, David Gray snuck across Long Island Sound under cover of darkness in advance of the British squadron. It was a route often traveled by the courier for British secret intelligence. He would depart British-occupied New York City, travel across Long Island, cross the Sound, and land either at the Rope Ferry, near the New London-Lyme border, or at Black Point in Lyme. Gray then rode towards Hartford, then Massachusetts, then to the Hampshire Grants, modern-day Vermont, delivering dispatches to his loyalist contact in Brattleboro. But tonight, as Gray crossed the Sound, he headed directly for New London. For unbeknownst to the British, Gray was an American double agent who worked directly for Washington. With him, he carried word of Arnold's planned attack.[1]

Gray sought to alert the commandant of the Department of New London and Groton—which included New London's harbor defenses—of the British approach. The current commandant was 42-year-old William Ledyard.[2]

---

1 John A. Nagy, *George Washington's Secret Spy War* (New York, 2016), 182–183; PA: David Gray (S.38776), NARA.

2 PA: Jeremiah Halsey (S.16845), NARA. Gray was not the only one seeking to warn of the impending British attack. Jeremiah Halsey observed the British squadron off Southold, New York, on Sep. 5, and took it upon himself to get the word out. Leaving Southold, he traveled three miles to Truman Beach at Oyster Point to get around the British ships, procured a boat and rowed across the Sound to Saybrook. There, Halsey warned Lt. Martin Kirtland, the commander of the fort on Sep. 6. However, it was too late; Halsey's warning did not reach New London in time. Halsey remained stuck in Connecticut for several months afterwards as travel across the Sound was "strictly prohibited" after the attack.

William Ledyard was born December 6, 1738, in Groton Bank, the third son of John and Deborah (Youngs) Ledyard. His father, John, had emigrated in 1727 from Bristol, England, to Southold, New York, on Long Island, intending to pursue teaching but instead taking up the law. As an apprentice, John met and married Deborah, the daughter of a prominent Southold judge, and the two moved across Long Island Sound, where they settled in the village of Groton Bank. There he worked his way up in society, becoming a prominent member of the community, serving as a representative in the General Assembly and as magistrate, or justice of the peace, for several terms. He also entered the merchant trade and established a successful merchant house, Ledyard & Company, trading almost exclusively with the West Indies.[3]

Deborah died in 1747, and John remarried a widower, Mary Austin Ellery, from Hartford. The two relocated with some of Ledyard's family to Hartford. There John retained his prominent status and continued his political career, serving as a representative in the General Assembly, an auditor for the colony, and a magistrate for Hartford County. Through these positions, John established relationships with several political leaders of the colony, including four colonial governors, one being Jonathan Trumbull. John died in 1771, but the relationships he had built during his lifetime proved invaluable for his family as the colonies headed to war with Great Britain.[4]

Not much is known about the early life of William, but he was described "as a man of fine form" who had a "good education for the times, [was] unassuming in his manners, possessed great executive ability, and could be depended upon in cases of emergency." Ledyard grew up in the family business, and he and his older brother Ebenezer assumed the duties of his father's merchant house in Groton when he moved to Hartford. These duties not only included running the business but piloting ships, as they traveled between New London and the West Indies.[5]

In 1774, the British Parliament passed the Coercive Acts in response to the Boston Tea Party the previous December. Also known as the Intolerable Acts, the acts stripped Massachusetts of its self-governance and judicial independence and closed the port of Boston. Feeling threatened by the actions of Parliament against a

3 Charles R. Stark, *Groton, Conn. 1705-1904* (Stonington, CT, 1922), 85; James Zug, *American Traveler: The Life and Adventures of John Ledyard, the Man Who Dreams of Walking the World* (New York, 2005), 2–4.

4 Zug, *American Traveler*, 2–4; *CCR*, 8:159, 224, 288, 367, 448, 514, 10:241, 290, 326, 352, 396, 405, 446, 457, 465, 487, 543, 10:286, 321, 334; Stuart, *Life of Trumbull*, 71.

5 Norman H. Burnham, *The Battle of Groton Heights: A Story of the Storming of Fort Griswold, and the Burning of New London, on the Sixth of Sep 1781* (New London, CT, 1903), 32; Zug, *American Traveler*, 2–4.

neighboring colony, a town meeting was convened at Groton in June. The purpose was to bring the community, primarily the merchants and traders, together to form a collective response to the acts. Immediately following the meeting, a proclamation was printed in the *Connecticut Gazette* which stated the meeting was to "[address] the dangerous situation of the British Colonies in North America, respecting the [Coercive Acts] particularly those of shutting up the port of Boston the metropolis of the Province of Massachusetts Bay, and abridging their chartered rights &c." Speaking on behalf of the town, the meeting attendees, including Capt. Ledyard, passed several resolutions.[6]

One resolution gave the town's support to the First Continental Congress in Philadelphia. Another resolution pledged support to boycott British goods traded from Great Britain and the West Indies, and another established a local committee of correspondence. Captain Ledyard served on this committee. Its purpose was to communicate with other like committees that were in other towns and colonies, to exchange information and collectively address their grievances. Additionally, it sought to rally collective opposition to British policy, and Ledyard's appointment openly showcased his support for the patriot cause.[7]

When war broke out in April 1775, Ledyard remained at home until the war came to him that summer. In July, three British warships suddenly appeared, briefly blockading the harbor and foraging on nearby Gardner's Island to help feed the British army, then besieged in Boston. Their appearance caused great consternation, and many feared it to be a precursor of an attack. The alarm was sounded, and the militia was called out.[8]

The effects of the incursion markedly changed Ledyard's feelings about the war. He became increasingly concerned about future British attacks. He also became very frustrated, since no political or military leader seemed equally concerned. Writing to the governor's son a couple of weeks later, Ledyard wrote, "no place lies more exposed than we do." As a result, Ledyard refused to play politics. Without official sanction he went ahead and supervised construction of defensive earthworks on Groton Heights two months before the second committee toured the harbor.[9]

---

6 Stark, *Groton*, 244–246. Ledyard was called a captain before he was commissioned one in the state troops, a rank he earned as a captain of a ship, or its pilot.

7 Ibid. Also serving on the committee were Thomas Mumford, Benadam Gallup, Dr. Amos Prentice, Charles Eldridge Jr., Deacon John Hurlburt, and Amos Gere.

8 Ledyard probably had no prior militia experience, as his profession meant he was exempt from normal militia service.

9 Caulkins, *New London*, 516–517; Ebenezer and William Ledyard to Joseph Trumbull, Aug. 10, 1775, Joseph Trumbull Papers, CHS.

In February 1776, the General Assembly was finally ready to act. Since July 1775, there had been three semi-independent militia companies, one stationed each at New London, Groton, and Stonington. Now they were ready to enlarge the garrison and begin creation of what would become a new military department, or district, encompassing New London, Groton, and Stonington. The Assembly authorized a new state regiment, consisting of four infantry companies under Colonel Erastus Wolcott of East Windsor, Connecticut, to garrison the three towns, to protect the adjacent coastline, and to improve the fortifications.[10]

That spring, Capt. Ledyard traveled to Hartford to serve as a representative for Groton in the General Assembly during its May session. It was only the second time Ledyard had served in this capacity. During the session, he became directly involved in the war effort when he was appointed to a committee established to purchase supplies for the use of the American army in Canada. The Assembly also authorized two matross or artillery companies to be attached to Wolcott's Regiment.[11]

Ledyard received an appointment to captain in the artillery company that was stationed at Fort Griswold, and with this came command of the fort. The assignment had been promised to him the previous February when the new department was established, but he was not officially given his commission until June. He owed his appointment to the citizens of Groton who nominated him, and to his older brother Ebenezer who helped lobby for it. Ebenezer would also serve as the commissary of the fort.[12]

In late June, Ledyard returned to Groton and officially took command of Fort Griswold from Capt. Oliver Coit, whose infantry company had been stationed there. Within a month, three additional infantry companies of Wolcott's Regiment arrived in the harbor area. Two remained in New London, while the third, under Capt. Jonathan Wells, was sent to Fort Griswold. There, Wells's Company fell under Ledyard's direct supervision, and joined Coit's Company in laboring on the fortifications and performing guard duty. Ledyard's Company was recruited throughout the remainder of the year, assisted with various duties, and trained

---

10 *CCR*, 15:238, 242–243. In 1775, Colonel Gurdon Saltonstall led the New London company, Captain Edward Mott led the Groton company, and Major Oliver Smith led the Stonington company.

11 Stark, *Groton*, 86; *CCR*, 15:422, 460, 510, 516.

12 *CCR*, 15:242–244; *Huntington Papers: Correspondence of the Brothers Joshua and Jedediah During the Period of the American Revolution* (Hartford, CT, 1923), 31. Ebenezer Ledyard to Jabez Huntington, Feb. 9, 1776, 31. Originally nominated by Thomas Mumford was 71-year-old Park Avery, as captain, and his son Park Avery Jr. as lieutenant. But this angered many in the community who, according to Ebenezer, considered it a "Party Plan."

with the fort's artillery, which in 1776 was primarily the river battery on the same earthworks begun earlier by Ledyard.[13]

Ledyard adjusted quickly to his new command. Although he had no formal training or experience in military matters, he did know about managing a ship's crew and operating a business, and adapted those peacetime skills to become an effective and well-respected company commander. He was able to remain close to his family, as his home and company office stood near Groton Ferry, only a short walk from the fort.[14]

As winter approached, enlistments for Wolcott's Regiment were set to expire. They had only been authorized to serve until December 1, 1776. As a result, the General Assembly had to reauthorize the units and re-commission the officers. The Assembly convened in mid-December and authorized a new, smaller battalion to replace Wolcott's Regiment for 1777. Because Wolcott was promoted to brigadier general in December, Capt. Wells was elevated to major and given command of the new battalion.[15]

The Assembly envisioned Wells's Battalion as comprising five companies—three infantry and two artillery—led by officers who resided in southeastern Connecticut. This "going local" was the case with most of Wolcott's officer corps. Out of his nine companies, six were led by officers who resided in southeastern Connecticut. Most officers who served in 1776, including Ledyard, were re-appointed, but recruitment for the companies proved to be a challenge, and would remain so in the coming years.[16]

The original intent was to recruit from the local militia companies. In Connecticut, in 1776, militia service was mandatory for all white males between the ages of 16-45, with certain occupational and religious exemptions, to serve in

---

13 *CCR*, 15:463; PA: David Fish (S.13019), NARA. There is no surviving record that indicates how Ledyard was trained in the artillery or how he was supposed to train artillerymen. The only experience he may have had would have been on merchant vessels before the war. According to Fish, the "gunner" played an important role in training and exercising the matrosses in artillery drill. They were also in charge of the cannon in the fort.

14 *CCR*, 15:500; Ebenezer Ledyard to William Williams, Feb. 12, 1778, Williams Family Papers, CHS. The Ledyard house and mercantile business office stood on the site of the present-day Avery Copp House Museum. On the opposite side of Thames Street stood Ledyard's storehouses and wharf.

15 *CSR*, 1:118–120.

16 *CSR*, 1:116–118; *CCR*, 15:128, 243. The Assembly authorized the infantry companies at Groton and New London to be at seventy men, plus a captain, lieutenant, and an ensign. The infantry company at Stonington was to have thirty men headed by a captain and lieutenant. Each artillery company was to consist of fifty men commanded by a captain, two lieutenants, and a lieutenant-fireworker. The Stonington fort had previously been garrisoned by a militia company under Maj. Oliver Smith. In 1776 Smith was replaced by Capt. Nathaniel Palmer, who retained command of the fort and the company in 1777.

Connecticut Militiaman, 1775-1783.

Don Troiani

local trainband (i.e. militia) companies. To increase available manpower, the Assembly, in December 1776, passed a resolution ordering those exempted from regular militia service to form into alarm list companies. It also increased the age limit in these companies to 60. These alarm list companies acted as "reserve militia units" and served primarily during local emergencies.[17]

Men could be temporarily released from their militia companies to serve in a state unit, such as Wells's Battalion. But this soon became impractical. Available manpower was already stretched thin during the latter part of 1776. Most of the militia in southeastern Connecticut and the eastern part of the state, including two of Wolcott's infantry companies, were mobilized in September. They were placed in the militia brigade under Brig. Gen. Gurdon Saltonstall and sent to the Continental army to assist with the protection of New York City.[18]

---

17 *CSR*, 1:92–94. Trainband companies were organized around sections of towns or even ecclesiastical societies. This determined membership in a specific company. Occupations granted exemptions were magistrates, justices of the peace, church officers, physicians, surgeons, schoolmasters, current representatives or deputies, sheriffs, constables, constant ferrymen, constant herdsmen or those seamen, sailors or "mariners who make their constant business to go to Sea." Also, those "lame persons or otherwise disabled." If a person objected to militia service due to religious reasons, they had to either hire a substitute or pay £5.

18 *CCR*, 15: 510, 516. The department saw much fluctuation during the fall of 1776. Wolcott's two immediate subordinates, Lt. Col. Oliver Smith, and Maj. John Ely, were transferred out, as were the infantry companies commanded by Capt. Oliver Coit and Capt. Martin Kirland. Smith took the 8th Regiment of Connecticut Militia, while Ely took the 3rd Regiment of Connecticut Militia, and reported to Saltonstall's Brigade. Captain Wells was elevated to major and took command of the department.

In November, George Washington wrote to Governor Trumbull, asking him for more troops from Connecticut. Obliging Washington, Trumbull pressed the General Assembly to authorize four additional state battalions to serve with the Continental Army until March 1777, which it did. This caused another conundrum with the recruitment of Wells's Battalion. One of these new units, the 4th Connecticut Battalion under Col. John Ely, the former major in Wolcott's Regiment, was recruited in eastern Connecticut and competed with Wells's officers recruiting for their companies.[19]

By mid-December, not enough men had signed up to fill Wells's Battalion. With the expiration of Wolcott's Regiment close at hand, the state was insufficiently prepared to replace them. At the December session, the General Assembly reacted swiftly. The recent British occupation of Newport, Rhode Island, may have influenced the Assembly's hastiness, as it greatly endangered the security of New London.

The Assembly appointed a committee of military officers, including Capt. Ledyard. It asked the committee to appeal to Maj. Wells, who had just assumed command, and the other officers in the regiment to persuade their men to stay another month. Some volunteered and remained on duty for the extra month, temporarily solving the problem.[20]

By mid-December, most of the militia had returned from New York, but desertion and sickness had plagued the ranks during the campaign, and many returned home unprepared for active service. Despite this, the Assembly ordered a draft of the militia and formed them into a battalion under Maj. Dyer Throop, of East Haddam. Throop's Battalion was to garrison and labor on the fortifications for two months to give Wells's companies additional time to recruit. But since Throop's Battalion needed time to be assembled, the 4th Connecticut State Battalion under Col. John Ely, currently enroute to Rhode Island to confront the British, was ordered to New London to temporarily take over for Wolcott's Regiment.[21]

In February 1777, after more than two months of lackluster recruiting, Wells's companies were still not filled, and Throop's men expected to be dismissed. Once

19 *CSR*, 1:69, 255-256. Ely's Battalion began recruitment in November and many of his officers came from either the 3rd or 8th Regiments of Connecticut Militia. In May 1777, Ely led the 2nd Connecticut State Regiment, and again competed with the department for recruits.

20 *CSR*, 1:127. According to several pension depositions, dozens remained with their companies in Wolcott's Regiment for an additional month.

21 Governor Trumbull to Washington, Oct. 21, 1776, Papers of George Washington, LOC; *CSR*, 1:118; Washington to Brigadier General Gurdon Saltonstall, Apr. 28, 1777, Papers of George Washington, LOC; *CSR*, 1:120. Throop's Battalion consisted of militia from the 3rd, 8th, 12th, 20th, and 25th Regiments of Connecticut Militia, many of whom had served in the 1776 New York Campaign.

again, the state was not prepared to replace them. The Council of Safety met in Lebanon in mid-February, to discuss their replacement. The only available troops nearby were Continental recruits being assembled in the eastern part of the state. The Council asked Brig. Gen. Samuel H. Parsons, who was tasked with sending them to the Continental Army at Morristown, New Jersey, to temporarily send part of them to replace Throop's Battalion. Another problem was momentarily solved.[22]

The Council then met with Captain Ledyard and Capt. Nathaniel Palmer, commander of the company in Stonington, to consult with them about the recruitment problem. Though no known records exist of what was discussed or what each officer suggested, the outcome was that Wells's Battalion was disbanded and the Council decided to reduce the regular garrison drastically. Instead of the planned five companies, members decided to recruit only two artillery companies, with a combined strength of just over 100 men, including officers. One artillery company was to be stationed in New London, the other was to be dispersed between Fort Griswold and the fort in Stonington. There would be no regular infantry force assigned to the department. Instead, the Council decided to rely on militia drafts to augment the garrison. This policy continued to be implemented throughout the war, both for the continued protection of the harbor and in times of alarm. Neither the General Assembly nor the Council of Safety would ever again authorize or attempt to raise anything close to what Wells's Battalion was supposed to resemble.[23]

It is unclear if Wells ever commanded the department beyond the winter, but by early summer 1777, possibly even earlier, Captain Ledyard effectively, though unofficially, led the department, as well as the artillery company stationed at Groton and Stonington and was responsible for its day-to-day operations.[24]

Recruitment continued to be an issue. One of Ledyard's first actions to address the problem was to press the political officials to increase the pay offered to potential recruits. After he met with the Council of Safety in February, a new pay table was laid out. And for the first time, the Council prepared to offer recruits a bounty, a significant change from past pay-tables. Ledyard always believed the lack of an attractive bounty hindered recruitment. He often brought it up, even more so when he officially became commandant, pressing for higher bounties each year. He argued that the lack of bounty deterred the "able-bodied men" needed to operate the cannon of the forts from enlisting. Absent a bounty, Ledyard argued,

22 CSR, 1:174–176. The recruits sent included men from the 1st and 4th Connecticut Regiments.

23 Ibid.

24 Ibid.

enlistment was most often attractive only to teenagers, many of whom lacked the strength to properly work the fort's cannon.

Ledyard discussed this problem at length with his brother, Ebenezer. In early 1778, Ebenezer urged William Williams, a member of the Council of Safety and a close advisor of Governor Trumbull, to lobby for the addition of a bounty to the regular monthly payment for the artillery companies, stating, "I dont believe they can enlist any but boys without a bounty, & boys are not fit for cannon—they can't do their duty," Ledyard wrote.[25]

A bounty was a powerful incentive to entice potential recruits. To help recruit for the Continental Army, Congress offered extra monetary amounts and, later, land grants. Prior to 1777, Connecticut offered no bounty to recruits to serve in its state units. But after the meeting with Ledyard, the Council added a small bounty of 20 shillings to any non-commissioned officer or private upon acceptance into the company. In 1778, when Ledyard officially assumed command of the department, the Council increased the bounty to £4 and doubled it the following year. In 1779, another incentive was added, exempting enlistees from the state poll tax.[26]

Unfortunately, even with added incentives, recruitment continued to be problematic. When Ledyard complained to Governor Trumbull that he did not have enough men to post guards around the harbor, Trumbull replied, "Keep out [your] recruiting officers til the two companies are filled. If not to be had near, send a greater distance." Unlike the original aim to recruit locally, efforts to recruit for the two companies stretched throughout eastern Connecticut and by 1781 Ledyard's recruiting officer, Lt. Benjamin Durkee, was traveling to Norwich, Hebron, Mansfield, and even Bolton, over forty miles away, looking for recruits.[27]

Competition in recruitment came not only from the Continental Army and other state units but from the privateer service that operated out of the harbor. It not only snapped up potential recruits, but also enticed existing soldiers away from re-enlisting. Men who served aboard a privateer could make more money from one cruise, which might last only a month, than from serving in an artillery company for an entire year. In mid-1781 Ledyard explained his dilemma to Governor

25 Ebenezer Ledyard to William Williams, Feb. 12, 1778, William Williams Family Papers, CHS.

26 William Ledyard to Governor Trumbull, Apr. 12, 1779, Governor Trumbull Papers, 9:174a–b, CSL; *CSR*, 1:175. If the recruit provided their own "good blanket and knapsack" and/or "sufficient fire-arm and accouterments," they would receive an additional one-time payment of 22 shillings. This latter incentive was probably more to help alleviate a supply issue then it was to encourage more men to enlist. Ledyard reported to Trumbull, "[there] is not the least probability of [the officers] filling up their companies upon the encouragement offered by the Honble General Assembly at their last Session."

27 *CSR*, 2:169, 380; William Ledyard to Governor Jonathan Trumbull, July 3, 1781, Governor Trumbull Papers, 14:322a–c, CSL.

Trumbull, writing that the companies did not fill up because "the great number of Privateers that have been fitted out this season with the great success they have had has taken almost all the men away that would leave home from this quarter."[28]

Though beneficial to the war, privateers sometimes harmed the state's efforts. For example, in early 1780, the privateer service had become so popular that it impeded Connecticut's ability to fill its quota for the Continental Army. The Continental Congress expected the state, in addition to protecting its borders, to fill established quotas to serve in the Continental Army, but this was a difficult balancing act. To address the situation at that time, with the approval of the governor and the Council of Safety, the General Assembly passed an embargo temporarily banning all privateers from sailing out of Connecticut until August.[29]

Command of both the department and an artillery company spread out over thirteen miles proved difficult for Ledyard. There was a never-ending stream of challenges, from recruitment problems to food shortages to the constant presence of the British navy in the Long Island Sound. Yet, Ledyard did his best to prepare the defenses of the harbor. During 1777, he assumed the additional role of engineer—voluntarily, without extra pay—which came with the hefty responsibility of superintending the construction of all the fortifications within the harbor. Ledyard traveled constantly, inspecting the fortifications, and directing the militia. He had little time for his own company. Esquire Philips, who served as his waiter, recalled, "I was backwards and forwards between the Forts with [Ledyard] frequently." According to his brother Ebenezer, Capt. Ledyard was "on duty every day" and "has no time to himself" and was near complete exhaustion by the end of the year.[30]

In early 1778, after performing these duties for the better part of a year, Ledyard expected to be promoted to major at some point within the coming year. This advancement meant an official appointment to department commander, and a pay increase. Ledyard would be able to focus his energy solely on the duties of commandant and not have to deal with the extra responsibilities of a company commander. But this expectation was dashed when, in early February, a dispatch arrived from Hartford instructing Ledyard to enlist and command a new artillery company, again spread out to garrison Fort Griswold and the fort at Stonington

28 William Ledyard to Governor Trumbull, May 27, 1781, Governor Trumbull Papers,14:257a–b, CSL; PA: Joseph Page (R.7866), Stephen Downing (S.29122), NARA. Page and Downing both served at Fort Trumbull, but both had left the company by 1778. Page joined the Continental Navy, while Downing enlisted in the privateer service.

29 *CSR*, 3:13.

30 PA: Esquire Philips (S. 14145), NARA; Ebenezer Ledyard to William Williams, Feb. 12, 1778, William Williams Family Papers, CHS.

Point. It also meant he would have to resume the responsibilities as commandant. This greatly disheartened Ledyard. The news also frustrated many local political and military leaders. Some, including John Deshon, then commissary of New London, advised Ledyard to decline the appointment.[31]

Ledyard wrote to the governor shortly after receiving his orders and officially declined the reappointment to captain. He had good reason. Besides being overworked, his company at Fort Griswold and Stonington suffered from a lack of discipline due to his constant absences. Every time Ledyard was away, "[his] Compy [as well as the officers] took the advantage of his absence and at times behaved very ill," his brother Ebenezer told a friend.[32]

Publicly, Ledyard wanted to retire from public service and return to his mercantile business. Privately, it was the exact opposite. He wanted to serve, but he wanted the promotion. Ledyard hinted this in his letter to Trumbull in which, though declining the commission, he offered advice on how to restructure the department to operate more effectively. Further, William asked Ebenezer to use his political connections to press for his promotion. Ebenezer wrote to William Williams, who served on the Council of Safety. In it, he laid out his brother's frustrations, pressed for his promotion, and brought to light the difficulties within the department, specifically recruitment. Ebenezer urged Williams to show the letter to Judge Richard Law, an assistant to the governor, to Benjamin Payne, a clerk to the speaker of the house in the General Assembly, and to "any other honest man."

He wrote:

> [Capt. Ledyard] is willing to serve to order the work on both sides [of the harbor] & command both forts, but to take charge of a Company & direct the works both as last year he can't. Last year he served as Engineer which made great saving to the public, but [he] thinks he ought to be allowed something extra. While others have been trading and making money he has served the public in many departments. But others that do very little are as much noticed as him & when any field officer of the militia comes in here they are over him. Yet they are obliged to go to him to set their men to work & he directs the whole. So he does the work & they have the credit—but if he is not put over both forts without taking a company—I believe he wont serve.[33]

---

31 Ebenezer Ledyard to William Williams, Feb. 12, 1778, William Williams Family Papers, CHS. Ledyard did not participate in his business throughout the war and relied solely on his military pay to provide for himself and his family.

32 *CSR*, 2:520; Ebenezer Ledyard to William Williams, Feb. 12, 1778, William Williams Family Papers, CHS. Ledyard would have lobbied himself, but he thought it improper.

33 Ebenezer Ledyard to William Williams, Feb. 12, 1778, William Williams Family Papers, CHS.

These efforts succeeded. Within a month, Ledyard received a promotion to major and was ordered to assume command of the department, a position he held for the next three years. The position included the command of the forts, the artillery companies, and any militia within the department; it also authorized Ledyard to distribute the military stores, such as gunpowder, ammunition, and other foodstuffs, to the companies, and he continued to oversee the construction of the forts.[34]

In 1779, the regular garrison of the department was enlarged to three artillery companies on Ledyard's advice. It was difficult for a commander to direct the day-to-day operations of Fort Griswold and the Stonington fort, which was more than ten miles distant. Ledyard understood this best. After some deliberation, the General Assembly authorized a third artillery company, which would be stationed at Stonington. The company, led by a lieutenant, was smaller than those at New London and Groton, but it allowed a more centralized command at each fort.[35]

Life in the Garrison

Daily life in the garrison was anything but monotonous. Activity was constant. The companies performed three everyday tasks in the forts: drill, guard duty, and fatigue duty. The latter two were shared when one or more drafted militia companies were present.

Each day had a set routine, which began at sunrise. The company was roused from the barracks onto the parade ground for morning roll call. There the orderly sergeant called off the names of men in the company, ensuring all members were either present or accounted for. Days ended with evening roll calls. After the morning roll call, duties for the day were assigned. The responsibilities were spelled out in the company orderly book kept by the first sergeant, sometimes called the orderly sergeant. Some would find themselves on guard or sentry duty. Those selected were paraded and then marched out to relieve the night guards. Depending on available manpower, guards were posted at several points around the fort, town, and along the coastline. Sometimes, it could mean being temporarily assigned to one of the garrison's whaleboats. They would patrol the harbor or out in Long Island Sound to counter illicit traders or, at times, sail out to reconnoiter suspicious activity on one of the small islands in the Sound.[36]

---

34 *CSR*, 1:574; Each company in New London and Groton was supposed to include fifty men, which included the officers, led by a captain. The company stationed at Stonington was designed to be much smaller, consisting of twenty-two men, commanded by a lieutenant.

35 *CSR*, 2:181–182.

36 PA: John Harris (S.10787), NARA.

If they were not assigned to guard duty, they could spend time drilling in the fort. Being a garrison unit, members of an artillery company were responsible for handling both muskets and cannon and maintaining their readiness in case of an attack. Working with artillery could be a dangerous task and required specialized training and skills. Yet these were not commonly taught to the militia, where most of the recruits originated.

To operate, the typical cannon in the fort would require, at the minimum, a five-man crew. Each of the five performed a specific job, which had to be practiced to ensure safety and efficiency. Each crew was under the direction of a non-commissioned officer. The other four crew members were stationed with the cannon to handle, load, and move it whenever required. A sixth member, who could serve more than one gun, sometimes referred to as a "powder monkey," was employed bringing up cartridges from the magazine and handing them to the crew.[37]

Additionally, each matross (the period rank in an artillery company equivalent to that of a private in an infantry company) was expected to know how to handle, load, and fire a musket properly. Fort Griswold was supplied with several "French Musquets." These muskets were probably the Model 1766 French "Charleville" musket, a .69 caliber muzzle-loaded firearm which, in 1777, was widely distributed to Continental and state units serving in the Eastern Department.[38]

Musket drill was more familiar to the soldiers as they would have done this with their militia companies. Still, they had to be drilled constantly to ensure they were familiar with basic marching formations, proper ways of performing guard duty, and handling, loading, and firing their weapons.[39]

37 PA: David Fish (S.13019), NARA. Fish served in Latham's Company as a "quarter gunner" between 1779 and 1780 and provided many specific details of his role at the fort in his pension application. His job was to carry the priming wire and the powder horn, which contained the gunpowder used to prime the gun. His duty required him to prick the cartridge with the priming wire and apply the matchstick to fire the piece.

38 Mackenzie, *Diary*, 2:628; James L. Kochan and Don Troiani, *Don Troiani's Soldiers of the American Revolution* (Mechanicsburg, PA, 2007), 167; Eric Schnitzer and Don Troiani, *Don Troiani's Campaign to Saratoga-1777: The Turning Point of the Revolutionary War in Paintings, Artifacts, and Historical Narrative* (Mechanicsburg, 2019), 38. The Eastern Department was a regional department within the Continental Army, headquartered in Boston. It was essentially the "New England Department," and included the states of Connecticut, Massachusetts, New Hampshire, and Rhode Island.

39 For infantry drill, the companies probably utilized either *The Manual Exercise, As Ordered by His Majesty, In the year 1764: Together with Plans and Explanations of the Method Generally Practis'd at Reviews and Field-Days, &c; or the 1778 Regulations for the Order of Discipline of Troops of the United States*, or another militia manual.

More Responsibilities

In 1779, Ledyard received more duties from the General Assembly. At its spring session assemblymen passed an act, with the governor's approval, which appointed Ledyard as a Commissary of Naval Prisoners. The act directed him to receive and care for all enemy naval prisoners brought into Connecticut by any naval vessel, including privateers belonging to or employed by the state. Many of these prisoners were housed in jails in either New London, Norwich, or Windham. The Assembly also charged Ledyard with negotiating and exchanging prisoners serving from Connecticut and held by the British, a duty formerly held by Nathaniel Shaw Jr.[40]

By 1780, illicit trade between Connecticut and British-occupied Long Island had become a serious problem. Because of these "ill minded people," acts were passed by the General Assembly in 1778 and strengthened in 1779 and 1780 to combat black market trading. The acts imposed strict regulations, requiring a trader or traders to obtain a license signed off by civil authorities before he could transport his goods. Additionally, the acts levied tough penalties if the person (or persons) was caught without a license. However, these penalties—which included a hefty fine, impressment into a military or naval unit without pay, or sometimes imprisonment—did not outweigh the financial benefits of smuggling, so the trade continued.[41]

By March 1780, the governor and Council of Safety empowered Major Ledyard to board and search, at his discretion, any vessel in New London Harbor that might be intending to trade with the enemy and prohibit them from traveling. By October, Ledyard's permission was needed before any vessel sailed into or out of the harbor, whether for trade or travel. Also, by this time, the harbor's defensive line had been extended into the Sound. Accordingly, Ledyard was authorized to recruit nine additional men into his garrison and use them to cruise the Sound in

---

40 *CSR*, 1:536, 2:287–288. During the Revolutionary War, prisoners taken by both sides were divided into two categories, those taken on the land and those taken on the sea. For the Americans, this was further broken down into which state the prisoners hailed from. Ledyard was primarily responsible, as his position stated, for naval prisoners or those taken on the sea, from Connecticut. Once prisoners were taken into New London, Ledyard was responsible not only for guarding them, but also housing, caring, and feeding them. In this position, Ledyard often communicated with his British counterpart, David Sproat in New York, to negotiate prisoner exchanges. When one was made, Ledyard hired a captain and vessel to transport British prisoners from New London to New York. This was referred to as "sending a flag."

41 *CSR*, 1:528, 2:222–223, 270, 3:15–17.

armed whaleboats "to prevent the ravages of the enemy and their cruizers and . . . illicit trade upon the coast."[42]

The following February, Ledyard, now a lieutenant colonel, received word of his reappointment to commandant. But with it came even more responsibilities. Colonel William Worthington, of Saybrook, commander of seven coast guard companies covering the coastline from Branford eastwards to New London, came under investigation for illicit trading. While the investigation was being conducted, the seven companies, and accompanying coastal surveillance, were given to Ledyard, whose responsibilities now stretched from Branford to Stonington, a coastline of over fifty miles.[43]

Though the responsibility must have been overwhelming, Ledyard never complained publicly. The coast guard companies were allowed to remain primarily independent as Ledyard's focus continued to be the safety of New London Harbor. By the spring of 1781, "Esquire Ledyard"—as he came to be called by the men— was served by an able staff. [44]

Jordan Freeman, a former slave belonging to the Ledyard family, served as the lieutenant colonel's waiter or orderly. First Lieutenant Enoch Stanton, nominally assigned to the artillery company at Fort Griswold, served as Ledyard's adjutant. In this role, Stanton assisted Ledyard with the administrative tasks of the department, such as conducting all official correspondence, maintaining official records, and publishing all orders.[45]

Ledyard maintained two officers as Assistant Commissary of Issues, one stationed at each town, with the responsibility to procure supplies for the artillery companies and any militia stationed there. At New London he had Guy Richards Jr., and at Groton his brother Ebenezer Ledyard. The post of Deputy Quartermaster General was occupied by John Holt Jr. and as a recruiting officer for the companies,

---

42 *CSR*, 2:384, 512, 3:180, 289, 292, 298. The General Assembly also ordered the garrisons of the forts at Milford and New Haven to take the same action against illicit trade. The Assembly had already provided Ledyard with a whale boat in 1779, and in Oct. 1780 approved the purchase of another.

43 *CSR*, 3:92–93, 317–319; Richard Buel Jr; *Dear Liberty: Connecticut's Mobilization for the Revolutionary War* (Middletown, CT, 1980), 269–271. In 1779, the General Assembly ordered the 8th Regiment to be split in two, to establish a new regiment, the 27th Regiment of Connecticut Militia. The regiment was comprised of the companies in Preston, North Groton, and North Stonington. The 8th Regiment's lieutenant colonel, Nathan Gallup, was elevated to colonel in the new unit. Ledyard was commissioned as lieutenant colonel to fill the vacancy in the 8th Regiment. Within a year the 27th was merged back into the 8th Regiment. Nathan Gallup returned to his old rank of lieutenant colonel in the 8th and Ledyard kept the rank (though not the office) of lieutenant colonel.

44 Ledyard utilized at least two buildings as his headquarters. In Groton, it was his home, while in New London he utilized an office owned by Marvin Wait on the Parade.

45 In the 18th century military, a waiter acted as an officer's personal assistant or valet.

Lt. Benjamin Durkee. As Barrack-Master, Lt. Green Plumb was responsible for finding quarters for the troops within the post. From 1780, Ledyard had access to the Continental Hospital which had been established at Gales Ferry in Groton. There he enjoyed the services of Dr. Philemon Tracy as Surgeons-Mate and Dr. John Turner as Ward-Master. Ledyard's staff remained without an engineer.[46]

In command of the artillery companies, Ledyard had two capable officers: Capt. William Latham, at Fort Griswold and Capt. Adam Shapley at Fort Trumbull. Described as "a very able young officer," Latham, like Ledyard, was a lifelong resident of Groton Bank. Born there in 1740, he was the son of Deacon Jonathan and Mary (Avery) Latham. He resided a half-mile south of the fort with his wife, Eunice (Forsyth), and their children. He had been active in the military since 1775, and by 1781 was arguably Ledyard's most experienced company commander.[47]

In 1775 Latham had served as an ensign in the 6th Connecticut Regiment, a state regiment raised to protect New London. However, in June, after a brief stay at Winthrop's Neck, the regiment, including Latham, marched to Massachusetts and took part in the Siege of Boston.[48] Latham returned home when his enlistment expired and accepted a commission as a second lieutenant in Capt. Samuel Mott's Company in Wolcott's Regiment, stationed at Fort Griswold. When Mott was promoted the following July, Lt. Oliver Coit assumed command. As Coit rose in rank, so did all his company officers, including Latham, who advanced to first lieutenant. Only a month later, another reorganization occurred.

When Coit's Company was ordered to New York, Lieutenant Latham did not go, but was instead promoted to captain-lieutenant and transferred to Ledyard's Company. The following year, Latham was supposed to serve in Wells's Battalion, but after the unit was disbanded, Latham was commissioned a first lieutenant in Ledyard's Company. Whenever Ledyard was away, Latham became the de facto commander of Fort Griswold. In September 1777, an artillery detachment from the department was sent to assist in the retaking of Newport and Latham was placed in command. But it saw no action and returned to New London.[49]

---

46 *CSR*, 3:116. The role of paymaster fell to each company commander. Ledyard had a third commissary, Nathaniel Miner, at Stonington with Sheffield's Company.

47 *Huntington Papers*, Ebenezer Ledyard to Jabez Huntington, Feb. 9, 1776, 31. The couple had at least five children in 1776 and seven or eight by 1781.

48 *Connecticut Men*, 78; Harris, *Groton Heights*, 257–258. According to Harris, Latham served with the American artillery at Dorchester Heights during the latter part of the Siege of Boston, but he does not cite the source of this information.

49 *Connecticut Men*, 78; *CCR*, 15:245, 463, 475; *CSR*, 1:118, 401; PA: Jonathan Waterhouse (S.18258), NARA.

When Ledyard was promoted to major, Latham was made a captain and given command of Fort Griswold. Like Ledyard before him, Latham encountered many challenges, including recruitment and morale. One of the worst challenges occurred during the winter of 1780–1781 when the department suffered a food shortage. According to John Harris, a 14-year-old member of the company who served as cook to the officers, the men were kept on half rations for several months. There was often no bread to eat. Instead, they were fed a substitute called "old sea bread" but it was often "full of worms & hardly fit for dogs to eat." As a result, members of Latham's Company met outside the fort and planned to mutiny over it, with some advocating desertion. Harris does not specify the date of the actual mutiny, but it occurred sometime during that winter. The mutinous soldiers demanded full rations, threatening not to go on sentry duty without them. The officer of the guard called on Lt. Enoch Stanton, who in turn ordered Harris to go fetch Captain Latham. According to Harris, when Latham entered the fort, he "ran out in a passion, with his hat off," knocked over one of the mutinous members, and "kicked [him] once or several times."[50]

When Ledyard learned of the quarrel, he wrote to the Council of Safety for assistance. Realizing the food shortage's impact on the effectiveness and readiness of his companies, Ledyard asked for permission to send part of his garrison home on furlough. The Council granted the request, fully knowing it was impracticable to supply the garrison. However, it advised Ledyard to retain enough men to do guard duty.[51]

On the other side of the Thames, Ledyard entrusted Captain Shapley with the command of the artillery company at Fort Trumbull. Shapley, only a few months older than Ledyard, was born in New London like several generations of his family before him. Like Ledyard, he made his living in the mercantile trade. He resided in a two-story home on Meetinghouse Hill in the northern part of town with his wife Mary, the daughter of magistrate Joseph Harris Jr., who was also lieutenant colonel of the 3rd Regiment of Connecticut Militia. The couple had one son, Daniel. By 1781, the elder Shapley had served as an officer in the militia for over fifteen years.[52]

Captain Shapley's military service in the current conflict had begun in the spring of 1776 when he served as first lieutenant under Colonel Saltonstall, whose company constructed the fort at Winthrop's Neck. When Saltonstall was made

---

50 PA: John Harris (S.10787), NARA.

51 *CSR*, 3:288.

52 *CG*, Nov. 17, 1781; *CCR*, 13:176. Shapley first earned his commission as ensign in mid-1769. He lived near his mother on Shapley Street. He also had a shop at the intersection of Shapley and Town Streets.

a brigadier general and sent with his militia brigade to New York, Shapley was elevated to captain and given command of the company for the duration of the year. In 1777 he expected to command an infantry company in Wells's Battalion, but it was dissolved, so he returned to his militia company until the following year when a vacancy as captain opened in the artillery company stationed in New London.[53]

The Threat Emerges

When David Gray entered the harbor, he was stopped by a sentry at Fort Trumbull, whose station acted as a checkpoint stopping all vessels entering the harbor. The sentry then brought Gray to Lt. Jabez Stow Jr. who was overseeing the company and the fort that night.[54]

Stow escorted Gray to Ledyard's headquarters across the river, where they arrived shortly after midnight. After waking Ledyard, Gray told him that a British force under Arnold "would soon pay him a visit if the wind was favorable the next morning." Ledyard took the news seriously but did not, at least initially, react decisively.[55]

Having served as commandant for the previous three years, Ledyard had to exercise caution before making major decisions, especially when sounding the alarm. For six years, the harbor area had grown accustomed to imminent warnings of an attack. Any time the British were spotted near the entrance of the harbor, even briefly, a landing was expected, and so the alarm was sounded.

Samuel Yeomans, of Stonington, had answered at least twenty-five of these alarms between early 1776 and September 1781. In his pension application, he meticulously listed each alarm he answered, when it happened and how long he was away from home. It provides one of the most detailed accounts known to survive, noting that alarms were usually raised between June and September. However, a few occurred in May and October and one in November. Ephraim

---

53 *CSR*, 1:118, 15:463.

54 "Lieutenant John Hempsted's Orderly Book," Council of Safety Papers, CHS. To cut back on illicit trade or enemy night attack, Fort Trumbull was designated as a check point. All friendly vessels during the daytime were supposed to approach the fort, using predesignated signal flags to communicate with the guard. A "ship" was supposed to raise a red flag, a snow or brig a "white flag," and a schooner a "blue pendant." If the vessels did not follow the rules, they risked either being fined or fired upon. If fired upon, they were responsible for reimbursing the state for the gunpowder used.

55 PA: David Gray (S.38776), NARA; *Connecticut Men*, 129, 272. Gray must have been escorted into a separate private room to meet with Ledyard. The family had recently celebrated both the marriage of Ledyard's oldest daughter Mary to Thomas Y. Seymour, a former captain in the 2nd Continental Light Dragoons, and the birth of the colonel's youngest son Charles born on August 27, and several members of the family were visiting.

Willey, of East Haddam, could sympathize with Yeomans. Willey claimed his militia company made the eighteen-mile trek to New London twenty times between 1776 and 1780.[56]

The sounding of an alarm constituted a major undertaking. Every time the alarm was sounded, militia members were obligated to leave what they were doing at home, shoulder their muskets, pack their equipment, gather with other members of their company, and march towards the coastline. They were typically away for at least a week, sometimes for multiple weeks. This made it difficult for them to provide for their families, especially during planting or harvest months.[57]

Each time no attack came, the calling up of the militia became less effective, and by 1781, readiness began to ebb. The cannon within the harbor, which were fired to signal the alarm, had been sounded so frequently and for so many different occasions that, as the Connecticut Gazette, reported, such discharges increasingly "answered little or no purpose."[58]

In addition to using cannon to call out the militia, Ledyard sent out post riders to alert individual commanders and move the militia along. However, this was a less effective time-consuming task, since post riders were limited; they had to travel overland by road and make individual stops, as opposed to the echo of the cannon fire, which could be heard over a greater distance in a shorter amount of time.

We can imagine how all these thoughts might have played out in Ledyard's mind as he listened to the information on Arnold's coming invasion. Ledyard faced a serious dilemma. Should he raise the alarm? Should he wake the town in the middle of the night, possibly causing panic? Or should he wait until he could see the threat before preparing the town, the militia, and his companies, for action? But if the British did attack in the morning, would the militia be able to reach the harbor in a timely manner?

---

56 PA: Ephraim Willey (R.11559), NARA.

57 Harris, *Groton Heights*, 123; "To Colonel McClellen, Commandant at the Posts of New London & Groton," Revolutionary War Records, Series I, Vol. XXII: 337, CSL. A petition was sent by local inhabitants in reply to the false alarms and the effects of being called into service during these months. It read in part, "the consequences had always been that great numbers of melitia are called from their labours & sent upon [the town], on so short a notice yet it was impossible for them to be compleatly equipped; and have been detained . . . greatly to their private loss."

58 *CG*, Sep. 7, 1781; Rufus Avery narrative in Harris, *Groton Heights*, 30; PA: John Harris (S.10787), NARA. According to a soldier in Groton, it was "customary, when there was a good prize brought into the harbor [by a privateer] or on the receipt of any good news, to rejoice by discharging cannon." On special occasions, such as the anniversary of the signing of the Declaration of Independence or the announcement of Burgoyne's surrender at Saratoga, the garrisons of Forts Griswold and Trumbull fired a total of thirteen cannon in honor of the thirteen states. Arrivals of notable dignitaries, such as a French general in 1780, also warranted cannon firing.

There is no surviving record of how Ledyard initially reacted to Gray's news, but his actions show that he yielded to caution. He chose to wait for the threat to become visible. In hindsight, it proved to be a tragic decision. However, it was not a decision born out of incompetence. Ledyard understood the situation of his post, and he was not one to ignore the threat of a British attack. He had addressed past rumors of attacks with quick, bold action. Because of this the governor and Council of Safety gave him the authority to call out entire militia regiments to come to his aid.

Instead, the decision was likely due to his reliance on reports from other militia leaders and his coast guard companies along the coast. He had not received reports from them about a British squadron, so he simply possessed no intelligence by which to corroborate Gray's information.

Ironically, on September 4 and 5 Governor Trumbull met with the Council of Safety and several high-ranking militia generals in Hartford. For two days, they discussed several intelligence reports gathered by various sources, including George Washington, that had been sent to them. These "various Accounts of the Movements and Designs of the Enemy" strongly suggested the British were about to launch a "hostile Attack upon or Invasion of [the] State." On the same day Gray arrived at Ledyard's headquarters, the governor and his generals agreed to conduct a review of the state's militia. Additionally, orders were already being sent out, with more forthcoming, to send detachments of militia to reinforce the coastline. If this intelligence had reached Ledyard, he might have acted more aggressively, but from surviving records it appears this information never reached him.[59]

One thing Ledyard could have done, but for reasons unclear chose not to do, was to send out precautionary orders to the two forts. No one except Lieutenant Stow knew of any possible threat. Neither Shapley nor Latham were at their respective forts that night. Neither commander appeared to be on the alert for anything out of the ordinary; they were at home, having left their posts in the hands of subordinate officers. They did not return to the forts until after the British were sighted.[60]

Even Ledyard did not seem to be on alert. He made no defensive preparations for the morning. The sentries were not notified or reinforced. The men from

---

59 Governor Trumbull to George Washington, Sep. 13, 1781, Papers of George Washington, LOC; *CSR*, 3:500–502.

60 PA: Gilbert Denison (S.15805), NARA. Neither captain appears to have resided at the forts, instead choosing to remain at their homes at night. Lieutenant Stanton was the highest-ranking officer who lived in the barracks at Fort Griswold.

Latham and Shapley's Companies who had been detached on foraging parties or were on furlough were not recalled.[61]

Besides his two artillery companies, Ledyard had two drafted militia companies attached to his command. One, under Capt. Peleg Noyes, was stationed with the artillery company under Lt. Acors Sheffield at the fort at Stonington Point. Noyes did not receive orders to move and remained at Stonington. Ledyard's other company, commanded by Capt. Griswold Avery, was much nearer. Having been on duty since July, some of Avery's Company was quartered at Fort Nonsense and operated out of there. The rest were spread out at various points along the coast in Great Neck, one being at Goshen Point. The 42-year-old Avery, a farmer, was commissioned as captain in 1777 and served as commander of the 7th Company Alarm List, 3rd Regiment of Connecticut Militia and had only served locally. This was his third tour in New London.[62]

Captain Avery was not on duty either, billeting at the James Thompson house in the center of town. Earlier, Avery had dispatched a picket guard to the lighthouse, four miles south of town. One sentry claimed they had been sent out because of a "rumor [that] prevailed that the enemy were coming from Gardiner's Bay that night." It is unlikely this was the sole reason because the information about Arnold's force did not arrive until much later. The lighthouse, built two decades earlier in an area known as "Harbour's Mouth," was a "picquet post," or a place where the militia was posted to look out for the enemy or to interdict illicit trade. Over the past four years, militia companies stationed at New London had rotated duty daily at the lighthouse and on the nearby Sarah Harris farm.[63]

That night, 11-year-old Benjamin Brown, whose father, Benjamin Sr, was a sergeant in Avery's Company, volunteered and shouldered "his fowling piece all night long [patrolling] with his older companions" along the river's edge. At least that's what Brown claimed eighty-five years later, at the age of ninety-six. He said he answered, "a call [that] was made for volunteers for a night patrol watch." So

61 PA: John Jones (S.31781), NARA. Jones, a member of Shapley's Company was home at Saybrook on furlough that night. See Appendix B for other furloughed soldiers.

62 PA: Griswold Avery Jr. (R.306), NARA; "From Waterford," *Mystic Pioneer*, Oct. 17, 1863. The elder Avery's commission does not survive, but he was the only captain of the company from 1777–1783. The 7th Alarm List Company was comprised of members from the districts of the 7th and 11th "trainband companies."

63 PA: Griswold Avery Jr. (R.306), NARA; Charles Allyn Papers, NLCHS; Caulkins, *New London*, 474; PA: Christopher Patton (S.8662), NARA; Revolutionary Rolls, Connecticut, Various Organizations, 264, LOC. This orderly book, which may have belonged to Capt. Elijah Avery's Company when stationed in the harbor in late 1777 shows how each of the different militia guards were broken down, between guard and fatigue duty and how they rotated duties. Sarah (Dyer) Harris was the widow of Thomas Harris, who died in 1778. The farm was operated by Sarah and her sons.

New London Harbor Lighthouse. The present-day lighthouse was built in 1801
on the site of the eighteenth-century lighthouse. *Author*

many years removed from the action, Brown's claim might be treated with some
skepticism but for the pension narrative of Griswold Avery Jr. written many years
earlier. Avery volunteered in his father's militia company and served as his waiter. In
his pension application, he claimed that on that same night, he was with Brown.[64]

After the meeting with Ledyard, Gray remained in Groton for the night at the
Ledyard house. Lieutenant Stow returned to Fort Trumbull. In a few hours, the sun
would rise and light up the horizon, revealing that the British had indeed arrived.

64 PA: Griswold Avery Jr. (R.306), NARA; "From Waterford," *Mystic Pioneer*, Oct. 24, 1863;
Charles Allyn Papers, NLCHS. Sergeant Brown was probably the sergeant of the guard, and in charge
of the patrol at the lighthouse.

Chapter Four

Another Alarm

Thursday, September 6, 1781, proved to be the most eventful day in Rufus Avery's entire military service. Perhaps his whole life. The night before, the 23-year-old orderly sergeant expected nothing more than another monotonous night of sentry duty, as he and the other sentries from Latham's Company walked their posts around Fort Griswold under the light of a bright moon.[1]

Avery recalled, "I had charge of the garrison the night before the enemy appeared anywhere near us or were expected by any one at that time to trouble." Already in his fifth year of wartime service, the native of Groton had been a member of Latham's Company since late 1780. He had been promoted to orderly sergeant a month earlier. Before his enlistment at Fort Griswold, he served in several locally organized militia companies. First, in the summer of 1776, he was drafted into a company assigned to the 4th Battalion, Wadsworth's Brigade. After the British landing at Kip's Bay, a rout of the Americans ensued and the 4th Battalion was caught up in the retreat, suffering many casualties and many others taken prisoner.

---

1 Revolutionary Rolls, Connecticut, Various Organizations, 264, LOC; PA: Edward Yeomans (W.11902), NARA. Avery was "sergeant of the guard," the senior non-commissioned officer in charge of the fort and sentries that night. When numbers allowed, on a typical day or night, a non-commissioned officer, such as a sergeant or corporal, with five other sentries, privates or matrosses, patrolled the grounds of the fort, the ramparts of the main fort and the river battery. This was called the "quarter guard." If more men were available, a second patrol called the "piquet guard," same makeup, was sent to Groton Point. There is no evidence that was the case at this time. It is more likely that with Latham's Company understrength, only two or three members stood sentry that night. "Letter extract from lieutenant."

Avery evaded capture and served out his term. Returning home, starting in 1777 and continuing for the next three years, Avery rotated through different militia companies raised to help augment New London Harbor defenses before he joined Latham's Company.[2]

As the first streaks of sunlight appeared over the horizon, Avery's dull expectations suddenly changed. The daylight revealed several British naval vessels at the entrance of the harbor. Avery remembered that at "about three o'clock in the morning . . . as soon as I had daylight so as to see the fleet, it appeared a short distance below the lighthouse." Stunned at the sight, he stared out towards the Sound and counted what he remembered to be "thirty-two vessels in number—ships, brigs, schooners, and sloops."[3]

From off Southold, the British squadron had weighed anchor at about 7:00 p.m. and stood for New London Harbor with a fair wind. Sailing northward for "about 10 leagues," they arrived, according to Arnold, "at 1 o'Clock the next morning . . . off the harbour, when the wind suddenly shifted to the Northward." He did not anticipate these wind conditions as he wanted to make a night landing to catch the garrison off guard, thereby delaying the appearance of the militia. The shift of the wind caused a lull that effectively eliminated the element of surprise. Bazely reported that "an unfortunate change of wind took place directly out of the harbour, which prevented my anchoring till ½ past 6." They were able to move toward the shore, but when the wind changed direction, they could not anchor their vessels but instead had to wait for favorable conditions, which took another four hours.[4]

After spotting the British squadron, Avery sent another sentry to rouse Captain Latham. Hearing the commotion outside, the enlisted men of the company quartered in the barracks building, started to come out onto the parade ground to investigate the noises. They climbed onto the ramparts to see the British

---

2 Rufus Avery narrative in Harris, *Groton Heights*, 29; PA: Rufus Avery (S.12939), Nehemiah Gallup (S.13110), NARA. Gallup was orderly sergeant before Avery and had been discharged in August. Gallup kept the company orderly book along with other papers in a trunk in the barracks with his brother Andrew when he was discharged. It was destroyed during the battle.

3 Rufus Avery narrative in Harris, *Groton Heights*, 29–30; Master's Log, HMS *Amphion*, ADM 52/2133, TNA. The *Amphion* reported being spotted about 3:30 a.m. The number of vessels was a little lower than Avery remembered years later, probably around 25.

4 Arnold report in Mackenzie, *Diary*, 2:623; Master's Log, HMS *Recovery*, ADM 52/2491, TNA; "Extract of a letter from Capt. John Forbes, an officer of the 40th regiment to a friend in Aberdeen, dated New York Sep. 20, 1781," CM, Nov. 14, 1781; "Extract from Capt. Bazely's Letter, dated *Amphion*, off New London, Sep. 8, 1781," *Saunders's News-Letter*, Nov. 13, 1781. According to Forbes, Arnold planned to land the 40th Regiment in Groton at night to take possession of Fort Griswold before the alarm could be sounded. Forbes believed this would have allowed the squadron to sail into New London Harbor and unload the other troops without opposition.

New London Harbor. A present-day view of the harbor from the southwest bastion of Fort Griswold.

Tad Sattler

squadron hovering over the entrance to the harbor. The excitement was heightened as Latham appeared a few minutes later. With Latham was his 10-year-old son, William Jr. and Lambert, the family slave. Latham climbed up onto the platform and viewed the British squadron himself. Seeing it, Latham sent a courier to notify Lieutenant Colonel Ledyard.[5]

Ledyard arrived a short time later, entering through the north gate, accompanied by David Gray and his aide, Jordan Freeman. Ledyard was greeted by his men as he walked across the parade ground and up onto the platform and joined Latham and his junior officers. Armed with a spyglass Ledyard looked south, scanned the entrance to the harbor, and saw the British vessels. He then scanned over to Fort Trumbull. They were signaling that they also saw the threat.

Matross Holsey Sanford, of Shapley's Company, was also on sentry duty that night. Walking the platform of Fort Trumbull at the same time as Sergeant Avery, Sanford saw the British squadron. Writing years later he recalled, "As daylight began to draw I espied a sail at the mouth of the river. I directly notified the Sergeant of the Guard—by the name of [Jeremiah] Harding." When Sergeant

5 Rufus Avery narrative in Harris, *Groton Heights*, 30; Harry Clinton Green and Mary Wolcott Green, *The Pioneer Mothers of America: A Record of the More Notable Women of the Early Days of the Country, and Particularly the Colonial and Revolutionary Periods*, 3 vols. (New York, 1912), 419–423. Latham's son's age is incorrect on the "Defenders of the Fort Griswold" memorial plaque. Vital records place his birth on Aug. 18, 1771.

South Wall of Fort Trumbull. It was from this location that the British squadron was sighted at the entrance of the harbor and fired upon by Shapley's Company. *Author*

Harding arrived at Sanford's post and saw the enemy, he sent word to Lt. Jabez Stow Jr., the only officer present. When he saw the British, he ordered the signal flags run up on the fort's flagpole, alerting Fort Griswold of the impending threat. Then, without Shapley or Ledyard present, they were forced to wait.[6]

Lieutenant Stow did not have to wait long. Ledyard was at Fort Griswold at that very moment, watching the British vessels. Once he saw the signal flags at Fort Trumbull, Ledyard pulled the spyglass away from his face, turned around, and ordered Latham to sound the alarm and prepare his company for action. The company, numbering only 21 that morning, sprang into action. The fort's Continental colors—a large, distinct flag consisting of thirteen alternating horizontal stripes of red, white, and blue—was attached to the halyard and run up the flagpole.[7]

6 Holsey Sanford, "Memoir of Holsey Sanford," Geni, Accessed Jan. 9, 2017, https://www.geni.com/people/Holsey-Sanford/6000000017267970162. The original copy of Sanford's memoir was believed to have been kept at the Huntington Historical Society in Huntington, Massachusetts, but according to Society officials has since been lost. It matches closely to his deposition in his pension application. Fortunately, a copy of it was added online by a descendant before the original was lost.

7 "Lieutenant John Hempsted Orderly Book," Council of Safety Papers, CHS; Map, Fort Griswold (unknown, 1781), LOC; William Ledyard to Governor Trumbull, July 3, 1781, Governor Trumbull

Garrison Colors. Known as the "Continental Navy Jack," this was the main garrison flag used by both Fort Griswold and Fort Trumbull during the Revolutionary War. *Author*

Lieutenant Obadiah Perkins, followed by Gray and other members of Latham's Company, went down to the parade ground and with key in hand Perkins unlocked and opened the powder magazine. The structure housed the garrison's supply of gunpowder, ammunition, and firearms. Once opened, Perkins could hand gunpowder charges to the runner or "powder monkey," who could then run up to the gun crews preparing to fire the alarm guns.[8]

Alarm guns were fired to alert the militia and call it out to assemble at designated alarm posts in New London and Groton. Two guns, presumably 12-pounders, one in the northeast part of the fort under Captain Latham, the other in the northwest bastion under Sergeant Avery, were prepared for action. "Heavy charges of good [black] powder" were loaded into each gun. The two crews then coordinated firing each gun every five minutes "so as to give a 'larum' to the country in the best possible manner." This was the predesignated signal for the militia to come to the aid of the forts.[9]

Once Stow saw the colors raised at Fort Griswold, he knew he had to prepare for action. He sent a runner to have Captain Shapley and Lt. Richard Chapman, his superiors, come to the fort. Until they did, he retained command and had a matross run up the fort's colors, the same one flown at Fort Griswold. If the company was not yet awakened, they were ordered up now. Like the other artillery company, Shapley's Company was also badly understrength. That morning, they only numbered 24 men, and half of them were borrowed from Fort Fenwick in

---

Papers, XIV:322a–c; CSL; PA: Humphrey Brown (W.18648), John Harris (S.10787), NARA. Both Fort Griswold and Fort Trumbull were provided with a large garrison flag made of "wool-bunting," along with other smaller signal colors, which were used for a variety of purposes. The only visual description of them is found in a sketch of Fort Griswold, in possession of the Library of Congress, supposedly drawn in 1781. The flag closely resembled the early Continental naval flag, sometimes referred to as the "rebel stripes," which flew over other forts such as Fort Stanwix (Schulyer) in New York and Fort Mifflin in Philadelphia. The universally recognized flag was probably used to indicate the port's friendliness to Continental shipping. The only part of the procedure not followed at either fort was the company drummer beating the "call to arms." Neither company had a drummer!

8 Perkins also held the rank of fire-worker and held direct command and responsibility over the powder magazine. The key to the magazine was also in his possession. PA: Robert Robinson (S.8914), Simeon Miner (S.14857), Gilbert Denison (S.15805), or John Harris (S.10787), NARA.

9 Rufus Avery narrative in Harris, *Groton Heights*, 30. The firing of two guns in the event of an alarm was pretty commonplace among all Continental posts.

Powder Magazine and Sally Port. After having fallen in disrepair, the powder magazine and sally port, both along the south wall of the fort, were reconstructed in 1881. The original powder magazine was much larger than the present-day reconstruction. *Tad Sattler*

Saybrook to help alleviate the manpower shortage. Next, the magazine was opened, and powder cartridges were brought out. Stow then directed two of the fort's guns, the garrison's heavier 18-pounders, readied to be used as alarm guns to work and fire in conjunction with those across the river. The "alarm guns [fired] every five minutes" and continued, according to Sanford, "till about 10 a.m."[10]

Each company distributed its supply of firearms to the men. At Fort Griswold, David Gray oversaw the removal of the muskets which were brought out of the magazine onto the parade ground. The garrison was equipped with upwards of 50 French muskets. On the parade ground, under Gray's direction, as they waited for the militia, members of Latham's Company checked the flints and fitted the muskets for action.[11]

10 Sanford, *Memoir*; Master's Log, HMS *Amphion*, ADM 52/2133, TNA. The *Amphion* confirmed both forts fired alarm guns, observing "at 4 the Rebel Forts firing Alarm Guns."

11 Mackenzie, *Diary*, 2:628; PA: David Gray (S.38776), NARA. The British reported finding "106 French Musquets" after the battle, but there is no way to distinguish how many were originally supplied to Fort Griswold or came with the militia or with members of Shapley's Company.

Also brought out of storage at Fort Griswold was the company's supply of pikes. These spear-type weapons, ranging "fifteen or sixteen feet in length," were used by ships crews in close combat situations, such as when they boarded an enemy vessel. Ledyard planned to distribute them among the garrison.[12]

Additionally, Ledyard dispatched two express riders. In Groton, Ledyard sent Matross Joseph Morgan and David Edgcomb, the latter a member of the 1st "Groton" Company who could not walk without the assistance of a cane. They were both to ride into the countryside and call out the militia.[13]

In response to the alarm guns, members of the 8th Regiment of Connecticut Militia started arriving atop Groton Heights, the designated alarm post, and were directed into the fort. They wore an assortment of civilian clothing, including an assortment of hats, varieties of different color frock coats, homespun stockings and overalls, and buckled cowhide shoes. Many came clad with canteens, haversacks, and blankets swung around their shoulders. They were equipped with their own firearms, short swords, and cartridge boxes or powder horns, some dating back to previous colonial wars. The men of Latham's Company were probably hardly distinguishable from them, as many artillerymen wore similar types of militia clothing.[14]

Most of the first volunteers lived in the immediate area. They belonged to one of two companies, the 1st "Groton" Company, under Captain John Williams or the 1st Company "Groton Alarm List," headed by Captain Elijah Avery. Throughout the morning, they were joined by their neighbors from four other militia companies in Groton.[15]

Some came from the 2nd "Groton" Company led by Capt. Simeon Allyn, some from the 2nd Company "Groton Alarm List" under his cousin Capt. Samuel

---

12 Barber, *Connecticut Historical Collections*, 309. Being large sized weapons, it is not clear where the pikes were stored when not in use at the fort; possibly tied under the platform. Two defenders, Elijah Bailey and Joshua Baker, assisted Barber and one of them told Barber, "Unfortunately [Latham's Company] lent the greater of the pikes . . . to a privateer a few days before."

13 Harris, *Groton Heights*, 234; "A Sixth of Sep Letter from the Son of one of the Fort Griswold Garrison," *New London Daily Chronicle*, Sep. 17, 1861.

14 PA: John Harris (S.10787), NARA. It is not known if Latham's or Shapley's companies were issued uniforms. They probably wore an assortment of civilian clothes, common with the militia. John Harris when he served in the company between 1780–1781 was sent on furlough, halfway through his term, to "get some clothes and necessaries."

15 *CSR*, 2:295; "Petition of Capt. John Williams showing his company is frequently called to answer alarms when the guard at Fort Griswold is not kept up & asking for exemption from other military duty," Revolutionary War Records, Series I, Vol. XIV:223, CSL.

Allyn.[16] Another group from the 3rd "Groton" Company, which was absent its captain, was led by Sgt. Daniel Eldridge, while the 3rd Company "Groton Alarm List," also absent its officers, was led by Sgt. John Stedman.[17] A small detail from the 5th "Stonington" Company under Sgt. Daniel Stanton traveled nearly thirteen miles to volunteer.[18] Many volunteers rode on horseback, but only as far as the Groton Meetinghouse where they tied their horses and walked the rest of the way to the fort in small groups.[19]

According to many pension applications, the militia arrived in a piecemeal fashion. There was no formal semblance of organization amongst them, at least initially. They expected to meet their company officers at the fort. Both Ledyard and Capt. Latham tried to keep the companies together in the fort. This is evident in the pension deposition of Caleb Avery, the younger brother of Rufus. He belonged to the 2nd "Groton" Company and arrived late in the morning. Caleb testified that as he entered the fort with his "arms and equipment [he] was stationed by order of one of the officers of the Fort at an embrasure" along the south wall, where he met other members of his company. The few surviving details of the men's placement in the fort or where they were killed or wounded, seem to imply that the south wall, especially between the southwest bastion and southeast angle, was manned by members of the 2nd "Groton" Company, both the trainband and

16 "Request of commissioned officers of the 4 companies to have Col. Avery form a fifth co. Col. Avery's orders for division & election of officers," Militia, Second Series, 823ab, CSL. The document, a unique find, described the boundaries of the five Groton companies based on the creation of the 5th Company. It provided a convenient method by which to assign militia men to their respective companies. The district of the 2nd Company ran northwest from the Groton Meetinghouse to the Thames River, then north to Gales Ferry, then east to and then south along the Norwich Road back to the meetinghouse. The boundaries of the 1st Company were directly south of the 2nd Company, running southeastward towards Capt. Jonas Belton's tavern, then south towards Long Island Sound.

17 The 3rd Company covered a large geographical area, mainly in eastern Groton. Its boundaries ran north from the Groton Meetinghouse to modern-day Church Hill Road in Ledyard, then east to the Stonington line, then south along the Stonington border to Long Island Sound, then westward along the Sound to the eastern boundary of the 1st Company at and including Belton's tavern, then northward back to the meetinghouse. The company's former commander, Hubbard Burrows, was present in the fort but his commission was not active, as he had retired in 1779. Therefore, his rank is not included here, nor is he even mentioned as their commander. Since he was below the age of 50, he would still legally have been considered a member of the 3rd "Groton" Company, but probably as a private. The current commander of the company, Capt. Nathan Crary, was later present at the meetinghouse with more of the company but was not at the fort when it was attacked.

18 "Description of wounds & pension allowed, May 1783–May 1784," Revolutionary War Records, Series I, XXVII:78, CSL; PA: Valentine Lewis (W.20431), Ezra Gallup (S.29168), NARA. Absent documentation, the boundaries of the 5th "Stonington" Company seem to encompass central Stonington, perhaps stretching from Pawcatuck to the Mystic section, in the western part of town. It remains a mystery as to how these members made it to the fort while the rest of the company did not.

19 CG, Oct 5, 1781. Abigail Palmer, widow of David Palmer, posted an ad looking for the horse her husband had ridden and left "some distance from the Fort," probably around the meetinghouse.

alarm list companies. Members of the two 3rd "Groton" Companies were placed along the south part of the east wall, and those of the 1st "Groton" Companies were positioned along the north wall and the upper part of the east wall.[20]

Other militia from the New London and Stonington companies and sailors from vessels in the harbor joined the garrison throughout the morning. Even if they arrived with their officers, they, like the militia, were directed by Captain Latham. Unlike the Groton companies, they were scattered about the fort. Especially sought amongst the sailors and even the militia were experienced artillerists, which the garrison desperately needed.

By all best estimates Latham, minus the officers, had 19 matrosses in his company who according to Ledyard were "not fit for cannon." At best, this was only enough to service three cannon without infantry support. In levying this critique, Ledyard was referring to the younger soldiers, who were just teenagers, such as 14-year-old Humphrey Brown or Sanford Williams, Azel Woodworth, Newbury Button, and Thomas Griffin, who were all only 15-years-old. These were the four youngest members and offered little or no experience working with cannon.[21]

Latham looked for sailors, especially those trained to operate cannon, to help make up for the inadequate number he had on hand. Several sailors strongly suggest this in their pension applications. This included Samuel Edgcomb, who had arrived home in Groton the day before aboard the prize ship *Syren* taken by *Randolph*, with Lt. Nathan Moore of the ship's marines, and Moore's younger brother Frederick. Edgcomb, at the request of Latham, was posted with the 18-pounder cannon, the main fort's largest gun, at its southeast corner.[22]

---

20 PA: Caleb Avery (W.25363), NARA; Harris, *Groton Heights*, 236, 239; "Death of A Survivor of the Groton Massacre," *Providence Evening Press*, Mar. 15, 1861; Rufus Avery narrative in Harris, *Groton Heights*, 34, 49. Hubbard Burrows, of the 3rd Company, was reported to have been killed along the east wall. Avery reported that two members of the 1st Company were forced to retreat along the west wall from the north wall. Charles Chester, another member of the 1st Company, with his brothers, was forced onto the roof of the barracks, from either the north wall or in the northeastern part of the fort. Moxley, Caleb Avery, and Luke Perkins were all reported to be along the south wall. Absent further documentation, the other sailors and the Stonington militia companies seem to have been intermixed.

21 See Appendix B; Ebenezer Ledyard to William Williams, Feb. 12, 1778, William Williams Family Papers, CHS; PA: Humphrey Brown (W.18648), Thomas Griffin (W.19537), Newbury Button (R.1563), NARA. Latham's effective strength was officially 29 including officers. But in early September only 22 were fit for duty. Seven others were either not present or on furlough, or their status is unknown. Griffin, Brown, and Button are three newly discovered members of the company and make no appearance on any of the earlier rosters. Griffin and Brown were captured during the battle and are noted in British naval musters. Button was able to escape the fort, being sent out by Ledyard at the very last moment to reach Lieutenant Colonel Gallup.

22 PA: Samuel Edgcomb (S.20743), Peter Vaill (R.10817), NARA; Avery narrative in Harris, *Groton Heights*, 33. Other members of the crew included Matross William Latham Jr, of Latham's Company,

Other pension applications, those of Cpl. John Morgan, and Jesper Latham, both members of the 1st "Groton" Company, suggest the same. Latham and Morgan had served at the fort several months prior, and Latham knew them both. Morgan even had privateer service. Morgan was singled out as an experienced artillerist and posted with a makeshift crew under Sgt. Elisha Prior, another member of the 1st "Groton" Company, at a 12-pounder on the east wall.[23]

Since Ledyard's responsibility encompassed the entire harbor, he needed to cross the river to help New London prepare its defense, as well as entice more volunteers to Fort Griswold. Leaving Latham in command, Ledyard, accompanied by Jordan Freeman and possibly Lt. Enoch Stanton, boarded a boat at the ferry landing, a short distance away from the shop and storehouse of Ledyard's mercantile business.

As he crossed the river, Ledyard must have felt anxious not only for the harbor but for his own family. Earlier, Ledyard had them moved to safety. Only days before they had celebrated the marriage of his oldest daughter Mary Ann and the birth of his son Charles. Now the family was fleeing. Ledyard's wife, Anna, their six children, and two slaves, Daph and Mingo, were placed aboard a barge belonging to Ledyard's mercantile company and were sent up the Thames to safety. Also aboard was Hannah Avery, the pregnant wife of Sergeant Avery, who resided in the Ledyard house. Captain Latham also had his family moved to safety. He ordered Lambert to return home and load a wagon with his wife Eunice and their children. Lambert drove them to the home of Eunice's uncle, three miles east of the fort. After doing so, Lambert returned to the fort to volunteer his services.[24]

Ledyard arrived in New London sometime around 5:00 a.m. By then, everyone was aware of the presence of the British squadron. Alarm guns from both forts continued to be fired. The patrol from Captain Avery's Company had spotted the British ships near the lighthouse through the lifting fog. Griswold Avery Jr. was then sent hurrying into town, three miles away, to notify his father, and raise the alarm to homes and farms along the way.[25]

---

and later Sgt. Stephen Hempstead, of Shapley's Company. Henry Halsey and Capt. Joseph Ellis, both Long Island refugees, may have also been part of the crew.

23 PA: John Morgan (S.17588), NARA. *Boston Evening Transcript*, Aug. 22, 1842.

24 Harris, *Groton Heights*, 213, 241–242; Carolyn E. Smith and Helen Vergason, *North Groton's Story* (Ledyard, CT, 2000), 40. As adjutant, Stanton's presence with Ledyard at this time would not have been out of the ordinary. It was his role to assist Ledyard and distribute the colonel's orders.

25 *CG*, May 2, 1783; Robert Hallam account of Sep. 6, 1781, undated, NLCHS; Charles Allyn Papers, NLCHS; PA: Griswold Avery Jr. (R.306), NARA. According to Robert Hallam, he met with Harris who was on his way to Brown's Farm at around 6:00 a.m. and by then Harris had already received his orders from Ledyard.

As Ledyard walked about in New London, he did so amid a perplexing situation. The townspeople were surprisingly, at first, hesitant to take the British threat seriously. Even with alarm guns echoing across the harbor, "[it] caused but little alarm," and some carried on like it was a typical day, according to one account. However, for some, the alarms definitely caused a certain amount of excitement and entertainment. Jonathan Brooks Sr., a member of the Independent Artillery Company, went to see the enemy ships for himself. He then returned home to retrieve his young son, Jonathan Jr. to show him the enemy flotilla before they could depart.[26]

Not much is known about the route Ledyard took through New London. He was only in town for an hour, most of which seemed to be spent near the waterfront and in frustration. After the attack, a petition submitted to the governor by over a dozen leading citizens of New London and Groton revealed this much. Ledyard was only one man and could only be in so many places. "He was," they said, "as a man without hands." While the petition focused on recommendations for improving the harbor's defenses, it also throws some light on Ledyard's plan for defending the harbor.[27]

Ledyard was not a trained military tactician. Even so, there is some evidence he thought about or was advised on what to do in the event of an attack. One objective of his visit to New London was to appeal to the volunteers, specifically sailors, to come to Fort Griswold, just like Captain Latham was doing at the fort. Most sailors were trained to handle and work cannon and Ledyard needed them to man the fort's guns. He reasoned if he could hold Fort Griswold, the British squadron could not enter the harbor or approach New London or Groton. According to the petition, "[Ledyard] gave his positive orders for all seaman to repair over to the Fort." That is, to Fort Griswold. As Ledyard understood it, Fort Griswold was the key to the harbor.[28]

---

26 Caulkins, *New London*, 546; Jonathan Brooks narrative in Harris, *Groton Heights*, 74; *CCR*, 12:25–26; Lieutenant George B. Hurlburt and Ensign Silas Church Jr. to Governor Trumbull, Dec. 19, 1776, Governor Trumbull Papers, 343a–c, CSL. The Independent Artillery Company, or simply the Independent Company, traced its origins to 1762. There was a necessity during the French and Indian War to regularly garrison the fort with trained artillerists, of which they had none. Local citizens, headed by Gurdon Saltonstall, were granted permission by the General Assembly to create a separate artillery company, comprised of members drawn out of the 1st and 2nd "New London" militia companies. They were specially uniformed and trained to handle the fort's cannon. Over time, as artillerists were not needed, membership became more a status symbol and its ranks contained mainly prominent citizens.

27 "To Col. McClellen, Commandant at the posts of New London and Groton," Revolutionary War Records, Series I, Vol. XXII:337, CSL.

28 Ibid.

There were over thirty vessels in the harbor that morning, including a variety of sloops, schooners, snows, brigs, and galleys. Of this, at least fifteen were privateers or letters of marque, perhaps eleven were prize vessels, with the others being merchant vessels. Most sailors Ledyard interacted with seemed indifferent to his requests. Some acquiesced, "[but] only by persuasion." We know that while in town, Ledyard visited at least one privateer.[29]

Ledyard stepped aboard the 18-gun sloop *Hancock*, tied up on Ephraim Miner's wharf, just south of the Parade, and asked to see its captain, Peter Richards, to obtain permission to address the crew. Most of the crew had already been dismissed after their return to the harbor four days earlier, but Ledyard was granted permission to speak to those that remained. Ledyard spoke about what was needed at the fort and asked for assistance. Several, including Captain Richards himself, volunteered.[30]

If Ledyard visited other ships, those visits went unrecorded. Most sailors considered the safety of their vessel and cargo their primary concern. They wanted to get them out of reach of the British, by heading upriver towards Norwich. In hindsight, this may appear a cowardly maneuver. Why retreat? Why not make some attempt to engage the British squadron and thus assist in the defense of New London? But even if they had wanted to, only some of the privateers were ready and equipped for action and could not have successfully resisted the British squadron. Nor did they have anyone to lead them in that action. Two vessels, the 4-gun schooner *Gamecock* and the 10-gun brig *Venus* had full crews as they were due to set sail that very day. The other crews varied in size. Several privateers, including the *Hancock*, the 18-gun sloop *Randolph*, and the 4-gun brig *Deane*, had only partial crews. All three had arrived within the last week, and as a result, most of their crews had been dismissed. A similar situation unfolded for the privateer brig *Minerva*, which was recruiting a new crew and fitting out for an upcoming cruise. The sloop *Active* had no crew as it was having its mast repaired.[31]

29 *CG*, Aug. 3, 10, 17, 1781, 24, 31, 1781, Sep. 7, 1781; "To the Honorable the General Assembly . . . ," Revolutionary War Records, Series I, Vol. XXII:80, CSL. Unfortunately for Ledyard, all he could do was appeal for help. Citizens suggested later that if Ledyard "had only fifty good men in the Fort under his absolute command" he could have "empress'd and compelled" upwards of 200–300 sailors. With both artillery companies understrength, Ledyard could hardly afford to spare anyone to try and impress the sailors into service.

30 PA: Ebenezer Averill (S.28625), Richard Tozer (R.10664), NARA; Harris, *Groton Heights*, 232–233; *CG* July 20, 1781, Sep. 7, 1781. Harris asserted the crew, which may have numbered at most 90–100, all volunteered. This is an overestimation, as the crew had been dismissed a day or two prior to the attack. It may have numbered around 20 sailors. Some remained in New London while others went to Fort Griswold.

31 *Naval Records of the American Revolution*, ed. Charles Henry Lincoln (Washington, D.C., 1906), 307, 323, 428, 486; *CG*, Sep. 7, 1781; "Captain Charles Bulkeley's Narrative of Personal Experiences in the War of the American Revolution from His Original Manuscript," in Rogers, *Naval Office*, 128;

Whatever the reasons, most sailors would not stay and fight it out with the British squadron. Ironically, some sailors may have seen this decision as helpful because as they left, they took onboard civilians with their personal belongings. Some ships were filled "with [the] effects of the inhabitants" as they set sail upriver to safety.[32]

Watching on the *Shuldham* offshore, Arnold was unable to strike his enemy. He watched in frustration as the privateers, a primary objective of the expedition, escaped before he had a chance to strike them. He reported to Clinton, "As soon as the Enemy were alarmed in the Morning, we could perceive they were busily employed in bending sails, and endeavoring to get their Privateers and other ships up River, out of our reach." Luckily for him, the wind conditions which had delayed the British also worked against the privateers. As they tried to go upriver, "the wind being small, and the tide against them, they were obliged to anchor again." But once the wind picked up, they carried on towards Norwich.[33]

The actions of the privateers angered Ledyard, so much so that he made a drastic decision, one that reveals how desperate he became to get volunteers. At that critical moment, he preferred the additional manpower more than the vessels themselves, so he ordered the privateers to be fired upon. The citizens in their petition explained, "[Ledyard] fired upon the shipping to stop them from running away." But it did nothing, he was still ignored. Even a militia officer commented, "there were a number of privateers in the harbor, and on the approach of the enemy's fleet [they] were making the best of their way up the river full of men, notwithstanding Col. Ledyard's orders to the contrary, and even [being fired] upon."[34]

Ledyard next turned to the defense of New London. To do this, he intended to hold the two forts south of town. To man them, he planned to use the militia, but its leisurely arrival confounded his intentions. Even with the firing of alarm guns and hours to prepare before the eventual British landings, they were slow to gather and organize. The constant false alarms had taken a toll on their readiness.

After the British attack, many refused to blame the militiamen for their delay. They instead looked to blame the British. One explanation first appeared several

PA: Ebenezer Averill (S.28625), Richard Tozer (R.10664), NARA. Both Averill of Norwich, a crew member on the *Randolph*, and Tozer of Colchester, a crew member on the *Hancock*, had returned to their homes by the morning of the attack.

32 *CG*, Sep. 7, 1781.

33 Arnold report in Mackenzie, *Diary*, 2:624.

34 "To the Honorable the General Assembly of the State of Connecticut to be convened at Hartford (by adjournment) on the 10th day of Jan Anno Dom 1782," Revolutionary War Records, Series I, Vol. XXII:80, CSL; *CG*, May 2, 1783.

decades later and has appeared in several histories, surprisingly without much scrutiny. This was the supposed hearing of a third cannon being fired. As discussed earlier, the pre-determined signal to call out the militia, known as "alarm guns," was to fire two cannon in quick succession every five minutes. Three cannon being fired was the signal for the return of a privateer.

At least two witnesses refer to how they heard this third gun. They believed this to be why the militia did not take the alarm seriously and attributed it to the British flotilla offshore. One witness, Avery Downer, the surgeon's mate of the 8th Regiment of Connecticut Militia, attempted to explain: "I well remember the morning of the alarm[.] [T]wo guns from the fort [being fired] in a given time was the alarm. This the enemy well understood, and they fired a third, by which we in Preston were deceived, being fourteen miles distant." Downer reasoned the British had played a dirty trick on the militiamen to confuse them.[35]

The claim of British interference has been published many times in histories of the raid and Fort Griswold without arousing any skepticism. Some authors have even gone so far as to assert that Arnold personally ordered the third gun to be fired. Yet, if he did, he never mentioned it in official or private correspondence or in his official reports. Both Captain Bazely's report and all surviving logs of British ships involved in the expedition are also silent. There simply is no contemporary evidence to back up this claim.[36]

So, if a third cannon was not fired, what exactly happened? And why would these two witnesses and others present say it happened? One possible theory that has never been previously offered is that Americans likely bore responsibility for this supposed "third cannon."

Past histories have asserted only Fort Griswold fired alarm guns. This was not the case. Fort Trumbull was also firing them. They were each firing two guns off every five or so minutes for most of the morning. Was the firing properly coordinated, so each fort's guns went off separately? Or did they possibly overlap? Did the witnesses hear guns from both forts? If the firing was not properly coordinated between the two forts, that alone could easily have caused confusion.

If the situation was not already confusing enough, the logbook of the *Amphion* revealed some additional information. It noted: "the Enemys small Craft in the

---

35 Avery Downer narrative in Harris, *Groton Heights*, 84.

36 Jerald P. Hurwitz, *Alamo of the Revolution: Benedict Arnold and Massacre at Fort Griswold* (New York, 2020), 24; Eric D. Lehman, *Homegrown Terror: Benedict Arnold and the Burning of New London* (Middletown, CT, 2014), 164–165; Smith, *North Groton's Story*, 26. All three books published in the last four decades continue to embellish the "third gun" story, some claiming Arnold knew the secret warning signals in advance of the raid. There is simply no evidence of any of this.

Mouth of the Harbour working [with] the Forts [and] firing Alarm Guns at the same time."[37]

So, in addition to the forts, the privateers also fired their guns. Were these guns coordinated with the forts? Probably not. Then why would they do this? The answer to that question could be traced back to almost three years earlier.

In 1779, sailors aboard an armed vessel, lying in the harbor, without reason, permission, or warning, fired two of the ship's guns in the middle of the night. Believing the harbor was under attack, civilians and militia panicked. To assure it never happened again, Ledyard published orders in the *Connecticut Gazette* stating, "All Commanders of armed Vessels, when lying in this Harbour, are desired to give the necessary Orders to all under their Command, not to suffer any Alarm Guns to be fired at any time, more especially not to suffer any Guns to be fired in the Night, unless it should appear that the Enemy are coming up the Harbour."[38]

The privateers at that time were doing precisely what Ledyard permitted them to do. But in hindsight, how could any military or political leader not have seen how this could be a problem? Unfortunately, we may never know the answer to that question. Maybe they thought it might hasten the militia? If there was one thing certain, there was a lot of cannon fire coming from the harbor. It would have been difficult for any member of the militia to determine what was going on in the harbor and whether he should rush to its defense.

The closest militia Ledyard could rely on for assistance was from the 3rd Regiment of Connecticut Militia. Its twenty-one companies—fourteen trainband and seven alarm list— were comprised of men from New London and the neighboring Lyme. Ledyard sought out their leadership while in New London. He wanted to issue his orders and then delegate the responsibility of organizing the defense of New London to its colonel while he returned to Fort Griswold.[39]

Ledyard knew that if the 3rd Regiment could assemble and hold the forts south of town, it could expect assistance by the afternoon from other militia units in the brigade, such as the 20th Regiment of Connecticut Militia from Norwich, and the 25th Regiment of Connecticut Militia from Colchester and East Haddam. By evening other militia units from the 5th Brigade, the 5th Regiment of Connecticut Militia from Mansfield and Windham, and the 12th Regiment of Connecticut Militia from Lebanon and Hebron could be expected to arrive.

---

37 Master's Log, HMS *Amphion*, ADM 52/2133, TNA.

38 *CG*, Jan. 29, 1779. Ledyard promised "that any Person or Persons guilty of the like disorderly Conduct, may depend on being treated according to the Nature of the Crime."

39 "A Return of the 3rd Brigade of Connecticut Militia in the State of Connecticut Aug 1, 1780," Governor Trumbull Papers, 24:123, CSL. On paper, in 1780, the regiment numbered up to 800 men.

To help move the militia along, while in New London Ledyard dispatched another express rider, Samuel Raymond, to gallop northward to Norwich, spreading the alarm along the way. Once in Norwich, Raymond was to alert Col. Zabdiel Rogers, commander of the 20th Regiment of Connecticut Militia, to assemble and bring his regiment to New London. Once accomplished, Raymond was to continue to Lebanon and give notice to Governor Trumbull of the British threat to the harbor. Trumbull, however, was not in Lebanon. Instead, he was in Hartford, and Raymond had to continue north, riding over sixty miles to deliver the first news of the impending British attack to the governor.[40]

Colonel Jonathan Latimer commanded the 3rd Regiment of Connecticut Militia. A native of New London, he was born in May 1724 to Jonathan and Borodell (Denison) Latimer. The Latimer family had made a considerable fortune in mercantile trade and shipbuilding, enjoyed strong political connections, and owned large tracts of land around New London. For most of his adult life, the colonel lived in Chesterfield, a small village in the North Parish of New London, where he and his wife, Lucretia, raised their fourteen children.[41]

Latimer's extensive militia service spanned over three decades. During the French and Indian War, Captain Latimer led his company in response to the Fort Willian Henry alarm and then led a company in the 3rd Connecticut Regiment under Col. Eleazer Fitch, which participated in the British expedition to capture Fort Carillon (later Fort Ticonderoga) but was held in reserve during the disastrous assault on the fort.[42]

In 1775, Captain Latimer was appointed a major in the 7th Connecticut Regiment and served at the Siege of Boston. The following year, he was elevated to lieutenant colonel in the 4th Battalion, Wadsworth's Brigade, during the 1776 New York Campaign, and led the battalion after its colonel was captured at Kip's Bay. Returning home, Latimer was promoted to colonel of the 3rd Regiment of Connecticut Militia. In August 1777 he commanded a battalion of Connecticut militia and played a vital role in the Saratoga Campaign, where he served under

---

40 *CSR*, 3:503; Rufus Avery narrative in Harris, *Groton Heights*, 30. Raymond was probably the express rider mentioned by Avery sent from New London.

41 Colonel Latimer's biographical information was gathered from descendant Dr. John Wilson and his brother.

42 *Rolls of Connecticut Men in the French and Indian War, 1755-1762*, 2 vols. (Hartford, CT, 1903), 1:232, 2:60. According to the family, Latimer returned home with a captured French sword and is supposed to have carried this sword throughout his service during the Revolutionary War. It is still in the possession of his family.

Benedict Arnold. Since Saratoga, Latimer's service had remained primarily within Connecticut.[43]

Since Latimer lived almost fifteen miles away and had not yet arrived on the scene, Ledyard was forced to seek out Lt. Col. Joseph Harris Jr., the regiment's second-in-command, who lived much closer. Harris resided in a three-story house on Town Hill just south of town, a short distance from Fort Nonsense. The 41-year-old lieutenant colonel was the son of Capt. Joseph and Phoebe (Holt) Harris. The Harris family had called New London home for four generations. Like his father, Harris was involved in politics and occupied various governmental offices; at the time of the attack he served as justice of the peace and as a selectman.[44]

Like Latimer, Harris's militia service was extensive, but his political responsibilities kept him close to home and away from service outside Connecticut. He was elected as a lieutenant under his father in the 1st Company in late 1766. Four years later, when his father retired, he rose to captain and led it at the outbreak of the war. He received a promotion to major in October 1776 but avoided serving with the regiment in the New York Campaign.[45]

In 1778, Major Harris went with the regiment, under Latimer, to Rhode Island. Though nearby, the unit was not involved in the climactic Battle of Rhode Island, but Harris managed to lose his horse by what he described as "inevitable providence." In early 1781, Harris was elevated to lieutenant colonel, filling a vacancy created by the resignation of the former lieutenant colonel.[46]

Ledyard managed to meet briefly with Harris. According to Harris, Captain Shapley was also present, and both officers received their orders from Ledyard. Harris recalled, "[Ledyard] issued out his orders directing me to man the garrisons ... to immediately procure some suitable person to send express to Col. Latimer."[47]

Despite Harris's rank and time of service in the militia, he lacked experience managing an entire regiment. Unlike Latimer, Harris had also never led troops in combat. Ledyard must have known this about him, and it probably concerned him. Harris was known as a "worthy member of society" and a "good citizen," but

---

43 *Connecticut Men*, 79, 403, 503–504.

44 Caulkins, *New London*, 143; Rogers, *Naval Office*, 29.

45 *CCR*, 12:507, 13:437; *CSR*, 1:28. At the time of his commission to lieutenant and captain, the 1st Company was the 1st "New London" Company. When Harris was promoted to major, he replaced Samuel Selden, who had resigned to take command of the 4th Battalion, Wadsworth's Brigade.

46 *CSR*, 2:207, 3:326. Harris was granted reimbursement by the General Assembly for the horse. According to Tinker, a member of the regiment, they "hurried on as fast as we could, and arrived at [Howland's] ferry ab[out] night—Orders came for us not to go upon the island until the next day," but the next night the American army retreated.

47 *CG*, Jan. 10, 1783.

it was not yet known how he might react to being under fire, nor was it clear how the militia would respond to Harris's leadership, especially in combat. Ledyard needed Latimer, but at that moment, he only had Harris.[48]

Harris's first task was to notify Latimer of the enemy's approach and bring him to the waterfront. In his account, Harris recalled, "I wrote a letter, dated at six o'clock that morning directed to Col. Latimer, and was about to send it when Captain John Hallam, then a captain in the regiment [commander of the Independent Artillery Company], informed me that he, with his brother [Robert], had sent an express to Col. Latimer." Harris explained "that I urged the expediency of this point and told him it was a matter of importance, he told me I might depend upon it that the Colonel had got the intelligence by then, and consequently would soon be in town."[49]

Unfortunately for Harris, his account was not entirely accurate. A witness, Robert Hallam, was called during Harris's court-martial to answer questions related to his delay in alerting Col. Latimer of the impending attack. Fortunately, Hallam's deposition survives, revealing what Harris did not want to admit. In it, Hallam testified, "As I was on my way towards the Harbour's mouth not far from 8 Oclock A.M. in company with Mr John Hallam & others to see where the Enemy was, I met Col. Joseph Harris between the Church and his House…[O]ne of the Company ask'd Col. Harris if he had sent an Express to Col. Latimer [and] he answer'd that he had not[,] that he was then about it but could not get a Horse." It is clear by Hallam's testimony that neither he nor his brother had sent for Latimer. However, it is unclear why they would have sent for the colonel. According to the chain of command, it was Harris's responsibility, not theirs.[50]

Instead, the most probable explanation for the mismanagement of the task falls on Harris's lack of experience, combined with the rapidly unfolding situation. Things were getting more stressful for him by the minute. He may have issued orders to send for Latimer around 6:00 a.m. and assumed they were executed without verifying it. When he did check on it, over two hours later, he found out his orders had not been carried out because of the lack of an available horse. It was not until around 8:00 a.m., shortly after the meeting with Hallam, that

48 *CG*, May 2, 1783.

49 Robert Hallam account of Sep. 6, 1781, undated, NLCHS; Book, "Connecticut Independent Company," NLCHS.

50 Robert Hallam account of Sep. 6, 1781, undated, NLCHS; PA: Hoel Huntley (S.18043), NARA. Huntley made the unsubstantiated claim that upon hearing the alarm guns, he went to Latimer's house and urged him to go to New London, but as Huntley asserted Latimer refused to go.

Harris finally procured a horse and sent Ens. Daniel Latimer, of the 2nd Company, hurrying towards Chesterfield.[51]

Besides sending for Colonel Latimer, Harris was consumed with other problems throughout the morning. Foremost was the absence of willing militia and volunteers. After meeting with Ledyard, Harris rode through town and attempted to locate his officers to get them to organize their companies. At least five captains either resided within or were billeted in town: Capt. Richard Deshon of the 2nd Company; Capt. John Deshon of the 1st Company Alarm List; Capt. Thomas Harding of the 2nd Company Alarm List; Capt. John Hallam of the Independent Artillery Company; and Capt. Griswold Avery of the drafted company currently assigned to the department. We know that Harris spoke with at least one, Capt. Richard Deshon, but lacking evidence to the contrary there is the probability he also met at least with Captain Avery and Captain Harding. The militiamen were expected to gather on the common on Manwaring Hill, the designated alarm post, where they would meet their officers. This was true for all except Captain Avery's company, which remained at Fort Nonsense.[52]

But members of the 3rd Regiment of Connecticut Militia were slow to respond, even in the defense of their own town. Most had been taken by surprise; even more did not take the situation seriously until it was too late. Earlier, Jonathan Brooks Jr. was brought to view the British squadron offshore, as if it was a source of entertainment. Brooks recounted how, when they reached a vantage point, the British vessels had not anchored but were coming closer to the shore. The boy's father, suddenly realizing the danger, yelled to him, "they are going to land; go home, take the bridle and get the horse from the pasture as quickly as possible." The rest of town reacted likewise, and in a short time the streets were thronged with people who were busily employed in taking care of their families and personal effects.[53]

One historian elaborated:

---

51 *CG*, May 2, 1783; Harris, *Groton Heights*, 115–116. Ensign Daniel Latimer was brought up on the charge of "being negligent of his duty in not seasonably forwarding intelligence to his colonel of the expected approach and attack of the enemy." He was found not guilty.

52 Parsons, *Life and Letters*, 219–220; John Hempsted narrative in Harris, *Groton Heights*, 62. Since 1779 the common on Manwaring Hill along the Colchester Road had been the designated alarm post. It had been noticed then that during an alarm the militia had no specified place to gather or assemble. They arrived piecemeal, often in small groups and with no officers, and wandered about looking for direction. The designation of the common was made to correct this. However, both Hempsted of the 1st Company, and Deshon of the 1st Company Alarm List, met and first spoke with Harris at Harris's house on town hill.

53 Brooks narrative in Harris, *Groton Heights*, 74; *CG*, May 2, 1783.

In the town, consternation and fright suddenly let loose [as many citizens] made haste to send away their families and their portable and most valuable goods. Throngs of women and children were dismissed into the fields and woods, some without food and others with a piece of bread or a biscuit in their hands. Women laden with bags and pillow-cases, or driving a cow before them with an infant in their arms, or perhaps on horseback with a bed under them and various utensils dangling at the side; boys with stockings slung like wallets over their shoulders, containing the money, the papers and other small valuables of the family; carts laden with furniture; dogs and other household animals, looking strange and panic struck; pallid faces and trembling limbs—such were the scenes presented on all the roads leading into the country.[54]

The militia were forced to decide: protect their families and property, or defend the town? Most members chose the former, at least at first. Even if greater numbers had rallied, there was soon another problem for Harris: a lack of firearms. Harris claimed, "I called upon the officers [of the 3rd Regiment] to embody their men; that many of those who turned out had no arms; that I applied to the select-men and other gentlemen for arms for those that had none; that I ordered ammunition for cannon and small-arms, as should be needed." A regimental muster from the previous summer revealed that out of the 765 men in the regiment, only 203 were properly armed and equipped and could be called to action.[55]

The 8th Regiment of Connecticut Militia across the river faced an even worse situation. Only about 229 out of 1229 men were properly armed and equipped. The lack of available firearms had been a problematic issue noted in previous alarms but, tragically, had never been corrected.[56]

Harris turned to the two other selectmen, Guy Richards Jr., and Joseph Packwood, to assist him in this matter. They may have given him the authority to pull additional muskets out of the town's supply kept in the cellar of the county courthouse. Lacking official documentation, we do not know how many, if any, came to Harris through them. However, we can speculate that the "other

---

54 Caulkins, *New London*, 547.

55 *CG*, May 2, 1783.

56 "A Return of the 3rd Brigade of Militia in the State of Connecticut Aug 1st, 1780," Governor Trumbull Papers, CSL; Revolutionary War Records, Series II, LIV:174; "To Col. McClellen, Commandant at the Posts of New London & Groton," Revolutionary War Records, Series I, Vol. XXII: 337, CSL. The 3rd Regiment of Connecticut Militia was the least equipped in the brigade. The 8th Regiment of Connecticut Militia, missing the records for the 3rd Company, "Groton Alarm List," were only slightly better at 229 equipped for action. No numbers were recorded for the 20th Regiment of Connecticut Militia. The 25th Regiment fared the best in the brigade, having 433 armed and equipped militia ready for action.

gentlemen," whose names went unrecorded, were probably the captains of two privateers: Peter Richards of the *Hancock* and Augustus Peck, of the *Randolph*, or the owners of both vessels. Both vessels contributed their supply of firearms to help alleviate the shortage.[57]

As the militia were gathering, Harris, without leaving guides, unilaterally moved the assembly point from Manwaring Hill to the Parade in the center of town, near the county courthouse. Harris never clarified why he risked confusing his militia by moving the assembly point. However, it may have been related to the issuing of muskets from the courthouse, a nearby storehouse, or a privateer vessel. Or maybe because that is where all the townspeople seemed to be at that moment. Harris did all he could to cope with the shortage of weapons, but it would take something more than the effect of Arnold's attack to draw real attention to the problem, with citizens still attempting to solve it a year later.[58]

In charge of the gathered militia and other volunteers, Harris appointed Capt. Richard Deshon, a 47-year-old, New Londoner who resided on Town Street. The decision was both tactically sound and logical. Deshon was a seasoned militia officer with combat experience. Besides having held his commission as captain of the 2nd Company since 1769, Deshon had led a company in the 4th Battalion, Wadsworth's Brigade, during the New York Campaign and had participated in the Battle of Kip's Bay. Since then, Deshon had periodically led drafted militia companies in and around the harbor. The members of his 2nd Company came from the central part of town. He was a sound choice to assemble them as they knew him and had elected him as their captain. He was also the most senior militia captain present. Also, he had his lieutenant, Samuel Latimer, there to assist him.[59]

---

57 "Copy of Flag of Truce Document," in Rogers, *Naval Office*, 29; "Protest Continued," *Morning News*, Oct. 25, 1845; *CG*, Jan. 4, 1782; Middlebrook, *Maritime Connecticut*, 2:107–108, 180. The owners of both vessels placed an ad in the *Gazette* looking for the return of guns they lent out the day of the battle. The *Hancock* was owned jointly by Joseph Packwood & Co., Thomas Mumford, and Howland, Coit & Co., while the *Randolph* was owned only by Howland, Coit, & Co.

58 Harris, *Groton Heights*, 124. The citizens complained that when the militia were called into action on "so short a notice[,] it was impossible for them to be compleatly equipped" and they also recommended that the magazine inside the fort on Town Hill "be provided with some arms, as many volunteers will run to the their assistance in time of alarm."

59 *CG*, May 2, 1783; *Connecticut Men*, 403; *CCR*, 13:176; Middlebrook, *Maritime Connecticut*, 1:82, 2:206. Deshon's ensign was Daniel Latimer, but he was sent to retrieve Latimer. Harris also claimed he continued sending expresses into the countryside to alert the militia. He also ordered Fort Hill, the old battery at the Parade, which he described as being "built to oppose the entrance of the enemy into the town, and garrisoned, by one man only, and much out of repair to be put in some of posture of defence." Harris might have done this based on the fear the British squadron might move upriver.

Before leaving New London, Ledyard made two requisitions from the Continental storehouses to be sent across the river. From Guy Richards Jr., the commissary in New London, Ledyard requested twenty-four barrels of beef, "well pak'd and pickled," and from John Holt Jr., the post's quartermaster, several barrels of gunpowder. The gunpowder and beef were rowed across the river. By gathering these additional supplies, Ledyard was thinking ahead. He did not know how long the threat would last or how many would gather at Fort Griswold. He endeavored to get enough foodstuff and gunpowder to sustain his command for as long as necessary.[60]

As Ledyard completed his visit, he walked with Freeman back towards the waterfront to the boat waiting to return them to Fort Griswold, where Ledyard decided he would watch the day's events unfold. According to Caulkins, Ledyard was followed by a crowd as he walked. As he stepped aboard the boat, he shook hands with friends and assured them, "If I must lose to-day, honor or life, you who know me, can tell which it will be." There at Fort Griswold, Ledyard would meet the British and his fate.[61]

---

60 *CSR*, 3:152; "Petition showing a quantity of gunpowder was taken for defense of Fort Griswold Sep 1781 from his store & asking for a like quantity from state. Account & certificate of officers to the amount," Revolutionary War Records, Series I, Vol. 24:380, 382, CSL.

61 Caulkins, *New London*, 548.

Chapter Five

The Battle of New London:
The Advance on the Town

*A*s the morning wore on, the situation for New London grew worse. According to Samuel Plumb, a member of the 2nd Company, "all, old and young [were] called to arms." But only about twenty militia and sailors joined Capt. Richard Deshon. Despite the lack of manpower, he was determined to take his company to meet the invaders. Forming them up into line on the Parade, as panicked others were fleeing town, Deshon's Company marched down the length of the Bank, then south out of town, and turned onto the Quagonapoxet Highway.[1]

Their first destination was Fort Nonsense, just under two miles away, where they were to join Capt. Griswold Avery's Company. After meeting with Harris, Captain Avery sent orders to his company to assemble and prepare for action and then left the Thompson house to join them. His son later stated the company was "drawn up very early in the morning" at Fort Nonsense.

As Captain Deshon moved his company onto Town Hill, sometime around 7:00 a.m., he brought Harris' orders to Captain Avery. These were to follow Deshon to Brown's farm where the British were expected to make their landing. It is unclear why Lieutenant Colonel Harris issued these orders to his militia officers as they clearly contradicted Ledyard's original orders to man the forts. Nonetheless, Avery dutifully obeyed and directed his company to follow Deshon's men down the Quagonapoxet Highway.

---

1 PA: Samuel Plumb (R.8287), NARA; "A Pay Role of Capt. Elijah Avery's Company for assisting the Sheriff of New London County when abused By a mob 7th Feb 1778," JSC; PA: Griswold Avery (R.306), Joshua Wheeler (R.11383), NARA; John Hempsted narrative in Harris, *Groton Heights*, 62.

Both militia companies, numbering around 40 men, trudged along the roadway, kicking up dirt and dust, for another mile and a half to the home of Jeremiah Brown. The two-story gambrel-roofed house, built about 1704, stood at a bend along the Quagonapoxet Highway, about a mile north of the Quagonapoxet salt marshes, Long Island Sound, and the lighthouse.

There the highway turned at a large, wooden gate, known as "Brown's Gate."

A short distance from the house, the gate stood at the entrance to the nearly 300-acre farm, which stretched southwestward towards Alewife Cove, southward towards the Sound, and then eastwards towards the lighthouse. A post and rail fence ran from the gate marking the northern edge of the property. Brown worked the farm with two of his brothers, John and James, his brother-in-law Benjamin Jerome, and cousin Francis Gardner.[2]

The two companies filed through the gate and marched southward across Brown's farm toward the river's edge. The farm was covered with orchards, woodlots, open fields, and pastures. The pastures, which might have been filled with grazing livestock on a typical day, were almost deserted. Earlier, Captain Avery had ordered his son, Griswold, along with Pvt. Joshua Hempstead, both of his company, to drive off Brown's livestock to safety.[3]

After crossing Brown's farm, both captains halted their companies on a ridgeline that overlooked the beach, and then dispersed the men to cover as much ground as possible. Some may have been sent to the home of Daniel Harris, the lighthouse keeper, which stood adjacent to the lighthouse. Volunteers continued to arrive, but not in numbers sufficient to resist the British landing. Harris eventually arrived, on horseback, accompanied by Capt. John Hempsted of the 1st Company and two other men.[4]

The nearly 40-year-old Hempsted lived three miles west of town. Upon hearing the alarm guns, he initially believed they were yet another false alarm. But as his company's commanding officer, Hempsted was legally obligated to answer the call. He downed a quick breakfast, grabbed his musket, slung his cartridge box over his left shoulder, and said goodbye to his wife. Mounting his horse, he rode along the Colchester Road towards Manwaring Hill, where he expected to find the members of his company and his orders. But, according to him, he "found nobody thare." Hempsted then walked to Town Hill, where Lieutenant Colonel Harris

---

2 New London Land Records, Volume 23:165, CSL.

3 John Hempsted narrative in Harris, *Groton Heights*, 62; Richard B. Wall, "Instructive Paper on Green Harbor by R.B. Wall," *The Day*, Apr. 2, 1908; PA: Griswold Avery Jr. (R.306), NARA.

4 Daniel Harris and his brother, Eliphalet, owned a small amount of property along the waterfront near to the lighthouse.

Jeremiah Brown House. The house still stands today at the intersection
of Ocean Avenue and Niles Hill Road. *Author*

lived, hoping to obtain orders. Along the way, he ran into Capt. John Deshon,
commander of the 1st Company Alarm List, and Michael Mellally, captain of the
privateer *Rochambeau* and a member of Deshon's Company, both without their
commands. Both were on a similar mission and with Hempsted sharing a horse
with one of them, all rode south. The men found Harris outside his home. Arriving
after the two militia companies had already marched by, they were anxious for
orders and leadership but found neither.[5]

Years later, Hempstead remembered his awkward meeting with Harris:

I saw him Standing on his Dore Stone. I slipt of the hors & met the Colo half
the way from his house to the highway with a Short willow Stick in his hand.
My reply to him was what is the news Colo? he replid the Enemy are landing att
Brown's farm. What is the order? his answer. go Down & make the defence you
Can gitt.[6]

---

5 *CG*, Sep. 7, 1781; John Hempsted narrative in Harris, *Groton Heights*, 61–62; "A List of the First
Alarm List Company in the 3d Regt of Militia in this State under the Command of Capt. John
Deshon," NLCHS; *Naval Records*, 446.

6 John Hempsted narrative in Harris, *Groton Heights*, 62.

Lieutenant Colonel Joseph Harris Jr. House. The house still stands today at the intersection of Willetts Avenue and Riverview Avenue where it was relocated during the nineteenth century. *Author*

"I hope you will go with me," Hempstead urged his commander. A moment of hesitation passed before, according to Hempsted, Harris agreed to go. Harris mounted his horse and rode with them toward Brown's farm. Once there, they took their places in line amongst the anxious militia and other volunteers. Hempsted noted that as they waited, it was "verry still."[7]

The stillness was soon broken by a party of militia, likely from Avery's Company, who moved closer to the river's edge. There, they concealed themselves among trees on property belonging to Sergeant Benjamin Brown Sr., of Avery's Company, and started shooting at the British offshore. One remembered, "[they] did all they could to annoy the enemy" as the British loaded their landing craft with troops.[8]

The *Amphion* recorded in its logbook that "the Rebels [were] firing muskets from the woods upon our boats." Captain Bazely reacted rapidly to the situation. He dispatched twenty marines from his ship's company under Lieutenants Thomas

7 Ibid., 62–63.

8 PA: Griswold Avery Jr. (R.306), NARA. The orchard likely belonged to Benjamin Brown Sr. as evidenced through a statement by Benjamin Jr. in Griswold Avery's pension application which stated, "many shot came into the orchard" and "were afterwards cut out."

Weston and George Edward Roby, along with twelve armed sailors, and sent them to shore to counter the threat. They landed quickly, the militia scattered, and the harassing fire ceased. Weston and Roby then remained to ensure the militia did not return.[9]

Temporarily untroubled, the landing craft continued to be loaded unimpeded and were ready to head towards shore an hour later. At that time, Capt. Henry Chads, the officer in charge of the landing, gave the signal to Captain Bazely, alerting him that he was ready to proceed to shore with the first wave.[10]

Two divisions of soldiers were to be landed on shore, one on the New London side, the other on the Groton side. The first division's objective, on the west side of the Thames River, was to secure Fort Trumbull, Fort Nonsense, and then New London. The objective of the second division, on the east side of the river, was to take possession of Fort Griswold.

Captain Chads only had enough landing craft, which consisted of several dozen flatboats and bateaux, to land on one side of the river at a time, and each division would require at least two waves. With enemy militia already sighted on the New London side, it would take some time. They would need assistance from the navy.

Acting in conjunction with the army were the armed vessels of the squadron, consisting of the *Recovery*, *Beaumont*, *Argo*, *Lurcher*, and *Hussar*, along with the Associated Loyalist vessels, *Colonel Martin*, and *Association*. Under the command of Capt. Edward Shepherd, of the *Recovery*, they were to bombard the shore to cover the landings, and then, once the forts were captured, move upriver "to aid in effecting the destruction of the port of New London" and attempt to capture or destroy the privateers.[11]

---

9 Arthur Bowler, *Logistics and the Failure of the British Army in America, 1775-1783* (Princeton, NJ, 1975), 25; Royal Navy Ship's Muster (Series 1), HMS *Amphion*, ADM 36/9561, TNA Master's Log, HMS *Amphion*, ADM 52/2133, TNA; "From Waterford," *Mystic Pioneer*, Oct. 24, 1863. Chads, a naval officer, had been appointed as a superintendent of vessels, or principal agent for transports, in Jan. 1777. This role was designed to reduce the burden on the army's quartermaster general's department and to oversee and command the naval transports that acted in concert with the army.

10 "From Waterford," *Mystic Pioneer*, Oct. 17, 1863. The militia from Avery's Company at Goshen Point watched the British prepare to land at Brown's Farm. One of them, Paul Rogers, remembered, "I was down on Goshen, when I saw a barge shoot off from one of their ships towards the shore, and as I saw a soldier in the boat raise his gun to fire I instantly jumped into the cart way that divided the bank, so the ball came whizzing near me, striking the water. A young man . . . Clark Crandall was on the other side of the creek, further east, and nearer to them. They also fired at him, as he stood on the wall. They missed him, and he swung his hat and called out to them to try it again, but I believe he did not wait long for them to fire again. The ships kept firing cannon balls at the houses during the day, while the army they had landed was up the river . . . One ball went over my head and struck a barn breaking one of the rafters."

11 Thomas Graves, *The Graves Papers and Other Documents Relating to the Naval Operations of the Yorktown Campaign July to Oct 1781*, French E. Chadwick, ed. (New York, 1916), 108–109.

Receiving the signal around 8:30 a.m., Shepherd's vessels, including the *Amphion* further offshore, opened fire on the militia positioned at Brown's farm. Shot and shell streaked through the air. A militiaman recounted: "they Opend there brode Sides . . . and all landed under ther Cannon whos balls flew over Our heads like hale stones." The noise was so loud it could be heard twenty miles away at Montauk Point on Long Island. A loyalist spy, according to a witness there, recalled, "there was a smart firing for some time, and soon after it was over, the ships and vessels appeared to close in with the Batteries, from which the people in the Neighborhood of the point conclude that the batteries were silenced and the troops landed."[12]

To the anxious militia, the ground seemed to be exploding all around them. Shot plowed into Brown's fields, smashing and breaking trees in one of his orchards. Even though the rounds missed their targets, the militia almost instantly panicked; men broke and ran back across the farm, heading in the direction of the Brown house. Harris's presence did not help, as he was among the first to leave. Without alerting anyone, he turned his horse around and galloped away.[13]

According to a witness, the "very heavy cannonade" lasted about nine minutes. It inflicted few, if any, casualties, but it worked its effect. Under the smoke landing craft carried the first wave—consisting of the combined force of the Associated Loyalists and Loyal Refugees under Lt. Col. Joshua Upham, and von Wangenheim's jaegers—towards the shore. They landed on the beach without incident just south of the lighthouse. There they linked up with the marines and sailors already onshore. Upham boasted to Governor Franklin, "we had the honor to be included in the first division, and I have the pleasure to add we were the first on shore."[14]

Reaching dry land, the 120 loyalist militia and 60 jaegers assaulted the ridgeline previously occupied by the militia. The armed vessels ceased firing, as Upham and von Wangenheim ascended the ridge and easily secured the now abandoned position. From there they deployed outward to protect the remainder of the division as it came ashore. Upham explained: "We advanced on the right of the whole to a height at a small distance from the shore, where we were ordered to cover the 38th regiment from a wood on our right until the second [wave] came up."[15]

---

12 Master's Log, HMS *Amphion*, ADM 52/2133, TNA; John Hempsted narrative in Harris, *Groton Heights*, 62; Mackenzie, *Diary*, 618.

13 Jonathan Brooks narrative in Harris, *Groton Heights*, 75; PA; *Griswold* Avery Jr. (R.306), NARA.

14 John Hempsted narrative in Harris, *Groton Heights*, 63; Master's Log, HMS *Amphion*, ADM 52/2133, TNA; Upham report in Harris, *Groton Heights*, 109.

15 Upham report in Harris, *Groton Heights*, 109; "State of the undermentioned Corps," Frederick Mackenzie Papers, WCL. The often-quoted number of 60 jaegers did not include the six sergeants, the horn-blower, or two officers who were with them.

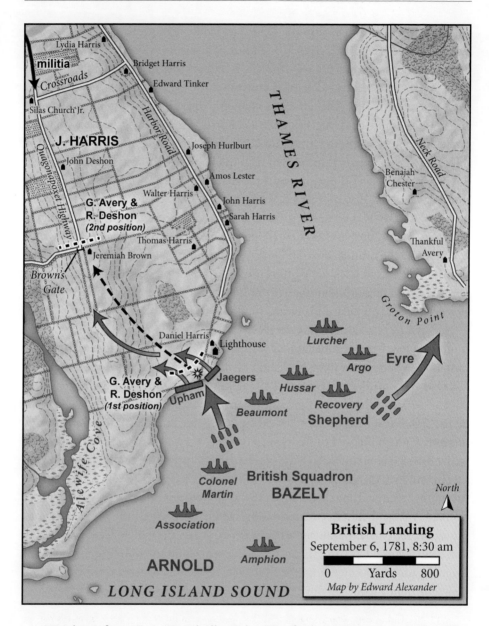

Watching from Fort Trumbull, Holsey Sanford, working one of the fort's 18-pounders, recalled: "We began to fire immediately on their landing." Nearby, Matross John Kilbourn claimed "[we] kept up an incessant firing," and the British were "much annoyed." The fire, however, did not affect Shepherd's vessels. After

Shepherd's ships ceased firing on Brown's farm, they repositioned themselves to fire on the Groton side of the river.[16]

After the ridgeline above the beach was secured, the 38th Regiment, the Loyal American Regiment, the American Legion, and a 6-pounder field piece with accompanying crew, under 1st Lt. William Horndon were all transported ashore. Horses were brought for the artillery, officers, and part of the American Legion.

Arnold soon joined them. As he stepped onto the sands of the beach, it marked his first time in his native Connecticut in over a year and the first time since his defection. With him were two staff officers, Capt. John Dalrymple, also known as Lord Dalrymple, and Capt. John Stapleton. Both served on the staff of Sir Henry Clinton, Dalrymple as aide de camp and Stapleton as assistant deputy adjutant general. During the expedition Stapleton acted as Arnold's brigade major and Dalrymple as his aide.[17]

Shortly after 9:00 a.m., the first division, almost 900 men, assembled on the southern end of the Brown farm and prepared to march for New London, three miles away. Arnold posted Captain von Wangenheim and his jaegers at the head of his column. Then, dispersed in skirmish order, they were pushed well out in front to screen Arnold's advance, scouting and probing ahead of the main column. A distance behind them, the 38th Regiment comprised the main column, followed by Horndon's artillery. The Loyal American Regiment brought up the rear.[18]

Arnold deployed a sizable force of flankers on both sides of the column as he anticipated the militia might try to ambush his column. According to Upham, the flankers fanned out "at a distance of two hundred yards from the main body." The task of the flankers was to keep the main column beyond the effective musket range of any militia that might try to spring a trap. Assuming the more significant threat would come from the left, not from the right closer to the river, the larger force of flankers was placed on the left: three companies, numbering almost 200 men. Two companies were from the Associated Loyalists under Upham, the third from

16 Sanford, *Memoir*; Payne Kenyon Kilbourne, *The History of and Antiquities of the Name and Family of Kilbourn, In its Varied Orthography* (New Haven, CT, 1856), 58–59.

17 Mackenzie, *Diary*, 2:662. Stapleton held his commission in the 17th Light Dragoons but was detached from the regiment and acted as Clinton's assistant deputy adjutant general. Arnold report in Mackenzie, *Diary*, 2:623, 627. A brigade major was in effect the chief of staff of a brigade. Captain Dalrymple held his commission with the 87th Regiment of Foot but was detached from it to serve in America.

18 Mackenzie, *Diary*, 2:611; "A Sketch of New-London & Groton, with Attacks made on Forts Trumbull & Griswold by the British Troops Under the Command of Brig. General Arnold Sepr 6th, 1781, by Captain Lyman of ye Prince of Wales American Volunteers," WCL. Lyman shows the two companies of Associated Loyalists followed by Wogan whose company brought up the rear of the flankers.

the American Legion under Capt. Samuel Wogan, a former lieutenant in the 44th Regiment of Foot. "This alteration," Upham explained, "derived its propriety from the circumstance of the rebels having gone over to the left, from an apprehension of being too much crowded between our troops and the river on their left."[19]

On the right flank, Arnold placed the remainder of the American Legion, one company, under Capt. Nathan Frink. Frink commanded one of the Legion's cavalry companies which, unlike Wogan's men, was at least partially mounted. Frink, a 22-year-old native of Pomfret, Connecticut, was the son of a former representative to the General Assembly. Once described as the town's "dashing young attorney and excise officer," by 1780 that reputation had drastically changed. Frink had been labeled as "a notorious traitor to the States" by Governor Trumbull and had been arrested and imprisoned.[20]

Before his trial, Frink broke out of jail and fled to British lines. Like Arnold, this was Frink's first time back in Connecticut since his escape. Now, only a day's ride from his old home, Frink's men protected Arnold's right flank and also helped keep a line of communication open with Shepherd's vessels, which were expected to sail upriver as soon as Forts Trumbull and Griswold were taken.[21]

Arnold's march towards New London commenced about 9:00 a.m. as the jaegers stepped off, followed a short time later by the entire column. The jaegers advanced effortlessly across the Brown farm. But waiting ahead of them, near the Brown house, were the remnants of Avery and Deshon's companies. The companies rallied along a bend of the Quagonapoxet Highway, near the Brown house. With the militia, Captain Hempsted remembered, "the Enemy adVanced with a Slow march untill they got upon high Ground," and then the fight began in earnest.

19 Upham report in Harris, *Groton Heights*, 109; "A Sketch of New-London & Groton, with Attacks made on Forts Trumbull & Griswold by the British Troops Under the Command of Brig. General Arnold Sep 6th, 1781 by Captain Lyman of ye Prince of Wales American Volunteers," Sir Henry Clinton Papers, WCL; Upham report in Harris, *Groton Heights*, 109. It appears Castles's small command joined one of the two companies under Upham, so one company now had 70 men and the other had 50.; Worthington Chauncey Ford, British Officers During the American Revolution 1774–1783 (Brooklyn, NY, 1897), 185. Wogan held a lieutenant's commission in the 44th Regiment of Foot but resigned and accepted a captain's commission in the American Legion, dated Dec. 10, 1780.

20 *CSR*, 1:2, 61, 90; Governor Jonathan Trumbull to George Washington, Feb. 13, 1781, Papers of George Washington, LOC; Larned, *Historic Gleanings*, 119–120. The presence of these mounted men caused quite a scare. Early American intelligence reports greatly exaggerated their strength at 300–500 troopers.

21 "State of various corps going on Benedict Arnold's Expedition against New London," Frederick Mackenzie Papers, WCL; Frink held a commission dated Nov. 1780 and Wogan held his dated Dec. 1780. Muster rolls, American Legion, British Military and Naval Records, RG 8, "C" Series, Volume 1871, PAC.

Sighting the jaegers, the militia fired a volley in their direction, then fell back onto the Walter Harris farm whose fields lay north of the Brown farm.[22]

The jaegers returned fire, then advanced towards the Brown house and the militia who were retreating up the Quagonapoxet Highway. Once at the highway, the jaegers, advancing in two platoons or wings, deployed on either side of the road and pursued the militia across the Harris farm. In what became a running firefight, the jaegers chased the militia, often moving "quick from one wall to another" as they exchanged shots with militia concealed behind stonewalls, fences, and outbuildings belonging to the farms along the highway. Few homes lined the road, as most of the land had been reserved for farming and pasturing livestock. The militia made good use of the ground. They fell back short distances, but maintained steady contact with the jaegers, often reloading and firing on the move, "Exchangen Shot every opportunity," as Hempsted recalled.[23]

As Deshon's and Avery's companies attempted to hold on, help was approaching from various parts of town. About a hundred militia and sailors gathered at the intersection of the Quagonapoxet Highway and a cross highway, about a mile south of Fort Nonsense. The cross highway, unnamed at the time, had been built only a decade earlier, spanning west to east and connecting the Quagonapoxet Highway to the Harbor Road. Included among those gathered there were members of the 1st and 2nd Companies, the 1st and 2nd Companies of the Alarm List, the Independent Artillery Company, and several sailors. Captain John Hallam organized these arrivals into a second company of volunteers. Joining Hallam's Company were elements of the 7th Company under Capt. Jabez Beebe, and parts of the 11th Company under Capt. Jonathan Caulkins from the western outskirts of New London.[24]

Since the volunteers came from various occupations, not one man was dressed the same as another. They wore an array of different styled and colored coats, pants, and hats. Most were equipped with military accouterments such as cartridge boxes, powder horns, haversacks, and canteens. Many, having served on other previous alarms and fully aware they might be away from home for an extended

---

22 John Hempsted narrative in Harris, *Groton Heights*, 63. Harris's farm encompassed almost seventy acres of land that extended from Alewife Cove to the river's edge. He resided in a small house by the river. By 1781, Harris's son-in-law Amos Lester had been given parts of the farm, where he constructed a house and farmed several lots.

23 John Hempsted narrative in Harris, *Groton Heights*, 63.

24 PA: Gurdon Flower Saltonstall (R.9159), NARA; Book, "Connecticut Independent Company," NLCHS; Brooks narrative in Harris, *Groton Heights*, 75. The cross highway was later known as Lewis Lane, and today is known as Thames Street. The Harbor Road was also known as "the road to Harbour's Mouth."

period, came bearing either blanket rolls or knapsacks containing extra food and a few other necessities. Their armament was just as varied as their appearance, men brandishing a variety of muskets, fowling pieces, and swords.

Just south of the intersection stood the Silas Church house. Residing there was Silas, his wife Anna, their two young daughters, Church's widowed mother, and two slaves, Cato and Jenny. To supplement the family's income, they had at least one tenant, Jabez Miner, living on the property. Church owned several dozen acres of farmland and orchards on both sides of the highway, though most, including his house and barn, lay just west of the intersection.[25]

The position at the intersection was crucial for the militia to maintain. Directly to the north was Fort Nonsense and to the northeast lay Fort Trumbull. Any further retreat put both forts in jeopardy. But despite the significant increase in numbers, the militia and sailors needed an overall commander to lead them. This caused immense frustration, and the men openly argued and disagreed with each other on how to proceed. Some even, according to a witness, "fell into [a] conversation about how they should manage." Without a leader and the enemy rapidly approaching, they attempted to choose a course of action democratically.[26]

Nearby, Jonathan Brooks Jr., who had retreated there with his father from Brown's farm, recalled how some "were for fighting at any odds" and wanted to form a line of battle "and contest the ground inch by inch." Nathaniel Saltonstall, who was also amongst them, vehemently disagreed. Saltonstall, a member of the 2nd Company Alarm List, and a veteran privateer captain, had commanded both the old fort on the Parade and Fort Trumbull. According to Brooks, Saltonstall was the most vocal as he tried to reason with the less combat-experienced men. Brooks wrote that Saltonstall told them, "[G]entlemen, whether I have as much courage as many who have given their opinion, I shall not undertake to say, but this I will say, for one I will not be such a fool to stand here open breasted and be shot down by the very first volley of the enemy's fire."[27]

Saltonstall understood the tactical situation well, perhaps more than anyone else in the group. He was not one to turn down the opportunity to fight—it was said of him that he was "a man of too much fire." However, even the aggressive Saltonstall realized that if they attempted to stand their ground, they would have

---

25 Connecticut, Wills and Probate Records, Hartford, Probate Packets, Christopher, Christopher-Cleveland, 1675–1850, Estate of Silas Church, Town of New London, 1786, No. 1234, CSL; Connecticut, Wills and Probate Records, Hartford, Probate Packets, Christopher, Christopher-Cleveland, 1675–1850, Estate of Rebecca Church, Town of New London, 1785, No. 1230, CSL.

26 Brooks narrative in Harris, *Groton Heights*, 75–76.

27 Ibid., 76.

difficulty with even the most rudimentary military formations, like forming into a line of battle. The group contained militia and sailors, and all differed significantly in their military experience and training and had never worked together as a unit.[28]

Even the militia had only limited training and combat experience. They had proven time and time again to be unreliable, almost unpredictable, under fire. They could not be expected to deal with British regulars face to face. When they did, they often broke and ran in the first moments of the battle. Therefore, they had to be carefully used on any battlefield. If they were to break, morale would plummet, making defense of the town impossible.

As the group debated, Lieutenant Colonel Harris came galloping up the highway, passing the Church house, ahead of Deshon and Avery's men "with his sword by his side." On sighting Harris, the group cheered and, according to Brooks, "were all much elated." He was their senior officer, and they believed he would lead them. Instead, they met a much-demoralized Harris, adversely affected by his experience on Brown's farm. He halted his horse near the group, where a relieved volunteer, according to Brooks, greeted him with these words: "Now, colonel, we have somebody to command us and are at your service." But instead of giving them orders or the direction they so desperately desired, Harris, showing obvious signs of extreme mental stress, according to a witness, blurted out: "You must excuse me, gentlemen, as I have a violent sick headache this morning and can hardly sit on my horse." Then, he rode on toward Town Hill. The group were enraged by Harris's abdication of command, some wanting to shoot "the d[amne]d rascal." Fortunately for him, their attention was drawn to the British column headed toward them.[29]

With Deshon's and Avery's men falling back toward them, the Americans at the crossroads realized they needed to act. After Harris's departure, the group looked to Saltonstall or perhaps Caulkins, Hallam, or Beebe, all militia captains, to decide what they were supposed to do. The individual captains took charge of their companies and ordered the men to fall in with Deshon's and Avery's men. One part joined Deshon's Company on the west side of the road, while the others augmented Avery's Company on the east side. The group on the west side of the highway ventured south across the Silas Church farm, while those on the east side

28 John A. McManemın, *Captains of Privateers During the Revolutionary War* (Spring Lake, NJ, 1985), 88.

29 Brooks narrative in Harris, *Groton Heights*, 76; Master's Log, HMS *Amphion*, ADM 52/2133, TNA; PA: Gurdon Flower Saltonstall (R.9159), NARA.

deployed onto a farm owned by John Deshon. From these positions, they were to maneuver and harass, to delay the British approach "as best [they] can."[30]

Despite their diligent efforts, this strategy was doomed to failure because there was no overall command and control. As a result, there was no way or time to coordinate attacks on the British column. Upham reported they were "constantly skirmishing with rebels, who fled from hill to hill, and from stone fences which intersected the country at small distances." For the next half a mile, the militia made a series of disjointed and uncoordinated attacks on the British flankers, annoying them but inflicting no real damage.[31]

West of the highway, at one point, Captain Hallam attempted to check Upham's men. According to Gurdon F. Saltonstall, a member of 2nd Company and now of Hallam's Company, "Capt. Hallam called on 12 of his men to follow him in order to check a flanking party, we deployed them, and after a few random shots, Capt Hallam ordered a retreat, sensing we were overpowered." Unfortunately, after making contact with Upham, some of the defenders had found themselves caught between the Associated Loyalists, the jaegers, and the fast-approaching 38th Regiment. Captain Hallam yelled for his men to pull back and the panicked men raced for their lives in a hasty, disorganized retreat. But Saltonstall was not with them. "I was left alone," he claimed, "& I was hemmed in between [the jaegers] and the main body of the British troops, I made my escape, [frequently fired upon by the enemy]."[32]

Just before 11:00 a.m., after almost two hours of skirmishing, the jaegers, under Captain von Wangenheim, had driven the militia back and reached the intersection. Already fanned outward, they moved forward a short distance and halted. Many crouched or dropped to the ground. With the enemy in front they remained alert. Behind them, the rest of the British column and flankers halted as well. A brief lull then descended upon the battlefield.

Arnold, accompanied by Stapleton, Lord Dalrymple, and Captain Millet galloped up past the Church house. Ahead of him, Arnold saw the first real obstacles on his trek northward, Fort Nonsense and Fort Trumbull. Both lay only a mile distant. Both needed to be secured before he could take the real prize, New London. From Arnold's vantage, he saw militia rallying about a half-mile ahead of him. He could not see Fort Trumbull, so had no idea what awaited him there.

---

30 Brooks narrative in Harris, *Groton Heights*, 76–77. The farm owned by Deshon was previously owned by William Rathbone, but after he died the family sold it. Deshon did not reside there but probably rented out the property.

31 Upham report in Harris, *Groton Heights*, 109.

32 PA: Gurdon Flower Saltonstall (R.9159), NARA.

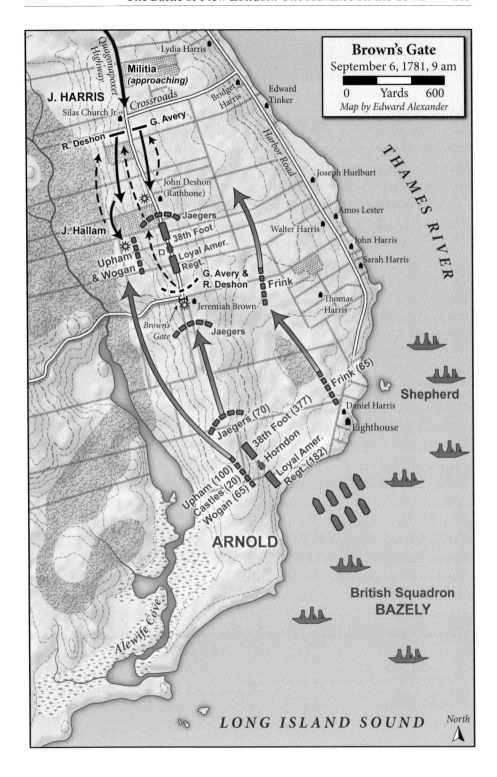

Brown's Gate
September 6, 1781, 9 am

0   Yards   600

Map by Edward Alexander

Quagonapoxet Highway

Lydia Harris

Militia
(approaching)

J. HARRIS

Crossroads

Silas Church Jr.

G. Avery

Bridget Harris

Edward Tinker

R. Deshon

Harbor Road

Joseph Hurlburt

John Deshon
(Rathbone)

Amos Lester

Jaegers

Walter Harris

38th Foot

John Harris

J. Hallam

Sarah Harris

**Upham
& Wogan**

**Loyal Amer.
Regt.**

**G. Avery &
R. Deshon**

Frink

Jeremiah Brown

Thomas
Harris

*Brown's
Gate*

Jaegers

Frink (65)

Shepherd

THAMES RIVER

Daniel Harris

Jaegers (70)

38th Foot (377)

Lighthouse

Horndon

Upham (100)

**Loyal Amer.
Regt. (182)**

Castles (20)

Wogan (65)

ARNOLD

**British Squadron
BAZELY**

Alewife Cove

LONG ISLAND SOUND   *North*

As a result of the brief reconnaissance, Arnold decided Fort Nonsense and Fort Trumbull would be assaulted simultaneously. The 38th Foot and Loyal American Regiment, Arnold's most experienced units, would be used to make the attack.

Without knowing what kind of force held Fort Trumbull, Arnold ordered Captain Millet to take four companies of the 38th Foot and move east from the crossroads towards the river, where they would link up with Frink's Company. Despite only being a captain, Millet was a seasoned officer with several years of combat experience. By 1781 he had been in America for about a decade, first serving in the 64th Regiment of Foot. He served with them through the New York Campaign until the summer of 1777, when he obtained a commission as captain in the 38th Regiment and led its Grenadier Company during the Battle of Rhode Island and the Siege of Charleston. Now he served as the regiment's commander.[33]

As Millet moved towards Fort Trumbull, Arnold with the Loyal American Regiment and the remaining four companies of the 38th, around 400 soldiers, would advance on Town Hill and capture Fort Nonsense. The rest of Arnold's force remained in reserve on or adjacent to the Church farm, remaining alert but getting some much-deserved rest.

As the British reached the crossroads, the militia fell back a half-mile to the expansive William Hempstead farm. There they were gradually rallied and posted in a skirmish line facing the approaching British. Hempstead's farm, situated on the west side of the Quagonapoxet Highway, lay a half-mile south of Fort Nonsense. While Hempstead and his immediate family resided in the adjacent house, his vast acreage was operated jointly by William and his two brothers, Thomas, and Stephen.[34]

This new militia line stretched for around a hundred yards, extending eastward from the Hempstead farm, across the highway, and onto fields belonging to Jeremiah Miller Sr. and John Harris. Captain Richard Deshon, the highest-ranking officer in the regiment present, held command over all the militia. This was due to Harris's continued absence. He was at Fort Nonsense, but never informed any of his militia commanders of his location. After leaving the group at the crossroads, Harris had ridden to the fort. Perhaps he intended to make a stand there, but again did so without notifying any of his militia commanders. Instead, he gathered any militia he could find and directed them to Fort Nonsense. The fort's magazine was

33 Arnold report in Mackenzie, *Diary*, 2:623.

34 Connecticut, Wills and Probate Records, Hartford, Probate Packets, Harris, William-Higgins, J, 1675–1850, 1051–1055, CSL.

opened, and militia ran up onto the platform, which lined the south wall, to await the British assault or, if they were trained to do so, man its cannon.[35]

South of the fort, on the west side of the highway, the militia took shelter behind the Hempstead barn and other outbuildings clustered about his farm. Then, clinging to their muskets, they awaited the approach of the Loyal American Regiment. William, in the process of evacuating his house, came out and offered several militia officers a drink of gin. The weather had grown increasingly humid as the morning wore on and had begun to take its toll on the militia, so the gin was well received.[36]

As Hempstead made his rounds, the British attack began anew. The first to move was Captain Millet. As ordered, Millett, accompanied by Captain Stapleton, took the four lead companies of the 38th Foot, just under 200 men, from the main column and upon reaching the intersection turned east toward the river.[37]

Advancing behind Millet's detachment, the remaining four companies of the 38th Foot, commanded by Capt. William Davies, prepared for action. Davies was a five-year veteran of the regiment who had seen his share of action. He now moved the roughly 180 redcoats beyond the intersection onto fields belonging to the widow Lydia Harris.[38]

Once all were in Harris's fields, Davies ordered his company commanders to deploy their men. With drums rattling, one by one the companies shifted from column formation into a line of battle. The order came to fix bayonets. Each soldier shifted his musket down to his left side and removed his bayonet from its scabbard with his right hand. The metallic clang was heard all up and down the line as the bayonets were fixed to the tip of the muskets.

As the 38th Foot formed, Lt. Col. Beverly Robinson Jr. advanced his 165 soldiers of the Loyal American Regiment onto the west side of the highway. After passing across the northern outskirts of the Church farm, Robinson moved them onto a pasture field owned by Robert Froud. Seven of Robinson's eight companies

---

35 Brooks narrative in Harris, *Groton Heights*, 77; Militia, Second Series, 1747–1788, 2581a, CSL.

36 John Hempsted narrative in Harris, *Groton Heights*, 63.

37 Ibid., 64; Matthew H. Spring, *With Zeal and With Bayonets Only: The British Army on Campaign in North America, 1775-1783* (Norman, OK, 2008), 78. Hempsted incorrectly believed that Millet's objective was to go around the militia line and cut them off from the fort. The companies taken by Millet were the four right companies of the battalion.

38 "State of various corps going on Benedict Arnold's Expedition against New London," Frederick Mackenzie Papers, WCL; Muster rolls, 38th Regiment of Foot, WO 12/5172, TNA; Spring, *With Zeal and With Bayonets*, 78; Ford, British Officers, 58. Davies was the second highest ranking officer present and therefore would have taken command of the left wing, or those left behind when Millet and the right wing of the regiment departed for Fort Trumbull.

were ordered into a line of battle with bayonets fixed. The eighth was deployed as flankers on the regiment's left to protect it as it advanced.[39]

Once deployed, the Loyalists faced northward towards Fort Nonsense, which was in line with the 38th Foot on the opposite side of the road. Arnold then signaled the advance and the two regiments advanced steadily up the hill towards the militia.[40]

The British line had almost 600 yards of ground to cover until they reached the Americans. As they neared, the militia emerged from their positions and began trading long-range shots with the advancing redcoats. Undeterred, drums pounding, Robinson and Davies pressed their commands forward. The militia on the Hempstead farm were compelled to fall back, firing as they gave ground to the fast-approaching Loyalists. The situation was the same on the other side of the road—pressed by the 38th Foot, the defenders were forced back across the Miller and Harris farms.

As the militia grudgingly retreated up the southern slope of Town Hill, gunners manning cannon at Fort Nonsense opened a "brisk fire" on the advancing British. In a normal situation, this would have been much-welcomed support and probably greatly assisted the militia. But in this case, it had the opposite effect.[41]

No communication or coordination between the fort and the militia had been established. Or at least, if there was, it was not recorded. Several rounds fell short or completely missed their targets. Their intended target appears to have been the Loyal American Regiment, as many of their rounds crashed into either the Hempstead farm or an adjacent pasture, which lay just north of the house. Some even fell dangerously close to the militia, and while they did not inflict casualties, caused turmoil in the ranks.

With the militia on his cousin's farm, Captain Hempsted recalled, "When the forte opened upon the Enemy the Shot fell Short, & wee ware between two fires." This greatly agitated the militia. On the skirmish line, William Coit ran up to Hempsted and started screaming at him. The "tall, portly [and] somewhat eccentric" New London native pleaded with the militia captain to go to the fort and order them to stop firing on the militia. Hempsted refused to leave the front

---

39 John Hempsted narrative in Harris, *Groton Heights*, 64, 69; Muster rolls, Loyal American Regiment, British Military and Naval Records, RG 8, "C" Series, Volume 1867, p. 71, PAC. Hempsted described them as advancing in "Indian file," which means they were moving in a long, single file line, much as flankers operated. Based on casualties, this was likely Capt. Christopher Hatch's Company.

40 Arnold report in Mackenzie, *Diary*, 2:611. This is in the area today around the Lawrence Memorial Hospital.

41 Arnold's report in Mackenzie, *Diary*, 2:623.

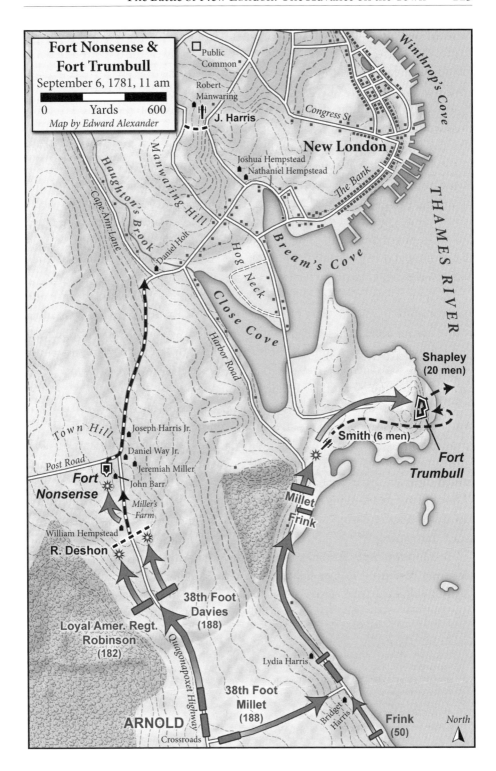

**Fort Nonsense &
Fort Trumbull**

September 6, 1781, 11 am

0   Yards   600

Map by Edward Alexander

Public Common

Robert Manwaring

J. Harris

Congress St

Winthrop's Cove

New London

Joshua Hempstead

Nathaniel Hempstead

The Bank

Manwaring Hill

Haughton's Brook

Cape Ann Lane

Daniel Holt

Hog Neck

Bream's Cove

Close Cove

Harbor Road

THAMES RIVER

Shapley
(20 men)

Smith (6 men)

**Fort
Trumbull**

Town Hill

Joseph Harris Jr.

Daniel Way Jr.

Post Road

Jeremiah Miller

**Fort
Nonsense**

John Barr

*Miller's
Farm*

William Hempstead

R. Deshon

**Millet
Frink**

**38th Foot
Davies**
(188)

**Loyal Amer. Regt.
Robinson**
(182)

Quogonapoxet Highway

Lydia Harris

**38th Foot
Millet**
(188)

ARNOLD

Crossroads

Bridget
Harris

Frink
(50)

North

and told Coit to do it himself. But, having "no Command," Coit held no authority to give that order. Hempsted then told Coit to go in the captain's name and do it. Coit complied, ran back towards the fort, and "the firing Seased." Hempsted took credit for it, but Colonel Harris was more deserving.[42]

Harris watched the British from Fort Nonsense as they passed across the Hempstead farm. He decided the fort could not be held and ordered it to abandoned. This surprised some of the militia at the fort. Israel Rogers, a member of the 1st Company, had just arrived and expected to help defend the fort. But instead it was being evacuated. He later testified in his pension application that upon his arrival, "all the guns had been spiked except one and the fort abandoned." Under Harris's direction, that single gun, an iron 12-pounder fieldpiece, was being moved to Manwaring Hill. Slinging his musket onto his shoulder, Rogers joined the gunners and helped pull the gun off the platform and out of the fort. Then with the crew and Harris, he fell back towards the town.[43]

Despite the militiamen's efforts, they could not stop the British advance and were forced back towards Fort Nonsense. At one point, as the militia was falling back, Captain Hempsted wanted to pull some troops from the line. So, he tried to move and put a force on the British left flank, allowing them to fire down the length of the advancing Loyal American Regiment. He believed this might be enough to stop them or inflict significant casualties.

Sprinting up and down the line, Hempsted called out for volunteers, but only three responded. Then, as the militia continued to exchange fire with the advancing British, Hempsted led his group back towards the fort. Reaching a farm lot just south of the fort, Hempsted led them westward across the lot and then turned them southward onto the western part of the Hempstead farm, owned by Thomas Hempstead. Along a stonewall, which marked Thomas's eastern boundary, Hempsted later recalled: "We posted Our Selves In a Very advatagos place" and awaited the enemy.[44]

In the meantime, Arnold's men continued advancing up Town Hill. Both regiments continued to face light, sporadic musket fire from the militia. As the Loyal Americans passed across the Hempstead farm, they became concealed in a cornfield, with only their bayonets visible over the stalks. The companies became

42 P. H. Woodward, "Captain William Coit," *Collections of the Connecticut Historical Society VII* (Feb. 1899): 5; John Hempsted narrative in Harris, *Groton Heights*, 63.

43 PA: Israel Rogers (S.14383), NARA.

44 John Hempsted narrative in Harris, *Groton Heights*, 64. Hempsted named only one of his volunteers, George Smith.

staggered as they moved through the cornstalks, unable to stay in line with each other. Hempsted watched them the whole way.

The flankers advancing in an "In[di]an file" ahead of the regiment soon reached a stonewall, which divided the cornfield from a potato field, only 30 yards from Hempsted. The obstacle caused the loyalist soldiers to slow down. Hempsted quietly signaled to his party to take aim as they passed over the wall. He then fired his musket, followed quickly by the three others. The shots caught the Loyal Americans entirely off guard.[45]

Reacting, some loyalists faced to the left and discharged a volley in Hempsted's direction. The shots all missed. But then, they faced to the front and continued to the fort, completely ignoring the small band of militia. A short time later, another of the Loyal American companies came into Hempsted's view. Reloaded, Hempsted's party again fired. The effect of the volley was the same as before and caused instant confusion amongst the loyalists. They had not expected it. But before Hempsted and his men could get off another shot, a group of jaegers suddenly emerged from the rear of the Loyal Americans. Ordered to clear out the militia, they came running in Hempsted's direction and scattered the party.[46]

Off to the east, the militia on Town Hill made its final stand near the John Barr farm, which lay just south of Fort Nonsense. Barr, a sailor, owned a small 2-acre plot of land with a house and a barn. The militia was dispersed on his property, taking shelter behind his house and barn. Some militia were still in the fort, others on the opposite side of the highway in an apple orchard, which lay at the northern of Miller's farm.[47]

Lieutenant Colonel Robinson cared little for the annoyance made by Hempsted and kept his men focused on their objective, Fort Nonsense. Coming within a hundred yards of the fort, Robinson halted the men, dressed their ranks, and ordered them to fire. A single volley of musketry erupted along his line towards the militia on the Barr farm. Before the smoke cleared, Robinson ordered a bayonet charge. The Loyal Americans surged forward towards the fort. They came on with shouts and drums rattling. One witness stated, "[they huzzahed]" as they stormed the fort. The psychological effects of the charge proved devastating to the militia. A few shots were fired, but most broke and ran. According to Samuel Plumb, of

45 Ibid., 64, 69. The Loyal American Regiment sustained three casualties during the expedition. According to Hempsted, his party inflicted at least two of them. William Hempstead later brought Hempsted to the site on his farm where blood covered a section of his potato crop.

46 Ibid. Hempstead described the jaegers as "men with grene Cotes and long fethers."

47 Parsons, *Life and Letters*, 218. While Miller resided in town, he owned a farm and house on Town Hill. His family later relocated there after his two other houses in town were destroyed by fire as the British departed.

Capt. Richard Deshon's Company, the British "dr[ove] all before them." Most fled northward to the Post Road and towards the town. Some bolted across the road. [48]

Reaching the fort without real opposition, Robinson's men scaled the walls and poured into it through the embrasures. As they breached the wall, at least one militiaman remained trapped inside. This citizen soldier is believed, at least locally, to have been 65-year-old Walter Harris, who resided near the lighthouse and had been fighting all day. Beyond the mandatory age for service in the militia, Harris was one of the oldest men who defended New London that day. Realizing the hopelessness of his situation, he surrendered himself as a prisoner.[49]

In the Miller orchard, the militia found themselves suddenly threatened on two sides. With the Loyal American Regiment in possession of Fort Nonsense and the 38th Foot rapidly approaching, their position became untenable. The militia, including Captain Hempsted, had escaped across the road. They exchanged shots from behind the orchard's trees with both British units. Then, as the 38th Foot approached the summit of Town Hill, they observed the militia in the orchard. The regulars closed, dressed their ranks, halted, and unleashed a volley. Hempsted remembered, "they gave Us a Shot in the orchard, but to no purpus." They then launched a bayonet charge, but before the full impact was felt, the militia abandoned the orchard and Town Hill, retreating towards the town.[50]

The 38th Foot and the Loyal Americans had experienced some desperate fights already in the American War—the 38th had been decimated at Bunker Hill, and the Loyal Americans had suffered substantial losses storming Fort Montgomery. Never had they seen the Americans give up so easily. The attack cost them about 1 killed and 4 wounded, the Loyal Americans suffering the brunt of the attack. On the other hand, the defense of Town Hill had been nothing spectacular. It had mostly been a show of force by the militia, and the only recorded casualties were one or two captured.[51]

Arnold followed the attack up the hill. The rest of his division followed at a short distance behind the two attacking regiments. Riding up the highway, Arnold

---

48 John Hempsted narrative in Harris, *Groton Heights*, 65; PA: Samuel Plumb (R.8287), NARA.

49 John Hempsted narrative, in Harris, *Groton Heights*, 65; Harris, *Groton Heights*, 272. It is believed Harris was either the only prisoner taken or one of two by the British on Town Hill.

50 John Hempsted narrative in Harris, *Groton Heights*, 64–65. Hempsted had no respect for the firing ability of the Loyal American Regiment. Years later he recalled running across the southern face of Fort Nonsense as the loyalists launched their attack. He remembered glancing over his shoulder toward the Loyalists "when their Guns flasht, but hapy for mee one of thir ball Struck a potato hill, clos by my feet, and the other whistled by my hed." Later in life, he jokingly commented, "I Rember what I thaught that they ware not Very good marks men."

51 Arnold report in Mackenzie, *Diary*, 2:627.

probably took time to view the wrecked John Barr farm as they passed as both the house and barn had been heavily damaged.[52]

Riding further, Arnold made his way to Fort Nonsense and inspected it. He was probably surprised the fort had been taken so quickly. The Americans left behind eight 12-pounders, all spiked. Little or no ammunition for the guns was found in the magazine. Instead, the barracks Avery's Company had occupied were filled with a variety of artillery accoutrements, cooking utensils, and other personal objects.[53]

Walter Harris, under guard in the fort, saw Arnold. According to a local legend, Harris recognized Arnold, and loudly hailed him as a traitor in front of his soldiers. This may have been the first time since his defection that Arnold had been recognized in person. Harris was quickly quieted by a guard as Arnold attempted to brush off the embarrassment.[54]

Riding out of Fort Nonsense, Arnold looked north where he could see the militia retreating in disorder. Then, satisfied with his soldiers' performance, Arnold prepared to resume the advance towards New London. He ordered Captain von Wangenheim to move his jaegers back to the head of the column. Their horn-blower sounded the call, and they swiftly redeployed in skirmish order, two platoons on either side of the road and then proceeded a short distance up the road. As the main column reformed behind them, Arnold looked east towards Fort Trumbull, wondering how Millet's men were getting on.[55]

As the British attacked Town Hill, Millet's men made good time marching across the cross highway. At its eastern end stood the home of the widow Bridget Harris, which faced the river. At 63-years-old, the widow operated much of the farm that ran south along the highway. Reaching the Harris house, Millet turned the column northward toward Fort Trumbull. He was probably unaware that, at that very moment, Fort Trumbull was in the process of being abandoned. Like Fort Nonsense, the Americans would give it to the British without much resistance. Once Captain Shapley realized he lacked a sufficient force to protect his rear his position became untenable and therefore he decided to retreat to Fort Griswold.

---

52 *CSR*, 7:466. Barr owned a two-acre property, which included a house and barn. There, in 1781, he resided with his wife, Elizabeth, and young son. Barr submitted a damage claim to the state for damages during the attack for £71, which translates to over $13,000.00 today.

53 Arnold report in Mackenzie, *Diary*, 2.628.

54 Harris, *Groton Heights*, 272; Royal Navy Ship's Muster (Series 1), HMS *Amphion*, ADM 36/9561, TNA.

55 Arnold report in Mackenzie, *Diary*, 2:623–624.

When Shapley and Harris had met with Ledyard earlier that morning, these were assuredly the orders Ledyard had given to Shapley: fight as long as you can, but once Fort Trumbull is found to be indefensible, spike the guns and retire across the river. The only flexibility Shapley had was when to evacuate it.[56]

According to Sgt. Jeremiah Harding, Shapley decided to evacuate at "Eleven oclock in the forenoon." Before leaving, Shapley needed to spike the fort's twelve guns to prevent the British from using them either against the militia or the shipping in the harbor. To accomplish this, Shapley needed time. He realized the British were fast approaching his position and he needed to delay them so his men could disable the cannon and then get to their waiting boats at the water's edge.[57]

Shapley needed a diversion, so he called upon Cpl. Josiah Smith, a native of New London and former member of the 1st Connecticut Regiment. Shapley ordered Smith and five men, along with a fieldpiece, to go out and delay the British approach. It was a bold decision. Corporal Smith took Elias and Levi Dart, John Kilbourn, Joab Wright, and Reuben Bushnell. The men dragged a 6-pounder fieldpiece out of the fort, and Smith positioned his makeshift battery in a pasture to the rear of the fort. From their position, they could see Frink's mounted men approaching. They loaded their gun and "commenced a brisk fire" on the approaching American Legion.[58]

A round or two from Smith's Battery exploded near the head of Frink's column as it approached, inflicting several casualties. As a result, Frink hesitated and halted his men to await the arrival of Millet. He may well have regretted this decision later, when he learned how few enemy he was facing. Seeing Frink halted, Millet sent Captain Stapleton ahead to find out why he had not yet pushed towards the fort. Frink would not move without help, so Stapleton rode back to Millet and reported

---

56 Stephen Hempstead narrative in Harris, *Groton Heights*, 47; "To Col. McClellen, Commandant at the Posts of New London & Groton," Revolutionary War Records, Series I, Vol. XXII: 337, CSL. The petition circulated afterwards suggested in the event of a British landing on the west side of the Thames River, the garrison of Fort Trumbull was not expected to remain there. Instead, the garrison at Fort Trumbull could abandon the fort and either man the field pieces to defend New London or retreat to Fort Griswold to help in its defense.

57 PA: Jeremiah Harding (S.13286), NARA; Master's Log, HMS *Amphion*, ADM 52/2133, TNA. Captain Bazely placed Shapley's evacuation a half hour earlier. The master's log recorded it when they "saw the Rebel Colours struck" at that time.

58 Stephen Hempstead narrative in Harris, *Groton Heights*, 48; Master's Log, HMS *Amphion*, ADM 52/2133, TNA; PA: Elias Dart (R.2673); Levi Dart (W.24046); Joab Wright (W.6598), NARA. Kilbourne, *Kilbourn*, 58–59. The position of the battery was probably near the intersection of present-day Nameaug and Trumbull Streets. Kilbourn's name in the official record has always been "— Kilbourn." Bushnell previously appeared as a defender of Fort Griswold, but the muster record of the *Amphion* grouped him with prisoners taken at Fort Trumbull.

the situation. Frustrated, Millet soon had his four companies rushing towards Frink. Once they arrived, Millett assumed overall command of almost 250 men.[59]

Millet made a quick observation of his front and realized that it was only a single field piece. All the while Smith's Battery kept up its fire, sending several additional rounds towards the British until Corporal Smith realized his ammunition had been depleted. One of the gunners, Joab Wright, stated, "Having fired away their ammunition . . . [Cpl.] Smith said he would go into the Fort & procure some more." Rushing back to the magazine, Smith saw Captain Shapley with the rest of the company crossing the river in the whaleboats *Griswold* and *Trumbull*. Smith knew it was time to leave but still rushed back to his battery with a box of cartridges. When Smith returned, he told Wright and the others that the company was gone. Having completed its mission, the crew agreed it was time for them to leave. They fired one more time. They then abandoned the 6-pounder and retreated towards the fort and their awaiting boat. Each man ran for the shore, except Wright, who rushed to the barracks to grab his blanket.[60]

It was at that same time that Millet launched his attack. He was not going to let a single 6-pounder deter him any longer. Using all four companies of the 38th Regiment, the redcoats filed up the road ahead of Frink's men and formed into line as they surged across the large, open, rocky pasture field. With Captain Stapleton riding with them they came on with cheers, some shooting, and rapidly overran Smith's former position, captured the 6-pounder, and rushed towards and over the rear wall into Fort Trumbull. As they came inside, several redcoats broke away and rushed for the magazine and barracks looking for Shapley's men or any militia. They found none.[61]

59 Parsons, *Life and Letters*, 218; "A Sketch of New-London & Groton, with Attacks made on Forts Trumbull & Griswold by the British Troops Under the Command of Brig. General Arnold Sepr 6th, 1781 by Captain Lyman of ye Prince of Wales American Volunteers," WCL; Arnold's report in Mackenzie, *Diary*, 2:623–624. Frink probably halted his company under the protection of the ledge of rocks, clearly shown in the Lyman map, along the Harbor Road, part of which may still exist near 50 Pequot Avenue today. The same ledges were noted by Parsons in his examination over the ground near Fort Trumbull. Arnold stated the fort was carried with "the loss of only 4 or 5 men killed and wounded" and an examination of his casualty figures points to the American Legion bearing the brunt of the casualties of the assault on Fort Trumbull.

60 PA: Joab Wright (W.6598), NARA. The third boat was an unnamed whaleboat recently captured from the Refugees on Long Island.

61 Master's Log, HMS *Amphion*, ADM 52/2133, TNA; PA: Asa Chapin (S.15775), NARA. Most past histories, even some written by veterans, claimed the fort "was open from behind," and had no rear wall. This is not entirely true. The fort had a low, rear earthen wall, which Capt. Solomon Wales's Company had labored on during their time there in 1777. The wall is clearly shown on the Lyman map.

First Sergeant Stephen Hempstead of Shapley's Company of Matrosses. Engraved about 1830 shortly before his death. *Charles Allyn*

Smith's men were in their boat, having been slightly delayed by Wright, and had just pushed off. They were "about ten rods" from shore when redcoats appeared on the bluff above them in the fort and, in the excitement "fired several platoons upon them" and the two other boats carrying Shapley's Company. First Sergeant Stephen Hempstead, of Shapley's Company, recalled, "The enemy was so near that they over-shot us with their muskets." The firing made Holsey Sanford, another of the company, nervous. He later wrote, "We crossed under fire of musketry, like hail. The balls skated the water and whistled about our ears."[62]

British officers rushed up and ordered their soldiers to cease firing, and then called out to Smith's party, demanding they surrender. Not wanting to risk his men, Corporal Smith surrendered his boat and it was rowed back to shore. There they were gathered up, disarmed, and marched back into the fort and placed under guard. About two hours later, they were placed back into the same whaleboat, sent downriver, and placed aboard the *Amphion*.[63]

On Town Hill, Arnold claimed he had watched the attack, though the details of his report suggest this may not have been entirely accurate. He told Clinton he had "the pleasure to see Captn. Millet marched into Fort Trumbull under a Shower of Grape shot, from a number of Cannon, which the Enemy had turned upon him; and I have the Pleasure to inform your Excellency, that by the sudden Attack, and determined Bravery of the Troops, the Fort was carried with the loss of only 4 or 5 men killed and wounded." Actually, by the time Millet attacked, the firing had ceased, and according to the muster, Frink's Company suffered the

62   PA: Joab Wright (W.6598), NARA; Kilbourn, *History*, 59; Stephen Hempstead narrative in Harris, *Groton Heights*, 26; Sanford, *Memoir*.

63   PA: Levi Dart (W.24046), NARA; Ship's Muster, HMS *Amphion*, ADM 36/9561, TNA. Dart stated they were transported to the *Amphion* as Fort Griswold was being attacked. Dart, with the others taken, are listed on the ship muster.

A present-day view of the ledges where members of the 38th Foot fired from as they attempted to stop Shapley's Company from escaping to Fort Griswold. *Author*

brunt of these casualties. Arnold also reported he was "greatly indebted to Capt Stapleton . . . for his spirited conduct and assistance" during the assault, of which he was well deserved.[64]

With the capture of Forts Trumbull and Nonsense, the march to New London could be resumed. Arnold recalled Millet back to the column. Frink's Company continued along the waterfront using the Harbor Road. Before Millet left the fort, he detached one company from his regiment, while the other three moved back to Town Hill. The company was to hold the fort and keep communication open with Captain Shepherd, who was supposed to be moving upriver. But they were still stalled, and for at least the first hour, the company did its best to attack American naval vessels in range. Watching from afar, Captain Bazely noted, "Our Troops from Fort Trumbull Open'd their Fire upon the Enemy Shipping in the Harbour." Their fire, perhaps from the captured 6-pounder, proved significant enough to attract the attention of Ledyard at Fort Griswold, who ordered his gunners to fire upon their sister fort, with the *Amphion*'s naval observers noting: "The Fort on Groton side firing in Opposition."[65]

---

64 Muster rolls, American Legion, British Military and Naval Records, RG 8, "C" Series, Volume 1871, PAC; Arnold report in Mackenzie, *Diary*, 2:623–627.

65 Arnold report in Mackenzie, *Diary*, 2:623–624; Master's Log, HMS *Amphion*, ADM 52/2133, TNA. We do not know who fired the cannon, whether a detachment from Lieutenant Horndon was sent to the fort, members of the 38th Foot, or whether they may have forced the captured prisoners to load the gun.

Though he incorrectly assumed Fort Griswold was their target, Rufus Avery described the exchange of artillery thus:

> [W]e were exchanging shots with the British at Fort Trumbull, of which they had got possession of said fort before the commencement of the battle at Fort Griswold. We could heave a shot into Fort Trumbull among the enemy without difficulty, but they could not raise a shot so high as to come into Fort Griswold. Having obtained possession of our good powder and shot left by Capt. Shapley in the fort, they used it against us.[66]

Under fire from Fort Griswold, the British at Fort Trumbull were overmatched and quickly ceased. Arnold greatly desired Shepherd to give chase to privateers instead, but Fort Griswold needed to be taken first. This still had not yet been done. From Town Hill, Arnold dispatched an officer to hurry Eyre. He reported, after taking Fort Trumbull, "I found the Enemy's ships would escape unless we could possess ourselves of Fort Griswold." Shepherd's vessels could not safely move upriver until the fort's guns were silenced. According to Arnold's report, he sent orders to Eyre "request[ing] him to make an attack on the Fort as soon as possible." The officer rode back to the lighthouse, where they signaled to the *Amphion* for assistance. Responding, Bazely dispatched a barge to shore, carrying the officer across the river ten minutes later.[67]

Before leaving Town Hill, Arnold ordered Millet to station another company from his regiment at Fort Nonsense. The Quagonapoxet Highway was the main British line of retreat. The fort provided an excellent position to act as an observation post, to continually observe all directions, and, most importantly, to observe the Post Road. If an American force moved from that direction to attempt to cut off Arnold's retreat, the company stationed here could give him the advance notice Arnold would need to shift his forces to protect this vital route.

Before marching with the column, Arnold scanned northward one more time with his spyglass. He could see New London, only a mile distant. He had become familiar with it before the war, and it was inhabited by many friends and several former business acquaintances. But his reason for coming today was not to visit but to destroy, and the road before him was open. New London was Arnold's for the taking.

---

66 Rufus Avery narrative in Harris, *Groton Heights*, 32.

67 Arnold report in Mackenzie, *Diary*, 2:624; Master's Log, HMS *Amphion*, ADM 52/2133, TNA. Arnold did not name this officer.

Chapter Six

The Battle of New London:
The Fight for the Town

After Fort Nonsense fell, the militia on Town Hill retreated towards town. Some drifted towards Manwaring Hill in the west-central part of the town, others towards the waterfront. Some took the opportunity to rest while new arrivals came onto the scene and looked for direction. Some, discouraged after being routed off Town Hill, deserted and left the field. Still others, defiant as ever, organized themselves and prepared to contest British entry into New London. Rough defensive works were constructed at the intersection of the Quagonapoxet Highway and Cape Ann Lane, facing southward, a route the redcoats would have to take. Cape Ann Lane, today's Jefferson Avenue, stretched only a half-mile and ran northwest.

On the north side of the lane lay a handful of houses and barns. Many of these dated to the town's original settlement, including a house owned by Daniel Holt, which sat at the intersection. Holt and his family occupied the house but rented part of it to the widow Mary Lewis and at least seven of her children.[1]

It is unknown if the Holt family remained on the property, but Mary stayed behind in the house. As the battle approached the town, Mary took her children and fled to the cellar, where they hid themselves. Militia gathered on the Holt

---

1 New London Land Records, Volume 19:267, CSL. The house no longer stands and is better known by its 19th century occupant, Betsey Coit. In 1781, the lane embraced at least five homes, from south to north, belonging to Daniel Holt, Robert Froud, Joseph Coit, Thomas Hill, and Christopher Christophers.

property, commandeered the house, ripped up fences and outbuildings and threw up a rudely constructed barricade to oppose the British column.[2]

The Holt property was only one place militia gathered to resist the British. Nearly 800 yards behind the Holt property rose Manwaring Hill, the militia alarm post. Named for the Manwaring family, who had resided on a greater part of the hill for over a century, it was a little over 100-feet in elevation. It overlooked the town and offered an unobstructed view of the harbor and the surrounding countryside and a direct view of the British route. The two-story home of Robert Manwaring and his family lay on its eastern summit. Earlier, Manwaring had evacuated it and escaped into the countryside with his family, as did the two other families who lived on the hill.[3]

In the road in front of the Manwaring house, Harris placed the 12-pounder fieldpiece taken from Fort Nonsense. The crew dragged the gun up and wheeled it around facing south. The caisson, which carried its ammunition and pre-filled cartridges of gunpowder, was taken to the rear of the fieldpiece, where one of the crew was assigned to bring the ammunition and gunpowder back and forth. The rest of the supplies taken from Fort Nonsense were transported further up the road to the meetinghouse.[4]

As soon as the British were in view Harris mounted his horse and ordered the gun crew to begin loading and firing. The echo of its fire was heard by many in town and for some militia it offered a desperately needed boost to morale. But the range being just short of a mile, it did little damage to the British, and simply revealed its location prematurely.[5]

Militia following the sound of the cannon gathered atop the hill. The new arrivals included men from other companies in the 3rd Regiment: the 4th Company under Capt. John Johnson, the 14th led by Lt. Manasseh Leech, and the 4th Alarm List under acting Capt. Moses Warren, all from neighboring Lyme, plus some late arrivals from the New London companies.[6]

2 James Lawrence Chew, "An Account of the Old Houses of New London," *Records of the NLCHS*, Vol. I (1890–1894), Part IV, 91. The Holt house was located at the northwest corner of the present-day intersection of Bank Street and Jefferson Avenue. The barricade was probably thrown up east of the house across Bank Street.

3 John Hempsted narrative in Harris, *Groton Heights*, 65.

4 Arnold's report in Mackenzie, *Diary*, 2:628. Arnold's men found "A quantity of Ammunition, Stores" in the meetinghouse, but none at Fort Nonsense. The meetinghouse remains the most likely place they moved the ammunition.

5 John Hempsted in Harris, *Groton Heights*, 65.

6 PA: John Tubbs (S.14730), Samuel Avery (R.307), Jacob Tillotson (W.25490), NARA; Muster Book, HMS *Amphion*, ADM 36/9561, TNA; Royal Navy Ships' Muster (Series 1), HMS *Beaumont*,

According to one witness, nearly a hundred militia gathered there by noontime. Unfortunately, most were unarmed. A seemingly reoccurring theme that day.

The artillery, the militia on Manwaring Hill, or even those in town did not concern Arnold and the British column, who simply kept coming. Ranging ahead of the column, Captain von Wangenheim's jaegers probed towards the southern outskirts. Approaching the Holt house, the jaegers traded shots with militiamen at the barricade, who grudgingly abandoned it as the riflemen neared the intersection. Then, as the jaegers took the barricade, they continued exchanging shots with the defenders and sent them scattering back up Truman Street or up the Bank. At one point, soldiers banged on the door of the Holt house. Mrs. Lewis came up from the cellar and met them at the door, and after giving them the food they demanded, the soldiers left.[7]

On the march, Arnold developed his plan to take and secure New London. He knew its layout and road structure, giving him a distinct advantage. The Post Road and Quagonapoxet Highway approached from the south and was already watched over by the company of the 38th Regiment of Foot at Fort Nonsense. The two other main roads, in the northern part of town, were commanded by adjacent hills. Occupying these heights would enable Arnold's troops to contest the movement of any American reinforcements coming to New London from those directions. So far, probably to his surprise, he had faced little real opposition. He assuredly knew the militia was commanded by Col. Jonathan Latimer. Latimer was a fighter. Compared to those he led at Saratoga, his militia had done a poor job defending New London. Arnold did not know of Latimer's absence and did not want to take their limitations for granted. He recognized the militia would grow in strength if given time and was determined not to provide the opportunity.[8]

In New London, parties of militia and sailors occupied three positions. Their retreat into town, and their desire to contest possession of it, drastically changed the nature of the fight, from a traditional battle fought on the fields south of town into one waged in an urban environment—something not commonly associated with the warfare of the period. Their westernmost position was on Post Hill,

---

ADM 36/9643, TNA. The 13th Company, having members from modern-day Waterford and East Lyme, might have been involved much earlier in the day. At least one soldier from the company, Samuel Tinker, was captured by the British, presumably in town.

7 "Additional City News," *The Day*, Sep. 5, 1881.

8 John F. Luzader, Saratoga: *A Military History of the Decisive Campaign of the American Revolution* (El Dorado, CA, 2008), 268. When Arnold threatened to resign after the battle of Freeman's Farm, due to conflict with the army commander Maj. Gen. Horatio Gates, Latimer, along with other officers who had served under Arnold, signed an "Address" which pleaded with him to stay with the army. The petition succeeded, and Arnold remained until he was seriously wounded during the battle of Bemis Heights.

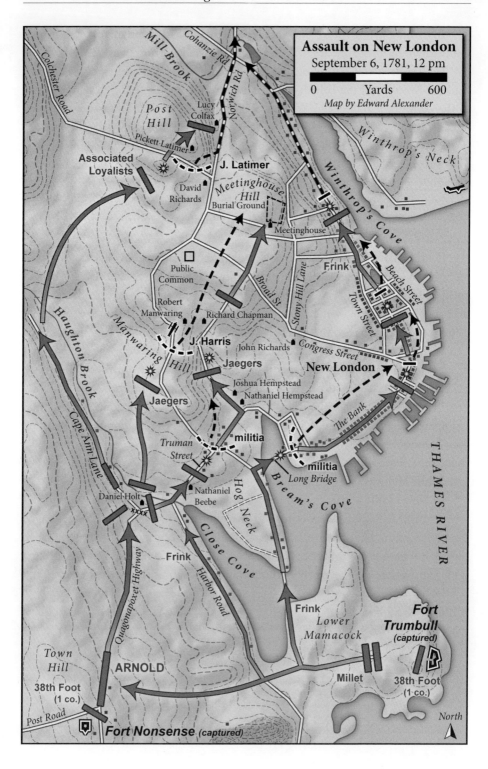

Assault on New London

September 6, 1781, 12 pm

0   Yards   600

Map by Edward Alexander

along the Colchester Road. In the middle, just south of Meetinghouse Hill, they supported Harris's makeshift battery on Manwaring Hill. To the east, militia and sailors were in the streets, closer to the waterfront.

The defense of the town relied on the ability of these groups to hold the British and trap them within the narrow and winding streets. It might have worked if there had been larger numbers and better leadership, but it was doomed from the beginning. They needed a leader to provide direction and coordination over the troops who were spread out across a front that stretched for nearly a mile. Lieutenant Colonel Harris remained on Manwaring Hill, and there is no evidence he attempted to coordinate the town's defense. As before, there was little established communication between the groups, and each group acted independently.

Arnold developed a sound plan to attack, occupy, and then hold New London. His strategy hinged on a three-pronged assault. First, the jaegers would advance northward from the Holt house, drive the militia and artillery off Manwaring Hill, and take possession of Meetinghouse Hill in the northern end of town. The hill commanded the Norwich Road, and its occupation would deter militia reinforcements from approaching from that direction.

Upham, with the Associated Loyalists and Loyal Refugees, would use Cape Ann Lane to make a wide, circuitous march to assault Post Hill, a mile distant. Securing the hill would give the British control of the other route into or out of town, the Colchester Road. Post Hill was also close enough to Meetinghouse Hill, where the Associated Loyalists could support the jaegers.

The American Legion formed the third prong of the attack. In a questionable move, the mostly untested Legion would press into the main part of town, along the waterfront, and clear out any resistance. The rest of the column, six companies of the 38th Foot, the Loyal American Regiment, and the artillery, some 550 men with Arnold, would follow behind as support.[9]

The attack began just after noon, the three forces moving simultaneously. The jaegers attacked using two platoons. One platoon advanced from the Holt property, splashed across Haughton's Brook, and moved against the southern slope of Manwaring Hill, drawing the attention of the American artillerymen and supporting militia. The second platoon crossed the nearby bridge, which spanned the brook, and moved up Truman Street, hoping to approach the hill from its eastern slope and outflank the defenders.

The defenders on Manwaring Hill noticed the British movements. They saw the column of redcoats, with their glistening bayonets, which one estimated to

---

9 Muster rolls, American Legion, British Military and Naval Records, RG 8, "C" Series, Volume 1871, PAC; Mackenzie, *Diary*, 2:611.

Manwaring Hill. Today, a nineteenth century naval howitzer marks the spot near where the militia attempted to defend the hill. *Author*

be "one thousand strong," approach the Holt house. The sight terrified many and most panicked and fled, even before the jaegers launched their attack. Captain John Hempsted, who rallied on the hill, recalled with disgust: "[A]s the Enemy appeard in Sight the people all fled." At a time when his leadership was needed, Harris was not there. Though he later contended he remained there during the assault, a witness placed him at the base of the hill, near the Richard Chapman barn, along Hempstead Street.[10]

The owner, Lt. Richard Chapman, served in Shapley's Company. He was, at that time, at Fort Griswold. Chapman's abandoned house stood near the barn at the base of the hill, in the rear of Manwaring's house. His property spanned nearly the entire eastern slope of the hill and included a second house, which the family leased, a short distance from the meetinghouse.[11]

Even as most of the militia deserted the hill, about 15 men remained and, as one member described, "Stuck By the Stuff," and prepared to meet the onslaught. They crouched behind the stonewall that ran along the road which passed over the

10 *CG*, May 2, 1783; John Hempsted narrative in Harris, *Groton Heights*, 65–66.

11 Harris, *Groton Heights*, 229–230.

hill and exchanged fire with the jaegers from there, seemingly unaware of those swinging around the rear of the hill.[12]

As the attack developed, the crew manning the 12-pounder fieldpiece kept loading and firing the gun. But they soon ran out of ammunition. No resupply came. They turned to gathering rocks and using them as a replacement, a hazardous practice. According to Israel Rogers, one of the gunners, they stood "against the advance guard of the right-wing of the Enemy" and "not having any shot [instead] charged the piece with stone and made several discharges."[13]

Despite the resistance from the Americans, the first platoon of jaegers advanced until they reached about 150 yards west of their position. Then, already spread out, they halted, dropped to the ground, and "commenced a severe fire" in the direction of the militia and gun crew. Bullets whistled through the air back and forth. The fire unnerved the artillery crew who soon abandoned their gun, dropped their gunner's tools, and fled.[14]

Their retreat disgusted Captain Hempsted. He turned to William Ashcraft, and Capt. Richard Deshon both of whom agreed, they could not hold back the jaegers alone and needed to withdraw. But as they did, they decided to make the 12-pounder of no use to the enemy. They hid the cartridges, the sponge, and the rammer. After hiding the cartridges in Manwaring's garden, Hempsted ran down towards the Chapman barn to find something that could be used to spike the gun. Unfortunately, his search was interrupted by the jaegers creeping around the hill.[15]

These flanking jaegers, or the second platoon, encountered little opposition in their movement around Manwaring Hill, except for a handful of the militia who, after retreating from the barricade, concealed themselves amongst houses and other structures along the road. As they had done earlier, militiamen hid in these positions, fired on the jaegers, and then hastily retreated northward towards Meetinghouse Hill. Residents returned home to find evidence of the skirmish inflicted on their houses. One man found several bullet holes through his front door. During the brief firefight up Truman Street, one civilian, indistinguishable in his dress from the militia, was tragically killed in the crossfire. Nathaniel Beebe, described as an "aged and infirm man," crept to the back part of his house where he stood in his garden when a soldier passing by shot him. Though assuredly unintentional, the incident made excellent propaganda, and the Continental press

---

12 John Hempsted narrative in Harris, *Groton Heights*, 65; PA: Joseph Plumb (S.31910), NARA.

13 PA: Israel Rogers, (S.14383), NARA.

14 PA: Joseph Plumb (S.31910), Israel Rogers (S.14383), NARA; *CG*, May 2, 1783.

15 John Hempsted narrative in Harris, *Groton Heights*, 65.

took advantage. Newspapers accused British soldiers of murdering Beebe. They reported "Old Mr. Beebe, was shot at his own door beging for mercy; he had not carried a gun for 20 years."[16]

With the militia falling back toward Meetinghouse Hill, the flanking jaegers reached the home of Nathaniel Hempstead, which still stands at the corner of Hempstead and Truman Streets. When the jaegers reached there, they wheeled west, passed the house, and pressed in a northwest direction across the property. Along the way, they passed the Joshua Hempstead house, owned by Nathaniel's older brother. Joshua Hempstead, the sheriff, belonged to the 1st Company Alarm List. While he was out fighting, his wife Anna remained behind. According to family lore, as the jaegers attacked, Mrs. Hempstead was inside with her children. When she heard the enemy, she called her children, took them, and ran outside. The jaegers did not shoot at them, though some headed for the house which they searched for militia and finding none, helped themselves to food on the dining room table. A few others ventured into the basement where they scavenged through the pantry, poking through cheeses and knocking over barrels of molasses.[17]

The rest advanced until they reached a pasture owned by the family, to the rear of the house. There they halted and unleashed a volley of rifle fire towards the militia near the Chapman house and barn. Captain Hempsted, standing near the barn, later wrote "I Rec'd a Volly of Shot" from 20 men, and it "cut thrugh the grass on Both Sid of me." Seeing the jaegers advancing on him, Hempsted ran.[18]

The jaeger pincer movement worked perfectly and without suffering any losses, converged on Manwaring Hill and drove off the militia. William Ashcraft was one of the last to leave. Ashcraft, according to a legend, got up on the 12-pounder, and shook his fist at the enemy. The jaegers responded with "a shower of bullets," convincing Ashcraft to flee. Not everyone was as fortunate, as at least one or two militia were taken prisoner. One was Joseph Plumb, of the 2nd Company. When Plumb applied for a pension, he remembered that he "discharged his Gun at the Enemy a number of times [and] the Americans did all they could, but were

---

16 Harris, *Groton Heights*, 226; *Independent Ledger*, Sep. 17, 1781; Caulkins, *New London*, 557; *Boston Gazette*, Sep. 17, 1781. Caulkins described him as living alone, when in fact Beebe's wife and son, Nathaniel Jr., still lived in the same house.

17 Katharine Abbott, *Old Paths of the New England Border: Connecticut, Deerfield, Berkshire.* (New York, 1907), 73; Sarah Hall Johnston. "Lineage Book," *National Society of the Daughters of the American Revolution.* Vol. 30, 29001-30000, (1899), 26–27. The elder Nathaniel and his son Nathaniel Jr. joined Deshon's Company earlier that morning and were out fighting for most of the day. See "A List of the First Alarm List Company in the 3d Regt of Militia in this State under the Command of Capt John Deshon," NLCHS.

18 John Hempsted narrative in Harris, *Groton Heights*, 65.

Nathaniel Hempstead House. *Author*

overpowered by numbers and discipline." "The whole party [on the hill]," Plumb wrote, was "completely routed."[19]

To the northwest, a short time later, the Associated Loyalists attacked Post Hill. "Having reached the southerly part of the town," Upham reported, "[Arnold] requested me to take possession of the hill north of the meeting house, where the rebels had collected." This was Post Hill. Arnold had faith in Upham's ability to take and hold the vital Colchester Road. After the jaegers advanced on Manwaring Hill, Upham moved his command from the left of the main column—which had now come up and halted near the intersection—and veered onto Cape Ann Lane, near the Holt house and from there advanced along its full length.[20]

Atop Post Hill, Col. Jonathan Latimer arrived on the scene, just as the British attack unfolded. Mounted on horseback, Latimer made his way into New London, riding down the Colchester Road accompanied by two of his sons, Witherel and

19 *Morning News* (New London), Aug. 12, 1845; PA: Joseph Plumb (S.31910), NARA.

20 Upham report in Harris, *Groton Heights*, 109.

Pickett Latimer House Site. The house stood here at the present-day
corner of Vauxhall and Williams Streets. *Author*

Robert, both members of the 5th Company. There, Colonel Latimer established
an observation post near the home of his cousin Lt. Pickett Latimer.[21]

At that time, Lieutenant Latimer, of the Independent Artillery Company, was
involved in the fighting along the waterfront. But he owned numerous acres across
Post Hill, which he worked as a farm. Unmarried, Latimer resided in a house that
stood near a bend in the Colchester Road.[22]

There, Colonel Latimer desperately tried to grasp the situation. As he scanned
southward, it did not look promising. Reports from militia and civilians passing by
were also not positive. The enemy was reported to be in heavy force. This Latimer
could plainly see. His regiment was never organized. The defense of the town was
not properly coordinated. Its leadership was scattered or conspicuously absent.
There was no way for Latimer to organize a defense now.

Some retreating militia from Manwaring Hill reached Post Hill before the
attack. There they were augmented into the small force the colonel gathered around
him, totaling no more than 12 or 15. Most, if not all, of them, were dispersed
outward along the south side of the road. There they used the fence, which lined
the roadway for some protection. Some may have been in the Latimer house and
barn, which stood on slightly higher ground a short distance away.[23]

21 PA: Witherel Latimer (S.31809), NARA; "Col Latimer's account for issuing orders, expresses,
&c; 1781–1782," Revolutionary War Records (1763-1789) Series I, XXXII:137a–b236, CSL. The
regimental adjutant was Lt. Elihu Wade who lived in Lyme and was not yet present.

22 *CG*, July 15, 1776, Aug. 18, 1780. Both issues of the *Gazette* include advertisements about
livestock which had wandered away from the Pickett Latimer farm.

23 PA: Israel Rogers (S.14383), Gurdon Flowers Saltonstall (R.9159), NARA. Latimer knew the hill
well. His grandfather had purchased many of the original house lots on the hill, which had then been
divided amongst the family, which caused some locals to call the area Latimer's Hill. In 1881, many

As the Associated Loyalists filed onto Cape Ann Lane, Upham formed them into a line of battle along the road. From the north end of the road, devoid of any houses, they advanced towards Post Hill. As they did, Latimer's men anxiously watched them the whole way, as the entire area was mostly open and devoid of trees. For a moment, they might have thought them to be friendly forces. Clad in mainly civilian clothing, the Associated Loyalists were hardly distinguishable from the militia. But, as Upham's 120 men came surging towards them, the militia, including Latimer, realized these were enemy troops.

At that moment, frustrated, Latimer may have quickly glanced back towards town. The jaegers were now in possession of Manwaring Hill. The 12-pounder field piece, which might have been of use elsewhere, was lost. Enemy musketry could be heard along the waterfront. Plumes of smoke could be seen rising as the British column pressed along the waterfront and clashed with small parties of militia and sailors. Outnumbered almost 9 to 1, Latimer decided it was foolhardy to try and hold Post Hill. He would withdraw towards the Norwich Road, where he hoped to meet reinforcements. But he needed to keep his small force intact. He could not risk it being routed or scattered, or worse, being captured himself. But he would not retreat without at least attempting to slow Upham's advance.

As the Associated Loyalists ascended the southern slope of Post Hill, they may not have known how many rebels awaited them. As Upham explained later, he believed "[Latimer] seemed resolved to hold [his position]." As Upham closed in on the Colchester Road, Latimer ordered his men to fire. The smoke had barely cleared before they turned and fell back over the hill. As the bullets whizzed through the air, an undaunted Upham pressed his men onward, only slowed by the fences and stonewalls which lined their path. Seeing the Americans retreating, the loyalists "soon gained the ground in contest."[24]

Upham's men pursued the retreating militia over the hill, exchanging shots with them along the way. On the opposite side of the hill lay the George Colfax farm. Colfax had died nearly two decades earlier and much of his farm was leased to David Richards Jr., but the two-story house, barn, and outbuildings at the farm's northeast corner were still held by Lucy Colfax, George's widow.[25]

---

spectators viewed the "mock battle" from Post Hill and commented how they could see the entire town and harbor from its summit.

24 Upham report in Harris, *Groton Heights*, 109–110; Caulkins, *New London*, 551–552.

25 New London Land Records, Vol. 26:30, CSL; *American Mercury*, July 8, 1802; Caulkins, *New London*, 62. Known locally as the "Post Hill House," the Colfax house was built in the late 17th century for Richard Post, one of the town's earlier settlers, who gave the hill its most familiar name. It went through a series of owners before it was demolished around 1895.

After passing the Colfax house and barn, Upham halted the loyalists before they reached Mill Brook. The brook, which ran along the northern base of the hill, originated several miles away in the North Parish. The waterway flowed southward and meandered around both the northern slopes of Post and Meetinghouse Hills, before it turned southward, running almost parallel to Town Street, and emptying into Winthrop's Cove.

The civilians who remained in town were aware of the transpiring battle around them, as its recognizable sounds drew nearer and nearer. But now it was upon them. A young boy recalled, "I heard the musketry going crack, crack on the whole westerly side of town." As he attempted to leave town, the boy had a difficult time moving along the streets, as many civilians were also trying to leave at the same time. The streets became so clogged with civilians, many laden with personal belongings struggling to get out through the only still open route out of town, Town Street. The boy wrote: "I, however, moved quickly on, and when I came to the head of [Winthrop's] Cove the street was so crowded with the fleeing women and children, all loaded with something, that I had to move slowly. They inquired where the enemy was. I said, 'they will be among you within five minutes if you delay.'" Hearing the loud echoes of musketry, followed by retreating soldiers and sailors, many civilians suddenly panicked.[26]

According to the boy, "Their loading was soon thrown down, and they started with a quick pace." No longer did personal belongings matter, they were thrown into the streets, and their owners fled to save themselves. Several ads were published in the *Connecticut Gazette* afterward by residents looking for numerous personal items that went missing during this time. One promised to "handsomely reward" the person who found their "red spotted silk handkerchief tied up full of shirts, stockings, and some other articles" that were lost on Town Street.[27]

Under the cover of the attacks in the west and central part of the town, the American Legion made its way into the eastern part. Initially, both wings of the Legion were on the flanks of the British column, but as they advanced closer to town, both wing commanders needed to form a junction. This junction was made, presumably, on the highway along Hog Neck.

Hog Neck was a peninsula that jutted outward in between Close Cove to its west, and Bream Cove and the harbor, to its south and east. Three public roads traversed it. Today, two of those, Truman, and Blinman Streets, still exist. Both

26 Jonathan Brooks narrative in Harris, *Groton Heights*, 79.

27 Ibid., *CG*, Sep. 14, 1781.

wound around the Neck's western and northern extremities. A third road, the Hog Neck Highway, ran north to south along its eastern edge along the Bream Cove.[28]

Lining the roads were several houses, barns, and farm lots. A green lay near its western edge, near Truman Street. A windmill stood at its southern tip where a small footbridge constructed during the war spanned the mouth of Close Cove. However, the bridge was only three feet across, stood high enough only to navigate the tides, and had no railing. Even so, a majority of Frink's dismounted soldiers probably crossed here as they advanced northward onto Hog Neck. Once on the opposite bank they trudged north along the Hog Neck Highway. Unable to cross, the mounted troopers were forced to circle back towards the Harbor Road and the main column.[29]

Concurrently, Wogan's redcoats moved to the head of the British column in anticipation of linking up with Frink's soldiers. In the process, the loyalist soldiers passed the Holt house, and following to the rear of the flanking jaegers, advanced up Truman Street onto Hog Neck, but only as far as the almshouse that sat at the intersection of Blinman Street. There, they turned eastward onto Blinman Street, heading in the direction of the bridge across Bream Cove. Known as Long Bridge, the wooden bridge had been constructed over a decade prior. The bridge, made of piling, was over 150 yards long and both large and sturdy enough to carry men, horses, and vehicles.[30]

Waiting at the opposite side of the bridge were numerous militia and sailors. Their exact identities and strength are not known. They had been hastily thrown together and were comprised of the remnants of seven different militia companies. Among them were also dozens of sailors and marines from various vessels, which had been or were still in the harbor. At least 62 belonged to the privateer brig *Deane*. After getting their vessel safety upriver, the sailors and marines were provided with arms, put ashore, and marched under Capt. Dan Scovell, to the

---

28 Current day Howard Street was built to replace the Hog Neck Highway but does not follow the same route. The highway originally followed a route much closer to the Cove.

29 "Lieutenant John Hempsted's Orderly Book," Council of Safety Papers, CHS; *People's Advocate* (New London), Nov. 19, 1845; Caulkins, *New London*, 287. The neck reportedly obtained its name due to the number of swine who went out there during low tide to root up clams. At various times, the neck was also known as Shaw's Neck, Morton's Point, and Windmill Point. The windmill was erected and owned by John Deshon and operated by John Shepherd.

30 James Lawrence Chew, "Facts and Reminiscences," *Records and Papers of the NLCHS*, Vol. II, Pt. 1 (1895): 86–100. Bream Cove was largely filled in during the mid-nineteenth century and today no longer exists. But in 1781, it covered an area between Coit Street to the north, Reed Street to the west, Brewer Street, to the east, and the water to the south. The bridge was roughly located along Blinman Street between Reed and Brewer Streets.

scene of action. One of these sailors remembered, "We had much hard fighting that day with the British."[31]

The lack of communication and overall military leadership, as well as chaos in town, caused these sailors and militia to remain in the lower part of town. They seemed to have been positioned there on their own initiative. Along the waterfront, they faced a unique challenge, as opposed to the defenders in other parts of town: the temptation to loot.[32]

Prior to and up until the British attack, numerous civilians, militia, sailors, and other vagrants freely roamed the streets. They had no interest in defending the town and took advantage to pillage storehouses and abandoned homes. A young civilian, who remained in his home on Bradley Street, observed sailors, whom he described as "five or six shabby looking fellows" at a full run from the direction of the British approach. He wrote, he heard them declare, "we'll have fine plunder by-and-by." Sometime later, he heard loud noises coming in the direction of Beach Street behind his house. Mounting a fence, he saw a group of thirty or forty break open one of Nathaniel Shaw's storehouses, and run in. The "goods," he said, "were flying out of the store."[33]

After the raid, most citizens blamed the British for the looting. Nowhere was this more so than in the *Connecticut Gazette*. But this was only part of the case. The British were responsible for some of it, but not all of it. A good deal was, in fact, done by the Americans. There were charges laid upon Colonel Latimer, which accused him of "not preventing the wanton plundering in the town, by the militia and others." Historian Frances Caulkins explored the subject in her 1852 book, *History of New London*. She interviewed witnesses, and in some cases, their immediate descendants, and documented some of these lesser-known stories. She acknowledged, "It was afterward well understood that most of the spoil and havoc in the private houses were the work of a few worthless vagrants of the town, who prowled in the wake of the invaders, hoping in the general confusion not to be detected." Despite this, many continued to blame the British and this is how it is still remembered today.[34]

The militia, sailors, and marines closest to the river gathered at the east end of Long Bridge near the homes of Joshua Starr and his sister-in-law, Lucy Starr. The homes stood along the eastern edge of Bream Cove on opposite sides of the road.

---

31 *CG*, Jan. 4, 1782; PA: Samuel Butler Spencer (S.23935), NARA.

32 PA: Samuel Butler Spencer (S.23935), NARA; *Robert Morris, Papers of Robert Morris, 1781–1784: Aug–Sep 1781*, 9 vols, ed. James Elmer (Pittsburgh, 1975), 2:194.

33 Brooks narrative in Harris, *Groton Heights*, 78.

34 Caulkins, *New London*, 556; *CG*, Nov. 15, 1782.

The men faced overwhelming odds. Not only did they have to deal with enemy soldiers, but also the confusion of a lawless town.

They dispersed themselves behind the protective cover of the two Starr houses. There, they anxiously awaited Frink's attack. They did not have to wait long; Frink's men soon came into view as they hurried towards the bridge. As they did, the defenders started shooting, but then pulled back as Frink's soldiers rushed over the bridge.

The position, which might have proved to be a suitable obstacle to the British, suddenly became untenable. At the same time Frink's men advanced across the bridge, the jaegers attacked up Truman Street, a short distance away. The noise of their rifle fire and the smoke would have been visible and heard by those at the bridge, causing some defenders to realize they were being outflanked.

Once over the bridge, the American Legion halted and returned fire. As on Town Hill, the American defense of the waterfront was no more than a show of force. Once the realization was made that there were other British soldiers moving throughout the town, the Americans attempted to slow the British advance by opposing them house by house and street by street. In a running skirmish, the Americans used the cover of whatever was available along the streets. From there, they waited for Frink's soldiers, fired, and then withdrew to a new position before the American Legion could catch up to them. This process was repeated until they were driven out of town.[35]

While forgotten in past histories, this intense firefight was certainly remembered by those who remained in their homes. It had come as a surprise to most. At the approach of the enemy, they took cover in their houses, or if they had not already, fled to their cellars. This included Mary Rogers. She later told descendants she took refuge to escape the "flying bullets." As she and her children rushed towards the cellar Mary, carrying her infant son, was nearly struck by a musket ball.[36]

After retreating from the bridge, the defenders fell back on the Bank. More than a dozen houses, workshops, storehouses, and other structures on both sides of the road provided cover. They took full advantage of this, and the skirmishing continued for the entire length of the street. Every so often, Frink's men halted so

---

35 Harris, *Groton Heights*, 226; S. Leroy Blake, "Two Hundred and Fiftieth Anniversary of the Settlement of New London, May 5 and 6, 1896," *Records and Papers of the NLCHS*, Vol. II, 1895–1904, 233. Battle damage throughout the town was noted by later generations. During the 250th anniversary of the settlement of New London, among the relics displayed was a portrait which hung in a house and had been pierced by a bullet. Also displayed was a cannon ball which was fired into the town.

36 James Swift Rogers, *James Rogers of New London, Connecticut, and his Descendants* (Boston, 1902), 233.

they could attempt to locate their concealed foes and fire back. Shots echoed and reverberated against the buildings.

The pursuit eventually reached the Parade. There, Frink's men managed to quickly clear the Americans out of the area, denying them from turning either the courthouse, St. James Church, or other structures which clustered the area into a citadel. But as they cleared the area, the Americans scattered onto Town, Bradley, and Water Streets. Halting near the courthouse, Captain Frink ordered detachments of his unit up each of the streets. This was both an effort to chase down the retreating Americans as well as ensure they were not ambushed as they continued the pursuit. As they did, they continued to exchange fire with the retreating Americans. As one detachment entered Bradley Street, it came under fire from a nearby house. The shot struck down at least one redcoat, wounding him. Comrades carried him into the safety of the nearby Joshua Potter house.

The redcoats asked the family to care for him, which they did. His identity has been lost to history, but, relying on a family story, it is believed to have been Capt. Samuel Wogan, the only British officer wounded on the New London side. Wogan was shot in the head. The wounding of this particular soldier proved so important that, according to the story, Arnold visited him at the Potter house. It is hard to believe Arnold would have taken the time to visit a wounded enlisted soldier. According to the same story, while there Arnold also ordered the house to be protected. The words "General Arnold's orders are to spare this house" were supposedly chalked on the front door as Arnold rode away.[37]

Further north, elements of the American Legion pressed onward, continuing to exchange fire with the retreating Americans. On Town Street, a party posted themselves around the Nathaniel Coit Jr. house. Once the American Legion troops came within view, they unleashed a volley and then withdrew again. The redcoats who had reached the Coit house searched the home. Inside, they found Nathaniel Coit and his teenage daughter Margaret. Coit, the tax collector and former merchant captain, was sick and confined to his bed. Earlier, Margaret had decided to remain with her father to care for him. She told the redcoats this when questioned. The two were left alone, but not Nathaniel's brother William whom they found hidden inside. He had been actively resisting the British since earlier that morning. Other redcoats rummaged through the house and found nearly £2,600 Coit had collected in taxes. They took the money and William and left.[38]

---

37 James Lawrence Chew, "An Account of the Old Houses of New London," *Records of the NLCHS*, Vol. 1, Part IV (1890-1894): 81.

38 "Houses of Historic Interest," *New London Day*, Aug. 31, 1881; James Lawrence Chew, "An Account of the Old Houses of New London," in *Records and Papers of the NLCHS*, Vol. 4 (1893):79; *CSR*, 4:40.

As the defending Americans fell back toward the northern part of town, some became separated from their groups. Some ran off. Others became trapped in the houses or buildings they were defending. This forced the redcoats, like those at the Coit house, to stop their advance to search buildings. Prisoners, such as Coit, were taken all throughout the town. Some, like Capt. Richard Deshon, who after leaving Manwaring Hill was captured, found in the confusion the means to escape. Some, like Deshon, were captured multiple times. This became a serious liability for the British. According to Joshua Smith, a member of the 2nd Company, Deshon and some of his men were captured three separate times during the fight in town but managed to escape each time. The last time, Captain Deshon was taken to his own house, where after he showed his captors his pantry full of food, slipped out the back door. With some of his men, he then managed to fight his way out of town. George Newcomb, of the 2nd Company, was also captured three times, twice during the fighting in the town, but managed to escape each time. Deshon's second-in-command, Lt. Samuel Latimer, was not so fortunate and ended up being captured and not able to escape.[39]

Marching behind the American Legion was the remainder of the British column: the 38th Foot, the Loyal American Regiment, and Horndon's Battery. They followed the same route as their swiftly moving loyalist counterparts, and as they did scooped up prisoners who had either been lost by the Legion or who had become separated from their captors in the confusion.

In the vanguard was a group of mounted soldiers from the American Legion. These troopers were not with their unit. As they trotted up the Bank, with swords and carbines clanging, they shouted to civilians who had remained behind, demanding they open their doors and windows. A man retelling the story to his grandchildren many years later recalled how fearful he was at that moment. At seven-years-old he was near the Parade when the mounted soldiers passed his

---

39 Charles Allyn Papers, NLCHS; Royal Navy Ships' Muster (Series 1), HMS *Amphion*, ADM 36/9561, TNA; Deposition, George Newcomb to Samuel Mott, Apr. 11, 1782, Governor Trumbull Papers, 16:88, CSL. "After a Considerable skirmish I was Taken prisoner by the British and kept about a half an hour when I found means to make my Escape, and in a Short time after was again made prisoner & held for a Short Space, when the party who had me in keeping being Intoxicated with Liquor I again attempted an Escape . . . but I was soon overtaken & Seized by another party of the Enemy." Newcomb was taken to a wharf. There "they Damned me for a Rebel & one of them Plungd a bayonet at me." Another soldier knocked Newcomb out with the butt of his musket, while another bound his legs with rope. Coming to his senses, Newcomb freed himself, jumped into the river, and swam out to a privateer where he was picked up by the crew. It is likely Newcomb was captured by the American Legion the first two times as they were attempting to clear the town. The third time, it appears he was captured either by members of the 38th Regiment or the Loyal American Regiment.

house. As they reigned their screeching horses to a halt, he heard them yelling out their instructions.[40]

The instructions were given because as Arnold's forces occupied New London, they were obligated to restore some sort of law and order. Like their counterparts in the American Legion, they were compelled to spend time searching homes and other buildings for lingering defenders who might disrupt their occupation.[41]

Further north, Frink's soldiers continued their pursuit along Town Street, pressing the retreating Americans in the direction of Winthrop's Neck. Along the way, they continued to receive sporadic fire. Their advance was much assisted by that of the jaegers on their left.

Further west, Upham's men were the first to take their assigned objective. They soon broke into Pickett Latimer's house and barn and searched for any hidden rebel militia, but more importantly, plunder. Entering, they found both filled with more items than they could ever hope to carry away. Numerous items, including clothing and other personal belongings, were left behind by civilians fleeing westward along the Colchester Road. To lighten their loads, they figured the Latimer farm was far enough away from the waterfront, and, therefore, a safe place to leave their personal effects. But this proved erroneous, as both the Latimer house and barn were set ablaze, the first structures to experience the torch that day.[42]

Soon after, off on their right, the jaegers under Capt. von Wangenheim captured Meetinghouse Hill. Along with the Associated Loyalists, they next formed the British outpost line, which stretched for over a mile and a half, from the Colchester Road on its left, to Town Street on its right. Its main purpose was to screen and provide security to the British force in town. The jaegers would also provide Arnold with intelligence, such as the size of the enemy force, whether they were being reinforced or were preparing to attack. If the latter, they would delay the attack, providing the main force time either to withdraw or take steps to resist the attack.

On Post Hill, Upham deployed one company on the north face of the hill, dispersed in skirmish order outward facing Mill Brook. The second company

---

40 Rogers, *James Rogers*, 146. The story was told by Orson P. Rogers whose father, Jedidiah Rogers, remained in town during the British occupation.

41 Ibid.,170. According to Rogers, the prisoners were detained in a house owned by the "elder Nathan Rogers," but it is not clear where this house was.

42 John Hempsted narrative in Harris, *Groton Heights*, 67; Eliza Pool to John Pool, Oct. 30, 1781, NLCHS. The Latimer house and barn were the first buildings set on fire. This is backed up by a letter written by a civilian almost two months later. Speaking speculatively, it is plausible both structures were burned under Upham's orders to ensure unit discipline after instances of looting in the middle of battle.

in the same formation was dispersed on the western slope, west from Pickett Latimer's house, perpendicular to the Colchester Road. They took advantage of cover provided by fences, hay bales, stonewalls, and trees.[43]

Between the Colfax house and Meetinghouse Hill ran a then-unnamed road, today's Williams Street. Built in the 17th century, the road was a part of a circular set of connecting roads which rounded the original settlement boundaries of the town. Near Upham's position, it went northward from the Colchester Road before it terminated a short distance north of the Colfax house. There, it intersected and terminated with Town Street and the Norwich Road.[44]

On Meetinghouse Hill, the jaegers' position extended eastward from near the Colfax house across the northern slope of Meetinghouse Hill towards Town Street, a short distance south of a stone bridge over Mill Brook. The 60 riflemen were dispersed outward in a skirmish line, allowing them to take advantage of available cover. Some took position in an orchard behind the Anne Adams house on Town Street.[45]

It did not remain quiet for long along the outpost line. Skirmishing erupted just after 1:00 p.m., a short time after the Latimer house and barn were set ablaze. The militia Upham initially encountered were a provisional company under Capt. Jonathan Caulkins, which deployed north of Post Hill.

After retreating across Mill Brook, Colonel Latimer halted his party near the Samuel Richards Jr. house, which stood on the west side of Norwich Road, almost 300 yards north of Mill Brook. The colonel realized he needed to organize his men so that they could better oppose the British. Unable to form their normal companies, he initially started with those closest to him. Gathering them with other nearby militia and armed volunteers, he formed them into this provisional company. Latimer placed Captain Caulkins in command and ordered them southward to engage the British outpost. Israel Rogers, one of Latimer's soldiers on Post Hill, remembered, "at [Samuel] Richards place [we] rec'd a considerable

43 Upham report in Harris, *Groton Heights*, 109–110. It is likely, based on Upham's own report, that Upham was with the right company positioned on the northern slope of the hill along Mill Brook, while Capt. Samuel Goldsbury was with the left company along the western slope of the hill. Upham specifically mentions being exposed to artillery rounds landing near his position coming at them "from the fort on the Groton side," almost a mile and a half away. They were likely fired from one or more 12-pounders in the barbette battery along the west wall. That was an impressive range of fire, over 300 yards over their effective range, and it is hard to imagine those rounds hitting any further west than near the Pickett Latimer house.

44 The road's original purpose was to provide easier access from Cape Ann Lane to Town Street and the grist mill on Winthrop's Neck.

45 Eliza Pool to John Pool Jr., New London, Oct. 30, 1781, NLCHS.

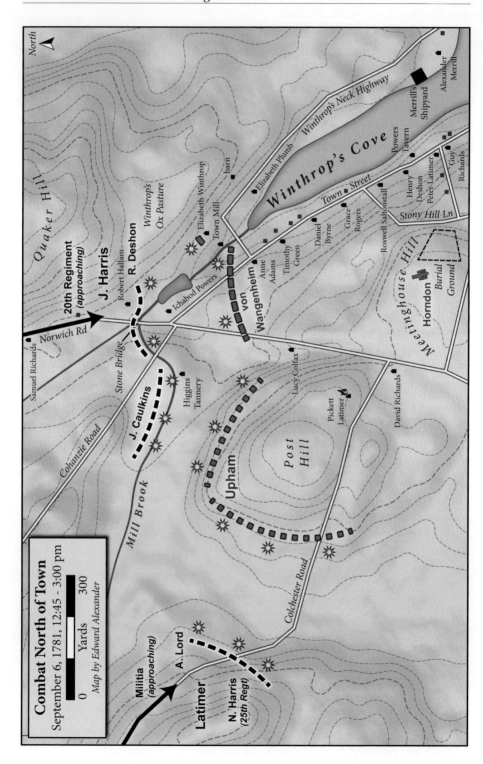

Combat North of Town
September 6, 1781, 12:45 - 3:00 pm

Yards
0   300

Map by Edward Alexander

addition to their numbers and Capt Caukins took the command [and] then [we] advanced towards [Post] Hill."[46]

Caulkins, at 44-years-old, was one of Latimer's most trusted subordinates. The two had known each other for several years. Like his colonel, Caulkins served in a variety of roles in colonial politics, including as selectman. He had over two decades of service in the militia. Currently, he commanded the 11th Company, 3rd Regiment of Connecticut Militia, a unit whose members hailed from western New London, near the Niantic River. Caulkins had seen much active service during the current war, most notably during the Saratoga Campaign in which he served in Latimer's Battalion, under Arnold, and was recognized for his bravery. He had been in action that day since Town Hill.[47]

As Caulkins's Company moved towards Mill Brook, Latimer rode off to find Lieutenant Colonel Harris. He found him, a short time later, not far from the Richards house. After the debacle on Manwaring Hill Harris had managed to evade capture. On horseback he escaped town, possibly passing along Stony Hill Lane, today's Huntington Street, to Town Street and then to the Norwich Road onto the southern slope of Quaker Hill. That is where Latimer presumably met him.

Quaker Hill, a large imposing height just north of town, was the highest elevation in the area. The summit, located roughly one and a half miles north of the county courthouse and today on the campus of Connecticut College, was almost 250 feet high. From there, the ridgeline extended northward towards the modern-day border of Waterford, then southward along the Norwich Road for a mile and a half towards the main part of town. At its southern end, two smaller rises overlooked both Winthrop's Neck and the Colchester Road. From anywhere on the hill, one could view the town, the harbor, and as far out as Long Island Sound.[48]

---

46 PA: Israel Rogers (S.14383), NARA; The place mentioned by Rogers where they gathered was "John Richards's place." The house is also mentioned by Captain Hempsted in his narrative, who passed it on his way to Quaker Hill. This appears to be a post-war naming reference. During the war, John Richards Jr. owned a house at the north end of Congress Street. After the war, he lived and died in a Richards house, which in 1781, was owned by Samuel Richards.

47 Harriet Caulkins Hill, "Reminiscences of Captain Jonathan Caulkins," *American Monthly Magazine*. Vol. VII (July–Dec. 1895): 226–229; John Hempsted narrative in Harris, *Groton Heights*, 63; *CCR*, 13:240; William W. Calkins, *The Calkins Memorial Military Roster* (Chicago, 1903), 18.

48 Caulkins, *New London*, 57. This Quaker Hill is not to be confused with the village of Quaker Hill in modern-day Waterford. Like many places in colonial Connecticut the hill was known by different names through the centuries. It was originally named Foxen's Hill, after Foxen the son of the Mohegan sachem Uncas. The Mohegan tribe inhabited the area both before and during the arrival of John Winthrop and his group of settlers. In some records it came to be called Bolles Hill after Thomas Bolles and his family. Bolles, at the invitation of Winthrop, came to New London from Massachusetts in the 17th century and purchased large tracts of land across the hill from the Mohegans. The hill

The initial meeting between Latimer and Harris, though short, must have been unpleasant for Harris. Things had not gone well for him that morning. His indecision and questionable tactical posture greatly impacted the course of the battle and with it the loss of New London.

At that time, the intentions of the British were not fully understood. Despite the defensive posture taken up the British, Latimer may have been concerned the British might advance towards Norwich. If they did, there was little at that moment to oppose them. Only Harris's recollections of the meeting, written eighteen months later, are known to exist. With the urgency of the situation, the two men only talked momentarily, but Colonel Latimer assumed command and gave Harris his orders.[49]

Latimer realized the British were in possession of New London, and the militia were so badly disorganized that they could not mount an attack. He needed to wait until reinforcements arrived. The closest reinforcements were the 20th Regiment of Connecticut Militia, from Norwich. The next closest was the 25th Regiment of Connecticut Militia, from the Colchester area. But neither had appeared. Latimer would be forced to remain on the defensive but would use the time to restore order to his regiment.

Latimer soon ordered the organization of a second provisional company under Capt. Richard Deshon. It was then ordered onto the southern slope of Quaker Hill to protect the Norwich Road, directly opposite Meetinghouse Hill and the jaegers. Once in position, Deshon anchored his company near the stone bridge that spanned Mill Brook. The bridge, situated at a bend in the brook, occupied the junction of Town Street and the Norwich Road. Over a century earlier, Mill Brook was the northern limits of John Winthrop's original settlement; now the brook was the boundary line between the two opposing sides. Most of Deshon's Company was drawn from those who had retreated from the town, plus new arrivals coming from the direction of Quaker Hill. Like the other companies organized, it included a mixed group of militia and sailors. While its strength is not exactly clear, according to one who was there the company included Capt. Thomas Harding, commander of the 2nd Company Alarm List, privateer Capt. Charles Bulkeley and "a small number of men."[50]

---

became known best as Quaker Hill. This was due to large numbers of Rogerene Quakers who resided on the hill, including many descendants of Thomas Bolles.

49 *CG*, May 2, 1783.

50 Charles Allyn Papers, NLCHS; Robert Hallam account of Sep. 6, 1781, undated, NLCHS. Inside the Allyn papers was a small note concerning the reminiscences of Joshua Smith. In it, he was a member of Deshon's Company, and placed his company along Mill Brook, near the bridge, with the

Latimer entrusted Harris with Quaker Hill. His orders were "to equip the men and send them forward." This meant Harris was to organize the militia as best he could, then direct them to one of the two provisional companies south of the hill.[51]

Harris and Deshon were fortunate the American Legion had not pursued the retreating militia toward Quaker Hill. It certainly gave Deshon's Company more time to organize. Frink did not even approach the bridge, instead allowing the jaegers on Meetinghouse Hill to confront the enemy. Most, if not all, of the American Legion only marched as far as the Adam's house, where they crossed Mill Brook at a bridge a quarter of a mile downstream of the stone bridge, near the Winthrop grist mill.

The small, wooden, one-story grist mill was owned by the Winthrop family. Originally constructed in 1650, it was one of the earliest industrial sites in southeastern Connecticut. The current mill, fed by the waters of Mill Brook, had been rebuilt in 1742, but contained some of its original features, including its elevated flume, wheel pit, and tailrace. The mill was used by citizens as well as the units stationed within the military garrison, making it a legitimate target for the British.

Overlooking the mill stood the impressive, two-story, gambrel-roofed, stone Winthrop mansion. With two large chimneys on both ends of the house, the large mansion overlooked Town Street, Winthrop Cove, and the northern end of the harbor. Built in the early 1750s, the "handsome dwelling house" belonged to the widow Elizabeth Winthrop. Her husband John Still Winthrop, the great-grandson of the founder of New London and an avowed loyalist, had died in 1776.[52]

A short time after crossing Mill Brook onto Winthrop's Neck, some of Frink's soldiers visited the Winthrop mansion. Entering, they searched the premises for militia or other armed rebels. Aware of her loyalties, no harm came to Mrs. Winthrop or any of her daughters who lived with her. A few soldiers even went up to the third floor, where they climbed out of a window and onto the roof. From there they could watch the Americans on Quaker Hill.[53]

The presence of Captain Deshon's Company at the bridge apparently caused the jaegers some concern. Sometime after the American Legion occupied the

---

enemy on the opposite bank at this time. The bridge no longer stands today but was located near the present-day intersection of Williams and Bragaw Streets.

51 *CG*, May 2, 1783.

52 American Loyalist Claims, 1776–1835, AO 13/42/637-640, TNA; *CSR*, 3:549.550. The mansion was leveled during the 1890's to make room for the Winthrop School. The school was demolished during the construction of Interstate 95 in the late 1960's.

53 John Hempsted narrative in Harris, *Groton Heights*, 66.

Winthrop's Mill. A reconstructed mill, built in the same style and on the same site as the one that there stood in 1781, stands today in a small park on Mill Street. *Author*

Winthrop mansion, Captain von Wangenheim ordered some of his jaegers to mount an attack against the bridge. Jonathan Chandler, a sailor from Hartford, who served with Deshon's Company, believed the purpose of the jaeger assault was to take possession of the Ichabod Powers house, which lay just opposite the bridge on the south side of the brook. He believed they wanted it so that they could burn and plunder it. Given the role of the jaegers in the British deployment, Chandler's reasoning seems unlikely. Its more practical tactical purpose was to scatter Deshon's Company before it could grow in strength to interfere with the British occupation.[54]

In typical fashion, the jaegers maneuvered and attempted to get closer to the bridge to disperse the militia. This, according to Chandler, "[they] attempted several times." Each time the jaegers advanced, they exchanged fire with the militia. But each successive time, Deshon's Company, as Chandler contended in his pension application, "drove them back." In the process, the Powers house, situated in the middle of the fighting, sustained significant damage.[55]

54 PA: Jonathan Chandler (R.21842), NARA; Robert Hallam account of Sep. 6, 1781, undated, NLCHS. The Powers house either became or stood on the site of the Ezra Dodge Tavern, a 19th-century local landmark.

55 PA: Jonathan Chandler (R.21842), NARA. Chandler was a sailor on the privateer *Deane.*

The militia, according to Joshua Smith of Deshon's Company, sustained casualties in the firefight. Smith remembered at one point turning to his right and seeing the soldier standing next to him killed. He never named the soldier, but the image of him falling was something Smith never forgot. Jaeger casualties, one militiaman, estimated were two or three killed and wounded. This is clearly an exaggeration as the jaegers did not suffer that many casualties that day, or it may point to the involvement of the Associated Loyalists in the action as well.[56]

After their failed attempts to disperse Deshon, the jaegers retired to their former position. There they remained, occasionally exchanging fire with those across the brook. Despite his success, Captain Deshon feared the jaegers would return later. Numerous attempts were made by those in his company to locate reinforcements.[57]

Robert Hallam, a member of Deshon's Company, testified, "Capt. [Thomas] Harding and theirs frequently went upon [Quaker] Hill to request a Reanforcement." Hallam, himself, eventually went looking for help. Hallam testified that he had found Harris, asked for reinforcements, and was promised help would soon be on its way—help that, Hallam elaborated at Harris's court martial, never came.[58]

Harris was all over Quaker Hill, often riding up and down the Norwich Road. At one point, Harris rode towards the Enoch Bolles farm. As he rode closer to the farm, he witnessed an overwhelming scene which complicated his task. The farm was covered with a crowd of men, women, and young children. Most had fled the town at the approach of the enemy. Some had nothing, others were encumbered with personal belongings in carts they dragged behind them. Most remained anxious. Many searched for missing family members who had become separated. Others found vantage points where they watched the British in town. Others looked for food, which caused owners or tenants of nearby farms to open their homes and barns to the evacuees. According to Frances Caulkins, one family opened their dairy, emptied their cupboards, and gave all they had to the people on their property.[59]

---

56 Charles Allyn Papers, NLCHS. Only one jaeger was wounded in New London. If Smith's casualty count is accurate, it may imply the Associated Loyalists were also involved in the skirmishing near the stone bridge.

57 "Losses of New London Sufferers By The Ravages of the British Army," Revolutionary War Records, Third Series, 1765–1820, I:95f, CSL; PA: Jonathan Chandler (R.21842), NARA. Powers submitted a damage claim to the General Assembly for £196, which in today's money is almost $31,000.

58 Robert Hallam account of Sep. 6, 1781, undated, Robert Hallam Papers, NLCHS.

59 *CG*, May 2, 1783; Caulkins, *New London*, 547–548.

Harris rode about Quaker Hill searching for his officers, he later asserted, so that they could help him organize their companies. Such delegating was not something he had done effectively that morning. As Harris remembered, he could not at first find any of his officers and therefore made attempts at collecting militia himself and ordering them separately or in small groups to join Caulkins's or Deshon's companies. Because of the general disorganization, this proved to be a difficult, time-consuming, and almost impossible task, one with which, according to a veteran Continental officer on the scene, even he would have had great difficulty. Though there were numbers of militia on the hill, they were scattered and intermixed with civilians and almost indistinguishable in their dress. It was a mess. Some arrived from the North Parish. Others had retreated from the town. Many could not find their companies or their officers. For reasons unknown, many militia, according to Harris, were unruly and refused to follow orders. Unfortunately, in his public letter, Harris was brief about this dire situation. Beyond stating his difficulties, we do not know how widespread the problem was, as Harris did not go into detail about how many refused to follow orders nor did he name any specific individuals. No individual members or officers of the regiment were ever brought up on charges of disobedience to Harris's orders. His solution was to forcefully disarm those who refused to follow orders. Weapons commandeered were then handed over to militia who were willing to fight but had no arms. According to Harris, the newly-armed men were then sent towards Mill Brook.[60]

Eventually, Harris located three officers: Capt. Griswold Avery, who in addition to his current drafted company also led the 7th Company Alarm List; Capt. John Deshon, of the 1st Company Alarm List; and Capt. Jabez Beebe, of the 7th Company. Harris ordered Captain Avery and Lieutenant Hillhouse, who had both escaped capture in town, to reform their company. But despite their best attempts, the company would not serve as a cohesive unit for the duration of the day, though some did serve with Deshon's Company at the bridge.[61]

Harris also told captains Deshon and Beebe to assemble their companies. Both tried to comply, but neither was able to do so. Both came to the same conclusion and testified, "it was not in their power to embody their companies, the surprise [of the British attack] being so compleat." Some had never reported for duty—the

---

60 *CG*, May 2, 1783.

61 PA: Griswold Avery Jr. (R.306), NARA. Avery helped drive away livestock, he "joined his company on the hill back of New London and continued with it during the day." The hill mentioned was Quaker Hill.

captain of the 1st Company, for example, recorded seeing only seven of his forty members the whole day.[62]

Harris was fortunate to find Christopher Darrow on Quaker Hill. Known as a "well approv'd [and] experienced officer," Harris met Darrow sometime after meeting with Latimer. Darrow was the antithesis of Harris in terms of military experience. He was a combat veteran and had seen much action during the war. He had been a major in the 1st Connecticut Regiment and saw action at Germantown, endured the winter at Valley Forge, and played a pivotal role at Monmouth. Despite such action, or perhaps because of it, Darrow had resigned his commission in 1780 and returned home.[63]

Darrow agreed to help Harris. On horseback, the former major went into action, seemingly without any hesitation, and periodically exposed himself to the enemy. At one point, he personally led militia down to join Deshon's Company. The group likely contained militia from the North Parish, who arrived with Darrow. Among them were the Whaley brothers, Samuel and Jonathan. Samuel was a sergeant in his company, as well as the son-in-law of Darrow.[64]

But like Harris, Darrow encountered difficulties. In one instance, he was riding towards the bridge and approached militia, which had been involved in the fighting in town and were retreating towards Quaker Hill. Darrow halted and told them to turn around and pointed back towards Mill Brook and the British. Most refused. One witness recalled hearing Darrow yell, "why the Devel dont [you] Go down & meet the Enemy?" Lieutenant Pickett Latimer, of the Independent Artillery Company, refused to go back, telling Darrow he would not risk his life to save other men's property.[65]

Around 12:30 p.m. Arnold entered New London. Riding with the main British column, and accompanied by Dalrymple and Stapleton, Arnold was not met by any governmental delegation. Nor did he ever receive a formal surrender of the

---

62 *CG*, May 2, 1783; John Hempsted narrative in Harris, *Groton Heights*, 69. While there, Harris testified, "I ordered a number of captains to march down the hill with parties of men to support our men that were ingag'd with the enemy at the north end of town; and that I sent every man forward that was armed." He does not name any of these captains. Nor does he distinguish if they were captains in his regiment or if they were captains of naval vessels. It is likely they were a combination of the two.

63 *Connecticut Men*, 18, 72, 99, 145; Caulkins, *New London*, 532; Christopher Darrow to George Washington, Aug. 23, 1780, George Washington Papers, LOC; *CG*, May 2, 1782.

64 PA: Samuel Whaley (R.11366), Jonathan Whaley (W.2739), NARA.

65 Hempsted narrative in Harris, *Groton Heights*, 66–67. What is probably more surprising, and revealing is Hempsted never attempted to help Darrow. In fact, in his memoir, Hempsted indirectly admitted that at that moment, he shirked his duties. Unmoved by Darrow's desperation, Hempsted made his way home and did not return until that afternoon.

town. The town's three selectmen, who headed the local government, had either left the town or opposed him in the militia. Arnold disregarded the formality, as there is no evidence he sought them out or looked for a formal surrender of the town.[66]

At least publicly, Arnold thought little of the resistance put up by the militia. As he reported to Clinton, "No time was lost on my part in gaining the town of New London. We were opposed by a small body of the Enemy with one field piece, who were so hard pressed, that they were obliged to leave the piece, which being Iron was spiked and left."[67]

Arnold proceeded with the column until it reached the Parade area. He then veered off, with at least one staff officer, to Bradley Street where he made his visit to the Potter house. After this, he proceeded in the direction of Meetinghouse Hill. Once there, they rode to the summit near the militia training field. The open field stood south of the town's burial ground and east of the hill's most prominent feature, the meetinghouse. Built in 1694, the two-story wooden structure was forty feet square and featured more than a dozen glass windows, at least three doors, and two galleries. The edifice contained a steeple with a large brass bell. Inside, the jaegers discovered the military stores removed from Fort Nonsense. With respect to the church, the stores were removed outside, where they were accounted and then destroyed.[68]

From the training field and burial ground, with a field glass, Arnold surveyed the harbor area. Local tradition has incorrectly surmised he remained there the whole afternoon and watched the burning of the town and attack on Fort Griswold. In fact, his own actions suggest he only used the hill as a temporary observation post. From there, Arnold had an excellent opportunity to observe the rebel privateers still in the harbor, as well as check the status of his own forces across the river. Nothing had changed since he left Town Hill.

Fort Griswold was still in rebel hands, and Captain Shepherd's advance up the river had not yet begun. This greatly agitated Arnold. What also frustrated him was Fort Griswold. It was much stronger than he had been led to believe. "From information I received before and after my landing," Arnold later stated, "I had reason to believe Fort Griswold . . . was very incomplete; and I was assured (by friends to [the] Government) after my landing that there were only 20, or 30 men

---

66 "Copy of Flag of Truce Document," in Rogers, *Naval Office*, 29. The three current selectmen were Lt. Col. Joseph Harris Jr., Guy Richards Jr., and Joseph Packwood.

67 Arnold report in Mackenzie, *Diary*, 2:624.

68 Caulkins, *New London*, 191, 574; S. Leroy Blake, *The Early History of the First Church of Christ, New London, Conn.* (New London, CT, 1897), 215; Mackenzie, *Diary*, 2:628.

Burial Ground. Present-day view of New London's oldest cemetery looking east towards Winthrop's Cove.

Author

inside the Fort." This led to him to believe the fort could be easily captured, but the information proved only partially true.[69]

The artillery company which was stationed at the fort consisted of only 20 men, but the garrison had been steadily increasing in size throughout the morning, by militia and by Shapley's Company which escaped from Fort Trumbull. Arnold admitted to Clinton he believed the locals would be more concerned with saving their own vessels and personal property than aiding in the defense of Fort Griswold or New London. This belief was further bolstered by the relative ease with which they had been able to march inland and secure New London, suffering only minimal losses. As to Fort Griswold being incomplete, the reality was quite the opposite. Arnold found it "much more formidable than [he] expected, or than [he] had formed any Idea [from] the information [he] had before received." He clearly had not expected this.[70]

---

69 Arnold report in Mackenzie, *Diary*, 2:624.

70 Ibid., 2:624. Arnold claimed that on Meetinghouse Hill he attempted to send an officer across the river to cancel the attack on the fort. But unfortunately, the officer, as Arnold put it, "arrived a few minutes too late." However, no contemporary evidence supports his claim, and he may have included it to save face after the high number of casualties sustained in the storming of the fort.

The delays that morning endured by the British allowed most privateers the chance to escape up the Thames River. It also gave the militia the opportunity to reinforce Fort Griswold. Arnold hoped the fort had already been taken, and Shepherd's vessels would be in pursuit of the privateers. But the fort was still flying American colors, and the British armed vessels were stalled at the entrance to the harbor unable to pursue the privateers. Because of this the success of the entire operation, or at least the task of destroying or taking the privateers, was in jeopardy.

Arnold looked towards Quaker Hill. He could see the civilians, and the militia dispersed about it as well as those along Mill Brook. All were in full sight. Aware the British occupation of New London depended on the outpost keeping the militia occupied, Arnold sent for Lieutenant Horndon. Horndon was ordered to bring his 6-pounder field piece onto the Meetinghouse Hill to strengthen the outpost.[71]

Horndon arrived on the hill a few moments before his crew. Only 18-years-old, Horndon was a graduate of the Royal Military Academy in London. He had served in America for the last two years and had been captured with the British garrison at Stony Point. After being exchanged, he was promoted to first lieutenant and returned to duty. Horndon may have spoken briefly with or received direction from Arnold as he determined where to place his fieldpiece. The militia to his front, specifically those near the bridge, were thought to be the most problematic, and his battery's attention was focused on them.[72]

Horndon's crew drove the fieldpiece onto the training field. There, under Horndon's direction, the crew members detached the 6-pounder from the horses, removed the side caisson containing its ammunition, and dragged the gun into position.[73]

The 6-pounder had a maximum range of up to 2,000 yards, though it was most effective up to 1,000 yards. The Americans at the bridge were only 850 yards from the training field, but Horndon had to be careful as he had only limited ammunition. Relying on solid shot ammunition for distance, Horndon's Battery

---

71 According to Hempstead family lore, William Hempstead saw Arnold from the bridge area. He is reported to have taken one or two shots at him. Both missed but they supposedly gained the attention of Arnold who shook his sword in Hempstead's direction.

72 "A Sketch of New-London & Groton, with Attacks made on Forts Trumbull & Griswold by the British Troops Under the Command of Brig. Gen. Arnold Sep 6th, 1781, by Captain Lyman of ye Prince of Wales American Volunteers," Sir Henry Clinton Papers, WCL. Lyman's map places Horndon's Battery adjacent to the meetinghouse in the training field, though pointed towards the harbor.

73 Caulkins, *New London*, 445. An attempt was made by an unnamed witness to identify the officer with Arnold as Lord Stair Park Dalrymple. While it may have been Dalrymple, it could have also been Stapleton, Horndon, or even von Wangenheim who commanded the outpost on the hill. The witness had no way to accurately identify the officers.

fired several rounds over the course of the next hour. Each time it went off the percussion rattled the meetinghouse but caused no serious damage to the building.

Horndon directed his fire mainly at Deshon's Company. At least one round struck the Robert Hallam house, just north of the bridge. Inside, Lydia Hallam was hiding with her infant son Orlando. She remembered years later how fearful she was as a round slammed into their house and destroyed the front door. Other rounds crashed into nearby fields, wrecking fences but inflicting, so far as is known, no casualties. The fire did help prompt Deshon and others in his company to believe, however, that even after they repulsed the jaegers, additional attacks might be forthcoming.[74]

The presence of British artillery on Meetinghouse Hill may have been the reason the outpost line was targeted by Ledyard's artillery at Fort Griswold. Or that Ledyard could not resist seeing British soldiers in the open and an opportunity to help his neighbors. The garrison had been observing British movements in New London as the panoramic view from Groton Heights allowed them to see everything across the river.

Once Holt arrived with his supply of gunpowder from the stores in New London, Ledyard had plenty to use. Ledyard's gunners utilized at least one 12-pounder along the west wall, loaded heavy charges of powder, and fired several times towards the British across the river. Unfortunately, Ledyard's cannon could not accurately hit their targets. Rounds either undershot or overshot their intended targets. Some crashed into and damaged buildings in the center and north of town. Others hit near the British outpost but inflicted no casualties. Upham explained his situation on Post Hill: "Here we remained, exposed to a constant fire from the rebels on the neighboring hills, and from the fort on the Groton side until it was [assaulted] by the British troops." The fire slightly unnerved Upham but did little else.[75]

---

74 Caulkins, *New London*, 552; PA: Robert Hallam (W.19731) NARA. Fire directed towards the house seems to suggest militia may have been using the house or other buildings on the property for cover. It is not clear how many rounds Horndon's battery fired. According to Francis Caulkins, several rounds were fired in the direction of Quaker Hill.

75 Upham report in Harris, *Groton Heights*, 109–110; "Ye Old Mechanics Hotel," *New London Daily Star*, Oct. 21, 1859; "Revolutionary Relic," *New London Democrat*, Sep. 30, 1848. Rounds were later discovered to have hit around Post Hill, at the north end of Congress Street, and along the upper part of Town Street, along Winthrop Cove. In the early 19th century repairs on a barn near the Mechanic's Hotel on State Street, then Congress Street, revealed a solid 12-pound cannon ball. It was said the ball was "fired from Fort Griswold at [a nearby] tavern." The tavern, formerly owned by Capt. Edward Palmes, was run in 1781 by David W. Richards. The article incorrectly assumed Benedict Arnold dined there during the occupation. Another round that came "from across the river" was found in 1848, along Winthrop's Cove on the upper part of Town Street, then Main Street, and was advertised as being on display at the nearby Smith and Beckwith store.

In Upham's front, to the north, was Captain Caulkins's Company. Caulkins moved from the Richards house towards the Cohanzie Road. From there, he dispersed the company into small parties and advanced and probed towards Mill Brook. There they maneuvered from behind rocks, trees, and fences, exchanging fire with the loyalists on Post Hill. One civilian who witnessed the skirmishing here commented "the bullets flew whistling . . . at no small rate." Over time, both sides took casualties.[76]

At least two members of Caulkins's Company, Jonathan Fox, and Isaac Birch, were killed. Fox and Birch both lived in western New London, near the Lyme border. Unfortunately, we only know details about Fox. He had participated in the Siege of Boston and the Battle of Bunker Hill. Fox was with a group of six men who attempted to get closer to the enemy, but as they did came under fire. In the words of one member of the party, Gurdon F. Saltonstall, "[we] took a ramble rather too near the enemy . . . Fox was killed, the rest escaped." Fox was struck in the chest by a musket ball and died almost instantly.[77]

Around 1:30 p.m. the Post Hill front widened, as Upham's men started encountering militia moving against the western slope of the hill. This was due in large part to Colonel Latimer. After leaving Harris on Quaker Hill, Latimer made a circuitous ride towards the Colchester Road, to the farm of his brother Ens. Daniel Latimer. Located a mile west of the Pickett Latimer house, Colonel Latimer designated it as an assembly point for the militia, both new arrivals and those who had retreated from town.

Fortunately for the Americans, once Latimer took command of the regiment, the situation began to change for the better. His presence seemed to increase the morale and resolve of the militia. Latimer remained close to the action, and relied on his son, Sgt. Witherel Latimer, his acting adjutant, to distribute his orders.[78]

On the Daniel Latimer farm, the militia rallied together into a third provisional company. Pieced together from the New London companies, as well as those arriving from Lyme, they were collected and placed under Capt. Abner Lord. At 48-years-old, Lord led the regiment's 12th Company, comprised of men from the 3rd Society of Lyme, sometimes known as either North Lyme or Hamburg. Captain Lord had served for several years as an officer in the militia, had seen

---

76 Jonathan Brooks narrative in Harris, *Groton Heights*, 79.

77 *CG*, Sep. 7, 1781; Charles Allyn Papers, NLCHS; *Connecticut Men*, 18; PA: Gurdon Flowers Saltonstall (R.9159), Thomas Bishop (W.17305), Peter Crocker (R.2493), NARA. Both Bishop and Crocker were friends of Fox and near him when he was killed. Bishop had been with Fox at Bunker Hill.

78 PA: Witherel Latimer (S.31809), NARA.

Grave of Jonathan Fox of Caulkins's Company, killed on September 6, 1781. *Author*

service during Spencer's Expedition to Rhode Island in 1777, and led several companies contributing to the defense of New London.[79]

Now, Latimer entrusted Lord to protect the Colchester Road. He was to do this by probing and harassing Upham's position on the western slope of Post Hill. Throughout the afternoon, the company continued to be augmented with men from other Lyme companies, specifically from its East Society, but all were placed under Lord. Lord's skirmish line was roughly a half-mile east of the Latimer farm. Fanned out on either side of the Colchester Road, both ends of Lord's line moved south until they made contact with Upham, then halted and skirmished with the loyalists all throughout the early afternoon.[80]

At around 2:00 p.m. Lord received reinforcements from the 25th Regiment of Connecticut Militia. These consisted of small detachments from the 3rd Company led by Sgt. Dan Worthington, and the 6th Company under Capt. Nathaniel Harris. John Cavarly, a member of the 3rd Company, recalled that upon arriving, "[we] were called immediately [into] the action" and joined in the skirmishing, but being part of a separate militia regiment, retained semi-independent status, under Captain Harris.[81]

79 PA: Hoel Huntley (S.18043), Seth Smith (S.14507), Isaac Sill (W.17358), William Greenfield (R.4283), Peter Way (W.18228), Joseph Lord (W.20517), NARA; *Connecticut Men*, 424, 620–621; Willahauer, *A Lyme Miscellany*, 103. After the alarm was sounded, Ezra Selden, a magistrate, from [North] Lyme went out riding and encouraging his neighbors to turn out. It is unusual that Lord was present, and it is not known how many members of his company were present, as the two other companies from the same geographical area, the 3rd Company under Capt. Daniel Lord, and 6th Company Alarm List under Capt. Seth Ely did not arrive until around midnight.

80 PA: John Tubbs (S.14730), (R.307), Jacob Tillotson (W.25490), NARA.

81 PA: Ebenezer Rogers (S.31941), John Cavarly (W.17593), Joel Bigelow (W.1535), NARA; *CSR*, 5:212. Sergeant Worthington was a member of Capt. Elijah Worthington's Company. The captain, Worthington's brother, does not appear to have arrived until the following day.

Both companies were the lead elements of the regiment. Harris's Company was from Paugwonk, a small hamlet fourteen miles away, and Sergeant Worthington's men were from Colchester, around twenty miles distant. The rest of their regiment, whose companies hailed from Colchester and East Haddam, should have been there with them. Their colonel, Elias Worthington, a native of Colchester, was at his home when a rider at midday alerted him of the British attack. But for reasons that are not understood, he failed to act.

It was revealed during his court-martial that instead of moving his regiment to the coast, Worthington "removed himself five Miles further Northward from the Town of New London, than his usual place of abode; and there set a Guard for his personal Security and continued there untill near [noon]" the following day. It was not until a full day later that his regiment began to make its way to New London.[82]

Frustrated at Worthington's inaction on September 6, numerous members of the regiment acted on their own. One militiaman recalled that he "went immediately to [New London's] defence without waiting the arrival of orders." The regiment's third-in-command, Maj. Daniel Cone, had also done the same. By 3:00 p.m. Major Cone had arrived at the Daniel Latimer farm with a company of militia from his native East Haddam. Along with Lt. Amasa Brainard of the 1st Company, Cone had collected as many militia as they could find, formed them into a provisional company, and then marched directly for New London.[83]

Arnold was soon made aware the Americans were converging on him, so he remained on Meetinghouse Hill for only a brief time. Apart from the escape of the privateers, the situation for the British could not have been better, though, at the time, Arnold probably did not fully understand that. He controlled New London, and the American force opposing him was in no condition to hinder his progress. They were in a disorganized mess. Even if Arnold did recognize this, he could not assume its continuance. Time was his biggest enemy. If the militia was given time, it would soon have enough men to launch an attack—or even worse, threaten his withdrawal back to the squadron.

---

82 PA: Simeon Ackley (S.18680), NARA; Hezekiah Bissell to Governor Trumbull, Oct. 22, 1782, Governor Trumbull Papers, 144a–b, CSL.

83 PA: Simeon Ackley (S.18680), Ebenezer Rogers (S.31941), Abraham Osborn (S.14061), Abraham Osborn (S.14061), Timothy Fuller (W.17974), John Tennant (R.10453), NARA. According to Rogers, Harris initially arrived with a small party from his own company; the rest, including Rogers, came later that day.

Chapter Seven

The Battle of Groton Heights:
Opening Phase

Lieutenant Colonel Edmund Eyre stood anxiously on the deck of his transport vessel anchored in view of Groton Point. From there he observed Arnold's force as it disembarked near the lighthouse. Though it "[was the] most delightful day, clear and still," Eyre was more concerned about landing on the enemy's shore than he was about the weather. When Arnold's force completed its disembarkation, the sailors rowed across the river to transport Eyre's command onto Groton Point. Eyre's second division consisted of the 40th Regiment, 54th Regiment, the 3rd Battalion, New Jersey Volunteers, 47 jaegers, and two pieces of artillery with accompanying artillerymen and horses.[1]

Eyre was a career army officer. Born in 1742 in Stambourne, in the county of Essex, in eastern England, Eyre was a member of a prestigious family with strong ties to the Anglican Church. His father was an archdeacon, and his uncle an influential bishop. Instead of following his father and uncle into the church, Eyre joined the army. By 1781 he was a 20-year veteran of the British army. First commissioned in 1760 as an ensign in the 24th Regiment of Foot, he purchased a commission to captain in the 54th Regiment two years later. As the 54th Foot embarked in

---

1 Barber, *Historical Collections*, 309. The actual place of the British landing is probably around modern-day Eastern Point and Shennecossett beaches. The oft-quoted number of 40 jaegers does not include the four sergeants, the horn-blower, or two officers, but they are included here.

Ireland for America in 1775, Eyre obtained the rank of major. After five years of service in the colonies he had earned the brevet rank of lieutenant colonel.[2]

With a force of about 950 men, Arnold ordered Eyre to secure Fort Griswold. It was an essential objective that could define the success or failure of the entire expedition. Eyre was up to the task. This was not the first time he had led an independent command into enemy territory. In 1778, when stationed in Newport, Rhode Island, he had been tasked with raiding Freetown, Massachusetts. This was an attempt by the British to slow down an anticipated American attack on Newport. Eyre's force sailed across Mount Hope Bay and initially met with success. They burned two mills, nine flatboats, and a large amount of lumber. As Eyre attempted to destroy more supplies he was forced to cross a creek, but found himself under attack by militia posted on the opposite bank. Worse, the planks on the bridge he intended to cross had been removed by the Americans. Unable to proceed further, Eyre withdrew.[3]

As they had on the New London side, Shepherd's armed vessels positioned themselves offshore and opened a six-minute bombardment on the landing area. But unlike at Brown's farm, no resistance awaited them. At 9:00 a.m. as the naval guns fell silent, Captain Chads began the landing of Eyre's force. Flatboats soon headed to the shore around Groton Point. The first units, presumably the jaegers, splashed ashore, onto the Thankful Avery farm, and advanced slightly further to set up a protective screen for the rest of the division.[4]

As more British troops came ashore, Eyre came with them. On shore Eyre was joined by Capt. Abiathar Camp, who was to act as a guide. Camp was the loyalist refugee who had delivered the request to Upham for his assistance, just days earlier. A sea merchant and presumably an acquaintance of Arnold from New Haven, Camp had been to New London before the war. He had knowledge of the harbor area and would help Eyre guide the British toward Fort Griswold. According to Capt. George Beckwith, who also assisted Eyre, Camp proved "[to be] very useful and often [himself] exposed to great Danger" all along the march.[5]

2 *Ipswich Journal*, Oct. 15, 1791; WO 65 Army Lists, 1760, 1762, TNA; Ford, *British Officers*, 67. Eyre's father was the Reverend Archdeacon Venn Eyre who served in many prominent positions within the Anglican Church. His uncle Edmund Keene was the Anglican bishop of the Diocese of Ely.

3 Christian M. McBurney, *The Rhode Island Campaign: The First French and American Operations in the Revolutionary War* (Yardley, PA, 2012), 66–69. The part of Freetown they struck is modern-day Fall River, Massachusetts.

4 Master's Log, HMS *Amphion*, ADM 52/2133, TNA.

5 American Loyalists Claims, 1776-1835, AO 13/41/102, 104,114-155, TNA; Beckwith also stated after the war that Camp "rendered every Service in his power to that cause in which he was engaged."

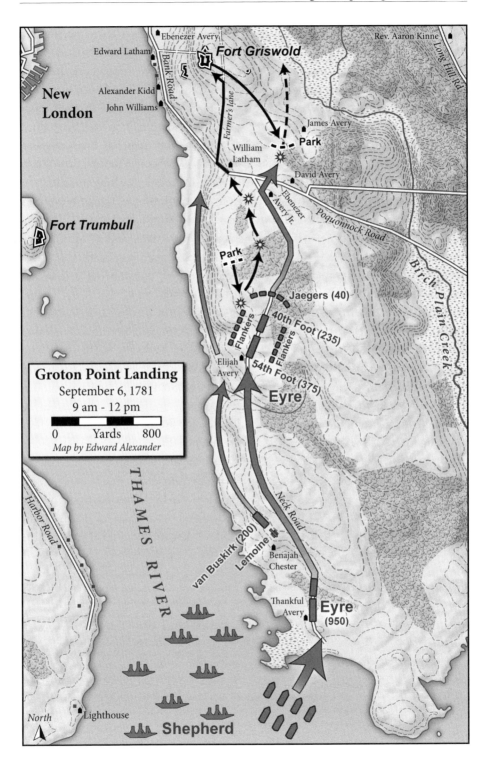

Ebenezer Avery

Rev. Aaron Kinne

Edward Latham

Fort Griswold

Long Hill Rd

New London

Alexander Kidd

John Williams

Bank Road

Farmer's lane

James Avery

Park

William Latham

David Avery

Fort Trumbull

Ebenezer Avery Jr.

Poquonnock Road

Park

Birch Plain Creek

Jaegers (40)

40th Foot (235)

Flankers

Flankers

Elijah Avery

54th Foot (375)

Groton Point Landing
September 6, 1781
9 am - 12 pm

0   Yards   800

Map by Edward Alexander

Eyre

THAMES RIVER

Harbor Road

Neck Road

van Buskirk (200)

Lemoine

Benajah Chester

Thankful Avery

Eyre
(950)

North

Lighthouse

Shepherd

As Eyre's troops waited for their comrades to come ashore, some ransacked the Avery house. Afterwards, Thankful submitted a damage claim, which included two tables, a desk, six chairs, chests, three bedsteads, a cradle, two wool wheels, farming equipment, and dozens of books, including a family bible. All had been burned.[6]

At around 9:45 a.m. Eyre called his division to attention and ordered them formed into column. The jaegers, led by Second Lieutenant von Reitzenstein of the 1st Ansbach Jaeger Company, were deployed in front to act as Eyre's advance guard. Behind them was the main column with flankers drawn from the two British regiments on both sides of the column to protect it from ambushing militia.[7]

The march toward Fort Griswold began just after 10:00 a.m., roughly an hour after Arnold's column had left Brown's farm. The column used the only public road available at the time, which connected Groton Bank and Groton Point. Sometimes called the Neck Road, it had been constructed years earlier and was not a smooth pathway but rather coarse and irregular, encumbered with many obstacles including rocks, small trees, and bulging thick roots from larger trees. It meandered north for two miles through several farm lots, most belonging to the Chester and Avery families, before it reached the intersection of the Bank and Poquonnock Roads.[8]

Deployed in skirmish order formation, the Ansbach jaegers moved first and probed a good, safe distance ahead into the woods before Eyre directed the column to follow. When the British entered the woods, the roughness of the highway became evident. Though not necessarily difficult for the veteran infantry soldiers to traverse the path was tough for the horse-drawn artillery, the unevenness of the road brought the column to a crawl. If Eyre continued at this pace, the column would become dangerously strung out. Moving into a wooded environment, which was ideal for ambushes set up by the militia, could prove disastrous.

Because of this, Eyre was forced to make a tough, but necessary tactical decision to speed the march. He divided his force. Eyre ordered Capt. John Lemoine, his

---

6 Harris, *Groton Heights*, 28. "An account of the losses of the Inhabitants of the town of Groton occasioned by the incursion of the British troops in the late war collected from the documents in the public offices distinguishing between such as consist of buildings and necessaries and such as consist of other articles with the advancements which have been made the Sufferers by the State," Revolutionary War Records, Series III, 79a–79e, CSL. Thankful was the widow of Elihu Avery. Avery had earlier served as a lieutenant in Latham's Company but died in 1779. The house was listed by Benadam Gallup as having been burned during the raid. The damage claim set by Thankful Avery for £265 was for "Buildings & necessaries destroyed" and was clearly meant for a large structure.

7 "A Sketch of New-London & Groton, with Attacks made on Forts Trumbull & Griswold by the British Troops Under the Command of Brig. General Arnold Sep 6th, 1781, by Captain Lyman of ye Prince of Wales American Volunteers," Sir Henry Clinton Papers, WCL. These were either drawn from the battalion companies or the two flank companies were used separately.

8 *CSR*, 3:233–238, 292. The road likely followed the modern-day route of Benham Road.

artillery commander, to take the artillery and locate another more suitable route toward the fort. Eyre also ordered the 3rd Battalion, New Jersey Volunteers, to go with Lemoine and act as an escort to ensure the safety of the guns. It was a difficult decision for Eyre since he would not want to divide his force in hostile territory or be without his artillery support if he had to attack the fort once he reached it. However, speed was of the essence. He could not afford the delays or the risks pulling the artillery up the road would entail.[9]

As the artillery and New Jersey loyalists departed from the main column, Eyre pressed onward with the remaining 750 men, and the march continued for a mile and a half without interruption. Then, unexpectedly, the column came under fire from an enemy force hidden in the woods and rocks around them. This was a group of armed sailors under Capt. Thomas Park. Park, commander of the privateer *Prudence*, had earlier armed his crew, which he said, "consisted of no more than ten men," and gone to Fort Griswold.[10]

They did not, however, remain at the fort. Rather, Park moved them south towards the Neck Road, the route the British were expected to take. There, he planned to watch, harass, and contest their approach towards the fort. Whether he acted on his own initiative or through Ledyard's order is unknown. Park's party may have been the scouts sent out by Ledyard referred to by William Harris in his book on the battle. In it, Harris named only one scout: Joshua Baker. Baker, a former member of Latham's Company, knew the area well. Unlike Baker, Captain Park

9 "A Sketch of New-London & Groton, with Attacks made on Forts Trumbull & Griswold by the British Troops Under the Command of Brig. General Arnold Sep. 6th, 1781, by Captain Lyman of ye Prince of Wales American Volunteers," Sir Henry Clinton Papers, WCL; "An account of the losses of the Inhabitants of the town of Groton occasioned by the incursion of the British troops in the late war collected from the documents in the public offices distinguishing between such as consist of buildings and necessaries and such as consist of other articles with the advancements which have been made the Sufferers by the State," Revolutionary War Records, Series III, 79a–79e, CSL; Barber, *Historical Collections*, 312. It is not clear as to what route the loyalists and artillery took, but they may have veered onto the Benajah Chester farm, and used a cart path which was used by neighboring farms to pasture their livestock along the riverbank. Lyman's map seems to imply this scenario, as does the fact that the Chester farm was reportedly burned by the British supports this as well. This may be the same path referred to by historian John Warner Barber when he wrote "a lame boy collecting cattle [was] compelled . . . to show them the cart path to the fort." The boy is sometimes identified as Bill Herron. However, no record can be found as to his existence or any Herron that owned property near Groton Point. They may have been tenants on one of the farms.

10 PA: Thomas Park (R.7932), NARA. Captain Park may have operated under Ledyard's orders though he never made that claim when he wrote about in his pension deposition. He was also a witness during the post-raid militia court martial and might have stated in them, but transcripts of the proceedings are not known to have survived.

was not from the immediate area. Park grew up in Stonington and lived in Lyme. If Baker did assist Park, Baker would have provided invaluable assistance as a guide.[11]

Park's mission to monitor and contest the British on their approach had been discussed at the fort that morning. But attempts to reinforce Park's men with militia never materialized, having been overruled by Ledyard. Ledyard consulted Henry Williams and Amos Stanton, both former officers in Sherburne's Additional Regiment, and arguably the two most combat-experienced volunteers to join the garrison. Stanton, a former captain, advised Ledyard that staying inside the fort was impractical and that they should meet the British troops closer to Groton Point, skirmish with them, and maneuver in such a way to make their numbers appear larger. This, Stanton and Williams argued, would give additional time for more militia to arrive.[12]

Despite their advice, Ledyard disagreed. His reasoning is not clear; it may have been he recognized that the British tactically needed the fort. Shepherd's armed vessels could not move into the harbor until the British secured Fort Griswold. If the fort held out, the Americans could hold the British navy at bay. The risk of losing the fort was too great if they attempted to defend it from the outside. Ledyard, like Captain Saltonstall across the river, understood the limitations of the militia and would attempt to hold Fort Griswold.

By doing so, Ledyard would force the British to attack his fortifications head-on, where his men would be protected by earthen walls and supported by cannon. It was a bold move, but it was not unlike Ledyard to make such a move. In 1779, when a British fleet approached the harbor, Ledyard ordered his companies to parade in full view "to make a display of as much strength as possible in order to deter the [British] from making an attack." The attack never materialized, and his bold actions probably earned his men's respect.[13]

As Ledyard readied the garrison for the coming battle, Park moved his small but highly mobile force of sailors south through the woods. He wanted to find the British column, not be surprised by it. Near the Capt. Elijah Avery house, the group of sailors "met a flanking party of 50 men" approaching in their

---

11 Harris, *Groton Heights*, 228; PA: Thomas Park (R.7932), NARA. Harris never revealed his source, but claimed Baker was shot at during his mission.

12 Harris, *Groton Heights*, 262; PA: Henry Williams (W.24163), NARA. After his death, Williams's wife sought a government pension and was awarded one with the help of Sgt. Rufus Avery, who claimed to have witnessed Williams's death. The pension application includes information about Ledyard consulting Williams about defending the fort; Francis B. Heitman, *Historical Register of Officers of the Continental Army During the War of the Revolution: Apr 1775–Dec 1783*, 514. Often misquoted as being home on furlough, Stanton resigned his commission in Apr. 1780 and returned home. Still of militia age, he resided in eastern Groton, the district of the 3rd "Groton" Company.

13 Harris, *Groton Heights*, 262; PA: Christopher Patton (S.8662), NARA.

direction. The British flankers were deployed in the woods away from the Neck Road and approached Park's position without being alerted to the presence of the sailors. When the flankers were judged in range, Park gave the word and his band "commenced a fire."[14]

Musket shots rang out and echoed through the woods. Reacting quickly, the British flankers halted, turned, and returned fire. But before they could attempt to flush Park's sailors out, the ambushers were gone. A few minutes passed and the British again found themselves under fire. A sharp firefight between the two sides developed, with the two sides exchanging shots as they chased each other through the woods. Park ordered them to conduct a fighting withdrawal for the next mile or so back in the direction of the fort. This, according to Park, they "kept up until their ammunition was exhausted" without the loss of a single man.[15]

The sailors returned to Fort Griswold, where they were resupplied with an additional "fifty-two rounds of ammunition each." Park's sailors may have hoped for a short respite but did not receive one. They soon headed south again to relocate the British and make more trouble. They met them again near Avery's Knoll, a half a mile south of the fort. The knoll was described by one of the participants as an "eminence of several acres of cleared land, skirted with woods and sloping moderately in each direction, with a tree upon its summit . . . all in plain sight of the fort." It was known locally as Packer's Rocks, for the large, tall rock cropping which ran across its southeastern slope, and was part of the James Avery farm operated by Avery, his wife Elizabeth, and up to five of their children. Two of Avery's sons were in the fort. The house, barn, and accompanying outbuildings were located behind the knoll's eastern slope.[16]

Park came onto Avery's Knoll, passed the house, and took position at the edge of a "cedar swamp." There Park dispersed his sailors amongst the rocks and trees while they waited for the approach of the enemy. From this position, it only

14 PA: Thomas Park Pension Application, (R.7932), NARA. As they passed the Elijah Avery house, the British set it ablaze.

15 PA: Thomas Park (R.7932), NARA. As the British passed the Elijah Avery house they plundered and burned it. Avery's widow Prudence submitted a damage claim for "Buildings & necessaries" of just over £300.

16 PA: Thomas Park (R.7932), NARA; "Surrender of Fort Griswold, Sep. 6, 1781," *The Boston Recorder*, July 15, 1847; "A Sketch of New-London & Groton, with Attacks made on Forts Trumbull & Griswold by the British Troops Under the Command of Brig. General Arnold Sep. 6th, 1781, by Captain Lyman of ye Prince of Wales American Volunteers," Sir Henry Clinton Papers, WCL. The James Avery house was one of the few houses included on the Lyman map. The map clearly shows the house as having been located behind the knoll. Though the house was destroyed sometime in the 19th century, its location was verified by discovery of its well by the author in 2016.

made sense that Park hoped to attack the British column from the right flank as it passed by.[17]

By then, Eyre's command was moving up the Neck Road in the direction of Fort Griswold, only a mile away. The roughness of the terrain and the sporadic skirmishing turned the roughly three-mile march into a two-hour-long ordeal. Approaching Groton Heights, they could see the colors of Fort Griswold in the distance as it fluttered in the breeze.

A detachment from the garrison, consisting of Cpl. Andrew Billings of the 3rd "Groton" Company, and Elijah Bailey of the 2nd "Groton" Company, occupied the outer redoubt. They were ordered to give advanced warning of any British movements beyond the eastern slope of the heights, which was not possible from the main fort. This redoubt was located on the lower summit of Groton Heights, three hundred yards east of the fort. From there, one could see a fair distance across the plain below the heights. The redoubt was equipped with three 4-pounder field artillery pieces mounted on traveling carriages.[18]

The detachment saw the approaching British column first as it advanced from the south, made visible by hundreds of bayonets glistening in the sunlight. Following Ledyard's orders, they fired one of the 4-pounders, then spiked the gun and retreated in the direction of the main fort. Only Corporal Billings made it into the fort. Bailey panicked and fled elsewhere.[19]

The echo of the gun and the sight of their comrades retreating from the redoubt brought the garrison quickly to its feet. Ledyard ordered "general quarters," or the call to arms. One of the two musicians in Latham's Company may have beaten the

---

17 PA: Thomas Park (R.7932), NARA. The cedar swamp is figured prominently in Lyman's map. It only makes sense that Park's men were at the edge of the swamp and not in it. Park could not have hoped the British would attempt to march through it.

18 "Extract of a letter from a lieutenant in the 40th regiment," *Saunders's News-Letter*, Nov. 24, 1781; PA: Asa Lester (S.16921), NARA; Smith, *North Groton's Story*, 28; Harris, *Groton Heights*, 234; Benson J. Lossing, *The Pictorial Field-book of the Revolution; or, Illustrations, By Pen and Pencil, Of The History, Biography, Scenery, Relics, And Traditions Of The War For Independence*, 2 vols. (New York, 1860), 1:617. There may have been a third man, with the last name Williams. But since there were five Williams in the fort, it is impossible to distinguish which one without further information. In a deposition for Lester, Bailey identified himself as a member of this company, as he was living on the farm deeded to him by his father. The British officer referred to their strength as "two pieces of cannon, and a small body of musketry." The placement of these 4-pounders in the outer redoubt was also to allow the militia opposing the British outside the fort access to them. This type of artillery was used to support infantry on a battlefield because its small size and mobility allowed easy maneuverability.

19 "Extract of a letter from a lieutenant in the 40th regiment," *Saunders's News-Letter*, Nov. 24, 1781; Smith, *North Groton's Story*, 28; Harris, *Groton Heights*, 234. Bailey claimed to have hidden in a nearby cornfield during the battle. Billings reached the fort, a rope was thrown down to him, and he climbed in through an embrasure.

Outer Redoubt Site. The redoubt has long since disappeared, but it once stood here along Mitchell Street. The land was donated in 1913 to the Fort Griswold Battlefield State Park. *Author*

long roll, the call to arms. The men who had not already done so grabbed their muskets and ran up onto the ramparts to observe the situation.[20]

The gunners along the south wall also stood at their stations. Two different gun crews, one manning the 18-pounder in the southeast corner another manning the 9-pounder in the southwest bastion, were able to direct their fire southward toward the approaching British. To fire the guns, each crew needed ammunition and gunpowder. Near each cannon stood, stacked like a pyramid, stood its primary ammunition, solid shot. Solid or "round shot," consisted of a solid iron ball that was used to batter the ranks of advancing troops. They were better used at longer ranges. Depending on the gun, each ball weighed either nine, twelve, or eighteen pounds.

20 PA: Humphrey Brown (W.18648), Newbury Button (R.1563), NARA. Latham was authorized by the General Assembly to have two musicians in his company, a drummer, and a fifer. However, the two musicians he had, Humphrey Brown and Newbury Button, who both survived and applied for pensions, claimed they were fifers. Button even included in his application a signed letter from his militia captain stating he was their company fifer. It is not hard to imagine at least one of them having some limited knowledge of drum playing.

The gunpowder needed to fire each gun came to the crews in pre-filled cartridges stored in the fort's powder magazine. During the battle the cartridges, weighing some 4-5 pounds each, were brought up to the crews by some of the younger members of the garrison, such as Daniel Williams of Shapley's Company, who was a "powder monkey" assigned to the 12-pounder on the east wall. The "powder monkeys" ran back and forth between the powder magazine and the platform bringing up cartridges to the gun crews. Once the crew had a cartridge, one gunner placed it into the muzzle of the gun. This was followed by ammunition. Both were then rammed down the barrel by another member of the crew handling a long rammer. From there, the cannon was sighted or aimed, then primed. Another gunner would then prick the vent of the gun, exposing the gunpowder, and place a match in it. Ready to fire, another gunner, typically called the bombardier, advanced with a lit linstock, lighting the match which fired the gun.

When Ledyard saw the approach of the British column, he gave his eager artillerists permission to open fire. Having already loaded their cannon with solid shot, they quickly sighted, then started firing their guns and, according to Sergeant Avery, "hove a number of shot" at them.[21]

The sound of solid shot whistled through the air toward the British column. Even though most of the rounds missed their targets, landing and bouncing harmlessly away from the column, the artillery did have some effect. It shook the nerves of Eyre enough that he directed the column to turn eastward in the direction of Avery's Knoll. As his orders were communicated down the length of the column, the officers and non-commissioned officers yelled and prodded their companies to move faster.

As the jaegers, under Lieutenant von Reitzenstein, moved toward Avery's Knoll, they encountered Park's sailors. Watching them, Park ordered his men to advance in their direction. Once the jaegers were within view, the sailors opened fire. As their shots rang out amongst the trees, the jaegers replied in kind and then pressed the sailors. Already heavily outnumbered, Park's sailors beat a hasty retreat across the Avery farm, running in the direction of the Post Road. As they did, the jaegers followed in hot pursuit.

As Park's sailors were chased away, the British column came up and disappeared from the eyes of the garrison. Ledyard ordered his gunners to cease fire. As the British moved behind the knoll, the head of the column sighted the James Avery house. Some broke out of the ranks and headed towards it where they broke into the house, and then into the barn. They may have been hunting for any lingering Americans, but in the process helped themselves to food stored there, especially

---

21 Rufus Avery narrative in Harris, *Groton Heights*, 31.

cheese in the dairy. According to an account, the redcoats "gratified their love of mischief by wantonly destroying the summer dairy, breaking the furniture, throwing the old clock out through the window."[22]

Eyre soon came up, order was restored, and he made the Avery house his headquarters. He had not been provided by Arnold with any type of sketch of the fort's design, but had been assured that Fort Griswold "was a plain redoubt or no strength" and that it "was very incomplete" and was garrisoned by a "few men," perhaps "only 20 or 30 men." The accuracy of this report now appeared to be questionable as the fort looked complete and armed with a number of cannon. Eyre saw no need to continue without obtaining more information.[23]

From the Avery house, Eyre dispatched Capt. George Beckwith, his volunteer aide, and two other officers to the fort under a flag of truce. Sending forward a flag was a commonly accepted practice in warfare during the 18th century prior to attacking an enemy fortification, and this tactic was used countless times by both sides throughout the Revolutionary War. When an opposing force approached an enemy behind enclosed fortifications, before launching an assault, the attacker would send forward a flag of truce to the fort in a last-ditch effort to avoid bloodshed. The officer approaching the fort would carry a small handkerchief or sometimes be accompanied by a drummer who would beat a parley and declare a temporary ceasefire. He would then meet with a representative of the fort and demand the surrender of the fort. If they refused, the attacking side usually responded that if they were forced to attack, no quarter would be given. Or they would simply attack and take no prisoners. This was more psychological than practical. On some occasions, such as the British attack on Fort Washington, the British issued the same threat but halted the assault before their men got out of control.

The mission of Captain Beckwith was threefold. One was to demand the surrender of Fort Griswold to see if the British could secure it without any serious casualties. This was unlikely since the Americans understood the value of the fort. The second, and more important aspect of the mission, was to get a close look at it, its armament, its approaches, and the size of its garrison. The third was to gain more time. If the fort was strongly garrisoned, as appeared from afar, Eyre needed his artillery and the New Jersey Volunteers, which had not yet come up.

---

22 PA: Thomas Park (R.7932), NARA; Rufus Avery narrative in Harris, *Groton Heights*, 31; Mabel C. Holman, "How Fort Griswold Looked Nearly Eighty Years Ago," *The Day,* Sep. 8, 1913; Harris, *Groton Heights*, 95. After the British dead were dug up, militia discovered several of them had cheese in their pockets.

23 Arnold report in Mackenzie, *Diary*, 2:624; Extract of a letter from a lieutenant in the 40th regiment," *Saunders's News-Letter*, Nov. 24, 1781.

Captain George Beckwith
New York Public Library

Beckwith was the perfect man for the task. The captain was a 10-year veteran of the British army, having first obtained a commission in the 37th Regiment of Foot in 1771. When the 37th Regiment arrived in America, Beckwith, now a lieutenant, was assigned to a grenadier battalion which he served as their adjutant and saw action at Brooklyn, White Plains, Brandywine, and Germantown. The following year, he transferred to a staff officer position and played a large role in the British military intelligence network. This was why Eyre sent him, so he could conduct an impromptu reconnaissance. The two officers who accompanied Beckwith, though never named, were likely the adjutants of the 40th and 54th Regiments, Lt. John Hall and Lt. James Campbell. Their primary role on the battlefield was to be able to place their regiments into a line of battle.[24] They needed to know their ground.

Along the south and east parapet walls of the fort, the garrison stood eagerly and anxiously on the wooden platform. Some men focused their attention on the approach of the British officers, others on the firing along the west wall. On the west wall, gunners manned one or more of the 12-pounders and fired several rounds across the river towards the British.[25]

Shapley's Company arrived at Fort Griswold just in time to see the British disappear behind Avery's Knoll. They added an additional 19 men to the

24 Glen P. Hastedt and Steven W. Guerrie, eds., *Spies, Wiretaps, and Secret Operations: An Encyclopedia of American Espionage* (Santa Barbara, CA, 2011), 79; Muster rolls, 40th Regiment of Foot, WO 12/5318, TNA; Muster rolls, 54th Regiment of Foot, WO 12/639, TNA.

25 Rufus Avery narrative in Harris, *Groton Heights*, 34; PA: Charles Martin (W.1978), NARA. The 12-pounder being fired at the British across the river was probably in the northwest bastion. We can place at least three sailors in this bastion during the battle, Capt. Edward Latham, and Christopher Latham Jr. placed by Rufus Avery. A third sailor, Charles Martin, placed himself there during his failed escape attempt as the north wall was breached. All three would have had some experience working with cannon and there would be no other reason to place sailors there.

understrength garrison, and entered the fort through the sally port, near the center of the south wall. Ledyard had already ordered the north gate, which consisted of two large thick wooden doors with iron hinges and bolts with a wooden bar in its rear, locked from the inside.[26]

Though small in numbers, Shapley's Company was "received by the garrison with enthusiasm, being considered experienced artillerists, whom they much needed, and we were assigned to our stations," 1st Sgt. Stephen Hempstead, a member of the company, remembered later. Upon his arrival, Hempstead was given command of the 18-pounder at the southeast corner, the fort's largest gun. The rest of Shapley's Company, minus those assigned to work other cannon, were stationed in the southwest bastion.[27]

Beckwith and the two British officers approached to a "little eminence before the fort" before the crack of a single musket shot, ordered by Ledyard, brought them to a halt. Ledyard "called a council of war to take the minds of his fellow officers and friends as to what was to be done" and it was agreed to send out three officers. Ledyard selected Amos Stanton of the 3rd "Groton" Company, Capt. Elijah Avery of the 1st Company "Groton Alarm List," and Capt. John Williams of the 1st "Groton" Company to be their representatives and hear the British demands, nothing else. The three men left through the sally port and walked out to meet them.[28]

Once there, Captain Beckwith sternly demanded, "the Surrender of the Fort to his Britannic Majestys Armies." One of the three American officers, presumably Stanton, replied he did not have the authority to surrender the fort. He explained that he had been tasked by Lieutenant Colonel Ledyard to meet with the flag and bring back their demands to the fort. They then requested to return to Ledyard which Beckwith granted, and the men returned to the fort.[29]

---

26 Rufus Avery narrative in Harris, *Groton Heights*, 32. The north gate was probably locked by the time Fort Trumbull was being evacuated. The sally port would have been the best gate to close last as its main purpose was to provide the garrison easy access in and out of the fort while under an attack.

27 This is where most documented members of Shapley's Company were later killed or were known to have participated in the battle.

28 Rufus Avery narrative in Harris, *Groton Heights*, 94–97; Stephen Hempstead to Governor Trumbull, Oct. 30, 1781, Governor Trumbull Papers,15:164b–d, CSL; *Royal Gazette* (NY), undated in *CG*, Sep. 21, 1781, in Harris, *Groton Heights*, 94–97. Considering the criticism that was received from the British high command regarding inaccurate statements, the only parts included here are ones that were corroborated by American accounts. Rufus Avery narrative in Harris, *Groton Heights*, 31. A search for the original article in the *Royal Gazette* could not be found, though reprints of it are found in several period Continental newspapers.

29 PA: Ziba Woodworth (R.11848), NARA.

Entering the fort, they went to the parade ground and brought Ledyard "the summons, which was to surrender the fort." A council of war was again convened. It is uncertain how long this council lasted, but a loyalist newspaper claimed it lasted "a considerable time." Whether the officers were having difficulty agreeing or if they were stalling for time for reinforcements to arrive is not known. But they would not surrender. It was an uncertain decision. Not only did the British outnumber them but they would likely be attacked on all sides. This presented the risk where they might be trapped and cut to pieces, but it was a risk Ledyard was willing to take.[30]

This was probably the time Ledyard sent his fourth and final messenger for help. He dispatched Newbury Button, a 15-year-old fifer of Latham's Company, on foot, hoping he could get around the British. Ledyard told Button where the militia were and handed him "a Letter & told him to run with it . . . & give it to the Colonel [Gallup]." Button then slipped down a rope and out of the fort. He eventually made it to Gallup, but by that time it was too late.[31]

When the Americans returned to Beckwith, he was surprised Ledyard was not with them. He had expected to meet with Ledyard himself. A loyalist newspaper later claimed that when Beckwith saw them, he stated that his "business was with the commanding officer of the fort." But Ledyard had refused to meet with him and sent Captain Shapley in his place, accompanied by Amos Stanton. This is corroborated by two sources, one from each side. The loyalist account claimed a new captain was now sent out. That captain, Shapley, told Beckwith for his "own part he was Colonel Ledyard, commanding officer of the fort." He said "the fort would not be given up" to the British forces.[32]

Beckwith then politely nodded and headed back with the two officers toward Avery's Knoll. He had to give Eyre the garrison's reply and the disappointing news that the fort was more formidable than had been expected. Later, Beckwith recalled how he respected Ledyard's decision and how he never anticipated them to surrender and had expected they would not give the fort up without a fight. Beckwith attested that Ledyard, "[t]he brave . . . commandant of Fort Griswold . . . knew the value of his post which he was determined to maintain."[33]

---

30 Rufus Avery narrative in Harris, *Groton Heights*, 32; *Royal Gazette* (NY), undated in *CG*, Sep. 21, 1781, in Harris, *Groton Heights*, 94–97.

31 PA: Newbury Button (R.1563), NARA. The author had a difficult time believing the story told by Button in his deposition. Had it not been for the deposition of Joshua Baker, who was part of the garrison, and included in Button's application, the story would have not been included in this book.

32 *Royal Gazette* (NY), undated in *CG*, Sep. 21, 1781, in Harris, *Groton Heights*, 94–97; Rufus Avery narrative in Harris, *Groton Heights*, 32.

33 *NY Journal*, June 16, 1787.

Birch Plain Creek

Ledyard knew time was running out. Even with Shapley's Company, the garrison only numbered some 176 men. Ledyard needed more militia, but as he looked in the direction of the Post Road, the main route to the fort, he saw none coming.[34]

As strategically important as Fort Griswold was to both sides, so was the Post Road. Both sides desired it. Eyre, to protect his rear during an attack on the fort, and Ledyard, because without it he was trapped in the fort.

The Post Road was the objective of the jaegers, not Park's men. The sailors had just gotten in their way. When the British first appeared south of the fort, Ledyard sent David Gray to hurry the militia, but also to protect his cover. Gray departed so abruptly he rode "with only his shirt and pantaloons on." The weather had grown warm and Gray, along with others, in the fort, had removed their frock coats. Galloping down the Post Road, Gray saw the jaegers approaching the road and was fired on, but their rounds overshot and Gray rode off.[35]

Once the jaegers reached the Post Road, von Reitzenstein performed a quick reconnaissance and discovered rising, tree-covered ground which overlooked Birch Plain Creek and commanded the road. He divided his force into two platoons of twenty riflemen each, and deployed them for action. One platoon occupied the north side of the road, the other occupied the slightly higher ground on the south side. They dispersed outward facing east, taking full advantage of the natural cover provided by the trees and rocks, thus creating a roadblock closing the Post Road.[36]

The ground was ideal for them. All afternoon, the jaegers displayed their prowess, keeping the militia, despite their gradually growing numbers, from breaking through their roadblock. The failure of the militia to achieve this

---

34 See Appendix H. Ledyard strength peaked at 181 men. However, by the time of the assault on the fort, four (Joseph Morgan, David Edgcomb, David Gray, and Newbury Button) were sent out for help and did not return, one more (Elijah Bailey) in the outer redoubt fled before the British attack and did not return, and one (John Clark) was in the village below and would come to the fort as it was being attacked and, but never actually entered the fort.

35 PA: David Gray (S.38776), NARA. Gray had good reason to fear for his cover: one of his contacts in British intelligence was Capt. George Beckwith!

36 "A Sketch of New-London & Groton, with Attacks made on Forts Trumbull & Griswold by the British Troops Under the Command of Brig. General Arnold Sep. 6th, 1781, by Captain Lyman of ye Prince of Wales American Volunteers," Sir Henry Clinton Papers, WCL. Both of Lyman's maps divides the jaegers into two groups and positions them on both sides of the Post Road, or as it was sometimes known as the Road to Stonington or the Country Road. One platoon consisted of jaegers from the 1st Ansbach Jaeger Company, while the second platoon consisted of jaegers from the 2nd Ansbach Jaeger Company. The ground today on the north side of the road is slightly west of the Motel 6, while the position on the south side is where Groton Towers apartment complex is located.

A present-day view of the area held by the jaegers along Bridge Street looking east toward Birch Plain Creek. *Author*

breakthrough is a subject which has been ignored by past historians. But it ended up playing a significant contributing role in the Battle of Groton Heights.

The militia coming to the aid of Fort Griswold was from the 8th Regiment of Connecticut Militia. The regiment was led by its second-in-command, Lt. Col. Nathan Gallup. The 54-year-old resided in North Groton, and served as representative in the General Assembly, the local Committee of Inspection, and on other wartime committees. He started the war as a captain and, by 1777, was a lieutenant colonel. The following year, he was appointed to serve in a militia battalion organized to protect Connecticut's southeastern coastline which augmented New London's defenses and assisted with guard and fatigue duties. In 1779, following Tryon's raid along the Connecticut coast, Gallup ably led a militia battalion assembled to protect the harbor.[37]

Gallup's actions that day have cast a shadow upon him. This was due in part to intense criticism from at least one veteran. Stephen Hempstead, in his memoir, bitterly attacked Gallup's lack of leadership and his inability to assist Fort Griswold. Hempstead never accused Gallup by name, instead referring to him as "a

37 *CCR*, 13:511, 571; 14:2; 15:2, 91, 134, 186; *CSS*, 1:409. 2:250; Stark, *Groton*, 246, 251, 253–254; *CSR*, 1:263, 2:91, 361. The reasons for Smith's absence are not known. Since no charges were brought against him, we can assume he had a good reason, possibly sickness or, due to the constant alarms, Smith and Gallup may have rotated command duties.

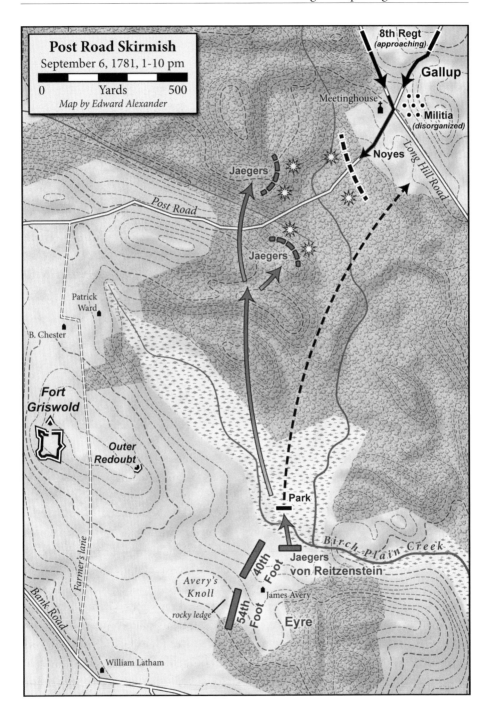

Post Road Skirmish
September 6, 1781, 1-10 pm

0   Yards   500
Map by Edward Alexander

8th Regt
(approaching)

Gallup

Meetinghouse

Militia
(disorganized)

Jaegers

Noyes

Long Hill Road

Post Road

Jaegers

Patrick
Ward

B. Chester

Fort
Griswold

Outer
Redoubt

Park

Birch Plain Creek

40th Foot

Jaegers
von Reitzenstein

Farmer's lane

Avery's
Knoll

James Avery

54th Foot

rocky ledge

Eyre

Bank Road

William Latham

Jaeger. *Don Troiani*

militia colonel," but did little else to hide about whom he was talking. Hempstead claimed Gallup was in the fort at the time the British demanded the surrender and promised Ledyard that if he would hold out, he would reinforce them with 200–300 men. Hempstead then criticized Gallup's leadership, writing that after he left the fort, he was "no more seen, nor did he even attempt a diversion in our favor." Sadly, this has been how most people remember his actions today.[38]

Hempstead's biggest mistake was that he attacked the wrong Gallup. It was not Lieutenant Colonel Gallup who was in the fort, but his older brother, Benadam Gallup, the regiment's former lieutenant colonel. Benadam Gallup rode to Fort Griswold that morning and met with Ledyard, probably on behalf of his brother. As commandant, Ledyard was Lieutenant Colonel Gallup's superior. Disappointed by the tardiness of the militia, especially the companies from eastern Groton,

---

38 Stephen Hempstead narrative in Harris, *Groton Heights*, 49.

Ledyard asked Benadam to ride east to Jonas Belton's tavern, five miles away, and hurry them. Gallup did this but by the time the militia arrived, the jaegers had closed the road.[39]

Hempstead's accusations infuriated Avery Downer, who served under Gallup during the battle, prompting Downer to write an editorial to "vindicate the character of a brave and worthy officer." Downer blasted Hempstead, writing "[Hempstead] did not publish his narrative until after he emigrated to the West, and when his memory must have been impaired, otherwise he never could have made the statement he has." Four years later, as Downer prepared an address for the anniversary of the battle, he again brought up Hempstead's treatment of Gallup, saying he was "correct in some things and very incorrect in others, particularly so in the case of Colonel Nathan Gallup."[40]

Unlike Hempstead, Downer knew why Gallup did not relieve the fort. He was simply unable. Enroute, he ran into Park's sailors and "a handful of men" near the Groton Meetinghouse and was told the Post Road was blocked by enemy soldiers.[41]

Despite this, Gallup did not remain inactive like he was later accused. He designated the meetinghouse as the assembly point for the militia, as well as his headquarters. Gallup chose it for two reasons. First, it was a recognizable and easily accessible location, as it was the focal point of the community; the militia knew it well. Secondly, it stood at the intersection of three main roads, the Post Road, the Preston Road, and the Long Hill Road. All three roads led into the interior of Groton, but the first two led to towns over which companies belonging to his regiment would travel; the Preston Road to Preston, and the Post Road continued east toward Stonington.

The intersection and the meetinghouse grounds had been bustling with activity all morning. Most of the militia who had joined Ledyard had passed by it earlier. Some left their horses hitched nearby while they walked the remaining way to the fort. The church's rector, Reverend Aaron Kinne, was also busy.[42]

---

39 PA: Newbury Button (R.1563), NARA. According to Button, Benadam Gallup, whom he identifies as a captain, was a recruiting officer who kept a rendezvous for recruits, possibly for Continental service, at the house of Simeon Button, Newbury's uncle.

40 Avery Downer narrative in Harris, *Groton Heights*, 86–87; *Norwich Courier*, Oct. 29, 1845, and July 22, 1854. Though the officer wrote under the pen name "A Soldier of the Revolution," his identity was assuredly Avery Downer.

41 "A Sixth of Sep Letter from the Son of one of the Fort Griswold Garrison," *New London Daily Chronicle*, Sep. 17, 1861; Avery Downer narrative in Harris, *Groton Heights*, 87. The meetinghouse was probably visible from the Jaegers' position, which was only about a half mile away.

42 *CG*, Oct. 5, 1781. Abigail Palmer, the widow of David Palmer, posted an advertisement in the *Gazette* looking for her husband's horse, which he left "some distance from the Fort," presumably near the meetinghouse, before he volunteered to join the garrison.

Groton Meetinghouse Site. A present-day view from the site along Kings Highway
looking west towards Birch Plain Creek. *Author*

Kinne awoke that morning to the sound of the alarm guns. He immediately
went to the fort and met with Ledyard, who told him he intended to hold the fort.
Kinne returned to his home, a short distance south of the meetinghouse, where
he and his wife Anna gathered their linens and cordials, which would be used as
bandages. Kinne then brought them to the church, which he intended to set up as
a hospital. Afterwards, Anna and their daughter, Lydia, fled inland to safety. Kinne
remained at the church.[43]

Despite assistance from civilians such as Kinne, Gallup faced many challenges.
The militia in Groton, like sister units in New London, was slow to arrive and for
practically the same reasons. There had been too many false alarms. No one seemed
to take it seriously, at least at first. Some of the regiment's companies, especially
from Stonington and Preston, were upwards of fifteen miles away and had further
distances to travel. Most would not arrive until later in the day.

Gallup only had one organized unit ready for action, Capt. Peleg Noyes's
Company from Stonington. Normally, Noyes led the 1st "Stonington" Company,
but currently led a drafted militia company raised earlier that spring. Attached
to the Department, it was doing duty in its native town. Primarily stationed at
Stonington Point, the company worked with Sheffield's Company at the fort in the
protection of the harbor and adjacent coastline.[44]

43 John A. Woodhull, *A Review of the Congregational Church of Groton, Connecticut: With Sketches of
its Ministers, 1704-1876* (New London, CT, 1877), 12.

44 The makeup of Noyes's company, other than from a few pension depositions, is not known. It
likely numbered around 30 men who were members of one or more Stonington companies. The

At the sound of the alarm guns, Noyes's Company marched to Groton. Along the way, Noyes picked up additional volunteers. Once there, Noyes's men were directed by Gallup to proceed west down the Post Road, towards Birch Plain Creek. There, they deployed in a skirmish line on both sides of the Post Road and began skirmishing with the jaegers. Noyes's men were joined by Captain Park's command, some other militia and together formed Gallup's main battle line. As senior captain, Noyes took command.[45]

Throughout the afternoon, as more and more militiamen arrived at the meetinghouse, Gallup "took the direction of those persons." The earliest arrivals came from the 1st, 2nd, 3rd, 4th, and 5th "Groton" Companies, both their "trainband" and "alarm list" companies, as well as the 4th "Stonington" Company. These members had not responded early enough to either enter the fort or had refused to join them, as they reportedly feared being trapped in the fort.[46]

Unfortunately, Gallup never wrote about his actions. So we must speculate as to his strategy or objectives. His skirmishers may have been an effort to create a diversion in favor of Ledyard. Perhaps Gallup hoped they could create a large enough distraction to draw British soldiers away from attacking the fort. Or maybe he could break through and fall upon the British rear. Combining forces with Ledyard, they might be able inflict significant damage to the British. Despite Gallup's intentions, he soon had other problems. Only a part of the newly arriving militia were properly armed.[47]

Then there was the lack of ammunition and gunpowder. The regimental supply was stored at Fort Griswold and they would not have access to it. Gallup would have to rely on his militia to bring their own with them. However, he was relieved when he met Captain Park and learned his ten sailors there had "fifty two rounds of ammunition each," and had used little of it. If that count was accurate, it meant the sailors were carrying around 500 valuable cartridges to share with the militia.[48]

---

company, like that of Griswold Avery, was probably spread up and down the coastline of Stonington, deployed there to protect it.

45 PA: Samuel Yeomans (S. 22612), Edward Clark (W.14671), Asa Chesebrough (R.1899), NARA. Noyes's Company may have been partially mounted, but even so, they were unable to reach the meetinghouse before the jaegers blocked the road.

46 PA: Thomas Park (R.7932), NARA.

47 "Commemoration of the battle of *Groton Heights*, 6th Sep. 1781," *New London Democrat*, Sep. 11, 1847. Besides being a participant in the battle, Downer sat on the military board that conducted Gallup's court martial and formally acquitted him of the charges. This gave Downer access to information the public, and even some veterans, did not know, or has been lost.

48 PA: Thomas Park (R.7932), Waters Clark (S.38612), NARA. The only recorded mention of any militia carrying ammunition that day was made by Hiram Clark, the grandson of Waters (or Watrous)

As the militia arrived, they were rounded up by their officers and sergeants. Gallup formed a provisional battalion. If they were armed and had ammunition, they were sent forward with those officers to Noyes's position along the creek. If they were unarmed, Gallup kept them in reserve near the meetinghouse. Most complied with his orders, except for one company.[49]

That company was the 4th "Groton" Company, which drew its members from the eastern half of North Groton. The problem stemmed from its commander, Capt. John Morgan. Morgan was the only person in the company court-martialed after the raid and was convicted of "neglect of duty" and "unofficerlike behavior." His commission was suspended for the duration of the war and pay he would have earned for his service during the alarm was refused.[50]

Unfortunately, transcripts of Morgan's court martial trial are not known to exist. He also never left any explanation, so we do not understand his actions from his perspective. The few surviving members from his company that submitted pension applications are also silent. Fortunately, the charges were printed in the *Connecticut Gazette*. Morgan neglected his duty and was found guilty on several counts. The court voted unanimously that he failed to assemble his company in an appropriate manner and to bring it either to or into the fort. Captain Morgan refused to order his company to follow Gallup's orders to engage the enemy and allowed them to stroll idly about the meetinghouse grounds for most of the afternoon.[51]

Throughout the afternoon, Noyes's Company, reinforced by elements of several other militia companies, maintained its position along Birch Plain Creek. Shots rang out and echoed throughout the woods as both sides continuously skirmished with each other. The militia companies there were unable to do much more than maintain their position. Better trained and occupying the higher ground, the jaegers had all the advantages.

As the skirmishing continued, the militia took casualties. Roswell Mattison joined Noyes's Company with others from the 2nd "Groton" Company. Mattison skirmished with the jaegers until he was struck by a ball in his left thigh, which

---

Clark. In it, Hiram stated he remembered how his father, Charles, took with him "24 rounds (of) ball cartridges" and went to New London.

49 *CCR*, 15:148. Of those captains present along Birch Plain Creek, Noyes, having received his commission in Oct. 1775, was senior to all of them.

50 *CG*, Nov. 15, 1782.

51 *CG*, Nov. 15, 1782; *Revolution Rolls and Lists* (Hartford, CT, 1901), 216; PA: Ezekiel Brown (W.16868), Ebenezer Morgan (W.17178), NARA. According to the company's pay roll, it numbered 45 officers and men. Morgan may have issued orders to the company to not obey Gallup. Neither his lieutenant and ensign attempted to correct the problem, but remained in the company and were afterwards promoted. Later, Lt. William Williams took command of the company.

exited below his knee. Toppling to the ground, he was unable to move on his own and had to be "carried off the field."[52]

Several other militiamen, including Benjamin Bill Jr. "and others" were also wounded throughout the afternoon. Bill, another member of the 2nd "Groton" Company, was shot in the ankle. Bill, Mattison, "and [the] others" were removed to the meetinghouse where their wounds were treated, likely by Reverend Kinne. Both Mattison and Bill survived, but, other than including it in their pension applications, received little recognition for their participation in the battle.[53]

The jaegers were successful in their mission that day. They effectively commanded the road and surrounding area and prevented any attempts to break into the British rear. Wyatt Palmer, of Latham's Company who had been on furlough, recalled because of the jaegers, "[we] did not go nearer to the [fort] than three fourths of a mile."[54]

Stalling For Time

As Beckwith returned to Avery's Knoll, he found both British regiments deployed in line of battle behind the knoll. Both faced northeast in the direction of the fort. The 40th Regiment, the lead regiment, had moved directly behind the knoll, while the 54th Regiment, second in line, formed to its left behind a small rocky ledge, which rose slightly higher than the knoll itself.[55]

As Beckwith met with Lieutenant Colonel Eyre, they were joined by Maj. William Montgomery, the commander of the 40th Regiment. Both Eyre and Montgomery had just finished up their own reconnaissance of the fort from afar. 28-year-old Montgomery was, like Eyre, a career soldier from a prestigious family. The son of a member of the Irish Parliament, Montgomery hailed from the northern part of Ireland in the town of Grey Abbey in County Downs where his family estate overlooked Strangford Lough. The major arrived in America in mid-1775 and served as a captain of a battalion company up through the Philadelphia Campaign until he took command of the Light Infantry Company following the action at Paoli. He retained command of the Light Infantry Company for the

---

52 PA: Roswell Mallison (W.9913), NARA.

53 Avery Downer narrative in Harris, *Groton Heights*, 84. Bill has long been believed to have been wounded at the fort and then escaped after its capture. However, it would have been impossible for him to have reached the meetinghouse due both to his leg wound and inability to get through the jaeger roadblock. Therefore, it is more likely Bill and the "others" mentioned by Avery were wounded at Birch Plain Creek.

54 PA: Wyatt Palmer (S.23357), NARA.

55 Rufus Avery narrative in Harris, *Groton Heights*, 31.

Avery's Knoll. The 54th Foot took shelter behind this rocky ledge on the knoll before assaulting Fort Griswold. *Author*

next three years while the regiment was stationed in the West Indies until he was promoted to major.[56]

Both Montgomery and Eyre hoped Beckwith would return with the surrender, but their instincts knew better. The best news Beckwith could bring back was better intelligence, specifically, information related to what the fort looked like, its armament, its approaches, and the approximate size of its garrison. From the start Eyre and Montgomery had no clear idea what they were up against and had eagerly awaited Beckwith's return. Now they had the information they needed to plan and launch the assault on the fort for which Arnold was so eager.[57]

When Captain Beckwith met with Eyre and Montgomery, he gave them Ledyard's answer. He also brought news that the fort was indeed much stronger than anticipated. A lieutenant recorded what he heard: "[the fort was] a strong work flanked every where, with a rampart 20 feet thick, and some places 16 feet

56 John Burke and John B. Burke, *A Genealogical and Heraldic Dictionary of the Landed Gentry of Great Britain & Ireland*, 2 vols. (London, 1847), 877; Muster rolls, 40th Regiment of Foot, WO 12/5318, TNA; "GENERAL RETURN of the NAMES, COUNTRY and AGE of H.M. 40th Regiment of Foot. Reviewed at Galway, 16th June 1772," Museum of the Queen's Lancashire Regiment. The author reached out to the Montgomery family and learned the family still occupies the same estate the major would have inherited had he not been killed during the battle. Montgomery had two younger brothers serving as officers in the military, one in the 67th Regiment of Foot the other in the navy.

57 "Extract of a letter from a lieutenant in the 40th regiment," *Saunders's News-Letter*, Nov. 24, 1781.

high, strongly frazed" on the north, south and east walls; and it was "defended by many cannon" and by a garrison under a commander who was "a man of extreme influence in the country." If the situation seemed bleak before, it now looked far worse. Even with both regiments, Eyre had only a combined strength of just over 750 men and officers. A frontal assault would be costly and perhaps not succeed at all.[58]

Eyre was anxious for the arrival of his artillery and uncomfortable about ordering an assault without it. If Captain Lemoine was there, he could deploy his two guns on the knoll and use them in conjunction with the infantry assault. His artillery consisted of two field pieces: a 6-pounder field gun and an 8-inch howitzer. The howitzer had been specially given to him with the expectation it would be useful during an assault. If the reports about the thickness of the fort's walls were accurate, a single 6-pounder would be useless in trying to take down the walls. But the howitzer, unlike the 6-pounder, could fire an explosive projectile at an angle and would be effective firing over the walls and into the fort.

Yielding to caution, Eyre decided to delay his attack to await his artillery. To stall, he sent Beckwith forward again under a flag of truce. This time Beckwith only made it to around 400 yards of the fort before he met an American officer whose identity remains unknown. The British demand now was more severe than the previous one. Beckwith brought with him the warning that if Ledyard did not surrender and the attack had to be made, then the British would give no quarter.

Sergeant Rufus Avery, a witness to both British demands, later wrote that when Beckwith came the second time, he "brought the demand if they had to take the fort by storm they should put martial law in force; that is, whom they did not kill with balls should be put to death with sword and bayonet." According to Avery, Ledyard's reply was another defiant response: "[T]hat he should not give up the fort to them, let the consequence be what it might."[59]

Beckwith again returned to Eyre with Ledyard's response. This time, Eyre was joined by a British officer sent by Arnold to hurry the attack. A lieutenant in the 40th Regiment recorded Beckwith's meeting with Eyre in a letter home, writing, "an officer [from Arnold] came over with orders to proceed, at the same instant that capt. Beckwith brought back a cavalier answer to the summons, from the rebel officer commanding in the fort." Eyre realized he had no other choice, no reason or cause to delay. The attack on Fort Griswold had to proceed without his artillery.[60]

---

58 Ibid. Pickets or fraize (or fraise) is an outer layer of defense on a fort consisting of pointed stakes driven into the ramparts at an inclined position to hinder an enemy's ability to scale the wall.

59 Avery narrative in Harris, *Groton Heights*, 32.

60 "Extract of a letter from a lieutenant in the 40th regiment," *Saunders's News-Letter*, Nov. 24, 1781.

Chapter Eight

The Battle of Groton Heights:
The Assault on Fort Griswold

Lieutenant Colonel Eyre recognized an assault on Fort Griswold from Avery's Knoll would be uphill over mostly open, rocky ground against a fortified enemy of unknown strength with artillery. In terms of casualties, it could be very costly. With this in mind, he developed a careful plan of attack. So long as the jaegers protected the British rear along the Post Road, there was no current threat from that direction. Thus Eyre could safely commit the entirety of the 40th and 54th Regiments in the attack. Utilizing the full force of both regiments, he would strike the fort in echelon, starting from the south, then the east, then the north. This would spread the garrison out and thereby limit the firepower the defenders could focus on the attackers at any one point.

The nearly 440 men of the 54th Regiment would be divided into two wings of four companies each. One would be led Eyre, the other by his second-in-command, Major Stephen Bromfield. Eyre's wing would begin the attack, advancing against the south wall to fix the garrison's attention. Simultaneously, Montgomery would move with the 40th Regiment, numbering around 200 men, and strike from the east. Then, as Montgomery's attack developed, the light and grenadier companies of the 40th Foot, roughly 100 men, would assault the north wall. Bromfield's wing would swing north of the fort, where they would remain in a support position. There they could assist the jaegers or exploit a breakthrough at the fort.[1]

---

1 "Extract of a letter from a lieutenant in the 40th regiment," *Saunders's News-Letter*, Nov. 24, 1781; Spring, *With Zeal and With Bayonets*, 76–89. According to regulations, when a British regiment

A half-mile away, the garrison of Fort Griswold anxiously awaited the British assault. Now numbering some 176 men, the defending force consisted mainly of militia and sailors, a motley group of varied ages and experiences. Many had seen some type of combat, likely during the 1776 New York Campaign five years earlier. But even so, they were not prepared for what was coming.[2]

Before the attack, Ledyard walked the platform of the fort, talking with many of his volunteers, inspecting the works and cannon, and giving direction—all to build up morale. Denison Avery of the 1st "Groton" Company witnessed Ledyard in action. Excused from duty due to a lame knee, Avery was bringing in a load of wood for cooking the rations Ledyard had requisitioned, after which he moved other goods out of the fort for safekeeping. He recalled, "[I] saw & spoke with Col Ledyard who was then walking on the platform encouraging his men."[3]

Despite having never seen combat, Ledyard did his best not to show his own anxiety. He was a strict leader but one who cared for his soldiers. Many who served under him during the war developed a deep affection for him. Henry Williams, the former lieutenant from Sherburne's Additional Regiment, and member of the 3rd "Groton" Company, also walked along the platform along the east wall encouraging members of his company and the gunners of Sgt. Elisha Prior's crew assigned to the 12-pounder. One of the artillerists remembered that Williams "saw that I felt bad and asked me what the matter was, and [I] said that I should be killed." Williams did his best to reassure him that everything would be okay.[4]

This encouragement was a helpful boost to morale since the prevailing feeling amongst the men, especially the younger boys, was anxiety. This seemed to be the case for Matross Ziba Woodworth. 18-year-old Ziba and his younger brother Azel were both from Norwich and had enlisted together earlier that year. Decades later, when Ziba applied for a pension from the Federal government, he compiled a lengthy account of his experiences during the battle. In it, he acknowledged that preceding the attack he was so scared that he cursed the moment he enlisted, referring to himself as an "ignorant child." His nervousness caused him to turn

---

divided into wings, the second-in-command led one wing, while the first-in-command led the other wing.

2 "Extract of a letter from a lieutenant in the 40th regiment," *Saunders's News-Letter*, Nov. 24, 1781; British accounts, written soon after the battle, place the garrison strength at about 200 men. Most American accounts and narratives, written years later, place the garrison at 150–175 men.

3 PA; Denison Avery (W.23474), NARA. Not remaining with the garrison, of which three of his brothers were part, was a decision Avery regretted for the rest of his life.

4 Sanford, *Memoir*; *Boston Evening Transcript*, Aug. 22, 1842. These qualities are evident in the dozens of pension applications of militiamen who served under Ledyard, which were reviewed for this study. His death seemed to cement this image for posterity.

his thoughts to eternity and he spent time in prayer. He asked himself if he was prepared to meet his maker that day and wrote, "I say how a Poor unreconsiled Soul must feel Expecting Every moment to appear marked before Jehovah's Tremendous Throne. These [were] some of the thoughts that occupied my Troubled mind." But he closed his deposition by assuring his reader that he was determined to obey his officers and do all he could to defend his life, his friends, and his country.[5]

Nearby, stationed with Prior's crew along the east wall, Holsey Sanford, three years younger than Woodworth, sympathized with him. Sanford, a member of Shapley's Company, was so terrified before the attack he could not bring himself to eat anything, even though he had not eaten for twenty-four hours. Upon their arrival, Shapley's men were offered a stew of pork and potatoes, but Sanford refused. He recalled years later, "I could not eat. My mind was on the scene before me in prospect," though afterward he admitted he gladly accepted a drink of rum.[6]

The rest of the militia and sailors attempted to ready themselves, each in their own way. Along the platform, the militiamen ensured their muskets were loaded and checked their flints. Some filled their cartridge boxes with cartridges from the powder magazine. Others talked and joked with each other. Some puffed on pipes. Others took swigs of rum, which was being passed around.

While the militia officers remained with their commands, the officers of the two artillery companies were scattered about the fort. Ledyard eventually made his way to the parade ground, where he remained during the attack. Nearby, Captain Latham, equipped with a fusil, as were all the officers of the artillery companies, walked along the interior of the south wall. Lieutenant Obadiah Perkins was at his station at the magazine, preparing to hand off powder cartridges for the cannon. Captain Shapley and Lt. Richard Chapman were in the southwest bastion.[7]

It was hard for anyone in the fort to ignore the reality that they were in the middle of something serious. Hundreds of British soldiers lurked in woods only a half-mile away. No one knew what to expect. The occasional boom from the guns along the west wall added to their anxiety. But the most anyone could do was wait.[8]

5 Sanford, *Memoir*; PA; Ziba Woodworth (R.11848), NARA.

6 Sanford, *Memoir*, PA: Holsey Sanford (W.586), NARA. According to Sanford, Shapley's Company carried a keg of rum with them across the river which was shared with the garrison.

7 *CSR*, 4:41; Deposition, Lieutenant Obadiah Perkins to Samuel Mott, Apr. 11, 1782, Governor Trumbull Papers,16:92a–b, CSL; Deposition, Captain William Latham to Samuel Mott, Apr. 11, 1782, Governor Trumbull Papers,16:90a–b, CSL. Perkins' role as fire-worker had him directly responsible for making and handing out the correct powder cartridges for each of the fort's cannon. This was a job assigned to someone trained for the task.

8 Sanford, *Memoir*; *The Boston Recorder*, July 15, 1847. As the rum was passed around, one participant claimed Ledyard said, "Come, my brave fellows, take something to drink, only do not drink too much."

The Attack Begins

Just before 1:00 p.m. Eyre gave the command to begin the assault. The officers of both regiments called their men to their feet. Drums rolled. Orders were barked. Following their officers, the three different contingents moved simultaneously to form for the attack. In column, Eyre's wing of the 54th Foot turned to the left and marched southward towards the Poquonnock Road. At the same time the light and grenadier companies of the 40th Foot and Bromfield's wing of the 54th Foot faced to the right, also in column, and marched northward in the direction of the Post Road. Following behind them was Major Montgomery with the rest of the 40th Foot.[9]

The three contingents marched northward across an open farm plain at the base of the heights, entirely out of sight of the garrison. After about a quarter of a mile, Montgomery's troops veered to the west. He then ordered his companies to deploy into a line of battle facing the west. The regiment's flank companies formed off to their right. From there, they advanced up the eastern slope of Groton Heights. Bromfield's men continued onward, heading toward the Patrick Ward house.[10]

As Montgomery and Bromfield marched their contingents, Eyre's wing reached the Poquonnock Road, then turned west moving at quick time. Whether Eyre realized it or not, his plan was already working. When his column emerged out of the cover of the knoll and onto the Poquonnock Road, it was readily observed by the garrison who focused their full attention on it. Those in the fort alerted their comrades that the enemy was approaching, and those not already on the platform rushed onto it. The artillerists along the south wall made last-minute preparations to "salute" the enemy. At the same time, the parapet and empty embrasures bristled with loaded muskets, each one held by a militiaman who carefully trained it in the direction of the approaching enemy.[11]

As Eyre's attackers advanced along the Poquonnock Road, the crew of the 18-pounder at the southeast corner and the 9-pounder in the southwest bastion directed their fire onto them. Solid shot hissed through the air as it hurtled toward

---

9 Muster rolls, 54th Regiment of Foot, WO 12/6399, TNA; "State of various corps going on Benedict Arnold's Expedition against New London," Frederick Mackenzie Papers, WCL. Eyre's wing consisted of Capt. Carr Thomas Brackenbury's Company under Capt. Brackenbury; Capt. John Breese's Company under Lt. Hugh Colvill; Capt. Peter Addenbrook's Company under Ens. John Hall; and Eyre's own Major's Company under Ens. Brandt Schuyler Lipton. Bromfield's wing was made up of his own company, under Lt. Thomas Frederick, the Lieutenant Colonel's Company under Lt. Thomas Palmer; Capt. Richard Powell's Company under Capt. Powell; and the Colonel's Company under Captain-Lieutenant Christopher Darby.

10 Sanford, *Memoir*.

11 Rufus Avery narrative in Harris, *Groton Heights*, 33.

the moving redcoats smashing into the ground but causing little damage. The gunners then called for more powder.

The powder monkey came running up onto the platform from the magazine carrying a pre-made linen-wrapped powder cartridges. He handed it to the wormer, who placed it into the end of the gun's barrel along with a solid iron ball. Another member, the rammer, using a large wooden shaft called the rammer, inserted it into the gun and pushed both the ball and powder down toward the breech. The rammer was pulled out, and the commander of the piece targeted the gun in the direction of the approaching British. When it was sighted, another member came forward carrying a powder horn and priming wire. Using the priming wire, he poked a hole in the loaded cartridge through the vent of the cannon and then, tipping the horn, inserted some powder. The gunner then took a lit linstock, touched it to the priming powder, and fired the gun.

After the cannon fired, the primer placed his thumb over the vent. Next, the crew member with the rammer turned his tool around and inserted its sponge side into the gun. The sponge, slightly dampened with water, was run down inside the gun to quench any lingering sparks. When he was finished, the wormer inserted his tool into the gun and quickly scraped out debris. Once done, those at the rear of the gun pulled the drag ropes or pushed the wheels to move the cannon back into firing position so that the loading process could begin again.[12]

The air was soon filled with sulfurous smoke, and the noise was deafening. Each time the gunners fired, the explosion's concussion shook the platform and rattled the windows of the barracks building. The noise was so loud it was distinctly heard several miles away. A civilian in North Groton remembered, "my ears heard, the death strife and the struggle. . . . It was awful to all who stand within hearing of this slaughter house."[13]

After Eyre's strung-out column approached the intersection with Bank Road, it was directed to turn onto an old narrow, fenced-in farmer's lane, which weaved northward up the heights, today's Smith and Cottage Streets. The lane, bounded by a stone wall topped with fence rails, dated back several decades, and ran nearly a mile from end to end. It had been built by farmers as a shortcut around the waterfront to the Post Road. Eyre's column showed remarkable discipline, continuing to trudge uninterrupted at great speed until it was within five-hundred yards of the fort. Eyre ordered his soldiers out of the lane and into line of battle. As the column divided into companies, they pushed over the fence rails, climbed

---

12 PA: David Fish (S.13019), NARA.

13 Sarah E. Sholes Nighman, "First News of an American Victory in 1782," *The Connecticut Magazine*, Vol. 11 (1907): 293.

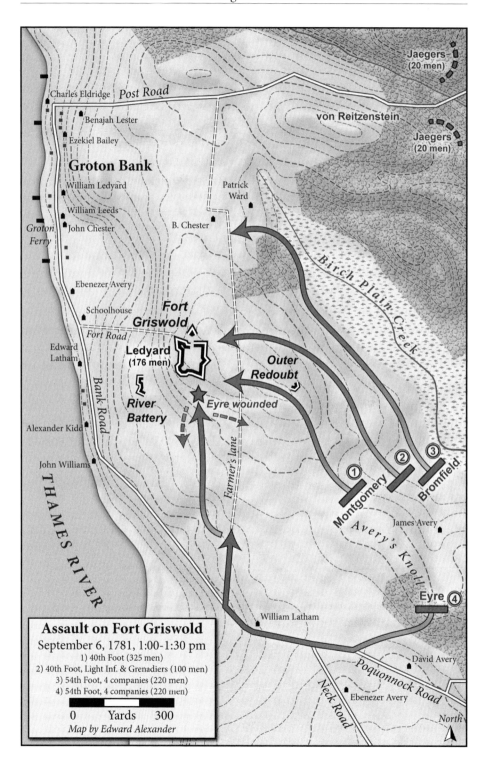

Jaegers
(20 men)

Charles Eldridge Post Road

Benajah Lester

Ezekiel Bailey

von Reitzenstein

Jaegers
(20 men)

Groton Bank

William Ledyard

Patrick
Ward

William Leeds

Groton
Ferry

John Chester

B. Chester

Ebenezer Avery

Schoolhouse

**Fort
Griswold**

Fort Road

Edward
Latham

Ledyard
(176 men)

**Outer
Redoubt**

**River
Battery**

Eyre wounded

Alexander Kidd

John Williams

THAMES RIVER

Bank Road

Farmer's Lane

①
Montgomery

②

③
Bromfield

James Avery

Avery's Knoll

Eyre ④

William Latham

Poquonnock Road

David Avery

Neck Road

Ebenezer Avery

Birch Plain Creek

Assault on Fort Griswold

September 6, 1781, 1:00-1:30 pm

1) 40th Foot (325 men)
2) 40th Foot, Light Inf. & Grenadiers (100 men)
3) 54th Foot, 4 companies (220 men)
4) 54th Foot, 4 companies (220 men)

0   Yards   300

Map by Edward Alexander

North

over the walls into the open, and, "rush[ing] furiously and simultaneously," formed into line as they advanced.[14]

On Eyre's approach, 1st Sgt. Stephen Hempstead, in command of the 18-pounder, ordered it to be reloaded. With the British coming into range, ammunition was changed from solid shot to case shot. Sometimes called canister, case shot consisted of a canvas bag packed with small iron balls. Once fired, the canvas disintegrated and scattered the little balls like a shotgun blast.[15]

Inserted down the 18-pounder was a double round of case shot, meaning two canvas bags instead of the normal one. It was intended to have maximum effect on the packed British. Once loaded, a gunner bent down and quickly sighted the gun in the direction of Eyre's approaching redcoats. With the piece sighted, the gunner yelled for the gun to be primed. Taking the lit linstock, Hempstead touched off the vent, and the gun fired. Screeching through the air, the round made a direct hit, exploding amid Eyre's men as they were deploying into line. "They fell like sheep lying down," one of Hempstead's artillerists recalled. It ripped apart several British soldiers, spewing dirt, rocks, and blood in the faces of their comrades as it "cleared a wide space in their solid column." Sergeant Avery, walking along the platform near the gun, estimated it took down nearly twenty men.[16]

Despite the carnage inflicted by the case shot, Eyre's men kept moving forward and eventually formed a rough line of battle. Part of the company on his extreme right, Capt. John Breese's then under Lt. Hugh Colvill, captured the abandoned outer redoubt. It looked to one defender as if Colvill's redcoats intended to use the cannon against the fort, but the redcoats found the guns spiked. Colvill's

---

14 Stephen Hempstead narrative in Harris, *Groton Heights*, 28; "Development and History of Ancient Streets of Groton," The Day, Apr. 12, 1913. The farmers' lane was later turned into Smith and Cottage Streets.

15 Frederick Gregory Mather, *The Refugees of 1776 From Long Island to Connecticut* (Albany, NY, 1913), 380; Rufus Avery narrative in Harris, *Groton Heights*, 33; Stephen Hempstead narrative in Harris, *Groton Heights*, 51; Peter Ross, *A History of Long Island: From Its Earliest Settlement to the Present Time*, 2 vols. (New York, 1902), 218, 1075. The gunner who sighted the 18-pounder, according to Stephen Hempstead, was Hempstead himself. Rufus Avery claimed it was Elias Henry Halsey, a Long Island refugee. Halsey, known simply as Henry Halsey, was also supposedly the captain of a privateer in the harbor. Rufus Avery attributed this rank to him. However, no trace of any naval or privateer record can be located for Halsey, so this might be a mistake. In most early lists of casualties, his name is next to a Captain Ellis which though being an entirely different person is often combined with him. Captain Ellis, or Capt. Joseph Ellis, like Halsey, fled to Connecticut after the British occupied the western half of Long Island in 1776. Prior to leaving Long Island, Halsey held the rank of lieutenant in the 6th Company, 2nd Battalion, Suffolk County Militia.

16 Rufus Avery narrative in Harris, *Groton Heights*, 33; Ensign Alexander Gray, Sketch, Sir Henry Clinton Papers, WCL. The round likely hit Eyre's and Brackenbury's companies as they were attempting to form into line of battle. They suffered the highest casualty rate of the regiment. Gray attributed the capture of the outer redoubt to "the 54th Regiment." It was his only specific mention of the 54th Regiment in his sketch and notes.

men found it difficult to move through the obstruction. Sergeant Elisha Prior saw them and directed his crew to fire on them. Having already loaded the gun with case shot, Prior sighted it toward the redoubt and ordered the crew to fire. The round hit its target. According to one defender, the "heavy charge of grape shot [exploded] among them" and "destroyed a large number." The round scattered Colvill's soldiers and sent them fleeing for the safety of the reverse slope.[17]

The rest of Eyre's men fared no better. They had the most difficult approach. Not only did they have the steepest climb, but they were exposed the whole way. There was no cover. Eyre ordered his men to charge. Halting to exchange fire would cause the advance to lose its momentum and expose his force and leave it open to annihilation.

When the order was given, the men quickly complied and the whole British line south of the fort rushed up the heights cheering loudly. The militia standing atop the platform along the south wall watched them the whole way. Taking their loaded muskets, the Americans propped them over the parapet walls and through the empty embrasures, which allowed them to take steady aim. Then with their eyes fixed on Eyre's advancing redcoats, they eagerly waited for the command to fire.

The militia officers waited until the British came within 100 yards to ensure their volley would have the maximum effect. When it was judged they were within range the officers yelled, "Fire!" The anxious men, mainly of the 2nd "Groton" Company, pulled their triggers, and a fierce volley like a sheet of flame erupted from the fort. Musket balls ripped into the advancing British ranks, dropping several redcoats.

Once they had fired, the militiamen quickly hunkered down behind the protection of the parapet wall, pulled out another cartridge, tore it open with their teeth, and emptied the ball and powder into the muzzle. Then pulling out their rammer, they jammed the ball and powder down the barrel. They poured a bit of powder into the pan, cocked the hammer back, reemerged from behind the wall, aimed, and pulled the trigger again. Soon a steady and continuous fire was being poured onto Eyre's men as the militia officers urged their men to keep up their fire.[18]

The musket fire stopped Eyre's charge. Within moments, Eyre's redcoats instinctively dropped to the ground and "fir[ed] volleys of small arms" through the

---

17 Rufus Avery narrative in Harris, *Groton Heights*, 33; "Extract of a letter from a lieutenant in the 40th regiment," *Saunders's News-Letter*, Nov. 24, 1781; "Surrender of Fort Griswold, Sep. 6th, 1781," *The Boston Recorder*, July 15, 1847; *Boston Evening Transcript*, Aug. 22, 1842.

18 Captain's log, *Amphion*, ADM 51/39, TNA. Sailors aboard the *Amphion* watched the assault and Bazely noted in his log "The Fort on Groton side keeping a brisk fire on our Troops, they advancing on a Charge."

A present-day view of the interior of the south wall of the fort. *Tad Sattler*

thick gray smoke. Frustrated, Eyre stepped forward with sword in hand and urged his men to press on. But as he did, a musket ball pierced him in the thigh, and he dropped to the ground. Some of his men saw him go down and managed to help him. They took Eyre back toward Avery's Knoll, where a hospital was set up at the James Avery house.[19]

Eyre's wounding stranded the redcoats south of the fort, leaderless. Without direction, the advance fell apart minutes after it commenced. Men began falling back individually, carrying wounded comrades with them and before long the rest joined the retreat down the heights. Sergeant Avery wrote, "the enemy's column was broken by the loss of officers and men [and they] scattered." The Americans grew jubilant and cheered loudly. Sergeant Hempstead was delighted to watch them run. He later joyfully recalled they were "repulsed with great slaughter."[20]

19 Master's log, *Amphion*, ADM 52/2133, TNA; Arnold's report in Mackenzie, *Diary*, 2:625; *Ipswich Journal*, Oct. 15, 1791; "State of various corps going on Benedict Arnold's Expedition against New London," Frederick Mackenzie Papers, WCL. Any battlefield would have had a designated collection point for the wounded once the fighting started. While not documented, it would be hard for there not to have been one here, as the British wounded began piling up. The 40th Regiment had Surgeon George R. Kittson, Surgeon's Mate Edward Shannon, and the 54th Regiment had Surgeon Robert Gordon with them.

20 Rufus Avery narrative in Harris, *Groton Heights*, 33; Stephen Hempstead narrative in Harris, *Groton Heights*, 49.

The victory was short-lived. As Eyre's men scattered, the rest of the British attack suddenly unfolded. Major Montgomery, advancing up the eastern slope of Groton Heights, had attempted to keep forward momentum in sync with Eyre's men. But as his force ascended the heights, they encountered difficulty maintaining their speed and formation because of the rocky terrain. As they pressed forward, they could hear and feel the percussion of the artillery barraging Eyre's men and what inevitably awaited them. Stragglers, wounded men from Breese's Company, soon appeared, approaching from the direction of the outer redoubt.

Sensing Eyre might be in trouble, Montgomery hurried his men forward. He ordered his regiment to dress to the left so that the center of the 40th Foot went through the outer redoubt. But Montgomery's men had difficulty performing the maneuver. As it rushed forward, the terrain broke up the regiment's cohesion. Each of its eight companies became staggered and lost its ability to stay in a compact line of battle. For a brief time, a hole was opened in the center of its formation. This was the "eighth battalion company," which was Capt. George Craigie's Company. As it attempted to pass through the redoubt, Craigie found it problematic to cross over it in a line of battle, so he rapidly redeployed the company "into a kind of column with open ranks and files" and rushed over it. As they did, several of Breese's Company, including Lieutenant Colvill, joined the 40th Foot as it moved forward.[21]

As Montgomery's men passed the redoubt, they came within full view of the fort. The militia soon realized their presence. With the repulse of Eyre's men, they could focus their full attention on this new group of attackers. According to Ens. Alexander Gray, a three-year veteran in the 40th Foot, advancing with the Colonel's Company, "the Enemy kept up a constant Fire of Round and Grape Shot, from the time the troops appeared in sight, till they got to the Fort, not a man was killed till they came within less than a Hundred Yards of the [fort]." Gray noted that as they moved toward the fort, three different cannon and small arms fire blasted away at them.[22]

---

21 "Extract of a letter from a lieutenant in the 40th regiment," *Saunders's News-Letter*, Nov. 24, 1781; Muster rolls, 40th Regiment of Foot, WO 12/5318, TNA. The layout of the 40th Regiment that day, from right to left was Capt. Edward Eyre's Company, under Lt. Arthur Law; the Colonel's Company, under Captain-Lieutenant William Hamilton; Capt. John Gason's Company, under Capt. Gason; the Lt. Colonel's Company, under Lt. Waldegrave Pelham Clay; Capt. Horace Churchill's Company, under Lt. John Moore; George Craigie, under Capt. Craigie; the Major's Company, under Ens. John Grant; and Capt. John Erasmus Adlam's Company, under Captain Adlam.

22 Ensign Alexander Gray, Sketch, Sir Henry Clinton Papers, WCL; "Extract of a letter from a lieutenant in the 40th regiment," *Saunders's News-Letter*, Nov. 24, 1781. The lieutenant agreed with Gray that the 40th Foot did not sustain casualties until they approached to within 100 yards of the fort. The lieutenant wrote, "It is worthy of being remarked, that we had no men hurt till we came within less than eighty yards of the fort though we were exposed to all of the enemy's cannon for near an English mile."

The crew of Prior's 12-pounder, which according to gunner Holsey Sanford, "continued to load and fire the round ball, and grape and canister and double headers and shots frequently filling the gun half full or more," making "great havoc" on the enemy. Hempstead's 18-pounder also continued to perform well. Sergeant Hempstead remembered, "our cannon . . . did great Execution as [the British] Dead and wounded spoke for them." The 9-pounder, likely under Gunner Jonathan Minor, in Shapley's Company, in the southwest bastion, directing its fire to the southeast, also annoyed the 40th Foot as it had advanced."[23]

Soon after the artillery opened, militia positioned up and down the platform along the east wall opened fire. Ziba Woodworth remembered, "the Carnage was . . . dreadfull," as "men [were] falling on the right hand & the Left[.] Some [were] Slain outright others Mortally wounded & groaning in Exquisite torture." Despite the overwhelming fire and increasing casualties, the men of the 40th Foot did not break. Company commanders, lieutenants, and sergeants took hold of their soldiers and kept them moving forward. In some cases, company formations broke apart and advanced in smaller platoons, groups of 20–25 men, some exchanging fire with the garrison as they rushed forward.[24]

With sword in hand, Montgomery led his men from the front. He did not know it at the time, but with Eyre's wounding, he was now in command. Not wanting his advance to stall, like Eyre earlier he ordered his regiment to charge. They were a well-trained, veteran unit that had shown their mettle on many battlefields over the past six years. This undeniably enhanced the quality of its enlisted men and officer corps and it would show its worth on this day. Arguably its most famous action had been at Germantown, where the regiment fortified itself in the Chew Mansion and helped halt an American attack. The 40th Foot's defense helped save the British army from defeat that day.[25]

Showing the same spirit and discipline, the 40th Regiment pressed onward "under a shower of grape shot and musquetry" toward the fort. As it did, it did not

23 Stephen Hempstead to Governor Trumbull, Oct. 30, 1781, Governor Trumbull Papers,15:164a–d, CSL; Ensign Alexander Gray, Sketch, Sir Henry Clinton Papers, WCL; Sanford, *Memoir*. Gray singled out three guns in the fort which fired on his regiment, one on the east wall, and two on the south wall.

24 Ensign Alexander Gray, Sketch, Sir Henry Clinton Papers, WCL; Rufus Avery narrative in Harris, *Groton Heights*, 33.

25 For a detailed look at the defense of the Chew mansion by the 40th Regiment, see Michael C. Harris, *Germantown: A Military History of the Battle for Philadelphia, October 4, 1777* (El Dorado, CA: 2020); Don Troiani, *Don Troiani's Soldiers of the American Revolution* (Mechanicsburg, PA, 2007), 20. Their participation was so valued that a "Germantown" medal was presented to surviving members. Silver ones were given to officers and bronze ones to enlisted men as an award of merit for faithful service. This is "the only general award produced for heroism for a specific Revolutionary War battle."

A present-day view of the approach of the battalion companies of the 40th Foot as they stormed the south and east walls of Fort Griswold. *Tad Sattler*

have its colors to guide the men forward, so Montgomery led them on himself. As the soldiers swept forward, they encountered the farmer's lane, which stood halfway between the fort and the redoubt, the same one the 54th Regiment had earlier utilized. The lane slowed the advance but did not stop it.

However, some redcoats were overwhelmed by the fire. These halted in the lane, took cover behind the rock wall, and started shooting through the smoke in the direction of the fort. The rest emerged from the lane and charged the last ninety yards toward the fort, according to one gunner, "with Vigor and Resolution." All seemed to be converging on the southeast corner of the fort. Some redcoats fired their weapons as they swept forward and hit their marks. 17-year-old Belton Allyn of Gales Ferry, who served in the 2nd "Groton" Company, was killed instantly when one of their musket balls struck him in the head.[26]

The artillery crews also sustained casualties. Daniel Williams, of Shapley's Company, working with Prior's crew, had just returned from the magazine with a powder cartridge in hand. The 40th Regiment emerged from the lane as he ran onto the platform. Williams reached the gun's position and was just about to hand the powder cartridge over to Matross Andrew Gallup, the wormer, when a musket ball struck him in the head, killing the boy instantly. Gallup was wounded when

26 Stephen Hempstead letter to Governor Trumbull, Oct. 30, 1781, Governor Trumbull Papers,15:164a–d, CSL; "Extract of a letter from a lieutenant in the 40th regiment," *Saunders's News-Letter*, Nov. 24, 1781; Harris, *Groton Heights*, 224–225, 259–260.

another musket ball passed through the embrasure, where the 12-pounder was positioned. The ball entered his hip and lodged itself in his groin. Dropping his worm, Gallup was taken to the parade ground, where the wounded were being gathered.[27]

The Lights and Grenadiers Hit the North Wall

As Montgomery's men neared the fort, their thrust allowed the remainder of the British attack to develop fully. The light infantry and grenadiers, known collectively as the flank companies, used Montgomery's men as a screen, emerged from behind them, and filed off toward the north wall as the battalion companies maneuvered through the lane. Behind them, and still slightly out of sight, approaching the Patrick Ward house, were the four companies of Major Bromfield's wing of the 54th Regiment. Once near the house, they halted and waited.[28]

In the thickening smoke and the deafening noise of battle, the grenadiers and light infantry cheered as they advanced. At the head of their commands, Capt. John Forbes of the Grenadier Company, and Lt. Henry William Smyth of the Light Infantry Company, guided their men directly toward the north wall without halting, except to pass through the lane near the modern-day intersection of Smith Street and Park Avenue.[29]

Waiting for them along the north wall were members of the 1st "Groton" Company and 1st Company, "Groton Alarm List." This new advance must have worried Ledyard. Now he had to contend with an attack on another front. Ledyard's lack of numbers had always been a serious concern. Thus far, he had been able to meet each advance. But as the British opened a third front, things started to get worse. One defender remembered "there were not enough men" and "[some were] obliged to run from one [point] to another."[30]

As the lights and grenadiers advanced, Sgt. Rufus Avery, who had been on the south wall, rushed to the north wall to move the militia to meet the attack. As the flank companies neared the wall, they encountered John Clark outside the fort.

---

27 PA: Andrew Gallup (S. 17430), NARA; Harris, *Groton Heights*, 224, 235; Sanford, *Memoir*. Gallup claimed he would have had one more shot if Williams had not been killed. But according to Sanford, the 12-pounder may have gone off prematurely. According to Sanford, when the gun fired "it broke herself [loose] from [its] fastenings and knocked me down and almost senseless."

28 PA: Henry Mason (W.17097), NARA. Mason revealed items from the fort, including his trunk of personal items, were taken to, and stored at the Ward house. Mason stated the house was plundered by British soldiers, presumably by soldiers of the 54th Foot as they waited to enter the battle.

29 Muster rolls, 40th Regiment of Foot, WO 12/5318, TNA. The commander of the Light Infantry Company, Capt. William Harris, was "gone to England on leave of the Commander in Chief."

30 "Surrender of Fort Griswold, Sep. 6th, 1781," *The Boston Recorder*, July 15, 1847.

A present-day view of the approach of the light and grenadier companies of the 40th Foot
as they charged towards the north wall of Fort Griswold. *Tad Sattler*

Clark had managed to escape from New London, probably because he had been assisting Holt in transporting gunpowder. Clark had no idea what he was walking into as he sprinted up the Fort Road with his musket and a sack of cartridges over his shoulder, heading for the north gate. By the time he reached the gate it was too late. It was locked, and because of the proximity of the British, a rope could not be thrown down to hoist him up. His comrades watched helplessly from the platform above as Clark was shot dead by the advancing redcoats.[31]

As Clark fell, the defenders along the north wall opened fire on the advancing British as they pressed through the fort's abatis. The abatis, which consisted of felled apple trees with their sharpened branches facing the direction of the attackers, had been placed around the entire exterior of the fort. It was the first of many obstacles

---

31 Rufus Avery narrative in Harris, *Groton Heights*, 32–34; Upham report in Harris, *Groton Heights*, 109; Harris, *Groton Heights*, 247. Avery described the lights and grenadiers as "some scattering officers and soldiers [who] came round to the east and north part of the fort." As mentioned in the previous chapter, there is evidence to suggest there was a crew manning a 12-pounder in the northwest bastion firing towards New London and Fort Trumbull. Avery may have rushed over to pull the crew off the gun and to make them aware of the attack along the north wall. They may have been some of those armed with muskets shooting down the length of the ditch along the north wall. Upham makes note that the firing from the fort stopped as soon as the attack on it commenced, which supports this possibility.

placed there, designed to keep an approaching enemy in the open and under fire for as long as possible.[32]

As the redcoats worked through the abatis, their clothing and accouterments became entwined in the tree branches, leaving them vulnerable to enemy fire. Some were shot down, their bodies falling onto the obstacles; others pressed onward and descended into the ditch.

The ditch, about fifteen to twenty feet wide and up to six feet deep, ran along most of the fort's exterior. Resembling a horseshoe shape, it started on the west side of the southwest bastion, proceeded along the west wall, then turned and continued along the north and east walls before ending at the southeast corner of the fort. The only break was an earthen ramp that provided access through the north gate. In place of a ditch along the south wall, the wall was raised an additional two feet. Along the base of the exterior walls, stone was stacked upwards for seven feet to support the walls. Fixed atop the stone, along the north, east, and south walls and projecting at a forty-five-degree angle were large sharpened wooden pickets that stuck out twelve feet into the air. Sometimes called fraize, they were made from cedar trees and were described by a British officer as "Fence Rails pointed & Incling upwards."[33]

Montgomery reached the line of abatis along the south and east walls at the same time the flank companies hit the north wall. They encountered the same difficulties pressing through the entanglements, and whatever organization Montgomery had left fell apart.

By now, the fort's artillerists had ceased firing the cannon as they could no longer depress their barrels low enough to fire below the walls. Even so, the gunners refused to abandon their positions and changed weapons. According to one, they grabbed muskets, pikes, or even their rammers "with a Resolution to repulse the enemy if possible."[34]

The militia armed with muskets continued to fire down on the British. But as the attackers were now below the walls, the defenders were forced to expose themselves more and come up over the walls, some onto the embrasures, to hit their targets. During the back and forth, several more defenders became casualties.

---

32 PA; Samuel Barstow (W.25196), NARA. Barstow, in 1779, testified his company "cut apple trees[,] Sharpened limbs and set [them] round the Fort."

33 Ensign Alexander Gray Sketch, Sir Henry Clinton Papers, WCL; PA: Jabez Hebard (S.18442), NARA. The pickets were made from cedar trees taken by the militia out of Cedar Swamp behind Avery's Knoll. Hebard, stationed at the fort in 1779, remembered, "working upon Fort Griswold. . . . I worked one day backing picket parts out of the cedar swamp near the fort."

34 Stephen Hempstead to Governor Trumbull, Oct. 30, 1781, Governor Trumbull Papers, 15:164a–d, CSL.

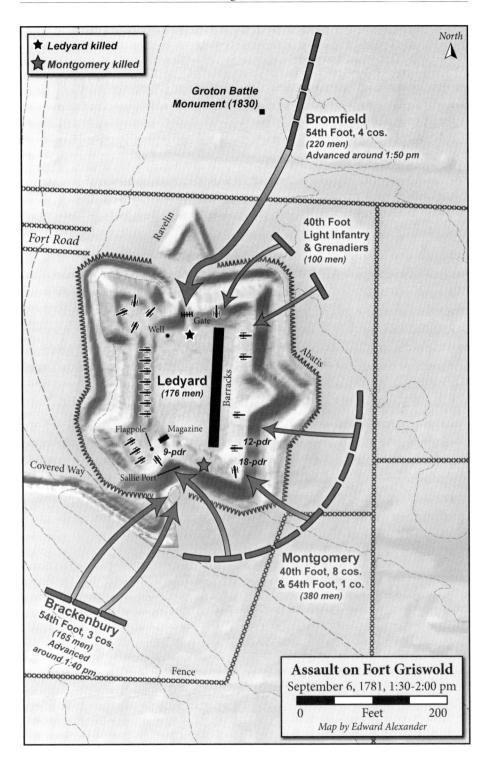

North

★ Ledyard killed
★ Montgomery killed

Groton Battle
Monument (1830)

Bromfield
54th Foot, 4 cos.
(220 men)
Advanced around 1:50 pm

Ravelin

Fort Road

**40th Foot
Light Infantry
& Grenadiers**
(100 men)

Gate
Well

Abatis

Ledyard
(176 men)

Barracks

Flagpole   Magazine

9-pdr

12-pdr

18-pdr

Covered Way

Sallie Port

Montgomery
40th Foot, 8 cos.
& 54th Foot, 1 co.
(380 men)

Brackenbury
54th Foot, 3 cos.
(165 men)
*Advanced
around 1:40 pm*

Fence

Assault on Fort Griswold
September 6, 1781, 1:30-2:00 pm

0   Feet   200
Map by Edward Alexander

Among them was Hubbard Burrows. Burrows was shot in the head as he exposed himself above the parapet along the east wall. Joseph Moxley Sr. faced a similar scenario. Moxley, with musket in hand, was at an embrasure along the south wall when a musket ball entered his thigh and passed out the opposite side. His son, Samuel, watched hm go down and rushed over to him and helped move him onto the parade ground. Holsey Sanford and John Morgan, another member of Prior's crew, picked up muskets and started shooting at the British. According to Morgan, he and another man got up onto the wall and started shooting down. Quickly, both men were hit. Morgan was struck in the left knee; his comrade was killed. Sergeant Prior was also eventually shot in the arm.[35]

Those not equipped with muskets or able to reload started throwing "sods of earth" and solid shot down onto the enemy. At the southeast corner, Samuel Edgcomb hurled 18-pound iron balls until a British musket ball struck him in the left hand. Nearby, Samuel Moxley was doing the same. After he helped his father, Moxley ran back onto the platform and attempted to fire his loaded musket, but when it misfired, he picked up solid shot and started lobbing them. Afterward, he claimed he "knocked at least one man down backwards." Initially, according to a defender, the iron balls terrified the redcoats, who thought they might be explosives. It caused them to temporarily scatter, but once they realized they were not explosives, the redcoats quickly returned and resumed their attack.[36]

Attackers assaulting an enemy fortification would typically have brought scaling ladders with them. The ladders would have been carried by lead soldiers who, upon reaching the fortification, would have placed them at the base so that the other attackers could use them to climb the wall. The plan had been to provide both regiments with ladders. Carpenters aboard the *Amphion* were ordered to construct them the day before, but for some reason they were never delivered or completed. As a result, the attackers were forced to do without them.[37]

---

35 Harris, *Groton Heights*, 248, 270; PA: John Morgan (S.17588), NARA; "Death of A Survivor of the Groton Massacre," *Providence Evening Press*, Mar. 15, 1861; Harris, *Groton Heights*, 236, 259; *CCR*, 15:206; *CSR*, 3:58. Burrows served as captain of the 3rd "Groton" Company from Dec 1775– May 1780.

36 "Death of A Survivor of the Groton Massacre," *Providence Evening Press*, Mar. 15, 1861; "Surrender of Fort Griswold, Sep. 6th, 1781," *The Boston Recorder*, July 15, 1847; PA: Samuel Edgcomb (S.20743), NARA; James A. Bacon, *Story of the Battle of Fort Griswold With A Description of the Monument On Groton Heights* (Groton, CT, 1894), 18; *Providence Evening Press*, Mar. 15, 1861. Most defenders wounded during this phase of the battle either report being taken to this area or to have been there after being wounded. The garrison had no medical staff and were forced to care for the wounded as best they could.

37 Master's Log, HMS *Amphion*, ADM 52/2133, TNA.

To get up the walls, the redcoats needed to ascend halfway up, then clear away the pickets and then climb several more feet to get onto the platform. It was a complex and physically demanding task under normal circumstances, made more problematic because the defenders were prepared to do anything to prevent them from coming up. Many redcoats were "butchered [as they tried] to scale the walls."[38]

Initially, the attackers attempted to scale the walls outright. This failed quickly. They then worked in teams, with one soldier lifting another onto their shoulders, and from there the top soldier worked either to break through or force out the large wooden pickets. This proved to be very difficult, but in the end it succeeded.

With almost 300 British soldiers clustering about the south wall and another 100 at the north wall, it was not long before cracks in the fort's defenses started to open. Three separate breaches were made along the south wall in the pickets between the southeast corner and the south gate. However, the holes were only big enough for a single soldier to pass through at a time.[39]

One by one, the attackers climbed up through the holes in the line of pickets, heading toward the empty embrasures and into the fort. This was attempted multiple times, according to a British lieutenant, but failed each successive time because "they rushed in at the embrazures before they could be properly supported from below, and they were more than once repulsed by the superior numbers of the enemy armed with musquetry and spears intermixed." A defender echoed the British lieutenant stating, "[the enemy] were beaten back by our soldiers with the breech of their muskets, or killed."[40]

Several artillerists, and others not equipped with muskets, were given pikes to defend the walls. Sixteen feet in length, they were used by defenders in every part of the fort. Matross Ziba Woodworth was armed with one, and during the battle, he remembered, "I thought to have slain 2 or 3 Bretons" in this manner.[41]

The initial British breakthrough occurred near the center of the south wall, as a small group of redcoats with fixed bayonets was led up by Major Montgomery. Hoisted up through the hole, Montgomery stepped into the fort through an empty embrasure. Once there, he turned around and waved his sword, urging his men to follow him. But a defender armed with a pike, believed to be Jordan

---

38 Sanford, *Memoir.*

39 Map, Fort Griswold (unknown, 1781), LOC. The map includes the three breakthrough points along the south wall, but incorrectly states they were the "Points where ye Light comps. & Grenrs. of ye 40th entered." This is where the battalion companies of the 40th Regiments broke through the pickets of the fort.

40 "Extract of a letter from a lieutenant in the 40th regiment," *Saunders's News-Letter,* Nov. 24, 1781.

41 PA: Ziba Woodworth (R.11848), NARA; Mackenzie, *Diary,* 2:628. For the artillerists, the pikes appear to be secondary weapons for use when they were unable to continue firing their cannon.

Major William Montgomery Monument. This monument marks the location of the mortal wounding of Major Montgomery along the south wall. *Tad Sattler*

Freeman, singled out Montgomery and, taking his weapon, jammed it into the major's chest and then ripped it back out. According to a British lieutenant, Montgomery was stunned and "had just time to retreat outside before he breathe[d] his last." The few soldiers that managed to follow him were killed, wounded, or knocked back out.[42]

The loss of Montgomery was deeply felt by his men. In a letter home, Captain Forbes, a close friend, openly expressed his personal feelings: "our dear Major Montgomery (my most intimate friend) fell . . . and [it will be] universally regretted by the whole army." Even some within the garrison respected the major; one later referred to him as "a Resolute and Spirited Officer."[43]

It is not known with full certainty who killed Montgomery. But credit is traditionally given to Freeman, Lieutenant Colonel Ledyard's waiter. The claim originated in 1836 when John Warner Barber, a Connecticut historian, included it in his brief history of Groton. Barber cited his source as Joshua Baker, who supposedly witnessed the act. Baker's claim, however, has been contradicted by other participants. Stephen Hempstead, whose narrative was published ten years earlier, asserted that Captain Shapley committed the act. Yet another source credits Henry Williams.[44]

A second breach was made near the southeast corner, where the 18-pounder was positioned. Here, the soldiers of the 40th Foot, together with Breese's Company of the 54th, clambered up the wall. A Scottish officer in the 54th Foot, likely

---

42 "Extract of a letter from a lieutenant in the 40th regiment," *Saunders's News-Letter*, Nov. 24, 1781. Montgomery's supposed last words were "put everyone to death, don't spare one." This is quoted in some form or another from American sources and is usually included to imply Montgomery ordered the garrison to be massacred, which is not true.

43 PA: Ziba Woodworth (R.11848), NARA.

44 Barber, Historical Collections, 309; George Middleton narrative in Harris, *Groton Heights*, 91–92; Stephen Hempstead narrative in Harris, *Groton Heights*, 28; Harris, *Groton Heights*, 102. Hempstead also claimed Montgomery ascended the southwest bastion, something period sources would dispute.

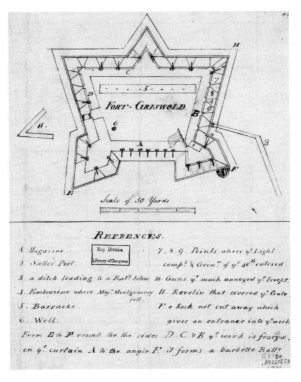

British Map of Fort Griswold. Though the map incorrectly identifies the soldiers who attacked the south wall of the fort, it does accurately show the three areas where the British breached the wall. The map also displays the colors of the fort as the "Continental Navy Jack."

Library of Congress

Colvill himself, recalled in a letter, "I had the honour to command a company, was the second man in the ditch, but fortunately received no hurt." The "besieged," he continued, "made every effort in their power to repulse us, with long lances and small arms."[45]

Most of the gun crew had been either killed or wounded by this point. First Sergeant Hempstead had been slightly wounded, a British ball having grazed his head as he sighted the gun. But he remained at his post, armed with a pike. The smoke was thick, the noise deafening, and confusion rampant. Soldiers had difficulty knowing or seeing what was happening around them, even feet away. This happened to Hempstead. He was busy jabbing at British soldiers in the ditch

---

45 "Extract of a letter from an officer of the 54th regiment, to his friend in Edinburgh, dated NY, Sep. 6," *Saunders's News-Letter*, Nov. 22, 1781.

to his left when other attackers broke through a picket to his right. They started to ascend through the hole, and Hempstead turned and attempted "to dispatch the intruder" when a ball struck him, this time in the left elbow. Clasping his wound, he dropped his pike and left the platform for the parade ground.[46]

A third breach was opened just above the south gate, near the southwest bastion. In the bastion was Captain Shapley and most of his company. They had been an annoyance to the soldiers in the 40th Foot. The 9-pounder in the bastion had repeatedly fired on them, and the supporting militia poured an enfilade fire each time they attempted to come up the south wall.

Once the third hole was made, soldiers, some with loaded muskets, were hoisted up through the breach aiming to take vengeance on those in the bastion. Once on the pickets, they started shooting in their direction. Those defenders were, according to a British officer, "instantly silenced by our musquetry." Lieutenant Richard Chapman, Matross John Whittlesey, both of Shapley's Company, and Capt. Peter Richards were killed. Captain Shapley himself fell seriously wounded when a musket ball pierced him in the hip. As he went down, his friend William Seymour, a nephew of Ledyard, rushed to him, but a musket ball struck him in the knee. Yet even as the British cleared much of the bastion, militia counterattacked and drove them back.[47]

Even though it initially met with defeat, the clearing of the southwest bastion proved to be a noteworthy action. It was credited with helping the British capture the fort. Arnold mentioned it in his report, writing, "the coolness and bravery of the troops was very conspicuous, as the first who ascended the fraize, were obliged to Silence a 9 pounder which enfiladed the place on which they stood."[48]

At some point, as musket balls whizzed back and forth at close range, a shot struck the fort's flagpole, which stood within the bastion and cut the halyard rope, which was used to raise and lower the colors up and down the pole, causing the garrison's colors to fall.[49]

Besides being symbolic to those fighting, flags, standards, or colors had a practical purpose on the battlefield. On a smoke-filled battlefield, colors were used to direct the placement of troops. On a ship or a fort, colors showcased ownership,

---

46 Stephen Hempstead narrative, in Harris, *Groton Heights*, 29.

47 PA: Stephen Hempstead (S.24612), NARA; Stephen Hempstead narrative in Harris, *Groton Heights*, 51–52; *Connecticut Mirror*, Sep. 4, 1826; "Extract of a letter from a lieutenant in the 40th regiment," *Saunders's News-Letter*, Nov. 24, 1781.

48 Arnold report in Mackenzie, *Diary*, 2:625; Ensign Alexander Gray, Sketch, Sir Henry Clinton Papers, WCL; The smoke was so intense that the British did not discover the rock face, which "gave an easy Entrance into the fort," until after the battle.

49 Stephen Hempstead narrative in Harris, *Groton Heights*, 49.

A present-day view of the ground south of Fort Griswold from the southwest bastion. *Tad Sattler*

and when they were lowered could mean surrender and cessation of hostilities. Corporal Luke Perkins of the 2nd "Groton" Company, armed with a pike, was nearby and watched them fall. Realizing the implications when he saw them drop, Perkins grabbed the fallen colors, hurriedly fixed them onto his pike, and defiantly raised them back into the air.[50]

As Montgomery's men struggled along the south wall, they took the pressure off Eyre's wing, which had retreated to the base of the heights. This had given Capt. Carr Thomas Brackenbury, the next senior ranking officer, time to reform the three companies. As soon as their battered ranks were reorganized, at around 1:40 p.m., Brackenbury rushed them to join the 40th Foot. With renewed anger, the 54th Foot pressed on at the quickstep, and its officers dressed the line at the "oblique step . . . inclining to the west" on the advance. Surging forward with "redoubled impetuosity," they passed the river battery and crossed over the bodies of their dead or dying comrades who fell during the first assault and then swept into and over the covered way.[51]

---

50 Harris, *Groton Heights*, 49; PA: David Fish (S.13019), NARA. There were two men in the fort named Luke Perkins from Groton. One was Corporal Perkins, the son of Elnathan and brother of Lt. Obadiah Perkins. The other remains a mystery but is sometimes misidentified as Luke Perkins Jr. This is an error. He is listed as "Luke Perkins Second" on contemporary records to distinguish him from Cpl. Luke Perkins. He is not a junior, just a second Luke Perkins. He may have been A tenant farmer in Groton. He may also have been the "Luke Perkins" Fish referred to in his pension who was the gunner in the company at the time he served in Latham's Company. There is no record of this second "Luke Perkins" in town at all. After the battle, a state committee visited the widows of both men, the second Luke was reported to have been married with one small child, but no estate.

51 Rufus Avery narrative in Harris, *Groton Heights*, 33.

A present-day view of the approach of Brackenbury's companies of the 54th Foot as they made their second attempt to storm the south wall of Fort Griswold. *Author*

The reappearance of the three companies of the 54th Foot shocked the defenders. Through the smoke, it appeared to one defender that these were new troops approaching from the village below. Reaching the south wall, they commingled with the 40th Foot and together, with almost 400 soldiers, made a concentrated push up the south wall.[52]

The redcoats of both regiments worked together, putting up as many men through the three holes and onto the pickets as possible. Montgomery's death and Eyre's wounding angered the soldiers and seemed to give them a renewed energy. "Nothing dispirited by the loss of their leaders, the two regiments obstinately continued the attack, and pushing up as many men as the fraize could bear," as one British officer penned, "they rushed in at three separate openings at once, and lodged themselves within the parapet without further loss." This time they would not be forced back.[53]

The British Breakthrough

Moments earlier, at the north wall, the flank companies had forced their way over the parapet wall at the northeast corner. Unlike those at the south wall, the defenders here had no artillery support during the initial British attack. They were

52 "Surrender of Fort Griswold, Sep. 6th, 1781," *The Boston Recorder*, July 15, 1847.

53 "Extract of a letter from a lieutenant in the 40th regiment," *Saunders's News-Letter*, Nov. 24, 1781; Map, Fort Griswold (unknown, 1781), LOC. The map of Fort Griswold identifies three points along the south wall where it claims the flank companies of the 40th Regiment entered the fort. This is an error. These are the points where the combined battalion companies of the 40th and 54th Regiments broke into the fort.

A present-day view of the exterior of the south wall where redcoats from the 40th Foot and 54th Foot broke into the fort. *Tad Sattler*

only equipped with muskets, swords, pikes, and solid shot which were piled next to each cannon. Nonetheless, the fight was brutal and desperate.[54]

The two flank companies intermixed as they descended into the ditch. Militia were constantly shooting at them; others jabbed pikes or threw solid shot down on them as they attempted to scale the wall. The most destructive fire came from the northwest bastion which poured a devastating fire down the length of the north wall. A British officer lamented how this flanking fire "did us a Great Deal of Mischief." The compact mass of redcoats made them especially vulnerable for a few moments. At such short-range, many bullets found their mark.[55]

The flank companies broke through the pickets at the northeast corner of the fort. Years later a member of the garrison explained, "The most successful breach that was made through the pickets, before the gate was opened, and where the rush from the trench was greatest, was on the northeasterly side of the fort, just by a jut in the wall, that projects to the east." Much blood was spilled taking possession of it. Most of it at close quarters.[56]

54 There were at least three cannon that could have been used to stymie an attack on this sector. None of them are believed to have been used or even manned during the battle. Ledyard simply did not have enough trained artillerists to man them.

55 Ensign Alexander Gray, Sketch, Sir Henry Clinton Papers, WCL.

56 "Surrender of Fort Griswold, Sep. 6th, 1781," *The Boston Recorder*, July 15, 1847. Light troops were often equipped with hatchets, but it is not clear if they used them here to break through the pickets.

North Wall of Fort Griswold. A present-day view of the exterior of the fort's north wall and ditch. *Tad Sattler*

Constable Parke Avery, of the 1st Company, "Groton Alarm List," was stationed there with his teenage son Thomas. A musket ball had already struck Thomas, killing him instantly, as he defended the wall. As British soldiers came inside, the elder Avery huddled down against the wall and attempted to defend himself with his sword, but as he did, two redcoats attacked him. One struck Avery in the head with the butt of his musket, while the other jammed his bayonet into Avery's skull, which came out his eye. Nearby, Daniel Chester, of the 1st "Groton" Company, was stabbed through the chest as the British came over the wall. His brother, Charles, nearly suffered the same fate, but was forced back onto the roof of the barracks.[57]

Coming with the redcoats was Capt. George Beckwith. Credited with being one of the first British officers into the fort, Beckwith found himself in the attack without sword or pistol, with the two flank companies. His "spirited conduct in the attack" won him praise from Arnold, then from Clinton, which was passed onto Lord Germain and earned Beckwith a promotion to major in the British army two months later. Behind Beckwith, more redcoats entered the fort and established a foothold on the platform.[58]

The assault took a high toll of the two flank companies as they fought fiercely. The heaviest reported British losses of the battle occurred here. Captain Forbes

57 Harris, *Groton Heights*, 238–239, 251–252.

58 Arnold report in Mackenzie, *Diary*, 2:624-625. How Beckwith ended up here during the attack or with the flank companies is not clear.

later mourned the loss of his grenadiers during the assault, "The men suffered very considerably. Of 48 I carried into the field, only 24 returned." Included was Archibald Willocks, who was killed. Willocks had only been with the regiment for a few months, having joined while it was stationed in the West Indies. Not able to purchase a commission, Willocks served as a volunteer with the Grenadier Company, hoping to earn a battlefield commission.

Writing about Fort Griswold, Forbes noted "The company of grenadiers I had the honour to command have been particularly fortunate with respect to [loss of] officers. Only one young man I brought from Antigua, particularly attached to me, who was doing his duty as a volunteer in my company . . . fell." Willocks had been hit on the head by an iron ball hurled at him by a defender. The ball fractured his skull and Willocks was thrown back into the ditch and died almost instantly.[59]

The Light Infantry Company also suffered considerably. Eight were killed, most notably their acting commander Lieutenant Smyth, who was mortally wounded and died the following day. To avoid his family from discovering his fate through the newspaper, Captain Forbes wrote directly to Smyth's father to communicate the "melancholy intelligence" of the "unpleasing account of the untimely death of his much-esteemed and worthy son." Forbes told him, "I must take the liberty of mentioning, that he fell in the field in a most gallant manner at the storming of Fort Griswold, in New England."[60]

Once the northeast corner was held, efforts were made to open the north gate. Once opened, it would allow the remainder of the flank companies outside the fort to come inside. A rash attempt was made by one redcoat as soon as he got over the wall. But as he did, he was shot and killed and there was, according to Sgt. Rufus Avery, "hard fighting" before another attempt was made.[61]

The fighting Avery spoke of was the clearing of the north, south, and east walls. Once the British gained a foothold on the north wall, they soon gained the

59 CM, Nov. 14, 1781; Muster rolls, 40th Regiment of Foot, WO 12/5318, TNA; *Boston Evening Transcript*, Aug. 22, 1842. The details surrounding Willocks's death came to light six decades later. A reporter from the *Transcript* visited Lebanon, Connecticut, and interviewed a veteran about his wartime experiences. As part of the militia, he was sent to Fort Griswold to assist with the cleanup. His company found the graves crudely marked and received permission to dig them up to investigate. They discovered Willocks's "scull badly fractured." Willocks was posthumously commissioned as an ensign in Capt. Edward Eyre's Company on the last 1781 muster, but next to his name is mentioned "never Joined."

60 "Copy of a genuine letter from Captain Forbes, of the 40th regiment, addressed to Dr Smyth, Rector of St Giles's in the Fields, on the loss of his son, Henry William Smyth, late Lieutenant of the same regiment," CM, Nov. 19, 1781; Muster rolls, 40th Regiment of Foot, WO 12/5318, TNA. The number also undoubtedly included several others wounded, but since the return does not specify individual wounded men, we cannot know how many with any degree of certainty.

61 Rufus Avery narrative in Harris, *Groton Heights*, 34.

A present-day view of the interior of the north wall and parade ground from the southwest bastion. *Author*

south wall, and the defenders inside the fort were now entirely exposed. They put up some resistance but were hopelessly overmatched. The southwest and then the northwest bastion were soon given up. Fire from their rear, front, and flank made the positions untenable. At least one defender there attempted to escape the fort. Aware there were few, if any, British attackers along the west wall, Charles Martin, a sailor from the privateer *Deane*, assumed he could jump onto the pickets and escape down the hill. He mounted the parapet through an embrasure and jumped onto the pickets but injured himself upon impact and could not move any further. Stuck, Martin was taken prisoner a short time later.[62]

The gaining of the platform by the British terrified the militia and sent them reeling into the fort's interior. Redcoats started shooting wildly at the retreating defenders, killing and wounding many. According to Rufus Avery, "The enemy mounted the parapet seemingly all as one, swung their hats around once, and discharged their guns, and them they did not kill with ball they meant to kill with the bayonet."[63]

62 PA: Charles Martin (W.1978), NARA; Harris, *Groton Heights*, 236, 241; Royal Navy Ships' Muster (Series 1), HMS *Amphion*, ADM 36/9561, TNA. From Nova Scotia and being a British subject, Martin was taken to Halifax where he remained confined until November 1782, the longest held prisoner taken at Fort Griswold. In his book, William Harris claimed several members of the garrison escaped by jumping out of the fort. This was not true. Those he listed, such as Henry Mason, were listed by the British as prisoners.

63 Rufus Avery narrative in Harris, *Groton Heights*, 34.

"[A]t last British bravery succeeded," Lt. Hugh Colvill wrote home, when but "we got upon the [pickets], and in at the embrasures." But to credit British bravery alone would be too simple an explanation. Nor would it give credit to the defenders. What tipped the battle in the favor of the British was numbers. No matter how determined the defenders were, there were not enough of them to hold the fort. In the words of Peter Avery, "That after the most desperate defence [we] were finally overpowered by the superior numbers."[64]

With nowhere to run, the militia instinctively sought cover wherever it could be found. Most members ran for the parade ground, the barracks, or the powder magazine, with the British attackers either above them or on their heels. The attack did not stop as adrenaline generated its own momentum. In a span of about five minutes, officers lost sight and control of their commands. This was something which often happened when the British broke enemy units on a battlefield. According to Matthew Spring, a British army historian of the period, "they maintained the full momentum of the advance, sometimes for considerable distances, nipping at the rebels' heels like a pack of hunting dogs." Usually, the momentum died on its own as the opposing force retreated, but this proved complicated within an enclosed fortification, like Fort Griswold.[65]

Ledyard had directed the fort's defense from the parade ground through the smoke. Except for the sword in his hand, he was hardly distinguishable from the rest of the militia. Despite holding the rank of lieutenant colonel, he wore no discernable military uniform. With the heat and humidity of the day, like several others, he had removed his frock coat. Now, he stood clad in a linen shirt covered by a white linen waistcoat drenched in sweat. He watched in horror as the walls were breached. His heart pounded, and his mind raced as he watched his panicked men run with the British at their heels. Bullets whistled through the air. The precarious situation forced Ledyard to make a quick decision. He could fight on, or he could attempt to surrender. He chose what was unthinkable an hour earlier: surrender. But was it too late?[66]

In retrospect, it is difficult to comprehend how Ledyard thought he could surrender in the heat of battle. Perhaps he thought if he could bring his men onto

---

64 "Extract of a letter from an officer of the 54th regiment, to his friend in Edinburgh, dated NY, Sep. 6," *Saunders's News-Letter*, Nov. 22, 1781; PA: Peter Avery (S.12024), NARA.

65 Rufus Avery narrative in Harris, *Groton Heights*, 37; Sanford, *Memoir*; Spring, *With Zeal and With Bayonets*, 238.

66 Deposition, Lieutenant Obadiah Perkins to Samuel Mott, Apr. 11, 1782, Governor Trumbull Papers,16:92a–b, CSL; Deposition, Captain William Latham to Samuel Mott, Apr. 11, 1782, Governor Trumbull Papers,16:90a–b, CSL. These are the only contemporary accounts known to exist that throw any light on Ledyard's decision.

the parade ground and if they ceased firing, the British from atop the platform would accept their surrender. It was a risky move and under the circumstances a complex task to perform. Even an experienced combat leader, which Ledyard was not, would have had difficulty performing it. Panicked soldiers, especially terror-stricken militia, were an uncontrollable and unpredictable force. To save their lives they would often not listen to reason or orders and would do things they would not do under normal circumstances. But to Ledyard it must have seemed worth the gamble. He wanted to survive, and many of his soldiers were close friends and family members.

Once the decision was made, Ledyard had to communicate it to his men quickly, another problematic task amid an ongoing battle. His men were not all in one place. Some remained on the platform; others were fleeing or had already fled to the barracks or the powder magazine. Even those near him on the parade ground were not guaranteed to hear, see, or even understand the order. Instead of yelling the order, which could not be done with any success, according to a witness, Ledyard walked from the south end of the parade ground to the north end, "raising and lowering" his sword. He probably grabbed the middle part of the blade and repeatedly raised and lowered it in front of his men to calm them but also tell them to cease fire.

Before moving, Ledyard communicated his order to Lieutenant Perkins and Captain Latham, who remained near the magazine. It took Latham a few moments to understand the order, but once he did, he ordered those around him to lay down their arms. Ziba Woodworth, who was near Latham, confirmed this in his pension narrative and recalled, without hesitation, that he threw his pike down. But not all complied. Whether this was due to the confusion, disobedience, or an instinct for survival telling them to keep fighting, we will never know. But shots continued to be fired at the British—one wounded Scottish-born Capt. George Craigie of the 40th Foot, as he stepped onto the platform near the southeast corner.[67]

Outside on the parade ground, the situation worsened by the second. Once the light infantry and grenadiers began pouring over the north wall, the militia stationed there, primarily from the 1st "Groton" Company and 1st Company, "Groton Alarm List," fled before them. This enabled British soldiers from the flank companies to gain the rear of the north gate. One or two went down towards it and

---

67 Deposition, Lieutenant Obadiah Perkins to Samuel Mott, Apr. 11, 1782, Governor Trumbull Papers, 16:92a–b, CSL; Deposition, Captain William Latham to Samuel Mott, Apr. 11, 1782, Governor Trumbull Papers,16:90a–b, CSL; PA: Ziba Woodworth (R.11848), NARA; Ford, *British Officers*, 53; "History of the Society," in *Transactions of the Royal Society of Edinburgh*, Vol. I (1788): 51–56.

removed the wooden bar in the gate's rear, and as they did, the doors swung open. Light infantry and grenadiers still outside the fort came pouring onto the parade.[68]

Sergeant Avery was crossing the parade ground, headed toward the barracks. As he did, he made his way through the militia retreating from the north wall. He saw Ledyard walking towards them, raising and lowering his sword, ordering them to lay down their arms. Some, among them Ens. Charles Eldridge and Youngs Ledyard, both from the 1st Company, "Groton Alarm List," and Sgt. Daniel Eldridge, of the 3rd "Groton" Company,' complied with the order. Others, perhaps up to six men with muskets in hand, went into the barracks. They intended to use the building as a blockhouse, a place to make one last stand. As Ledyard attempted to bring order to the parade, they leveled their weapons out through open windows and waited for an opportunity to shoot. They would not have to wait long. In an adjacent room, Peter Avery, terrified, passed the men and three other wounded soldiers looking desperately for a place to hide. Avery entered a fireplace and managed to climb up into the chimney, where he hid.[69]

Ledyard kept advancing. Writing to Governor Trumbull, Avery provided the only known contemporary eyewitness account of Ledyard's final moments. Avery wrote, "[once the gate was opened] the Enemy Rusht in [and came] to one of our men[,] he askt them for Quarters they dam'd him and put him to death, Likewise Colonel Ledyard fair'd his fait in the Same manner." Ledyard walked towards the enemy and attempted to surrender himself. But not recognizing Ledyard in the heat of battle, the redcoat went after him and thrust his bayonet at him. Ledyard instinctively turned his body to the left to avoid it, possibly even swinging his sword toward his attacker. As he turned, the British soldier made a second thrust and drove his bayonet into the colonel just below the right armpit, puncturing his lungs and heart and killing him almost instantly. Ledyard's body was thrown to the ground. The garrison, now leaderless, was in a hopeless situation.[70]

---

68 Holman, "How Fort Griswold Looked Nearly Eighty Years Ago," *The Day*, Sep. 8, 1913; "Report giving inventory of articles at Fort Griswold belonging to the state, Oct. 1781," Revolutionary War Records, Series I, XXVII:348, CSL.

69 Deposition, Daniel Eldridge to Samuel Mott, Apr. 12, 1782, Governor Trumbull Papers,16:93c, CSL; Deposition, Charles Eldridge to Samuel Mott, Apr. 12, 1782, Governor Trumbull Papers,16:93a–b, CSL; Harris, *Groton Heights*, 221; PA: Peter Avery, (S.12024), NARA.

70 Rufus Avery to Governor Jonathan Trumbull Sr., undated, in Dr. Walter L. Powell, *Murder or Mayhem: Benedict Arnold's New London, Connecticut Raid* (Gettysburg, PA, 2000), 64. Most depictions of Ledyard's death indicate it was caused by his own sword being thrust through his chest after he surrendered it to a British officer. However, Ledyard's waist coat and shirt, which he wore the day of the battle, refute this. Both pieces of clothing are kept today at the CHS. When examined both pieces show two holes, an entrance hole on his right side, and an exit hole on his left. The entrance hole is clearly triangularly shaped and reflects the shape of a bayonet, such as those carried by British soldiers at the end of their musket. According to the historical society's own description of

Ensign Charles Eldridge Jr. of the 1st Company, "Groton Alarm List." *Charles Allyn*

When the gate was opened, Bromfield's men, upwards of 220 soldiers, came to their feet, suddenly on the move. Major Bromfield had remained near the Patrick Ward house with his four companies and had watched the fighting from there. Bromfield, like Eyre and Montgomery, was a veteran army officer, having served nearly two decades by 1781. Born about 1741 in southern Scotland, he had served most of his military career in the 54th Regiment. Between 1778 and 1780, Bromfield commanded the regiment's Grenadier Company, which saw action at the Battle of Rhode Island in 1778 and again during the Siege of Charleston, South Carolina, in 1780. After that action, Bromfield returned with his company to New York. There, he obtained the brevet rank of major within the army but retained his regimental rank of captain and transferred back to one of the regiment's battalion companies.[71]

Bromfield's men were fresh and had grown anxious, waiting for their chance to enter the battle. At around 1:50 p.m., with a terrifying yell, they advanced in column through the smoke, with muskets loaded and bayonets fixed. Whether this new advance was ordered by Maj. Bromfield or was a spontaneous movement by the troops themselves or their officers is not known. Though because of their eventual actions and the absence of Major Bromfield from actively leading it, the latter seems entirely plausible.

Rushing forward, Bromfield's men worked themselves into a frenzy as they passed over the dead and wounded bodies of their comrades and were cheered on by their comrades atop the platform along the north wall. Nothing but the

---

the clothing, to have the holes on both pieces of clothing match up, Ledyard would have had to have been turning when the deadly blow came at him.

71 *Records of the 54th West Norfolk Regiment* (Roorke, India: 1881), iii–iv; Muster rolls, 54th Regiment of Foot, WO 12/6399, TNA; Ford, *British Officers*, 33. Other biographical data was obtained from his gravestone in Scotland.

Today, a stone marks the site that has been traditionally believed to have been the site of Lt. Col. William Ledyard's death. *Author*

ON THIS SPOT
COL. WILLIAM LEDYARD
FELL BY HIS OWN SWORD IN THE HANDS
OF A BRITISH OFFICER TO WHOM HE HAD
SURRENDERED IN THE MASSACRE OF
FORT GRISWOLD, SEPT. 6, 1781.

ravelin outside the north gate slowed them and this proved only a minor hindrance. The redcoats moved around it and then exploded into the fort. Surrounded atop them on the platform and on the parade ground, there was, as Sergeant Avery recalled, "about six of the enemy to one of us."[72]

Next occurred some of the most brutal and vicious fighting of the war. An officer in the 54th Foot described the "horrid scene of carnage" which only "succeeded for a few minutes" and could "not . . . be described" with words. Holsey Sanford agreed. He depicted these moments as "indescribably fierce and bloody, for it was life or death."[73]

As Bromfield's men advanced, they came under fire, which only enraged them more. Ensign Gray noted that after the British "carried the Work, the Enemy fired from their Barracks & wounded several men." Those in the barracks had found their opportunity. Bromfield's wing suffered four men killed and lost at least eight wounded in the subsequent melee. Volunteer James Boyd of the Lieutenant Colonel's Company was shot multiple times. Welsh-born Capt. Richard Powell was shot in the jaw, and his ensign William Rainsforth was also severely wounded. This left Powell's Company without any officers at a crucial moment when their leadership was needed the most.[74]

The head of Bromfield's column entered the fort and then "discharged" what Sergeant Avery described as "the volleys of three platoons" across the parade ground. Then they charged. Musket balls zipped through the air, barely missing the sergeant, but struck down several others, including Ensign Eldridge who was shot in the knee. His brother Daniel fared worse. A musket ball struck him in the neck, and another hit him in the face, wounding him grievously. The colonel's

---

72 Rufus Avery narrative in Harris, *Groton Heights*, 37. A ravelin is a two-faced detached fortification forming a salient intended to blunt an attack against the main gate.

73 Sanford, *Memoir*; "Extract of a letter from an officer of the 54th regiment, to his friend in Edinburgh, dated NY, Sep. 6," *Saunders's News-Letter*, Nov. 22, 1781. Depending on the person asked, the duration of the melee varies. A British officer stated a "few minutes," Rufus Avery said, "a minute," and Holsey Sanford remembered it as "ten minutes."

74 Ensign Alexander Gray, Sketch, Sir Henry Clinton Papers, WCL; Mackenzie, *Diary*, 2:627.

A present-day view of the parade ground through the north gate where
Bromfield's redcoats entered the fort. *Tad Sattler*

nephew, Youngs Ledyard, was shot down, as was Henry Williams, who clenching his chest, fell dead onto the ground. Those not struck, or those able to move, retreated toward the barracks or the magazine.[75]

Captain Latham, who had set out to follow Ledyard moments earlier, turned and retreated across the parade when he was attacked from behind. According to a family story, Latham was saved by Lambert, who was stabbed in the hand as he blocked a British bayonet from his master's back. Lambert was subsequently stabbed in the chest and killed. Latham tripped and fell, whereupon he was stabbed in the thigh by a British soldier.[76]

The Barracks

Bromfield's men continued across the parade and as they did, broke into two contingents: one drove southward across the parade, the other rushed the barracks building. On the parade ground, it was wholesale destruction. The fight was up close and personal. Heavily outnumbered, the militia bore the brunt of the brutality and the casualties. Men were shot down at close ranges. Others were

75 Rufus Avery narrative in Harris, *Groton Heights*, 37; PA: Henry Williams (W.24163), NARA; Sanford, *Memoir*.

76 Harry Clinton Green and Mary Wolcott Green, *The Pioneer Mothers of America: A Record of the More Notable Women of the Early Days of the Country, and Particularly of the Colonial and Revolutionary Period*, 3 vols. (New York, 1912), 3:419–423.

The exterior of the barracks at Fort Griswold probably closely resembled those reconstructed here at the Fort Stanwix National Monument. *Author*

bayonetted. Some were stabbed several times by multiple soldiers. Others had their brains splattered with the butt of a musket.

In the chaos, Bromfield's redcoats could not distinguish the wounded and non-wounded defenders. Many on the parade had been wounded earlier, like Matross Andrew Gallup or Pvt. Daniel Stanton who had been shot in the foot. Many were now bayonetted or trampled over. Gallup was bayonetted twice. Stanton was stabbed almost two dozen times. Others, like Matross Robert Gallup, attempted to fight back. Already wounded earlier on the platform, Gallup was bayonetted. Somehow, he managed to grab a spontoon from another redcoat, whom Gallup then stabbed with it. Another redcoat whacked Gallup in the head with the breech of his musket, knocking him unconscious. Before he was killed, Amos Stanton used his musket as a club and fought with it until the barrel broke off its stock.[77]

During this time, several militiamen on the parade ground attempted to surrender and pleaded for quarter. Most, but not all, were refused. After being wounded, Captain Latham was taken prisoner by a British sergeant who grabbed him and held him down by the shoulder. Some of Bromfield's line officers, such as

---

77 PA: Ebenezer Brown (R.1270), NARA; Harris, *Groton Heights*, 32, 133, 224; PA: Daniel Stanton Jr. (S.20978), NARA; Deposition, Edward Latham to Samuel Mott, May 6, 1782, Governor Trumbull Papers,16:127e, CSL; "Another Fort Griswold Survivor," *Alexandria Gazette*, Aug. 7, 1854.

captains, lieutenants, ensigns, and his sergeants, realized that once in the fort, the battle was over and tried to reign in their men.[78]

Sergeant Hempstead described their actions to the governor about two months after the battle. He noted how these officers got between members of the garrison and their own men, sometimes at the risk of their own lives, to curtail the violence. John Daboll, of the 3rd "Groton" Company, had earlier been wounded in the hand along the east wall. He was on the parade when Bromfield's men entered the fort. Daboll was knocked over by the butt of a musket and was about to be bayonetted when a British officer intervened and ordered the soldier to stop.[79]

Despite these examples, there were many heinous acts committed by British soldiers before they were brought under control. Latham attested, "[I] saw Numbers shot down, then Bayonetted . . . Men Butchered on every side while begging for Quarter and were Answered '"Damn you Rebels, there is no Quarter for you."'"[80]

Edward Latham, of the 1st Company, "Groton Alarm List," and privateer captain, saw much of the same. Testifying later, he stated, "I saw them kill and butcher numbers whole Begging For Quarter, and many who were wounded and fallen to the Ground, they would Blow them through with whole Charges into the Body, the Head & other Parts, and Plunge them through with Bayonets." He continued, "they came at me and push'd their bayonets into my body in Six places and I constantly Lay'd Hold of their Bayonets & Swords every pass they made which prevented the wound [from] Being so Deep." At one point, a bayonet came off a musket, and Latham attempted to pull it out to defend himself, but another soldier came, drew his sword, and struck him on the head. Latham had barely pulled himself to the door of the barracks before he passed out.[81]

Ziba Woodworth remembered "the enemy were so Exasperated that no surrendery would answer" and reasoned the British anger was based upon the deaths of their comrades by the Americans, and the killing continued because, as he thought, "life must go for life."[82]

This was evident in the barracks. No quarter was given to the militia there, especially those who had fired at Bromfield's men. Redcoats took their loaded

---

78 Deposition, William Latham to Samuel Mott, Apr. 11, 1782, Governor Trumbull Papers,16:90a, CSL.

79 Stephen Hempstead to Governor Trumbull, Oct. 30, 1781, Governor Trumbull Papers,15:164a–d, CSL; Harris, *Groton Heights*, 231–232; PA: John Daboll (S.19950), NARA.

80 Rufus Avery narrative in Harris, *Groton Heights*, 38.

81 Deposition, Edward Latham to Samuel Mott, May 6, 1782, Governor Trumbull Papers,16:127e, CSL.

82 PA: Ziba Woodworth (R.11848), NARA.

muskets, pushed them into the windows from which the militia had fired at them, started shooting into the structure, and then stormed the building. Entering the barracks, they bayonetted anyone they encountered.[83]

In a room further south, Solomon Perkins, a former militia captain, led a group of defenders off the parade and into the building. He testified, "[Having perceived] the British were not giving quarter," he and several others "Retir'd Into a Room in one of the Barracks in hope of Escaping their fury." Inside, Perkins stated that a British officer approached the doorway and demanded Perkins and his group lay down their arms. Perkins testified they did and asked for quarter. The British officer granted the request, and another officer came up with more soldiers and "Damn'd Us and told us we Ought to be put to death," Perkins later recalled. This group pushed the first officer aside and fired into the room, and according to Perkins, "some they kill'd, some they wounded." Perkins attempted to escape into the next room but was shot twice and bayonetted three times.[84]

Ziba Woodworth shared a similar fate. In his post-war pension application, Woodworth described the incident in great detail:

> I reached the Barracks . . . into which I Entered in hope of finding some weapon of Defence but could find none, One [Briton] who met me on the Parade followed me to the Door & then Called to Some of his fellows to fire in at the windows and kill the d[amne]d Rebel as he calld one but all were Employd in butchering . . . so he ventured in himself & made a Pass at me with his bayonet which I fended off with my hand, he again Repeated the stroke and I warded off the force of it by striking it aside, he then turned the breech of his gun & struck at my head & spoke as he struck, there you d[amne]d Rebel lay there, I at the same time seized his gun by the breech & held fast telling him I had as good a chance as he then struck me in the left Ear with his fist and stunned me for a little time but I being so closed so fast in with him did not break my hold and I was conscious if I did he would have his bayonet through me immediately. [T]hus we strove for some time but I found my antagonist too strong for one and my Nature & strength failing. So I took [hold of him and] so confined him to the corner of the room that his efforts to clear himself proved abortive [but soon] Another Briton Came in & in an instant Cocked his gun at my head[.] I turned & begged of him for god sakes to spare my life & I would go with him & serve him as long as I lived [but] there was no mercy for me the Enemy's gun was lowered to my thigh and went off.

---

83 Rufus Avery narrative in Harris, *Groton Heights*, 35.

84 Deposition, Captain Solomon Perkins to Samuel Mott, May 6, 1782, Governor Trumbull Papers,16:127c, CSL. Perkins was the former captain of the 2nd "Groton" Company.

As Woodworth fell, he cried out and soon went unconscious, due to loss of blood. He was later accounted among the dead. When he awoke several hours later, he was in terrible pain with two agonizing wounds. His right thigh bone had been shot away, and a bayonet had cut into his chest.[85]

Holsey Sanford was one of the fortunate ones in the barracks. He managed to climb into and then hide in one of the straw-filled mattresses of an upper bunk.[86]

The Powder Magazine

A similar bloody scenario unfolded at the powder magazine only twenty yards away. Being the only other place where some cover was available, several defenders ran for it. According to one, about 30 men were holed up inside, where they were crammed in, knocking over gunpowder and other supplies as they attempted to shield themselves from the British onslaught.

The fact that there was a struggle for the powder magazine showcases both the desperation of the defenders and how unruly the redcoats had become. It was the most volatile location in the fort, where even a simple, small spark could cause an explosion. Common sense would have told either side that firing muskets near barrels of gunpowder was not a smart decision. But with the heightened adrenaline, all sense of reason for a time was gone.

A Continental army general reflecting on the reported atrocities at Fort Griswold wrote, "[I]n all attacks by assault, the assailants, between the feelings of danger on the one hand, and resolutions to overcome it on the other, have their minds worked up almost to a point of fury and madness, which those who are assailed, from a confidence in their works, do not feel." Continuing his analysis, he continued, "[T]hat consequently when a place is carried, and the assailed submit, the assailants cannot simultaneously curb their fury to reason, and in the interval many are slain in a way which cool bystanders would call wanton and barbarous, and even the perpetrators themselves, when their rage subsided would condemn; but while the human passions remain as they now are, there is scarcely a remedy."[87]

After clearing a bloody path across the parade, the second group of redcoats went for the magazine. On the platform just above the magazine, Lt. Enoch Stanton was either pushed or fell off. As he clung to the platform, his body dangling, Stanton had redcoats with their bayonets pointing at him from atop and below.

---

85 PA: Ziba Woodworth (R.11848), NARA.

86 Sanford, *Memoir.*

87 William Heath, *Memoirs of Major General William Heath,* ed. William Abbatt (New York, 1968), 284.

According to Henry Mason, the lieutenant was pulled down, but it is just as likely that he fell, and once Stanton landed outside the magazine doors, several redcoats bayonetted him.[88]

Another party of British soldiers approached the magazine, intent on firing into it. One defender, Sgt. Ezekiel Bailey, of the 1st Company, "Groton Alarm List," stood near the door weeping and begged the British not to fire as it would blow them all up. But the soldiers refused to listen to reason and opened fire. Sergeant Rufus Avery, who had also been chased toward the magazine, wrote of this group: "A platoon of about ten men marched up near where I stood, where two large outer doors to the magazine made a space enough for ten men to stand in one rank. They discharged their guns into the magazine among the dead and wounded, and some well ones, and some they killed and wounded." Among those killed was Sergeant Bailey.[89]

Sergeant Daniel Eldridge, of the 3rd "Groton" Company, also testified to the incident. He recalled, "myself and a number of others Sought for Shelter in the Entrance of the Magazine[.] But they pursued us and fired in upon us where some of us Were Killed, the People of the Fort all the Time being begging for Quarter & that they would Spare their Lives, but they were Answered only with firing & with Bayonets & Insults of the Most Barbarous Kind." Eldridge was shot twice, in the face and the neck. The same volley wounded Sgt. William Starr, the regimental quartermaster, a musket ball entering his chest and passing into his left arm. After firing, the party went to bayonetting before falling back, so "another platoon came forward to discharge their guns into the outer part of the magazine, where the others did." But before they were able, they were interrupted by Major Bromfield.[90]

Shortly after Bromfield's soldiers advanced, the major grew wise. With the north gate opened and his soldiers inside, the British were clearly in possession of the fort. The fighting needed to cease before order was lost amongst his troops. Tragically for many of the defenders who tried to surrender, Bromfield's assumption of command would come too late.

---

88 PA: John Harris (S. 10787), NARA. Harris served with Mason prior to the attack. The two remained friends after the war. The details about Stanton's death were shared with Harris by Mason as the two talked about their time at the fort.

89 "A Sixth of Sep Letter from the Son of one of the Fort Griswold Garrison," *New London Daily Chronicle*, Sep. 17, 1861; Rufus Avery narrative in Harris, *Groton Heights*, 38.

90 Harris, *Groton Heights*, 226–227, 243–244; *CSR*, 4:295; Rufus Avery narrative in Harris, *Groton Heights*, 38; Deposition, Daniel Eldridge to Samuel Mott, Apr. 12, 1782, Governor Trumbull Papers,16:93c, CSL. Starr is often identified as a lieutenant, which in 1781 he was not. He received his commission in 1782.

In Bromfield's defense, by their sudden advance, and with Bromfield being at the rear of them, he probably never ordered his men to advance into the fort. Neither could he have been aware of Eyre's wounding or Montgomery's death. Hence there was no way at that moment for Bromfield to know that he was now in command of the entire British force. But at that moment, Bromfield rushed into the fort to end the fighting and more importantly restore order amongst the troops of both sides. Along the way, he found a drummer and ordered him to start beating the long roll, which was a long beat that signaled the soldiers to cease fighting and fall into formation. The long roll was heard by many as it echoed over the battlefield. Several defenders, such as Peter Avery, attested "that soon after the drum beat . . . the firing ceased." Most redcoats recognized it, and along with their officers prodding, finally stopped fighting.[91]

Bromfield did not stop there but went across the parade, bringing his orders directly to his soldiers, often yelling and swinging his sword at them. Those who disobeyed, he chastised. This was observed when he saw soldiers firing into the powder magazine. Incensed, he at once rushed over as they were about to fire a second volley into the magazine, Bromfield waving his sword, screaming at them. Years later, Sergeant Avery, who was nearby, claimed he heard the major yell, "Stop firing! You'll send us all to hell together!" The soldiers complied and lowered their weapons without firing them.[92]

Governor Trumbull, though not naming Bromfield, credited him with saving the lives of over a hundred men. In a letter to Washington, Trumbull explained that if not for "the interpositions of a British who entered the fort too late," the garrison would have been entirely wiped out.[93]

When the fighting ceased, the redcoats in the fort pointed their muskets upward, discharged a celebratory volley into the air, and gave a loud cheer. By just after 2:00 p.m., the battle was over. Fort Griswold and New London Harbor belonged to the British.[94]

91 Rufus Avery narrative in Harris, *Groton Heights*, 38; PA: Peter Avery (S.12024), NARA.

92 Rufus Avery narrative in Harris, *Groton Heights*, 38, 40. Avery was one of the few Americans who could identify Bromfield, as he was introduced to him when he came to talk to the prisoners.

93 Trumbull to Washington, Sep. 13, 1781, Governor Trumbull Papers,15:121a, CSL.

94 Deposition, Obadiah Perkins to Samuel Mott, Apr. 11, 1782, Governor Trumbull Papers,16:92a–b, CSL.

Chapter Nine

The Battle of New London:
The Occupation and Burning of the Town

At around 1:00 p.m. black smoke began to billow over New London Harbor. The town was on fire. The thick, dark cloud of smoke became so large it was seen by numerous witnesses, some as far as forty miles away. In Preston, more than twenty miles from the harbor, one recalled that "the smoke of New London appeared like a cloud." If the militia were hesitant to respond to the alarm guns earlier or thought it was another false alarm, the smoke was an ominous sign that something was not right. But by the time most arrived, it was too late to save the town.[1]

When Arnold left Meetinghouse Hill, he ordered Captain Stapleton to oversee the occupation and to implement his orders to destroy the remaining privateers, the storehouses, wharves, and any other military or economic targets—and to do so as quickly as possible. The Americans had already started their work; at least two privateers, the 10-gun brig *Venus* and the prize brig *Syren* were already on fire, burned by retreating militia to prevent their capture.[2]

In the northern part of town, the American Legion scoured the upper part of Town Street and the southern part of Winthrop's Neck. The Winthrop mansion was at least structurally left intact, but the gristmill was set ablaze. Nearly opposite

---

1 Master's Log, HMS *Amphion*, ADM 52/2133, TNA; Avery Downer narrative in Harris, *Groton Heights*, 84; PA: Reuben Phelps (W.15214); Valentine Lewis (W.20431), NARA. The noise of battle was heard many miles away. Elias Rood, of Hebron, nearly forty miles away, remembered "cannonading was distinctly heard, and smoke was distinctly seen."

2 *1781 Groton Heights and New London, Letters from Zabdiel Rogers, and Thomas Mumford* (Brooklyn, NY, 1881), 4.

Nineteenth century engraving of mercantile storehouses on Beach Street in New London. *Charles Allyn*

the mansion and overlooking the cove, the two-story John Plumb house, occupied by his elderly widow Elizabeth, as well as her barn, was set on fire. Nearby, the old shipyard, previously operated by Alexander Merrill at the southwestern part of the Neck along Winthrop Cove, was destroyed.[3]

During the war, Merrill had constructed a few small privateers and part of a Continental naval ship here. In 1777, Nathaniel Shaw had his 20-gun privateer *General Putnam* built in Merrill's yard. Launched that fall and commissioned the following spring, it was the largest recorded vessel constructed in New London during the war and took many prizes.[4]

Merrill died in 1779 and it is not clear what became of his shipyard. Whatever had been left there, which may have included piles of timber, rigging, ropes, and

3 *CG*, May 5, 1775, June 24, 1779, Oct. 12, 1781; R. B. Wall, "When The Traitor Arnold Burned New London Town, Part 1" *The Day*, Dec. 2, 1914; "Nathaniel Shaw, Jr.'s Account Against The Connecticut Privateer Ship General Putnam," Ledger No. 9, Nathaniel and Thomas Shaw Papers, YUL, YU; Harris, *Groton Heights*, 24. Merrill constructed coasting vessels, such as fishing boats, Moses boats, and oared barges.

4 "Nathaniel Shaw, Jr.'s Account Against The Connecticut Privateer Ship General Putnam," Ledger No. 9, Nathaniel and Thomas Shaw Papers, YUL, YU. "Nathaniel Shaw, Jr.'s Account Against The Connecticut Privateer Sloop *American Revenue*," Ledger No. 4, Nathaniel and Thomas Shaw Papers, YUL, YU; "Accounts of the Continental Navy Brigantine Resistance," Ledger No. 26, Nathaniel and Thomas Shaw Papers, YUL, YU; Rogers, *Naval Office*, 54–56.

other tools, was set ablaze. The soldiers visited Merrill's house, where they found his widow Hannah, but left her and the house alone.[5]

Across the street from the Merrill house stood the home of Brig. Gen. Gurdon Saltonstall Jr. whose estate stretched eastward to the Thames River. A member of one of New London's most prominent families, Saltonstall enjoyed a long record of public service. In addition to being involved in the mercantile trade, he served as collector of customs and judge of the court of probate for the district of New London and served several terms as a representative in the General Assembly.

In 1775, then Colonel Saltonstall led the 3rd Regiment of Connecticut Militia and the following year as a brigadier general led a brigade of Connecticut militia during the New York Campaign. The following spring he retired from the militia and semi-retired to private life, but continued to be active in politics and allowed his large estate to be utilized as an encampment site by the militia sent to protect New London. Because of his patriot-leaning loyalties, Saltonstall's mansion, barn, and workshop were burned. Just south of the mansion along the waterfront two of his storehouses and a cooper shop owned by his son were also set aflame.[6]

Hours earlier, Saltonstall had attempted to assist in the defense of the town. But the old general grew frustrated at the inability of the militia to assemble in more than what he termed "a single company of soldier[s]." Saltonstall was probably referring to Capt. Richard Deshon's Company. It is not clear how involved the general was in the fighting that morning. No other eyewitness account mentioned the general's involvement and his participation appears to have been limited primarily to helping collect volunteers to oppose the British. Saltonstall did, however, ride out as the militia and others were falling back into town, and claimed he was within musket range of the British. But he then returned home to move some property to safety. He managed to load a couple of carts containing a few feather beds, some clothing, and a pillowcase full of personal papers and get them out of town, believing the rest of his property was safe and that the British would not burn the town. He was wrong.[7]

The unfinished fort on Winthrop's Neck stood on the eastern end of the Saltonstall property. The fort had been a personal project for Saltonstall and he freely offered his property for its placement. He had supervised its construction

5 New London Land Records and Deeds, Vol.23:16–17, CSL; Caulkins, *New London*, 197–198, 552; *CSR*, 3:131, 171, 253.

6 PA: John Harris (S.10787), NARA; R. B. Wall, "When Traitor Arnold Burned New London Town, Part 3," *The Day*, Dec. 4, 1914. It was located near the intersection of Congdon and 16th Streets.

7 Gurdon Saltonstall to Governor Trumbull, New London, Oct. 10, 1781, Governor Trumbull Papers, 15:182, CSL. When Saltonstall explained the loss of the town's probate files, he wrote, "I had no Idea the Enemy would burn the Town."

and led the militia company which built and initially garrisoned it. Subsequently abandoned due to lack of resources, the fort contained a barracks building, and a wooden platform, which were fitted to have mounted "10 heavy cannon" behind its earthen walls. The loyalist soldiers set it all on fire.[8]

On Town Street, Frink's men terrorized civilians who remained in their homes. When they visited the Adams house, they found Anne Adams, her daughter Elizabeth Pool, and two of Elizabeth's young children inside. The soldiers' appearance alone was frightening. They forced their way into the house and started indiscriminately breaking dishes, much to the disdain of the women. Elizabeth attempted to describe the encounter, writing "It would be demeaning my pen to describe their childish destruction of crockery wherever they went, as they seemed to show a particular dislike to female trappings."[9]

While they refrained from burning the Adams house, most of the neighbors were not so fortunate. Pool explained "There is not a Building standing from my Mothers to Robert Latimores," she told her brother "there was not one in that distance; a few [along Town] Street purchased their houses for trifling sums of the mercenary wretches and by that paltry means escaped the general wreck." At least fifteen houses were burned along the upper part of Town Street, including the one occupied by Peter Latimer Jr., which he lost along with his cooper shop.[10]

The Ichabod Powers tavern, operated by Powers and his wife Meribeth, was picked through by the loyalist soldiers. Located on the east side of the street, the tavern was a popular privateer recruiting station. Henry Deshon's wharf, located on the cove behind the tavern, was frequently used by privateers. The wharf was often where a sea-going vessel was tied up or a place where goods could be temporarily stacked and stored while they were either being loaded onto or unloaded from

8 "The Plan of New London Harbour by Samuel Mott," Letters from Joseph Carleton and Thomas Hutchins, Papers of the Continental Congress, NARA; Gurdon Saltonstall to Governor Trumbull, Apr. 1, 1776, Governor Trumbull Papers, 5:26a–b. It is estimated that 60–90 men labored for around 6–8 months, between Nov. 1775 and July 1776 on the fort. When writing to the governor, Saltonstall clearly envisioned his fort would later be enclosed and strengthened with bastions. The fort survived until the late 1800s, when its remaining earthworks were removed by the New London and Northern Railroad.

9 Eliza Pool to John Pool Jr., New London, Oct. 30, 1781, NLCHS.

10 Eliza Pool to John Pool Jr., New London, Oct. 30, 1781, NLCHS; PA: Jonathan Chandler (R.21842), NARA. The Adams family may have bribed the soldiers with money to spare their home. Hannah Merrill may have done the same. While Pool does not identify any individual houses, she does mention in her letter, "a few in that Street . . . purchased their houses for trifling sums" The Adams and Merrill houses were two of three within reach of the British not burned either on this part of Town Street or on Winthrop's Neck. According to Chandler, some homes on Town Street were burned as the American Legion withdrew from town, to mask their withdrawal as it would deter or impede any use of Town Street as a means of pursuing the retreating British column.

a vessel or being moved to a storehouse. There were numerous wharves, usually named after their owners, up and down the waterfront. At least one vessel, the privateer *Minerva*, was tied at Deshon's wharf that morning but had escaped.[11]

Frink's soldiers broke into Powers's Tavern, and if they were still there threw the family out and then wrecked the place. In the process they discovered alcohol. Casks were broken open and soldiers consumed large amounts of rum and wine. One provincial soldier became so intoxicated that he passed out on Town Street near the tavern and was later picked up by the Americans as a prisoner.[12]

On the west side of the street, near the Adams house, the British targeted the home and property of Timothy Green Jr., a printer. Green operated two print shops, one next to his residence, another on Congress Street. Touted as the "Printer to the Governor and Company," Green printed books, pamphlets, rebel currency, official documents, and broadsides, as well as the weekly *Connecticut Gazette*, a Continental-friendly newspaper, which enjoyed a wide circulation throughout eastern Connecticut. Soldiers ransacked the house and print shop before setting them ablaze.[13]

Soon, it appeared that the whole street was on fire. Homes belonging to Christopher Prince, James Pittman, Daniel Byrne, Grace Rogers, Joseph Hurlbut, James McEvers, and Roswell Saltonstall were all set on fire. Saltonstall, his wife Elizabeth, and their two small children resided in his grandfather's house on the west side of the street. Like his father, Gurdon, Roswell was engaged in the family mercantile business. He worked with his father, and his brother, Winthrop. The family owned a wharf, several storehouses, a distillery and various workshops and stores along Beach Street. Despite being the son of the general, Roswell refused to take the oath of allegiance to the state and remained a loyalist. He made a sizable claim to the British government after the war, and in it stated he believed that if he remained in his house and did not interfere with the British, the family would be left alone. He was unfortunately wrong. In his deposition, Roswell stated soldiers came and forced him, his wife (who was "Extremly weak and sick"), and children out "into the open fields." The house, as well as that of Saltonstall's neighbor, Henry Deshon, was set ablaze.[14]

---

11 *CG*, Sep. 7, 1781, Oct. 12, 1781.

12 Brooks narrative in Harris, *Groton Heights*, 81. Brooks claimed to have found a drunken soldier in front of Timothy Green's home, located a short distance from Powers tavern.

13 *CSR*, 2:166. The former home of Henry Latimer sat in between Adams and Green. It was currently owned by or leased to George Newcomb.

14 Harris, *Groton Heights*, 24; American Loyalist Claims, 1776–1835, AO 13/83/346-347, TNA; *CSR*, 3:548–549; "Losses of New London Sufferers By The Ravages of the British Army," Revolutionary War Records, Series III, June 1765–May 1820, 95a–l, CSL; *CG*, Feb. 3, 1786. Saltonstall's claim was

The American Legion committed some of the most grievous acts during the occupation. The Continental press persuaded their readership that this was the behavior of the entire British force. The *Norwich Packet* printed "the soldiery seemed to be under no regularity, and everyone was at liberty to commit what devastation he thought proper." Later, the paper claimed Arnold's soldiers threatened to burn women and children in their homes and asserted, "notwithstanding the earnest cries and intreaties of the women and children in them, who were threatened with being burnt up in their houses if they did not instantly leave them."[15]

The lack of discipline in the American Legion contributed to the unruly behavior, as did the consumption of alcohol. The rawness of its officers also did not help. This was the first time Capt. Nathan Frink had led soldiers into action. He had no previous experience as an officer in either the colonial militia or provincial forces and had not been on the Virginia expedition. Frink deserves most of the blame for their actions. He had hesitated at Fort Trumbull, and now he had lost control of his soldiers. It did not help him that his most experienced officer, Captain Wogan, was out of action. Arnold also deserves his share of the blame, as both commander of the expedition and organizer of the American Legion. It was his unit. He selected its officers and should have known its limitations. We are left to wonder why they were given a position so far from the main force and why they were not placed under a tighter discipline. It was probably no accident that this was the American Legion's last action of the war.

Further south on Town Street at the intersection with Richards Street stood the home of Guy Richards Sr., an influential citizen as well as a prosperous merchant. Richards co-owned a profitable mercantile business with his son Guy Jr., the commissary of New London. Both were avowed patriots.[16]

According to Caulkins, the Richards house was marked for destruction. Led by an officer, the soldiers attempted to enter the front door but were greeted by a group of women. Mrs. Richards was assuredly among them. The women, according to Caulkins, implored "the English officer" to spare their house as they had remained behind to care for one of Richards's daughters who was ill and

---

made by Joseph Chew. Saltonstall also lost "A Large Well," "A Wharehouse store & Part of a Wharf" with a variety of West Indian and European goods. He attempted to procure "several articles of household goods and clothing for the use of his family" from friends in New York, but when they arrived in the harbor he was denied them because of his "dubious character with respect to his political principles, and not having taken the oath of fidelity to this State." James McEvers is not on any previous lists, but his family submitted a house damage claim of £600 and the empty lot with ruins of the house was sold in 1786. Daniel Byrne resided in the John Prentis house, which was leased to him by the heirs of Prentis who had died.

15 *Norwich Packet*, Sep. 13, 1781, Oct. 11, 1781.

16 *CSR*, 2:444; *CG*, Dec. 26, 1780, July 6, 1781, Aug. 17, 1781.

confined to bed. After listening, the officer ordered his soldiers to leave, and the house was left intact.[17]

This was a radical shift in behavior by the occupiers, especially considering what was going on along the upper part of Town Street. This might indicate the soldiers at the Richards house were not members of the American Legion. Caulkins's mention of an "English officer" suggests they were soldiers of the 38th Regiment, which in line of march was behind the American Legion. This would have placed them in occupation of the Beach Street area. If the 38th Regiment was in this area, then the Loyal American Regiment was probably on the Parade and along the Bank.[18]

The 38th Foot and Loyal American Regiment performed much better during the occupation than their counterparts in the northern part of town. Most documented plundering occurred in areas held by either the American Legion, the jaegers, or the Associated Loyalists. We only know about the plundering along the outpost line because it involved soldiers who were later captured and searched. One soldier, likely an Associated Loyalist, loaded his knapsack with several items including plates, jewelry, a pair of scissors, and a prayer book. Another prisoner was found with an "American ensign," or flag, on him.[19]

There was only one report of drunken soldiers in the Parade area. There an American prisoner, George Newcomb, accused his captors of being drunk and mistreating the prisoners. There were only a few reports of civilians or houses, along either Beach Street or the Bank, being robbed or burned without cause. This may have been for a couple of reasons. In comparison to the American Legion, the 38th Regiment and Loyal American Regiment contained seasoned veterans. Their officers had more experience at handling their troops. These soldiers seemed to be after food more than plunder. Soldiers in each of Arnold's units, including the 38th Foot and Loyal American Regiment, visited several locations where they either asked, demanded, or took food from civilians or their gardens. Only

---

17 Caulkins, New London, 552; *CG*, Oct. 5, 1781. Like the Adams house, money may have played a role in saving the Richards house. According to the *Gazette*, and Elizabeth Pool, the redcoats would only refrain from burning homes in this area if the occupiers offered them money. The *Gazette* reported that at least two houses in this area were spared because they "were bought off for Ten Pounds each, after an officer, who appeared to be a Captain, had ordered them fired." The only two houses on this part of Town Street spared were those belonging to the Adams and Richards families.

18 *James Rogers*, 146. This speculation of the Loyal American Regiment being in the Parade/Bank area is supported by a civilian who contended that he watched a building on the parade set ablaze by a "tory" soldier.

19 *CG*, Sep. 14, 1781.

provided with two days of rations, the expedition was now on its fourth day; the soldiers were hungry.[20]

Also helpful in keeping the soldiers under control was Captain Stapleton. Stapleton remained active throughout the occupation, often riding up and down the streets monitoring the two regiments and enforcing Arnold's order not to harass civilians or destroy private property. The brigade major's supervisory actions earned special praise from Arnold. In his report, Arnold wrote "I am greatly indebted to Capt Stapleton (who acted as Major of brigade) for his spirited conduct and assistance [for] his endeavors to prevent plundering, (when the publick stores were burnt) and the destruction of private buildings." When any soldier in the 38th Regiment or Loyal American Regiment attempted to plunder a storehouse or rob and pillage citizens, they were chastised by either Stapleton or their own regimental officers. It remains unclear, however, why Stapleton did not keep an eye on the behavior of the American Legion.[21]

Frances Caulkins asserted she uncovered several examples of positive interactions between the occupiers and citizens while working on her book, but only mentioned three. Unfortunately, she never cited names. One example involved a woman whose house was broken into by a soldier who stole clothing. The angry woman came outside, found an officer, and complained directly to him. The officer then found the soldier, publicly chastised him, and ordered the clothing to be returned, which was done. Another example involved a different woman who, seeing buildings around her house being set ablaze, moved an elderly relative, unable to walk, into her garden. An officer saw them, went over, and calmed the anxious women, assuring her that her house would not be entered, as he would watch over it himself.[22]

A third example involved a woman who lived in a house on the Bank overlooking Bream Cove. Though Caulkins did not identify the woman, she was probably Elizabeth Crocker. Crocker and her husband John, a sea captain, had, in 1781, at least three small children and lived in a house which matched Caulkins's details. The woman, after watching redcoats enter the town, sent her teenage son to hide in the cellar and took her two youngest children out onto the street. Upon seeing an officer, she begged him to spare her home. She claimed her husband was

---

20 James Lawrence Chew, "An Account of the Old Houses of New London," in *Records and Papers of the NLCHS*, 3 volumes (New London, CT, 1890), 1:91; George Newcomb deposition to Samuel Mott, Apr. 11, 1782, Governor Trumbull Papers,16:88, CSL. Newcomb claimed to have escaped a short time later because his guards were intoxicated.

21 Mackenzie, *Diary*, 2:627.

22 Caulkins, *New London*, 552, 556.

gone, and she lived alone with her small children. The officer approached the grief-stricken woman and told her to return home and assured her that none of his men would touch her house.[23]

While Guy Richards's home had been spared, his mercantile company was not as fortunate. Most of the company's property was clustered in between the customs house and the town wharf on Beach Street. This wharf was normally the scene of much activity. Along with Beach Street, which ran south of it, it was the commercial heart of New London.

Located at the wharf was the ferry which carried passengers, animals, and goods back and forth across the river to Groton. Nearby, passage boats operated almost daily. Most transported passengers, mail, and goods between Norwich and New London. Others traveled back and forth to New Haven. Before the war, additional passage boats ran between New London and Long Island. The frequent commercial and privateer activity left the town wharf routinely stacked with hogsheads, barrels, and crates containing sugar, coffee, rum, or Irish butter. These were either set on fire or cracked open and thrown into the river.

Nearby, at the northern tip of Beach Street, sat the Tavern of the Sun. Advertised as a "good house of entertainment," it was operated by Zebulon Elliott. Elliott capitalized on the constant traffic of the area. In addition to running the ferry house, he operated his own passage boat, as well as a store on the bottom floor of the tavern. His death in 1779 left the management of the ferry house and tavern to his widow Abigail. The tavern fell victim to the flames.[24]

North of the town wharf, Guy Richards had three additional storehouses. They were utilized to store goods or military stores brought in either by merchant vessels or privateers until they could be sold or transported elsewhere. The company also owned and operated a slaughterhouse, and a store from which they sold their goods. Nearby, the company wharf serviced the company's merchant vessels and the occasional privateer. It was all set ablaze, as was the customs house, the customs officer's residence.[25]

Goods stacked atop Adam Shapley's wharf which lay on the cove opposite Shapley Street were likewise burned. Shapley's store and the home of his widowed mother, Elizabeth, which stood close to the intersection of Shapley and Town Streets, were destroyed. Joseph Packwood & Company, which financed several

---

23 Ibid., 554–555; *CG*, Aug. 13, 1790.

24 *CG*, Nov. 7, 1766, Oct. 12, 1781.

25 Ibid., Aug. 17, 1781.

privateers, lost a storehouse near Shapley's wharf. The shop of John Hertell, an agent who gathered supplies for Nathaniel Shaw, was set ablaze.[26]

South of the town wharf, the British continued their trail of destruction. Most of the property of Edward Hallam & Company stood opposite that of Guy Richards. Since 1777 he had co-owned the company with his three brothers. Hallam's company had its own wharf, barn, and three storehouses filled with "European and West India Goods." Business had been good that summer. Investing in at least two privateers had paid off. In June, Hallam advertised at his store "5 Pair 4-Pound Cannon, with Carriages," cutlasses, blunderbusses, and "Excellent French Muskets." A week before the raid, he was promoting "English (Prize) Goods, directly from London" at the store. Like Guy Richards, Edward Hallam lost everything in the flames.[27]

Further south along Beach Street, but north of the Parade, the British destroyed eight more storehouses. Windows were smashed, doors broken open, and lit torches thrown inside. One was owned by John Springer, who operated a passage boat at the town wharf, another by Thomas Wilson who operated a boarding house on Town Street.[28]

The Saltonstall family continued to suffer considerably. Already having lost much on Winthrop's Neck and Town Street, on Beach Street the family owned two additional storehouses and a cooper shop which had been improved into a house and leased out to a family. The storehouses were filled with linens, clothing, silverware, tobacco, and a variety of medicines. They also operated a distillery complex which distilled molasses into rum and covered much of the land between Bradley and Beach Streets. Everything was lost in the flames.[29]

Slightly down the street, two more storehouses which lay opposite Douglass Street belonged to Nathaniel Shaw Jr. & Company, who also owned an adjacent wharf. Tied up at Shaw's wharf was the British letter of marque *Hannah* and the schooner *Arbuthnot*. Both were captured during the summer by the privateer *Minerva*. Both vessels had been abandoned during the retreat. Particularly prized

26 Middlebrook, *Maritime Connecticut*, 2:5, 158, 107–108, 243; *Naval Records*, 323, 388, 492. Packwood was a merchant and associate of Nathaniel Shaw Jr. who owned at least three privateers during the war.

27 "Losses of New London Sufferers By The Ravages of the British Army," Revolutionary War Records, Series III, June 1765–May 1820, 95a–l, CSL; *CSR*, 1:351, 3:444; *CG*, July 3, 1772, Feb. 24, 1774, Feb. 14, 1777, June 22, 1781, Aug. 31, 1781, Oct. 12, 1781; Middlebrook, *Maritime Connecticut*, 2:70, 159, 171, 204.

28 Winthrop also served as the registrar of the New London County Maritime Court. The involvement of the two other sons of Gurdon, Nathaniel and Dudley, in the family company is not quite clear as they were often away in either the privateer service or Continental navy.

29 *CG*, Dec. 26, 1780, Apr. 29, 1785; *People's Advocate* (New London), Nov. 12, 1845.

was the *Hannah*. Over the last few weeks much of its former cargo, valued by one British newspaper at £80,000 sterling, had been unloaded and placed into one of Shaw's nearby storehouses. Unable to move the vessels, soldiers set them on fire, cut their moorings, and allowed them to drift into the harbor.[30]

South of Shaw's wharf lay the property of John Deshon & Company. Captain John Deshon was one of the largest landowners in town. He owned two houses in town, one on Beach Street the other on the Bank, which served as his main residence. Here on Beach Street, the company owned two storehouses and a wharf, which stood near Wilson's storehouse. Deshon was an avowed patriot and a particular annoyance to the British. He had been involved in the war since its outset and often used his own business to supply Continental and Connecticut forces. Besides being captain of the 1st Company Alarm List, he also served as the first Deputy Commissary of Issues at New London from 1776 until 1777. In May 1777, the Continental Congress appointed him to the Continental Naval Board in the Eastern Department. In that position, which he held for the duration of the war, he directed the recruitment of sailors and the procurement of supplies and armament for vessels in the Continental navy, as well as overseeing naval stores kept in New London. Additionally, he was often sought after for advice by the governor and other government and military leaders. John Deshon & Company owned three or four privateers during the war. One, the 4-gun schooner *Gamecock*, tied at their wharf, was due to set sail that morning, but instead was abandoned. When the British arrived at Deshon's property, they broke open the storehouses, and set them ablaze. The *Gamecock* was cut loose and set on fire. Deshon's house on the west side of the street, which he leased to a family, also fell victim to the flames.[31]

As the fires were being started, Arnold made his way to the Bank. As he rode down Beach Street, he observed his soldiers busy at work setting much of the area ablaze. According to a local story, as he rode past them, he drew his sword and

30 R. B. Wall, "When The Traitor Arnold Burned New London Town, Part 3," *The Day*, Dec. 4, 1914; Caulkins, *New London*, 553; Arnold report in Mackenzie, *Diary*, 2:626; *Royal Gazette* (NY), Aug. 4, 1781, Aug. 22, 1781; *CG*, Aug. 24, 1781. The *Minerva* was owned by Samuel Broome & Company out of Wethersfield, Connecticut. Broome was a close business associate of Shaw. It is likely Broome rented space from Shaw for the cargoes of captured privateers. Commanded by Capt. Dudley Saltonstall, the general's son, it was arguably the most valuable capture by a Connecticut privateer during the war. The schooner *Arbuthnot*, which was also taken by the *Minerva* during the same cruise, loaded with salt and tobacco, was probably tied up here and as such burned with the *Hannah*. After its arrival in New London, it disappears from the records. Both the *Hannah* and *Arbuthnot* had just been condemned by the maritime court. The *Hannah* was bound to New York from London. The *Arbuthnot*, loaded with tobacco, was headed to Newfoundland from New York when it was captured.

31 *Naval Documents*, X:331; *Naval Records*, 79, 307, 333, 410; *CG*, Oct. 12, 1781; *CSR*, 1:83, 127, 212, 351; "A List of the First Alarm List Company in the 3d Regt of Militia in this State under the Command of Capt John Deshon," NLCHS.

repeatedly called out to them, "Soldiers! Do your duty!" Time was of the essence. They needed to keep on task.[32]

Reaching the Bank, Arnold rode as far south as the home of Jeremiah Miller Sr., a long-time acquaintance. The two had known each other for years before the war. But Arnold's visit was not for personal reasons. Rather, Miller was the main loyalist contact in town. In 1781, Miller was 62-years-old and resided with his wife Margaret, and several of their children, in a large two-story mansion on the Bank. On the property Miller also had a barn, chaise house, a corn crib, a chicken coop, and a dairy outhouse. Born in New London, Miller had strong connections to the community. He was the grandson of a colonial governor of Connecticut, and his father once headed the first school in New London. Miller, like many others, had grown considerably wealthy in the mercantile trade. He owned two houses on the Bank. His main residence stood near Nathaniel Shaw's at the lower end, while his second house, rented to William Constant, lay up the road closer to the Parade. Additionally, Miller owned a 60-acre farm and a house on Town Hill. His wealth, along with his family connections, led to his prominence in town. But that prominence had somewhat declined in the last few years over the suspicion of his disloyalty to the patriot cause.[33]

Miller's disloyalty had not always been in question. In 1767, he supported a public condemnation of the British government in response to the Townsend Acts. But after that, his attitude began to change and his loyalty to the crown strengthened throughout the war. In 1777, he had been the naval officer at the customs house, and a judge of the county court. When the General Assembly required those who held those positions to take an oath of allegiance to the state, Miller refused and as a result lost both positions. Loyalty to the crown was a hallmark of his whole family, including his son-in-law, James Tilley. The family remained largely unbothered by local officials.[34]

Miller's situation was unique, and quite unlike that of other loyalists in town, who were often harassed and jailed. While many suspected Miller's loyalties might lean towards the crown, the only harassment he endured was when the militia carried loads of timber, firewood, and hay from his Town Hill farm without payment. Town officials allowed Joshua Coit, the town clerk of probate, to rent a room in Miller's house which was utilized as an office and storage space for most

32 Caulkins, *New London*, 552; Harris, *Groton Heights*, 25.

33 *CG*, Oct. 12, 1781; American Loyalist Claims, 1776–1835, AO 13/7/130–132, TNA; American Loyalists Claims, 1776–1835, AO 13/42/92–146, TNA. The location of the Miller house was at the present-day intersection of Bank and Tilley Streets opposite the New London Fire Department.

34 Caulkins, *New London*, 398–399, 477, 509.

of the town's vital records. After the war, Miller even managed to successfully file damage claims done to his properties from both Connecticut and Great Britain.[35]

Miller's family did not abandon the town, but eagerly awaited the arrival of the British troops, and expected to meet with their commander. Miller may even have known they were coming. Arnold had been asked by Joseph Chew, the British Secretary for Indian Affairs, to visit Miller while he was in New London.

Chew had lived in New London before the war and served as surveyor at the customs house, while Miller was naval officer. Captured on Long Island in 1777, Chew was brought back to New London and billeted at Miller's house. There, he "privately received many civilities" from Miller. Chew knew Miller as a "Zealous Loyalist" and after his release kept up a secret correspondence with Miller, as well as other loyalists in New London. Miller's son, Jeremiah Jr., often fed information to British intelligence in New York through Chew.[36]

Prior to leaving New York, Arnold met with Chew and was handed a list of those in New London who were loyalists and those who "were the most violent [patriots]." Jeremiah Miller was at the top of the loyalist list. Chew received Arnold's guarantee that he would protect loyalist citizens and their property while he was there. Arnold assured the anxious Chew that he had "Sir Henry Clinton's orders to protect all Such Persons."[37]

Once Arnold reached the Miller residence, he dismounted. Still suffering from the effects of his Saratoga leg wound, Arnold hobbled as he approached the front door. He was greeted by the elder Miller, his son Jeremiah Jr., and James Tilley, who then took the general inside where they went into the dining room. Unfortunately, no transcript or records exists of the roughly one-hour meeting. But it can be presumed Miller provided Arnold with dinner and some local intelligence. This seems to match Arnold's brief reminiscence of it, recalling, "[I was] cordially received and entertained by [Miller] and that aid was given by Him in favour of His Majestys cause."[38]

North of the Miller house, the Parade area was pretty much left alone by the British. With the limited time they had, destroying most of these buildings made no military sense. This was especially true with St. James Church. However, some

---

35 American Loyalist Claims, 1776–1835, AO 13/7/130–132, TNA; American Loyalists Claims, 1776–1835, AO 13/42/92–146, TNA; Gurdon Saltonstall to Governor Trumbull, New London, Oct. 10, 1781, Governor Trumbull Papers, 15:182, CSL.

36 Caulkins, *New London*, 477; American Loyalist Claims, 1776–1835, AO 13/42/96-106, 126-132, TNA At one point, Jeremiah Miller Jr. served as the postmaster.

37 American Loyalist Claims, 1776–1835, AO 13/42/96-106, 126-132, TNA

38 American Loyalist Claims, 1776–1835, AO 13/7/250–251, TNA. Arnold testified for Miller when he applied for compensation to the British government for damage done to his property.

military targets were set ablaze, such as the powder magazine which served the town, and the remnants of the old fort.[39]

South of the Parade, along the Bank, the British destroyed at least thirteen more storehouses and just as many wharves which belonged to over a dozen merchants and mercantile companies. Most of these were situated on the east side of the street, closer to the waterfront. On the opposite side were mainly homes, some owned by members of New London's oldest and wealthiest families. These were mostly left alone, but included in the destruction were several mercantile stands, some in separate buildings, others inside homes—as a result of which the house was also consumed. Merchant William Stewart, an associate of Nathaniel Shaw, was among those who lost the most property. Stewart sold a variety of items such as "Choice Muscorvado Sugar," rum and horses, or everyday items such as crockery, molasses, tea, and even nails. During the war he also advertised a couple of sea-going vessels. Stewart's neighbor, merchant Samuel Belden, who sold "European Goods" and ship chandlery from two stores along the Bank, lost both storehouses. Two doctors involved in the privateer trade, Simon Wolcott, and Cornelius Cunningham, who also sold a variety of medical supplies, had their stores burned. Dr. Cunningham ran a store in the home of Charles Chadwick, where he openly recruited for privateers as well as advertised items in his store which were "fit for a Privateer." This too was burned.[40]

The British targeted two taverns along the Bank, probably due to their privateer connections. The first was operated by Ephraim Miner, the second by Nathan Douglass. Both were located near the courthouse and had adjacent wharves which were used by merchant vessels and privateers. The privateer *Hancock* operated from Miner's wharf and was tied there the morning of the attack, before it escaped upriver. Douglass, a former merchant captain, opened his establishment in 1774; he promised his customers "oysters, fry'd and otherwise dres'd, in the best Manner." At times, Douglass rented rooms to Continental army and navy officers that they utilized to recruit volunteers.[41]

At the south end of the Bank, at Tongue Rock, lay the Coit shipyard. Established decades earlier, the yard was owned by Joseph Coit. Coit also operated his own mercantile business and owned four houses, two barns, and at least one wharf in

---

39 *CG*, Oct. 12, 1781; "Lieutenant John Hempsted Orderly Book," Council of Safety Papers, CHS.

40 *CG*, Nov. 1, 1771, Nov. 15, 1771, Sep. 1, 1775, Sep. 15, 1775, Sep. 29, 1775, Sep. 8, 1780, Mar. 16, 1781, Sep. 8, 1780, Mar. 16, 1781.

41 *CG*, June 3, 1775, May 9, 1777, Jan. 30, 1781, Apr. 13, 1781; July 27, 1781, Oct. 12, 1781, Apr. 21, 1786. Miner's tavern is named as John Erving's house. Erving, a Boston merchant, owned the house, storehouse, and wharf, but rented it to Miner.

town. Before the war, Coit constructed merchant vessels, but in 1776 Coit was nearly eighty years old and could not deal with the increased stress caused by the heightened demands placed on his shipyard. He stepped aside from management of the yard and removed to Norwich, but the shipyard continued to operate.[42]

Records are unclear as to how many, if any, wartime vessels were constructed at the Coit yard. But what appears likely is that it was used primarily for fitting out vessels. Fitting out could mean one of two things. For new vessels it was the final stage of construction. After the hull was finished and launched into the water it was brought to the Coit yard where it was fitted out. This involved bringing on board a variety of tradesmen, such as carpenters, joiners, and painters. While some finished the interior of the vessel, others on deck fitted out their masts, bowsprit, rigging, sails, and finally its cannon. For completed vessels, fitting out meant preparation for a cruise— receiving any necessary repairs and taking on supplies before putting to sea. Coit's yard was able to do both types of fitting out. Dozens of vessels, including privateers and Continental vessels, were fitted out in New London Harbor during the war. Nathaniel Shaw and John Deshon played integral roles, mainly supervisory, in most of them.[43]

Coit's yard was a top target for the British. The entire complex, including the spar yard and company buildings and sheds, many containing tools, piles of lumber, rigging, and sails was set ablaze. Nearby, the British targeted the workshops and wharves of others involved in shipbuilding or the fitting out of vessels, like Joshua Starr a merchant and shipwright, Jonathan Starr a carpenter, Jonathan Douglass a cooper, Clark Elliott a nautical instrument maker, and John Way who operated a small candle and soap factory on his waterfront property, as well as his own store —from both of which he provided supplies to privateers.[44]

Incidentally, James Tilley, despite being a loyalist, was targeted. The British set his ropewalk, which stood near Tilley's house, ablaze. The large, wooden, shed-like structure, spanning the entire length of present-day Starr Street, was used to construct the massive amount of rope needed by sea going vessels. Ironically,

---

42 Robert Owen Decker, *Whaling City: A History of New London* (Guilford, CT, 1976), 20–22; *CG*, Oct. 12, 1781. All but one of Coit's houses were located on the Bank, the fourth was on Cape Ann Lane. Today, though filled in, Sparyard Street passes over the area the shipyard once encompassed.

43 Decker, *Whaling City*, 46–49; Caulkins, *New London*, 555–556. According to Caulkins, a part of Coit's shipyard was designated as a spar-yard, where masts and bowsprits were constructed.

44 Caulkins, *New London*, 554–555; "Accounts of the Continental Navy Brigantine Resistance," Ledger No. 26, Nathaniel and Thomas Shaw Papers, YUL, YU; *CG*, Oct. 12, 1781; James Lawrence Chew, "An Account of the Old Houses of New London," in *Records and Papers of the NLCHS*, 4 volumes (New London, CT, 1893), 4:95. Elliott lived in the house listed in the *Gazette* as the "Andrew Palmes house." Palmes died in the 1750s and willed the house to Elliott.

even as a loyalist, Tilley supplied rope for many privateers, and Continental naval vessels. At other times, he also sold them other items, like tar.[45]

Across from the Coit shipyard stood Nathaniel Shaw's mansion. Shaw was, however, not home. A few days prior, he went out on a fishing trip on Long Island Sound with Dr. Simon Wolcott. The two planned to return home that day, but upon discovering the British squadron, ran their schooner into Poquonnock Creek, in Groton, two miles east of the entrance to the harbor—and hid there. Soldiers visited Shaw's residence and probably would have burned it had it not been for Shaw's wife, Lucretia, who remained there during the British occupation. As leading patriots, Shaw and his brother, Thomas, suffered the highest financial losses that day.[46]

Initially, the British only burned Shaw's office and an adjacent storehouse, which was being used as a slaughterhouse. Both stood on the property, just east of the house. Out of the office, Shaw conducted much of his pre-war mercantile business, and during the war his responsibilities as a naval agent. Lucretia had earlier ordered the family's slaves to remove her husband's personal papers and account books out of town. They were able to save all but one chest, which was destroyed when the office was burned.[47]

In addition to those on Beach Street, Shaw lost two storehouses that stood opposite his house on the Bank. He also lost the privateer *Rochambeau*, a 16-gun snow, which lay tied to Coit's wharf. *Rochambeau* was set ablaze and cut loose, and then floated into the harbor.[48]

At the lower end of the Bank, along Bream Cove, the tannery owned by Peter Christopher and John Deshon was set ablaze. The leather manufactured at the tannery was sold to craftsmen who turned it into a variety of leather goods for both civilian and military usage, which included shoes, saddles, belts, sword

45 "Nathaniel Shaw Jr.'s Account Against The Connecticut Privateer Ship *General Putnam*," Ledger No. 9, Nathaniel and Thomas Shaw Papers, YUL, YU; "Accounts of the Continental Navy Brigantine *Resistance*," Ledger No. 26, Nathaniel and Thomas Shaw Papers, YUL, YU.

46 Caulkins, *New London*, 548; "Losses in New London during the British raid," Revolutionary War Records, Series III, Vol. I:95a–l, CSL. After the raid, their mercantile company placed a sizeable damage claim with the General Assembly of over £2,800 in property damage and £11,400 in destroyed merchandise.

47 Rogers, *Connecticut Naval Office*, 21–22; Charles M. Holloway, "Historic New London," *New England Magazine and Bay State Monthly*, Vol. 5, No. 1 (Nov. 1886): 136; *Morning News* (New London), Dec. 11, 1845. According to Brooks, the slaughterhouse sat on the eastern edge of Shaw's property and was operated by William Brooks.

48 Caulkins, *New London*, 555; *CG*, Oct. 12, 1781; *Naval Records*, 446; McManemin, *Captains of Privateers*, 92. The *Rochambeau* was formerly known as the *Le Despencer*, sometimes called the *Lady Spencer*, and was a former British packet vessel captured in 1778.

Nathaniel Shaw Jr. House. The house still stands today on Blinman Street. *Author*

scabbards, and cartridge boxes. All around the cove area, British soldiers set fire to wharves, boats, or fishing craft they could locate. This despite an elderly fisherman who ventured out and pleaded with the soldiers to spare his boat. According to Caulkins, they apologized, but they had their orders.[49]

As much damage as the British inflicted, they did spare large parts of the town. While some homes were damaged along Beach Street and the Bank, the majority were not set on fire, at least initially. Most of Congress Street, and the lower end of Town Street do not even seem to have been touched. This seems perplexing considering they contained the homes of some of New London's most well-known rebels, including Richard Law, who served as a county judge and a representative to the Continental Congress. Timothy Green's second print shop, on Congress Street, also survived the raid. In fact, Green resumed publication of the *Gazette* the following day. Bradley Street also remained largely untouched. This is largely believed because it was known as "Widow's Row"—a designation which was only partially true. Several widows did indeed reside there, but it also contained the

49 Caulkins, *New London*, 554; *CG*, Oct. 12, 1781, Aug. 13, 1790.

Bradley Street. Today most of what remains of the street is now Atlantic Avenue. *Author*

homes of notable merchants, including Jonathan Brooks and William and Joseph Packwood, the latter two of which were heavily involved in the privateer service.[50]

50 *CG*, Sep. 7, 1781.

Chapter Ten

The Battle of New London:
The Evacuation of the Town

At around 2:00 p.m. the British started their evacuation of New London. Arnold emerged from the Miller house and mounting his horse, thanked Miller, and began to supervise the withdrawal. Forming up outside the house along the Bank, the 38th Regiment led the column, followed by Horndon's artillery, then the Loyal American Regiment, and the American Legion. The jaegers and Associated Loyalists were assigned to the rear guard.

Marching with them were 22 American prisoners, a number which included thirteen militiamen, eight sailors and one civilian. Seven additional prisoners, those taken at Fort Trumbull and Fort Nonsense, would meet them on the *Amphion*. The militia were mainly members of the 1st and 2nd Companies, and the Independent Company of Artillery. But also included were members of the 7th Company and at least one member from the 14th Company from eastern Lyme.[1]

The sailors in custody included mariners from both the Continental navy and the privateer service. Among them were William Tyrone and William Bell, both of whom had served in the Continental navy. Tyrone had served with John Paul Jones on the sloop *Providence* and ship *Alfred*, while Bell had served on the frigate

---

1 Royal Navy Ships' Muster (Series 1), HMS *Amphion*, ADM 36/9561, TNA; Book, "Connecticut Independent Company," NLCHS; "A List of the First Alarm List Company in the 3d Regt of Militia in this State under the Command of Capt John Deshon," NLCHS; "A List of Towars [Tours] Off Duty Dun by the Oficrs And Privete Belonging to the furst Comy In the 3d Rigment," NLCHS; *CG*, Feb. 14, 1772.

Confederacy. Bell was an indentured servant to Joshua Starr, who lived near Long Bridge and was assuredly captured during the fight through the town.[2]

The British also took with them Benajah Donham, who had just been released from British captivity. Donham had been employed by the commissary department in Rhode Island and been captured just prior to the British evacuation of Newport. He was passing through on his way home to Plainfield, Connecticut, when he joined in the defense of the town. But now he was headed back into captivity.[3]

Elisha Beckwith, a loyalist from Lyme, also joined the British as they withdrew, but for his own safety. Beckwith had been on his way home from Rhode Island, where he had been employed by British intelligence to gather information on the French navy. Having escaped authorities in New London in the past on charges of spying for the enemy, Beckwith was not about to risk it again. Rightly fearing brutal reprisals, he fled town under Arnold's protection.[4]

The British left most of their wounded behind in New London. In 1785, a petition was submitted to the General Assembly on behalf of the selectmen of Norwich asking for reimbursement for the care and guarding of British prisoners. The petition stated "that on the 6th of September 1781 Twenty one prisoners of war taken at New London and some of them wounded" were sent to Norwich. This was roughly the same number of British wounded and missing. There they were housed and cared for by the town in a storehouse owned by Ebenezer Backus at Norwich Landing.[5]

As far as we know, there were few, if any, wagons containing any captured public or military stores with the column. The same went for plundered property belonging to civilians. There is no evidence of any large-scale effort made by Arnold to take with him anything. None of Shepherd's vessels, which would have assuredly

---

2 *Connecticut Men*, 601; New London Land Records, Volume 25:207, CSL; *Naval Documents* VIII:43, 47. Bell was described in the land record as a "servant to Joshua Starr," and he was granted permission by Starr to purchase a piece of land, near Long Bridge, in 1787.

3 Middlebrook, *Maritime Connecticut*, 2:164; PA: Benajah Denham (S.30379), NARA. Denham's last name is listed at times as Donham or Dunham.

4 American Loyalist Claims, 1776–1835, AO 13/26/37-38, TNA; *CG*, Nov. 30, 1781. He was employed by Capt. George Beckwith and Col. Beverly Robinson. Beckwith returned home in November where he was captured by soldiers of Capt. John Johnson's Coast Guard Company, under Ensign Andrew Griswold. He was held for several months at New-Gate Prison, in Simsbury (now East Granby), CT, but eventually escaped and returned to British lines.

5 "Petition showing 21 prisoners of war taken at New London Sep 1781 & a part of them cared for in Norwich by Ebenezer Backus;" Revolutionary War Records (1763–1789) Series I, XXVIII:265, CSL. It is unclear why, but the word British is crossed out in the original petition.

carried these goods or stores, ever approached the town. If any British soldier took anything, they carried it on their person during the march out of town.[6]

In a letter, Governor Trumbull revealed "the enemy had reembarked with precipitation and without any great booty." This was an interesting revelation and unusual for Arnold, especially considering his actions during the Virginia expedition. Then, there were numerous documented instances of pillaging not only by the soldiers but by Arnold himself. A German officer stated the expedition "resembled those of the freebooters, who sometimes at sea, sometimes ashore, ravaged and laid wasted [to] everything. Terrible things happened on this excursion; Churches and holy places were plundered." When Richmond was captured, Arnold sent over forty vessels downriver to Portsmouth loaded with all kinds of items meant for resale. Even Major Mackenzie privately penned in his diary, "The love of money, [Arnold's] ruling passion, has been very conspicuous in Virginia." For reasons that are not understood nothing to that extant happened in New London. Perhaps Arnold felt something for his former friends. We shall never know for sure.[7]

After the British column re-crossed Bream Cove at the Long Bridge, Arnold again ordered flankers to protect the main force as it moved south towards the light house. The task was again assigned to the American Legion. As soon as Frink's Company crossed the bridge, it turned southward down the Hog Neck Highway, as it would protect the left of the column, closest to the river. As the redcoats passed over Hog Neck, they set at least one more house ablaze. It was later identified by New London historian, R. B. Wall, as belonging to Isaac Fellows.[8]

Wogan's Company, now under a lieutenant, remained with the main column until it crossed Haughton's Brook near the Holt house. There, moving in a column,

6 There is nothing to suggest the march back to the squadron was hindered by the transportation of any large amount of plunder. The initial march from the lighthouse to the Parade, four miles, took three hours and the return march on the same route took roughly the same amount of time.

7 Jonathan Trumbull Sr. to Jonathan Trumbull Jr., Sep. 10, 1781, Governor Trumbull Papers, 15:120, CSL; Ewald, *Diary*, 268–269; Heath to Governor Trumbull, Sep. 23, 1781, Governor Trumbull Papers, 15:150a–b, CSL; Mackenzie, *Diary*, 2:540. Heath told Trumbull the same, writing, "I have from a person who saw them-Arnold brought back little plunder."

8 R. B. Wall, "When The Traitor Arnold Burned New London Town: Part 3" *The Day*, Dec. 4, 1914; Caulkins, *New London*, 554; Hempstead narrative in Harris, *Groton Heights*, 56; *CG*, Oct. 12, 1781; "Losses of New London Sufferers By The Ravages of the British Army," Revolutionary War Records, 3rd Series, June 1765–May 1820, 95a–l, CSL. It was presumed that Isaac Fellows did not reside in the house at the time. He never submitted a damage claim to the General Assembly. It was probably either occupied by family members of his family, possibly, his son-in-law, Daniel Tinker, his wife, and family. Tinker did submit a house damage claim. Another scenario is that Sgt. Stephen Hempstead rented the house or that both Tinker and Hempstead shared the house. Caulkins referenced a house and shop at the south end of town being burned, and assured her readers it was lived in by someone who held a commission at Fort Trumbull. Sergeant Hempstead lost his house and submitted a damage claim.

it deployed to the right of the main column. As Wogan's and Frink's companies protected the main column, they did so without any interference from the militia. As such, some took the opportunity to wreck and plunder farms along their route of march.

From available information, much of the plundering was done by soldiers in the American Legion, as most of the recorded destruction occurred on farms along the Harbor Road. This was the same route taken by Frink's soldiers to and from New London. Almost every family who lived along the road submitted substantial claims to the General Assembly for damage done to their homes and properties. This appears to back up the assertion of the militia captain, whose members resided in that part of town, when he said these families "ware exposed to the ravagis of the Enemy." The *Connecticut Gazette* told a similar story: "At the Harbour's Mouth the Houses of poor Fishermen were stripped of all their Furniture of every kind: The poor People having nothing left but the Cloths they had on." The *Gazette's* account was somewhat embellished, as not all were fishermen, nor were their homes set ablaze.[9]

The hardest hit was the widow Sarah Harris, who presented the General Assembly with a damage claim of £186 for her home, a very substantial amount of money for the time. Harris resided in the house with her son, Ezra, a half-mile north of the lighthouse. Her house lay east near Brown's farm, overlooking the mouth of the harbor. Frink's soldiers broke into the house and ransacked and rummaged through every room. Numerous items, including furniture, were stolen and eventually strewn along the road. One item, a desk, displayed later during the centennial of the raid, was believed to be an item left behind by the Frink's men. According to the New London County History Society, which was in possession of the desk at the time, a soldier entered the Harris house, picked through the items in the desk, and then removed it from the house. After he carried it outside, he abandoned it in the road a short distance from the house. Fortunately, the Harris house was not burned, and Sarah later operated a tavern out of it. It was not only furniture left behind by the soldiers, but horses stolen from pastures and barns. Unable to take them aboard the vessels in the squadron, they were set loose.[10]

9 *CG*, Oct. 5, 1781; "Losses in New London during the British raid," Revolutionary War Records, Series III, Vol. I:95a–l, CSL. An examination of these records reveals that at least seven heads of household, including Lydia Harris, John Harris, Bridget Harris, Edward Tinker, Amos Lester, Walter Harris, and Sarah Harris, submitted claims of £25 or more.

10 *CG*, Sep. 14, 1781, June 6, 1783; *Catalogue of Articles Shown At The Groton Heights Centennial Loan Exhibition, Groton, CT; Sept. 6, 7, and 8, 1881* (Groton, CT, 1881), 19. The Harris house, no longer standing, was located opposite where the Pequot house was later built.

The Explosions

As the British column trudged uneventfully up Town Hill, several successive explosions were heard coming from along the Bank. According to witnesses, the explosions "shook the whole country round." The cause, Arnold reported, was "a large quantity of powder unknown to us." That quantity of gunpowder was kept in a storehouse, near or at the Coit shipyard, opposite Jeremiah Miller's house. When the storehouse was set on fire, it had not been thoroughly searched. The barrels of gunpowder had not been removed or dumped out. Instead, when the flames reached the part of the structure where the barrels were stacked, the building exploded. [11]

The blast sent smoke, debris, and flames in every direction. Aided by an easterly breeze coming off the river, combined with the already set fires, the flames rapidly spread so that the entire Bank and nearby areas, which included thirty-eight more homes, were either instantly engulfed in flames or imminently threatened by them.

These fires do not appear to have been intentionally set but rather resulted from the explosion of gunpowder in one of the storehouses. The fires lay unattended for almost an hour between the British evacuation of the town and the American reoccupation of it. Most of these were situated on the east side of the street, closest to the waterfront. On the opposite side stood many homes. Frantic civilians inside started panicking, throwing furniture, clothes, and other valuables out through doors and windows onto the street in a desperate attempt to save them. Many of these items were later looted by militia and other vagrants.[12]

Sparks hit the roof of the Nathaniel Shaw mansion, which set it on fire. Fortunately, for Shaw, a neighbor rushed to the assistance of Lucretia in the house and went into the attic, and reportedly, put it out with either a cask or a scuttle of vinegar, and saved the house.[13]

The same flames also spread to the homes of Jeremiah Miller and James Tilley. Arnold's visit with Miller had not gone unnoticed. The *Massachusetts Spy* printed, "We hear that Arnold when he landed at New-London, dined at a gentleman's

11 Master's Log, HMS *Amphion*, ADM 52/2133, TNA. The log reports "several Explosions of Powder in the town" at 2:30 p.m.

12 Arnold report in Mackenzie, *Diary*, 2:626; Caulkins, *New London*, 556; Harris, *Groton Heights*, 26–27; *CG*, Sep. 28, 1781. The cause of the explosions was either negligence or the pressure the British were under to destroy as much as they could as fast as possible, leaving no time to conduct a full search.

13 Rogers, *Naval Office*, 73; Caulkins, *New London*, 555. The neighbor who lived in the Christopher house has often been identified as someone who lived next-door to the Shaw mansion. It afterwards earned the name, the "Vinegar house." Owned by the Christopher family, it is unclear who resided in the house at the time. The c. 1746 house was demolished sometime in the late 20th century.

house with whom he was formerly acquainted. After dinner, he ordered the house to be plundered and set on fire." Even though this was not the case, the Continental press used the incident to further demonize Arnold by telling its readers Arnold even burned the homes of his friends.[14]

The truth was quite the opposite. When Arnold later discovered Miller's house had been destroyed, he secretly sent Miller money through the lines to help him. After the war, when Miller applied to the British government for compensation for his losses during the raid, Arnold testified for him. Arnold explained, "[W]hen the Public Stores on Wharfs opposite [Miller's house] were Set on Fire, by my orders . . . [t]he Flames by an Explosion of Gunpowder, not known to be in the Stores were communicated to [Miller's] houses, Stores in which the Greatest part of their Contents were consumed." Miller even defended Arnold, stating, "I dont mean to blame Genl Arnold for it, the circumstances of the winds was such that on firing the Stores, the houses took fire also."[15]

As the flames spread, they consumed the entire Parade area. The county courthouse, St. James Church, the jail, the jailer's house, and even a barber shop, were all ablaze. One witness stated, "[one] could not pass that way . . . the smoke was so dense . . . no object whatever could be discovered. From there the flames spread northward onto Beach Street and consumed three buildings at its south end—a tavern operated by Abigail Potter and the homes of her neighbors, Bathsheba Smith, and Elijah Richards. Had it not been for a group of militia and citizens who came out to fight the fires, they would have consumed the homes on Bradley and Congress Streets.[16]

It was not only the land that was on fire but also the harbor. Observing from the *Amphion*, Bazely saw "several vessells in the Harbour on Fire." These were the privateers and other vessels set ablaze. Arnold's troops moved so fast there was no attempt made to account for each vessel destroyed, as was often done during such

---

14 *Massachusetts Spy*, Sep. 13, 1781; *New London Daily Star*, Apr. 25, 1866. The American version worsened and within a century, it was believed "[Arnold] had the effrontery to enter a house where often he had been honorably entertained as a guest, and there satisfy his hunger from the plunder of the pantry; and when he had finished his repast, he ordered the house to be fired."

15 American Loyalist Claims, 1776–1835, AO 13/42/96-106, 126-132, TNA. After the raid, in addition to Arnold's help, Miller also received monetary donations from Col. Beverly Robinson. Miller also successfully played both sides after the war. He made two property damage claims, one to the Americans and the other to the British and received compensation from both sides. Most of the documentation included in his British claim consisted of copies of the information submitted during his American claim.

16 Arnold report in Mackenzie, *Diary*, 2:626; *Norwich Packet*, Sep. 13, 1781; Harris, *Groton Heights*, 25–27; Caulkins, *New London*, 556; Brooks narrative in Harris, *Groton Heights*, 81–82. The *Norwich Packet*, a newspaper not friendly to the British, corroborated Arnold's statement, and printed "the wind being something high, soon communicated [the fire] to the dwelling houses."

expeditions. Arnold estimated "Ten or twelve of the Enemy's ships were burnt: among them three or four armed vessels, and one loaded with Naval Stores." As of today, twelve vessels which were damaged or destroyed can be identified with some certainty.[17]

Five of the vessels destroyed were privateers. Two, the brig *Venus* and the prize brig *Syren*, were owned by Thomas Mumford & Co. and had been burned by retreating Americans. The schooner *Gamecock*, owned by John Deshon & Co., and the 16-gun snow *Rochambeau*, owned by Nathaniel Shaw, were both burned by the British. Likewise the 10-gun sloop *Active*, owned by John Wright & Co., which lay at a wharf with one of its masts out for repair, fell to British flames.[18]

The remaining seven ships destroyed were prize vessels. Two have already been mentioned: *Hannah* and *Arbuthnot*; an unnamed sloop, captured by the *Hancock*, *Active* and *Deane*; the brig *Margaret & Mary*, a prize to the brig *Jay*; the brig *Jenny*, a prize to the *Deane*; the pettiauger *Betsey*, a prize to the galley *Black Joak*; and the brig *Hope*, a prize to the Pennsylvania letter of marque *Navarre*. The *Hope* was in the harbor and caught fire from flying debris and was partially damaged, though only the awning above its quarter-deck was burned.[19]

These burning vessels presented a legitimate danger to the squadron. If they drifted too far downriver, they could damage Shepherd's vessels. The *Hannah* drifted without direction into the harbor, but fortunately for the British, it sank near the entrance to Winthrop Cove. At least one vessel, the *Rochambeau*, however, drifted southward towards Shepherd's vessels. Captain Bazely reacted by ordering the *Amphion* to run up the hazard signal, warning the squadron to stay alert. While the "fire ships" caused a scare, none damaged any British vessel.[20]

17 Master's Log, HMS *Amphion*, ADM 52/2133, TNA; Arnold report in Mackenzie, *Diary*, 2:626.

18 McManemin, *Captains of Privateers*, 92; Middlebrook, *Maritime Connecticut*, 2:48–49, 93, 239–240; *CG*, July 20, 1781, Sep. 28, 1781; 1781, 4. The *Active* was severely damaged but did not sink. Deemed unrepairable, it was auctioned off in pieces in Oct.

19 *CG*, Aug. 17, 1781, Aug. 21, 1781, Aug. 24, 1781, Aug. 31, 1781; *Pennsylvania Packet*, Sep. 29, 1781; McManemin, *Captains of Privateers*, 96–97. The *Siren* (or *Syren*) was formerly a Massachusetts privateer from Marblehead which had been captured sometime in Aug. When the British frigate chased her, the crew attempted to increase her speed by throwing her guns overboard and was still unarmed when she was taken by the *Deane* off New York and arrived in New London just days before the attack. The unnamed sloop was carrying wood when it was captured in the Fire Island Inlet. It presumably belonged to or was hired by the British Quartermaster Department to gather wood for use by the garrison in New York. The *Margaret & Mary* was captured in July bound from Waterford, Ireland to NY. The *Jenny* was a copper-bottom brig bound from Jamaica to England with a cargo of rum and sugar. The *Betsey* was set to be auctioned on Aug. 31 but disappears from the historical record after the attack.

20 Caulkins, *New London*, 553; Rogers, *Naval Office*, 24; Master's Log, HMS *Amphion*, ADM 52/2133, TNA.

The Pursuit of the British Column

As the British withdrew amidst the rapidly spreading flames, a courier reached Col. Jonathan Latimer, near the Daniel Latimer farm. The courier carried with him word of the 20th Regiment of Connecticut Militia fast approaching on the Norwich Road. Receiving the news, Latimer left the Latimer farm and rode back to Quaker Hill. When he reached the spot, he found Col. Zabdiel Rogers, in command of the 20th Regiment. The two had known each other for years. Rogers, a 44-year-old shopkeeper and merchant was, like Latimer, an experienced militia commander though he had not seen much combat. In 1776, then a major, Rogers led the regiment when it was sent to New York to aid Washington's army. For the next five years, his service kept him within Connecticut's borders. Rogers received promotion to lieutenant colonel in 1777 and then to colonel in mid-1781.[21]

The 20th Regiment was from Norwich, which then included the towns of Bozrah, Franklin, Sprague, and Lisbon. The regiment consisted of ten trainband companies, eight alarm list companies, two independent companies—the Norwich Light Infantry and Veteran Guards—and an artillery company. In all, on paper, the regiment numbered 500 to 700 men. The regiment was unique in one aspect: it also had an artillery company. That company garrisoned the Norwich fort, which overlooked the Thames River at Waterman's Point, just south of Norwich Landing. But in cases of alarm, the company—numbering around 30 men and officers—was equipped with two wrought-iron four pounders mounted on field carriages, which, pulled by horses, could march with the regiment.[22]

Rogers was home, at around 10:00 a.m., when he received word from a rider, probably Samuel Raymond, of the impending British attack. Rogers immediately sent out orders through Lt. Simeon Huntington, his adjutant, to his commanders to gather their companies. Most companies gathered on the Norwich Green, outside the Congregational Meetinghouse, a short distance from Arnold's birthplace. According to one, the regiment was mustered with "hot haste & with as much military order as the occasion would admit." Marching with Rogers were most of his ten trainband companies, including the Norwich Light Infantry, led by Capt.

---

21 Zabdiel Rogers to Governor Trumbull, Sep. 7, 1781, Governor Trumbull Papers, Vol. 4, Folder 6, CHS; *CSR*, 1:264, 3:54.

22 Francis Manwaring Caulkins, *History of Norwich, Connecticut: From Its Possession by the Indians to the Year 1866* (Hartford, 1873), 388; "A Return of the 3rd Brigade of Militia in the State of Connecticut Aug 1, 1780," Governor Trumbull Papers, 24:106, 123, CSL; Hinman, *Historical Collections*, 469, 494, 529. The fort was constructed during the summer of 1775 to protect the riverway approach to Norwich. It no longer exists but was located somewhere along modern-day West Thames Street.

Norwich Green. Present-day view of the site where the 20th Regiment of Connecticut Milita assembled before they marched to New London. *Author*

Christopher Leffingwell, and the Artillery Company, under Captain-Lieutenant Isaac Abel, with a 4-pounder fieldpiece.[23]

The regiment's route southward was along the Norwich Road. At the time, the road was "little better than an Indian trail. Its numerous windings, fords, and precipitous hills made it both inconvenient and hazardous." The regiment took some three or four hours to cover the roughly ten miles but began arriving on Quaker Hill about the same time the British were retreating.[24]

In the weeks following the attack, Rogers was criticized for the time it took to get his regiment to New London. He was later investigated for his supposed tardiness, as was his second-in-command, Maj. Benajah Leffingwell. Both were eventually acquitted, the charges being determined as having no merit.[25]

23 PA; Joshua Yeomans (W.20145); Isaac Williams (S.15719), NARA; L.H. Sigourney, *Life and Letters* (New York, 1866), 16; Rogers to Governor Trumbull, Sep. 7, 1781, Governor Trumbull Papers, Vol. 4, Folder 6, CHS; "Account of distributing regimental orders, 1781–82," Revolutionary War Records, Series I, XXV:176, CSL. *Life and Letters* is a collection of reminiscences from Sigourney whose father was Ezekiel Huntley and a member of the 3rd Company under Capt. Isaac Johnson.

24 Caulkins, *Norwich*, 529–530; PA; Elijah Waterman (S.7825); Dyer Crocker (S.22710); Obadiah Hudson (R.5337), NARA. Waterman belonged to the 7th Company and arrived to see the British retreating. Crocker was part of the 6th Company under Capt. Nehemiah Waterman and witnessed the town in flames. Hudson was in the 9th Company under Capt. John Waterman and arrived somewhere between 2:00 p.m. and 4:00 p.m.

25 Harris, *Groton Heights*, 116–117; *CG*, Jan. 10, 1783; PA; Daniel Kingsbury (W.20324), NARA. The one detail Kingsbury's wife Martha remembered of the raid was how her husband came home and complained bitterly about Rogers's sluggishness.

Upon their arrival, Dyer Crocker, of the 6th Company, stated "[they] found the town in flames." They were prepared for action, but the march had been tough. With the heat, distance, and terrain, they were exhausted. During the last few miles, they were motivated when a rider passed along the column, shouting, "New London is in flames!" Even so, stragglers continued to catch up into the following day.[26]

Atop Quaker Hill, the regiment worked its way through the mass of refugees. It was truly a heart-wrenching scene, as one soldier remembered, to see so many "sobbing children [clinging] to their bewildered mothers." Reaching the summit, Rogers halted the regiment and allowed soldiers time for rest and for stragglers to catch up, while he and Lt. Simeon Huntington, rode to find Colonel Latimer.[27]

When Rogers found Latimer, the two were happy to see each other. Watching the two colonels converse, Jonathan Brooks waited impatiently a short distance away. He desired to speak with Latimer because, as he later claimed, he wanted to get back into town and thought the colonel might help him. When he last saw his mother, she asked him to find his two missing brothers who were thought to be at the family home on Bradley Street. Whether he embellished his reasoning years later is not known, but Brooks wrote he attempted to "enter the town at all hazards." At one point, as Brooks remembered it, "I . . . pushed for the town, but was immediately stopped by a sentinel, who inquired where I was going. I replied, 'into New London.'" The sentinel was a member of either Caulkins's or Deshon's Companies.

He told Brooks, "you cannot go, the enemy are there." The soldier, sensing Brooks's resolve, grabbed the bridle of his horse and brought him to Latimer.[28]

Brooks thought he could speak with Latimer as the two colonels were about to make a reconnaissance. But as Brooks approached Latimer, the colonel told him to go away, he was busy, and not to go into town. Latimer and Rogers rode off towards high ground, east of the Norwich Road, onto the northern part of the Winthrop estate. However, without any documentation, we are left to speculate as to the exact purpose of the reconnaissance. It was presumably to confirm reports which by then had reached Latimer of a supposed British withdrawal and if it was feasible to attack them.[29]

---

26 Dyer Crocker Pension Application, (S.22710), NARA; Sigourney, *Life*, 16.

27 Brooks narrative in Harris, *Groton Heights*, 80; Sigourney, *Life*, 16.

28 Brooks narrative in Harris, *Groton Heights*, 80; *CSR*, 5:192; "Account of distributing regimental orders, 1781–82," Revolutionary War Records, Series I, XXV:176, CSL.

29 The area from where they conducted their reconnaissance was likely near today's Riverside Park.

As Arnold withdrew, he was concerned the militia might mount a pursuit of his retreating force. He realized that until he reached the lighthouse, where he would be under the protection of the squadron, his force was vulnerable to being attacked. Even though he had defeated the militia earlier, Arnold had no clear knowledge of current rebel strength or organization and had to prepare for the likelihood that he was now outnumbered.

Arnold had ordered the jaegers and the Associated Loyalists to form as his rearguard. Their task was to protect the withdrawing British force. If the militia launched a pursuit, the rearguard units would stand in the way, skirmishing, and maneuvering, attempting to slow it down. This would give the main force more time either to reach the squadron or to prepare to resist an attack.

After giving the main force an hour's time, the rearguard began to withdraw at around 3:00 p.m. On Post Hill, Upham's two companies gradually started pulling their dispersed commands back over the hill, but as they did the militia watched their every move. Captain Lord, Captain Harris, and Sergeant Worthington ordered their companies to advance. As they did, Maj. Daniel Cone and Lt. Amasa Brainard's Company joined them. Together, the four companies followed the Colchester Road eastward up Post Hill. Concurrently, Caulkins's Company moved across Mill Brook so that it was moving almost perpendicular to the militia moving on its western slope.[30]

The two opposing sides continued to exchange gunfire, but the sudden pursuit by the militia and the fact they were coming at them from two sides made some loyalist soldiers nervous. As they passed the Colfax house, they decided to leave their wounded behind.[31]

Upham then continuously fell back in the direction of Cape Ann Lane. The militia easily recaptured the hill. A party from Lord's Company was sent into the Colfax house, where, according to one militiaman, they found three wounded enemy soldiers who were taken prisoner.[32]

As the militia moved towards Post Hill, Capt. Richard Deshon realized the jaegers were also withdrawing. Atop the hill, Captain von Wangenheim returned

---

30 *CG*, Sep. 7, 1781; *CT Journal*, Sep. 13, 1781; PA: Abraham Osborn (S.14061); Timothy Fuller (W.17974), NARA. Osborn, a member of Cone's Company, stated they arrived "as the British were retreating to their shipping."

31 Charles Allyn Papers, NLCHS; James Lawrence Chew, "An Account of the Old Houses of New London," in *Records and Papers of the NLCHS*, 3 vols. (New London, CT, 1890), 1:87. Blood stains from the wounded loyalists remained on the floors of the Colfax house for several decades.

32 PA: Hoel Huntley (S.18043), NARA. It is not known with any certainty the exact strength of either company, but by this time both companies included a mix of militia from New London, Lyme, and Colchester.

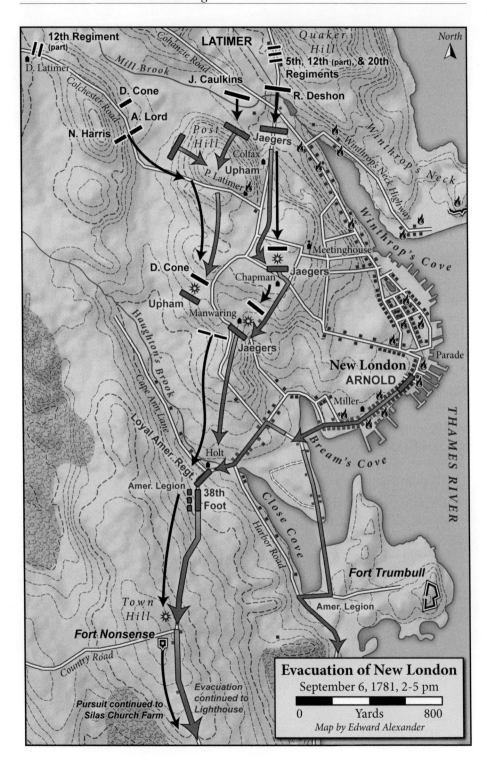

Evacuation of New London
September 6, 1781, 2–5 pm

0   Yards   800

Map by Edward Alexander

to maneuvering his riflemen in two platoons, which enabled him to stagger their withdrawal and leave the hill without being molested. Deshon's men pursued them, advancing across Mill Brook and doing their best to advance in unison with Caulkins's Company as it moved on Post Hill. Deshon's Company passed through the burial ground without opposition, but as it entered the town the jaegers were waiting for them.

One platoon of jaegers halted a quarter mile south of the meetinghouse, inside a two-story wooden house owned by Richard Chapman, in later years known as Belcher's Tavern. The house occupied by the jaegers stood at the beginning of the Colchester Road, where it intersected with modern-day Hempstead Street, known then as "the road to the meetinghouse." The remaining jaegers retreated towards Manwaring Hill.[33]

Deshon's militia spotted the jaegers and approached cautiously. Once they were in view, the jaegers opened fire. Joshua Smith of Deshon's Company thought that since they were so well-positioned they intended to make a stand. Once Deshon realized, however, that the jaegers only occupied a single building, he ordered his company to storm it. Deshon's men complied and swept down the hill, some even halting to exchange fire with the enemy. But as Deshon's men neared the house, the jaegers fled. It was a quick fight, according to Smith, who stated the "[jaegers] were soon driven from there by Deshon."[34]

Deshon continued in pursuit. A few minutes later, the company spotted more jaegers a short distance away and prepared to engage them. This platoon of jaegers had broken into the main Chapman house where Richard and his family lived. There, they rummaged through the first floor and before leaving, planned to set it on fire. As Deshon's Company approached them, a few jaegers were removing "two large crocks of lard" out of the cellar. They cracked open the canisters and planned to use their contents to fuel the fire. But as they did, Deshon's men attacked. The jaegers quickly dropped the canisters and retreated towards Manwaring Hill.[35]

Atop Manwaring Hill, more jaegers occupied the Robert Manwaring house, the scene of fighting earlier that afternoon. Having halted there for some time, they plundered and wrecked the house. Caulkins, in her *History of New London*, described the scene: "[T]hey ransacked [the house], and having wantonly

33 James Lawrence Chew "Famous Old Taverns of New London," in *Records and Papers of the NLCHS, Part I, Vol. 2 (1895-1904)* (New London, CT 1890), 84. Hempstead Street is often called the "road to the meetinghouse" in period documents.

34 Charles Allyn Papers, NLCHS.

35 R. B. Wall, "When Traitor Arnold Burned New London Town, Part 1," *The Day*, Dec. 2, 1914. Wall incorrectly places the event happening earlier in the afternoon, but this clearly occurred during the British retreat.

Chapman House Site. The house occupied by the jaegers once stood here at the
present-day intersection of Broad and Hempstead Streets. *Author*

destroyed some of the furniture, set fire to it, by leaving heaps of burning brands
and combustibles upon the floor."[36]

Deshon saw these jaegers and again yielded to prudence before sending his
men forward. He briefly halted near the Chapman house, and after a scan of the
situation, ordered Sgt. Samuel Whaley to take a party and storm the Manwaring
house. The rest of the company would provide cover. Despite being a veteran of
Saratoga, Whaley remembered this attack as one of the proudest moments of his
military service.[37]

By now, the jaegers atop Manwaring Hill knew the Americans were
approaching. The sides exchanged fire and then most of the jaegers, not wanting to
risk being captured, fled towards the Holt house, leaving a trail of items from the
Manwaring house strewn across the property. Also left behind was the abandoned
12-pounder cannon from earlier.

36 Caulkins, *New London*, 551.

37 PA: Samuel Whaley (R.11366), NARA.

Sergeant Whaley and his party raced up the hill and headed directly for the Manwaring house, where a few jaegers lingered, attempting to set the house ablaze. As the Americans advanced, they were fired upon by retreating jaegers, but this did little to hold Whaley's men back. They soon reached the house and burst in through the door. Behind the door, a jaeger waited with his loaded rifle. But as Whaley led the way into the house, the jaeger, unable to discharge his weapon, was tackled onto the floor. He was one of two jaegers taken prisoner during the brief assault. From one prisoner Thomas Rogers, a member of Whaley's party, secured a powder horn and cartridge box, which he took home as souvenirs. After putting out the fires, the militiamen resumed the pursuit.[38]

While Deshon's men attacked Manwaring Hill, the militia on Post Hill, some under Lt. Amasa Brainard of the 25th Regiment of Connecticut Militia, moved in pursuit of Upham. In fact, according to contemporary sources, the militia acted independently and formed themselves into parties and set out in pursuit of the retreating enemy, whom they reported "gauled them sorely."[39]

However, again, there seemed to be no overall coordination between the parties. They may well have acted on their own initiative, as there is no evidence any orders came from Latimer to pursue the retreating British. To the contrary, Latimer had one of his officers, Capt. John Hempsted, arrested as the captain attempted to join the pursuit on his own.[40]

Latimer had other problems. As the day wore on, reinforcements continued to arrive, and they needed direction. First, it was the 20th Regiment. Then the 5th Regiment of Connecticut Militia and 12th Regiment of Connecticut Militia arrived throughout the afternoon. Later, they were joined by the 21st Regiment of Connecticut Militia. They were all from the 5th Brigade of Connecticut Militia and were without their brigade commander. So was the 7th Regiment of Connecticut Militia, of the 2nd Brigade of Connecticut Militia, which began arriving that evening. Latimer could not have undisciplined militia wandering around without orders.[41]

---

38 Ibid., PA: Thomas Rogers (S.14343), NARA.

39 *Norwich Packet*, Sep. 13, 1781.

40 "Russell Smith Deposition," NLCHS. Hempsted may have been arrested because Latimer had not seen him all day and he may have appeared to have shirked his duty. Hempsted's guard at the Daniel Latimer house was seen by members of the 12th Regiment of Connecticut Militia.

41 John Hempsted narrative in Harris, *Groton Heights*, 67. Hempsted recalled, "[I] Sett out agane to follow the Enemy, but passing Daniel Latimers, whare I suppose thare was a hundred men, I past them and had gott 20 or 30 Rods By, Colo. Latimer Cauld me to Cum back. I Repl'd I could not, I was In Persute of the enemy. His Reply to me was, I command You to com back . . . he Detaned mee abot [one half hour] & Sent with me 2 other men."

Nevertheless, the pursuit continued with or without orders from Colonel Latimer, as Upham later wrote: "We took the same route in our return as in going up, equally exposed, though not so much annoyed." The militia pursued Upham's men southward across the farm and house lots, often running from stonewall to stonewall and exchanging fire with Upham's soldiers who were doing the same a short distance away, staggering their withdrawal by company. A member of Caulkins's Company, Israel Rogers, remembered, "the enemy continued to retreat, and some skirmishing took place . . . as they advanced from wall to wall on the retreating foe." Another militiaman, Pierce Mobbs, of East Haddam, who was involved in the pursuit, became a celebrity when he returned home. It was said of Mobbs, "he would dodge so quick the British could not hit him."[42]

At one point, militia sent from Post Hill caught up with a company of Associated Loyalists on a farm lot 300 yards west of the Robert Manwaring house, owned by Samuel Gardiner, and as the two sides exchanged fire, at least one loyalist was wounded and dropped to the ground. Unable to carry him away, he was left behind as the others continued to withdraw. The advancing militia took the 18-year-old prisoner and transported him to the Manwaring house where he was carried inside and laid on a bed. The family found him when they returned home that night "piteously calling out for water." Before he died several hours later, the soldier gave his name, and requested his family, then in Nova Scotia, be notified of his fate. He was later buried near the property.[43]

By retaking Manwaring Hill, the Americans had effectively recaptured the town, but the pursuit continued. As it did, the number of pursuers gradually decreased, probably due to exhaustion, the continued shortage of available ammunition and gunpowder, and militia breaking away to help contain the fires.[44]

---

42 Upham report in Harris, *Groton Heights*, 110; PA: Timothy Fuller (W.179/4); Israel Rogers (S.14383), NARA. In Fuller's pension application, Aaron Gates Jr. made a statement on Fuller's behalf. Gates implies that his father, Aaron Sr., Timothy Fuller, Jonathan Fuller, Pierce Mobbs, and Lieutenant Brainard, participated in the pursuit of the British. Rogers also stated, "they succeeded in killing several officers & men," but this cannot be substantiated.

43 American Loyalist Claims, 1776–1835, AO 13/45/347-349, TNA; John Hempsted narrative in Harris, *Groton Heights*, 67; Caulkins, *New London*, 551; R. B. Wall, "When Traitor Arnold Burned New London Town, Part 1," *The Day*, Dec. 2, 1914. The name of the soldier was unfortunately lost to history. While never identified as a field hospital, the Manwaring house bears all the characteristics of one, such as wounded soldiers laid on beds, burials on the property, etc. This might be the reason why within twenty years, the family demolished the house and rebuilt a new one on the same lot.

44 Arnold report in Mackenzie, *Diary*, 2:628; Jonathan Brooks narrative in Harris, *Groton Heights*, 82; PA: Timothy Fuller (W.17974), NARA. According to Fuller, the militia, the day after the battle, wanted to un-spike and fire one of Fort Griswold's cannon at the British in the harbor. In the process of planning it, Fuller stated they did not have gunpowder and had to send to Norwich for it. The cannon was never fired.

The running skirmish continued southward towards the Holt house and then down the Quagonapoxet Highway. As one militiaman recalled, "Our militia hung upon their flank and rear and picked off here and there a man." As it went down the highway, it was in full view to sailors on the *Beaumont*. Its commander, Lt. William Scott, watching it, noted in the ship's master's log "the Rebels following and firing on [our] Rear[guard]."[45]

At around 4:00 p.m. somewhere near Fort Nonsense, the two sides exchanged fire and the jaegers inflicted at least two casualties on their pursuers. Samuel Booth Hempstead, of the 1st Company Alarm List, and Jonathan Whaley, of the 5th Company, and brother of Sergeant Whaley, were both wounded. Hempstead was shot in the hip, and Whaley in the thigh. Blankets were retrieved and turned into makeshift stretchers and both men were carried back towards town. Sergeant Whaley, one of those carrying his wounded brother, remained with him until the next day, eventually transporting him to their father's house.[46]

Near Town Hill, the pursuers were joined by Abijah Rogers, commander of the armed boat *Defiance*, and his crew of five men. They had been cruising the coastline for illicit traders when they spotted the British squadron. Rogers put his crew ashore to investigate. They encountered the British rearguard, near Town Hill, and captured two more prisoners.[47]

According to Robert Hallam, who had been under Capt. Richard Deshon, but now served under Lt. John Griswold Hillhouse, the pursuit of the British ended south of Town Hill on the Silas Church Jr. farm, near his house at the crossroads. There the exhausted militia and other volunteers halted and dispersed outward to keep watch over the British. They had chased the rearguard for nearly three miles and most of those present had been marching and fighting all day. Any further movement and they would not just be up against the jaegers, but the entire British force supported by their armed vessels. So, they remained where they were until fresh militia replaced them.[48]

---

45 "From Waterford," *Mystic Pioneer*, Oct. 24, 1863; Master's Log, HMS *Beaumont*, ADM 52/2192, TNA.

46 Jonathan Whaley Pension Application, (W.2739), NARA; Samuel Whaley Pension Application, (R.11366), NARA; Samuel Booth Hempstead Pension Application, (No Number), NARA; John Hempsted narrative in Harris, *Groton Heights*, 67–68.

47 Abijah Rogers Pension Application, (W.11160), NARA.

48 Robert Hallam account of Sep. 6, 1781, undated, Robert Hallam Papers, NLCHS; "From Waterford," *Mystic Pioneer*, Oct. 24, 1863. According to Benjamin Brown, Griswold Avery Jr. joined Deshon's Company during the pursuit and shot a "straggling jager" and took his rifle home as a prize. Avery in his many interviews never mentioned this event.

Later, Lieutenant Colonel Harris, who remained on Quaker Hill, rode to Town Hill and then down to Church's farm. There he spoke briefly with Robert Hallam, who was still frustrated with Harris's performance that day. Hallam testified Harris came up to him, asked about the enemy, and then rode away. Hallam's annoyance with Harris was just the beginning of the lieutenant colonel's problems. Soon after, Harris was temporarily relieved of command so he could face a court-martial for his actions. Harris faced public scrutiny as well as five charges alleging negligence. Among these were not notifying Colonel Latimer of the approach of the enemy, not opposing the British advance into New London, not supporting the fight north of town, allowing the militia to remain unorganized on Quaker Hill, and not doing enough to pursue the retreating British. He was found guilty on all charges and subsequently dismissed from the militia. But when the ruling was issued, the court was careful to state that Harris's neglect of his duty was not due to any secret British sympathies, which might cause severe reprisals against him or his family. Harris was described as a "worthy member of society" and a "good citizen in private life," but one not suited for military service. Though embarrassed by the court martial, Harris continued to serve in the local government until his death in 1798.[49]

Arnold's force reached Brown's farm at around 5:00 p.m. A short time later his column moved towards the beach near the lighthouse, where they signaled to the squadron, they were ready for re-embarkation. Fortunately for them boats from the *Beaumont* and *Recovery* were already there to meet them, and more soon came from the *Amphion*. So, the re-embarkation started immediately upon their arrival and for the next hour and a half, boats went back and forth between the beach and the squadron, bringing the redcoats back to their assigned transport vessels.[50]

The total British casualties sustained at New London were 3 killed, 16 wounded, and 7 missing.[51] The most were sustained by the American Legion which reported a loss of 1 killed, 6 wounded, and 2 missing.[52] Among the wounded was

49 Robert Hallam account of Sep. 6, 1781, undated, Robert Hallam Papers, NLCHS; *CG*, Nov. 15, 1782.

50 Master's Log, HMS *Beaumont*, ADM 52/2192, TNA. The boats were sent by Lieutenant Scott who had watched the skirmishing between the militia and the British rearguard.

51 *CG*, Sep. 7, 1781; Zabdiel Rogers to Governor Jonathan Trumbull, Sep. 7, 1781, Governor Trumbull Papers, vol. 6, CHS. The *Gazette* reported British casualties in New London at 5 killed, 20 wounded, and 7 prisoners. One prisoner reportedly taken was a Hessian captain. This seems to be in error, as only one Hessian captain accompanied the expedition, and he is not reported as wounded or missing. It may in fact, be Capt. Samuel Wogan, though incorrectly referred to as an ensign in Rogers's letter.

52 Master's Log, HMS *Amphion*, ADM 52/2133, TNA; Arnold report in Mackenzie, *Diary*, 2:627; Muster rolls, American Legion, British Military and Naval Records, RG 8, "C" Series, Volume 1871–

Captain Wogan, who due to the seriousness of his head wound was left behind at the Potter house. He was captured by the militia once the town was retaken. He died within a month from the effects of his wounds. Also included in the wounded was Cpl. Ichabod Beckwith, of Frink's Company, who was wounded in the leg. He was a native of New London and had served in the Continental Army since 1777. In 1776, he had even served in a militia company stationed at Fort Trumbull. But in May 1781, he deserted and enlisted in the Legion. His role in the attack is not fully known, but his knowledge of New London and its forts would likely have proved invaluable.[53]

The next heaviest losses came from the combined force of the Associated Loyalists and Loyal Refugees. Unfortunately, neither Upham nor Castles filed an official casualty report. Upham only stated his losses at one moment in the battle, so we must use a few different sources to approximate casualties in these units, which were 1 killed and 5 wounded, the latter all being taken prisoner.[54]

The Loyal American Regiment reported losses at 1 killed, 2 wounded, while the 38th Regiment recorded a loss of 2 wounded and 1 missing. The jaegers in New London lost 1 wounded and 4 missing. Horndon's artillery reported no losses.[55]

When the jaegers reached Jeremiah Brown's house, Captain von Wangenheim formed them nearby to cover the re-embarkation area. They remained there until the main force was back aboard the squadron. The property had been ransacked as British soldiers passed by twice. Brown even remembered seeing Arnold on his property. Soldiers entered the house and removed one of Brown's feather beds, carried it outside, and then emptied its contents into the well. A nephew of Brown elaborated further, recalling, "they plundered [him] of every thing they could use, and then destroyed, most wantonly, feather-beds, furniture and farming utensils, stabbing his hogs and shooting his cattle, even where they did not want for

1872, pages 236, 252, PAC; Peter Wilson Coldham, *American Migrations 1765–1799: The Lives, Times, and Families of Colonial Americans who Remained Loyal to the British Crown Before, During, and After the Revolutionary War, as Related in Their Own Words and Through Their Correspondence* (Baltimore: 2000), 14.

53 Arnold report in Mackenzie, *Diary* 2:627; Hibernian Journal, Dec. 28, 1781; *Royal Gazette* (NY), Oct. 6, 1781. Compiled Service Records of Soldiers who Served in the American Army During the Revolutionary War; Record Group Title: War Department Collection of Revolutionary War Records, RG 93, Series Number: M881, NARA; Roll Number 257, NARA. Wogan's obituary noted him as a captain of grenadiers in Arnold's regiment and lamented him as "a young Man who was an Honour to his Country." The exact date of his death remains a mystery.

54 Upham report in Harris, *Groton Heights*, 110; PA: Hoel Huntley (S.18043); Zebulon Brockway (S.31565), NARA; John Hempsted narrative in Harris, *Groton Heights*, 67; Zabdiel Rogers to Governor Trumbull, Sep. 7, 1781, Governor Trumbull Papers, Vol. 4, Folder 6, CHS.

55 Arnold report in Mackenzie, *Diary*, 2:627; Muster rolls, Loyal American Regiment, British Military and Naval Records, RG 8, "C" Series, Volume 1867, page 71, PAC.

commissary purposes. They even stole his hard earned coin which was concealed under the floor of his house." The incident earned the British the lifetime hatred of Brown, who referred to their actions "as bad as [the] ill fated denizens of Sodom and Gomorrah."[56]

By 6:30 p.m. the jaegers were withdrawn from the Brown property and placed aboard their transport vessel, and Arnold's entire force on the western side of the Thames, including the general himself, was safely aboard the transport vessels. Arnold did not know it then, but this would be the last time he would ever step foot in his native state, and it had been quite the exit.[57]

56 "Instructive Paper on Green Harbor by R. B. Wall," *The Day*, Apr. 2, 1908; "From Waterford," *Mystic Pioneer*, Oct. 24, 1863.

57 Master's Log, HMS *Amphion*, ADM 52/2133, TNA.

Chapter Eleven

The Battle of Groton Heights:
The Evacuation of Fort Griswold

Tactically, the battle of Groton Heights was a British victory. The capture of Fort Griswold, Fort Trumbull, and New London gave the British complete control over the harbor. But success, especially at that hour, reaped few benefits. While most storehouses were destroyed, most privateers escaped upriver to Norwich.

The capture of Fort Griswold a couple of hours earlier would have enabled the British armed vessels under Captain Shepherd, which remained at the entrance of the harbor, a chance to move against the privateers. But now that was impossible. Even as Fort Griswold "displayed English Colours" just after 2:00 p.m. Shepherd did not move. Ledyard's defiant stand had delayed Shepherd's attack for nearly eight hours.[1]

But that stand was costly. Ledyard's entire force at Fort Griswold was gone. When the numbers were calculated, 79 had been killed, 58 wounded, and only 40 remained unhurt, making Ledyard's total losses at 177.[2]

---

1 Master's Log, HMS *Amphion*, ADM 52/2133, TNA; *History of Middlesex County, Connecticut, With Biographical Sketches of Its Prominent Men* (New York, 1884), 403. The colors were seen for a distance. On his way from the Gales Ferry hospital, Jonathan Clark spotted them and did not approach the fort.

2 See Appendix II; Arnold report in Mackenzie, *Diary*, 2:625. The total number engaged in the battle was about 944 men. 356 or 37.7% of those engaged became casualties making this one of the bloodiest battles of the war, considering the number of men engaged. The British reported "85 men were found dead [five of these were wounded but unconscious at the time of the count] in Fort Griswold, and 60 wounded, most of them mortally." They did not specify the number of prisoners taken at the fort, but rather clumped them in with those also taken at New London.

The British had suffered just as much. The almost hour-long battle cost the two British veteran regiments just under 180 casualties, roughly one-fourth of their total numbers engaged, including 43 killed and 136 wounded. This number included ten commissioned officers. The 54th Foot suffered the brunt, especially those companies in Eyre's wing, losing a reported 93 men, which included 15 killed and 78 wounded. The 40th Foot, now under Capt. John Erasmus Adlam, lost a combined 86 men, including 31 killed and 55 wounded.[3]

Bromfield did not concern himself with the missed opportunity afforded to the navy. He had other, more immediate matters to oversee. His command was spread all over Groton Heights. His position, despite the victory, was very precarious. Off to the east lay unknown numbers of hostile militia. Sporadic gunfire could be heard in the distance along the Post Road. Preparations needed to be made to complete the mission. This meant the evacuation of his force and its wounded, including the prisoners it had taken, the burial of its dead, and the destruction of the fort.

The situation in and around the fort was very unsettling. Blood was everywhere. The sounds of battle were replaced by the wailing and crying of the wounded on both sides. One member of Latham's Company vividly described the haunting sounds: "Nothing but the keenest anguish & the infinite Despare Reign[ed] throughout the gloomy Coast and no other music to Salute the Ear but hideous yells of Devils & Shrieks of Damned ghosts."[4]

One of the first decisions Bromfield made was to change the embarkation point to the ferry landing in Groton Bank. This was done because of the large number of British wounded and American prisoners that would have to be transported back to the squadron. Bromfield had originally intended to take both wounded and unwounded American prisoners back to New York. This number totaled 97 men. Adding to Bromfield's own wounded, the number exceeded 200 men. Furthermore, if the enemy attempted to attack Bromfield's column as it moved southward towards Groton Point, it might prove to be very problematic and was a risk Bromfield did not want to take. It would be much easier and far safer to transport them down to the waterfront, load them onto boats, and ferry them back to the squadron.[5]

---

3 Arnold report in Mackenzie, *Diary*, 2:627; Ford, *British Officers*, 15. Militia claimed to have uncovered 61 British bodies. Adlam was senior captain present after Montgomery, having obtained his commission in Dec. 1775.

4 PA: Ziba Woodworth (R.11848), NARA.

5 The ferry in Groton Bank was sometimes referred to as the New London Ferry or South Ferry to distinguish it from the North or Gales Ferry, upriver.

After the battle concluded, the 3rd Battalion, New Jersey Volunteers arrived at the fort along with Captain Lemoine's artillery. Both units watched the battle from Avery's Knoll. They relieved the 40th and 54th Regiments, which were pulled out of the fort and sent down the Fort Road, where they secured the waterfront area, including the ferry landing, which lay a short distance northwest of the fort. There, still under the protective screen provided by the jaegers, they engaged in the central part of their overall mission, destroying the privateers and storehouses. Detachments were sent toward the northern edge of Bank Road, nearly a half mile from the fort. Homes and properties of some of Groton's most notorious rebels were singled out, ransacked, plundered, and set on fire. These included the homes, wharves, storehouses, and workshops of Thomas Mumford, Ens. Charles Eldridge, Dr. Amos Prentice, and Edward Jeffery, whose home operated as a tavern.[6]

Immediately following the battle, the wounded and unwounded prisoners were corralled onto the parade ground. Peter Avery and Thomas Griffin were removed from the chimney in the barracks where they had hidden. They were guarded by soldiers of the 3rd Battalion, New Jersey Volunteers, who armed with loaded muskets and fixed bayonets, were under orders to shoot any man who tried to escape. As the prisoners were gathered, they were searched. Weapons and other accouterments, such as cartridge boxes, powder horns, swords, and personal sidearms were taken from them. Some captors took other personal items; especially prized were silver knee and shoe buckles.[7]

Peter Avery had his hat, coat, watch, money in his pocket, and shoe buckles taken. Sergeant John Prentis, of Shapley's Company, had his hat, shoe, and knee buckles taken. A handful of prisoners, including Lt. Jabez Stow Jr. and Sgt. Jeremiah Harding, also both of Shapley's Company, were stripped as their captors looked for loot. Harding remembered, "[I] was stripped of [all my] clothing by the British soldiers." Stow fared worse. The British found on him "Seven pounds in hard money," roughly a month's pay, and took it.[8]

The dead were picked over for anything deemed valuable or for items to be kept as souvenirs. This was commonly done by both sides after most battles. The corpse of Amos Stanton was searched, and a soldier found a state note for £25 and took it. After stripping Capt. Samuel Allyn, soldiers took his sword, belt, and

---

6 "Names of the Owners of Houses Burned," in Harris, *Groton Heights*, 28.

7 Avery narrative in Harris, *Groton Heights*, 38–39.

8 PA: Peter Avery (S.12024); Thomas Griffin (W.19537), NARA; Harris, *Groton Heights*, 226; "Petition with others, in behalf of the survivors of garrisons of Fts. Trumbull & Griswold, showing that though fortunate in escaping death, they suffered from wounds, loss of clothing &c & being captive to N.Y.," Revolutionary War Records, Series I, Vol. XXII:198, CSL; *CSR*, 3:199; PA: Jeremiah Harding (S.13286), NARA.

Bank Road. A present-day view of the upper part of the road, known today as
Thames Street, looking south in the direction of the fort. *Author*

shoe buckles. Ledyard's body was moved from near the main gate to the barracks
building, where his head was propped up against the outside wall. His sword was
left with him. The bodies of Jordan Freeman and Lambert Latham were placed on
either side of him.[9]

According to Lt. Obadiah Perkins, the prisoners were taunted by their captors.
One guard accused them of breaking the rules of war. Perkins remembered the
soldier told them, "[E]very Man ought to be put to the sword, for (says he) This
is a proper Storm & you fought us after your Colours were struck." Perkins
replied, "They were not struck, but cut away with your shot," to which the British
soldier begrudgingly replied, "that might be." Shortly after, Capt. Abiathar Camp
entered the fort, unaware Ledyard was dead, took a personal shot at him, and said,
according to Perkins, "Col Ledyard was the man that ought to Die."[10]

9 PA: Jason Stanton (W.505), NARA; Harris, *Groton Heights*, 258; Revolutionary War Records,
Series I, 28:198–200, CSL. It seems odd Ledyard's sword was not taken as a souvenir by any British
soldier. It would have been a highly prized trophy.

10 Deposition, Obadiah Perkins to Samuel Mott, Apr. 11, 1782, Governor Trumbull Papers, 16:92a,
CSL. Perkins referred to Camp as a commissary "who formely liv'd at New Haven."

Despite the taunts, some guards showed compassion towards the prisoners. Lieutenant Colonel Abraham van Buskirk, commander of the 3rd Battalion, New Jersey Volunteers, supervising his unit, and a surgeon by trade, also helped. He discovered Edward Stanton, of the 5th "Stonington" Company, amongst the wounded. Stanton was still bleeding after being shot in the stomach. The lieutenant colonel bent down, removed his linen cap from his haversack, applied it to Stanton's chest, and stopped the bleeding. Afterward, van Buskirk gave Stanton a cup of water to drink. This act, Stanton contended, saved his life. Throughout his remaining years, nearly five decades, Stanton never forgot the kind act.[11]

Other prisoners were allowed water from the fort's well. Unwounded, Sgt. Rufus Avery did his best to help his wounded comrades. Youngs Ledyard and Lt. Nathan Moore, both seriously wounded, lay near Avery and he tried to comfort them. He asked a guard for water for the two and himself to drink. The request was granted. It may be safe to assume other prisoners asked for water and were granted it. However, the ever-bitter Sergeant Hempstead did not feel the same way. Hempstead complained bitterly about how the British put their wounded under the shade of the platform of the west wall and how the Americans were left exposed to the sun. Hempstead even claimed the prisoners were refused water, a claim Sgt. Avery would have refuted.[12]

Except for a few exceptions, as was common during war, the victors prioritized their own wounded over their enemies'. As the American prisoners were collected, two dozen British soldiers went to work retrieving their wounded. Not provided with stretchers, they pried off the six outer doors to the barracks and, with four men to a door, converted them into makeshift stretchers. They then scoured the interior and exterior of the fort, picking up and moving their wounded. Most were placed under the platform of the west wall, as it was, according to one prisoner, "the most comfortable place they could find." From the fort, they were transported to the Ezekiel Bailey house, which lay next to Jeffery's tavern near the ferry, and was set aside by the British as a field hospital.[13]

---

11 PA: Edward Stanton (W.2481), NARA.

12 Stephen Hempstead narrative in Harris, *Groton Heights*, 53–55; Rufus Avery narrative in Harris, *Groton Heights*, 39; PA: Peter Vaill (R.10817), NARA. Stephen Hempstead resented the British and would not have agreed with Avery. He claimed we were "within a few steps of a pump in the garrison, well supplied with water, and, although we were suffering with thirst, they would not permit us to take one drop of it, nor give us any themselves. Some of our number, who were not disabled from going to the pump, were repulsed with the bayonet; and not one drop did I taste after the action commenced although begging for it after I was wounded."

13 Avery Downer narrative in Harris, *Groton Heights*, 84; *New London Democrat*, Mar. 17, 1849. Downer mentions this hospital twice. In the *New London Democrat*, he describes it as a "small house" and in his narrative written the same year he attributes the house to James Bailey. This may have been

Ezekiel Bailey House. Built around 1700, the house still stands today on Thames Street in Groton Bank.
Author

There, British medical staff worked diligently to dress wounds and perform surgeries as best as possible. The wounded officers, including Eyre, were assuredly brought there. Among the others was John Gibson, a 30-year-old cordwainer from Cambridge, serving in Capt. Peter Addenbrook's Company, who had been shot through the throat. He survived but would earn his discharge because of it, as would John Goodall, a 32-year-old laborer from Wiltshire. Goodall served in Eyre's Company and suffered his second serious wound in his left leg, the other having been at Charleston two years earlier.[14]

a mistake based on what he heard from his father afterwards, because no James Bailey is known to have lived along the riverfront. The only traceable James Bailey in Groton lived north of the village in the district of the 2nd "Groton" Company. Only one Bailey resided near the ferry, Ezekiel Bailey, whose home, and blacksmith shop was a short distance north of it. This was the house used as a hospital.

14 "State of various corps going on Benedict Arnold's Expedition against New London," Frederick Mackenzie Papers, WCL; Muster rolls, 40th Regiment of Foot, WO 12/5318, TNA; Muster rolls, 54th Regiment of Foot, WO 12/6399, TNA; Rufus Avery narrative in Harris, *Groton Heights*, 39; Pension Records, John Goodall, WO 121/14/457, TNA; Pension Records, John Gibson, WO 121/7/96, TNA. It is not clear if the British surgeons came ashore earlier in the morning or later in the afternoon. The medical staff may have included up to five men.

At least two wounded Americans were also brought there, William Seymour, Lieutenant Colonel Ledyard's nephew, and Ens. Charles Eldridge. When Captain Beckwith walked among the prisoners in the fort, he recognized Seymour. The two had met during a prisoner exchange in New York in 1780. Beckwith ordered Seymour to be carried to the Bailey house and that a surgeon attend to him. In a similar situation, Ens. Charles Eldridge, also wounded in his knee, managed to pull out his gold watch and bribe a British soldier to carry him to the same hospital, where his wound was dressed.[15]

Unlike the American dead, who were left where they fell, the British dead were gathered, accounted for, and given as proper a burial as possible under the circumstances. Most of the 43 redcoats were placed into the ditch which surrounded the western and eastern faces of the ravelin, just outside the north gate. Others were buried around the fort. They were then, "buried . . . in a heap promiscuously, and covered . . . up slightly" with dirt.[16]

Major Montgomery and Archibald Willocks were given separate, distinct graves. Montgomery's corpse was carried from the base of the south wall to outside the north wall to the inside part of the ravelin, where a grave was dug. A second adjacent grave was prepared for Willocks after carrying his body from the ditch around the fort's northeast corner. After burying the two men, a crude memorial was placed atop their graves.[17]

When the militia discovered the memorial, one remembered it read, "Here lies a couple of british men who have fought well for their country . . . and if they should be dug up which they supposed would be[,] they desired they might be buried again decently." Another militiaman said it read, "[here are] the bodies of Major Montgomery and a gentleman volunteer from Antigua [Willocks]." The

---

15 Harris, *Groton Heights*, 242; "A Revolutionary Reminiscence," *New London Democrat*, Mar. 17, 1849; Avery Downer narrative in Harris, *Groton Heights*, 84.

16 George Middleton narrative in Harris, *Groton Heights*, 92; *Norwich Packet*, Sep. 13, 1781; Arnold report in Mackenzie, *Diary*, 2:627; *CG*, Sep. 21, 1781. Arnold totaled his dead at Fort Griswold at 43, though the *Connecticut Gazette* claimed 61 bodies were found.; Avery Downer narrative in Harris, *Groton Heights*, 85; An archeological study was done by Boston University in 1985, headed by Ricardo J. Elia. Elia made it a point to investigate the possibility of human remains being along the outer edge of the ravelin. Using ground-penetrating radar, his study concluded that there was "No evidence of burial pit or burials," which leads to the likelihood all the bodies were removed to a location that research still has not revealed. However, the study was focused on the enlisted British and not the two officers. See Ricardo J. Elia, *The Fort on Groton Hill: An Archaeological Survey of Fort Griswold State Park in Groton, Connecticut* (Boston, 1985).

17 George Middleton narrative in Harris, *Groton Heights*, 92. He was placed "on the right of the gate as we pass out, which I well remember;" Avery Downer narrative in Harris, *Groton Heights*, 84–85; Deposition, William Latham to Samuel Mott, Apr. 11, 1782, Governor Trumbull Papers, 16:90a, CSL. As he was taken out of the fort, Latham claimed, "the Enemy who were Paraded out on the Hill[,] Shout'd and Huzza'd." Latham may have witnessed an impromptu funeral for Montgomery.

militia were curious about the note's validity and received permission from their officers to open the graves. Inside, they found two bodies and, after examining them, reburied them there.[18]

At around 5:00 p.m. Bromfield signaled to the squadron that his force was ready to begin its re-embarkation aboard its transports. However, they were forced to wait as Arnold's force had also simultaneously requested to re-embark. In any case, the landing craft would not be ready for almost two more hours. To assist Bromfield in the meantime, Captain Bazely sent the *Lurcher* and the *Argo*, along with several small vessels which operated close to the shore, to help retrieve Bromfield's wounded. So, from 5:30 p.m. onwards, the British wounded from Groton were steadily transported to the squadron. Some were placed on their assigned transport vessels; others went aboard the *Amphion* and the *Beaumont*. Most wounded officers, except Eyre, were brought to the *Amphion*. These included Captain Craigie, Lieutenant Smyth, Ensign Hyde, and Volunteer Boyd. Once aboard, Captain Bazely opened his cabin to them and provided them with as much assistance as possible.[19]

Near 6:00 p.m. Major Bromfield ordered the prisoners out of the fort. The major was very blunt to them, as Samuel Edgcomb remembered. Bromfield stated he intended to blow up the fort, and they needed to remove themselves from it. Those either not wounded or slightly wounded marched under guard through the main gate down the Fort Road to the waterfront. Other wounded were seated on planks and transported down the heights.[20]

The most seriously wounded prisoners were the last to leave. To transport them, the British intended to use one of the two large, heavy ammunition wagons they had found inside the fort. The wagon was emptied, and then loaded with the wounded. The British planned to use the horses, which had pulled Lemoine's guns, to move the wagon. But according to two Americans, the British could not figure out how to rig the horses to the wagon. Finally, an officer ordered twenty of his men to pull the wagon down the road. As the soldiers started down the hill, the chain broke, and the wagon's weight became so much that all but three of them abandoned the wagon for fear of being run over by it. But then they too gave up and the wagon was allowed to career down the hill. As it rolled, the wagon picked up speed and would have rolled into the river had it not struck a large apple stump.

18 *Boston Evening Transcript*, Aug. 22, 1842; PA: Wyatt Palmer (S.23357), NARA.

19 Muster Book, HMS *Amphion*, ADM 36/9561, TNA; Royal Navy Ships' Muster (Series 1), HMS *Beaumont*, ADM 36/9643, TNA; Arnold report in Mackenzie, *Diary*, 2:626; Master's Log, HMS *Amphion*, ADM 52/2133, TNA.

20 PA: Samuel Edgcomb (S.20743), NARA.

A present-day view of the remains of the Fort Road near the outside of the north gate of the fort. *Author*

Once it hit the stump, "both shafts of the wagon struck very hard, and hurt the wounded men very much."[21]

While the British never intended it, the Continental press accused them of purposely allowing the wagon to roll recklessly down the hill. The *Connecticut Gazette* headed their description, "The following savage action committed by the troops who subdued Fort Griswold on Groton hill . . . ought to be recorded to their eternal infamy." Describing the incident, the paper claimed the British "loaded a wagon with our wounded men, by order of their officers, and set the wagon off from the top of the hill, which is long and very steep; the wagon went a considerable distance with great force, till a tree suddenly stopped it: The shock was so great to those faint and bleeding men, that part of them died instantly." As if that was not exaggerated enough, they went as far as to claim their officers ordered their men to fire on the wagon while it was running down the hill. One Continental newspaper claimed Captain Shapley, one of the wounded in the wagon, told them the "officers dam'd the soldiers and bid them set the waggon agoing."[22]

While the crash inflicted great pain inside the wagon, it had not been purposely pushed, and no British soldier fired upon it or was ordered to do so. Andrew Gallup stated, "I had the honor to ride down-hill in that wagon. Some of them

---

21 Avery narrative in Harris, *Groton Heights*, 40–41; Deposition, William Latham to Samuel Mott, Apr. 11, 1782, Governor Trumbull Papers, 16:90a, CSL; Stephen Hempstead to Governor Trumbull, Oct. 30, 1781, Governor Trumbull Papers, 15:164b–d, CSL; PA: Samuel Edgcomb (S.20743), NARA.

22 *New-Hampshire Gazette*, Sep. 29, 1781; *CG*, Sep. 14, 1781.

meant well enough, and chained the wheel; but the chain broke, so they let us go." Even after a survivor told the governor less than two months after it happened "[they] did not fire on us as reported," neither the governor nor the press deemed it necessary to correct their version.[23]

The other prisoners could do nothing for their stricken comrades but watch and listen as they cried for help. Fortunately, according to Sergeant Avery, "A great number of the enemy," probably the guards, "were where the wagon stopped, and immediately ran to the wagon" and assisted them. From there, they were brought to the larger group of prisoners sitting along Bank Road near the riverbank. Major Bromfield approached them, and talking to most of them, compiled a list of their names and ranks. Their names and ranks were noted because once they were in New York they would be held until they were exchanged for a British soldier of equivalent rank.[24]

The plan had been to take all the prisoners, including the wounded, back to New York. This would have happened had it not been for a deal worked out between Bromfield and Ebenezer Ledyard. Ledyard emerged sometime during the afternoon, as it is not believed he was in the fort. He realized the wounded prisoners might not survive in captivity, and that they stood a better chance if they remained behind and were attended to by their own medical staff.[25]

Ledyard convinced Bromfield to parole those 53 wounded prisoners, meaning they promised not to fight until they were properly exchanged. Ledyard probably had ulterior motives: his 18-year-old son, Jonathan, was among those wounded. After agreeing, Bromfield compiled their names and had Ensign Eldridge sign the parole certificate.[26]

---

23 Harris, *Groton Heights*, 20; Stephen Hempstead to Governor Trumbull, Oct. 30, 1781, Governor Trumbull Papers, 15:164b–d, CSL.

24 Rufus Avery narrative in Harris, *Groton Heights*, 40–41.

25 John A. Woodhull, *A Review of the Congregational Church of Groton, Connecticut: With Sketches of its Ministers, 1704–1876* (New London, CT, 1877), 12; *Connecticut Men*, 577–578. It is not clear as to Ebenezer Ledyard's role in the battle. Nor is it known when or how he arrived and made the deal with Bromfield. He may have remained at home in Groton Bank or come through the line under a flag of true. Perhaps the same one mentioned by Rev. Kinne's relative who stated that "[Kinne was] carrying a flag of truce, going to and fro, ministering to the suffering." The number was compiled from counting the number of wounded men left behind in addition to those mortally wounded. Many of those mortally wounded were alive when the British left them at the Avery house. Also added in were a number of those men who claimed to have escaped during the battle. None of these supposed escapees proved to be speaking the truth according to their own pension applications and British ship musters which list them as prisoners.

26 *Norwich Packet*, Sep. 13, 1781; PA: Samuel Edgcomb (S.20743); Joseph Eldredge (S.2323), NARA. At least four other wounded men (Ziba Woodworth, Parke Avery, Daniel Stanton Jr., and Elisha Morgan) were left for dead in the fort and were not included in this count. All survived.

Bromfield also released William Latham Jr., Captain Latham's son. He was let go on account of his youth. "What are you going to do to me?" Latham supposedly asked before being let go, to which the British officer, allegedly replied, "Let you run home to your mother, sonny if you'll promise not to grow up to be a damned rebel."[27]

After the parole certificate was signed, those paroled were moved to the property of Ens. Ebenezer Avery, just south of the ferry. The property had been pillaged and the house partially set on fire. But before they arrived, the fire was put out. "With great exertion and by assisting each other," Samuel Edgcomb recalled, the wounded, among them Ensign Avery, reached the property. Some occupied the house, while the rest were placed in the barn. Blood from their wounds soaked into the wooden floorboards of the house and remained visible for over a hundred years.[28]

The British occupied Groton Bank for around eight hours and, like their comrades in New London, foraged for badly needed food and livestock. Their efforts were focused primarily on the north and central parts of Bank Road. Over a dozen structures, including two storehouses, the schoolhouse, four barns, two workshops, and twelve homes faced the torch.[29]

Some fires were set in retaliation. An officer in the 54th Regiment admitted rather crudely in a letter home, "We expected to have been able to take off all the public stores, which would have entitled every officer to a considerable sum of prize money; but [in New London] the rebels set fire to their ships themselves, to prevent their falling into our hands, and [Groton] was set on fire by some of the soldiers in resentment." Some looting may have been attributed to the vengeful attitude of the Associated Loyalists, whom Arnold requested and Upham sent over after they returned to the squadron. In several whaleboats, one company of Associated Loyalists, or as they were termed by one prisoner, "our renegade countrymen," assisted with the evacuation.[30]

---

27 Rogers, *Sesquicentennial of the Battle of Groton Heights*, 136; Harris, *Groton Heights*, 227; *Providence Evening Press*, Mar. 15, 1861.

28 Rufus Avery narrative in Harris, *Groton Heights*, 41; PA: Samuel Edgcomb (S.20743), NARA.

29 Master's Log, HMS *Amphion*, ADM 52/2133, TNA; Rufus Avery narrative in Harris, *Groton Heights*, 42; *CG*, Sep. 7, 1781; Harris, *Groton Heights*, 28. Avery mentioned the prisoners were served "hog's brains" from livestock taken by Upham's men which suggests the British also collected livestock.

30 "Extract of a letter from an officer of the 54th regiment, to his friend in Edinburgh, dated NY, Sep 6," *Saunders's News-Letter*, Nov. 22, 1781; Upham report in Harris, *Groton Heights*, 110; Stephen Hempstead narrative in Harris, *Groton Heights*, 55. The company numbered 40 men. Upham wanted to send his vessels *Association* and *Colonel Martin* as well, probably to carry off captured stores, but was not allowed to. Reporting, "Captains [Nathaniel Gardiner] and [Charles] Thomas would have gladly

Ebenezer Avery House. In 1971, the house was moved from its historic location, at the intersection of Thames and Latham Streets, and moved to the Fort Griswold Battlefield State Park. *Author*

After the British wounded were transported downriver, 42 American prisoners followed. According to Sergeant Avery, it was the most depressing moment of his life, even more so as he and his wife, Hannah, were soon expecting their first child. Only five of the Americans were wounded, and their wounds were not considered life-threatening.[31]

Among them was John Newson, a native of Groton, who had spent time in the privateer service.[32] Another was Shoram Stanton, a free black man from Groton, who the previous year had served six months in the Continental Army.[33]

gone up to the town, but were not permitted" by Arnold. Upham's men were the worst, according to Hempstead who wrote, "the cruelty of our enemy cannot be conceived," and these loyalists, "surpassed in this respect, if possible, our British foes."

31 See Appendix H; Royal Navy Ships' Muster (Series 1), HMS *Amphion*, ADM 36/9561, TNA; Royal Navy Ships' Muster (Series 1), HMS *Beaumont*, ADM 36/9643, TNA.

32 Middlebrook, *Maritime Connecticut*, 2:59, 80. Newson later became a sea merchant and moved to Wethersfield, Connecticut, where he is buried today.

33 PA: Giles Tracy (S.30748), NARA; *Connecticut Men*, 156; "Appropriations to Groton Sufferers," Revolutionary War Records, Series III, I:79b, CSL. In 1762, Shoram, described as a "negro boy," was owned by Capt. John Stanton, the father of Amos Stanton. He may have been in his late 20's at the

Fort Griswold Prisoners Monument. This monument inside a small park on Thames Street marks the departure point of the American prisoners taken during the battle. Though it incorrectly numbers the prisoners as only being 38. *Author*

Yet another was Aaron Perkins, also of Groton, a former carpenter's mate aboard the Continental brig *Resistance* and the son of Solomon Perkins, who had been wounded in the barracks. Aaron had volunteered with his father and younger brother, Simeon, who had been killed.[34] The British also took three teenagers from Latham's Company with them: Humphrey Brown, a 13-year-old fifer, Matross Thomas Griffin Jr. and Sanford Williams, both 15-years-old. Griffin's brother-in-law, Elnathan Mason, who also served in Latham's Company, was taken as well.[35]

---

time of the battle. After Captain Stanton died in the Siege of Havana, according to his will, Shoram was given to Stanton's son, Robert. Even though we have no concrete proof of his emancipation, the author believes by 1781 he had been freed. Stanton served in the 1st Connecticut Regiment as a hired substitute for Tracy in 1780. Tracy specifically mentions hiring Shoram, not paying his master as he would have if he were still enslaved. He was freed by the time of Robert's death in 1783, as he is not mentioned in his will. Nor is he mentioned in the will of Amos in 1782. Shoram likely remained close to the Stanton family, possibly on their farm, and volunteered with Amos. Shoram survived the war and submitted a damage claim of £6.

34 *Naval Documents*, IX:855.

35 PA: Humphrey Brown (W.18648); Thomas Griffin (W.19537); Elnathan Mason (W.15842), NARA.

With the assistance of Upham's men as oarsmen and guards, prisoners were gathered into groups of twelve and formed into two ranks, six men in each rank. Then, under guard, they waded into the river, directly opposite the Fort Road, until the water reached their knees. There, a boat met them. The two ranks were then divided on each side of the boat, where they were ordered to get in at the point of the bayonet. Once inside, they were rowed downriver and dispersed between the *Association* and *Amphion*.[36]

When the prisoners were gone, the 40th and 54th Regiments, and the 3rd Battalion, New Jersey Volunteers, evacuated Groton. As the latter units were ferried out into the harbor, Lieutenant von Reitzenstein pulled the jaegers back from the Post Road to a position east of the fort to cover Lemoine's artillerists. With them, they carried the wounded jaeger Wolfgang Muller, their only combat casualty on September 6. Captain Lemoine's men were among the last to leave the area. After sending their two fieldpieces back to the squadron, Lemoine had been busy all afternoon, compiling a detailed inventory of the main fort, the river battery, and outer redoubts. His artillerist accounted for each of the fort's cannon. As each gun was inventoried, it was spiked and its trunnions—the medal rods connecting it to the carriage—were knocked off, making them inoperable.[37]

In addition to the fort's cannon, the artillerists counted 80 pikes, 106 French muskets (presumably the Model 1766 Charleville), and accompanying accouterments. Several older, obsolete muskets carried by the militia were also collected. These were smashed and broken. Inside the magazine they found 10,000 pre-made musket cartridges, 67 artillery cartridges, and 150 barrels of gunpowder. They also discovered over 4,000 rounds of solid shot and almost 900 rounds of grapeshot. Additionally, they counted spare gun carriages, a gyn triangle, and an ammunition wagon. These needed to be destroyed.[38]

To accomplish this, Lemoine planned to blow up the powder magazine. His artillerists carefully trailed gunpowder out of the magazine across the Parade out through the north gate. There, at a safe distance, they set a fuse with a slow match.

36 Rufus Avery narrative in Harris, *Groton Heights*, 41–42; Royal Navy Ships' Muster (Series 1), HMS *Amphion*, ADM 36/9561, TNA; Royal Navy Ships' Muster (Series 1), HMS *Beaumont*, ADM 36/9643, TNA; PA: Caleb Avery (W.25363), NARA.

37 Muster of the Brandenburg-Ansbach Corps of Chaussers, TO 38/812-814, TNA; John Tyler to Governor Trumbull, Sep. 10, 1781, Governor Trumbull Papers, 15:116a–b, CSL; Ernest E. Rogers, *Sesquicentennial of the Battle of Groton Heights and the Burning of New London, Connecticut, Sep. 6 and 7, 1931* (New London, CT, 1931), 136.

38 Arnold report in Mackenzie, *Diary*, 2:628. A gyn triangle was a three-pole pulley used to raise and lower cannon onto the platform.

The artillerists and then the jaegers made a hasty retreat down the hill to their waiting boats.[39]

If Lemoine's plan had worked, the explosion would have been massive. It would have leveled the fort's walls and destroyed its artillery, magazine, and barracks building. Lemoine positioned himself at a safe distance in the harbor as he anxiously waited for the explosion that would assuredly have lit up the night sky. But after a time, nothing happened. Arnold ordered a second attempt, but Lemoine was unable to comply.[40]

Fort Griswold is Retaken

A short time earlier, around 10:00 p.m., almost a mile away at the Groton Meetinghouse, Lieutenant Colonel Gallup ordered a party of militia, under cover of darkness, to attempt to make a reconnaissance of the fort. Gallup's battle line along the Post Road, which had been continuously reinforced, had been unable to break through the jaegers to Fort Griswold. But now, this was about to change.[41]

Major Nathan Peters, the brigade major of the 3rd Brigade of Connecticut Militia, was now on the scene. The 33-year-old major, a native of Preston, had arrived sometime after the capture of Fort Griswold. Peters enjoyed an extensive record of military experience, a record that would rival almost any other militia leader on the field that day. He was known as a "gentleman of courage and skill and a good officer." After leading a company of Preston militia in response to the Lexington Alarm, Peters had served as a captain in the 4th Massachusetts Regiment (also known as the 3rd Continental Regiment), fighting at the Battles of Brooklyn, White Plains, Trenton, and Princeton before returning home in early 1777. Once home, he received a promotion and was assigned as the brigade major in the 3rd Brigade. In 1778, he saw service at Rhode Island, one junior officer so impressed that he later testified "[Peters] was much exposed to the fire of the British, the duty which he had to do, perhaps [making] him [more] exposed to danger than any other Man in the Brigade."[42]

39 George Middleton narrative in Harris, *Groton Heights*, 92.

40 Arnold report in Mackenzie, *Diary*, 2:626.

41 Governor Trumbull to George Washington, Sep. 13, 1781, Governor Trumbull Papers, 15:121a, CSL. Trumbull reported, "together with the increasing number of ye militia & some small skirmishes between some scattering Parties & [the] advanced Guards [or jaegers] & prevented the enemy from fully executing their savage design."

42 PA: Nathan Peters (W.21937), NARA. The officer quoted, Lt. Samuel Capron, noted an incident at Rhode Island, where a company of American soldiers were going out to replace another company on the picket line. Each group took the other for the enemy and opened a "brisk fire" upon them. Peters rode out at the risk of his life, bringing order to the two companies without firing a shot.

Peters was ordered by Gallup to lead the party. The reconnaissance was probably prompted by a German prisoner who had been brought to the meetinghouse by Capt. Thomas Park. As the jaegers withdrew, Park and others managed to capture Wolf Andreas Eichorn, of the 1st Ansbach Jaeger Company, who was deserting, and brought him back to Gallup. This may have led Gallup to believe the jaegers had withdrawn, but he wanted to find out for sure.[43]

Peters picked twenty men from along Noyes's skirmish line. Included was Capt. Lemuel Lamb and a detachment from his 4th Troop, 2nd Regiment of Light Horse, a mounted militia unit from New London County. Armed with pistols and cutlasses, it is not clear if Lamb's men advanced mounted or dismounted. Also selected was Wyatt Palmer, a member of Latham's Company on furlough, and Capt. William Whitney of the 1st Company "Preston Alarm List."[44]

In the darkness Peters led them westward towards the fort. His route is not known, but it may have been on the Post Road until they reached the farmer's lane, which would have led them directly towards the fort. As they continued to get closer to the fort, they found no enemy. The jaegers, unlike their counterparts across the river, had escaped without detection. As Peters approached Groton Heights, from a distance he saw flames and smoke billowing over the fort and homes and other structures along the waterfront.

Perhaps near the Ward house, Major Peters halted the party and advanced alone towards the fort, a decision which came with great risk. He knew the powder magazine could explode at any moment. Nonetheless, Peters needed to see if the fort, and its cannon, could be saved.

Peters reached the fort and entered through the north gate and found it deserted. Then according to a friend whom he told about the incident, Peters scanned the interior and saw "a large train of powder which led directly from [the] fire to the magazine." Peters ran over, and kicked the train of powder with his boot, cutting off the charge. He then yelled out, ordering the men to come quickly, and put out the fire. He needed help putting out a few small fires set by the British. Rushing up, the militia went right to work. With no buckets, the men, according

---

43 PA: Thomas Park (R.7932), NARA; Muster of the Brandenburg-Ansbach Corps of Chasseurs, TO 38/812-814, TNA. Park escorted Eichorn a day or two later back through Groton. The two stopped at Thomas Eldridge's home about three to four miles east of the fort, where the prisoner was seen by Eldridge's daughter Helena, who testified to it in Park's pension application.

44 PA: Jason Stanton (W.505); Wyatt Palmer (S.23357); William A. Morgan (W.1308); David Bennett (S.12201), NARA. Lamb's Company was organized in 1779 and charged with patrolling the coastline between Narragansett in Rhode Island and New London, with the purpose of intercepting illicit trade. Two others testified in their pension applications to being part of Peters's group, William A. Morgan of Groton and David Bennett of Stonington.

to Thomas Wells, turned to filling their hats with water drawn from the fort's well and throwing it on the fires, containing them, and eventually putting them out.[45]

Peters's courageous actions saved Fort Griswold, bravery much appreciated by the militia leadership. Brigadier General Tyler mentioned Peters in his report to Governor Trumbull, noting, "the [design] of the Enemy . . . was happily prevented by the Vigilence of Majr Peters." Captain Isaac Gallup, adjutant of the 8th Regiment of Connecticut Militia, wrote of Peters's actions, "I considered it to be a bold and Dangerous undertaking," but "the fort was saved with its contents." Newcomb Kinney, a friend of the major's, said that the feat was so hazardous [it] could not have been done without the "assistance of Divine Providence."[46]

Major Peters was the reason Captain Lemoine could not make his second attempt to blow up the fort, as ordered by Arnold. The British had left only minutes before Peters's arrival and remained close enough to know militia were in the immediate area. But they could not have known it was only a handful of men, especially in the darkness.

Officially, the abandonment of the fort intact was attributed to the approach of a large force of Americans. A West Yorkshire newspaper reported, "The Reason given for Gen. Arnold abandoning Fort Griswold without destroying it is that he had received Advice that [a] very superior Force was coming upon him, which might have rendered his Retreat impracticable." Another British newspaper stated, "[I]t has, however, unluckily transpired, that Continental militia assembled in such numbers, as rendered the attempt impracticable, and compelled the troops to retreat with the utmost precipitation."[47]

After retaking the fort, Peters sent word to Gallup about the British withdrawal. Gallup began moving some of his militia, including his medical staff, towards the waterfront. The regimental surgeon, Dr. Joshua Downer, had already been on the scene for a couple of hours when the call from Gallup came to him. The 46-year-old Downer, a native of Preston, was a prominent physician in southeastern Connecticut and had been the regimental surgeon since at least the previous year. Downer arrived in Groton accompanied by Maj. Samuel Tyler, also of Preston, the

---

45 PA: Jason Stanton (W.505), NARA; John Tyler to Governor Trumbull, Sep. 10, 1781, Governor Trumbull Papers, 15:110a–b, CSL; PA: Ebenezer Morgan (W.17178), NARA; Harris, *Groton Heights*, 247–248. Wells's statement is included in Morgan's pension application, placed there to verify Morgan's presence at the battle. Wells was a member of the 3rd Company, "Groton Alarm List." Elisha Morgan, a member of the garrison, is also believed to have helped Peters. According to Harris, Morgan played dead inside the fort and heard Lemoine planning the destruction of the fort. When Peters arrived, Morgan assisted. This is the only place this claim appears.

46 John Tyler to Governor Trumbull, Sep. 10, 1781, Governor Trumbull Papers, 15:110a–b, CSL; PA: Nathan Peters (W.21937), NARA.

47 *Norfolk Chronicle*, Nov. 10, 1781; *Leeds Intelligencer*, Nov. 13, 1781.

regiment's third-in-command, with the Preston militia companies. With Downer was his 18-year-old son Avery, who served as the surgeon's mate, and Cyrus Tracy, his apprentice.[48]

After Dr. Downer arrived at the Groton Meetinghouse, he met with Reverend Kinne and took charge of the makeshift hospital. Avery Downer recalled encountering several wounded already at the meetinghouse: "On [our] arrival near the meeting-house [we] met Benjamin Bill and others who had escaped from the enemy slightly wounded," he recalled. These were from the action along Birch Plain Creek. Eventually, Dr. Downer received assistance from two more local physicians, Amos Prentice and Prosper Rose.[49]

At around 11:00 p.m., Dr. Downer received orders from Gallup to proceed to the waterfront. Leaving his son, Prentice, and Rose behind to take care of those at the meetinghouse, Downer headed out. Lieutenant Colonel Gallup and Capt. Isaac Gallup accompanied Downer with a single company of militia. This was probably Capt. John Morgan's 4th "Groton" Company, the company whose commander had refused to follow orders earlier. Led now by Lt. William Williams, the 42-man strong company towards Groton Bank where they would spend a restless night doing picket duty south of the fort. The British were still near, and Gallup did not know what they might do next.[50]

It appears only Morgan's Company, along with Peters's men, were near the fort as evening fell. The remainder of the regiment remained near the meetinghouse and bivouacked there for the night. Gallup wanted to wait until morning to move the rest of his regiment. Daylight would allow for better command and control, as well as ensuring the protection of the private property the British had not destroyed. In hindsight, it was a smart decision, especially since two of Gallup's officers and one of his soldiers were found plundering "divers[e] valuable goods and effects [from] the property of the distressed inhabitants of [Groton]," the following day, misconduct which could have been greater under cover of darkness.[51]

48 Avery Downer narrative in Harris, *Groton Heights*, 83–84; PA: Cyrus Tracy (S.19130), NARA.

49 PA: Cyrus Tracy (S.19130); Prosper Rose (S.35), NARA; Avery Downer narrative in Harris, *Groton Heights*, 84; *Norwich Packet*, July 17, 1790.

50 *Rolls and Lists of Connecticut Men in the Revolution, 1775–1783* (Hartford, 1901), 216; PA: Ebenezer Morgan (W.17178), NARA; Avery Downer narrative in Harris, *Groton Heights*, 84; *CG*, Nov. 15, 1782. Captain Morgan was court martialed and found guilty on six charges, which include not supporting the garrison at Fort Griswold, disobeying orders, not organizing his company, and not attempting to attack the enemy as they evacuated. He was subsequently dismissed from the militia. Morgan was not even paid for his time served during the alarm.

51 *CG*, Nov. 15, 1782; Harris, *Groton Heights*, 113–117. The two officers were Capt. Thomas Wheeler and Lt. John Williams, both from the 4th "Stonington" Company. Both men were found guilty of passing through a guard post on September 7 to plunder private property. They were cashiered and

Guided through the darkness down the Post Road, Gallup, Downer, and the others made their way to the house of Benajah Lester at the intersection of the Post and Bank Roads, which had escaped serious damage from the British. As the road turned south towards the ferry, they immediately discovered several houses ablaze. Only the Bailey house at the north end was not on fire. Searching the property, they discovered the house's interior was a mess. Furniture and personal items were thrown about, and blood could be seen everywhere. Inside they also found two wounded Americans, William Seymour and Ens. Charles Eldridge, who had been treated there and then left behind.[52]

Downer went inside and attended to them. According to a witness, Seymour was in great pain. While a British surgeon had stopped the bleeding, he had tied the bandage too tight, which increased the pain. Seymour's leg was later amputated, but he survived, as did Eldridge.[53]

The militia found more destruction further down the road. At least four more homes were ablaze; these belonged to Michael Jeffery, Capt. William Leeds, Lt. Nathan Moore, and Youngs Ledyard. The schoolhouse, standing opposite the ferry, was destroyed. The structures, storehouses, wharf, and shops which made up the mercantile businesses of William and Ebenezer Ledyard were gone, as was their nephew Youngs's wharf. A quarter mile south of the Bailey house, the militia heard cries of wounded soldiers coming from the Ebenezer Avery property. Once there they discovered forty-nine more wounded Americans.[54]

Immediately, they sent for Dr. Downer, who was still at the Bailey house. Downer was overwhelmed by the number of wounded soldiers, so a call for help was sent to the meetinghouse. Joining Downer after midnight was his son, Avery, and Dr. Prentice. The three worked tirelessly by candlelight throughout the night. But all they could do was comfort, and attempt to clean, bandage, and dress wounds as well as possible. It was impossible to perform surgeries, as they did not have either sufficient light to see by or the necessary medical equipment. Fortunately, almost miraculously, only three wounded soldiers died that night—Youngs Ledyard, Lt.

---

barred from holding any future commissions. Warham Williams, of the 5th "Stonington" Company, was also convicted of stealing three muskets. Ironically, Williams managed to acquire a military pension for his service during the war, though any mention of his involvement in the battle is not mentioned.

52 Avery Downer narrative in Harris, *Groton Heights*, 84; New London Democrat, Mar. 17, 1849.

53 "A Revolutionary Reminiscence," *New London Democrat*, Mar. 17, 1849. The story was told by Avery Downer, who talked with William Seymour at the laying of the cornerstone of the Groton monument.

54 PA: Samuel Edgcomb (S.20743), NARA; Stephen Hempstead narrative in Harris, *Groton Heights*, 54–55. Hempstead placed their number at 51, of which 35 were in the house, and 16 in the barn.

Nathan Moore, and Joseph Moxley Sr. Such good results were due in large part to the efforts of the American medical personnel. But as the sun rose over the harbor, the real horrors of war were about to be revealed.[55]

55 Avery Downer narrative in Harris, *Groton Heights*, 84; Stephen Hempstead narrative in Harris, *Groton Heights*, 55; Rufus Avery narrative in Harris, *Groton Heights*, 39; Harris, *Groton Heights*, 24. It is not known how many, if any, civilians remained in their homes along the waterfront in Groton. It is possible there were a few. One may have been Fanny Ledyard, a niece of Lieutenant Colonel Ledyard, who had been visiting her uncle at the time. Hempstead singled her actions out in his narrative. He claimed she was the first person he met after the British departed, and not the medical staff. Hempstead remembered, "The first was . . . Miss Fanny Ledyard . . . who held to my lips a cup of warm chocolate, and soon after returned with wine and other refreshments, which revived us a little."

Chapter Twelve

Reclaiming New London Harbor

$\mathcal{A}$s the sun rose on September 7 it revealed the horrors of the previous day. Evidence of the conflict was visible everywhere. The sights and smells at Fort Griswold were ghastly and impossible to evade. Early that morning, Gallup moved his battalion onto Groton Heights. Along the way they met civilians looking for loved ones. Most had never seen a battlefield. Some found it unbearable to remain, others became physically ill. To have seen the battlefield that morning, one militiaman recalled years later, "sickens my heart [even to this day.]"[1]

Near the north gate they encountered the British dead hastily buried in the ditch of the ravelin and "in different places round [the fort]," some with limbs sticking out of the ground. One had to be careful walking the exterior of the fort, as well as the ditch, both of which, according to a witness, "[were] completely covered and slippery with blood."[2]

The interior was gruesome. Even a week later, militia assigned to clean the fort recalled "the blood . . . flowed so freely." The dead Americans lay all about the platform, some on it, some hanging from it. Others were strewn about the barracks,

---

1 PA: Timothy Carpenter (S.12675), NARA. Gallup's decision to send his regiment onto *Groton Heights* probably had an ulterior motive. The presence of so many militia around Fort Griswold, which the British were undoubtedly watching from their naval vessels, would have acted as a deterrent and made the British think twice about renewing their attack. They would be facing far greater numbers than the previous day.

2 PA: Willard Davis (BLWt.67513-160-55), NARA; *Norwich Packet*, Sep. 13, 1781.

some on the parade ground, or in and around the powder magazine. Their corpses lay in every gruesome position, some with their mouths hanging open.[3]

Dr. Prentice entered the fort but upon seeing the body of his friend, William Ledyard, he left, emotionally broken. Ledyard lay outside the barracks, near the north gate. His body had been discovered by Major Peters's men the previous night. It was something Trumpeter Jason Stanton, of Captain Lamb's Troop, who was with Peters, never forgot. Stanton recalled, "The dead all lay as they were slain except a row drawn with their heads against the Barracks—Colonel Ledyard was drawn up against the North End of the Barrack-between two negroes, one on each side of him."[4]

From the Parade, they could see the bodies "[and] the blood on the platform at the fort and also the Bullet holes and the places where the enemy had kindled fires." One militiaman who entered the partially burned barracks stated, "The barracks were a shocking sight to behold. The partitions had been broken down in the melee, and the inequalities in the floor were filled with the blood of our men, so that we were often over the soles of our shoes in gore."[5]

Gallup did not allow the militia to wander the battlefield, as the continued presence of the British squadron made the situation tense. The militia were kept under arms, meaning they were to remain alert, continue to wear their accouterments, and keep their muskets on them or close by because if the British renewed their attack they needed to be ready to assemble at a moment's notice. Gallup then dispersed them about the heights performing a variety of tasks. The most important was security.[6]

Early on, Gallup recalled Morgan's Company from picket duty and replaced it, presumably, with Capt. James Morgan's 5th "Preston" Company. With the sun up, Gallup deployed militia beyond the fort. Using the Neck Road, Morgan's Company marched southward to Groton Point, where soldiers monitored the British squadron. They remained on the same duty for the duration of their tour. For almost two weeks, Cpl. James Tyler remembered, all his company did was stand guard on the beach, watching and preparing to contest another British

---

3 PA: Frederick Brewster (S.15346), NARA. Brewster probably served in Capt. Nathan Crary's Company, a drafted company formed from the 3rd Brigade of Connecticut Militia, which occupied the fort until the end of September.

4 Harris, *Groton Heights*, 258; PA: Jason Stanton (W.505), NARA; Avery narrative in Harris, *Groton Heights*, 84.

5 PA: Thaddeus Gage (R.3860), NARA; *Boston Evening Transcript*, Aug. 22, 1847.

6 PA: Nathan Geer (S.16126), NARA.

landing. They were eventually joined by a detachment from the 2nd Regiment of Light Horse which assisted them and increased the area in which they patrolled.[7]

Gallup also rotated militia companies to perform guard duty at various points. They were to ensure the protection of places not ravaged by the British the previous day. Not all had been unfortunate to lose their homes. Several homes south and east of the fort, including those belonging to Capt. John Williams and Capt. William Latham, were not destroyed.[8]

Militia assisted the medical staff at the Ebenezer Avery house, which continued to function temporarily as a makeshift hospital. The medical staff, assembled the previous evening, continued to serve in these capacities. Having already worked several hours, the task proved exhausting. They were joined in the afternoon by Dr. Hezekiah Clark of Lebanon, who arrived in New London with the 12th Regiment of Connecticut Militia. Clarke found a "rickety skiff," one of the few surviving boats, and he and a volunteer crossed the river and joined the medical staff.[9]

Female civilians, including Eunice Allyn, sister of Capt. Samuel Allyn of the 2nd Company "Groton Alarm List" and Frances Ledyard, a niece of Lieutenant Colonel Ledyard, volunteered. The assistance was gratefully appreciated not only by the medical staff but the wounded soldiers themselves. Sergeant Hempstead remembered the women as "ministering angels to our relief."[10]

A better-organized hospital, in Groton Bank, was eventually established on the Patrick Ward property. The militia helped transport the wounded soldiers there from both the Avery house and the Groton meetinghouse. A modest story-and-a-half home constructed in 1717 belonging to Patrick and his young wife Elizabeth sat on an acre-and-a-half lot. Patrick, a former Continental naval lieutenant, had been killed during the battle, and Elizabeth found her house pillaged by the British and now commandeered by the militia. Dr. Philemon Tracy, acting superintendent of the Continental Hospital at Gales Ferry, five miles upriver, arrived by mid-morning. Tracy, a hospital surgeon's mate with the Eastern Department of the Continental Army, had been directed by the former surgeon general of the

7 PA: James Tyler (W.19479); Jason Stanton (W.505), NARA.

8 Harris, *Groton Heights*, 235; *CG*, Nov. 15, 1782. Two officers from the 8th Regiment were found guilty of using their authority to plunder property protected by militia guards.

9 W. W. Clayton, *History of Onondaga, New York With Illustrations and Biographical Sketches of Some of Its Prominent Men and Pioneers* (Syracuse, NY, 1878), 403–404. Clark was the former surgeon's mate of the 3rd Connecticut Regiment. He had a difficult time getting across the river. The skiff he found was described as "utterly unseaworthy" and he had a hard time compelling a volunteer help him get across the river. Finally, when he did, that person rowed while Clark continuously bailed water out of the boat. Clark's efforts were greatly appreciated, and three survivors whom he helped following the battle thanked him in person thirty years after the battle.

10 Stephen Hempstead narrative in Harris, *Groton Heights*, 55.

Patrick Ward House. A witness to both the battle and its aftermath.
The house still stands today on Meridian Street. *Author*

department, Dr. Philip Turner, also of Norwich, to repair to Fort Griswold the previous night. Dr. Turner was already on the scene by the time Tracy arrived. Dr. Tracy's assistant, Dr. John Turner, the hospital's ward master and Dr. Turner's son, also accompanied him. Their help was especially needed since the militia medical staff did not possess the necessary medical supplies, nor were they able to perform the necessary surgeries some of the wounded required.[11]

In the weeks following the battle there was a need for constant additional medical care for the wounded.

On September 9, to ensure they continued to receive proper care, Dr. Philip Turner was ordered by Brig. Gen. John Tyler, commander of the 3rd Brigade of Connecticut Militia, to supervise the care of all the wounded at both New London and Groton. Tyler had arrived by the night of September 6 and assumed overall command of New London's defenses.

A native of the Second Society of Preston—modern-day Griswold—Tyler had served in the militia for over three decades. In 1775, he was the lieutenant colonel of the 8th Regiment of Connecticut Militia. He rose to colonel in October

---

11 PA: James A. Smith (R.9750), NARA; Harris, *Groton Heights*, 258; *Middlesex County*, 403; *Naval Documents*, IX:855, XI:116; PA: Philemon Tracy (W.3625), NARA. Ward is listed as a lieutenant, but this was a Continental naval rank.

1776, then to brigadier general of the 3rd Brigade in May 1777, replacing the aging Saltonstall.[12]

Brigadier General Tyler's choice of Tyler was a sound one. He knew Turner was both a seasoned physician and army surgeon who enjoyed a prodigious professional reputation. In 1777, the Continental Congress appointed him surgeon general of the Continental Army's Eastern Department. He held the office until 1780, when Congress dissolved it and reassigned Tyler as a hospital physician and surgeon. The following year, Turner resigned and returned home.[13]

Turner was well prepared for the task at hand. His new responsibilities included much of the same he held as surgeon general, though on a smaller scale. Tyler also appointed Dr. Avery Downer and Dr. Amos Prentice to assist Turner. Turner was also entrusted with the procurement of food, medicines, and other necessary supplies, as well as to assist and supervise Downer and Prentice, ensuring they were attending to the needs of the wounded, such as cleaning and dressing their wounds.[14]

For many of those cared for by Turner, it was a long road to recovery, both physically and mentally. Most survived their wounds, but each carried with them scars for the rest of their lives. Robert Gallup, of Latham's Company, had suffered two serious wounds. He was deemed well enough the following February to return to duty at Fort Griswold. However, unable to perform most duties, he spent the rest of his enlistment filling musket and artillery cartridges. Years after the war, he continued to suffer not only from the physical effects of his wounds but also the psychological effects. This was no more evident than when he talked about the battle. For years, Gallup was sought to talk about his experiences, and upon starting to talk, even decades later, his mood suddenly changed, and his lips quivered with agitation.[15]

12 *Connecticut Men*, 72, 99, 430, 434; *Rolls of Connecticut Men in the French and Indian War, 1755-1762*, 2 vols. (Hartford, CT, 1903), 1:9, 142, 231–232, 2:168, 218, 366; *CSR*, 1:264. Tyler's exact arrival time is not known, but likely occurred between the night of the attack or early the following morning.

13 Brig. Gen. John Tyler's Orders, Sep. 9, 1781, Governor Trumbull Papers, 15:103, CSL. Tyler used this home as his headquarters in 1779. It is not clear if or where there was a hospital set up in New London.

14 Brig. Gen. John Tyler's Orders, Sep. 9, 1781, Governor Trumbull Papers, 15:103, CSL; "Wounded at New London, Sep 1781, physician's bill," Revolutionary War Records, Series I, XXV:214, CSL. Once the British departed, Nathaniel Shaw and Dr. Simon Wolcott returned to New London. Wolcott also assisted with the care of those wounded in New London, primarily Capt. Adam Shapley and Elijah Richards.

15 PA: Robert Gallup (S.23651), NARA; John D. Gallup. *The Genealogical History Of The Gallup Family In The United States, Also Biographical Sketches Of Members Of The Family* (Hartford, CT, 1893), 72–73.

Ziba Woodworth was long haunted by the memories of his experience. After spending several months in hospital, he went home to Norwich, but never walked right again. In a long handwritten and repentant statement included in his pension application, Woodworth recalled how he was proud to have served during the war and thanked God for allowing him to survive. But he could never get over the fact that his participation in the battle resulted in the killing of another human being, referring his actions to having "so broken gods holy law & so injured his justice." To make up for it, he moved to the Hampshire Grants, what later became Vermont, and dedicated the last thirty years of his life to "the service of god."[16]

According to the daughter of Samuel W. Jacques, a sailor from Exeter, Rhode Island, who had volunteered at Fort Griswold, the experience traumatized her father. Jacques often recalled how he had killed a redcoat in a hand-to-hand fight and how the image of the soldier always remained on his mind.[17]

From many veterans' pension applications, we learn Gallup assigned most of his regiment the day after the battle to the grisly task of burial duty. Right away, priority was given to the American dead. With the continued presence of the British squadron, the fort needed to be put into some temporary state of defense. Later, it would need a complete rehabilitation, but this would not begin until the British departed.[18]

Until it did, the British dead were left where they had been buried by their comrades. Their bodies in the ditch were not dug up for several more days, during the repair of the outer ravelin. All were removed, that is, except Major Montgomery and Archibald Willocks, whose bodies remain unmarked there today.

While most of the British were buried in the ditch or "in different places round [the fort]," the *Norwich Packet* claimed a week after the battle that the militia discovered "a considerable number" of bodies "at some distance" from the fort. All the enlisted soldiers were unburied, counted, and loaded onto carts and then transported to a local cemetery where they were reinterred in unmarked graves.[19]

---

16 PA: Ziba Woodworth (R.11848), NARA.

17 Harris, *Groton Heights*, 236.

18 PA: Ezekiel Brown (W.16868), NARA. Brown explained that after Morgan's Company was pulled off picket duty, where they spent the entire night, they were assigned to burial duty.

19 *Norwich Packet*, Sep. 13, 1781; *CG*, Sep. 7, 1781. The newspaper was dated Sep. 7 but was not printed until Sep. 10; "How Fort Griswold Looked Eighty Years Later," *The Day*, Sep. 8, 1913; John Steward, "Dead British Soldiers A Link To Our Past," Tossing Lines, *The Day*, Jan. 12, 2023. The Packet reported 40 bodies were found near the fort and that more were found "at some distance." If this is true, they were more than likely buried on the James Avery farm where a temporary British hospital had been set up before the attack on the fort. The author worked with Steward on this article to track down the location of the British dead from Fort Griswold but was unsuccessful. There are

Burial duty proved to be an exhausting, all-day task. Many of the same soldiers assigned burial duty had also been assigned to keep grieving and curious civilians at a safe distance away from the fort but did their best to help them find their loved ones and friends. Rather than have civilians enter the fort, the bodies appear to have been carried out of it by the militia and laid out somewhere adjacent for people to identify and claim.

For some, it proved deeply emotional, especially when they discovered friends or family members. Denison Avery had a difficult time as he recovered the bodies of his three brothers. He returned to the fort in the same wagon in which he had left the previous day. He carted away the bodies along with those of some friends and recalled it being "a most sad and heart rending office."[20]

Some corpses were so bloodied and disfigured it made them difficult to identify. The weather, like the previous day, was warm and humid, making the task even more difficult. Flies buzzed around as corpses began to decompose, eventually leaving ghastly imprints upon the ground in the shape of fallen soldiers, which were not easily removed. The "impressions on the ground where the dead bodies lay were distinct, and the quantity of clotted gore which we scraped up and carried away sickens my heart," a member of the militia recalled.[21]

Hubbard Burrows's son found his father's body only after turning over almost thirty corpses. Esther Chapman, wife of Lt. Richard Chapman, of Shapley's Company, sent her sons across the river to find their father's body. They found it, but it was so unrecognizable they were forced to identify him by a missing toe.[22]

Deacon Joseph Allyn, the father of Belton, was so upset at his son's departure for the fort, he set out after him and arrived at the meetinghouse to find the road blocked and endured "long hours of dreadful suspense," only to discover his son had been killed. The elder Allyn found his son's body, fixed it onto his horse, and carried him home to his awaiting mother.[23]

Stephen Avery, a member of the 2nd "Groton" Company, arrived too late to join his company in the fort. He was sent on burial duty when he learned the three officers of his company had been killed. Avery sent word home of their

---

two possible locations where they may lie: Smith Lake Cemetery or the Avery-Morgan Cemetery in Groton.

20 Pa: Denison Avery (W.23474), NARA.

21 PA: Timothy Carpenter (S.12675), NARA. Carpenter, of Tolland, served in Capt. Solomon Wales's Company. The company, comprised of drafted members of the 22nd Regiment of Connecticut Militia, was assigned to the fort in the aftermath of the attack.

22 Harris, *Groton Heights*, 230, 236, 258.

23 Ibid., 259–260.

deaths, and his younger brother Punderson came with a cart pulled by oxen. They retrieved the bodies of Capt. Simeon Allyn, Lt. Joseph Lewis, Ens. John Lester, and Cpl. Simeon Morgan, and transported them, like so many others, back to their homes for burial.[24]

Sometime during the morning, men from East Haddam under Maj. Daniel Cone were ordered across the river to Fort Griswold. Their task was to bring the dead and wounded from New London and Saybrook back across the river. Among the dead they brought back were Capt. Peter Richards, John Clark, John Holt Jr., Daniel Williams, and 69-year-old James Comstock, the oldest volunteer in the fort. Captain Adam Shapley, Sgt. Stephen Hempstead, and Sgt. John Prentis were among the wounded they retrieved. Abraham Osborn, a member of Major Cone's command, remembered listening to their groans, as they drifted across the river, but nothing was more heartbreaking than hearing the moaning of friends and family awaiting the return of the slain.[25]

The wounded were carefully moved either to their homes, if unburned, or to the homes of relatives. Shapley was taken to his home on Shapley Street, which was damaged but survived. There, his wife and Dr. Simon Wolcott attended to him, dressing and cleaning his wound until he succumbed to its effects on February 14, 1782.[26]

Sadly, not all the bodies at Fort Griswold were claimed. In some cases, families could either not bring themselves to come to collect them, or those killed did not have any local connections. Given the humidity, the militia were in a hurry to remove them as the stench was overwhelming. According to historian William W. Harris, who researched the biographies of individual defenders, the location of at least 21 of the dead remained unknown or uncertain at best. Many of these were probably unclaimed and buried in unmarked graves.[27]

As difficult as burial detail was, there were a few happy surprises. Some of the bodies were not, actually, dead. Parke Avery, left for dead on the platform along the north wall, suddenly arose. The loss of blood caused him to drift in and out of consciousness. As his supposed corpse was carried away, Avery suddenly regained

---

24 PA: Stephen Avery (S.12026), NARA; Harris, *Groton Heights*, 258. The funeral of Capt. Samuel Allyn occurred at his sister Eunice's house. He was subsequently buried in his brother-in-law's family cemetery.

25 PA: Abraham Osborn (S.14061), NARA.

26 "Wounded at New London, Sep 1781, physician's bill," *Revolutionary War Records*, Series I, XXV:214, CSL.

27 Harris, *Groton Heights*, 223–265. They were likely interred at the Starr Burying Ground or what is now Colonel Ledyard Cemetery. Several others appear to have been buried in either cemetery yet having no family connection to the town or the cemetery.

Gravestone of Lieutenant Ebenezer Avery Jr. of the 1st "Groton" Company, killed on September 6, 1781. Many of those killed at Fort Griswold and New London are buried locally throughout New London County. *Author*

consciousness. Then according to a witness, he shouted, "Keep step, damn it, keep step boys! You shake me." This startled the men carrying him, and they almost dropped him.[28]

Moses Smith, of Stonington, found his friend Daniel Stanton Jr. who had also been left for dead in the fort. But Stanton, though he'd been shot in the leg and suffered multiple bayonet wounds, was still holding onto life. Smith received permission from his captain and transported Stanton home himself. There, Stanton defied the odds, recovered, and lived for another forty-five years.[29]

The most poignant event following the battle was the funeral of Lt. Col. William Ledyard. Occurring on September 7, the funeral service was attended by members of the militia, local citizens, and Ledyard's widow Ann and his young children. Ledyard was well-known and almost universally respected. His tragic death greatly affected the community. Ledyard's corpse was carried out of the fort and prepared for burial. A wooden coffin with brass handles was procured, and Ledyard was laid in it. With Captain Lamb's Troop in the vanguard, the coffin was escorted by at least four militia companies from the 8th Regiment of Connecticut Militia to Avery's Knoll. There near the rock outcropping, a short distance from the James Avery house where the British attack began, Ledyard was buried with the "honors of war."[30]

28 Harris, *Groton Heights*, 251–252. Avery recovered and survived for another forty years.

29 PA: Moses Smith (W.22235), NARA; Harris, *Groton Heights*, 264–265. Though Smith recounted finding Stanton inside the fort, Harris noted Daniel as being one of those removed by the British in the wagon.

30 "Reinternment of the Remains of Col. Ledyard," *New London Weekly Chronicle*, Aug. 13, 1855; PA: Jason Stanton (W.505); John Eells (S.29132), NARA. Ledyard was interred there until 1855 when the state legislature allocated money for a larger monument. They opened the graves of the Ledyard family and moved them about fifty yards to the west where they lie today. Present

Lieutenant Colonel William Ledyard Monument. In 1854, the state of Connecticut appropriated funds for a new monument over Ledyard's grave at the Colonel Ledyard Cemetery to commemorate his death. *Author*

In New London, the fires were still burning, and smoke continued to hover over the harbor, causing the smell of burned charcoal to hang in the air. Militiamen marching along the waterfront were aghast at the sights. Never had they seen so much destruction. One militiaman remembered, "The place was in ruins, the fires smoldering, the chimneys standing at intervals marked the site of the destroyed habitations. Among other things we noticed [was] where the fire had burned a warehouse containing large quantities of butter, a stream of the liquid article had flowed down the street, to the distance of several rods, and two or three in width."[31]

Over 140 structures, mainly along the waterfront, had either been severely damaged or destroyed. In a somber letter to the governor, a militia officer in New London wrote, "The Loss Sustain'd in [New London] In Goods, Provisions[,] Stores[,] Shipping &c is Very Great." Over thirty storehouses were destroyed and several wharves were damaged. A ropewalk, at least five cooper shops, a tannery, three slaughterhouses, a shoemaker shop, and a distillery were all destroyed. Additionally, around twenty barns, one print shop, the post office, the county courthouse, the town jail, and St. James Anglican Church and a variety of other smaller structures, including a barbershop, were all consumed in the flames. What had been a flourishing waterfront a day earlier was "all in ashes." The local economy would not recover for several years.[32]

Half the structures burned or damaged were homes, leaving at least 100 families homeless. Some escaped the town on the day of the battle, most only carrying with them a few personal belongings. Others, especially those with small children, left with only the clothes on their backs. When they returned, many found their homes along with everything they owned suddenly gone. Distressed

---

at the funeral were Nathan Geer, of the 3rd "Preston" Company, Ezra Gallup, of the 5th "Stonington" Company, Asa Cheesebrough, of Captain Noyes's Company, and Jason Stanton, of the 4th Troop.

31 *Boston Evening Transcript*, Aug. 22, 1847.

32 John Hempsted narrative in Harris, *Groton Heights*, 68; Zabdiel Rogers to Governor Jonathan Trumbull, Sep. 7, 1781, Governor Trumbull Papers, Vol. 4, Folder 6, CHS; *CG*, Sep. 12, 1781.

and overwhelmed with grief, civilians wandered the streets throughout the day. Most looked for food for themselves or their families.

This greatly saddened Brig. Gen. John Tyler. On September 7, he toured the harbor area, inspecting its defenses. Part of the day was spent riding through New London, and what he saw was heartbreaking. He later reported to Governor Trumbull, "I found many bereav'd [widows] and Fatherless Children who had lost their all & Left without the Least substance wandering in the streets." To help alleviate some of their sufferings, Tyler issued orders releasing the public stores kept in nearby towns and directed them to New London so they could be distributed to citizens in need.[33]

If a family was fortunate to find its home still standing, it was more than likely broken into and ransacked. Thousands of soldiers, both British and American, had been through the town in a matter of hours. Since the town had been retaken, citizens, militia, and sailors were everywhere with no recognizable organization or command structure, and as a result there was no law and order. This would take another day or so to reestablish. The streets were littered with sundries, including furniture and clothing, which had been thrown out from homes as they caught fire. Without law and order there were those "evil-minded persons who took the opportunity to [carry off] many valuable Articles, especially Clothing," as well as vandalize abandoned homes.[34]

Even as Tyler attempted to restore order, other concerns vexed him. The British squadron still hovered about the entrance of the harbor. Their intentions were not yet clear. Were they headed back to New York? Were they headed towards another target along the Connecticut coast? Or would they strike at Norwich?

Many in the militia believed Norwich was the next British target. They recognized that the British had come to either capture or destroy the privateers, but they had escaped upriver to Norwich. There was also the news that Arnold was in command. This was confirmed by citizens who had remained and recognized

---

33 John Tyler to Governor Trumbull, Sep. 10, 1781, Governor Trumbull Papers, 15:110a–b, CSL; *CG*, Oct. 12, 1781; Rogers, *Naval Office*, 30–31. About a week prior to the raid, the prize ship *Hope* arrived in the harbor. Captured by the letter of marque, *Navarre*, of Philadelphia, the *Hope* carried flour, beef, pork, butter, candles, soap, porter, and other articles which were desperately needed by the local population. The owners petitioned Governor Trumbull and the Council of Safety to hurry the legal process so they could auction the goods for the benefit of the local population.

34 "From Connecticut Gazette, Sep. 28, 1781," Charles Allyn Papers, NLCHS. Captain Michael Mellally returned to his home on Bradley Street and found a variety of household items had been stolen from his garden. Items included "7 pair sheets, 5 pair pillow-cases, [several pieces of fabrics], 1 crimson ratten coat, 1 blue ditto, large number of waistcoats of different colours, and a number of shirts." They had been stolen, according to him, *after* the British had departed.

Arnold as he rode about the town. It seemed the next logical step for the Norwich native was to give chase to the privateers, especially since he knew the area so well.[35]

Arnold's actions had already unleashed a new and stronger wave of hatred against him. Even while it made strategic sense that Arnold would continue the attack up the Thames River, some believed he would attack Norwich for a different, far more sinister reason—personal retribution. According to a member of the 20th Regiment of Connecticut Militia, he heard a rumor circulating that while Arnold was in New London he had threatened "to go and burn the town of Norwich and his uncle's property" where he had formerly lived. Another soldier in the regiment believed "British forces were about to ravage the country."[36]

This belief was so strongly held that in the following weeks town officials in Norwich instituted a nine o'clock curfew and ordered a nighttime militia patrol to keep watch over Norwich Landing (today's downtown Norwich) and its harbor. Special express riders were also privately contracted to ride between Norwich and New London to ensure the quickest flow of information between the two towns.[37]

Most in the harbor area grew relieved when, by mid-morning, the British squadron lifted sail and drifted out into Long Island Sound. All throughout the previous night, sailors aboard each of the vessels had been busy preparing to set sail that morning. The expedition was for all intents and purposes over. It was time to return to New York. It took until around 7:30 a.m. for wind conditions to become favorable. Captain Bazely then ordered the *Amphion*, which was anchored at the entrance of the harbor, to weigh anchor and make sail westward. Signal flags were run up, alerting the rest of the convoy to follow suit. The *Amphion*, accompanied by the brigs *Argo* and *Lurcher*, and the rest of the squadron, sailed westward for about two hours along the coast towards Lyme.[38]

As they did, they remained under the watchful eyes of the militia, as well as the coast guard company under Lt. Josiah Burnham, which were stationed at various points at Lyme. Burnham's Company employed two whaleboats which patrolled day and night between Lyme and New London to intercept illicit trade. One boat, commanded by Sgt. Zebulon Brockway, was out the night of September 5-6 and watched the British squadron approach New London Harbor. But for some reason

35 PA: Solomon Welch (W.14664), NARA. Welch stated some companies of the 5th Regiment of Connecticut Militia on their way to New London were diverted to Norwich.

36 PA: Elijah Waterman (S.7825); Obadiah Hudson (R.5337), NARA.

37 Christopher Leffingwell to Samuel McClellan, Oct. 17, 1781, "Christopher Leffingwell's Letter Book," Leffingwell Family Papers, YU.

38 Master's log, HMS *Amphion*, ADM 52/2133, TNA.

crew members never sounded the alarm. Instead, they took their boat closer to the coastline, and the crew went ashore.[39]

To ensure the British squadron remained together in case the privateers might suddenly descend the Thames River and threaten the convoy, Bazely ordered the entire squadron to turn back towards New London. As it did, the British brig *Keppel* approached the squadron. The 14-gun brig, under Lt. Robert Steel, had been patrolling Long Island Sound. Steel ordered his vessel towards the Connecticut coast to join the squadron.[40]

The *Keppel* was the first vessel to reach the lighthouse, where it anchored around noon. The rest of the squadron arrived over the next several hours, all returning close to shore and anchoring by 5:00 p.m. Bazely, again anxious about the privateers, ordered his armed vessels, among them the *Recovery*, the *Beaumont*, the *Hussar*, and the *Keppel*, to enter the harbor. There, throughout the remainder of the day and into the night, the armed vessels were strung out near the lighthouse, to cover the troop transports.[41]

The return of the British squadron put more pressure on Tyler and assuredly helped fuel the rumors of a renewed attack. Sometime during the day, Tyler was joined by Maj. Gen. Joseph Spencer, who arrived from Hartford, accompanied by his son and aide-de-camp, Maj. Isaac Spencer. The general was a member of the Council of Safety, and the state's senior ranking militia general.[42]

Spencer had been sent by Governor Trumbull. Both men had been in Hartford attending a meeting with the Council of Safety when news of the attack arrived about sunrise on September 7. The news came from Samuel Gay of Lebanon, who was sent to Hartford by William Williams, the governor's son-in-law. Upon hearing the news of the attack, Williams sent Gay on to Hartford, who rode to New London and arrived as the British were withdrawing, covering 23 miles in about three hours.

Unfortunately, when Gay arrived in Hartford, he only brought the governor limited information. Confiding in his diary, Trumbull summarized: "N. London

---

39 PA: Joseph Bloss (S.21071); Zebulon Brockway (S.31565), NARA.

40 Winfield, *British Warships*, 320; Mackenzie, *Diary*, 2:602; Master's Log, HMS *Amphion*, ADM 52/2133, TNA; Royal Navy Ships' Muster (Series 1), HMS *Amphion*, ADM 36/9561, TNA. The *Keppel* was formerly the privateer *New Broome*, which operated out of New Haven. On his arrival, Steel secured from the *Amphion* a supply of freshwater for his vessel. The *Amphion* also dispersed a supply of fresh water to all the transports, nearly seven tons of it.

41 Captain's Log, HMS *Keppel*, ADM 51/503, TNA; Master's Log, HMS *Keppel*, ADM 52/2367, TNA; Master's Log, HMS *Recovery*, ADM 52/2491, TNA; Master's Log, HMS *Beaumont*, ADM 52/2192, TNA.

42 *CSR*, 2:294.

attacked by 2000 men, 3 ships, and in the whole 30 sail." Another report came from Levi Wells, of Colchester, a report that struck a more dramatic note. Wells wrote, New London is "in flames which is Plain to be seen hear [sic] by Large Quantities of Smoke." With these reports, Trumbull dispatched Spencer to take command of the militia at New London and figure out what was going on.[43]

More intelligence arrived the next day, and the situation continued to look bleak. In a somber letter written early the previous day, Col. Zabdiel Rogers informed Trumbull, "The Enemy were under the Command of The Infamous Genl Arnold & by the Best Accounts Consisted of from 1500 to 2000 Men. They have Burnt The Greatest Part of the Towns of New London & Groton, Near the Water." And as of this writing, Rogers continued, "The Enemy This Morning were at the Harbour Mouth On Board there Shipping and Came to Sail about Eight O Clock. They are Still but Just out Beyond The Light House as the Wind is Against them[.] The Enemy's Shipping Consists of about Thirty Sail, Two of which appear to be about 20 Guns Each." The only comforting news was that most of the privateers had escaped upriver.[44]

Trumbull had every reason to worry. For him, the attack on New London confirmed warnings he had received from various sources in the Continental Army of the possibility of a British incursion into Connecticut. For two weeks in August, Trumbull had been in Danbury with his Council of Safety. The governor's visit to western Connecticut had coincided with the initial movements of the armies under Washington and Rochambeau southward towards Yorktown. On August 22, three days into their march south, Washington warned Trumbull he had received intelligence of the strong possibility of "a hostile Attack" or even an "Invasion of [the] State." Washington pressed Trumbull to prepare his militia and that any "valuable Effects" stored along the coast "be removed to Interior Parts."[45]

The same day, the governor's son, Jonathan Jr., a secretary to Washington, also suggested the same possibility attacks against Connecticut to his father. The younger Trumbull wrote, "The withdraw of the troops, & the absence of [Washington from the Hudson Highlands], will render it necessary for the States to keep a very watchfull eye of the motions of the enemy on the sea coasts, & to

43 I. W. Stuart, *Life of Jonathan Trumbull, Sen; Governor of Connecticut* (Hartford, CT, 1878), 542; PA: Isaac Spencer (S.15653), NARA; Levi Wells to Governor Trumbull, Sep. 6, 1781, Governor Trumbull Papers, Vol. 4, Folder 6, CHS.

44 Zabdiel Rogers to Governor Jonathan Trumbull, Sep. 7, 1781, Governor Trumbull Papers, Vol. 4, Folder 6, CHS.

45 Jonathan Trumbull to George Washington, Sep. 13, 1781, Papers of George Washington, LOC. The original letter written by Washington does not seem to have survived, but Trumbull's reply to Washington still exists.

keep themselves as well guarded at all points possible. I am very apprehensive they may find leisure to vent their mischievous humour on our shores."[46]

Additional warnings came from Maj. Gen. Samuel H. Parsons who, in 1781, commanded troops in the Hudson Highlands. Parsons told Trumbull he had learned from his spies in New York that if Washington moved his army away from the Hudson River Valley, the British were prepared "to undertake desultory expeditions upon the coasts of some of the States." Where or when they might strike was not known.[47]

Following their meeting in Danbury on August 23, the governor heeded the warnings, and he and his Council of Safety returned to Hartford. From there, they were in a better position to deploy the state's militia and other resources to defend the town in the event of a British attack. Fortunately, Connecticut was not entirely defenseless. The close presence of the British army and navy at New York City and on Long Island, along with the hard lessons learned because of the British attacks in 1777 and 1779, had forced the state to set up regular defenses along its coastline and borders.

As early as 1777, shortly before the British attack on Danbury, the General Assembly organized several coast guard companies and positioned them at points along the coastline. In the event of an attack, these companies sounded the alarm and then acted as the first line of defense, giving the other militia companies time to mobilize. As an incentive to enlist, the coast guard companies drew their recruits from militia companies raised in towns they protected and allowed the soldiers the opportunity to protect their own homes and enjoy the assurance they would never serve far from home. By 1781, there were eighteen sectors dispersed among fifteen coastal towns, spreading eastward from Stonington, on the Rhode Island border, towards Greenwich, on its western border with New York.[48]

Additionally, Trumbull, that summer, had a militia brigade under Brig. Gen. David Waterbury. Consisting of two infantry battalions, it numbered some 500

---

46 *The Trumbull Papers: Early miscellaneous papers related to the Narragansett country. Letters of William Samuel Johnson. Letters of Jedediah Huntington -pt. II. Correspondence between General Washington and Governor Trumbull and others. Letters of John Hancock, Joseph Warren, Thomas Gage, James Warren and Governor Trumbull. List of Washington's letters. List of Trumbull's letters to Washington. -pt. III-IV. Letters and documents relating to the revolution, 1777-1783* (Boston, 1902), 264–265.

47 Parsons, *Life and Letters*, 396–397.

48 *CSR*, 1:116–118; "A Return of a Brigade of Connecticut State Troops commanded by Brig. Gen. Waterbury," Stamford, June 19, 1781, Governor Trumbull Papers, 24:153, CSL; William Ledyard to Governor Trumbull, July 3, 1781, Governor Trumbull Papers, 322a–c, CSL. Each company had a main station within their sector, but hardly remained just there. Small detachments were often dispersed, especially during the nighttime hours, to patrol beaches along their assigned areas. This was done to keep watch as well as counter the illicit trade.

men. Ordered by the General Assembly the previous fall, Waterbury's Brigade was the largest organized militia force in Connecticut. Its primary function was the protection of the Lower Post Road, the main route into Connecticut from the direction of New York City, which passed through Greenwich.[49]

Directly over the border in New York was Westchester County. Known during the war as the "neutral ground," it was one of the most divided and volatile regions in the country. By 1781, the chaos had spilled over into Connecticut. Waterbury's men were kept busy. They constantly clashed with British irregular troops, as well as the loyalist Westchester County Militia, led by Col. James Delancey, who foraged throughout Westchester County and frequently crossed into Connecticut, where they stole cattle, horses, and other livestock. Then, there were the Associated Loyalists at Fort Franklin or other Refugee forces on Long Island, which regularly harassed coastal towns. That summer the situation had worsened so much in Greenwich that civil authority was almost non-existent. Waterbury was forced to withdraw eastward, where he took up a position along the Mianus River in neighboring Stamford.

The other forces protecting Connecticut's borders were also kept busy throughout the summer months. They combated illicit trade and defended against several small enemy incursions, which occurred quite frequently. These attacks targeted vulnerable farms and other areas away from the larger, better-defended towns and more than once occurred under cover of darkness. Most of these attacks solely involved the Associated Loyalists.

A week before the raid on New London, the Associated Loyalists mounted their largest attack into Connecticut. This alone would have confirmed the warnings sent to Trumbull of an attack on Connecticut. During the night of August 31-September 1, 150 Associated Loyalists in several whaleboats, accompanied by the sloops *Association, Colonel Martin*, and the brig *Sir Henry Clinton*, attacked the parish of West Haven in New Haven.

New Haven was Connecticut's largest town by population and the state's second-largest port. Because of its strategic importance, a regular garrison, like in

---

49 *CSR*, 3:317–319; "A Return of a Brigade of Connecticut State Troops commanded by Brig. Gen. Waterbury," Stamford, June 19, 1781, Governor Trumbull Papers, 24:153, CSL; *Connecticut Men*, 564–574. The brigade was organized from the state's militia and up until August had served with Washington's army in Westchester County, even participating in the feint attacks against New York City. But with the march southward, it returned to Connecticut. Waterbury also oversaw the nine coast guard companies, which protected the coastline from Greenwich to New Haven. If he desired, he had the authority to call on them for assistance.

New London, was organized to protect it. Lieutenant Colonel Aaron Austin was appointed its commandant.[50]

The loyalists came ashore at Savin Rock, near the western entrance of New Haven harbor, about five miles from the center of town, the same place a British force had landed two years earlier. They landed and surprised the sentries, captured them along with guards who were asleep. With the alarm unsounded, the loyalists marched inland for almost two miles. Facing no opposition, they freely plundered farms and houses. Before dawn, the Associated Loyalists withdrew, taking with them prisoners and about 30 head of cattle and horses.[51]

The raid shocked residents as it was reminiscent of the attack in 1779, and the population remained on edge. One resident stated, "Our situation, in this town, has been such that but little business has been done this day or two, occasioned by [the enemy's attack]." Exaggerated accounts strengthened the belief that the next target was New Haven. One enemy deserter told officials, they "may expect another visit in 10 days for the Purpose of Ruin." When one resident learned of the attack, he kept anxious watch over the movements of the loyalists, noting them in his diary.[52]

Major General Parsons, on leave from his post in the Hudson Highlands, was riding from Milford to New Haven. Hearing of the attack, Parsons detoured to West Haven. Once there, he took command of the militia which assembled to contest the loyalists. Parsons, also aware of the possibility of attacks on Connecticut, remained in the area, a decision Governor Trumbull came to appreciate.[53]

With the knowledge of a possible attack on Connecticut for almost two weeks, Trumbull had not remained idle. He realized that even with the coast guard companies, protecting 120 miles of coastline was no simple task, especially when the British had the ability to land almost anywhere. Until late August, the presence of the French naval squadron under Admiral de Barras in Rhode Island provided some cover to the coastline. Now, with its departure, other than the privateers there was no major naval force to counter British naval movements in Long Island Sound. So, with the advice of the Council of Safety, the governor came up with a plan.

---

50 *CSR*, 3:318.

51 PA: Deliverance Painter (S.15567), NARA; *Newport Mercury*, Sep. 8, 1781.

52 Timothy Jones and Charles Chauncey to Governor Trumbull, Sep. 1, 1781, Governor Trumbull Papers, 15:87a–b, CSL; Ezra Stiles, *The Literary Diary of Ezra Stiles, D.D.; LLD. President of Yale College*, 3 vols., Franklin B. Dexter, ed. (New York, 1901), 2:552. Stiles incorrectly believed that 100 prisoners were taken.

53 Stiles, *Literary Diary*, 2:552.

The plan involved using privateers to fill the void left by the departure of the French navy. They would act as an exterior line of defense in Long Island Sound. The governor's plan would benefit both parties. The privateers were still allowed to prey on vulnerable enemy shipping, but at the same time, their presence in the Sound would deter the British from making sudden incursions into the state or, at the very least, act as an early warning system for the militia. The militia needed all the help it could get in the event of an attack. It was already stretched thin. Besides Waterbury's Brigade, another Connecticut militia regiment of 800 men was sent to reinforce West Point.[54]

Governor Trumbull turned to his counterpart in Massachusetts for assistance. Writing to Governor John Hancock, Trumbull informed him of his plan and asked the Massachusetts governor for his support, in the form of militia from his western counties and for the use of "one or more frigates [which] could be sent to New London to assist the Privateers lying there, and to Cruise with them in the sound." Their presence, Trumbull told Hancock, "would be of [excellent] service & Effectually prevent the future Incursions of the Enemy by Water, & be a greater security to our sea port Towns which constitute a 5th part of this State than many thousands of Militia." Trumbull closed by expressing his fear that since Long Island Sound was so largely unprotected, "the Enemy At New York have nothing to fear and may employee their whole force upon this State."[55]

Unfortunately, Trumbull's plan never went into effect. His letter to Hancock, along with two subsequent letters, went unanswered for about a week. By then, the British had already accomplished what they planned. Even if Trumbull had received assistance, it would have arrived too late to have stopped the British attack on New London. However, if it had been arranged earlier, it might have worked. Trumbull's plan was sound and quite feasible. The presence of one or more Continental frigates, which were larger naval vessels built for combat and typically mounted with 24–32 guns, working with the privateers could have matched the strength and firepower of Bazely's squadron. Bazely would have had a more difficult time convoying Arnold's troops if there had been this type of opposition in his way.[56]

54 *CSR*, 3:462. This was Canfield's Regiment of Connecticut Militia under Lieutenant Colonel Samuel Canfield.

55 Trumbull to John Hancock, Sep. 11, 1781, Governor Trumbull Papers, CHS. By the time this third letter was written, Trumbull was clearly irritated and growing impatient. Hancock had not replied to his two previous letters, written on Sep. 6 and Sep. 10.

56 John Hancock to Trumbull, Sep. 9, 1781, Governor Trumbull Papers, 15:106a–b, CSL. In his reply, Hancock pledged his support to Trumbull. He also ordered several of his militia regiments, primarily from his western counties, to be ready to march to the aid of Connecticut. Hancock never

Unlike the first part of Trumbull's plan, the second part, prompted by Washington's urgings to ready the state's militia, reinforce the coast guard companies, and remove "valuable Effects" away from the coastline, did go into effect, but it was too late.[57]

During the last week of August, Trumbull directed several militia regimental commanders to draft companies to reinforce key points on the coast. There is strong evidence to suggest at least six militia companies were being organized and deployed the week of Arnold's attack.[58]

The day following the attack on New London, Trumbull issued preparatory orders to at least one militia colonel to ready his entire regiment in order that it could be moved to the coastline at a moment's notice. Trumbull told Col. Comfort Sage, of the 23rd Regiment of Connecticut Militia, whose companies were drawn from Middletown and Chatham, in the central part of the state, "Being advised that the Enemy landed yesterday Morning at New London and probably design to ravage the Sea Coast or penetrate the Country . . . you are hereby directed to issue your Orders immediately for the Regt under your Command to be in Readiness to march on the shortest Notice."[59]

In what best could be described as tragic irony, the Council of Safety had spent most of September 6 discussing how to improve the defenses of New London. By the end of the day, the Council, with Trumbull's approval, had given Lieutenant Colonel Ledyard the authority to move any goods or merchandise lying in storehouses or vessels within the harbor which might attract the attention of the British to be moved inland.[60]

Days before the attack, Dr. Philemon Tracy was ordered to remove the hospital's stores, such as blankets, bedding, medicines, and furniture to the Continental hospital in Norwich. The hospital's proximity to New London was judged too vulnerable, so as a precaution, it was ordered evacuated. The hospital

---

brought up naval support, though at the time, there was at least one Continental frigate, the *Alliance*, refitting in Boston Harbor. However, repairs did take longer than expected due to lack of available funding.

57 Jonathan Trumbull to George Washington, Sep. 13, 1781, Papers of George Washington, LOC.

58 Companies under Capt. Alexander Catlin (14th, 17th, and 18th Regiments of Connecticut Militia), Capt. Charles Norton (10th Regiment of Connecticut Militia), Capt. Daniel Brainard (23rd Regiment of Connecticut Militia) were ordered to New Haven. At least one company under Capt. Joseph Garnsey (10th and 28th Regiments of Connecticut Militia) was headed to Milford.

59 Trumbull to Comfort Sage, Sep. 7, 1781, Council of Safety Papers, 201, CHS. It is hard to imagine the governor only sent a single directive to one commander, but since only one survives we do not know how many units were ordered to do the same.

60 Stuart, *Life of Trumbull*, 541; *CSR*, 3:502.

was established to tend sick sailors, both American and British, brought into the port, as well as provide smallpox inoculation for recruits who had not yet received it. The Gales Ferry site was chosen specifically because the ferry provided the ability to shuffle men and supplies across the river. On the west bank, a road connected it to the Norwich Road, which provided access to New London or Norwich. Tracy had completed the establishment, and the hospital was partially operational when the orders came to evacuate it along with its stores.[61]

News of the attacks on West Haven and New London caused Trumbull to fear the entire state was under attack. Perhaps his only comfort during this trying time was the promise of a successful outcome to the campaign against Lord Cornwallis at Yorktown, a campaign which he believed, if successful, promised great results. His son eagerly wrote to his father of the arrival of the French fleet in the Chesapeake Bay. Trumbull replied, "[I] hope Lord Cornwallis may soon be in as safe custody as Ld Rawdon," referring to Lord Francis Rawdon, a British brigadier general who had been captured at sea on his way back to England. Closing, he told his son, "[W]e may trust that the supreme director of all events will give our enemy's into our hands. Our Eyes are to be up to him to bless & prosper our aims and enterprizes." But even so, he could not take it for granted.[62]

While the prospects of an American victory at Yorktown looked promising, Trumbull could not be distracted. No one then knew the effects the eventual victory would have. Initially, Trumbull's focus was on the protection of New London. He knew he could rely on the state's militia, which was collecting there to defend it. But they would only serve for a short duration of time, especially since it was the fall harvest season. There was an urgent need for a longer-serving force to New London and Groton. So, Trumbull ordered the formation of a new state regiment to be stationed there. It would be comprised of 500 men drafted from the state's militia who would serve for one month.[63]

The governor hoped this regiment would protect the harbor, but also put its forts back into a posture of defense. Appointed to command was Col. Samuel McClellan, of Woodstock, and commander of the 11th Regiment of Connecticut Militia. The 51-year-old McClellan, the great-grandfather of the famed Civil

---

61 PA: Philemon Tracy (W.3625), NARA; *Middlesex County*, 403. Timothy Clark, wounded aboard the privateer Sampson, was taken to the hospital the day of the raid.

62 Governor Trumbull to Jonathan Trumbull Jr., Sep. 13, 1781, Governor Trumbull Papers, 15:120, CSL.

63 *CSR*, 3:507, 514. Their time of service commenced the day they arrived in New London, and while only required to serve one month, many testified in their pension applications that they served longer.

War general George B. McClellan, would also be appointed to serve as Ledyard's replacement as commandant of the harbor, a post he held until the end of the war.[64]

When Major General Spencer arrived, he probably carried with him orders related to the formation of McClellan's Regiment. Soon after his arrival, officers were appointed, and the militia present began to be drafted into its companies. Present in the New London area were seven militia regiments from two different brigades. McClellan's companies would be drawn from two of them. From the Third Brigade, the 3rd, 20th, and the 25th Regiments of Connecticut Militia; and from the Fifth Brigade, the 5th, 12th and 21st Regiments of Connecticut Militia. Once organized, they marched to their duty stations, which were primarily at Fort Trumbull and Fort Griswold.[65]

The new companies could not be formed fast enough. The disarray in the face of a hostile British squadron was a serious liability for both Spencer and Tyler. When the 12th Regiment arrived, one member immediately recognized the disorder. The regiment, under Col. Jeremiah Mason, began arriving during the evening of September 6 along both the Norwich and Colchester Roads. One member, halted on Quaker Hill, and observed, "The troops or militia which were out . . . were ordered or stationed at different points in & about the [town] & the whole scene was attended with so much hurry and compulsion." If the British renewed their attack, the militia might have difficulty resisting it.[66]

Not only was McClellan's Regiment organizing on September 7, but the other militia present, most of which would be dismissed home within a week, took the day to better organize themselves. With the lull, officers were able to collect their commands, many of whom arrived by themselves or in small groups. Several militiamen testified to this fact.[67]

---

64 Selah Norton to Governor Trumbull, Sep. 8, 1781, Council of Safety Papers, CHS; *CSR*, 3:507. The regiment was ordered by Trumbull on Sep. 8, but not sanctioned by the Council of Safety until four days later. Lieutenant Colonel Joshua Huntington, of the 20th Regiment of Connecticut Militia, was originally appointed to command, but declined for personal reasons.

65 PA: Samuel Emmons (W.7106), NARA. Spencer only stayed until September 9. Until McClellan's arrival in the last week of September Maj. Richard Wait of Lyme, and third-in-command of the 3rd Regiment of Connecticut Militia, assumed command of the new regiment. This gap of time caused the unit to be referred to as Wait's Battalion.

66 PA: John Eells (S.29132); Ezekiel Avery (S.5261); Stephen Barber (S.12030), NARA. Barber, of Capt. Samuel Jones "2nd Veteran Company," stated they moved from Hebron to Colchester to modern-day Montville, and then onto Quaker Hill, where they remained for a few days before moving "below the town" where they kept guard and performed the "various duties of a soldier."

67 PA: Peter Way (W.18228), NARA. Way, from Lyme, owned a small lot of land on Town Hill just south of Fort Nonsense and his brother Daniel's lot.

Tyler took advantage of the better organized 12th, 20th and 25th Regiments of Connecticut Militia and utilized them right away. The balance of the 25th Regiment, under Col. Elias Worthington, arrived throughout the morning. As the fires died out, Tyler moved all three units from their position north of town. A few days following the attack, the 12th Regiment was marched to Fort Trumbull, where they bivouacked in the area around the fort, and Colonel Mason assumed temporary command of the fort. Rogers's men were moved from Quaker Hill down the Norwich Road onto Town Street, where they were quartered for the next several days. Their role was to help re-establish law and order in the town, and in detachments they cleared and patrolled the streets, put out lingering fires, and assisted civilians.[68]

The 25th Regiment was ordered to Meetinghouse Hill, where it bivouacked on the militia training field. Since the town's supply of tents had been destroyed, the men were forced to do without or with whatever they carried with them from home. Most militiamen carried knapsacks and blankets. But still, a member of Capt. James Ransom's Company on the hilltop remembered "[he] got no sleep for three nights."[69]

Companies from the 25th Regiment rotated guard duty around the harbor. Their duty posts were in areas south of town. From available sources, we know that at least three companies from the regiment, under Capt. James Ransom, Capt. Stephen Brainard, and Capt. Elijah Worthington spent about a week along the river and Long Island Sound. They were dispersed along the river from Fort Trumbull southward to the Sarah Harris farm, near the lighthouse. While Captain Ransom's command was deployed along the river, Brainard's command was stationed near the lighthouse. Brainard's men were eventually joined by Capt. Richard Deshon's Company from the 3rd Regiment. Eventually a detachment from Capt. Abraham Fitch's Troop in the 2nd Regiment of Light Horse was sent to assist the infantry.[70]

---

68 Jeremiah Mason, Memoir, *Autobiography and Correspondence of Jeremiah Mason* (Kansas City, MO, 1917), 3; PA: John Frisbie (W.17921); Bezaleel Bristol (W.20781); Samuel Churchill (R.1953); John Newtown (S.17602), NARA. Other various companies from the 2nd Regiment of Connecticut Militia, formed in New Haven, 6th Regiment of Connecticut Militia, organized in the Wethersfield and Glastonbury area, and the 7th Regiment of Connecticut Militia, organized in Saybrook, Haddam, and Killingworth, also served in New London during this time. Most veterans testified to helping civilians during this time of service. Unfortunately, lacking any official returns we do not know how many companies arrived or the strength of the regiment. Though according to John Newton, a member of Capt. James Ransom's Company, the "whole regiment was called out," which, according to a 1780 return meant close to 700 men.

69 PA: John Newton (S.17602), NARA. Newton, of Capt. James Ransom's Company, marched on New London upon hearing the alarm guns and without official orders.

70 PA: David Treadway (S.11578); Eldad Sabin (S.14395), NA; Joel Bigelow (W.1535), NA; Charles Allyn Papers, NLCHS; PA: Daniel Dewey (S.17926); Charles Wattles (S.14799), NARA. Sometime

As at Fort Griswold, burial parties were sent out to collect and bury the dead. At least two companies, one from the 12th Regiment under Sgt. Christopher Crouch and another from the 25th Regiment under Capt. Elijah Worthington, were sent out. Compared to Fort Griswold, the Americans in New London suffered significantly fewer casualties. The *Connecticut Gazette* reported the day after the battle that they suffered four killed and ten or twelve wounded. Most casualties seemed to have occurred in the fighting north of town and during the pursuit of the British rear guard. Strangely absent were the number of American prisoners taken by the British.[71]

Bodies were scattered on Post Hill, throughout the town, and on Town Hill. More care was given to the dead American soldiers, as most were buried in marked graves. The British dead were not given the same courtesies; no effort was made to identify or even mark their graves. The dead loyalists found on Post Hill were hastily buried near where they fell. According to Charles Allyn, a local historian, burial parties discovered at least one of the Associated Loyalists buried under an ash tree near the intersection of modern-day Vauxhall and Channing Streets. This would have been just yards away from where the Pickett Latimer house stood.[72]

Other British bodies were reportedly buried along modern-day Williams Street, near the Manwaring House. The loyalist who died at the house was believed to have been buried opposite the house. Militia found the body of Pvt. Stephen Islick, of the Loyal American Regiment, in a potato field just south of Fort Nonsense. "It was as Evident as that there had been two hogs kild, By the blood & whare they Draged them away through a feald of potoes, & ther Shoulders tore up the potatoes out of the hills," a militia officer on the scene remembered. But where the body was removed to remains unknown.[73]

---

during their week of service, Captain Worthington turned over his command to Capt. David Kilbourn. Fitch's Troop of the 2nd Regiment of Light Horse, a mounted militia unit, arrived with the 12th Regiment. It was very active during this time, as it had also provided dispatch riders to help with the flow of information between all the militia commanders. Wattles explained the breakdown of dispatch riders and assigned duties.

71 *CG*, Sep. 7, 1781. Oddly, they made no mention of the number of prisoners taken by the British, which at the time was probably undetermined.

72 PA: John Cavarly (W.17593); Joel Bigelow (W.1535); Abijah Dewey (S.22725), NARA. Harris, *Groton Heights*, 110. After burial duty, Worthington's Company was sent south of town on guard duty.

73 R. B. Wall, "When the Traitor Arnold Burned New London Town, Part 1" *The Day*, Dec. 2, 1914; Muster rolls, Loyal American Regiment, British Military and Naval Records, RG 8, "C" Series, Volume 1867, page 71, PAC; John Hempsted narrative in Harris, *Groton Heights*, 69. Islick was the only soldier killed from the Loyal American Regiment. The amount of blood convinced Hempsted there was a second soldier killed. There were also 2 or 3 other reported burials near the Manwaring

Since the town jail had burned, there was no place to keep British prisoners. Colonel Latimer had in his possession almost thirty prisoners, both enemy combatants and a loyalist civilian. It is probable they were kept for a time at the Daniel Latimer house. The one loyalist civilian, arrested for illicit trading, was kept there in the immediate aftermath of the attack. The 21 British prisoners taken by the militia would not remain in New London. They were soon escorted to Norwich where they were kept in a storehouse owned by Ebenezer Backus until a prisoner exchange could be arranged. While there the wounded prisoners received treatment for their wounds.[74]

Efforts were made almost immediately to use these prisoners and exchange them for American prisoners taken by Arnold's force. The downside was that there were not enough British prisoners to exchange for even half the numbers Arnold had with him. And due to the rules of the prisoner exchange, they could only exchange army personnel for army personnel and naval personnel for naval personnel. So, despite a significant number of British naval prisoners in Norwich awaiting an exchange, these could not be utilized.

On September 9, things had calmed down enough that Brig. Gen. Tyler was ready to open an exchange with the British. The British prisoners were returned to New London, along with six other naval prisoners held in the town prior to the attack. They were placed aboard Nathaniel Shaw's schooner the *Queen of France*, which had just returned to port and immediately set sail. Aboard was Nathaniel Shaw Jr. and Ebenezer Ledyard who carried a letter to Arnold drafted by Tyler with permission to go between the lines. It was a flag of truce document signed off by the selectmen of Groton and New London to their appointment as "Flag Officers" to negotiate the release of the prisoners taken at Fort Griswold and New London. However, by the time they departed, the British squadron was gone, and the delegation had to continue to Whitestone.[75]

---

house, on modern-day Williams Street. Human remains were reportedly discovered in nearby Williams Park in 2000.

74 John Hempsted narrative in Harris, *Groton Heights*, 67. Muster Book, HMS *Keppel*, ADM 36/10026, TNA. The civilian was Thomas Fitch, of Chesterfield Society, New London, who had been arrested at Black Point in Lyme, as he attempted to send "a Drove of Sheep" over to the British on Long Island. Tensions were so high that the militia standing guard over Fitch had to protect him from local citizens bent on revenge. The number also included six British naval prisoners, probably a prize crew from the brig *Syren*, who were held in town just prior to the attack.

75 Muster Book, HMS *Keppel*, ADM 36/10026, TNA; "Copy of Letter from David Sproat to Nathaniel Shaw," in Rogers, *Naval Office*, 30; "Copy of Flag of Truce Document and Letter Written by Brig. Gen. John Tyler to Brig. Gen. Arnold," in Rogers, *Naval Office*, 29–30. The *Queen of France* met with the *Keppel* in Long Island Sound, and handed over the six naval prisoners, Joseph Sommers, William McGee, Richard Griffith 2d, Richard McKee, Robert Waddel, and Richard Tryman. These

From there, using the land prisoners, Shaw, with the help of Ebenezer Ledyard, was able to successfully exchange some prisoners, including Rufus Avery, William Latham Jr., Thomas Griffin, and Jabez Pembleton, all from Latham's Company, who left with Shaw on September 14. The rest would unfortunately have to wait. Upon his return to Fort Griswold, Sergeant Avery finished his one-year enlistment, receiving his discharge in November. Afterward, he decided he was done with the war and did not reenlist again.[76]

After Shaw's departure, Ledyard remained behind in New York until the other prisoners were exchanged. Once in New York, the prisoners disembarked at Peck Slip, under the escort of a company of Hessians, and marched down Crown Street, there confined in Livingston's Sugar House. They remained incarcerated in the six-story stone structure for several weeks and suffered in deplorable, wretched conditions with shortages of both food and clothing. Peter Avery recalled the most delicious morsel he ever ate during his entire life were two raw potatoes he stole from a cook during his captivity. When fellow prisoner Ebenezer Fish returned home to Groton he was wearing the same clothes he had been captured in.[77]

Ebenezer Ledyard negotiated the exchange of the remaining prisoners by the first week of November. This was due in large part to the large number of British prisoners taken at Yorktown. While Ledyard returned home a short time later, the prisoners did not. According to Ledyard, he arranged to have them transported directly to New London aboard a flag vessel. This should have proceeded, except that Abraham Skinner, the Commissary of American Land Prisoners, stepped in and had them instead transported to Elizabethtown, New Jersey, the prisoner exchange point for both armies. There they were released, and, according to Joseph Plumb and Levi Dart, marched to Morristown, New Jersey, where they received rations and then continued north to King's Ferry, where they crossed the

---

were later accounted for in the naval prisoner exchange worked out between Shaw and David Sproat, British Commissary of Naval Prisoners in New York.

76 Rufus Avery narrative in Harris, *Groton Heights*, 43; PA: Rufus Avery (S.12939); William Latham (S.13688); Thomas Griffin (W.19537); Jabez Pendleton (W.2557), NARA; Rogers, *Connecticut's Naval Office*, 29–33. The *Queen of France* left Whitestone, accompanied by the British schooner *Mifflin*, sometimes known as the *General Mifflin*, which was designated as a flag of truce vessel and carried 72 naval prisoners back to New London.

77 PA: Jesper Latham (S.13707); Joseph Plumb (S.31910), NARA. Harris, *Groton Heights*, 254–255; Rogers, *Naval Office*, 30. Ebenezer Ledyard fared better than the prisoners as he was billeted in a private residence. Part of his time was spent with David Sproat, the British commissary of naval prisoners. Despite popular lore, no prisoners taken at either New London or Groton, were kept on any prison ship. Only prisoners taken at sea were kept on a prison ship like the *Jersey*, while prisoners taken on land were kept at Livingston's Sugar House.

Livingston Sugar House Prison. One of three former sugar houses in Manhattan converted into prisons by the British for captured Americans during the Revolutionary War. *New York Public Library*

Hudson River and continued to Connecticut, some 200 miles.[78]

Watching and Waiting

Back in New London, the two sides spent September 7 watching each other. Neither side made any movement to engage the other. The privateers had not returned, remaining safely upriver. The Americans, while significantly reinforced, were in no condition to withstand another British attack. On the other hand, the British had not planned to still be there that day. Arnold and Bazely both believed they would be on their way back to New York. Instead, that day, the sixth day of the expedition, found the British squadron still at the entrance of New London Harbor. The wind did not cooperate, and the overall weather was getting worse. The humidity of the two previous days brought on a heavy rainstorm. All throughout the morning of September 8 a driving rain poured down, and when it finally passed, the humidity returned. At 7:00 a.m. Bazely ordered the *Amphion* to make the signal for the squadron to sail. They were underway an hour later, not to New York but to Gardiners Bay at the easternmost tip of Long Island. The expedition faced yet another delay.[79]

78 Ebenezer Ledyard to Governor Trumbull, Feb. 14, 1782, Governor Trumbull Papers, 16:37a–b, CSL. PA: Joseph Plumb (S.31910); Levi Dart (W.24046); Charles Martin (W.1978), NARA. It is suspected Ledyard remained in New York to be able to negotiate the prisoners the first chance he got. When the Dart brothers returned home to Bolton, they were ordered back to Fort Trumbull. Martin, born in England, was suspected of being a British deserter and was eventually taken to Nova Scotia where he was held until October 1782.

79 Master's Log, HMS *Amphion*, ADM 52/2133, TNA.

Chapter Thirteen

Panic Along the Coastline

As Bazely's squadron sailed towards Gardiners Bay, British headquarters in New York was anxiously awaiting its return. Nothing had been heard for four days. This was causing a headache for Major Mackenzie. For three successive days, beginning on September 6, Mackenzie looked intently for Arnold's return or even word of the progress of the expedition, but received none. He daily noted in his diary, "No account yet from General Arnold." By September 8, word reached the Kennedy mansion. Clinton received the news from a loyalist informant who had come to the city from Oyster Pond Point, the easternmost point of Long Island. According to Mackenzie, the informant stated, "Arnold arrived off New London the 5th at night, that early the next morning there was smart firing for some time, and soon after it was over the ships and vessels appeared to close in with the Batteries, from which the people in the Neighbourhood of the Oyster-pond-point conclude that the batteries were silenced and the troops landed." But beyond that, no one knew anything else.[1]

The military situation for the British had greatly changed since Arnold's departure. By September 8, Clinton realized he had been deceived by Washington. New York was not his target, but rather Cornwallis's army at Yorktown. This realization was something that had not come easily to Clinton.

A week earlier, on September 1, two days after Clinton gave Arnold his orders, the commander-in-chief received word that French and Continental soldiers were

---

1 Mackenzie, *Diary*, 2:616–618. Mackenzie watched daily for Arnold's return, beginning on Sep. 6 through Sep. 9.

marching towards Philadelphia. This was brushed off as a small detachment, being sent "to reinforce the Corps under [the Marquis de Lafayette] in Virginia," not the two armies. The following day, as Arnold's Corps was being assembled on Long Island, the news got worse. Intelligence clarified that it was not a small force, but the entire French and most of the Continental Army and its lead elements were already crossing the Delaware River at Trenton, New Jersey.[2]

Despite this report, Clinton remained obstinate. He was not yet convinced the allies were headed to Virginia. Even if they were, British naval forces were believed to be far superior in numbers to the French. This overconfidence led Clinton to believe he could move whatever force he desired without interference from the French navy.[3]

Despite Clinton's belief that Washington and Rochambeau were not moving towards Cornwallis, the pressure was mounting on him not to let them move unmolested. Clinton's two senior military commanders in New York urged him to move against them. On September 2, Clinton, according to Mackenzie, reluctantly agreed to meet with Lieutenant General Wilhelm, Baron von Knyphausen, second-in-command of British forces, and Maj. Gen. James Robertson, the royal governor of New York and military adviser to Clinton. Neither general shared their commander's optimism, as both believed Cornwallis was in imminent danger. In Mackenzie's diary he revealed that the two generals intended to put pressure on Clinton, either to assist Cornwallis or to do something to counter the allied movements. Robertson and von Knyphausen "had a long conference with The Commander in Chief . . . in consequence of which an arrangement was made for moving two Corps to the Southward under certain circumstances, leaving between Six and 7000 men" in New York. No minutes of the meeting are known to have survived, so we are left to guess as to what those "certain circumstances" might have been, but they were more than likely related to the developing naval situation.[4]

The combined British naval squadrons of Admirals Graves, Hood, and Drake, under Graves' overall command, and consisting of up to forty vessels including many larger ships of war, set sail from Sandy Hook on August 31-September 1 to locate, intercept, and defeat the two French squadrons. The location of the first squadron under Admiral de Barras, which had escaped Clinton's grasp at Newport, was still not known. But it was believed to be somewhere on the coast.

---

2 Ibid., 2:610.

3 Ibid., 2:606, 610–613; Clinton, *Narrative*, 20. Mackenzie expressed a similar opinion in his diary on Sep. 1: "[T]he British fleet is so much superior . . . there is every reason to expect a most Glorious Victory at last over the French fleet."

4 Mackenzie, *Diary*, 2:610–611.

The whereabouts of Admiral de Grasse's squadron, which had operated in the Caribbean, was about to become problematic for the British.

During the late hours of September 3, a dispatch arrived for Clinton from Cornwallis. Written on August 31, Cornwallis informed him that the day before, a large French fleet numbering between thirty and forty vessels had arrived at Cape Henry, just outside the Chesapeake Bay. This was Admiral de Grasse's squadron. The presence of de Grasse in the Chesapeake came as a complete surprise to Clinton. It was the piece of information that finally convinced the commander-in-chief that New York City was not in danger, but Cornwallis was. De Grasse's squadron was there to bottle Cornwallis up by water, while Washington and Rochambeau were headed south to block Cornwallis by land.[5]

The British could ill afford to lose another army. The loss of Burgoyne's army at Saratoga four years earlier had brought the French, and eventually, the Spanish and Dutch, into the war. The loss of Cornwallis's army might lose the British the war. Justice Smith confessed the same sentiment in his diary: "This is an Hour of Anxiety! [This] Week will decide perhaps the Ruin or Salvation of the British Empire."[6]

British success now depended on two factors—the first on the British navy. Graves needed to defeat the two French squadrons, preferably separately. If the French were defeated, it would leave the way open for Clinton either to reinforce Cornwallis or, if need be, evacuate his force by sea. A French naval victory would leave Cornwallis trapped. Whatever happened between the two navies would impact the second factor: where and how Clinton would assist Cornwallis. Clinton could either reinforce Cornwallis directly, which was preferred, or as some at British headquarters suggested, launch a large-scale diversionary expedition into New Jersey. This would threaten Philadelphia, which might pressure Washington and Rochambeau to march north to protect the rebel capital.[7]

Despite the anxiety, spirits at British headquarters remained high. They were optimistic that the British navy would succeed. Not only would the navy succeed, but it would deal a decisive blow to the French navy, which would undoubtedly be followed by a decisive British victory over Washington and Rochambeau. Mackenzie believed the victory would be large enough to bring an "end to the Rebellion."[8]

---

5 This information confirmed reports of the presence of the French navy near the Chesapeake that was received earlier.

6 Smith, *Historical Memoirs*, 438; Mackenzie, *Diary*, 2:613. Mackenzie believed, "The defeat of the [French] fleet will in all probability decide the fate of America."

7 Mackenzie, *Diary*, 2:610–611.

8 Ibid., 2:619.

The following day, September 4—the same day Arnold sailed from Whitestone—Clinton reacted swiftly to Cornwallis's dispatch. He ordered Mackenzie to assemble "a Corps of near 4000 men" from the New York garrison. The new expeditionary force contained a combination of British regulars and Hessian forces, including some of his most experienced and combat-tested soldiers. Clinton would lead them.[9]

Its planned embarkation date was set for September 6, but the exact departure time was not yet determined. That time would be chosen based on the outcome of the battle between the British and French navies, as well as the return of Arnold and Bazely. Clinton wanted to take the 54th Foot and the jaegers, then with Arnold, to Virginia with him. He also required the troop transports and two horse vessels which were with Arnold, and the sailors from the 74-gun *Robuste*, which was being repaired, and who were temporarily serving on the *Amphion*.[10]

On September 4 Clinton met with Major General Robertson, and the two discussed the New London expedition. According to Chief Justice Smith, Clinton expressed his desire to cancel it and to recall Arnold. With attention being shifted southward, an attack on New London or Connecticut's coastline was no longer strategically useful. An attack there would not divert Washington and Rochambeau's movement southward, as it was too far away. The most an attack might do was to pull Continental troops away from the Hudson River.[11]

But according to Smith, Clinton was persuaded, presumably by Robertson, to allow the expedition to proceed. Their exact reasoning is not known, but it was probably based on the assumption that Arnold would return to New York in a few days, a week at the latest. Clinton would have to wait just as long for word from Graves. Therefore, the New London expedition would not hinder the newly planned British operation. It was no longer considered a diversionary attack, but an attack solely limited to New London— a place Clinton and other British commanders had long desired to visit to destroy the privateers which operated out of its harbor. It remained a sensible target.[12]

That same day, Clinton drafted a letter to Lord Germain in which he explained the aim of the New London expedition. The letter is revealing because Clinton never mentioned Arnold's attack, initially, as being diversionary. Nor was the

9 Ibid., 2:613–615.

10 Ibid., 2:613–615, 620; Royal Navy Ships' Muster (Series 1), HMS *Amphion*, ADM 36/9561, TNA. Seventy sailors from the *Robuste* were assigned to *Amphion* while the latter vessel was being repaired. They transferred back to the *Robuste* after their return to NY.

11 Mackenzie, *Diary*, 2:620.

12 Smith, *Historical Memoirs*, 440.

expected attack on New York mentioned either. Clinton was unwilling to admit he had been fooled by Washington. Instead, Clinton told Germain how Arnold's operation fit directly into his orders to seize and/or destroy rebel shipping and stores, and to deprive the Americans of the means to fit out privateers. Clinton stated, "I propose[d] sending immediately a small Expedition under the Orders of Brigadier General Arnold to endeavor to bring off or destroy the Privateers, and Naval and other Stores collected at New London."[13]

Arnold may never have been told of the original aims of the expedition. He appears to have known as little as Clinton revealed to Lord Germain. Though the attack had been limited to New London, the military and political leadership of Connecticut had no idea that was the case. The general fear and anxiety was that New London was only the beginning. Additional attacks on the coastline, or as Governor Trumbull termed it, "desultory expeditions," seemed imminent.[14]

Within two days of Arnold's attack on New London, militia in Connecticut were marching on almost every coastal town. The attack and continued presence of the British squadron in Long Island Sound started a chain reaction up and down the coastline. Beginning at New London, it reverberated eastward towards Rhode Island and then westward towards Greenwich. Hundreds of citizen-soldiers were mobilizing, not only from the coastal or central regions of the state but from towns along the Massachusetts border. Supplies, ammunition, gunpowder, foodstuff, and horses were hastily collected to be sent to the coast to assist the militia. Outside New London, this was no more clearly seen than at New Haven.

New Haven was 50 miles west of New London by way of the Post Road. Citizens in town received word of Arnold's attack on September 7 at around 3:00 a.m. and it threw them into a state of alarm. Many were still apprehensive about the Associated Loyalists attack, which had occurred only a week earlier. Then there was the memory of the larger British invasion in 1779. Many citizens did not want to risk waiting for the arrival of the British, and set about evacuating themselves, their families, and personal belongings out of town.[15]

In town was Lieutenant Governor Matthew Griswold, who was also the chief justice of the state's Superior Court. Griswold was about to attend to the business of the court, but instead convened an emergency meeting with the judges and several

13 Lord Charles Germain to Sir Henry Clinton, Jan. 23, 1779, *American Rebellion*, 398–399; Sir Henry Clinton to Lord Germain, Sep. 4, 1781, Sir Henry Clinton Papers, WCL.

14 *CSR*, 3:504; *Providence Gazette*, Sep. 15, 1781. In response to the attack on New London, officials in Rhode Island ordered a review of the militia to ensure they were properly armed and equipped, so if the British attacked the state, "an effectual Opposition may be made."

15 Stiles, *Literary Diary*, 2:553.

inhabitants of the town. They wanted to determine what to do in response to the hostile British force present in Long Island Sound. Griswold assured Trumbull they were preparing to defend New Haven. Griswold had ordered Lieutenant Colonel Hezekiah Sabin, of the 2nd Regiment of Connecticut Militia, and Colonel Thaddeus Cook, of the 10th Regiment of Connecticut Militia, to both call out a hundred men each from their regiments for the defense of New Haven.[16]

Brig. Gen. Andrew Ward, commander of the 2nd Brigade of Connecticut Militia, was ordered to "fix Posts of Intelligence between New Haven and New London" to ensure eyes were kept on the British. If they attempted to land troops, militia commanders would know where to direct their units. Further, Griswold informed the governor he had already alerted Brigadier General Waterbury, in Stamford, and Brig. Gen. John Mead of the 4th Brigade of Connecticut Militia, of the attack on New London and the presence of the British in Long Island Sound. The dispatch urged Mead to prepare the 4th and 9th Regiments of Connecticut Militia of his brigade for possible action.[17]

Bazely's squadron arrived in Gardiners Bay at around noontime on September 8, the roughly ten-mile journey from New London having taken almost four hours. The armed vessels covering the rear of the squadron arrived a couple of hours later. The bay was often visited by the British navy to refit their vessels. Several nearby islands, as well as Southold and Oyster Pond at the easternmost point of Long Island, offered places to forage for supplies.

Most transport vessels, including the *Shuldham*, anchored off Plumb Island, located at the northern entrance of Gardiners Bay. Onboard with Captain Stapleton, Arnold spent the early hours finishing his report of the expedition. Concurrently, Bazely compiled his report to Admiral Graves. Both wanted to send word back to their commanders of the progress of the expedition, and once done the reports were given to Captain John Dalrymple and 1st Lt. Joseph B. Bunce of the *Amphion*. Both officers, together with Capt. George Beckwith, went aboard the *Lurcher* and set sail for New York. The brig, unlike the other ships, was fast, maneuverable, and could manage, even with the contrary winds, to get back to Whitestone.[18]

---

16 Matthew Griswold to Governor Jonathan Trumbull, Sep. 7, 1781, Governor Trumbull Papers, Vol. 4, Folder 6, CHS. The militia called out were from the 2nd and 10th Regiments of Connecticut Militia.

17 Ibid. Additionally, Lt. Col. Hezekiah Sabin, of the 2nd Regiment of Connecticut Militia, was ordered to prepare to call out his entire regiment if the British landed near New Haven.

18 *Derby Mercury*, Nov. 8, 1781; *Northampton Mercury*, Nov. 12, 1781; *Connecticut Journal*, Nov. 29, 1781; Smith, *Historical Memoirs*, 440.

Of great concern to Arnold was the number of wounded, specifically those seriously wounded at Fort Griswold. They were in much larger numbers than had been anticipated. The expeditionary force had not been provided with a hospital ship to care for the wounded on the return trip. Forced to improvise, the transport brig *Sally*, which had carried around 150 soldiers from the 38th Foot, including Captain Millet, was selected and repurposed into a hospital ship to accommodate the most seriously wounded. The soldiers from the 38th Foot were dispersed onto the *Amphion*, *Recovery* and *Beaumont* to make room, while the wounded, primarily of the 40th and 54th Foot, moved onto the *Sally*.[19]

Several had already succumbed to their wounds before the transfer. These were given impromptu funerals and thrown overboard. Captain George Craigie, of the 40th Regiment, along with at least one other soldier who died aboard the *Amphion*, were treated slightly better. Sailors from the *Keppel* rowed their bodies to Plumb Island where they were buried.[20]

That same day, a British force of around 400 men, mainly from the 40th and 54th Regiments, landed in Southold at Ashmomogue Beach. They headed for the village of Oyster Pond, nearly two miles away, where they intended to forage for food. Some visited Jeremiah Vail's tavern. The owner's wife Elizabeth recalled how the soldiers looked: "awful—having not slept probably within the last forty-eight hours and . . . besmeared with . . . blood." They searched every room, for "something to drink." Realizing they might be looking for liquor, Elizabeth went to the cellar and dumped out two large barrels of cider. The British never found them. The *Connecticut Gazette* was the only newspaper to cover the event. "Arnold's burning fleet, after leaving this harbour, plundered [a] great part of the inhabitants on Long Island; 400 of them landed at Southold, and plundered and carried off to the value of £3000."[21]

Like the British soldiers, the American prisoners had had nothing to eat for nearly three days. According to Sgt. Rufus Avery, aboard the *Association*, the

19 Master's Log, HMS *Amphion*, ADM 52/2133, TNA; Royal Navy Ships' Muster (Series 1), HMS *Amphion*, ADM 36/9561, TNA; Royal Navy Ships' Muster (Series 1), HMS *Recovery*, ADM 36/9910, TNA; Royal Navy Ships' Muster (Series 1), HMS *Recovery*, ADM 36/9643, TNA; Master's Log, HMS *Beaumont*, ADM 52/2192, TNA. According to the muster rolls of the *Amphion*, *Recovery*, and *Beaumont*, the men of the 38th Foot were transferred to the three vessels the same day the *Amphion* and *Beaumont* transferred the British wounded they had carried to the *Sally*.

20 Master's Log, HMS *Amphion*, ADM 52/2133, TNA; *CG*, Sep. 21, 1781. Three bodies washed up on the Groton shore and another 7–8 washed up "on the Great Neck," probably at or near today's Harkness Memorial State Park.

21 Augustus Griffin, Griffin's Journal. First Settlers of Southold; The Names of the Heads of Those Families, Being only thirteen at the time of their landing; First Proprietors of Orient; Biographical Sketches, &c. &c. (Orient, NY, 1857), 193–194; *CG*, Sep. 21, 1781.

prisoners suffered from hunger and thirst. They had been stuffed into the hold and were dehydrated and, as a result, "could hardly swallow." Avery remembered how his captors took pity on them and they were offered a chance to come up on deck, under guard, a couple at a time to get some air. They were also offered "a mess made of hogs brains," which came from the plunder carried out of Groton Bank. Afterward, Avery noted some weapons which had been left out in the open by their captors and the prisoners whispered amongst themselves and planned to take over the vessel. But before they could, their plan reached the crew, and the prisoners were forcibly locked in the hold. However, they did not remain there long. They were soon moved to either the *Keppel*, *Beaumont* or *Amphion*.[22]

The following morning, September 9, just after 6:30 a.m. with the wind conditions proving favorable to move to Whitestone, the *Amphion* fired a single gun, which signaled the squadron to weigh anchor and begin the day's movement down Long Island Sound. Headed out of Gardiners Bay, the squadron navigated its way through the tempestuous waters of the Plumb Gut and then veered westward around Oyster Point.[23]

The Battle of Killingworth

As the *Beaumont* navigated through Plumb Gut at around 9:00 a.m. and into the Sound, lookouts spotted "several Strange Sail to the northwest" of the squadron. The *Recovery* spotted the same vessels, describing them two hours later as "3 Sail under the Rebel Shore." They lay in the Sound off Saybrook, thirty miles west of New London. From available American sources, two of the vessels were identified as smaller boats, presumably whaleboats. The third, according to the same sources, was either a sloop or schooner, which according to one witness "belong[ed] in the Connecticut River." It was probably an unarmed or lightly armed merchant vessel.[24]

22 Royal Navy Ships' Muster (Series 1), HMS *Beaumont*, ADM 36/9643, TNA; PA: William Latham (S.13688), NARA; Rufus Avery narrative in Harris, *Groton Heights*, 42. Aboard the *Beaumont*, the prisoners were not trusted. Avery remembered they were guarded with "a sentry to nearly every man, with orders to shoot any one that offered to move." The marines guarding them were from the 3rd Battalion, Delancey's Brigade, under Sgt. William Irwin. Several prisoners, including Latham, remained on the *Association* until they returned to Huntington Bay and then were moved to the *Shuldham*, called by Latham "Arnold's sloop."

23 Captain's Log, HMS *Amphion*, ADM 51/39, TNA.

24 Middlebrook, *Maritime Connecticut*, 2:81, 266; Master's Log, HMS *Beaumont*, ADM 52/2192, TNA; Master's Log, HMS *Recovery*, ADM 52/2491, TNA; PA: James Smith (S.11426); Peter Spencer (W.7198), NARA. CSR, 3:500. The sloop's identity remains a mystery. It may be the sloop *Elizabeth*, a merchant vessel out of Middletown, owned by Benjamin Henshaw. Just five days earlier, Henshaw, in conjunction with Wensley Hobby, had been given permission by the Council of Safety to transport

Captain Shepherd ordered the *Recovery* to "[give] chase" and the sloop raced back northward towards the Connecticut shore. Shepherd's decision resulted in a small battle forgotten by historians, but whose effects helped strengthen the fear of further British depredations in the coming week. The exact reason for the offensive movement is not clear. It may have been precautionary, or the lure of capturing three seemingly vulnerable vessels and the potential prize money involved may have proved too tempting for Shepherd.[25]

The *Recovery* chased the American vessels for about three hours. As the better armed British vessel approached the Connecticut shore, the sloop and the two whaleboats had no choice but to fall back towards the shore. The sloop made for the Connecticut River but was forced back towards the West Parish of Saybrook, with the intention of getting up the Menunketesuck River to some sort of safety, while the two whaleboats sailed towards Kelsey Point in Killingworth.

Killingworth, established in 1663, had at the time of the war a population of just over 1,800 people. It was at the time bounded on the south by Long Island Sound, on the west by Guilford, on the east by Saybrook, and in the north by Durham and Haddam. Killingworth Harbor lay just south of the Post Road, which ran through the southern part of town. Along the eastern edge of the harbor a peninsula jutted for a mile out into the Sound, where at its farthest eastern point was Kelsey Point. Just east of the point lay two small islands, Duck Island and Menunketesuck Island.

Killingworth was garrisoned by a coast guard company under Ens. Joab Wright. Wright had been assigned to the post the previous April. A native of Killingworth, Wright was in 1781 only 35-years-old. He held the militia rank of captain and had served extensively in the militia in command of the 4th Company, 7th Regiment of Connecticut Militia. But since the coast guard company was only comprised of 23 men, it did not warrant a captain to command it, so Wright, as its commander, held the rank of ensign. However, he was hardly ever referred to by the lower rank.[26]

Wright's responsibility was the protection of the Killingworth coastline. Its main enemy was illicit trade. His company, divided into small groups, routinely patrolled a sector stretching nearly four miles long. Besides its small strength, Wright's Company was not well armed nor were they supplied with enough

---

nearly four tons of wheat flour from Middletown to Newport. The only surviving records of the *Elizabeth* are from mid to late 1777, which state that she mounted 6 swivel guns and a crew of 12.

25 Master's Log, HMS *Recovery*, ADM 52/2491, TNA.

26 *CSR*, 3:363–364. The 4th Company was comprised of members from the South Parish of Killingworth, today's Clinton.

ammunition. Inspected the previous July, it was found the muskets provided to the company were "indifferent, and not more than 4 rounds to a man." Though they lacked firearms and proper ammunition, the company was equipped with two 3-pounder field pieces. On the Sound, the company was supported by one armed whaleboat, commanded by Capt. John Wilcox. This was probably one of the smaller boats spotted by the British squadron.[27]

In addition to the whaleboat attached to Wright's Company, other whaleboats regularly operated out of nearby Killingworth Harbor. So, it is likely the second small boat spotted by the British was also a whaleboat. Whaleboats were used extensively during the war by Connecticut authorities to cruise the Sound to counter illicit trade. The whaleboats, crewed typically by 7–10 men, were open rowboats, generally thirty feet long, equipped with a single mast. The crews were usually armed with swords or firearms. Armament varied from boat to boat: some relied solely on weapons carried by the crew, others were equipped with small light cannon and/or swivel guns.

Wright's men had been on high alert since being notified of the attack on New London. When the *Recovery*, at around 2:00 p.m., suddenly pulled away, the short respite allowed Wright to catch his breath. But within two hours, the situation worsened. The *Association* and the *Colonel Martin*, with accompanying whaleboats carrying the Associated Loyalists and Loyal Refugees, resumed the chase and headed towards the coastline.[28]

It is not clear when Wright learned of the renewed approach of the enemy. He probably remained within view or kept eyes on the waterfront for most of the afternoon. In light of the renewed threat, the situation turned perilous. Would the enemy do to Killingworth what had reportedly been done to New London and Groton? Badly outnumbered, Wright needed help and sent couriers galloping towards both New Haven and New London.

Most of the nearby companies belonging to the 7th Regiment of Connecticut Militia had gone to New London. Some were already on their way home, or so they thought. However, since the threat level was deemed high with the British presence in Long Island Sound, they were detained in Saybrook, where they were gathered under Lt. Col. Abraham Tyler, commander of the 7th Regiment. There

---

27 "Account for cannon & guard granted [to] town of Killingworth," Revolutionary War Records, Series I, XVI:267–268, CSL; *CSR*, 2:353, 3:363–364; PA Hiel Williams (W.6513), NARA; William Ledyard to Governor Trumbull, July 4, 1781, Governor Trumbull Papers, 14:323b–d, CSL. At the time they were supplied with 200lb of gunpowder, 50lb of grapeshot, and 100lb of lead, which could make around 50 rounds of ammunition.

28 PA: Peter Spencer (W.7198), NARA; Master's Log, HMS *Recovery*, ADM 52/2491, TNA.

they would be kept for the protection of that town as well as to assist Lt. Martin Kirtland's Company at Fort Fenwick.[29]

Fortunately for Wright, reinforcements were already on their way, although unintentionally. Well before Upham and his men began their approach to the shore, at least one company, the 1st Company under Capt. Giles Meigs of the 23rd Regiment of Connecticut Militia and another, Capt. Jeremiah Bacon's 4th Troop of the 1st Regiment of Light Horse, were marching westward towards Killingworth from New London. Upon learning of Arnold's attack, Bacon's Troop and Meigs's Company, both from Middletown, had gone directly to New London. But upon nearing the town they learned the British had already departed. As a result, they were directed to Guilford. There they would rendezvous with the rest of the 23rd Regiment, which was also headed in that direction.[30]

On September 7, Governor Trumbull ordered the 23rd Regiment to prepare to deploy in response to the British presence in Long Island Sound. A day or so later, they were directed to Guilford to help protect the coastline there. Already there was a coast guard company under Capt. Peter Vail. Vail's Company, numbering around 55 men and officers, was spread out over nearly ten miles of coastline covering both the towns of Guilford and modern-day Madison, then called East Guilford.[31]

As the 23rd Regiment, led by Lt. Col. John Penfield, reached Guilford, Brig. Gen. Andrew Ward, who was also there, received word of the enemy incursion towards Killingworth. Ward ordered Penfield to move his regiment to Wright's aid.[32]

Fortunately for Wright, not all the militia from Killingworth had gone to New London. Some remained at home and volunteered to assist Wright. Local militia assembled with Wright's coast guards at the town arsenal, located just south of the town green along the eastern edge of the harbor. The arsenal housed the coast guard company, its cannon, ammunition, and other supplies. After gathering, the militia and coast guards, with at least one cannon, marched southward from the arsenal. They followed a route that proceeded down modern-day Waterside Street, continuing onward for almost the entire length of the eastern edge of Killingworth Harbor before turning eastward toward Kelsey Point. There, according to a militia

---

29 PA: Bezaleel Bristol (W.20781); Nathan Buel (S.23558); Joseph Pelton (W.26303), NARA.

30 PA: Noadiah Rockwell (S. 18181); William Bacon (S.23525); Daniel Southmayd (S.14547), NARA.

31 William Ledyard to Governor Trumbull, July 4, 1781, Governor Trumbull Papers, 14:323b–d, CSL; PA: Caleb Chapman (W.16209), NARA. Vail's Company had already tangled with the Associated Loyalists in July at Leete's Island in Guilford.

32 PA: Noadiah Rockwell (S. 18181), NARA.

volunteer Zadock Wellman, the British "had driven two of our vessels on shore." These were the two whaleboats.[33]

The point, named for the Kelsey family whose members had resided in town since its founding, overlooked Long Island Sound to the south and Duck Island Roads to the east. Just over a mile and a half due east from the point stood Duck Island. The island was tiny, a mere five acres, and less than a quarter of a mile from north to south. It was owned by John Ely, a doctor and former colonel. There were at least two small wooden buildings on the island, which were used as a smallpox hospital before the war. A mile north of the island lay what one militiaman referred to as "Saybrook Beach," which was probably located around today's Grove Beach near the entrance of the Menunketesuck River in Westbrook. This is where the sloop had been forced ashore and abandoned by its crew. Saybrook Beach connected with Kelsey Point by way of a near mile-long open stretch of beach.[34]

Also aware of the situation unfolding at Killingworth was Capt. Simeon Lay. Lay, a resident of Saybrook, led a company from the 7th Regiment that was drafted the previous May to serve on coast guard duty. They were stationed in what was then the West Parish of Saybrook, today's Westbrook. They were nearly five miles from Killingsworth, just across the Menunketesuck River. They remained in place at their station, "Saybrook Beach," and did not depart for New London.[35]

It is not clear if Wright and Lay communicated before the attack, but it is likely they did because they came to the same decision: to gather their companies and place them to protect the three vessels and prevent the enemy from coming ashore. It was a daring move to make. Both companies were outnumbered and could easily have abandoned or burned the boats and then withdrawn inland to safety. Instead, they dared the British to attack. If they wanted the vessels, or to come ashore, they would have to fight.

Arriving at Kelsey Point, Wright positioned his cannon facing eastward towards Duck Island. The militia was deployed nearby to cover and protect both the cannon and the whaleboats. Peter Spencer, a member of Lay's Company, stated Lay did the same, and positioned them near the sloop. Lay soon received reinforcements. Word had reached Saybrook of the impeding attack and the 3rd Company, 7th Regiment, under Capt. John Ventres, came rushing over. They had just crossed back to the west bank of the Connecticut River in Saybrook when

33 PA: Zadock Wellman (R.11306), NARA.

34 PA: Peter Spencer (W.7198), NARA.

35 Ibid. Lay led the 10th Company, 7th Regiment of Connecticut Militia, which drew its members from the West Parish of Saybrook. It is likely Lay's drafted company was comprised of 20–25 men drawn from the 10th Company.

they were ordered over to "Saybrook Beach." When Ventres' Company arrived at the beach, they were moved in the direction of the sloop. This led James Smith of Ventres's Company to believe they were going to burn the sloop to prevent its capture, but instead he was shocked to find they were being sent to defend it.[36]

As Upham closed in on the coastline, the *Association* and *Colonel Martin* with accompanying whaleboats headed in the direction of Duck Island. As they did, Lieutenant Colonel Upham, Captain Thomas, and Captain Gardner all studied the situation in their front. The decision to attack Killingworth had been made only a short time earlier. After the *Recovery* withdrew, it became solely an Associated Loyalist operation. Upham held overall command. Before that afternoon, there had been no plan by them or Arnold to attack anywhere else along the Connecticut shore. This operation was not like any other that summer. Almost all were launched in secret in the dead of night using darkness as a cover. This time was different, it was daytime, and the Americans were waiting for them onshore.

Nearing the coastline, Upham saw Wright's Company and its cannon at Kelsey Point. He could also see Lay's and Ventres's companies coming into position along the Killingworth/Saybrook border. While Upham could see his opposition, he had no idea of their strength, of how many more Americans there were hidden from view. Nonetheless, he made the decision to attack. He decided to move the *Association* and *Colonel Martin* to the front so they could bombard the shore. Upham hoped this would clear away the militia, after which whaleboats carrying his soldiers would be sent in to capture the American vessels.[37]

The *Association* and *Colonel Martin* approached Duck Island. Around 5:00 p.m. they veered, turning their broadsides towards the shore, and opened fire. This was quickly returned by Wright's men on Kelsey's Point. Further south, cruising around Rocky Point, which lay directly across the Sound from Killingworth, the crew of the *Amphion* watched the action with great interest. The *Amphion* reported, "[the Associated Loyalists were] in with the Rebel firing Guns which was return'd from the Shore." A half-hour later, the same crew "saw Several Houses on Fire suppos'd to be set on fire by the above Vesells."[38]

After a short bombardment, the Associated Loyalists approached the shore. Moving through the smoke, militia on shore watched as they advanced on both

36 PA: James Smith (S.11426), NARA.

37 PA: Samuel Smith (S.31971), NARA. Attempting to capture American vessels by dragging them out into the Sound was something the Associated Loyalists excelled at. At West Haven, they nearly captured Smith's galley *Adventure*. To try and save the vessel, Smith ran it aground, but the loyalists hooked it to the brig *Sir Henry Clinton* and attempted to drag it away. Had it not been for a change of wind, which sank the *Sir Henry Clinton*, they would have captured the *Adventure*.

38 Master's Log, HMS *Amphion*, ADM 52/2133, TNA.

Duck Island. Present-day view of the island from Clinton but what was in 1781 still part of Killingworth.
Author

sides of Duck Island, some headed in the direction of Kelsey's Point, others towards Saybrook Beach. Along the way some loyalists landed on Duck Island where, after scouring the buildings for plunder or militia, they soon departed leaving Ely's property in flames. To the north, as the Associated Loyalists neared Saybrook beach, they met significant resistance. As the "Barges [sent] in pursuit of the sloop" neared the shore, Lay's and Ventres's men opened fire and drove them back. In what was termed by one of Lay's Company as a "small engagement," "they drove the British boats back and saved the sloop." James Smith proudly recalled, "this is about the only valuable service I recollect doing in the militia."[39]

At Kelsey's Point, Wright's men were partially successful. An attack was made in the same manner as at Saybrook. Upham's soldiers reached close enough to exchange fire with Wright's, who, according to one defender, also sustained casualties. According to Hiel Williams, "the Americans fired from the land, the British from the vessels. Six of the British were killed." Before the Refugees were repulsed, they managed to capture and then successfully drag off one of the smaller vessels.[40]

After being repulsed at Kelsey's Point, Upham and Captains Gardner and Thomas called off the attack and withdrew out into Long Island Sound. The

39 PA: Peter Spencer (W.7198); James Smith (S.11426), NARA.

40 PA: Hiel Williams (W.6513), NARA. The captured vessel does not appear to have been the one under Capt. John Wilcox.

decision to retreat was a sound tactical decision. As they departed, the lead elements of the 23rd Regiment of Connecticut Militia were arriving near the center of Killingworth, two miles north of Kelsey's Point. The regiment, besides bringing additional militia to Wright's aid, also brought its artillery company, which was equipped with two field pieces.[41]

Killingworth was effectively a draw, though each side could claim a small victory. The Americans had successfully repulsed what they believed to be an imminent invasion of their town and saved two of three vessels. The Associated Loyalists, while driven away, managed to take with them one of the whaleboats, which could be used in future operations. Compared to the fighting and devastation in New London and Groton, the attack on Killingworth was minuscule. No contemporary newspaper even made mention of it. Over time, as the veterans died off, it would essentially be forgotten.[42]

Only one book, *A History of Middlesex County, Connecticut*, published in 1884, made any mention of it. And the author only gave it one sentence and was not even certain he had the correct date, writing, "They [the British] landed on Duck Island, which is opposite Westbrook, and burnt the buildings; I believe it was in 1781." Other historians, while making an even briefer mention, misplaced the attack as having occurred during the War of 1812, mistaking it for a similar attack that occurred in 1813.[43]

Panic Along the Coastline

Word of the action at Killingworth traveled fast. West Haven, New London, Groton, and now Killingworth. All in just over one week. In New Haven, Ezra Stiles noted in his diary on September 9, "The Fleet from N. London arrived by [5] P.M. off against Killingworth. Very threat[ing] & alarmg!" The following day, Stiles again noted, "Last Eveng the fleet seen off Killingworth. Alarm. Militia flocking into New Haven, & ordered in along the whole Sea Coast of Connect. From N. London to Stam[ford]."[44]

---

41 *CSR*, 3:43. The artillery company was organized in 1780 and equipped with either 6 or 12 pounder fieldpieces.

42 PA: Hiel Williams (W.6513), NARA. There were locals who conducted tours of where the battle occurred. According to Joseph Wilcox's deposition, included in Williams's pension application, Wilcox was shown by "persons where the battle . . . was fought."

43 *Middlesex County*, 469. The placing of the attack during the War of 1812 was not entirely random. The British attacked Killingworth harbor in 1813 for the same reasons they had in 1781. They chased American vessels towards the coastline and then made an unsuccessful attempt to capture them. Both times they were beaten off by local militia equipped with artillery.

44 Stiles, *Literary Diary*, 2:553.

Learning of the attacks, Trumbull continued to fear the worst. His state, as Washington had warned, was under attack. With the British squadron heading down Long Island Sound the governor, like many others, expected additional attacks on the western part of the state. The governor was particularly concerned about New Haven. On September 10, the day after Killingworth, Trumbull wrote to Major General Parsons, still in the New Haven area, "The desultory expeditions on the coast of this State requiring the immediate attention of the Council of Safety, to oppose the designs of the enemy, and if possible compel them to desist from the present system of carrying on the war." Trumbull wanted Parsons to take charge of the defense of the western part of the state and granted the major general complete strategic flexibility to repel the enemy in any way he saw fit without fear of direct interference from political officials.[45]

The governor, with the consent of the Council of Safety, also directed Parsons to assume command over all the state troops, coast guards, and militia called into service within that geographical area, from New Haven to Greenwich. Parsons also had the authority, if he needed it, to call out additional men from three militia brigades in the western part of the state as well as the powers "to seize or impress any vessels, boats, or other craft to transport men, artillery, or military stores for any enterprise you may undertake." Furthermore, Parsons would also assume command of all Continental troops who might operate within the borders of Connecticut.[46]

The closest Continental troops to Connecticut were those in the Hudson Highlands. When Washington departed for Virginia, he took with him only part of the main Continental Army, giving Maj. Gen. William Heath command over the Hudson Highland Department. Heath's department consisted of the river defenses of the Hudson River, including those at West Point and Peekskill, some 45 miles upriver from New York City. Washington told Heath, "The Security of West Point and the Posts in the High Lands is to be considered as the first Object of your Attention." But Washington gave Heath the liberty, as long as it did not jeopardize the safety of West Point and the other posts along the Hudson River, to use detachments from his force to protect the countryside and prevent the British from harassing the inhabitants, specifically along the coast of Connecticut.[47]

45 *The Heath Papers, Collections of the Massachusetts Historical Society*, Series 7, Vol. 5. (Boston, 1905), Heath to Parsons, Sep. 19, 1781, 3:220–221. Parsons was about to return to his division, but Trumbull asked him to remain in Connecticut until the British threat dissipated.

46 *CSR*, 3:504.

47 George Washington to William Heath, Aug. 19, 1781, Papers of George Washington, LOC; F. B. Heitman, *Historical Register of Officers of the Continental Army During the War of the Revolution, Apr,*

The first indication that something might be happening in Connecticut reached Heath on September 5. While he was drafting a letter to the Continental Congress, an informant arrived at his headquarters at Peekskill. The informant reported that the previous afternoon a "fleet of 26 sail, some of them large vessels, passed by Stamford to the eastward, but whether they were merchant ships or transports with troops," was not known. Neither were their exact intentions. This fleet proved to be Bazely's squadron. But at the time, Heath did not know this and disregarded it.[48]

Three days later, on September 8, a dispatch, sent by the selectmen of Killingworth, made its way to Heath's headquarters. It revealed the likely destination of the vessels that had been spotted days earlier and the real possibility of trouble in Connecticut. It read:

> To all Civil & Military Officers   6 September 1781
>
> This may certify, this moment an Express arrived from New London informing that the British Fleet—about 2500 men landed at New London—Delancey and Arnold command—have shut in the Inhabitants—was plundering & burning the Town—the truth of which we have no doubt of—Some have heard the Magazines blow up and a large smoak has been seen to rise at this Town.
>
> —Dated at Killingworth the 6th
> Sepr 1781.
>
> Signed—Willm Worthington
> Benjamin Gale
> Aaron Eliot

The message revealed the British had landed at New London, as well as the possibility the British had plundered the town and set it ablaze. But Heath had to be prudent. Despite it coming from a trustworthy source, Heath deemed the report as unconfirmed. One piece contained within it that caused Heath to hesitate was the inclusion of Delancey. This was Col. James Delancey, the same opponent of Brigadier General Waterbury in southwestern Connecticut. While it was plausible to Heath that Arnold commanded, it was odd that Delancey was also there.

1775–Dec, 1783 (Washington D.C., 1893), 216. Peekskill was 40–50 miles from Hartford, and some 130 miles from New London.

48 Heath to Governor Trumbull, Sep. 10, 1781, Governor Trumbull Papers, 15:109a–c, CSL. Heath admitted he thought this was Hood's squadron headed to sea to escape the French navy believed to be cruising about Sandy Hook.

Delancey commanded loyalist troops in Westchester County. Heath knew this because his troops often clashed with them. How could he be there? Heath decided to await official word from Governor Trumbull to confirm the attack. But even so, Heath could not afford to remain idle. If the British had attacked New London, Heath had to consider the possibility of further attacks along the Connecticut coastline. Acting on Washington's orders to protect the coastal inhabitants, Heath, even as a precaution, needed to send troops to Connecticut.

The day after receiving the Killingworth dispatch, Heath wrote to Col. Rufus Putnam, who commanded an advanced outpost along the Croton River in northern Westchester County, thirty miles from the Connecticut border. The outpost consisted of an assortment of troops, including New York militia, Continental infantry primarily from Massachusetts regiments, cavalry from the 2nd Continental Light Dragoons, and a detachment from the Continental artillery. After informing Putnam of events transpiring in Connecticut, Heath instructed the Massachusetts colonel to detach a force of 20 mounted dragoons and 200 infantry and send them to Stamford, Connecticut, early the following morning. Selected to command was Maj. Benjamin Tallmadge, of the 2nd Continental Light Dragoons. The native of Setauket, New York, was later known for his role as Washington's director of military intelligence and for having organized the Culper Spy Ring. Tallmadge's selection to lead the detachment made a great deal of sense, as he had spent a lot of time patrolling Westchester County and knew the area, as well as the quickest and most direct route to Connecticut.[49]

On September 10, the day following the Battle of Killingworth, Tallmadge marched for Connecticut. That same day, Heath received confirmation of the attack on New London from Governor Trumbull. Trumbull wrote on September 7, "The enemy yesterday made a descent upon…New London, and by the advices I have received are about 2,000 men, besides a body of light horse, perhaps 300, about 40 ships of war & transports. By this enterprize they have posses'd of the only harbour of importance within this State and property to a very great amount, perhaps 400,000 pounds."[50]

---

49 William Heath, *The Revolutionary War Memoirs of Major General William Heath.* Sean M. Heuvel, ed. (Jefferson, NC, 2014), 279. Major Lemuel Trescott, 9th Massachusetts Regiment, also accompanied the detachment. A commissary was also sent with Tallmadge with additional supplies and the expectation that they would be gone for more than two days.

50 Heath, *Heath Papers*, Governor Trumbull to Heath, Sep. 7, 1781, 3:237–238. The inclusion of 300 light horse on the raid surprised Heath. It was a high number to be included on a raid. They had only brought 10 with them during the Danbury expedition, a much larger operation. Heath knew with certainty where all the British light horse were stationed about New York, and the report caused Heath to spend time attempting to figure out their identify and where they had been stationed.

Trumbull's letter took three days to travel from Hartford to Peekskill. By the time it reached Heath, it contained outdated information. At the time it was written, Trumbull was in Hartford and being fed a continuous stream of information by couriers. Some of the information was accurate, some was inaccurate, and the rest was greatly exaggerated. As Trumbull wrote the letter, the British were still off New London, and he greatly feared Norwich was about to "be destroyd." This fear was not unfounded as discussed earlier; many in New London feared the same scenario. The most exaggerated intelligence in it was the British naval strength, which was nearly doubled in size. This meant to the governor that the British intended not only to attack New London, but assuredly had plans to devastate the entire coastline. The governor then pleaded with Heath to send help, writing, "As desultory expeditions are without a doubt meditated upon different parts of this State, I must beg you to order part of the troops under your command to such stations as will give some protection to the western parts of the State. New Haven is an object of great consequence, and I have every reason to fear an attempt will be made to destroy it." Trumbull requested at least 300 Continentals be sent towards New Haven, to support the local militia, which would be organized to resist the British. He also asked that the 2nd Continental Light Dragoons, as well as Colonel Putnam's detachment, be ordered to Connecticut where they "may render essential service on the western coast of the State."[51]

Heath did not delay in his reply, writing to the governor the same day. He assured the anxious Trumbull that help was already on its way. Heath told him he had received word two days earlier in "a very vague manner" that the enemy had gone to New London, blown up the magazine, and plundered the town. But he could not confirm the report until the governor's letter arrived. Even so, the general told the governor, though the information was not yet confirmed, he had already acted on it. He had the same worries as the governor, believing that if the British had attacked New London with the numbers they were reported to have, they would not remain in New London but probably had designs on New Haven, Stamford, and other coastal towns. He reasoned these places would probably be attacked by the British on their return to Whitestone.[52]

Heath told Trumbull that Tallmadge, with a force of Continentals, was marching towards Connecticut where they could "give countenance and support

51 Heath, *Heath Papers*, Governor Trumbull to Heath, Sep. 7, 1781, 3:237–238. Of Norwich, Trumbull wrote, "I fear [it] will be destroyed. We shall use our utmost efforts to save that town, which is the most we can expect to accomplish."

52 William Heath to George Washington, Sep. 9, 1781, Papers of George Washington, LOC. The information which came in "a very vague manner" was assuredly the dispatch sent by the selectmen of Killingworth and was included in Heath's Sep. 9 letter to Washington.

to the militia." Furthermore, Heath told Trumbull the 1st Connecticut Brigade, under Brig. Gen. Jedidiah Huntington, was on standby. The brigade consisted of the 1st, 3rd, and 5th Connecticut Regiments, and had orders to be ready to march to Connecticut at a moment's notice.[53]

But Heath had to be careful. His department only consisted of about 3,000 Continentals plus some 2,000 militia. He could not afford to spread them out. Their sole responsibility was the protection of the Hudson River. Heath, along with other officers under his command, believed that the movement of Washington and Rochambeau's forces to Virginia might induce Clinton to attempt something drastic. He predicted to a subordinate officer, "Mr Clinton will be in a great fury for a few days" and will probably try something desperate to divert attention away from Cornwallis. This belief was furthered when Heath learned British troops had embarked aboard transports in New York. These were the troops mentioned earlier that Clinton planned to send south. But at the time Heath did not know their destination and continued to remain uncertain of it.[54]

Heath reasoned the troops would be used in one of two ways. One, judged to be the more likely, was that Clinton was preparing to launch a large-scale diversion into New Jersey with the intention of threatening Philadelphia. The second, thought less likely but still plausible, was that Clinton might advance up the Hudson River to capture West Point. If the latter, the real reason for Arnold's presence along the Connecticut coastline might be to cause Heath to pull troops away from his posts along the Hudson River. Heath could not afford the risk of sending too many of his troops to Connecticut.[55]

---

53 Heath to Governor Trumbull, Sep. 10, 1781, Governor Trumbull Papers, 15:109a–c, CSL. Heath also had plans, if necessary, to move Putnam's entire outpost to the aid of Connecticut. Huntington's Brigade consisted of some 300 men.

54 Heath to Governor Trumbull, Sep. 15, 1781, Governor Trumbull Papers, 15:131a–b, CSL; Mackenzie, *Diary*, 2:610. Before leaving, Washington had called for 4,100 militia from Connecticut, Massachusetts, New Hampshire, Rhode Island, and New Jersey to augment his department. According to Heath, at this point they were arriving daily, but had not reached the number requested. There is no official American return which can be located of the department at this time, but British intelligence placed their strength at around 3,000, which seems only to include the Continentals and not the militia that Washington had requested or those yet to arrive.

55 William Heath to Rufus Putnam, Sep. 11, 1781 in Putnam, *The Memoirs of Rufus Putnam and Certain Official Papers and Correspondence*, ed. Rowena Buell (Cambridge, MA, 1903), 194; Heath to Washington, Sep. 12, 1781 in Heath, *Heath Papers*, 3:246–248; Heath to Washington, Sep. 9, 1781, Papers of George Washington, LOC; Heath to Governor Trumbull, Sep. 16, 1781, Governor Trumbull Papers, 15:131a–b, CSL. It is also important to note that Heath was not only watching the British in New York City or even in Connecticut. His headquarters was flooded with dispatches from the Northern Department, which lay just to the north of his own department. Heath had what he believed were reliable reports of a possible British movement into northern New York from Canada with the intent of burning Albany. Heath detached some of his militia to bolster the defenses

Acting on Trumbull's confirmation of the British attack on New London and the speculation that New Haven was likely their next target, Heath made some adjustments to the original disposition of the troops he was sending to Connecticut. On September 11, the day after Trumbull's letter arrived, Heath sent orders to Tallmadge to march for New Haven. That same day, Huntington's Brigade left its camp at Gallows Hill, three miles from Peekskill, bound for Connecticut. Before departing, according to one soldier, Huntington informed his brigade that the British had burned New London, and they were headed to their native state to repel them.[56]

The action at Killingworth, despite being small, had strengthened the speculation New Haven was the next British target. Though not recorded, some in the militia may have seen the Killingworth action as a diversion to draw militia away from New Haven. Some companies from the 2nd Regiment of Connecticut Militia, upon hearing of the attack on New London, were ordered there. But these were immediately turned around and directed back towards New Haven as the British squadron passed down the Sound. In addition to the artillery company and those militia companies already on service in town. But as the British neared, another call for additional militia went out.[57]

Some militia heading to New Haven came from the Waterbury area, nearly twenty miles northwest of New Haven. Sometime between September 9 and 10, Lt. Col. Hezekiah Sabin Jr., commander of the 2nd Regiment of Connecticut Militia, wrote to Col. Phineas Porter, commander of the 28th Regiment of Connecticut Militia. In the letter Sabin requested Porter to order his regiment to the defense of New Haven. Sabin's original letter has been lost, but Porter wrote to Governor Trumbull about it, and this document has survived. In it, Porter stated, "Informed [by Lt. Col. Sabin] the Enemies Fleet late from New london where within about 15 miles of New haven Harbour Standing in for land and Requested the Assistance of my Regt." Porter promptly responded by calling out his regiment, placing them under Lt. Col. Benjamin Richards, and sending them towards New Haven.[58]

---

of that town. Other reports came in of another possible British incursion from Canada down the Connecticut River into modern-day Vermont.

56 Tallmadge to Heath, Sep. 13, 1781 in Heath, *Heath Papers*, 3:249–251; PA: Jehiel Munger (S.31875), NARA; Heath to Governor Trumbull, Sep. 15, 1781, Governor Trumbull Papers, 15:130a–b, CSL. Heath's original orders to Tallmadge have been lost but in his reply Tallmadge tells Heath how he adapted them to the changing situation.

57 PA: William Grinnell (S.29843), NARA.

58 Phineas Porter to Governor Trumbull, Sep. 10, 1781, Governor Trumbull Papers, Volume 4, Folder 6, CHS; PA: Eben Hotchkiss (S.36582), NARA. According to Eben Hotchkiss, the 28th Regiment never reached New Haven. They only marched to Woodbridge, where orders came to draft

Throughout most of September 10 and 11, those in New Haven held their breath. Militia and citizens, including Parsons, watched intently as the British squadron passed within view. The *Connecticut Journal* reported, "30 sail, one of them a frigate, and two other ships of considerable force passed our harbour."[59]

Even sailors in Bazely's squadron believed they would attack New Haven. John Kimball, a native of Rhode Island who had been pressed into British service aboard the *Amphion* during the New London expedition, recalled the anticipation. The frigate's crew saw the militia assembled onshore. Kimball testified, when the *Amphion* "arrived before New Haven, the American Militia had collected, and Arnold dared not land his troops."[60]

To the surprise of many, the British squadron passed harmlessly through on September 10 and 11, except for the *Keppel* and three troop transport vessels. But even these four vessels caused anxiety for those onshore. For some, it just appeared that the squadron had become dispersed and spread out. Ezra Stiles remembered watching "Arnold & his fleet returned in a scattering matter to Long Isld." What Stiles probably saw was the *Keppel* and the three transport vessels, a brig, schooner, and a sloop, all carrying troops. While most of the squadron proceeded towards Whitestone, the three transports had a difficult time keeping up. The *Keppel* remained in the rear of the squadron to escort them and passed New Haven the day after the rest of the squadron. Still, no attack on New Haven came. On September 11–12, the squadron passed Huntington Bay, headed in the direction of Hempstead Bay, directly threatening Stamford and neighboring Greenwich. Again no attack came, but this did little to calm anyone's nerves.[61]

---

one company from the regiment and then to send them to Milford, while the rest of the regiment was ordered home.

59 *Connecticut Journal*, Sep. 13, 1781.

60 PA: John Kimball (S.13657), NARA; Royal Navy Ships' Muster (Series 1), HMS *Amphion*, ADM 36/9561, TNA. Kimball was captured on Aug. 7, 1781, aboard the Massachusetts privateer *Belisarius*. He was pressed into British service eight days later. Though he wrongly identifies the vessel as the *Amphitrite* in his pension application, the muster books of the *Amphion* state otherwise. His date of impressment, and his being on board during the New London expedition is clearly seen. Using the harbor boat of the *Amphion*, Kimball escaped with another pressed American sailor on Sep. 11, 1781. The two managed to reach American lines near the New York/Connecticut border and were brought to Gen. Waterbury who provided the two escapees with food and medical care. Kimball continued eastward and returned to his home in Rhode Island by winter. Kimball's pension narrative, specifically his service and escape story, are both verified by the muster book of the *Amphion*.

61 Master's Log, HMS *Amphion*, ADM 52/2133, TNA; Tallmadge to Heath, Sep. 13, 1781 in Heath, *Heath Papers*, 249–250; *CSR*, 3:512–513; Stiles, *Literary Diary*, 2:553. Tallmadge heard rumors that the British had landed near Stamford early on the morning of Sep. 12. He had his detachment on the road from Bedford at 2:00 a.m. and advanced to the outskirts of Stamford before he learned the British had not landed and had sailed for Long Island. Preparations to defend New Haven did not end

Parsons was among those not yet convinced the British threat had entirely subsided. He prepared, much to the angst of Heath who wanted him back with his command, to remain longer in Connecticut. Thinking back to 1779, when he led Continental troops to Connecticut in response to Tryon's raid, the British had done something similar. After destroying Fairfield, the British took a brief respite in Huntington Bay before they returned to attack Norwalk. Parsons refused to dismiss any of the militia in New Haven or along the coastline before he knew what the British intended to do. Writing early on September 13, Parsons told the governor, "I shall not dismiss Such . . . until I can Satisfy myself of the Enemys further Intention."[62]

Even so, that same day, Huntington turned his brigade back to Peekskill. The brigade only reached as far as Pound Ridge, New York, some three miles north of the Connecticut border. Tallmadge's detachment, only a short distance ahead of Huntington's men, was about to do the same. Tallmadge's men were on their way to New Haven but had reached Bedford, New York, by the night of September 11. Very early the following morning, Tallmadge was alerted to a British attack on Stamford. So he hurriedly had the detachment on the road again, but instead of New Haven he now decided to detour to Stamford.

As Tallmadge's command approached Stamford, he was made aware the British squadron had already passed by. When the attack failed to materialize, Tallmadge's command, per orders from Colonel Putnam to return once the British appeared to be gone, once again turned back and were on their way back to their original post. Having reached Bedford, Tallmadge ran into Huntington. Huntington recommended, with Tallmadge in complete agreement, that while Huntington's Brigade would return to Peekskill, Tallmadge should remain in the area "until the enemies' intentions will be fully discovered."[63]

Tallmadge, like Parsons, was also not entirely convinced the British were finished with Connecticut. Reporting to Heath of his meeting with Huntington, Tallmadge told Heath he was "at a loss to conjecture what the next movements of the enemy will be; some suppose the warm reception they met at New London will induct them to give [up] any further attempts on the coast, while others are full in opinion that they have retired a little to the westward to give time for the militia to

---

as the British squadron passed by. About a week later, 300 French muskets were sent to New Haven, as well as horses so that Warner's Company could function as a mobile field artillery unit.

62 Parsons to Governor Trumbull, Sep. 13, 1781, Governor Trumbull Papers, 15:119a–c, CSL.

63 Tallmadge to Heath, Sep. 13, 1781 in Heath, *Heath Papers*, 3:249–251.

return home, and then prosecute the original plans of their expedition, which I am well convinced was to burn the towns on the seacoast of this State."[64]

To meet this expected threat, Tallmadge chose a new location where he could receive intelligence in a timely manner, communicate with forces already on the coast, and have access to roads by which he could easily move his force to wherever a threat materialized. Bedford would not suffice. He needed what he termed "a more centrical position," and decided to move back into Connecticut. Tallmadge chose Canaan, today's New Canaan, four miles south of the New York border. Canaan was the ideal location to position his command. Roads from the hamlet provided easy access to both Stamford and Norwalk. The roads not only provided a way to move troops, but also communication links with Waterbury in Greenwich and Parsons, who was soon to be in Stamford.[65]

Parsons remained in New Haven until September 13. That same day, he notified the governor that he would be riding towards Stamford. Along the way, Parsons inspected the readiness of the other coastal towns to ensure they were prepared to counter any British threat. In his absence, Parsons recommended the militia present in New Haven should be "formed into One Battalion, that the whole shall be under one direction." If the British attacked the town, Parsons recognized the difficulties in leading this body of militia effectively. Difficulties involving jurisdiction and the personalities of their individual commanders would undoubtedly rear their ugly head, especially since the militia present in and about the town were from at least four different militia regiments from two militia brigades. Officially placing them in one organized unit with an appointed commander would help alleviate these issues.[66]

Parsons' request to Trumbull for the formation of a new unit to protect New Haven and its vicinity appears to have been made only as a formality. Without waiting for a response, Parsons invoked the authority given to him by the governor and Council of Safety and organized the new battalion on his own from the militia gathered. In command, he placed Lt. Col. James Arnold, of Durham, (no relation to the general), of the 10th Regiment of Connecticut Militia. Arnold was entrusted with the protection of New Haven, as well as the adjacent towns of Guilford and Milford.[67]

---

64 Ibid.

65 Ibid.

66 Parsons to Governor Trumbull, Sep. 13, 1781, Governor Trumbull Papers, 15:119a–c, CSL.

67 *Connecticut Men*, 406, 614.

In New Haven, Parsons, at the time, estimated Arnold's Battalion to be around 300 men. Warner's Company, which garrisoned the town, increased it by another 100 men. This number does not appear to include the militia gathered concurrently at Milford or Guilford. Parsons believed the 400 men would be enough to act as an effective delaying force. Concurrently, they were also preparing to equip Warner's Company with horses to convert it into a field artillery unit. When and wherever the enemy attacked, "this Body of Men with the Coast Guards would be able in Conjunction with the Militia who could collect in a Few Hours to give [the British] such opposition as would retard their Operations till a greater force should arrive."[68]

Even as Parsons organized the militia gathered in New Haven, there were other issues. They lacked an adequate supply of ammunition, something which they would desperately need if the British returned. Parsons estimated the militia only had enough ammunition to fight for a half-hour before the supply would be completely expended. He requested from the governor and Council of Safety, "at least 100,000 cartridges." The lack of ammunition had not been just limited to Groton or New London or New Haven; the commanders of the 4th and 9th Regiments of Connecticut Militia, as well as Waterbury's Brigade, also found their units lacking and requested from state officials over 3,000 flints and thousands more cartridge papers to supply their commands.[69]

Additionally, Parsons discovered provisions in New Haven were also in short supply. When they had responded to the alarm, most militia had only brought with them enough food for a day or two. As their time of service extended beyond two days, the food began to run dangerously low. If not properly supplied, Parsons would be forced to dismiss them. This was something he did not want to do. The alarm had been so sudden that state officials, specifically the quartermaster department, had not had time to prepare a regular flow of provisions. This included not only foodstuffs but also rum. Parsons knew provisions had been collected in New Haven County to be sent to Connecticut's Continental regiments, so he asked the governor to divert the provisions directly to New Haven. This was done to keep the militia in service.[70]

After finishing his letter, Parsons left Lieutenant Colonel Arnold in command at New Haven and rode westward along the coast. Unknown to Parsons and

---

68 Parsons to Governor Trumbull, Sep. 13, 1781, Governor Trumbull Papers, 15:119a–c, CSL.

69 *CSR*, 3:505–506.

70 Ibid. On Sep. 11 the Council of Safety ordered Col. Henry Champion, Superintendent Commissary of Purchases for Connecticut, to ready and deliver, as needed, supplies for the militia stationed on the coast.

Tallmadge, as both prepared to defend the state, by September 13 the New London expedition was over, as was the threat to the Connecticut coast.[71]

---

71 *CSR*, 3:505–506; Stiles, *Literary Diary*, 3:556–557, 562. Due to the constant threats and alarms, Arnold's Battalion (later Regiment) was on duty until the winter months of 1781–1782. On September 15, a rumor spread of a large British squadron of nearly 40 sail headed back up the Sound. Parsons believed it was Arnold again, and his objective was either New Haven or Newport, RI. In New Haven, on September 17, at around 2:15 a.m. alarm guns were fired in anticipation, and according to Ezra Stiles, "2000 militia flocked in this day at this & adjacent Towns." Citizens again moved their goods out of town, but church services were not cancelled. When the sun rose there were no British in sight, and the mood calmed considerably. The alarm and fear of additional attacks caused Arnold's Battalion to be enlarged to a regiment and by the end of October it numbered 600 men.

Chapter Fourteen

Arnold the Traitor

The vanguard of Bazely's squadron, consisting of the *Beaumont*, *Shuldham*, and transport vessels carrying four companies of the 40th Foot, along with the *Sally* carrying the wounded, reached Whitestone on September 12, a day ahead of the rest of the squadron. While the *Beaumont* remained off Whitestone, the *Shuldham* and other transport vessels continued into the East River. The wounded were disembarked at Harlem and transported to the military hospital at King's College, while the four companies of the 40th Foot landed in the city.[1]

The following morning, under orders from Lt. Gen. Henry Clinton, the rest of the transport vessels bypassed Whitestone. The exception was the American Legion, which disembarked at Whitestone and returned to Flushing. The transport vessels carrying the remainder of the 40th Foot, the 38th Foot, and the 54th Foot, went down the East River and were landed in the city, while the Loyal Americans disembarked at Albany Pier and were marched to the redoubt at McGowan's Pass in northern Manhattan. The 3rd Battalion, New Jersey Volunteers returned to Staten Island. The jaegers went briefly into the city but were reembarked aboard transport vessels bound for the Chesapeake by the afternoon.[2]

Publicly, the New London expedition was a British success. A Scottish newspaper reported, "We thought the rebel navy received a deadly blow by the spirited stroke at Penobscot, but the attack made by General Arnold at New London

---

1 Mackenzie, *Diary*, 2:629; Heath to Trumbull, Sep. 23, 1781, Governor Trumbull Papers, 15:150a–b, CSL.

2 Mackenzie, *Diary*, 2:629.

is of far greater consequence." An Irish newspaper praised Arnold's generalship in the New London and Virginia expeditions saying, "The two expeditions on which general Arnold has command have done more mischief to the rebels than almost all the other operations of the war. Much of this is owing, no doubt, to his own good conduct, activity, and courage, of all which he has given such manifest specimens; but part must be referred to his accurate knowledge of the country, and especially of those places from which the enemy draw their chief resources. That points out where they are most vulnerable, and where a blow may be struck with most effect; and that alone independent of his military talents, renders him a valuable acquisition to the royal cause."[3]

When Arnold's report was published in the newspapers, it included, as an addendum, Clinton's General Orders of September 17, 1781, which touted the operation's success. It read, "BRIGADIER-GENERAL ARNOLD having reported to the commander-in-chief the success of the expedition, under his direction, against New London . . . His Excellency has the pleasure of signifying to the army the high sense he entertains of the very distinguished merit of the corps employed upon that service." The *Royal Gazette* was so thrilled that it boasted, "The breast of every honest loyalist can not help emotions of joy on finding that the most detestable nest of pirates on the continent have at last . . . attracted the notice of his Excellency the commander-in-chief." "It was, in fact, the magazine of America, and the blow now given will affect the sensitive nerves of every staunch rebel on the continent," explained the paper. The following month, several dozen newspapers across Great Britain, Scotland, and Ireland carried the same reports.[4]

However, as positively as the newspapers portrayed the expedition, privately amongst the British high command it was a different story. Three days before Arnold's return, Lieutenant Bunce, Captain Dalrymple, and Captain Beckwith returned and brought the first official word of the expedition. A meeting was held that day at the Kennedy mansion and in in attendance were Clinton, Major General Robertson, Beckwith, Dalrymple, and Chief Justice Smith. Beckwith told them, "They landed at that place the 6th Instant, Stormed all the Enemies Redoubts and batteries, burnt the Stores, and some shipping." But Beckwith noted, "The greatest part of the Shipping . . . [and] escaped up the River to Norwich." The losses suffered were "near 200 killed and wounded." After learning of the casualties,

---

3 CM, Nov. 10, 1781; *Saunders's News-Letter*, Nov. 20, 1781.

4 "From Rivington's *Royal Gazette*," in *CG*, Sep. 21, 1781. Arnold's report was printed by the *Gazette* twice by the end of September.

according to Smith, the generals charged Arnold "with intemperate Heat" and judged him to be too aggressive.[5]

Beckwith's report made it clear that Arnold had captured the forts and New London and had destroyed the storehouses. But he had failed to bring off any public or naval stores, nor had he managed to capture any of the privateers or prize vessels. If that had been all, Clinton might have judged the expedition a small victory. But the high number of British casualties significantly diminished any success brought during the expedition. Smith asserted that the army "lament[ed] the Loss as exceeding the Purchase."[6]

Arnold returned on September 12 and walked right into a firestorm of criticism. Most came from the British headquarters. The first and most grievous point was the number of casualties sustained by the force under his command. The second was his failure to destroy Fort Griswold. The third was the burning of New London. Already disliked by most British officers in New York, the New London expedition only seemed to worsen Arnold's reputation.

The New London expedition was the bloodiest British incursion into Connecticut during the entire war. The raid on Danbury in 1777, which lasted four days, cost the British 171 casualties. That in 1779, which spanned a week but only involved three days of skirmishing at New Haven, Fairfield, and Norwalk, cost the British 147 casualties. The single-day action at New London and Groton cost 201 casualties. The storming of Fort Griswold alone, which only lasted an hour, cost 179 men, among whom were ten commissioned officers.[7]

Not since Bunker Hill had the army suffered so many casualties in such a short period. This assuredly shook Clinton—so much so, one can almost feel the emotions when reading his General Orders. Even as he praised the actions of the two regiments, he expressed much grief, writing, "[I] can not but lament with the deepest concern the heavy loss in officers and men sustained by the [two regiments], who had the honor of the attack; and no words can do justice to the discipline and spirit which they shewed on that occasion."[8]

In Arnold's defense, the casualties suffered at Fort Griswold were not directly his fault. That was Eyre's responsibility. But as commander of the expedition,

---

5 Mackenzie, *Diary*, 2:619; Smith, *Historical Memoirs*, 440.

6 Smith, *Historical Memoirs*, 440.

7 Mackenzie, *Diary*, 2:627; *Newcastle Courant*, June 12, 1777; *Saunders's News-Letter*, Sep. 29, 1779; Clinton, *American Rebellion*, 415.

8 Master's Log, HMS *Amphion*, ADM 52/2133, TNA; *Proceedings of a Board of General Officers of the British Army at NY, 1781*, 208; Robertson, *Twilight*, Robertson to Lord Jeffrey Amherst, Sep. 25, 1781, 216; "General Orders, Headquarters, NY, 17th Sep 1781," *Royal Gazette* (NY), Sep. 19, 1781. The 8-inch howitzer and six bateaux were lost in Long Island Sound on the return to New York.

Arnold bore ultimate responsibility. Eyre was a veteran commander and knew the risks of a frontal assault. That is why he delayed the attack twice to give his artillery time to come up. Artillery support would presumably have lessened the casualties the attacking force sustained. But time was of the essence. Eyre was under pressure from Arnold to take the fort as quickly as possible. Even so, he developed a sound plan of attack. By spreading his soldiers out, the defenders were also stretched out, which resulted in their being overwhelmed. The tactics worked, but at a high cost. The defenders had done well. An officer in the 54th Foot wrote, "To do the rebels justice, they defended the garrison bravely. You will see the loss we sustained in the papers. We suffered much."[9]

Despite being reported in American newspapers as having died of his wounds on the return to New York, Eyre survived. He ended the war as a lieutenant colonel in the 64th Regiment of Foot. But in the coming years, the effects of the Fort Griswold wound lingered and attributed to his eventual death in October 1791. Eyre had served in the British army for over thirty years, but his participation at Fort Griswold is what followed him for the rest of his life. His obituary read, "He was a very able officer, and particularly distinguished himself in the American War, by his gallant conduct in the attack upon Fort Griswold, which was strongly garrisoned, and made a most obstinate defence; but at last was carried by the superior valour and perseverance of the British troops under his command. In the assault, he received a dangerous wound from a musket ball, which brought on a gradual decline, and at length occasioned his death."[10]

Arnold may have anticipated a negative reaction from Clinton when he learned of the casualties suffered at the fort. This was probably why he reported that he attempted to cancel the assault on the fort but was thwarted by an unnamed officer arriving a few minutes too late to carry out his orders. Unlike the first officer Arnold sent to expedite the attack, there is no evidence outside his report that a second officer was sent.[11]

American spies operating within New York City were able to pick up on the tension between Arnold, Clinton, and the other British generals. Most of it was unfavorable towards Arnold. The information the informants collected left the city, went to Long Island, then across Long Island Sound to Connecticut, and to Major General Heath's headquarters. In one letter relaying the intelligence to John

---

9 "Extract of a letter from an officer of the 54th regiment, to his friend in Edinburgh, dated NY, Sep 6," *Saunders's News-Letter*, Nov. 22, 1781.

10 Ford, *British Officers*, 66; *Ipswich Journal*, Oct. 15, 1791; *CG*, Sep. 7, 1781. Eyre's rumored death is one of those oft-repeated myths of Fort Griswold.

11 Letter extract from a lieutenant; *Saunders's News-Letter*, Nov. 24, 1781.

Hancock, Heath wrote, "Arnold is generally blamed for his conduct at N. London. His loss has been great." The same agent also conveyed, "[The British] rate their whole loss at near 400, some say five hundred, a Bunker Hill expedition they say. The British say if Arnold has the command they will be able to make but few more expeditions."[12]

Arnold's force suffered greatly, but not to the extent Heath's informants reported. Nevertheless, because of the difference in casualty numbers printed in British newspapers and those being fed by American spies, Heath believed Clinton was up to something. Moreover, Heath thought the British commander was concealing the actual numbers from his army, the public, and the Americans. This belief was furthered when Heath learned the British wounded were not landed in the city but instead in Harlem, some nine miles away.

Writing to Governor Trumbull, Heath reported the British wounded "were landed in boats at Harlem, and conveyed to the Hospital in waggons, carts, & sleds, this being done to prevent their being seen by the troops and inhabitants of the city." It is unclear why the informant conjectured that this somehow was being done to prevent them from being seen. Harlem was not a deserted area. People lived there. Hundreds of British and Hessian soldiers were stationed there. A Hessian officer at nearby Kingsbridge even noted their passage in his diary.[13]

Arnold also faced condemnation because Fort Griswold, its barracks, and magazine were left intact. This aggravated Clinton so much Arnold was called to Kennedy house to explain how this happened. Unfortunately, no transcripts or notes survive of the meeting, so we do not know how Arnold attempted to defend his actions or decisions. But there was assuredly tension. Major General Robertson, who was at the meeting, admitted in a private letter, "[Fort Griswold] . . . that cost us 200 Men killed and wounded. [Arnold] left this dear bought place without burning [the barracks] for 300 men and setting fire to a large Magazine that would have blown up the Fort and are now [quarreling] how this happened."[14]

---

12 Heath, *Heath Papers*, "Secret Intelligence from NY," 3:265–266. The numbers were slightly higher than the official casualty figures released in the *Royal Gazette*.

13 Heath to Trumbull, Sep. 23, 1781, Governor Trumbull Papers, 15:150a–b, CSL; Johann Charles Philip von Krafft, Journal of Lieutenant John Charles Philip von Krafft of the Regiment Von Bose, 1776–1784. Thomas H. Edsall, ed. (New York, 1868), 149; "State of the undermentioned Corps" Frederick Mackenzie Papers, WCL; Mackenzie, *Diary*, 2:637. It is unlikely Clinton was attempting to conceal anything. Examining the regimental returns taken by the 40th and 54th Regiments before and after the expedition does not reveal any casualty reporting abnormalities.

14 Either Robertson misspelled or the editor mistakenly transcribed quarreling as "qarreling." The barracks were designed to house a company of around 50 men. It is unlikely it was large enough to house 300.

There would be much quarreling between Arnold and the other generals. From the information collected in New York, Heath assured John Hancock, "Every account confirms the loss of the enemy to have been great at New London, and Arnold's conduct in burning, &c, almost universally detested by the British officers."[15]

Arnold refused to take responsibility for not destroying Fort Griswold, its cannon, or munitions. He blamed Capt. Lemoine, his artillery commander. He made no attempt to meet with Lemoine in person, as they lay off Plumb Island, to discuss what happened so it could be included in his report. Instead, Arnold criticized Lemoine, writing, "Captain Le Moine . . . had my positive directions to destroy; an attempt was made by him but unfortunately failed; he had my orders to make a second attempt: the reasons why it was not done, Captain Le Moine will have the honor to explain to Your Excellency."[16]

When Lemoine discovered he had been blamed, he was livid. It is not clear when he found out, but he certainly knew of it when Arnold's report was published in the *Royal Gazette*. Everyone in the city saw it. A British officer mentioned it in his diary, writing, "[T]he Barracks & Magazine in Ft. Griswold was order'd to be burn't by Capt. Lemoine of the artillery but by some mistake or neglect of his it was not done the reason of which he is to account for."[17]

By mid-November, over two-thousand miles away in Europe, people were asking the same questions. A British newspaper published, "There is something very mysterious in that part of General Arnold's letter, which relates to the magazine of powder and barracks found in Fort Griswold. If the troops were in the entire possession of the fort, as it appears they were, what should have hindered them from destroying every thing they should think proper; yet it appears that two attempts were made for this purpose."[18]

It was an embarrassment for Lemoine. Within days of Arnold's report being printed, Lemoine met with Clinton and explained the situation. Lemoine "had received advice that [a] very superior force [of American militia] was coming upon, which might have rendered retreat impracticable." This "superior force" was Major Peters's party, whose strength, in the darkness, had been overestimated by the British. Lemoine had yielded to prudence. He believed he could not make another attempt to destroy the fort's magazine without jeopardizing his command's

---

15 Heath, *Heath Papers*, Heath to John Hancock, Sep. 22, 1781, 3:262–263.

16 Mackenzie, *Diary*, 2:626.

17 Peebles, American War, 475.

18 *Stamford Mercury*, Nov. 15, 1781.

safety and called it off. Clinton accepted Lemoine's explanation and restored the artilleryman's public reputation in his General Orders of September 25. But that was not enough for Lemoine, and he requested and was granted permission to have the correction published in the *Royal Gazette*. It was subsequently published in several other British and Irish newspapers. Lemoine's honor was restored, and, in the coming years, as a lieutenant colonel of artillery, he served with distinction during the Napoleonic Wars.[19]

The third point of contention with Arnold was the destruction wrought against New London and Groton. Arnold was instructed to bring off the privateers and the military and public stores collected there. If he could not, he was to destroy them. He was not to burn the towns. As commander-in-chief, Clinton favored conventional warfare. He did not want to make war on the civilian population. Moreover, Clinton realized it did little to bring about the end of the rebellion. Past abuses only increased the colonists' resolve for continued resistance against the Crown.[20]

When Clinton discovered New London was largely burned, it was clear that Arnold had disobeyed his orders. Of all three charges, this was the only one for which Arnold could be personally held responsible, because he oversaw the British occupation of New London. For unclear reasons, Arnold spent little time overseeing his troops and spent most of it at Jeremiah Miller's home. The burning of the privateers, storehouses, and management of the occupation was given to his brigade-major Captain Stapleton.

Why did Arnold leave Stapleton in charge of accomplishing the most important objective of the raid? The answer may lie in Arnold's feelings about his personal safety. According to the opinion of an officer who served with him in Virginia, Arnold was not the same type of aggressive fighter he had been before his defection to the British. Instead, he now seemed more cautious than ever before. This was because, according to the same officer, Arnold feared being captured by the Americans.

Whether or not this was true, Arnold had a genuine concern for his safety. The Continental Congress had placed a bounty on his head. In Virginia, people knew of his treachery but few knew him by face. In Connecticut people knew both his

---

19 Reading Mercury, Nov. 11, 1781; *Royal Gazette* (NY), Sep. 29, 1781; George Tancred, Historical Record of Medals and Honorary Distinctions Conferred on The British Navy, Army & Auxiliary Forces, From the Earliest Period (London, 1891), 68–70.

20 Clinton, American Rebellion, 131. The only exception was when Clinton ordered Tryon to raid the coast of Connecticut. Tryon favored what we might call total warfare and believed the only way to successfully conclude the conflict was to make war on anyone, including civilians who opposed royal policies.

treachery and his face. This was especially true in New London. We know at least one person, Walter Harris, recognized Arnold and openly hailed him as a traitor. This probably unnerved the usually cocksure Arnold. Supposedly because of his fear of being captured, Arnold concealed two small pistols in his inside coat pocket to cheat the gallows if captured. He was still reportedly carrying the pistols when he visited England the following winter.[21]

Two stories exist of individuals who attempted to kill Arnold while he was in New London. These reinforce the idea that he should have been concerned for his safety. The most famous involved Abigail Hinman, a friend of Arnold's before the war. Several versions of the story are known to exist. The shortened version, which appeared in a Hinman family history, stated that Abigail remained in her house the day of the attack. Seeing Arnold ride past, there was a quick, polite exchange of words, but when Arnold turned, Abigail pulled out a musket and aimed it at him. Then, depending which version you read, the gun either misfired or was not loaded, and Arnold got away.[22]

A second, lesser-known story also exists. It involves three unnamed men who "full of resentment at [Arnold's] villainous conduct" conspired to kill him while he was in New London. Instead, the account claims, they killed one of Arnold's aides, wounded another, and shot the general's horse. The same story was retold to the president of the Continental Congress by the governor of New Jersey. But the story was either not true or exaggerated.[23]

However, even under Arnold's supervision, New London would likely have endured the same fate. The reason was the result of a tactical decision made by Arnold. It had to do with time. His plan was to land the night of September 5–6 and secure the forts and New London before the militia could come up. Had the wind not interfered with his plan, the raid might have produced greater results. The forts and New London would have been more vulnerable, and privateers would not have escaped. Arnold may have returned to New York with a few of them. But by the time he and the rest of his force landed, the entire country was alarmed. The delay had given the militia time to gather and organize. Arnold did not want to provide them with the opportunity to jeopardize his escape. British soldiers were

---

21 *Norfolk Chronicle*, Nov. 24, 1781; Harris, *Groton Heights*, 272; Ewald, *Hessian Journal*, 295.

22 R. R. Hinman, A Family Record of the Descendants of Sgt. Edward Hinman who first appeared in Stratford in CT about 1650 Collected From State, Colony, Town, And Church Records Also From Old Bibles and Aged People (Hartford, CT, 1856), 820.

23 *Salem Gazette*, Nov. 8, 1781; William Livingston to Thomas McKean, Sep. 14, 1781, State Papers-PA, 2:396–397, Papers of the Continental Congress, NARA. Livingston told McKean, "[Arnold's] Horse was shot under him, and his Servant killed next to his side." This story cannot be verified.

hurried during the occupation and were not allowed time to search every corner of each storehouse. They were to set them on fire and move on.

Arnold anticipated Clinton's criticism. In his report, Arnold explained he never intended to burn the town, and its cause was accidental. As discussed earlier, Arnold, as well as loyalists in town, attributed the fires to an explosion in a storehouse caused by a supply of gunpowder his soldiers had failed to locate. Once the storehouses were aflame, they were left unattended by both sides. After the British withdrew, the Americans did not reoccupy the town for about an hour and thus could not contain the fires. According to Arnold, the wind "communicated the flames to part of the town, which was, notwithstanding every effort to prevent it, unfortunately, destroyed."[24]

When Clinton learned of the destruction, he realized the implications of it. While he never publicly admitted his feelings, his adviser Chief Justice Smith predicted New London's destruction would have no impact on the war. Instead, Smith concluded, it would only make the Americans angrier. He confided in his diary on September 12 that "the Destruction of New London awakens Attention and adds to Fear and Revenge." Clinton attempted to play damage control. In his General Orders of September 17, he proclaimed he "was convinced [Arnold] took every precaution in his power to prevent the destruction of the town, which is a misfortune that gives him much concern." But it was too late; the damage was done.[25]

Smith was only partially correct. The Americans were angry, not about New London, but about Fort Griswold. It was the bloodiest battle fought in Connecticut during the entire war. Southeastern Connecticut had not seen something so horrific since Pequot War of 1637, when a combined force of Connecticut colonists and their native allies attacked a barricaded Pequot village in eastern Groton and killed over 400 people, including men, women, and children, an attack remembered as the "Mystic Massacre." According to historian John Warner Barber, it was in this way that many in southeastern Connecticut viewed and remembered Fort Griswold. It became "an Aceldama," a biblical term meaning a place of slaughter and bloodshed, where "the flower of [their] sons were sacrificed to the vengeance of an infuriated enemy."[26]

The immediate reaction of the community to the raid was shock. For many, it was beyond comprehension. In its most brutal fashion, the war had come to their

---

24 Arnold report to Clinton in Mackenzie, *Diary*, 2:626.

25 CM, Nov. 10, 1781.

26 Barber, Historical Collections, 309. Aceldama was the place Judas purchased with the thirty pieces of silver gotten for his betrayal of Jesus.

doorsteps. So many men were lost in such a short amount of time. Everyone felt its effects, and its memory left an indelible impression on the population, which still resonates to this day. Almost everyone knew someone who had fought or been killed there. Forty women were suddenly widows, while dozens of children were now fatherless. It was equally devastating for families who sometimes relied on each other for survival.

Even the militia, though many of them had seen some combat, were significantly impacted by it. None of them had seen or witnessed anything so vicious and brutal as they had at Fort Griswold. The entire experience was traumatic, and for most, its psychological effects haunted them for the rest of their lives. Battles of the period were not typically so up close and personal. Many saw the faces of the enemy they killed or wounded. Others watched family members or friends being shot, bayonetted—sometimes repeatedly—to death, even as they attempted to surrender. Many, even in the heat and confusion of battle, saw this as nothing less than cold-blooded murder.

Eventually, shock turned to anger and a desire for revenge. Governor Trumbull recognized these heightened emotions and planned to use them to his own advantage. In a carefully orchestrated propaganda campaign, Trumbull sought control over the public narrative of the attack. He hoped to stoke the fires of public opinion and thus generate continued anger against the British. He had good reason to do so because, by the summer of 1781, the state was bankrupt. As a result, public morale for the continuation of the war was at its lowest point during the conflict. This, in turn, negatively impacted recruitment for all of Connecticut's units, both Continental and state. With the memory of the Pennsylvania Line Mutiny—where Pennsylvania Continental soldiers rebelled over lack of pay—still fresh in everyone's memory, Trumbull, in August, sent a large amount of "silver and gold" to pay Connecticut's Continental soldiers. As the fear of additional attacks was raised, Trumbull desperately needed something to unite his citizens.[27]

Capitalizing on the often-uncontrollable hatred of Arnold, the governor focused his attention on Fort Griswold, specifically the death of Ledyard and the treatment of the garrison. The governor explained this to Thomas Mumford two days after the attack. Trumbull wrote his friend, while in Groton, to "carefully collect and state those Transactions and all material circumstances, more especially the Treatment of Col. Ledyard, the unfortunate Garrison, procure the same to be authenticated and forwarded to me, for Such Improvement as may be here after

---

27 Richard Buel Jr., *Dear Liberty: Connecticut's Mobilization for the Revolutionary War* (Middletown, CT, 1980), 239–281; *CSR*, 3:488–492; Stuart, Life of Trumbull, 540–541. In modern terms it was as if a person had $1,000 in 1777, but by 1780 it was only worth $25.

thought proper." After reading the governor's instructions, it is hard to imagine how the governor might improve the participants' accounts. Were the events not tragic enough on their own? Apparently not.[28]

Before writing to Mumford, the only information Trumbull had of the attack and death of Ledyard came from Col. Zabdiel Rogers. Reporting from New London on September 7, Rogers explained, "Ledyard Made a Noble Defence [and] Repuls'd The Enemy Two Or Three Times But at Last was Oblig'd To Surrender the Fort to [a] Superior Force. The enemy After Colo Ledyard had Surrendered [they] Murder'd him & A Number of Others."[29]

However, the conditions under which Ledyard had acted are missing from Rogers's account. Rogers was neither a participant nor a witness to the battle and did not know the details. It can be assumed that the information came to him secondhand without knowing his source, which is not revealed in the letter. If it is read as-is, without considering the circumstances under which Ledyard was operating, it appears the fighting at the fort ceased, and when it did, Ledyard formally surrendered. As he did, he was killed, and the fighting flared up again, with several dozen more defenders being killed or brutally wounded.

As discussed in Chapter 8, the fighting did not end until Major Bromfield entered the fort a few minutes after Ledyard was killed. Nor was there a formal surrender. No survivors who testified within a year of the battle ever made mention of such a ceremony. But to Trumbull, these details did not matter. He did not even wait to verify Rogers's information through "additional sources," or await the conclusion of an investigation, which occurred a year later. Instead, Rogers's letter was given to the Hartford-based, Continental-friendly newspaper, *Connecticut Courant and Weekly Intelligencer*, who published an excerpt of it in their September 11 issue. From there, Trumbull's version of Fort Griswold spread like wildfire.[30]

As was common during the period, stories printed in one newspaper would be frequently published verbatim in other newspapers. Often, this was done without any fact-checking. The same was with Rogers's excerpts. They were republished in several other Continental-friendly newspapers, reaching New Jersey by the end of September. In their coverage of the raid, newspapers focused attention on Fort Griswold and Ledyard, just like Trumbull's directions to Mumford. While some touched on the destruction of New London, most attention was paid to the former. There, as the tragic events were spelled out, the editors, like those at the

---

28 Trumbull to Thomas Mumford, Sep. 8, 1781, Governor Trumbull Papers, Vol. 4, Folder 6, CHS.

29 Rogers's letter was probably the first written account of Ledyard's death.

30 *Connecticut Courant and Weekly Intelligencer*, Sep. 11, 1781.

Gazette, manipulated and sensationalized the narratives, carefully choosing words to evoke an emotional response from readers.

Typical descriptions of the raid started by mentioning Arnold's involvement. Arnold was never just another British general: He was "Traitor Arnold" or, in one case, "that fiend and dog of Hell Arnold." When the excerpts were published in Massachusetts, a week after the *Courant*, the editors took liberties and modified parts of the letter. Rogers had initially referred to Arnold as the "infamous General Arnold." That was not bad enough, and the *Gazette* changed it, so the same line read "the infamous Judas Arnold." The New London expedition was not just another British operation but "[Arnold's] satanic expedition into Connecticut." When describing the events, those opposing the British were "brave and worthy citizens" while the British were "inhuman banditti."[31]

It was not only the language that fueled the propaganda campaign, but anonymous accounts that appeared in various American newspapers. One such was a letter, supposedly written on September 12 from New London. It read in part:

> The next assault was made upon [Fort Griswold], where they were repulsed several times by a bravery unequalled, for about three hours. A flag was then sent, demanding a surrender, accompanied by a threat of giving no quarters in case of refusal. The commandant consulted with his brave garrison, who refused to submit. The action was then renewed, when the flag staff was unfortunately shot away; not withstanding which the defence was gallantly continued until five or six hundred of the enemy having forced the pickets had entered through the breach. At this time there were but *four* of the garrison killed, and it was thought prudent to submit, to preserve the lives of the remainder.[32]

The same anonymous letter introduced aspects, many of which cannot be found or are contradicted in contemporary accounts, such as the length of the battle and that only four defenders had been killed by this point. However, some of these details made numerous appearances in many of the participants' post-war pension applications.

---

31 *Connecticut Courant and Weekly Intelligencer*, Sep. 11, 1781; Boston Gazette, Sep. 17, 1781; *CG*, Nov. 23, 1781; *Connecticut Courant* and Weekly Advertiser, Oct. 2, 1781; New-Jersey Gazette, Sep. 19, 1781; Pennsylvania Journal, Sep. 26, 1781; Pennsylvania Gazette, Sep. 26, 1781; Maryland Journal, Oct. 9, 1781.

32 "Extract of a letter from New-London, dated Sep 12," Maryland Journal, Oct. 9, 1781. Often these narratives, like the one presented above, used techniques like italicized words to draw attention to them.

No description was more consequential in the letter than the details surrounding Ledyard's death and the subsequent massacre of many in the garrison. Its depiction read, "The officer who at the time commanded the assailants . . . inquired who commanded the garrison? Col. Ledyard informed him he had had the honour, but was unfortunate in being obliged to surrender it, at the same time delivered up to him his sword, and asked for quarter for himself and people; to which the infamous villain replied, 'yes, ye rascals, I'll give you quarter,' and then plunged the sword into his body. The inhuman banditti, taking this as a signal, drove their bayonets up to the muzzles of their pieces into the breasts of all that were taken, except one or two who made their escape." The letter's publication marked the first time a dialogue between Ledyard and a British officer to whom the colonel supposedly surrendered was revealed, as well as the first time it was publicly stated that Ledyard had been killed with his own sword.[33]

The letter's focus on Fort Griswold, Ledyard, and the treatment of the garrison strongly suggest Mumford was its source. The dialogue and manner of Ledyard's death were some of the "improvements" suggested by the governor. Three days before the anonymous letter was supposedly written, Mumford wrote to the governor, telling him the same thing. Mumford wrote, "[Ledyard] tho't proper to Surrender himself with the Garrison prisoners, and presented his Sword to an officer who Rec'd the same and immediately lunged in thro the Brave Commandant, when the Ruffians (no doubt by order) pierced him in many places with Bayonets."[34]

There are two major problems with Mumford's description of Ledyard's death. First, he gave no source from where he obtained his information. Seven survivors, among them Captain Latham and Lieutenant Perkins, gave testimony about their involvement, and none of them indicated any formal surrender or the specifics of Ledyard's death. The second issue is the manner of Ledyard's death. Mumford stated Ledyard was killed with his own sword, thrust through his chest, and then bayonetted multiple times. Since Ledyard's sword was not taken as a trophy, it would be expected that the militia who discovered Ledyard's body after the battle may have found it still lodged in his chest. Jason Stanton, one of those who first entered the fort, wrote a detailed description of where they discovered the colonel's body but found no such sword. Silent witnesses to the affair, Ledyard's waistcoat and shirt, further contradict Mumford's description. Both pieces of bloodstained

33 Philadelphia Packet, Sep. 26, 1781.

34 Thomas Mumford to Governor Trumbull, Sep. 9, 1781, Governor Trumbull Papers, 15:105a–c, CSL. The "surrender dialogue" disappeared from the overall story after the war, only to reappear in a slightly different form in Stephen Hempstead's 1826 narrative, a detail he'd left out of his two previous accounts of the battle. Hempstead's inclusion of the dialogue probably prompted two others, George Middleton and Thomas Hertell, to include two more variations of it in their own narratives.

Lieutenant Colonel William Ledyard's Sword. The sword that is believed to have been carried by Ledyard during the battle of Groton Heights. *Tad Sattler*

clothing were removed from the colonel's body before he was buried. They were saved by the family and donated to the Connecticut Historical Society in the mid-nineteenth century, where they remain today. Dr. Walter Powell examined both pieces while researching his book, *Murder or Mayhem? Benedict Arnold's New London, Connecticut Raid, 1781*. Powell realized that the clothing shows no evidence of being "pierced . . . in many places with Bayonets," as Mumford told Trumbull. Instead, both pieces only contain two corresponding holes, one on each side, about six inches below the armpit. The fatal blow to Ledyard came not from his front but from his right side. The entrance hole is also triangular-shaped, which corresponds to the exact shape of a British bayonet. Also revealing was that in order for the holes to match up on both pieces of clothing, Ledyard could not have been motionless in his final moments. He was actively turning the upper part of his body. As he did, he was assuredly attempting to defend himself when he was killed.[35]

The propaganda campaign waged by Trumbull did not end with the war. The claim that a British officer murdered Ledyard unleashed a public manhunt for the culprit. Hempstead's 1826 narrative identified Ledyard's killer as Captain Beckwith. This was not an original accusation. It probably originated about forty years earlier, a short time after the battle. Over the decades, many American authors have accused Beckwith of committing the act. Major Bromfield and Lt. Col. Abraham van Buskirk were also accused of killing Ledyard, though their names were only known to their accusers through their inclusion

---

35 Some have taken this information into consideration and argued that the mortal wound was delivered by a hanger sword, such as the one carried by Ledyard. A hanger sword has a triangular blade, like that of a bayonet. But if this were the case, when Ledyard was attacked he would have been awkwardly standing perpendicular to his attacker. There would also have been at least a moment where the fighting suddenly stopped so that Ledyard could give over his sword. This, according to most American sources written during the war, did not occur.

Lieutenant Colonel William Ledyard's Waistcoat. This was the waistcoat worn by Ledyard during the battle of Groton Heights.

Don Troiani

in contemporary newspapers. Van Buskirk did not even participate in the attack.[36]

Beckwith was the most vilified of the British officers. On his way to a government post in Quebec, he visited New York City in 1787. Once it was known he was in the city, he was publicly harassed in several editorials printed in the *New York Journal*. These editorials, all written under the pen name "AN AMERICAN," accused Beckwith of being both a "S P Y" and the "ASSASIN" of Ledyard. They "commanded B[eckwith] depart!—reasons forbids, justice will never permit you to remain here, in the presence of those men, who feel the loss of their friends and relations, occasioned by your hands." Another editorial taunted Beckwith and demanded he reveal "[the] secret horrors of LEDYARD's unnatural death."[37]

Aware of the editorials, Beckwith attempted to ignore them as he continued onto Quebec. But upon reaching the city he decided to release a public response to address the matter. This would be the only public response about Ledyard by any British officer involved in the battle. In it, Beckwith revealed his admiration for Ledyard and the American commander's decision to hold the fort. But Beckwith also revealed something more telling. He defended himself by stating he could not have killed Ledyard because he went into the battle unarmed; he did not know of the claims that Ledyard had been killed with his own sword or even that he

---

36 Samuel F. Wilson, History of the American Revolution with a Preliminary View of the Character and Principles of the Colonists and their Controversies with Great Britain (Baltimore, 1834), 338–339. Wilson's book is one of numerous examples. He wrote, "Ledyard finally surrendered his sword to Major Bromfield, who instantly plunged it in the heart of the prisoner, and the bloody example was followed so mercilessly, that nearly every man of the garrison was butchered. The Groton Massacre is another horrible stain on the British arms and was fitly perpetrated under the lead of Arnold."

37 *New York Journal*, Mar. 15, 1787, Mar. 29, 1787. Beckwith is never named but instead referred to as Major B***.

surrendered. Beckwith continued, "The brave, although unfortunate commandant of Fort Griswold, was regularly summoned, but he knew the value of his post which he was determined to maintain; and I have uniformly understood, that he fell fighting for its preservation, scorning to bestow one moment's reflection about himself I am of opinion, that the manner of his death never was known. Such are usually the consequences when strong field forts are stormed, and defended at noon day, by men of resolution."[38]

A month later, an unnamed member of the Ledyard family, who resided in New York City, joined the editorial fray. They responded both to the original editorials and Beckwith's statement. In their lengthy reply, they publicly accepted Beckwith's innocence of the charge and encouraged the public to put the matter to rest. But it did not.[39]

Most people have continued to accept that Ledyard formally surrendered and was killed with his own sword by one of the three named British officers. It is even commemorated as such on the battlefield today. In 1826, the citizens of Groton lobbied the state legislature to fund a monument to commemorate the "Memory of the Brave Patriots who fell in the massacre at Fort Griswold." Around this time, many veterans, but not all, started claiming they all saw Ledyard being killed. This could have been because, as Dr. Powell concluded, "it was easy to imagine the aging veteran . . . putting himself at every point where the important events took place." Most claims came through the veteran's pension applications or interviews with news reporters. A majority were new, as many had not said anything publicly about the battle, least of all Ledyard's death until now. And not surprisingly, not all the veterans agreed, either on the surrender or on the details of Ledyard's death.[40]

In the 1840's some historians started openly questioning the accepted version of the battle. They pointed out the lack of credible primary sources involving both the surrender and death of Ledyard. Most sources being used thus far were written decades later. One researcher, doing research in the state library in 1847, was shocked when he could not find one contemporary source from any witness detailing the surrender or Ledyard's death. When addressing them, he dismissed

---

38 *New York Journal*, Jun. 16, 1787.

39 The identification of the member of the Ledyard family remains unknown, but two of the colonel's nephews, sons of his brother Youngs, lived in New York at the time: Major Benjamin Ledyard who served in the Continental Army, and his brother Isaac Ledyard, a prominent New York city doctor and politician.

40 PA: Ziba Woodworth (R.11848), NARA. The most colorful description of Ledyard's death was given by Ziba Woodworth, who claimed that after Ledyard surrendered his sword the British officer beat him over the head with it, after which the British officer pulled his own sword and drove it into Ledyard.

Groton Monument. Completed in 1830, the monument commemorates those who were killed during the battle of Groton Heights. *Tad Sattler*

them as "common tradition." Two decades later, William Harris, a historian of the raid, was equally frustrated at the lack of a contemporary eyewitness account of such a seminal event. Without any such accounts, he referred to the manner of Ledyard's death as "merely a conjecture, at the most."[41]

Apart from historical mythmaking, what resulted from the battle and continued through the last two years of the war was anger, which resonated with the public, governmental officials and among the rank and file in the Continental Army. In October, a mixed force of Continentals under Major Tallmadge mounted a successful attack on the Loyal Refugee-held Fort Slongo. Among the prisoners was Lt. William Castles, who had participated in the New London expedition. Writing to Trumbull afterward, Tallmadge reported, "The Recollection of Fort Griswold . . . occasioned a more severe Treatment that they otherwise would have rec'd."[42]

Days before the assault on Fort Slongo, word of the attack on New London reached Washington's army outside Williamsburg, Virginia. In all, Washington received five letters about it. Three from Major General Heath, one from Thomas McKean, the president of the Continental Congress, and another from Governor Trumbull. Heath and McKean's letters probably reached Washington first but only provided the commander-in-chief with knowledge of an attack with little details. It was not until Trumbull's letter reached Washington in early October (though written on September 13) that he learned of the extent of the attack.

---

41 "Massacre at Fort Griswold, Sept. 6, 1781," *Connecticut Courant*, Aug. 28, 1781; Harris, *Groton Heights*, 35.

42 Tallmadge to Governor Trumbull, Oct. 5, 1781, Governor Trumbull Papers, 15:174a–c, CSL; *CG*, Nov. 9, 1781. The Associated Loyalist sloop Colonel Martin was captured two months later by the privateer *Sampson* and brought into New London Harbor.

Trumbull's letter confirmed the attack and Arnold's involvement in it. It also explained the overwhelming damage done to New London. But it was Ledyard and Fort Griswold Trumbull wanted the focus on and most of the letter was about them. Writing to Washington, "Yet what is more to be regreted is the unhappy Fate of that worthy Officer Col. Ledyard & those brave Men (many of whom sustained respectable Characters & were esteemed the Flower of that Town[)]who so gallantly fought & unfortunately fell with him, victims to British Cruelty."[43]

Heading into the final climactic stages of the Yorktown campaign, Washington and the soldiers of his army were led to believe Ledyard and his men at Fort Griswold had been butchered by Crown forces after they had surrendered. The soldiers instinctively wanted revenge. This was stated by the Marquis de Lafayette, the commander of the army's light infantry battalions, when he wrote to the French minister to the United States on the siege, "We had promised ourselves to avenge the New London affair."[44]

It is not known how or when Washington told his army. According to an officer on the general's staff, the senior leadership was told on September 28 the British had burned New London, and the "Infamous Arnold headed the party." It is unclear how far the news went, but from available sources, it stayed within Washington's headquarters for the time.[45]

The withholding of the news from any of his General Orders released during the siege seems to imply that Washington wanted to use the New London story for maximum propaganda impact. It would be used to galvanize the troops at the most critical moment of the siege, the storming of Redoubt 10, during the night of October 14. John Patten, a Connecticut light infantryman in Lt. Col. Alexander Hamilton's Battalion of Light Infantry, implied this scenario. Just before

---

43 Governor Trumbull to George Washington, Sep. 13, 1781; Journals of the Continental Congress, 1774–1789 (Washington D.C., 1912), 21:978, 1017–1018. Washington forwarded the letter to Congress, where it was given to the Congressional Committee on Retaliation. The committee's ruling was harsh. First, it decided to publicly execute, if captured, any of the British officers behind the atrocities reported at Fort Griswold. Additionally, it was recommended a similar number of British prisoners be executed for those at Fort Griswold. Lastly, the committee resolved if the British continued such attacks in "burning defenceless villages, or houses, or in murdering inoffensive citizens or prisoners of war," all persons involved, if captured, were to be put to death." It is unclear if any such policies were either adopted or carried out.

44 Marquis de Lafayette to Anne-Cesar, Chevalier de la Luzerne, Oct. 16, 1781, in Letters from Lafayette to Luzerne, 1780–1782, ed. Waldo G. Leland (Bloomingdale, IN, 1915), 610–611.

45 Henry Dearborn, Revolutionary War Journals of Henry Dearborn, 1775-1783, Lloyd A. Brown and Howard H. Peckham, eds. (Chicago, 1939), 218.

the assault, Patten remembered how the officers exhorted the light infantrymen, "Remember New London!"[46]

Overall, the British attack on New London did very little militarily for the British, especially at that point in the war, though it did cause chaos along the Connecticut coast for over a week. Very few privateers were destroyed. None were captured. Even though the waterfront was devastated, the raid could not deter American privateers and other vessels from continuing to operate out of the port. An Irish newspaper probably put it best: "General Arnold's Attack on …New London… appears to have scorched the Snake, as Macbeth says, not killed it; she'll close and be herself again; as a Proof of this, Arnold had scarcely left that [place], when two of the American Privateers carried in two prizes…both valuable Prizes to the Captors." Despite the continued harassment of vessels operating out of the port, the British never again returned. [47]

Fort Griswold, Fort Trumbull, and Fort Nonsense would all be repaired and regarrisoned. Most of the cannon were fixed and put back into service. The attack had definitely demonstrated the limitations of a small permanent garrison. In April 1782, fourteen leading citizens of New London petitioned Col. McClellan for changes. Among a host of things, they asked for a larger garrison, stiffer penalties for militia who did not respond to the alarm guns, and to make it illegal for ships to abandon the harbor during an attack. But nothing changed.[48]

The only noticeable difference was made to the alarm sequence, recognizing the confusion caused by the "promiscuous firing of cannon" by the privateers and other vessels, most notably during the morning of the attack, which greatly confused the militia. Shortly after taking command, Col. McClellan requested the commanders of such vessels "to discontinue the Practice, and on no Pretence" were they "to fire a Cannon while riding" in the harbor.[49]

If there was any one group that was the most impacted by the raid, it was the local citizens. The community was devastated. The destruction of the raid reduced

46 PA: John Patten (S.19745), NARA; Alexander Hamilton, Papers of Alexander Hamilton Volume XXVI May 1, 1802–Oct 23, 1804, Additional Documents 1774-1799 Addenda and Errata, ed. Harold C. Syrett (New York, 1979), XXVI:30–32; New-Jersey Gazette, Nov. 7, 1781. In a widely circulated story afterward, "Remember New London!" was taken to mean the light infantrymen were ordered to retaliate against the British for Fort Griswold—that in the assault on Redoubt 10, they were to take no prisoners and to kill every redcoat they encountered. Hamilton later publicly refuted this popular notion and wrote "that no such order, nor any intimidation nor hint resembling it, was ever by me received or understood to have given.

47 Hibernian Journal, Nov. 30, 1781.

48 "To Col. McClellan, Commandant of the Posts of New London & Groton," Revolutionary War Records, Series I, XXII:337, CSL.

49 CG, Oct. 26, 1781.

the local maritime economy to shambles. Dozens of families found themselves homeless. Financiers and owners of privateers and other maritime merchants lost their storehouses and valuable inventories contained therein. The town would not see prosperity return for decades.

The General Assembly attempted to relieve those who suffered. Recognizing the devastation caused by the British during their multiple excursions into Connecticut, legislators appointed several committees the following May to investigate the damages. These committees visited the impacted areas and compiled a catalog of property claims. But unfortunately, lacking sufficient funds to indemnify them, the state instead provided citizen tax abatements for 1782. After the war, they again tried to provide relief. This time the compensation was land. Over 500,000 acres of land in Connecticut's vast Western Reserve, in modern-day Ohio, were distributed and appropriated to those affected, but very few took the offer.[50]

The attack on New London did little to impact the war's outcome or the eventual Franco-American victory at Yorktown. But it proved to be a mindful distraction. It drew British attention, resources, time, and energy away from the real threat in Virginia. Most notably, the sailors, transport, and horse vessels would have been necessary to perform any large-scale operation, whether diversionary or relief. What is clear is that over the course of the New London expedition, things started going from bad to worse for the British. Washington had masterfully played and, as Major Tallmadge described, "entirely deceived" Clinton. Believing an attack on New York by the allies was imminent, Clinton remained, apart from the Rhode Island and New London expeditions, almost paralyzed in the city. While Arnold was gone, Washington and Rochambeau moved their armies southward through New Jersey, Pennsylvania, and Maryland entirely unmolested. By the time Arnold returned to New York on September 12, the allies were approaching Annapolis, Maryland.[51]

On the morning of September 5, the day before Arnold landed in New London, Admiral Graves located Admiral de Grasse near the entrance to Chesapeake Bay. That afternoon, elements of both fleets were locked in a nearly three-hour battle over control of the entrance to Chesapeake Bay. When the Battle of the Chesapeake ended, Graves was unable to break through, but despite the setback remained in the area for a little over a week—but never renewed the engagement. This was due to the arrival on September 10 of the squadron of Admiral de Barras, the

---

50 "Appointment of committee to make abatements of taxes of those in New London & Groton who suffered from the British invasion, May 1782," Revolutionary War Records, Series I, XXII:304, CSL.

51 Benjamin Tallmadge, Memoirs of Col. Benjamin Tallmadge, Prepared by Himself, at the Request of his Children (New York, 1858), 4.

same squadron which had escaped Clinton's grasp at Newport. His appearance increased French strength to 40 ships and destroyed Graves's hopes of renewing the engagement. Graves's 23 ships, now greatly outnumbered, were ordered back to New York.[52]

Clinton received word of Graves's setback on September 13 and called for a council of war the following day. At least eight additional councils followed over the next four weeks. The main point of discussion was Cornwallis and his army. Arnold was present for two meetings, on September 14 and 15, but was excluded from all others, contributing to the ongoing friction between Arnold and Clinton.[53]

During the initial meeting, it was decided unanimously, according to Clinton, to wait for Graves's return and the arrival of naval reinforcements from England under Admiral Robert Digby, which was due any day, before making an attempt to relieve Cornwallis. In the meantime, Clinton conceived the idea of entering New Jersey with "some intention of making a push at Philadelphia" to take the pressure off Cornwallis's army. Major Mackenzie predicted the tactic "by making a Sudden movement into Jersey, with all the force we can collect, and marching directly to Philadelphia . . . would throw the Rebels into the utmost consternation, and possibly make an important diversion in favor of [Cornwallis]." However, upon consultation with Admiral Graves, Clinton was dissuaded.[54]

Cornwallis could be relieved by sea. But this could only be done once the navy was ready. When Graves returned, he needed time to complete repairs on his damaged vessels. When the fleet moved again, it would carry Clinton and a detachment from his army.[55]

Arnold remained anxious throughout September. Despite the intense criticism he faced for his leadership during the New London expedition he desired to return to combat. It is not clear if Arnold knew about the discussion of the diversionary action against Philadelphia. Still, on October 2 he submitted a plan of his own to Clinton, targeting the rebel capital. Two days later, Clinton summoned Arnold to the Kennedy mansion for a meeting about his plan with Robertson and von Knyphausen. Considering the problematic relationship between Clinton and Arnold, the meeting may have been only a ploy to silence Arnold. After Arnold presented his plan, Clinton told him he would consent to it only if the two other generals present did not object. Both von Knyphausen and Robertson objected.

---

52 Mackenzie, *Diary*, 2:634–635. After the battle, Admiral de Grasse disembarked 3,200 French soldiers. Upon his arrival de Barras landed siege artillery and other equipment.

53 Clinton, American Rebellion, 569–580; Mackenzie, *Diary*, 2:631.

54 Mackenzie, *Diary*, 2:235–236; Clinton, American Rebellion, 570–572,

55 Mackenzie, *Diary*, 2:614.

The generals feared there were insufficient troops to send to Virginia, protect New York, and send with Arnold. According to Chief Justice Smith, Arnold was "displeased" at their response but refused to take no for an answer. Arnold argued that there were more than enough troops in New York to accomplish all three tasks. Clinton then stepped in and told Arnold he had been misinformed and that there were insufficient troops. Even when they asked him to postpone the plan until Clinton landed in the Chesapeake, Arnold grew irritated. He realized they no longer trusted his ability to lead an independent command. But his desire to return to action was strong. For a moment, Arnold decided to cast aside his ego. He again proposed to attack Philadelphia but agreed to serve under Robertson or any other general. Again, the request was denied. Arnold left the meeting exasperated. Immediately following it he met with Smith and accused Clinton of lying about the strength of his army to prevent Arnold from returning to action.[56]

Nearly two weeks later, as the second relief force for Cornwallis was being organized, Arnold again went to Clinton's headquarters. He expected to be appointed to command troops on the relief expedition. But Clinton had no intention of including Arnold. Instead, the commander-in-chief appointed a junior brigadier general. Arnold again grew embittered at being passed over. To calm him, Clinton promised to employ Arnold once reinforcements arrived in New York from Charlestown. It was an empty promise.[57]

On October 17, after over a month of delays, Clinton set sail for Yorktown with around 6,000 troops accompanied by 32 warships under Admiral Digby. But the relief expedition proved to be in vain. Cornwallis had by that time already been locked in a siege for nearly four weeks. Three days earlier American and French troops had captured Redoubts 9 and 10. This brought their artillery close enough to make the main British line untenable, and as a result on October 19, 1781, Cornwallis surrendered.[58]

Word of Cornwallis's surrender reached New York within a week. The news brought great agitation to the city, but it emboldened Arnold. Frustrated with Clinton, whom he blamed for the defeat, Arnold was granted leave to depart for England. He would not wait for Clinton to send him back into action; he would go to London in person to ask for it. Arnold was not imprudent. He realized the implications of Cornwallis's surrender, not only for the war but for himself and his

---

56 Smith, *Historical Memoirs*, 455.

57 Ibid., 457–459. According to Smith, Clinton was going to allow Arnold to strike at Philadelphia. It is not clear how honest Clinton was about the operation or how it would fit any strategic goals of the British at that time.

58 Mackenzie, *Diary*, 2:662–665.

reputation. He made no attempt to hide the purpose of his trip. His sole purpose was to push for the continuation of the war. As Arnold's biographer Clare Brandt stated, he did this because, "[For Arnold] it was a matter of life and death. Benedict Arnold's deeds would be vindicated if the British won the war, and his stature would be affirmed. If they lost, he would be nothing." A British victory was his only hope of vindication.[59]

When Arnold arrived in London in January 1782, the effects of the British surrender at Yorktown had reverberated across the Atlantic. Support for the war in Parliament was dwindling. Despite this, Arnold met with Lord Germain, Lord Frederick North the prime minister, and eventually with King George, and assured them most Americans supported the royal cause and were waiting for the British to demonstrate their will to protect them. All three had been promised this many times before but had never seen anything come of it.

Arnold lobbied his plan for a British victory in which he hoped to play a significant role. He claimed Yorktown was only a "French victory" and would only prove fatal to the cause if England ended the war. Arnold called for a new commander-in-chief and an additional 15,000-20,000 troops to be sent to America. With these, Arnold promised he could subjugate the Americans in a single campaign. This final campaign, Arnold believed, would be his greatest victory.[60]

Arnold's proposals went nowhere. His most enthusiastic supporter, Lord Germain, resigned in early February. Three weeks later, Parliament voted against continuing the war. The following month, Lord North resigned. This brought a change to the leadership of the British government. North's replacement, Charles Watson-Wentworth, the Marquess of Rockingham, was sympathetic to the Americans. Upon his appointment, he sent an envoy to meet with the Americans to discuss peace terms. Arnold was undoubtedly displeased with the turn of events. The only good news was that Clinton had been replaced as commander-in-chief. His successor was Sir Guy Carleton. Arnold expected to sail with him to New York, but Carleton sailed without him. Arnold remained in London and was there when the Treaty of Paris formally ended the war in February 1783.

---

59 Brandt, *Man in the Mirror*, 253.

60 Benedict Arnold to Lord Germain, May 13, 1782, Lord Shelburne Papers, WCL; *Reading Mercury*, Jan. 28, 1782; *Stamford Mercury*, Jan. 31, 1782, Feb. 7, 1782; *Ipswich Journal*, Jan. 19, 1782; CM, Jan. 26, 1782. Arnold brought with him his disdain for Clinton. It was so well known that the *Ipswich Journal* reported, "Brigadier General Arnold brings home with him a string of serious charges against the commander-in-chief at New York." According to the CM, Arnold remained upset with Clinton for not allowing him to attack Washington and Rochambeau as they crossed the Hudson River.

Its end brought Arnold searching for a new livelihood and ways to restore his reputation and financial standing. He sought positions within the British government and the East India Company, but these failed as did most of his claims for compensation as a loyalist refugee. In 1785, Arnold left England with his family for New Brunswick in Canada and settled with thousands of loyalists who had relocated there after the war. Arnold speculated in land and attempted to re-establish himself in the mercantile business as he had before the war. This time, however, he did not meet with much lasting success and ended up losing most of his investments. After several years in Canada, Arnold, struggling to provide for his family, went back to England, where he again attempted to recuperate his losses during the war. Once again, he failed.

In 1793, with the outbreak of war between Napoleonic France and Great Britain, Arnold sensed an opportunity and tried to use the conflict to his advantage by resuming his mercantile operations. During one voyage to the West Indies, the French briefly captured him. After escaping, Arnold lobbied for an appointment to brigadier general and return to combat. But he was refused and sat out the rest of the war.

Toward the end of 1800, Arnold's health began to decline. He had suffered from gout since 1775. Initially, it had only impacted his left leg, but now it spread to his right. No longer able to go to sea, the effects of gout spread to his lungs and his throat, making it difficult for him to breathe, swallow, or talk. He retired to his London home, where he lingered until he died on June 14, 1801.[61]

By that time, nearly twenty years had passed since Arnold sailed on the *Shuldham* for New London. Just as many years had passed since he departed New York for England. Departing, Arnold was confident that upon his return to America, he would help suppress the rebellion and restore his tarnished reputation. But it was not to be. He did not know it yet but his involvement in the war was over. All his feats, which had gained him legendary status in the Continental Army—Fort Ticonderoga, Quebec, Valcour Island, Ridgefield, Compo Hill, Fort Stanwix, and Saratoga—were all for naught. Instead, treason and treachery followed him and his name. New London sealed that legacy forever.

---

61 Brandt, *Man in the Mirror*, 254–273.

Order of Battle:
Ledyard's Regiment
September 6, 1781

Captain William Latham's Company of Matrosses
(Stationed at Fort Griswold)

Capt. William Latham
1st Lt. Enoch Stanton
2nd Lt. Obadiah Perkins

Captain Adam Shapley's Company of Matrosses
(Stationed at Fort Trumbull)

Capt. Adam Shapley
1st Lt. Richard Chapman
2nd Lt. Jabez Stow Jr.

Captain Griswold Avery's Company of Militia
(Stationed at New London & Great Neck)[2]

Capt. Griswold Avery
Lt. John Griswold Hillhouse

Lieutenant Acors Sheffield's Company of Matrosses
(Stationed at the Stonington Fort)

Lt. Acors Sheffield

Captain Peleg Noyes's Company of Militia
(Stationed at Stonington Point)[3]

Capt. Peleg Noyes

1 "A General Return of the Troops Under the Command of Brigadier General Tyler in The Department of New London Groton &c;" Governor Trumbull Papers, Aug. 17, 1779, 24:80, CSL; William Ledyard to Governor Trumbull, July 3, 1781, Governor Trumbull Papers, 14:322a–c, CSL. Sometimes called "Ledyard's Battalion."

2 PA: Griswold Avery Jr. (R.306); Joshua Wheeler (R.11383), NARA.

3 PA: Samuel Yeomans (S. 22612); Edward Clark (W.14671); Asa Chesebrough (R.1899), NARA.

Coast Guard Stations[4]

"Lyme" Company of Guards (Stationed at Black Hall)[5]	Lt. Josiah Burnham Ens. Zechariah Marvin Jr.
Company of Flying Guards (Patrols coast between the Connecticut River & the Niantic River)[6]	Ens. Andrew Griswold
"Saybrook" Company of Guards (Stationed at Fort Fenwick)[7]	Lt. Martin Kirtland
Captain Simeon Lay's Company of Militia (Stationed at Patchogue)[8]	Capt. Simeon Lay
"Killingworth" Company of Guards (Stationed at Killingworth)	Ens. Joab Wright
"Guilford" Company of Guards (Stationed at Guilford & East Guilford)[9]	Capt. Peter Vail Lt. Timothy Field Ens. Jonathan Todd Jr.
"Branford" Company of Guards (Stationed at Branford)	Lt. Enoch Staples

Armed Boats[10]

Chatham (Schooner)	Capt. Joshua Griffith
Griswold (Armed Whaleboat)	
Hawke (Armed Whaleboat)	Capt. Daniel Hale
Trumbull (Armed Whaleboat)	
Weazel (Schooner)	Capt. Edward Johnson
Defiance (Armed Boat)	Capt. Abijah Rogers

4 William Ledyard to Governor Trumbull, July 3, 1781, Governor Trumbull Papers, 14:322a–c, CSL.

5 PA: Joseph Bloss (S.21071); Zebulon Brockway (S.31565), NARA.

6 PA: Andrew Griswold (W.21205), NARA.

7 *CSR*, 3:364. Kirtland is sometimes referred as lieutenant-commandant.

8 PA: Peter Spencer (W.7198), NARA. Patchogue was the West Parish of Saybrook, now Westbrook.

9 A detachment, under Todd, was stationed in East Guilford, today's Madison.

10 *CSR*, 3:292, 298, 342; PA: John Comstock (W.25434); Abijah Rogers (W.11160), NARA. All armed boats served under the direction of Ledyard. This does not include other whaleboats attached to coast guard companies. Most went undocumented. The armed whaleboats *Trumbull* and *Griswold* were manned by the two artillery companies at New London harbor.

Reconstructed Rosters:
Department Staff, Latham's and Shapley's Companies of Matrosses

Department of New London, Groton &c.[1]
September 6, 1781

Department/Regimental Staff

Last	First	Rank/Role	Residence	Age[2]	Status
Ledyard	William	Lt. Col.; Commandant; Commissary of Naval Prisoners[3]	Groton	42	
Stanton	Enoch	1st Lt.; Adjutant[4]	Stonington	36	
Ledyard	Ebenezer	Commissary; Asst. Commissary of Issues at Fort Griswold[5]	Groton	45	
Richards Jr.	Guy	Commissary; Asst. Commissary of Issues at New London[6]	New London	34	

1 Surviving rolls of the department and/or either of the two companies were believed to have been destroyed in a fire in the War Department building in Washington set by the British army on Aug. 24, 1814, during the War of 1812.

2 All ages are at the time of the battle.

3 *CSR*, 2:182, 287–288.

4 PA: Thomas Park (R.7932), NARA.

5 *CSR*, 1:244. Ledyard held a state rank and was the chief commissary at the fort and any troops assigned to it.

6 *CSR*, 2:444. Richards held a state rank and was the chief commissary at New London and any troops assigned to it or any of its forts.

Holt Jr.	John	Qtrmaster; Deputy Qtrmaster General[7]	New London	34	
Tracy	Philemon	Sgn. Mate; New London Continental Hospital[8]	Norwich	24	
Turner	John	Ward-Master; New London Continental Hospital[9]	Norwich	17	
Durkee	Benjamin	Lt.; Recruiting Officer[10]	Windham	37	Recruiting
Plumb	Green	Lt.; Barracks-Master[11]	New London	46	
Plumb	Samuel	Waiter; Asst. to Barracks-Master[12]	New London	16	
Freeman	Jordan	Waiter; Asst. to Lt. Col. Ledyard	Groton	49	

Latham's Company of Matrosses

Last	First	Rank	Residence	Age	Status
Latham	William	Captain	Groton	39	
Stanton	Enoch	1st Lt.	Stonington	36	
Perkins	Obadiah	2nd Lt. Fireworker	Groton	36	
Avery	Rufus	1st Sgt.	Groton	23	
Darrow	Nathan	Sgt.	Groton	22	
Swift	John	Sgt.[13]	Mansfield	20	Furlough
Judd	Jehiel	Cpl.	Colchester	18	
Sholes	Nathan	Cpl.	Groton	26	
Brown	Humphrey	Fifer[14]	Groton	13	
Button	Newbury	Fifer[15]	Groton	15	
Beaumont	Samuel	Matross	Lebanon	26	
Billings	John	Matross	Preston	20	
Brice	Robert	Matross[16]	Groton	26	Unknown

7 *CSR*, 3:113. Holt held the state rank of Deputy Quartermaster General and was the chief quartermaster of the department.

8 PA: Philemon Tracy (W.3625), NARA.

9 PA: John Turner (W.3625), NARA.

10 William Ledyard to Governor Jonathan Trumbull, July 3, 1781, Governor Trumbull Papers, 14:322a–c, CSL. Lieutenant Durkee was recruiting in the East Haddam area during the battle.

11 PA: Samuel Plumb (R.8287), NARA.

12 Ibid.

13 PA: John Swift (S.22353), NARA.

14 PA: Humphrey Brown (W.18648), NARA.

15 PA: Newbury Button (R.1563), NARA. Button was from Voluntown, but in 1781 was living with his uncle Simeon Button in Groton. Simeon was drafted to serve for three months in Latham's Company, but had his nephew serve in his place.

16 *CSR*, 4:112–113; PA: Asa Lester (S.16921), NARA; *Belfast Newsletter*, June 3, 1774. Brice was a British deserter. He enlisted in the Continental Army in 1781 but was rejected by the muster master and sent to serve in Latham's Company.

Eldredge	Joseph	Matross[17]	Groton	17	Furlough
Gallup	Andrew	Matross	Groton	20	
Gallup	Robert	Matross	Groton	20	
Griffin	Thomas	Matross[18]	Stonington	15	
Kingsley	William	Matross[19]	Norwich	17	Detached
Lamb	Thomas	Matross	Groton	21	
Latham	William	Matross	Groton	16	
Mason	Elnathan	Matross[20]	Groton	27	
Morgan	Joseph	Matross	Groton	18	
Palmer	Wyatt	Matross[21]	Stonington	17	Furlough
Sholes	Jabish	Matross[22]	Groton	27	Furlough
Smith	James A.	Matross[23]	Groton	18	
Wheeler	Joshua	Matross[24]	Stonington	19	Furlough
Williams	Sanford	Matross	Groton	15	
Woodworth	Azel	Matross	Norwich	15	
Woodworth	Ziba	Matross	Norwich	17	

Shapley's Company of Matrosses

Last	First	Rank	Residence	Age	Status
Shapley	Adam	Capt.	New London	43	
Chapman	Richard	1st Lt.	New London	46	
Stow	Jabez	2nd Lt.	Saybrook	31	
Minor	Jonathan	Gunner[25]	New London	32	
Hempstead	Stephen	1st Sgt.	New London	27	
Harding	Jeremiah	Sgt.	New London	21	
Prentis	John	Sgt.[26]	New London	44	

17 PA: Joseph Eldredge (S.23213), NARA.

18 PA: Thomas Griffin (W.19537), NARA.

19 PA: William Kingsley (W.768), NARA. On Sep. 5, Kingsley was given permission by Ledyard to help a Samuel Denison move goods out of Winthrop's Cove. His enlistment ended on Sep. 7.

20 PA: Elnathan Mason (W.15842), NARA.

21 PA: Wyatt Palmer (S.23357), NARA.

22 PA: Jabish Sholes (S.11378), NARA. Sholes was on sick furlough.

23 PA: James A. Smith (R.9750), NARA.

24 Harris, *Groton Heights*, 251. On sick furlough, due to broken arm.

25 PA: Stephen Miner (W.25710), NARA; "The Petition of the Subscribers . . . were non-commissioned officers in a Military Company lately raised by said State for the defence of the same which said company was stationed in the Garrison at Fort Trumbull, and commanded by Capt. Adam Shapley," Revolutionary War Records, Series I, XXIV:123, CSL. Stephen verified in his pension application that his brother was the company's "Gunner."

26 "The Petition of the Subscribers . . . were non-commissioned officers in a Military Company lately raised by said State for the defence of the same which said company was stationed in the Garrison

Comstock	Elisha	Corporal[27]	Saybrook	22	Furlough
Smith	Josiah	Corporal	New London	22	
Bushnell	Jordan	Matross[28]	Saybrook	34	
Bushnell	Reuben	Matross	Saybrook	40	
Butler	Jonathan	Matross	Saybrook	20	
Comstock	William	Matross	Saybrook	15	
Dart	Elias	Matross[29]	Bolton	22	
Dart	Levi	Matross	Bolton	17	
Jones	Eliday	Matross	Saybrook	16	
Kilbourn	John	Matross[30]	Bolton	18	
Kirtland	Charles	Matross	Saybrook	18	
Rowley	Isaac	Matross[31]	East Haddam	?	
Sanford	Holsey	Matross	Saybrook	14	
Stillman	Samuel	Matross	Saybrook	18	
Whittlesey	John	Matross	Saybrook	23	
Whittlesey	Stephen	Matross	Saybrook	16	
Williams	Daniel	Matross	Saybrook	14	
Wright	Joab	Matross	Saybrook	22	
Williams	Henry	Matross[32]	East Haddam	16	Not Yet Joined

at Fort Trumbull, and commanded by Capt. Adam Shapley," Revolutionary War Records, Series I, XXIV:123, CSL.

27 PA: Elisha Comstock (S.12570), NARA.

28 George Eleazar Bushnell, *Bushnell Family Genealogy: Ancestry and Posterity of Francis Bushnell, (1580-1646), of Horsham, England and Guilford, CT, Including Genealogical Notes of Bushnell Families, Whose Connections with This Branch of the Family Have Not Been Determined* (Nashville, TN, 1945), 54.

29 PA: Elias Dart (R.2673), NARA; *Connecticut Men*, 588.

30 Payne Kenyon Kilbourne, *The History of and Antiquities of the Name and Family of Kilbourn, In its Varied Orthography* (New Haven, CT, 1856), 58–59.

31 "Petition with others, in behalf of the survivors of garrisons of Fts. Trumbull & Griswold, showing that though fortunate in escaping death, they suffered from wounds, loss of clothing &c & being captive to NY," Revolutionary War Records, Series I, Vol. XXII:198, CSL.

32 PA: Henry Williams (W.2889), NARA. He enlisted on Sep. 5 and was enroute the day of the attack.

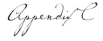

British Order of Battle:
New London Expedition
September 4–13, 1781

Arnold's Expeditionary Corps[1]
Brig. Gen. Benedict Arnold

Capt. John Stapleton, Brigade Major
Capt. John Dalrymple, Aide de Camp
Capt. George Beckwith, Volunteer Aide
Capt. Abiathar Camp, Associated Loyalists, Volunteer Guide

38th Regiment of Foot[2]
Capt. Mathew Millet

40th Regiment of Foot[3]
Maj. William Montgomery (k)
Capt. John Erasmus Adlam

54th Regiment of Foot
Lt. Col. Edmund Eyre (w)
Maj. Stephen Bromfield

Loyal American Regiment[4]
Lt. Col. Beverly Robertson Jr.

---

1 Mackenzie, *Diary*, 2:623–628; American Loyalists Claims, 1776–1835, AO, 13/41/102, 104,114-155, TNA.

2 Mackenzie, *Diary*, 2:623.

3 Muster rolls, 40th Regiment of Foot, WO 12/5318, TNA; Mackenzie, *Diary*, 2:662.

4 "State of various corps going on Benedict Arnold's Expedition against New London," Frederick Mackenzie Papers, WCL.

3rd Battalion, New Jersey Volunteers
Lt. Col. Abraham van Buskirk

American Legion[5]
Capt. Nathan Frink

4th Battalion, Royal Artillery (detachment)
Capt. John Lemoine

Jaeger Company[6]
Staff Capt. Friedrich Adam Julius von Wangenheim

Associated Loyalists[7]
Lt. Col. Joshua Upham

Loyal Refugee Volunteers[8]
Lt. William Castles

Naval Escort[9]
Captain John Bazely

Vessel	Type	Guns	Commander	Crew
Amphion	Frigate	28	Capt. John Bazely	220
Recovery	Sloop	16	Commander Edward Shepherd[10]	80
Beaumont	Brig-sloop	14	Lt. William Scott[11]	90
Argo	Brig	10	Lt. John Consett Peers[12]	80
Lurcher	Brig	12	Lt. James Taylor[13]	80
Hussar	Galley	2	Lt. John Skinner[14]	40
Association	Sloop	10	Capt. Charles Thomas[15]	80

5 Ibid.; Muster rolls, American Legion, British Military and Naval Records, RG 8, "C" Series, Volume 1871, PAC. Return shows two captains present; Frink's commission was dated Nov. 1780, Wogan's Dec. 1780.

6 "Journal of the Hesse-Cassel Jaeger Corps," in *Enemy Views: The American Revolutionary War as Recorded by the Hessian Participants*, Bruce E. Burgoyne, ed. (Berwyn Heights, MD, 2019), 459.

7 Upham report in Harris, *Groton Heights*, 108–110.

8 American Loyalist Claims, 1776–1835, AO 13/80,77–78, TNA.

9 Arnold's report in Mackenzie, *Diary*, 2:626; Ship's Muster Book, HMS *Amphion*, ADM 36/9561, TNA; Ship's Master's Log, HMS *Beaumont*, ADM 52/2192, TNA; Ship's Master's Log, HMS *Recovery*, ADM 52/2491, TNA.

10 Ship's Muster Book, HMS *Recovery*, ADM 36/9910, TNA.

11 Ship's Muster Book, HMS *Beaumont*, ADM 36/9643, TNA.

12 *Naval Chronicle*, 1:261–262.

13 *Proceedings of a Board of General Officers*, 62.

14 Ship's Muster Book, HMS *Hussar*, ADM 36/10213, TNA.

15 Upham report in Harris, *Groton Heights*, 108–110.

Colonel Martin	Sloop	10	Capt. Nathaniel Gardiner[16]	80
Keppel	Brig-sloop	14	Lt. Robert Steel[17]	120

Crew numbers are approximate.

Transports[18]
Capt. Henry Chads, Agent of Transports

Vessel

Amazon	*Antelope*
Baker & Atley	*Betsey*
Charming Nancy	*Fathers Desire*
Minerva	*Molly*
Polly	*Raynham-Hall*[19]
Regard	*Shuldham*
Sally[20]	*William*
Unknown (Horse transport)	Unknown (Horse transport)

A Note on the British Transport Vessel Makeup

No two British sources, agree on the number of transport vessels. The closest count which could be verified was from the *Recovery*, whose log counted "17 transports." One must be careful when counting, as the number seemed to change every day. At least two sloops belonging to the Associated Loyalists joined the squadron on the second day of the expedition. The following day around 20 Loyal Refugees aboard up to three whaleboats or batteaux joined the squadron. Were these smaller vessels counted as transports? We do not know for sure. Most, if not all, the transports used by the British army were privately contracted vessels and their names and involvement in specific actions were often not recorded. Fortunately, Mackenzie's diary for 1781 lists the names of forty-five transports used by the British out of New York during that period. He lists those by name scheduled to accompany the Rhode Island expedition and the first and second planned Yorktown relief expeditions, but he does not list those intended for the New London expedition. Fortunately, the transports scheduled for the first Yorktown

---

16 Ibid.

17 Ship's Muster Book, HMS *Keppel*, ADM 36/10026, TNA. The *Keppel* joined the squadron on September 7.

18 Mackenzie, *Diary*, 2:515, 604, 608, 614, 666; *Proceedings of a Board of General Officers*, 66–67; John Stapleton, acting as Major of Brigade, on board the *Shuldham*, Sep. 8, 1781; *The Bath Chronicle*, Nov. 8, 1781; "J. Lemoine, Captain of Artillery, Betsey sloop, New-London Harbour 6th Sep, 1781"; *The Derby Mercury*, Nov. 1, 1781; Master's Log, HMS *Beaumont*, ADM 52/2192, TNA; Master's Log, HMS *Recovery*, ADM 52/2491, TNA.

19 Also known as the *Rainham-hall*. It was formerly an East India Company ordnance vessel.

20 The *Sally* originally carried some 150 men of the 38th Regiment, but was converted, mid-expedition, into a hospital ship. According to the muster rolls of *Amphion*, *Recovery*, and *Beaumont*, these men were transferred to the three vessels the same day the *Amphion* and *Beaumont* transferred the British wounded they had carried to the *Sally*.

expedition, listed in Mackenzie's diary, were scheduled to set sail September 6, and remained in New York harbor, thus excluding them completely from the New London expedition. Cross examining the lists of the transports of the second Yorktown expedition, scheduled to set sail on October 12, with those supposed to go on the cancelled Rhode Island expedition leaves the above fourteen transports available for the New London expedition. At least two, the *Betsey* and *Shuldham*, were mentioned in British reports, one, the *Raynham-Hall*, is referred to in Mackenzie's diary and a third, the *Sally*, is found in the log of *Beaumont*. Mackenzie explained the transports comprising the first Yorktown expedition could not leave New York harbor until Arnold returned with the horse vessels, implying at least two of them were sent to Connecticut. According to records of the British quartermaster department, there were four horse transports available at that time, the *North*, *Jupiter*, *Mary*, and the *Escape*. Unfortunately, we cannot distinguish which ones participated in the New London expedition.

Appendix D

American Order of Battle:
Battle of New London
September 6, 1781

Units are only cited when they first appear

Morning Phase: Fight South of Town
7:00 a.m. -11:30 a.m.

Department of New London, Groton, &c
Lt. Col. William Ledyard

Ledyard's Regiment

Capt. Griswold Avery's Company[1]
Capt. Griswold Avery

Shapley's Company of Matrosses[2]
Capt. Adam Shapley

3rd Regiment of Connecticut Militia
Lt. Col. Joseph Harris, Jr.

Capt. Richard Deshon's Company[3]
Capt. Richard Deshon

Capt. John Hallam's Company
Capt. John Hallam

1 PA: Griswold Avery Jr. (R.306), NARA.

2 PA: Jeremiah Harding (S.13286), NARA; Master's Log, HMS *Amphion*, ADM 52/2133, TNA; PA: Joab Wright (W.6598), NARA.

3 *CG*, May 2, 1783.

The above two companies were augmented by detachments of:

1st Company[4]
Capt. John Hempsted

2nd Company
Capt. Richard Deshon

7th Company[5]
Capt. Jabez Beebe

11th Company[6]
Capt. Jonathan Caulkins

Independent Artillery Company[7]
Capt. John Hallam

1st Company Alarm List[8]
Capt. John Deshon

2nd Company Alarm List[9]
Capt. Thomas Harding

7th Company Alarm List
Capt. Griswold Avery

Sailors/Marines (detachments from the privateers)[10]

Gamecock[11]
Capt. David Roberts

Minerva

Hancock

4 John Hempsted narrative in Harris, *Groton Heights*, 61–69.

5 PA: Paul Beebe (W.17274); Josephus Lovett (W.21584), NARA.

6 John Hempsted narrative in Harris, *Groton Heights*, 63; PA: Peter Crocker (R.2493), NARA.

7 Robert Hallam account of Sep. 6, 1781, undated, Robert Hallam Papers, NLCHS; *CG*, May 2, 1783; Jonathan Brooks narrative in Harris, *Groton Heights*, 74–77; Connecticut Independent Company, NLCHS; *CG*, May 2, 1783. Brooks named Pickett Latimer as captain, but Harris, in his contemporary letter, named Hallam as captain. According to the roster book Hallam was captain and Latimer was lieutenant.

8 John Hempsted narrative in Harris, *Groton Heights*, 62.

9 Robert Hallam account of Sep. 6, 1781, undated, NLCHS.

10 Privateers are added based on being abandoned or ones that are known ran up the Thames River and their crews returned to defend the town.

11 Middlebrook, *Maritime Connecticut*, 2:93; Hempsted narrative in Harris, *Groton Heights*, 67. The schooner *Gamecock*, having a crew of 30 men, was abandoned. To what extent Capt. Roberts and the crew participated in fighting is not known, but Roberts remained in New London.

Hunter[12]

Randolph

Venus[13]

Capt. Joseph Conkling

Young Cromwell[14]

**Early Afternoon: Fight for the Town
12:00 p.m.-1:30 p.m.**

**Department of New London, Groton, &c
Lt. Col. William Ledyard**

Ledyard's Regiment

Capt. Griswold Avery's Company
Capt. Griswold Avery

3rd Regiment of Connecticut Militia
Col. Jonathan Latimer[15]
Lt. Col. Joseph Harris, Jr.
Sgt. Witherel Latimer, Acting Adjutant[16]

Capt. Richard Deshon's Company
Capt. Richard Deshon

Capt. John Hallam's Company
Capt. John Hallam

The above two companies were augmented by detachments of:

1st Company[17]
Capt. John Hempsted

2nd Company
Capt. Richard Deshon

3rd Company[18]
Capt. John Johnson

---

12 PA: Wilmot Munson (R.7501), NARA. The *Hunter* was not in the harbor. Munson served on a prize vessel, the schooner *Hibernia*, taken by the *Hunter*, which was in the harbor. The *Hibernia* was abandoned, and its crew fought in defense of the town.

13 Middlebrook, *Maritime Connecticut*, 2:239–240. The *Venus* was abandoned and burned; the crew, numbering about 60 men, remained on shore.

14 PA: John Dilleber (S.12747), NARA.

15 PA: Gurdon Flowers Saltonstall (R.9159); Witherel Latimer (S.31809), NARA.

16 PA: Witherel Latimer (S.31809), NARA. Latimer was acting adjutant.

17 John Hempsted narrative in Harris, *Groton Heights*, 61–69.

18 PA: John Tubbs (S.14730), NARA.

7th Company[19]
Capt. Jabez Beebe

11th Company[20]
Capt. Jonathan Caulkins

14th Company[21]
Lt. Manasseh Leech

Independent Artillery Company
Capt. John Hallam

1st Company Alarm List[22]
Capt. John Deshon

2nd Company Alarm List[23]
Capt. Thomas Harding

4th Company Alarm List[24]
Capt. Moses Warren

7th Company Alarm List
Capt. Griswold Avery

Sailors/Marines (detachments from the privateers)

Deane
Capt. Dan Scovell

Gamecock[25]
Capt. David Roberts

Minerva

Hancock

Hunter

Randolph

Venus
Capt. Joseph Conkling

Young Cromwell[26]

19 PA: Paul Beebe (W.17274); Josephus Lovett (W.21584), NARA.

20 John Hempsted narrative in Harris, *Groton Heights*, 63; PA: Peter Crocker (R.2493), NARA.

21 PA: Samuel Avery (R.307); Hoel Huntley (S.18043); Isaac Sill (W.17358); Jacob Tillotson Jr. (W.25490), NARA.

22 Ibid., 62.

23 Robert Hallam account of Sep. 6, 1781, undated, NLCHS.

24 PA: Benjamin Cobb (W.10661), NARA. Warren, the former captain, was acting commander until Capt. Samuel Mather Jr. arrived later.

25 Ibid., 67.

26 PA: John Dilleber (S.12747), NARA.

Afternoon: Fight North of New London and British Withdrawal
1:30 p.m.-12:00 a.m.

Department of New London, Groton, &c
Lt. Col. William Ledyard (k)

Ledyard's Regiment

Capt. Griswold Avery's Company[27]
Capt. Griswold Avery

3rd Regiment of Connecticut Militia
Col. Jonathan Latimer
Lt. Col. Joseph Harris, Jr.
Sgt. Witherel Latimer, Acting Adjutant

Capt. Richard Deshon's Company
Capt. Richard Deshon

Capt. Jonathan Caulkins's Company[28]
Capt. Jonathan Caulkins

Capt. Abner Lord's Company[29]
Capt. Abner Lord

The above two companies were augmented by detachments of:

1st Company
Capt. John Hempsted

2nd Company
Capt. Richard Deshon

4th Company
Capt. John Johnson

5th Company[30]
Unknown

7th Company
Capt. Jabez Beebe

9th Company[31]
Capt. Nathaniel Comstock Jr.

27 PA: Griswold Avery Jr. (R.306), NARA.

28 PA: Israel Rogers (S.14383), NARA.

29 PA: Abner Ely (W.21056); Hoel Huntley (S.18043); Seth Smith (S.14507); Isaac Sill (W.17358); William Greenfield (R.4283); Peter Way (W.18228), NARA.

30 PA: Samuel Whalcy (R.11366); Jonathan Whaley (W.2739), NARA.

31 PA: Thomas Bishop (W.17305), NARA. Bishop could not remember if Nathaniel Comstock or Nathaniel Waterhouse was captain. Captain Comstock served until 1782, when Lt. Waterhouse was elected captain.

11th Company
Capt. Jonathan Caulkins

12th Company
Capt. Abner Lord

14th Company
Lt. Manasseh Leech

Independent Artillery Company
Capt. John Hallam

1st Company Alarm List
Capt. John Deshon

2nd Company Alarm List
Capt. Thomas Harding

3rd Company Alarm List
Capt. Seth Ely

4th Company Alarm List
Capt. Moses Warren

7th Company Alarm List
Capt. Griswold Avery

Sailors (detachments from the privateers and armed vessels)

Deane
Capt. Dan Scovell

Randolph

Hancock

Gamecock
Capt. David Roberts

Venus
Capt. Joseph Conkling

Minerva

Young Cromwell

Defiance[32]
Capt. Abijah Rogers

---

32 PA: Abijah Rogers (W.11160), NARA.

20th Regiment of Connecticut Militia
Col. Zabdiel Rogers
Maj. Benajah Leffingwell
Lt. Simeon Huntington, Adjutant

1st Company[33]
Ens. Seth Minor

2nd Company
Capt. Samuel Wheat

3rd Company[34]
Capt. Isaac Johnson

4th Company[35]
Capt. Moses Stevens

5th Company[36]
Capt. William Pride

6th Company[37]
Capt. Nehemiah Waterman

7th Company[38]
Capt. Joshua Smith

8th Company[39]
Capt. Daniel Rose

9th Company[40]
Capt. John Waterman

10th Company
Capt. Samuel Lovett

---

33 PA: Joshua Burnham (R.1480), NARA. Burnham incorrectly named his commander as Capt. Joseph Carew. Carew had been detached since July and was serving at West Point.

34 PA: John Tracy (W.16448), NARA.

35 PA: Enoch Baker (S.17250); Prosper Wheeler (W.22604); John Jackson (S.22851), NARA.

36 PA: Uriah Corning (S.15262), NARA. Corning named Jabez White (Wight) as his captain, but he only served until 1780. That same year, Lt. William Pride was elected captain.

37 PA: Dyer Crocker (S.22710); Daniel Rudd (W.22137), NARA.

38 CCR, 14:400; PA: Elijah Waterman (S. 7825), NARA.

39 CSR, 2:298. PA: Darius Fitch (W.1162); John Jackson (S.22851); Aaron Bennett (R.748), NARA.

40 PA: Obadiah Hudson (R.5337), NARA.

Norwich Light Infantry[41]
Capt. Christopher Leffingwell

DeWitt's Company of Matrosses[42]
Capt.-Lt. Isaac Abel

25th Regiment of Connecticut Militia
Maj. Daniel Cone[43]

Maj. Cone's Provisional Company[44]
Lt. Amasa Brainard

3rd Company[45]
Sgt. Dan Worthington

6th Company[46]
Capt. Nathaniel Harris

Fifth Brigade of Connecticut Militia[47]
Col. Jeremiah Mason

5th Regiment of Connecticut Militia
Col. Experience Storrs[48]

1st Company[49]
Capt. William Young

2nd Company[50]
Capt. Eleazar Huntington

3rd Company[51]
Capt. Jonathan Rudd

41 PA: Isaac Williams (S.15719), NARA.

42 PA: Ebenezer Averill (S.28625); Libbeus Webb (R.11250), NARA.

43 PA: Abraham Osborn (S.14061), NARA.

44 Ibid.

45 PA: John Cavarly (W.17593), NARA. Sergeant Worthington led the company until the arrival of Capt. Elijah Worthington later that day.

46 PA: John Tennant (R.10453); Ebenezer Rogers (S.31941), Moses Rathbone (W.22040), NARA.

47 *Connecticut Men*, 433, 436. There is no record of Brig. Gen. John Douglass being present. By default, the senior colonel, Mason, would have assumed command responsibilities.

48 The regiment was drawn from Ashford, Coventry, Windham, and Mansfield. Examining dozens of pension depositions revealed only companies from Windham, Mansfield, and Coventry were called out.

49 PA: Roswell Hurd (R.5431), NARA.

50 PA: Phinehas Parker (S.9964), NARA.

51 PA: Elisha Lillie (S.15509), NARA.

4th Company[52]
Capt. Jeremiah Ripley

6th Company[53]
Capt. William Howard

7th Company[54]
Ens. Eliphas Hunt

14th Company
Capt. Lemuel Barrows

2nd Company Alarm List[55]
Capt. Nathaniel Hall

6th Company Alarm List[56]
Capt. Ebenezer Moseley

11th Company Alarm List[57]
Capt. Nathaniel Linkon

12th Regiment of Connecticut Militia
Col. Jeremiah Mason[58]

1st Company[59]
Capt. William Huntington

2nd Company[60]
Capt. Daniel Dewey Jr.

3rd Company[61]
Capt. Roger Phelps

---

52 PA: Jeremiah Ripley (R.8835), NARA.

53 PA: James Burnham (W.17380), NARA.

54 PA: Joseph Waldo (S.11649), NARA.

55 PA: Solomon Welch (W.14664), NARA; marched to Norwich Landing.

56 PA: Thomas Utley (W.19565); Joel Greenslit (S.10765), NARA.

57 PA: Nathaniel Linkon (S.17546), NARA; marched to Norwich Landing.

58 Mason, *Memoir*, 3. Mason remembered his father was credited with rallying and bringing his entire regiment, which would have meant the trainband companies, not necessarily the alarm list companies, to New London with "commendable speed." While many pension applications verify the presence of individual companies, this source was used to place those trainband companies which could not be verified through individual applications or other sources.

59 Ibid.

60 Mason, *Memoir*, 3.

61 PA: Daniel Phelps (S.14143); Andrew Mann (S.16934), NARA.

4th Company[62]
Lt. Daniel Dunham

5th Company[63]
Capt. Andrew Waterman

6th Company[64]
Capt. David Miller

7th Company[65]
Capt. Daniel White

8th Company[66]
Capt. John Skinner

9th Company[67]
Sgt. Christopher Crouch

10th Company[68]
Capt. Daniel Clark

'2nd Veteran Company'[69]
Capt. Samuel Jones

2nd Company Alarm List[70]
Capt. Stephen Palmer

4th Company Alarm List[71]
Capt. Denison Wattles

6th Company Alarm List[72]
Capt. John H. Wells

21st Regiment of Connecticut Militia
Commander Unknown

---

62 PA: Joseph Rood (R.8980); Daniel Ashley (S.14928); Abner Ashley (S.18298), NARA.

63 PA: Nathan Clark (W.17635); John Kaple (S.13593), NARA.

64 PA: John Eells (S.29132); John Huxford (S.13504), NARA.

65 PA: Benjamin Jones (S.45428), NARA.

66 PA: James Brown (W.21701); David Bliss (W.5829); Ralph Mack (S.29313), NARA.

67 PA: Abijah Dewey (S.22725) NARA. Dewey named Crouch (or Cronk) as captain, but as a sergeant in 1781 Crouch was presumably "acting captain."

68 PA: Jacob Clark (S.10453), NARA.

69 PA: Stephen Barber (S.12030), NARA. Jones's Company arrived on September 7 and remained on Quaker Hill "for a few days."

70 PA: Elijah Graves (S.44173); Amasa Archer (S.17242), NARA.

71 PA: Dan Wattles (W.3743), NARA.

72 PA: Jeremiah Brown (W.25283), NARA.

1st Company[73]
Capt. Joshua Bottom

2nd Company[74]
Capt. Ephraim Lyon

5th Company[75]
Capt. Benjamin Bacon

7th Company[76]
Capt. Samuel Robbins

8th Company[77]
Capt. William Hebbard

Second Brigade of Connecticut Militia

7th Regiment of Connecticut Militia
Commander Unknown

3rd Company[78]
Capt. John Ventres

10th Company[79]
Unknown

12th Company[80]
Capt. Bezaleel Bristol

13th Company[81]
Capt. Abraham Waterhouse Jr.

73 PA: John Gallop (S.10721); Jacob Patrick (W.19960), NARA.

74 PA: Ephraim Lyon (W.17366), NARA.

75 PA: John Brown (S.22660); John Burt (W.3653), NARA.

76 PA: Britnal Robins (W.7150), NARA.

77 PA: Eliphalet Farnan (W.24175), NARA.

78 PA: James Smith (S.11426), NARA.

79 PA: Selah Griswold (S.17454), NARA.

80 PA: Bezaleel Bristol (W.20781), NARA.

81 PA: Joseph Pelton (W.26303), NARA.

Appendix E

American Order of Battle:
Battle of Groton Heights
September 6, 1781

Fort Griswold

Lt. Col. William Ledyard

Ledyard's Regiment
Lt. Col. William Ledyard
1st Lt. Enoch Stanton, Adjutant
Jordan Freeman, Waiter to Lt. Col. Ledyard

Latham's Company of Matrosses
Capt. William Latham

Shapley's Company of Matrosses
Capt. Adam Shapley

3rd Regiment of Connecticut Militia[1]
(Detachment)
Ens. Japhet Mason Jr.

8th Regiment of Connecticut Militia
(Detachments)

1st "Groton" Company[2]
Capt. John Williams 3rd

---

1 Includes all militia in fort from New London. These may have come over with Holt or on their own. Ensign Mason of the 1st Company came with Shapley's Company and was the most senior officer of the regiment present at the fort.

2 *CSR*, 2:144.

2nd "Groton" Company
Capt. Simeon Allyn

3rd "Groton" Company[3]
Sgt. Daniel Eldridge

1st Company "Groton Alarm List"
Capt. Elijah Avery

2nd Company "Groton Alarm List"[4]
Capt. Samuel Allyn

3rd Company "Groton Alarm List"[5]
Sgt. John Stedman

4th "Stonington" Company
No Commander

5th "Stonington" Company[6]
Sgt. Daniel Stanton

2nd Company "Stonington Alarm List"
No Commander

Sailors/Marines (Detachments)

Hancock[7]
Capt. Peter Richards

Deane

Randolph

Minerva

---

3 Harris, *Groton Heights*, 244–245. Eldridge lived in the district of the 3rd "Groton" Company which was in the Mystic area.

4 *CSR*, 3:402.

5 *CG*, Sep. 21, 1781; *Boston Gazette*, Sep. 17, 1781. Stedman resided in the district of the 3rd Company. Some lists assign him the rank of ensign, though this might have been a temporary rank assigned to him earlier in the war.

6 Harris, *Groton Heights*, 261.

7 Harris, *Groton Heights*, 232–233.

Birch Plain Creek

Gallup's Provisional Battalion

Lt. Col. Nathan Gallup

Ledyard's Regiment

Capt. Peleg Noyes's Company[8]

Capt. Peleg Noyes

Latham's Company of Matrosses (detachment)[9]

Sailors[10]

Prudence

Capt. Thomas Park

8th Regiment of Connecticut Militia

(Detachments)

Lt. Col. Nathan Gallup

Capt. Isaac Gallup, Adjutant[11]

Rev. Aaron Kinne, Chaplain

Benadam Gallup, Volunteer aide[12]

1st "Groton" Company[13]

Sgt. John Barber

2nd "Groton" Company

Unknown

3rd "Groton" Company[14]

Capt. Nathan Crary

4th "Groton" Company[15]

Capt. John Morgan

5th "Groton" Company[16]

Capt. Oliver Spicer

---

8 PA: Samuel Yeomans (S. 22612); Clark Edwards (W.14671); Asa Chesebrough (R.1899), NARA.

9 PA: Wyatt Palmer (S.23357); Newbury Button (R.1563); John Swift (S.22353), NARA.

10 PA: Thomas Park (R.7932), NARA.

11 PA: Isaac Gallup (W.26032); Nathan Peters (W.21937), NARA.

12 "List of Court Martial Witnesses," Charles Allyn Papers, NLCHS. Benadam Gallup was the former lieutenant colonel of the 8th Regiment of Connecticut Militia but had retired from militia service. He served as a volunteer aide to his brother.

13 "List of Court Martial Witnesses," Charles Allyn Papers, NLCHS; *Connecticut Men*, 452. Barber assumed temporary command and appeared as a witness at the court martial.

14 PA: Joseph Eldridge (S.23213), NARA.

15 "A Pay abstract of Capt. John Morgan's Company in Col. Oliver Smith's Regt who Marched upon the Alarm the 6th Sep 1781," Revolutionary War Records, Series 1, XXV:517, CSL.

16 "List of Court Martial Witnesses," Charles Allyn Papers, NLCHS.

1st Company "Groton Alarm List"
Unknown

2nd Company "Groton Alarm List"[17]
Lt. Samuel Williams

3rd Company "Groton Alarm List"[18]
Lt. Isaac Wightman

4th Company "Groton Alarm List"[19]
Capt. Abel Spicer

1st "Stonington" Company
Capt. Peleg Noyes

4th "Stonington" Company
Capt. Thomas Wheeler

2nd Regiment of Light Horse

4th Troop[20]
Capt. Lemuel Lamb

September 7-10, 1781
Fort Griswold and Groton Bank

Third Brigade of Connecticut Militia
Brig. Gen. John Tyler
Maj. Nathan Peters, Brigade Major

8th Regiment of Connecticut Militia[21]
Lt. Col. Nathan Gallup
Maj. Samuel Tyler[22]
Capt. Isaac Gallup, Adjutant

---

17 PA: Stephen Avery (S.12026), NARA.

18 "List of Court Martial Witnesses," Charles Allyn Papers, NLCHS; PA: Ebenezer Morgan (W.17178), NARA. Wells, a member of the company, testified for the widow of Morgan. Wells resided in east Groton. Several other pension applications testify to serving under Capt. John Avery Sr. and Lt. Isaac Wightman. Both resided in the district of the 3rd "Groton" Company. However, only Wightman testified in the court martial, making him likely the only officer in the company present. In 1787, Wightman was elected ensign of the 3rd "Groton" Company, but multiple pension applications testify him as a lieutenant as early as 1777.

19 PA: William Avery Morgan (W.1308), NARA.

20 PA: Jason Stanton (W.505), NARA.

21 The 8th Regiment followed an older Connecticut militia regimental organizational pattern. Unlike the 3rd Regiment which, in 1781 numbered their companies in sequential order 1–14 regardless of town, the 8th Regiment numbered its companies in successive order by town.

22 PA: James Tyler (W.19479), NARA. According to Tyler, Major Tyler arrived at the meetinghouse accompanied by all the Preston companies during the evening of Sep. 6.

Dr. Joshua Downer, Surgeon[23]
Avery Downer, Surgeon's Mate[24]
Dr. Prosper Rose, Aide to Dr. Downer[25]
Cyrus Tracy, Aide to Dr. Downer[26]
Dr. Amos Prentice, Volunteer[27]
Dr. Hezekiah Clark, Volunteer[28]
Rev. Aaron Kinne, Chaplain

1st "Groton" Company
Sgt. John Barber

2nd "Groton" Company
Unknown

3rd "Groton" Company
Capt. Nathan Crary

4th "Groton" Company[29]
Lt. William Williams

5th "Groton" Company
Capt. Oliver Spicer

1st Company "Groton Alarm List"
Unknown

2nd Company "Groton Alarm List"
Lt. Samuel Williams

3rd Company "Groton Alarm List"
Lt. Isaac Wightman

4th Company "Groton Alarm List"
Capt. Abel Spicer

1st "Stonington" Company
Capt. Peleg Noyes

2nd "Stonington" Company[30]
Lt. Sanford Billings

---

23 Avery Downer narrative in Harris, *Groton Heights*, 83–84.

24 Ibid.

25 PA: Prosper Rose (S.35), NARA.

26 PA: Cyrus Tracy (S.19130), NARA. Tracy was a medical student studying under Dr. Downer.

27 Avery Downer narrative in Harris, *Groton Heights*, 83–84.

28 Clayton, *History of Onondaga*, 403–404.

29 "A Pay abstract of Capt. John Morgan's Company in Col. Oliver Smith's Regt who Marched upon the Alarm the 6th Sep 1781," Revolutionary War Records, Series 1, XXV:517, CSL.

30 PA: Peres Main (S.2720), NARA.

3rd "Stonington" Company[31]
Lt. Joshua Brown

4th "Stonington" Company[32]
Capt. Thomas Wheeler

5th "Stonington" Company[33]
Capt. William Stanton

6th "Stonington" Company[34]
Capt. Christopher Brown

1st Company "Stonington Alarm List"[35]
Lt. Sand Niles

2nd Company "Stonington Alarm List"[36]
Capt. Amos Hallam

3rd Company "Stonington Alarm List"[37]
Capt. Oliver Grant

1st "Preston" Company[38]
Capt. Ebenezer Witter

2nd "Preston" Company[39]
Capt. Eleazar Prentiss

3rd "Preston" Company[40]
Lt. David Green

4th "Preston" Company[41]
Capt. Jesse Starkweather

31 PA: Jephthah Brown (S.12340); Stephen Breed (W.16511), NARA. Brown testified that Capt. Amos Main, the company commander, was sick the day of the attack, and Lieutenant Brown assumed command.

32 *CG*, Nov 11, 1782; PA: Isaac Williams (W.6500), NARA.

33 "List of Names," Charles Allyn Papers, NLCHS; PA: Ezra Gallup (S.29168); Valentine Lewis (W.20431); Nathan Stanton (R.10061), NARA.

34 PA: James York (S.17218), NARA.

35 PA: James Palmer (W.19969), NARA.

36 This is speculation, as it was the closest Stonington Alarm List Company to Fort Griswold and two members of the company were in the fort. Hallam was the only officer at home as its lieutenant, Henry Denison, was detached and serving in Canfield's Regiment at West Point.

37 PA: Daniel Smith (S.11416), NARA.

38 PA: Giles Tracy (S.30748), NARA; *CG*, Nov. 11, 1782.

39 PA: James Tyler (W.19479), NARA. According to Tyler, Major Tyler arrived accompanied by all the Preston companies.

40 PA: Amos Hutchinson (W.18088); Nathan Geer (S.16126), NARA.

41 PA: James Tyler (W.19479), NARA.

5th "Preston" Company[42]
Capt. James Morgan

1st Company "Preston Alarm List"[43]
Capt. William Whitney

2nd Company "Preston Alarm List"[44]
Capt. Ezra Kinney

2nd Regiment of Light Horse
4th Troop
Capt. Lemuel Lamb[45]

Sailors
Prudence[46]
Capt. Thomas Park

---

42 Ibid.

43 PA: Jason Stanton (W.505), NARA. Stanton did not serve in this company, but testified to its officers being present.

44 Jason Stanton (W.505), NARA.

45 *CSR*, 2:374; PA: Jason Stanton (W.505), NARA.

46 PA: Thomas Park (R.7932), NARA.

British Casualties:
New London and Groton[1]
September 6, 1781

40TH REGIMENT OF FOOT[2]

Colonel's Company

Drummer James Wright	Killed
Pvt. James Frill[3]	Wounded
Pvt. Thomas Lloyd	Killed
Pvt. James Twitt	Killed

Lt. Colonel's Company

Cpl. Mark Snow	Killed
Pvt. Thomas Hunter[4]	Wounded
Pvt. Joseph Leach	Wounded

---

1 There are two names of wounded men on the Beaumont, John Miller, and Robert Cantling (or Cantlin) which though identified as 40th or 54th Foot cannot be placed into these individual regiments or any other British unit which participated in the expedition. This is an almost complete list of those killed, but an incomplete list of those wounded as many of those still remain unknown.

2 Muster rolls, 40th Regiment of Foot, WO 12/ 5318, TNA; Muster Book, HMS Amphion, ADM 36/9561, TNA; Muster Book, HMS Beaumont, ADM 36/9643, TNA; Mackenzie, Diary, 2:627. All casualties from the 40th Regiment come from above sources unless otherwise noted. This list contains the names of all the soldiers killed in the regiment but is missing 17 names of the wounded.

3 Royal Hospital, Chelsea: Disability and Royal Artillery Out-Pensions, Admissions Books, WO 116/7/241 (hereafter Chelsea Disability). TNA. Sometimes the location of where a British soldier was wounded is not listed in his pension records, and one must resort to conjecture. Those included from WO 116 were selected based on the following criteria: (1) Their "present" status with the regiment at the time of the battle, (2) their discharge or invalided status immediately following the battle, and (3) the discharge being due to wounds. Frill was treated with the wounded on the Beaumont and later pensioned due to his wounds.

4 Chelsea Disability, WO 116/7/218, TNA. Hunter was treated on the *Beaumont*, presumably for an arm. He was invalided in December when he received a pension for a lost arm.

Major's Company

Maj. William Montgomery	Killed
Drummer Edward Dawe	Wounded
Pvt. John Broom[5]	Wounded
Pvt. Richard Collard	Wounded
Pvt. James Harriott	Killed
Pvt. Richard Hewlett[6]	Wounded
Pvt. Duncan Smyth	Killed
Pvt. Simon Starr	Killed

Capt. John Erasmus Adlam's Company

Sgt. William Fisher	Wounded
Cpl. William Irwin	Killed
Pvt. Donald Cameron[7]	Wounded
Pvt. John Cox[8]	Wounded
Pvt. George Nottingham	Killed

Capt. Edward Eyre's Company

Pvt. Thomas Binding[9]	Wounded
Pvt. William Cahill[10]	Wounded
Pvt. Michael Donnelly	Wounded
Pvt. Jonathan Roberts[11]	Wounded

Capt. Horatio Churchill's Company

Cpl. Alexander Gregory	Killed
Cpl. John Rudd[12]	Wounded

5 Chelsea Disability, WO 116/7/243, TNA. Broom originally enlisted in the 33rd Regiment but was transferred prior to the New London expedition. No record exists of his being a member of the 33rd Regiment. He was probably a recruit who arrived in NY while the 33rd Foot was in the southern theater and was assigned to the 40th Regiment just prior to joining the New London expedition. He was discharged on June 25, 1782, and received a pension for his wound.

6 Hewett was placed with the seriously wounded aboard the *Amphion* after the attack on Fort Griswold. The regimental muster recorded his death on Dec. 13, 1781, presumably of those wounds.

7 Chelsea Disability, WO 116/7/218, TNA. Cameron was placed with the seriously wounded on the Beaumont. Upon his return to New York, he was invalided in December 1781, when he was pensioned for his wound.

8 Ibid., WO 116/7/218, TNA. Cox was invalided shortly after the expedition and pensioned for a wound.

9 Binding died of his wounds enroute to New York on September 7. He might be one of those who were thrown overboard and washed up on Goshen's Neck or one of those buried on Plumb Island.

10 Cahill was treated on the *Beaumont*. The regimental muster reported his death on September 29, presumably of those wounds.

11 Chelsea Disability, WO 116/7/218, TNA. Roberts was invalided in December 1781 where he was pensioned for his wound.

12 Ibid., WO 116/7/218, TNA. Corporal Rudd was invalided in December 1781 where he was pensioned for his wound.

Pvt. John Carpenter	Killed
Pvt. David Hommel[13]	Wounded
Pvt. Daniel Johnston[14]	Wounded
Pvt. John Kelly	Wounded

Capt. George Craigie's Company

Capt. George Craigie[15]	Wounded
Ens. Thomas Hyde[16]	Wounded
Cpl. Donald McDonald	Killed
Pvt. Martin Heavy[17]	Wounded
Pvt. James Moore[18]	Wounded

Capt. John Gason's Company

Pvt. Alexander Lindsey	Wounded
Pvt. Thomas Brown	Wounded
Pvt. John Hill	Wounded

Grenadier Company[19]

Sgt. Duncan Campbell	Wounded
Pvt. Robert Anderson	Wounded
Pvt. Thomas Dearing	Killed
Pvt. John Dunford	Killed
Pvt. James Eggelston[20]	Wounded

13 Chelsea Disability, WO 116/7/243, TNA. Hommel was reported in the hospital immediately following the return to New York. He remained there until he was discharged in June 1782 and the subsequently pensioned due to his wound.

14 Ibid., WO 116/7/243, TNA. Johnston was discharged in June 1782 and immediately obtained a pension for a wound.

15 Master's Log, HMS *Amphion*, ADM 52/2133, TNA. Craigie was placed on board the *Amphion* for medical treatment, where he died sometime on September 7. According to the master's log of the *Amphion*, a captain, Craigie, was buried on Plumb Island.

16 Hyde died of his wounds on the night of September 6–7.

17 Chelsea Disability, WO 116/7/218, TNA. Roberts was invalided in December 1781 where he was pensioned for his wound.

18 Moore was aboard the *Amphion* where he is listed as having been wounded. He died on board on September 8. He may have been one of those thrown overboard and washed ashore.

19 Extract of a letter from an officer of the 40th regiment to a friend in Aberdeen, dated New York, Sep. 20, 1781, *Caledonian Mercury*, Nov. 14, 1781. Captain Forbes reported the only specific loss of any British company during the expedition. He wrote, "The men suffered considerably. Of 48 I carried into the field, only 24 returned." This list names just half of those grenadiers who were wounded.

20 Chelsea Disability, WO 116/7/243, TNA. Eggelston was shortly afterwards transferred out of the grenadier company to Eyre's Company. He did not remain there long and was sent home by the time the next regimental muster was completed. There, he was discharged and obtained a pension.

Pvt. Samuel Garland[21]	Wounded
Pvt. Richard Kinders	Killed
Pvt. William Knox	Wounded
Pvt. Alexander McPherson	Wounded
Pvt. Thomas Mawhor	Killed
Pvt. Alexander Murphy	Wounded
Pvt. George Palfrey	Wounded
Pvt. Thomas Ross	Killed
Pvt. John Serogay	Wounded
Pvt. William Sinclair	Wounded
Pvt. John Smilie	Killed
Pvt. Samuel Taylor	Wounded
Vol. Archibald Willocks[22]	Killed

Light Infantry Company

Lt. Henry William Smyth[23]	Wounded
Sgt. Adam Thompson	Killed
Cpl. William Constable[24]	Wounded
Pvt. John Algrove	Wounded
Pvt. Thomas Bishop	Killed
Pvt. John Bowine[25]	Wounded
Pvt. William Conroy	Killed
Pvt. William Dunbar	Killed
Pvt. James Green	Killed
Pvt. John Graham	Killed
Pvt. Thomas Lewis	Killed
Pvt. Daniel Moore	Killed
Pvt. John Oage[26]	Wounded

---

21 Garland was treated for his wound aboard the *Beaumont*. He subsequently died of those wounds Oct. 29, 1781.

22 Willocks served in the Grenadier Company as a volunteer and was killed serving in that company. Though on the regimental muster rolls, he was officially listed as a volunteer in the Major's Company. According to the muster rolls, taken on Dec. 24, 1781, he appears to have been commissioned posthumously as ensign in Capt. Edward Eyre's Company.

23 Smyth died of his wounds on Sep. 7, 1781.

24 On the *Beaumont*, he was incorrectly listed as Cpl. Joseph Constable.

25 Bowine died of his wounds on Sep. 7, 1781.

26 Oage was treated on the *Beaumont* and was transferred to a battalion company in Oct. 1781.

54TH REGIMENT OF FOOT[27]

Colonel's Company

Sgt. William Wilson[28]	Wounded
Pvt. William Goulding	Killed

Lt. Colonel's Company

Cpl. Edward Beckwith	Killed
Pvt. Samuel Childridge	Killed
Pvt. Thomas Hargrove[29]	Wounded
Vol. James Boyd	Wounded

Major's Company

Lt. Col. Edmund Eyre[30]	Wounded
Sgt. John Jagger[31]	Wounded
Cpl. William Simpson	Killed
Pvt. William Anson[32]	Wounded
Pvt. John Bartlam	Killed
Pvt. Edward Blackburn[33]	Wounded
Pvt. Owen Connelly[34]	Wounded
Pvt. Richard Dowling[35]	Wounded

27 Muster rolls, 54th Regiment of Foot, WO 12/6398/2, 6399, TNA; Ship's Muster Book, HMS *Amphion*, ADM 36/9561, TNA; Muster Book, HMS *Beaumont*, ADM 36/9643, TNA; Mackenzie, *Diary*, 2:627. The names of casualties from the 54th Regiment come from the above sources unless otherwise noted. The names of all those killed are complete, but the list is missing the names of 45 wounded soldiers.

28 Listed on the *Amphion* as wounded but on regiment muster as killed. He was probably mortally wounded and died on board the ship.

29 Hargrove previously served in the 24th Regiment of Foot and was probably captured at Saratoga and then escaped to New York. He joined the 54th Regiment in Jan. 1781.

30 In the regiment, Eyre ranked as a major.

31 Chelsea Disability, WO 116/7/211, TNA. Jagger was invalided in Feb. 1782, where he was pensioned with several others in the regiment for wounds.

32 Royal Hospital, Chelsea: Discharge Documents of Pensions, WO 121/14/444, TNA. According to Anson's discharge papers, he was "[wounded] by a shot in the Throat, received in the attack and storm of Fort Griswold . . . and by being ruptured, is unfit for further service."

33 Chelsea Disability, WO 116/7/244, TNA; Chelsea Discharge, WO 121/140/670, TNA. Blackburn was aboard the *Beaumont* with a wound in the right arm. He was sent home by June, where he received a pension for his arm wound.

34 Chelsea Discharge, WO 121/7/212, TNA. Connelly was discharged from the regiment in June 1782 and immediately obtained a pension for a wound. Even though it does not specify where the wound was received, this was his first and only action of the war as he had joined the regiment from the Additional Company on Oct. 8, 1780.

35 Dowling is noted on the muster as having died of wounds on Sep. 9, 1781.

Pvt. John Fenn[36]   Wounded
Pvt. James French   Killed
Pvt. John Garrick[37]   Wounded
Pvt. John Goodall[38]   Wounded
Pvt. Thomas Nicholls   Wounded
Pvt. John Wormwood[39]   Wounded
Pvt. James Whittle[40]   Wounded

Capt. Richard Powell's Company

Capt. Richard Powell   Wounded
Ens. William Rainsforth   Wounded
Cpl. William Higgins   Wounded
Pvt. Charles Russell   Killed

Capt. Stephen Bromfield's Company

Sgt. William Bucklys[41]   Wounded
Pvt. John Scott   Killed
Pvt. Peter Fisher[42]   Wounded

Capt. Carr Thomas Brackenbury's Company

Lt. Thomas Daunt   Wounded
Pvt. John Cork   Wounded
Pvt. Daniel Thursfield   Killed
Pvt. James Higgins   Killed
Pvt. Robert Davis   Killed
Pvt. William Sutton[43]   Wounded
Pvt. John Jack[44]   Wounded

36 Chelsea Discharge, WO 121/7/212, TNA. Fenn was discharged from the regiment in Feb. 1782 and immediately obtained a pension for a wound that resulted in the loss of his leg. Even though it does not specify where the wound was received, this was perhaps Fenn's first action of the war, having only appeared on the regimental muster the previous June.

37 Garrick is noted on regimental muster as having died of wounds on Sep. 9, 1781.

38 Chelsea Discharge, WO 121/14/457, TNA. According to Goodhall's discharge papers, he was "wounded through the left thigh at the storm of Fort Griswold."

39 Noted on regimental muster of having died of wounds on Sep. 9, 1781.

40 Whittle was treated on the *Amphion* for his wound. He presumably died of it on Oct. 2, 1781.

41 Chelsea Disability, WO 116/7/211, TNA. Even though the place of his wound is not stated, Bucklys was invalided and sent home at the Dec. muster. Once there, he immediately obtained a pension for a wound.

42 Chelsea Disability, WO 116/7/212, TNA. Even though the location of Fisher's wound was not specified, he was immediately invalided after the expedition and granted a pension for a wound.

43 Chelsea Discharge, WO 121/13/76, TNA. According to Sutton's discharge papers, he was "wounded through both Thighs at the Storming of Fort Griswold."

44 Chelsea Disability, WO 116/7/211, TNA. Jack was invalided in Feb. 1782 and received a pension with several others of the regiment. Jack was reported as being wounded in the arm.

Pvt. William West[45]   Wounded

Capt. John Breese's Company

Pvt. William Bunney   Killed
Pvt. John Carey[46]   Wounded
Pvt. James Duncan[47]   Wounded
Pvt. William Dowling[48]   Wounded
Pvt. William McKinzie   Killed

Capt. John Peter Addenbrook's Company

Sgt. Thomas Strangahan   Killed
Pvt Benjamin Payne[49]   Wounded
Pvt. John Gibson[50]   Wounded
Pvt. William Lee[51]   Wounded
Pvt. Roger McCormack[52]   Wounded
Pvt. Edward Smith   Killed
Pvt. Thomas Stebbins   Wounded

LOYAL AMERICAN REGIMENT[53]

Capt. Christopher Hatch's Company

Pvt. Stephen Islick   Killed

Capt. Lemuel Wilmot's Company

Pvt. Josiah Burrell[54]   Wounded

---

45 Ibid., WO 116/7/211, TNA. West was invalided in Feb. 1782 and received a pension with several others of the regiment for wounds.

46 Listed on the *Beaumont* incorrectly as Cpl. John Corey. No such name exists in either the 40th or 54th Foot.

47 Chelsea Discharge, WO 121/14/452, TNA. According to Duncan's discharge papers, he was "wounded in the right thigh at the storm of Fort Griswold."

48 Chelsea Disability, WO 116/7/211, TNA. Dowling was invalided in Feb. 1782 and received a pension with several others of the regiment. He reported being wounded in the hand.

49 Payne was treated aboard the *Amphion* and the *Sally* hospital ship. He died in New York, presumably of that wound, on Oct. 4, 1781.

50 Chelsea Discharge, WO 121/7/96, TNA. According to Gibson's discharge papers, he was "[wounded] by a shot in the Throat, received in the storm of Fort Griswold."

51 Chelsea Discharge, WO 121/12/288, TNA. According to Lee's discharge papers, he was "wounded at the storm of Fort Griswold." No further details were provided.

52 McCormack was wounded in the thigh.

53 Ship's Muster Book, HMS *Amphion*, ADM 36/9561, TNA; Arnold report in Mackenzie, *Diary*, 2:627; Muster rolls, Loyal American Regiment, British Military and Naval Records, RG 8, "C" Series, Volume 1867, page 71, PAC.

54 Ship's Muster Book, HMS *Amphion*, ADM 36/9561, TNA; Arnold report in Mackenzie, *Diary*, 2:627. On the ship's muster, his name is listed as Robert. Upon examination of the regimental muster rolls, the only Burrell in the regimental hospital following the attack is one named Josiah.

Capt. William Howison's Company

Pvt. Robert Ward[55]   Wounded

JAEGER COMPANY[56]

Jaeger Wolfgang Muller[57]   Wounded
Jeager Wolf Andreas Eichorn[58]   Missing

AMERICAN LEGION[59]

Capt. Nathan Frink's Company

Cpl. Ichabod Beckwith   Wounded
Trooper James Higgins[60]   Wounded

Capt. Samuel Wogan's Company

Capt. Samuel Wogan[61]   Wounded
Pvt. Patrick Rowland[62]   Missing

---

55 Mislabeled on the *Amphion* as having been a member of the 54th Regiment. Ward was reported to be in the regimental hospital on the Nov. muster.

56 The list below is missing the names of one wounded, and four missing jaegers.

57 Treasury Office Papers, Muster of the Brandenburg-Ansbach Corps of Chasseurs, T38/812-814, TNA. Muller was a member of the 2nd Ansbach Jaeger Company and died of his wounds in Oct. 1781.

58 Ibid.

59 Muster rolls, American Legion, British Military and Naval Records, RG 8, "C" Series, Volume 1871, PAC; Ship's Muster Book, HMS *Amphion*, ADM 36/9561, TNA. The names are listed below in the company they served in the day of the attack with notations to which company they belonged to in the unit. The list is missing the names of the soldier who was killed, three of those wounded, and one who was missing. These remain unknown at this time.

60 American Loyalist Claim, 1776–1835, AO 13/41/366-367, TNA. Higgins was wounded twice. He normally served in Capt. Gilbert Livingston's Troop.

61 Wogan normally led the regiment's Grenadier Company.

62 Rowland, assigned to Capt. Richard Ness's Company, was listed as having "Deserted New London."

American Casualties:
New London[1]
September 6, 1781

Department of New London, Groton &c.

Shapley's Company of Matrosses[2]

Cpl. Josiah Smith	Taken Prisoner
Matross Reuben Bushnell	Taken Prisoner
Matross Levi Dart	Taken Prisoner
Matross Elias Dart	Taken Prisoner
Matross John Kilbourn	Taken Prisoner
Matross Joab Wright	Taken Prisoner

3rd Regiment of Connecticut Militia
1st Company[3]

Robert Frazer	Taken Prisoner
Nathan Miner	Taken Prisoner
John Shepherd	Taken Prisoner

2nd Company

Lt. Samuel Latimer	Taken Prisoner
Giles Mumford[4]	Wounded

1 All names of casualties are from *Connecticut Men*, 575–579, Royal Navy Ships' Muster (Series I), HMS *Amphion*, ADM 36/9561, TNA; Royal Navy Ships' Muster, (Series I), HMS *Beaumont*, ADM 36/9643, TNA unless otherwise noted. Those taken to New York are noted only as "Taken Prisoner."

2 PA: Elias Dart (R.2673); Levi Dart (W.24046); Joab Wright (W.6598), NARA.

3 "A List of Towers [Tours] off Duty Dun by the Ofiers And Privets Belonging to the furst Comy In the 3d Rigment," NLCHS.

4 Governor Trumbull to Thomas Mumford, Sep. 8, 1781, Governor Trumbull Papers, Vol. 4, Folder 6, CHS.

----- Nelson[5]	Killed
Joseph Plumb	Taken Prisoner
Elijah Richards	Wounded
Samuel Smith	Taken Prisoner

5th Company

Robert Latimer[6]	Wounded
Jonathan Whaley[7]	Wounded

7th Company

Thomas Durfee	Taken Prisoner
John Soper	Taken Prisoner

11th Company

Isaac Birch[8]	Killed
Jonathan Fox[9]	Killed

14th Company

Samuel Tinker	Taken Prisoner

Independent Artillery Company

William Coit[10]	Taken Prisoner
Jonathan Holt[11]	Taken Prisoner
David Richards[12]	Taken Prisoner

1st Company Alarm List[13]

Ephraim Brown	Taken Prisoner
Samuel B. Hempstead[14]	Wounded

5 *Boston Gazette*, Sep. 17, 1781. Nelson's first name is unknown. An extensive search of vital and land records revealed that he was probably the husband of Mary (Beebe) Nelson.

6 "Col Latimer's account for issuing orders, expresses, &c; 1781–1782," Revolutionary War Records (1763–1789) Series I, XXXII:137a-b236, CSL.

7 *Connecticut Men*, 578; PA: Samuel Whaley (R.11366); Jonathan Whaley (W.2739), NARA.

8 PA: Peter Crocker (R.2493), NARA.

9 Harris, *Groton Heights*, 208

10 Ibid.

11 Book, "Connecticut Independent Company," NLCHS.

12 Ibid.

13 "A List of the First Alarm List Company in the 3d Regt of Militia in this State under the Command of Capt John Deshon," NLCHS.

14 Hempstead served as a marine onboard the Continental frigate *Deane*, at the time docked in Boston. He was on furlough from the ship in New London. This ship is not to be confused with the Connecticut privateer brig *Deane*.

25th Regiment of Connecticut Militia

6th Company

John Tennant[15]   Wounded

Sailors/Marines

Unknown Vessel

William Bell[16]   Taken Prisoner
John Evans[17]   Taken Prisoner
John Saunders[18]   Taken Prisoner
Thomas Summers[19]   Taken Prisoner
William Tyrone[20]   Taken Prisoner
Ben Uncas[21]   Killed
Joshua Winslow[22]   Taken Prisoner

Volunteers/Civilians[23]

Nathaniel Beebe   Killed
Benajah Denham[24]   Taken Prisoner
Walter Harris   Taken Prisoner

Unknown[25]

Francis Burwash   Taken Prisoner
George Wellevey   Taken Prisoner

---

15 PA: John Tennant (R.10453), NARA.

16 Middlebrook, *Maritime Connecticut*, 2: 201; *Connecticut Men*, 601.

17 Royal Navy Ships' Muster (Series I), HMS *Jersey*, ADM 36/8573, TNA. Evans was aboard the prize vessel *Hunter* when he was captured in June 1779 and held aboard the *Jersey* prison ship until August 1779 when he was exchanged.

18 Middlebrook, *Connecticut Maritime*, 2:201; *Connecticut Men*, 601. Saunders served on the privateer *Recovery* which sailed out of New London in February 1780 and was captured the following month by the *Galatea*. He also served on the Connecticut warship *Oliver Cromwell*, also out of New London, in 1779.

19 Royal Navy Ships' Muster (Series I), HMS *Royal Oak*, ADM 36/9522, TNA. Summers was captured sometime in 1780, kept on the *Royal Oak*, and was exchanged in December 1780.

20 *Naval Documents*, VIII:43, 47.

21 Middlebrook, *Maritime Connecticut*, 1:123. Uncas served under the name Benjamin Uncas on the *Oliver Cromwell*.

22 Royal Navy Ships' Muster, HMS *Royal Oak*, ADM 36/9522, TNA. Winslow was captured in February 1780 aboard the sloop *Washington*, which sailed out of New London, and held on the *Royal Oak* prison ship until being exchanged in February 1781.

23 Beebe and Harris were over 60 years old and were thus exempted from militia service and would not have belonged to any militia company.

24 PA: Benajah Denham (S.30379), NARA. Listed on British records as Benjamin Donham. He was a resident of Plainfield.

25 Likely, but unconfirmed, sailors.

Appendix H

American Casualties:
Groton Heights and Birch Plain Creek[1]
September 6, 1781

Note: All company rosters are listed as follows: officers, enlisted, and volunteers. Italicized names were casualties along Birch Plain Creek.

Department of New London, Groton &c.

Lt. Col. William Ledyard, Commandant	Killed
1st Lt. Enoch Stanton, Adjutant	Killed
John Holt Jr., Dep. Asst. Quartermaster	Killed
Jordan Freeman, Waiter to Lt. Col. Ledyard	Killed
William Seymour[2]	Wounded
Horatio Wales, Express Rider for Payroll Committee[3]	Taken Prisoner

1 *Connecticut Men*, 575–579; Royal Navy Ships' Muster, HMS *Amphion*, ADM 36/9561, TNA; Royal Navy Ships' Muster, HMS *Beaumont*, ADM 36/9643, TNA. All wounded men, except those along Birch Plain Creek, were taken prisoner and with the exception of one, paroled. Those carried to New York are only noted as "Taken Prisoner." All names of casualties are from *Connecticut Men*, 575–579, unless otherwise noted.

2 "Petition, with list of notes, show he held 4 notes issued by the Treasurer which William Seymour was about to carry to Hartford for renewal. Seymour entered Ft. Griswold Sept. 6 as volunteer & notes were lost with his clothing in the raid," Revolutionary War Records, Series I, XXIII, 1, 8, 9, CSL. Seymour was from Hartford and was visiting his uncle, Colonel Ledyard. He was carrying several state notes that he was to bring to the state treasurer in Hartford but were lost during the battle.

3 "State of Connecticut to Horatio Wales, March 31, 1781," Revolutionary War Records, XVII: 487, CSL; "State of Connecticut to Horatio Wales, December 1781," Revolutionary War Records, Series I, XXV:134, CSL. Wales was an express rider from Hartford, whose father sat on the payroll committee. This might be why he was in Groton at the time of the battle. He may have been meeting with Ledyard.

Latham's Company of Matrosses

Capt. William Latham	Wounded
2nd Lt. Obadiah Perkins	Wounded
1st Sgt. Rufus Avery	Taken Prisoner
Sgt. Nathan Darrow	Taken Prisoner
Cpl. Jehiel Judd	Wounded
Cpl. Nathan Sholes	Killed
Fifer Humphrey Brown	Taken Prisoner
Matross Samuel Beaumont	Taken Prisoner
Matross John Billings	Killed
Matross Andrew Gallup	Wounded
Matross Robert Gallup	Wounded
Matross Thomas Griffin	Taken Prisoner
Matross Thomas Lamb	Killed
Matross William Latham Jr.	Wounded and Taken Prisoner
Matross Elnathan Mason	Taken Prisoner
Matross Jabez Pembleton	Wounded and Taken Prisoner
Matross James A. Smith	Wounded and Taken Prisoner
Matross Sanford Williams	Taken Prisoner
Matross Azel Woodworth	Wounded
Matross Ziba Woodworth[4]	Wounded
Lambert Latham	Killed
William Latham Jr.[5]	Taken Prisoner and Released

Shapley's Company of Matrosses[6]

Capt. Adam Shapley[7]	Wounded
1st Lt. Richard Chapman	Killed
2nd Lt. Jabez Stow Jr.	Taken Prisoner
Gunner Jonathan Minor	Taken Prisoner
1st Sgt. Stephen Hempstead	Wounded
Sgt. Jeremiah Harding	Taken Prisoner
Sgt. John Prentis[8]	Wounded
Matross William Bolton	Killed
Matross Jordan Bushnell	Wounded
Matross Jonathan Butler	Killed
Matross William Comstock	Killed

---

4 Left for dead. Not included in prisoner count.

5 Captain Latham's son. Not to be confused with a matross of the same name.

6 The Petition of the Subscribers . . . were non-commissioned officers in a Military Company lately raised by said State for the defence of the same which said company was stationed in the Garrison at Fort Trumbull, and commanded by Capt. Adam Shapley," Revolutionary War Records, Series I, XXIV:123, CSL.

7 Died of wounds on February 14, 1782.

8 Left for dead. Not included in prisoner count.

Matross Eliday Jones	Killed
Matross Charles Kirtland	Taken Prisoner
Matross Isaac Rowley	Taken Prisoner
Matross Holsey Sanford	Taken Prisoner
Matross Samuel Stillman	Wounded
Matross John Whittlesey	Killed
Matross Stephen Whittlesey	Killed
Matross Daniel Williams	Killed

8th Regiment of Connecticut Militia
1st "Groton" Company

Capt. John Williams	Killed
Lt. Ebenezer Avery Jr.	Killed
Ens. Daniel Avery	Killed
Sgt. Christopher Avery[9]	Killed
Sgt. Jasper Avery	Killed
Sgt. Solomon Avery	Killed
Sgt. Elisha Prior	Wounded
Sgt. William Starr[10]	Wounded
Cpl. Ebenezer Avery	Wounded
Cpl. Elisha Avery[11]	Killed
Cpl. John Morgan	Wounded
Amos Avery	Wounded
Thomas Avery	Killed
Joshua Baker	Wounded and Taken Prisoner
Walter Buddington Jr.	Taken Prisoner
Charles Chester	Taken Prisoner
Daniel Chester	Killed
Eldridge Chester[12]	Wounded
Jedidiah Chester	Killed
Gilbert Edgcomb	Taken Prisoner
Jonathan Havens	Taken Prisoner
Jesper Latham	Taken Prisoner
Jonathan Latham Jr.	Wounded
Jonathan Ledyard	Wounded
Henry Mason	Wounded and Taken Prisoner
Elisha Morgan[13]	Wounded

9 *CG*, Sep. 21, 1781.

10 Starr also served as the regimental quartermaster.

11 *CG*, Sep. 21, 1781. Avery was a former Continental commissary captain, though here he is listed with his militia rank.

12 Died of wounds on Dec. 31, 1781.

13 Left for dead. Not included in prisoner count.

James Morgan Jr.	Wounded
Frederick Moore	Wounded
John Starr	Wounded
Thomas Starr Jr.	Killed
Patrick Ward[14]	Killed
Joseph Woodmansee[15]	Wounded

2nd "Groton" Company

Capt. Simeon Allyn	Killed
Lt. Joseph Lewis	Killed
Ens. John Lester	Killed
Sgt. Rufus Hurlbut	Killed
Sgt. Elisha Perkins	Killed
Sgt. Nicholas Starr	Killed
Cpl. Luke Perkins	Killed
Cpl. Simeon Morgan	Killed
Belton Allyn	Killed
Benadam Allyn	Killed
Caleb Avery	Taken Prisoner
Andrew Baker	Killed
James Bailey	Wounded
Benjamin Bill	Wounded
John Brown[16]	Killed
Daniel Davis[17]	Killed
Samuel Hill	Killed
Benajah Holdridge	Wounded
Moses Jones	Killed
Jonas Lester	Killed
Peter Lester[18]	Wounded
Wait Lester	Killed
Roswell Mattison[19]	Wounded
Thomas Mallison	Wounded
Thomas Miner	Killed

14 *Naval Documents*, 9:855. Ward was previously listed as a lieutenant. This was a Continental naval rank and was not current at the time of the battle. He had previously served aboard the Continental brig Resistance.

15 Previously listed as an ensign. However, he did not receive his commission to ensign until October 1782.

16 Brown was the former fife major in Sherburne's Additional Continental Regiment. He served from 1777–1780.

17 Davis was a member of the 3rd Connecticut Regiment and was on leave from his unit. His death caused him to be listed as a deserter for a short time until it was confirmed.

18 *Norwich Packet*, Sep. 13, 1781. Lester is a previously unknown defender.

19 PA: Roswell Mattison (W.9913), NARA.

Isaac Morgan[20]	Taken Prisoner
Joseph Moxley Jr.	Wounded
John Newson[21]	Taken Prisoner
Aaron Perkins	Taken Prisoner
Asa Perkins	Killed
Luke Perkins[22]	Killed
Simeon Perkins	Killed
David Seabury[23]	Wounded
Josiah Widger	Killed
Christopher Woodbridge	Killed
Henry Woodbridge	Killed
Samuel Moxley[24]	Wounded
Elnathan Perkins[25]	Killed

3rd "Groton" Company

Sgt. Daniel Eldridge	Wounded
Cpl. Andrew Billings	Killed
Cpl. Edward Mills[26]	Wounded
Cpl. David Palmer[27]	Killed

20 It has been previously believed Morgan was Cpl. Isaac Morgan, of the 4th "Groton" Company, but this is now doubted. Corporal Morgan was later paid for three days of service during this alarm. The Morgan captured at the fort did not serve for three days. His service combined with his prison time lasted at least three months. It is rather Isaac Avery Morgan, who was a Groton mariner who survived his imprisonment and later died at sea in 1782. It appears he placed a damage claim afterwards under Jos[ep]h and Isaac Morgan.

21 Middlebrook, *Maritime Connecticut*, 2:59, 80. Newson actively served on privateers on other naval vessels both before and after his capture.

22 "A Pay Role of Capt. Elijah Avery Avery's Company for assisting the Sheriff of New London County when abused By a mob 7th Feb 1778," JSC. Perkins was the second militia volunteer in the fort with this name. Original records name him "Luke Perkins 2nd" which some have wrongly interpreted to mean "Luke Perkins Jr." which was not the case. He is attributed to having resided in Groton and left a widow named Margaret and a child with no estate when he died. This was a slight conjecture as a Luke Perkins was on the above cited payroll as having lived two miles from the Groton Ferry, the other Cpl. Luke Perkins lived another mile or so further away. He may have also been in the 1st "Groton" Company.

23 *Norwich Packet*, Sep. 13, 1781. Died sometime before September 13.

24 *Providence Evening Press*, Mar. 15, 1861. Samuel was with his father Joseph, brother Joseph Jr; and brother-in-law Moses Jones working on a house in Groton Bank. Being under the minimum age to serve in the militia, he was a volunteer. All four met their respective companies at the fort. Samuel claimed that he was bayonetted twice near the magazine, where he ran after the north gate was forced open, once in the arm and another in the side. The latter wound was "prevented from killing him . . . by striking a rib." He is a previously unknown defender.

25 Perkins was 62 years old and above militia age. He was the father of Obadiah, Asa, Luke Jr., and Elisha Perkins and joined the fort with the latter three as a volunteer.

26 Died of wounds on Sep. 7, 1781.

27 *CG*, Sep. 21, 1781. Palmer's rank was listed in the newspaper.

Nathaniel Adams Jr.	Killed
Peter Avery[28]	Taken Prisoner
John P. Babcock	Killed
Elisha Burrows	Taken Prisoner
Hubbard Burrows[29]	Killed
Nathan Burrows	Taken Prisoner
Frederick Chester	Killed
John Daboll	Wounded
Ebenezer Fish	Taken Prisoner
John Miner Jr.[30]	Taken Prisoner
Amos Stanton	Killed
Henry Williams	Killed
Thomas Wells	Taken Prisoner
James Comstock[31]	Killed
Capt. Joseph Ellis[32]	Killed
Henry Halsey	Killed
Shoram Stanton[33]	Taken Prisoner

4th "Stonington" Company

| Samuel Abraham[34] | Taken Prisoner |

28 PA: Peter Avery (S.12024), NARA. Avery identifies his company in his pension application.

29 Burrows, usually listed as Capt. Hubbard Burrows, was the former captain of the company, but retired from command in May 1780. At only 42-years-old and a farmer by occupation, he was still of age to serve in the regular trainband company. He may have served as an acting captain the day of the battle.

30 Mather, *Refugees* of 1776, 302, 312, 374, 380, 385, 425, 427, 463, 479, 507, 603, 632–633, 734, 802, 808, 830, 857–858; *CG*, July 6, 1781, May 24, 1782. Listed on the *Beaumont* as "John Minner." He and his father John Miner served together in Capt. Seth W. Holmes's Company in Chapman's Regiment of Connecticut Militia during the battle of Rhode Island in 1778. According to the *Connecticut Gazette*, John Sr. was an innholder in Groton, and died in July 1781 without any personal real estate. Earlier in the war, Captain Miner made a business transporting refugees, livestock, and other materials across the Sound to Connecticut from Long Island. It is believed that the family resided in a tavern near the Mystic River and therefore made Miner a member of this company.

31 Smith, *North Groton's Story*, 107. Comstock was 69 years old and resided in New London. Well above militia age, Comstock was visiting his daughter and son-in-law, Nathaniel Adams Jr., the day of the attack. He went as a volunteer with Nathaniel.

32 *CG*, Sep. 21, 1781; "List of Men Killed at Fort Groton, 1781," American Revolution Collection, Box 1, Folder 11, CHS; "Mrs. Waty Fitch," Mystic Pioneer, June 20, 1863. He was probably a merchant marine captain, as he transported Refugees across the Sound earlier in the war. Previously unknown defender. Mentioned in Fitch's obituary was the notation that on her father's property in Mystic was a "hospitable retreat" for refugees from Long Island. As such, Ellis, and Halsey, being refugees from Long Island, are placed as volunteers under the 3rd "Groton" Company.

33 *Connecticut Men*, 156.

34 "The Memorial of the Subscribers, Inhabitants of the Town of Groton & Towns adjacent . . . December 1781," Revolutionary War Records, Series I, XXII:80, CSL; *Connecticut Men*, 403; "Rolls of the Milage Money belonging to Capt. Witter's Company," Revolutionary War Service

5th "Stonington" Company

Sgt. Daniel Stanton	Killed
Daniel Stanton Jr.[35]	Wounded
Edward Stanton	Wounded

1st Company "Groton Alarm List"

Capt. Elijah Avery	Killed
Ens. Charles Eldridge	Wounded
Sgt. David Avery	Killed
Sgt. Ezekiel Bailey	Killed
Parke Avery Jr.[36]	Wounded
Edward Latham	Wounded
James Latham	Taken Prisoner
Youngs Ledyard[37]	Wounded
Cary Leeds[38]	Wounded
Ebenezer Perkins	Wounded

2nd Company "Groton Alarm List"

Capt. Samuel Allyn	Killed
Ens. Amos Lester	Wounded
Joseph Moxley Sr.[39]	Wounded
Solomon Perkins	Wounded

3rd Company "Groton Alarm List"

Sgt. John Stedman	Killed
Samuel Billings	Killed
Philip Covil	Killed

Records, NARA. Abraham was part of a group of petitioners from "the Town of Groton & Towns adjacent" who had been part of the garrison and in January 1782 asked the state government for relief from wounds and other sufferings. A search of vital and property records in Groton revealed Abraham probably did not reside in Groton. His only recordable service during the war was under "Samuel Abrams" in Capt. Ebenezer Witter's Company in the 4th Battalion of Wadsworth's Brigade during the fall of 1776. The company was comprised of militia from Preston and Stonington. Since the militia from Preston did not arrive until after dark, it is strongly believed Abraham came from a Stonington militia company, near the Mystic River. One of the company commanders, Ens. John Williams, was part of the 4th "Stonington" Company, the others were companies in North Stonington. He was probably the only member of his company who served in the fort. The rest remained near the meetinghouse.

35 Left for dead. Not included in prisoner count.

36 Elroy McKendree and Catherine Hitchcock (Tilden) Avery, *The Groton Avery Clan*, 2 vols. (Cleveland, 1912), 1: 260. Avery is listed as lieutenant on records related to the battle, but this appears to be a rank he held in the state battalion, earlier in the war, not his rank at the time of the battle. As town constable, he would have served with the alarm list company.

37 Died of wounds on Sep. 7, 1781. Ranked as captain on previous lists. This is his mercantile business rank.

38 Died of disease, as a result of his wounds on Dec. 28, 1781.

39 Died of wounds on Sep 7, 1781.

Sylvester Walworth	Killed

3rd Company "Stonington Alarm List"

Christopher Eldridge	Wounded
Thomas Williams	Killed

3rd Regiment of Connecticut Militia
1st Company

Ens. Japhet Mason	Taken Prisoner

2nd Company

John Clark[40]	Killed
Elias Coit	Killed

Sailors/Marines
Deane

Charles Martin[41]	Taken Prisoner

Hancock

Capt. Peter Richards	Killed
Christopher Latham Jr.[42]	Wounded

Minerva

John King	Taken Prisoner

Randolph

Lt. Nathan Moore[43]	Wounded
Samuel Edgcomb[44]	Wounded

Unknown Vessel

James Caheen[45]	Taken Prisoner
Samuel W. Jacques	Wounded

---

40 Might have actively been a sailor aboard a privateer or been assisting John Holt transport gunpowder and other supplies across the river. Had previously served on the *Hancock* in 1780.

41 PA: Charles Martin (W.1978), NARA. Martin was originally a British soldier who arrived in Quebec in 1776. He hinted to this in his pension application deposition. Upon his arrival in Quebec, he deserted and joined the American forces besieging the city. Eventually, Martin made his way to Rhode Island. In 1777, he assists in the capture of British Brig. Gen. Richard Prescott. In 1780, he joined the *Deane* and served on her throughout the summer of 1781. After his capture at the fort, he was transported to Halifax, where he is refused an exchange until late-1782, the last prisoner taken at New London and Groton to be exchanged. Martin blamed his long captivity based on his "having been born in Great Britain." This is probably only part of the reason as he was probably recognized as a deserter in New York.

42 Also, a member of the 1st "Groton" Company, but actively serving on the *Hancock*.

43 Also, a member of the 1st Company "Groton Alarm List," but actively serving on the *Randolph* as a lieutenant of marines.

44 Also, a member of the 1st "Groton" Company, but actively serving on the *Randolph*.

45 The name on the muster roll is hard to distinguish. No local connection could be found, so he is attributed to a privateer crew.

Barney Kinne[46]	Killed
Benoni Kenson	Killed
Charles Owen	Taken Prisoner
Zachariah Riley	Taken Prisoner
Nathaniel Sibil[47]	Taken Prisoner
Tom Wansuc[48]	Wounded

46 Royal Navy Ships' Muster (Series I), HMS *Royal Oak*, ADM 36/9522, TNA. Kinney, also known as Barnabas Kinney and/or Barney Kane, had been previously captured by the British frigate *Triton* as part of prize crew of the brig *Betsey* in the summer of 1780. He was exchanged on Dec. 29, 1780.

47 No local connection could be found, so he is attributed to a privateer crew.

48 Wansuc was from Groton and a member of the Pequot tribe. He was not legally allowed to serve in the militia and is traditionally believed to have been a member of a privateer.

Appendix I

Notes on the Jaeger Company During the New London Expedition[1]

Detachments of jaegers sent on short expeditions were common throughout the war. That September in New York around 700 jaegers in eight companies were organized into two battalions and made up the Feldjaegerkorps. The first battalion consisted of six companies from Hesse-Kassel, while the second battalion consisted of two companies from Ansbach and Bayreuth. Often, detachments were made up of jaegers from both battalions, and according to treaties with their rulers, in the field they only served under their own officers. This led to detachments being comprised of officers from both Hesse and Ansbach companies to accommodate this provision.

Each assigned officer led his own platoon (20-40 jaegers), made up of jaegers from their own companies. Arnold's jaeger detachment consisted of a captain, three lieutenants (one first lieutenant and two second lieutenants), two horn-blowers, a surgeon's mate, ten sergeants, and 100 rank and file, the perfect complement of a jaeger company. 60 jaegers, accompanied by 6 sergeants, and a horn-blower, attacked New London, under Staff Captain Friedrich Adam Julius von Wangenheim and a currently unknown first lieutenant. The remaining 40 jaegers, with 4 sergeants, and a horn-blower, under 2nd Lieutenant Julius von Reitzenstein and, a currently unknown second lieutenant, attacked Groton.

The presence of von Wangenheim, of the Lieutenant Colonel's Company of the Hessian Battalion of the Feldjaegerkorps, indicates his platoon, if not all his jaegers, were from his own company. The jaegers in Groton were from the two Ansbach companies. Their December 1781 muster roll revealed their casualties. Wolf Andreas Eichorn of the 1st Company deserted, and Wolfgang Muller of the 2nd Company was wounded. Eichorn's desertion is the only documented jaeger deserter, and his capture was included in the pension application of Capt. Thomas Park. The likely scenario is each Ansbach

---

1 Treasury Office Papers, TO 38/812-814, TNA; *Diaries of Two Ansbach Jaegers: Lieutenant Heinrich Carl Philipp von Feilitzsch and Lieutenant Christian Friedrich Bartholomai.* Translated and edited by Bruce E. Burgoyne. (Westminster, MD: Heritage Books, 2007), 49; Rosengarten, J.G. *The German Allied Troops in the North American War of Independence, 1776–1783.* Translated by Max von Eelking. (Albany, NY: Joel Munsell's Sons, Publishers, 1893), 342; PA: Thomas Park (R.7932), NARA.

company provided 20 jaegers, and two sergeants, both led by a second lieutenant. According to its muster roll, the 1st Company had only one lieutenant, 2nd Lt. Julius von Reitzenstein, present in New York during this time; the other two lieutenants were either in the hospital or in Virginia. The 2nd Company is more complicated. It had two second lieutenants present at this time, Christian Friedrich Bartholomai and Jakob Ernst Kling. Either one of these two lieutenants could have been present. According to Rosengarten, Bartholomai and von Reitzenstein had the same commission dates to second lieutenant. Bartholomai's diary, though the editor incorrectly annotates von Reitzenstein as a different officer of the same name, indicates the two arrived in America on the same day. Even if Bartholomai was present with the group from the 2nd Company, von Reitzenstein from the 1st Company—the senior company—would have outranked him.

Bibliography

Primary Sources

Manuscript Collections

Hessian Archives (Arcinsys Hessen), Marburg, Germany
    Bickell Estate and Family Papers (Nachlass und Familienarchiv Bickell)

Connecticut State Library, Hartford, Connecticut
    Connecticut, Wills and Probate Records, Hartford, Probate Packets, 1675–1850
    Governor Jonathan Trumbull Papers
    Groton, Land Records, and deeds, 44 vols.
    Militia, Series II, 1747–1788
    Militia, Series III, 1728–1820
    New London, Land Records, and deeds, 94 vols.
    New London Town Papers, 1674–1925
    Revolutionary War, Series I, 1763–1789
    Revolutionary War, Series II, 1756–1856
    Revolutionary War, Series III, June 1765–May 1820

Connecticut Historical Society, Hartford, Connecticut
    Council of Safety Papers
    Governor Jonathan Trumbull Papers
    Tyler Family Papers, 1777-1811
    Joseph Trumbull Papers
    William Williams Family Papers
    Woodward Family Papers, 1778-1948

James Steelman Collection
"A Pay Role of Capt. Elijah Avery's Company for assisting the Sheriff of New London County when abused By a mob 7th february 1778"

Library of Congress, Washington, D.C.
George Washington Papers

Museum of the Queen's Lancashire Regiment, Preston, Lancashire, United Kingdom
Regimental Returns

National Archives, Washington, D.C.
Papers of the Continental Congress
Pension Office Records

New London County Historical Society, New London, Connecticut
Charles Allyn Papers
Robert Hallam Papers
"Connecticut Independent Company" Notebook

Public Archives of Canada, Ottawa, Ontario, Canada
RG 8, British Military and Naval Records

British National Archives, Kew, United Kingdom
CO 5: Board of Trade and Secretaries of State: America and West Indies, Original Correspondence
ADM 36, Admiralty: Royal Navy Ships' Musters (Series I)
ADM 51, Admiralty: Captains' Logs
ADM 52, Admiralty: Masters' Logs
AO 11, American Office, American Loyalists Claims, Series I
AO 12, American Office, American Loyalists Claims, Series I
T 38, Treasury Office Papers, Accounts of Hessian Troops Engaged in America
WO 12, Commissary General of Musters Office and successors: General Muster Books and Pay Lists
WO 65, War Office: Printed Annual Army Lists
WO 121, Royal Hospital, Chelsea: Discharge Documents of Pensioners

William Clement Library, University of Michigan, Ann Arbor, Michigan
Frederick Mackenzie Papers
Lord Shelburne Papers
Sir Henry Clinton Papers

Yale Library, Yale University, New Haven, Connecticut
Nathaniel and Thomas Shaw Papers
Leffingwell Family Papers

Printed Original Sources

A Historical Collection from Official Records, Files, &c., of the Part Sustained By Connecticut During the War of the Revolution With an Appendix, Containing Important Letters, Depositions, &c., Written During the War. Edited by Royal R. Hinman. Hartford, CT: E. Gleason, 1842.

Clinton, Henry. *The American Rebellion: Sir Henry Clinton's Narrative of His Campaigns, 1775-1782, with an Appendix of Original Documents.* Edited by William B. Willcox. New Haven, CT: Yale University Press, 1954.

Clinton, Henry. *Narrative of Lieutenant-General Sir Henry Clinton, K.B. Relative to His Conduct During Part of His Command of the King's Troops in North America, Particularly to that which reflects the unfortunate Issue of the Campaign in 1781, With an Appendix Containing Copies and Extracts of those Parts of his Correspondence with Lord George Germain, Earl Cornwallis, Rear Admiral Graves, &.* 2nd ed. London: J. Debrett, 1783.

Curfew, Samuel. *Journal And Letters Of The Late Samuel Curfew, Judge Of Admiralty, Etc., An American Refugee In England, From 1775 To 1784, Comprising Remarks On The Prominent Men And Measures Of That Period.* Edited by George Atkinson Ward. New York: C. S. Francis and Co., 1842.

Dearborn, Henry. *Revolutionary War Journals of Henry Dearborn, 1775–1783.* Edited by Lloyd A. Brown and Howard H. Peckham. Chicago: The Caxton Club, 1939.

Dohla, Johann Conrad. *A Hessian Diary of the American Revolution.* Translated and edited by Bruce E. Burgoyne. Norman, OK: University of Oklahoma Press, 1990.

Enemy Views: The American Revolutionary War as Recorded by the Hessian Participants. Edited by Bruce E. Burgoyne. Berwyn Heights, MD: Heritage Books Inc., 2009.

Ewald, Johann. *Diary of the American War, A Hessian Journal.* Edited by Joseph P. Tustin. New Haven, CT: Yale University Press, 1979.

Graves, Thomas. *The Graves Papers and Other Documents Relating to the Naval Operations of the Yorktown Campaign July to October, 1781.* Edited by French E. Chadwick. New York: Naval Historical Society, 1916.

Hamilton, Alexander. *The Papers of Alexander Hamilton.* 27 vols. Edited by Harold C. Syrett and Jacob E. Cooke. New York: Columbia University Press, 1961–1975.

Heath, William. *Memoirs of Major General William Heath.* Edited by William Abbatt. New York: Arno Press, Inc., 1968.

The Heath Papers, Collections of the Massachusetts Historical Society, Series 7, Vol. 5. Boston, Massachusetts: 1905.

Hempstead, Joshua. *Diary of Joshua Hempstead of New London, Connecticut, Covering A Period of Forty-Seven Years, From September, 1711, To November, 1758 Containing Valuable Genealogical Data Relating To Many New London Families, References To The Colonial Wars, To The Shipping And Other Matters Of Interest To The Town And The Times,*

With An Account Of A Journey Made By The Writer From New London To Maryland. New London, CT: New London County Historical Society, 1901.

Hood, Samuel. *Letters Written by Sir Samuel Hood (Viscount Hood) In 1781-2-3.* Edited by David Hannay. n.p.: Navy Records Society, 1895.

Huntington Papers: Correspondence of the Brothers Joshua and Jedidiah During the Period of the American Revolution. Hartford, CT: Connecticut Historical Society, 1923.

Jones, Thomas. *History of New York During the Revolutionary War and of the Leading Events in the Other Colonies at that Period.* Edited by Edward Floyd de Lancey. New York: New York Historical Society, 1879.

Journals of the Continental Congress, 1774–1789. Washington D.C.: Government Printing Office, 1912.

Journal of the Hesse-Cassel Jaeger Corps and Hans Konze's List of Jaeger Officers. Edited by Bruce Burgoyne and Marie E. Burgoyne. Berwyn Heights, MD: Heritage Books Inc., 2008.

Journal of the Hessian Jager Corps, 1777–1779. Translated and Edited by W. Steedman and Ian Steedman. Surrey, UK: Grosvenor House Publishing Limited., 2018.

Diaries of Two Ansbach Jaegers: Lieutenant Heinrich Carl Philipp von Feilitzsch and Lieutenant Christian Friedrich Bartholomai. Translated and edited by Bruce E. Burgoyne. Bowie, MD: Heritage Books, 1997.

Letters from Lafayette to Luzerne, 1780–1782. Edited by Waldo G. Leland. Bloomingdale, IN: American Historical Review, 1915.

Life and Letters of Samuel Holden Parsons Major General in the Continental Army and Chief Justice of the Northwestern Territory 1737–1789. Edited by Charles S. Hall. Binghamton, NY: Otseningo Publishing Co., 1905.

Lists And Returns of Connecticut Men In The Revolution, 1775–1783. Hartford: Connecticut Historical Society, 1906.

Lloyd's Register of Shipping For the Year 1779–1780. London: The Gregg Press Limited, 1963.

Lloyd's Register of Shipping For the Year 1781. London: The Gregg Press Limited, 1963.

Lloyd's Register of Shipping For the Year 1782–1783. London: The Gregg Press Limited, 1963.

Mackenzie, Frederick. *Diary of Frederick Mackenzie: Giving a daily narrative of his military services as an officer in the regiment of Royal Welsh Fusiliers during the years 1775-1781 in Massachusetts, Rhode Island, and New York.* 2 vols. Edited by Allen French. Cambridge, MA: Harvard University Press, 1930.

Mason, Jeremiah. *Memoir, Autobiography and Correspondence of Jeremiah Mason.* Kansas City, MO: Lawyers' International Publishing Co., 1917.

Morris, Robert. *Papers of Robert Morris, 1781–1784: August–September 1781.* 9 vols. Edited by James Elmer. Pittsburgh: University of Pittsburg Press, 1975.

Narrative of Jonathan Rathbun With Accurate Accounts Of The Capture Of Groton Fort, The Massacre That Followed, And The Sacking And Burning Of New London, September 6, 1781, by the British Forces, under the command of that Traitor Benedict Arnold. n.p.: Jonathan Rathbun, 1840.

Naval Documents of the American Revolution. 11 vols. Edited by William Bell Clark. Washington D.C.: United States Government Printing Office, 1970.

Naval Records of the American Revolution. Edited by Charles Henry Lincoln. Washington D.C.: Government Printing Office, 1906.

The Papers of General Nathaniel Greene. 13 vols. Edited by Dennis M. Conrad and Roger N. Parks. Chapel Hill, NC: University of North Carolina Press, 1976–2015.

Peebles, John. *John Peebles' American War: The Diary of a Scottish Grenadier.* Edited by Ira D. Gruber. Stroud, UK: Sutton Publishing Ltd., 1998.

Proceedings of a Board of General Officers of the British Army at New York, 1781. New York: New York Historical Society, 1916.

Proceedings of a general court martial of the line, held in Raritan, in the state of New-Jersey, by order of His Excellency George Washington, Esq. and commander in chief of the Army of the United States of America, for the trial of Major General Arnold, June 1, 1779. Major General Howe, president.: Published by order of Congress. Philadelphia: Francis Bailey, 1780.

The Public Records of the Colony of Connecticut. 15 vols. Hartford, CT: Case, Lockwood, & Brainard Co., 1850-1890.

The Public Records of the State of Connecticut. 23 vols. Hartford, CT: Case, Lockwood, & Brainard Co., 1894–2021.

Putnam, Rufus. *The Memoirs of Rufus Putnam and Certain Official Papers and Correspondence.* Edited by Rowena Buell. Cambridge, MA: Riverside Press, 1903.

The Record of Connecticut Men in the Military and Naval Service During the War of the Revolution, 1775–1783. Edited by Henry P. Johnston. Hartford, CT: Case, Lockwood, & Brainard Co., 1889.

Robertson, James. *The Twilight of British Rule in Revolutionary America: The New York Letter Book of General James Robertson 1780–1783.* Edited by Milton M. Klein and Ronald W. Howard. Cooperstown, NY: The New York State Historical Association, 1983.

Rolls of Connecticut Men in the French and Indian War, 1755–1762. 2 vols. Hartford, CT: Connecticut Historical Society, 1903.

Rolls and Lists of Connecticut Men in the Revolution, 1775–1783. Hartford: Connecticut Historical Society, 1901.

Smith, William. *Historical Memoirs From 26 August 1778 to 12 November 1783 of William Smith: Historian of the Province of New York; Member of the Governor's Council, and Last Chief Justice of that Province Under the Crown; Chief Justice of Quebec.* Edited by William H. W. Sabine. New York: Arno Press, 1971.

Stiles, Ezra. *The Literary Diary of Ezra Stiles, D.D., LLD. President of Yale College.* 3 vols. Edited by Franklin B. Dexter. New York: Charles Scribner Sons, 1901.

Tallmadge, Benjamin. *Memoirs of Col. Benjamin Tallmadge, Prepared by Himself, at the Request of his Children.* New York: Thomas Holman, Book, and Job Printer, 1858.

Von Krafft, Johann Carl Philipp. *Journal of John Charles Philip von Krafft, Lieutenant in the Hessian Regiment von Bose, 1776–1784 with Six Illustrations Reproduced by Artotype Process and Biographical Sketch and Index.* Edited by Thomas H. Edsall. New York: Printed for Private Distribution Only, 1888.

1781 Groton Heights and New London, Letters from Zabdiel Rogers and Thomas Mumford. Brooklyn, NY: Privately Printed, 1881.

Secondary Sources

Abbott, Katharine. *Old Paths of the New England Border: Connecticut, Deerfield, Berkshire.* New York: Knickerbocker Press, 1907.

Askwith, A. H. *List of Officers of the Royal Regiment of Artillery from the Year 1716 to the year 1899. To Which Are Added The Notes On Officers' Services.* London: William Cloves and Sons Ltd., 1900.

Avery, Elroy McKendree and Catherine Hitchcock (Tilden) Avery. *The Groton Avery Clan.* Cleveland: n.p., 1912.

Avery, John Reverend. *History of the Town of Ledyard: 1650–1900.* Norwich, CT: Noyes and Davis, 1901.

Bachan, Robert L. *An Illustrated History of the Town of Waterford.* Waterford, CT: Bicentennial Committee, Town of Waterford, Connecticut, 2000.

Baker, Henry Augustus. *History of Montville, Connecticut Formerly The North Parish of New London From 1640 to 1896.* Hartford, CT: Press of the Case, Lockwood, & Brainard Company, 1896.

Banks, Elizabeth V. *This is Fairfield 1639–1940, Pages from Three Hundred One Years of the Town's Brillant History.* New Haven, CT: The Walker-Rackliff Company, 1960.

Barber, John Warner. *Connecticut Historical Collections, Containing A General Collection of Interesting Fact, Traditions, Biographical Sketches, Anecdotes, &c. Relating to the History of Antiquities of Every Town In Connecticut with Geographical Descriptions.* New Haven, CT: Durrie & Peck and J. W. Barber, 1836.

Bayles, Richard M. *Historical And Descriptive Sketches Of Suffolk County, And Its Towns, Villages, Hamlets, Scenery, Institutions And Important Enterprises; With A Historical Outline of Long Island, From Its First Settlement By Europeans.* Port Jefferson, NY: Richard M. Bayles, 1874.

Billias, George Athan, ed. *George Washington's Generals and Opponents: Their Exploits and Leadership.* New York: De Capo Press, 1994.

Blake, S. Leroy. *The Early History of the First Church of Christ, New London, Conn.* New London: Press of the Day Company, 1897.

Bowler, Arthur. *Logistics and the Failure of the British Army in America, 1775–1783.* Princeton, NJ: Princeton University Press, 1975.

Braisted, Todd W. *Grand Forage 1778 The Battleground Around New York City.* Yardley, PA: Westholme Publishing, 2016.

Brandt, Clare. *Man in the Mirror: A Life of Benedict Arnold.* New York: Random House, 1994.

Brown, Richard H., and Paul E. Cohen. *Revolution: Mapping The Road To American Independence 1755–1783.* New York: W. W. Norton & Company, 2015.

Buel, Richard, Jr. *Dear Liberty: Connecticut's Mobilization for the Revolutionary War.* Middletown, CT: Wesleyan University Press, 1980.

Burke, John. *A Genealogical And Heraldic History Of The Commoners Of Great Britain And Ireland, Enjoying Territorial Possessions Or High Official Rank; But Unvested With Heritable Honours.* 4 vols. London: Henry Colburn, 1838.

Burke, John, and John B. Burke. *A Genealogical and Heraldic Dictionary of the Landed Gentry of Great Britain & Ireland.* 2 vols. London: Henry Colburn Publisher, 1847.

Bushnell, George Eleazer. *Bushnell Family Genealogy: Ancestry and Posterity of Francis Bushnell, (1580–1646), of Horsham, England and Guilford, Connecticut, Including Genealogical Notes of Other Bushnell Families, Whose Connections with This Branch of the Family Tree Have Not Been Determined.* Nashville, TN: G. E. Bushnell, 1945.

Brumwell, Stephen. *Turncoat: Benedict Arnold and the Crisis of American Liberty.* New Haven, CT: Yale University Press, 2018.

Burnham, Norman H. *The Battle of Groton Heights: A Story of the Storming of Fort Griswold, and the Burning of New London, on the Sixth of September, 1781.* New London, CT: Bingham Paper Co., 1903.

Calkins, William W. *The Calkins Memorial Military Roster.* Chicago: M. A. Donohue & Co., 1903.

Catalogue of Articles Shown At The Groton Heights Centennial Loan Exhibition, Groton, Conn., Sept. 6, 7, and 8, 1881. Groton, CT: Groton Centennial Commission, 1881.

Caulkins, Frances Manwaring. *History of New London, Connecticut from the First Survey of the Coast in 1612, to 1852.* New London, CT: H. D. Utley, 1895.

Caulkins, Frances Manwaring. *History of Norwich, Connecticut From Its First Settlement in 1660, To January 1845.* Norwich, CT: Thomas Robinson, 1845.

Chopra, Ruma. *Unnatural Rebellion: Loyalists in New York City during the Revolution.* Charlottesville, VA: University of Virginia Press, 2011.

Clement, Justin. *Philadelphia 1777: Taking the Capital.* Westminster, MD: Osprey Publishing Ltd., 2007.

Coldham, Peter Wilson. *American Migrations, 1765–1799: The Lives, Times, and Families of Colonial Americans who Remained Loyal to the British Crown Before, During, and After the Revolutionary War, as Related in Their Own Words and Through Their Correspondence.* Baltimore: Genealogical Publishing Company, 2000.

Crofut, Florence S. M. *Guide to the History and Historic Sites of Connecticut.* 2 vols. New Haven, CT: Yale University Press, 1937.

Decker, Robert Owen. *The Whaling City: A History of New London.* Guilford, CT: Globe Pequot, 1976.

Dexter, Franklin B. *New Haven Loyalists.* New Haven, CT: New Haven Colony Historical Society, 1918.

Elia, Ricardo J. *The Fort on Groton Hill: An Archaeological Survey of Fort Griswold State Park in Groton, Connecticut.* Boston: Boston University Press, 1985.

Ford, Worthington Chauncey. *British Officers During Serving in the American Revolution, 1774–1783.* Brooklyn, NY: Historical Printing Club, 1897.

Gallup, John D. *The Genealogical History Of The Gallup Family In The United States, Also Biographical Sketches Of Members Of The Family.* Hartford: Press of The Hartford Printing Company, 1893.

Gipson, Lawrence H. *Jared Ingersoll: A Study of American Loyalism in Relation to British Colonial Government.* New Haven, CT: Yale University Press, 1920.

Gooding S. James. *An Introduction to British Artillery in North America.* Alexandria Bay, NY: Museum Restoration Service, 1988.

Green, Harry Clinton, and Mary Wolcott Green. *The Pioneer Mothers of America: A Record of the More Notable Women of the Early Days of the Country, and Particularly of the Colonial and Revolutionary Periods.* 3 vols. New York: G. P. Putnam's Sons, 1912.

Griffin, Augustus. *Griffin's Journal. First Settlers of Southold; The Names of the Heads of Those Families, Being only thirteen at the time of their landing; First Proprietors of Orient; Biographical Sketches, &c. &c. &c.* Orient, New York: Augustus Griffin, 1857.

Hagist, Don N. *British Soldiers American War: Voices of the American Revolution.* Yardley, PA: Westholme Publishing, 2012.

Hallam, Robert A. *Annals of St James's Church, New London, For One Hundred and Fifty Years.* Hartford: M. H. Mallory & Co., 1873.

Harris, Michael C. *Brandywine: A Military History of the Battle that Lost Philadelphia but Saved America, September 11, 1777.* El Dorado Hills, CA: Savas Beatie, 2017.

Harris, Michael C. *Germantown: A Military History of the Battle of Philadelphia, October 4, 1777.* El Dorado Hills, CA: Savas Beatie, 2020.

Harris, William Wallace. *The Battle of Groton Heights: A Collection of Narratives, Official Reports, Records, Etc. of the Storming of Fort Griswold, The Massacre of Its Garrison, and the Burning of New London by British Troops Under the Command of Brig.-Gen. Benedict Arnold on the Sixth of September, 1781.* Edited by Charles Allyn. New London, CT: Charles Allyn, 1882.

Hastedt, Glen P. and Steven W. Guerrie, eds. *Spies, Wiretaps, and Secret Operations: An Encyclopedia of American Espionage.* Santa Barbara, CA: ABC-CLIO Inc., 2011.

Heitman, Francis B. *Historical Register of Officers of the Continental Army During the War of the Revolution: April, 1775–December, 1783.* Washington D.C.: The Rare Book Shop Publishing, Inc., 1914.

Hillhouse, Margaret Prouty. *Historical and Genealogical Collections Relating to the Descendants of Rev. James Hillhouse.* New York, NY: Tobias A. Wright, 1924.

Hinman, Royal R. *A Family Record of the Descendants of Sergt. Edward Hinman who first appeared in Stratford in Connecticut about 1650 Collected From State, Colony, Town, And Church Records Also From Old Bibles and Aged People.* Hartford, CT: Case, Lockwood, & Brainard Co., 1856.

Hinman, Royal R., ed. *A Catalogue of the Names of the Early Puritan Settlers of the Colony of Connecticut With the Time of their arrival in the Country and Colony, Their Standing In Society, Place of Residence, Condition In Life, Where From, Business, &c., As Far As Is Found On Record.* Hartford, Case, Tiffany, and Company, 1852.

History of Middlesex County, Connecticut, With Biographical Sketches of Its Prominent Men. New York: J. B. Beers & Co., 1884.

Hurd, D. Hamilton. *History of New London County, Connecticut: With Biographical Sketches of Many of Its Pioneers and Prominent Men.* Philadelphia: J. W. Lewis & Co., 1882.

Hurwitz, Jerald P. *Alamo of the Revolution: Benedict Arnold and Massacre at Fort Griswold.* New York: Knox Press, 2020.

Katcher, Philip R. N. *King George's Army, 1775–1783, A Handbook of British, American, and German Regiments.* Harrisburg, PA: The Stackpole Company, 1973.

Kilbourne, Payne Kenyon. *The History of and Antiquities of the Name and Family of Kilbourn, In its Varied Orthography.* New Haven, CT: Durrie & Peck, 1856.

Larned, Ellen D. *Historic Gleanings in Windham County, Connecticut.* Providence, RI: Preston and Rounds Company, 1899.

Lehman, Eric D. *Homegrown Terror: Benedict Arnold and the Burning of New London.* Middletown, CT: Wesleyan University Press, 2014.

Lender, Mark Edward, and Gary Wheeler Stone. *Fatal Sunday: George Washington, the Monmouth Campaign, and the Politics of Battle.* Norman, OK: University of Oklahoma Press, 2016.

List of Congregational Ecclesiastical Societies Established in Connecticut Before 1818 with Their Changes. Hartford, CT: Connecticut Historical Society, 1913.

Lossing, Benson J. *The Pictorial Field-book of the Revolution; or, Illustrations, By Pen And Pencil, Of The History, Biography, Scenery, Relics, And Traditions Of The War For Independence.* 2 vols. New York: Harper & Brothers, Publishers, 1860.

Luzader, John F. *Saratoga: A Military History of the Decisive Campaign of the American Revolution.* New York: Savas Beatie, 2010.

Martin, James Kirby. *Benedict Arnold, Revolutionary Hero. An American Hero Reconsidered.* New York: New York University Press, 1997.

Mather, Frederic G. *The Refugees of 1776 from Long Island to Connecticut.* Albany, NY: J. B. Lyon Company, 1913.

McBurney, Christian. *The Rhode Island Campaign: The First French and American Operation in the Revolutionary War.* Yardley, PA: Westholme Publishing, 2012.

McCullough, David. *1776.* New York: Simon and Shuster, 2005.

McGuire, Thomas J. *The Philadelphia Campaign: Brandywine and the Fall of Philadelphia.* Mechanicsburg, PA: Stackpole Books, 2007.

McManemim, John A. *Captains of Privateers During the Revolutionary War.* Spring Lake, NJ: Ho-Ho-Kus Publishing Company, 1985.

Middlebrook, Louis F. *History of Maritime Connecticut During the American Revolution, 1775–1783.* 2 vols. Salem, MA: Essex Institute, 1925.

Morrissey, Brendan. *Yorktown 1781: The World Turned Upside Down.* London: Osprey Publishing, 1997.

Mullen, Jolene R. *Connecticut Town Meeting Records during the American Revolution.* 2 vols. Southampton, MA: Heritage Books, 2011.

Nagy, John A. *George Washington's Secret Spy War: The Making of America's First Spymaster.* New York: St. Martin's Press, 2016.

Nafie, Joan. *To the Beat of a Drum: A History of Norwich, Connecticut During the American Revolution.* Norwich, CT: Old Town Press, 1975.

O'Shaughnessy, Andrew Jackson. *The Men Who Lost America: British Leadership, the American Revolution, and the Fate of the Empire.* New Haven, CT: Yale University Press, 2013.

Philbrick, Nathaniel. *Bunker Hill: A City, A Siege, A Revolution.* New York: Penguin Books, 2013.

Philbrick, Nathaniel. *In The Hurricane's Eye: The Genius of George Washington and the Victory at Yorktown.* New York: Viking Press, 2018.

Powell, Walter L. *Murder or Mayhem? Benedict Arnold's New London, Connecticut Raid, 1781.* Gettysburg: Thomas Publications, 2000.

Randall, Willard Sterne. *Benedict Arnold Patriot and Traitor.* New York: Barnes and Noble, Inc., 1990.

Records and Papers of the NLCHS. 3 vols. New London, CT: Press of the Day Publishing Company, 1881–1912.

Records of the 54th West Norfolk Regiment. Roorkee, India: Thomason Civil Engineering College Press, 1881.

Reid, Stuart. *Redcoat Officer 1740–1815.* Long Island City, NY: Osprey Publishing Ltd., 2002.

Rogers, Ernest E. *Connecticut's Naval Office at New London During the War the American Revolution.* New London, CT: New London County Historical Society, 1933.

Rogers, James Swift. *James Rogers of New London, Connecticut, and His Descendants.* Boston: James Swift Rogers, 1902.

Root, Mary Philothea, ed. *Chapter Sketches Connecticut Daughters of the American Revolution: Patron Saints.* New Haven, CT: Connecticut Chapters, Daughters of the American Revolution, 1901.

Rosengarten, J. G. *The German Allied Troops in the North American War of Independence, 1776–1783.* Translated by Max von Eelking. Albany, NY: Joel Munsell's Sons, Publishers, 1893.

Ross, Peter. *A History of Long Island: From Its Earliest Settlement to the Present Time.* 2 vols. New York: The Lewis Publishing Company, 1902.

Schaefer, Patricia. *A Useful Friend: A Companion to the Joshua Hempstead Diary, 1711–1758.* New London, CT: New London County Historical Society, 2008.

Schellhammer, Michael. *George Washington and the Final British Campaign for the Hudson River, 1779.* Jefferson, NC: McFarland & Company, Inc., 2012.

Schnitzer, Eric and Don Troiani. *Don Troiani's Campaign to Saratoga—1777: The Turning Point of the Revolutionary War in Paintings, Artifacts, and Historical Narrative.* Guilford, CT: Stackpole Books, 2019.

Sigourney, L. H. *Life and Letters.* New York: D. Appleton & Company, 1866.

Smith, Carolyn E., and Helen Vergason. *September 6, 1781: North Groton's Story.* Ledyard, CT: Ledyard Historical Society, 2000.

Smythies, Raymond Henry. *Historical Records of the 40th (2nd Somersetshire) Regiment, Now 1st Battalion The Prince of Wales's Volunteers (South Lancashire Regiment) From its Formation, in 1717, to 1893.* Devonport, UK: A. H. Swiss, 1894.

Spring, Matthew H. *With Zeal and Bayonets Only: The British Army on Campaign in North America, 1775–1783.* Norman, OK: University of Oklahoma Press, 2008.

Stark, Charles. *Groton, Conn. 1705–1904.* Stonington, CT: The Palmer Press, 1922.

Stedman, Charles. *The History of the Origin, Progress, and Termination of the American War.* 2 vols. London: J. Murray, 1794.

Stewart, William. *Admirals of the World: A Biographical Dictionary, 1500 to the Present.* Jefferson, NC: McFarland & Co. Inc., 2009.

Story of the Battle of Fort Griswold September 6, 1781, with a Description of the Monument on Groton Heights. Groton, CT: James M. Bacon, 1894.

Stuart, Isaac William. *Life of Jonathan Trumbull, Sen., Governor of Connecticut.* Boston: Crocker & Brewster, 1859.

Syrett, David. *Shipping and the American War 1775–1783: A Study of British Transport Organization.* London: The Athlone Press, 1970.

Tancred, George. *Historical Record of Medals and Honorary Distinctions Conferred on The British Navy, Army & Auxiliary Forces, From the Earliest Period.* London: Spink & Son, 1891.

Townshend, Charles Hervey. *The British Invasion of New Haven, Connecticut: Together with Some Account of Their Landing and Burning the Towns of Fairfield and Norwalk, July, 1779.* New Haven, CT: Tuttle, Morehouse & Taylor, 1879.

Troiani, Don. *Don Troiani's Soldiers of the American Revolution.* Mechanicsburg, PA: Stackpole Books, 2007.

Trumbull, Jonathan, Jr. *Jonathan Trumbull, Governor of Connecticut, 1769-1784.* Boston: Little, Brown & Company, 1919.

Van Dusen, Albert E. *Connecticut.* New York: Random House, 1961.

Wall, Caleb A. *Reminiscences of Worcester from the Earliest Period, Historical and Genealogical, With Notices of Early Settlers and Prominent Citizens, and Descriptions of Old Landmarks and Ancient Dwellings, Accompanied By a Map and Numerous Illustrations.* Worcester, MA: Tyler & Seagrave, 1877.

Warshauer, Matthew. *Connecticut in the American Civil War: Slavery, Sacrifice, & Survival.* Middletown, CT: Wesleyan University Press, 2011.

Wilson, Samuel F. *History of the American Revolution with a Preliminary View of the Character and Principles of the Colonists and their Controversies with Great Britain.* Baltimore: Cushing and Sons, 1834.

Winfield, Rif. *British Warships in the Age of Sail, 1714–1792: Design, Construction, Careers and Fates.* Barnsley, UK: Seaforth Publishing, 2007.

Woodhull, John A. *A Review of the Congregational Church of Groton, Connecticut: With Sketches of its Ministers, 1704–1876.* New London: Press of the New London Telegram, 1877.

Wright, Esther Clark. *The Loyalists of New Brunswick.* Hantsport, Nova Scotia: Lancelot Press, 1981.

Zug, James. *American Traveler: The Life and Adventure of John Ledyard, the Man Who Dreamed of Walking the World.* New York: Basic Books, 2005.

Newspapers

British

Caledonian Mercury

Derby Mercury

Ipswich Journal

Leeds Intelligencer

Norfolk Chronicle

Northampton Mercury

London Gazette

Reading Mercury
Scots Magazine
Stamford Mercury

Irish
Hibernian Journal
Saunders's News-Letter

American
American Journal and General Advertiser (Providence)
American Mercury (Hartford)
Boston Evening Transcript
Boston Gazette
The Boston Recorder
Connecticut Courant
Connecticut Courant and Weekly Advertiser (Hartford)
Connecticut Gazette (New London)
Connecticut Journal (New Haven)
Connecticut Mirror
Evening Post and General Advertiser (Boston)
Independent Ledger (Boston)
Maryland Journal
Massachusetts Spy
Morning News (New London)
Mystic Pioneer
New Hampshire Gazette
New Jersey Gazette
New London Daily Chronicle
New London Daily Star
New London Democrat
New London Weekly Chronicle
Newport Mercury
New York Gazette and the Weekly Mercury
New York Journal
Norwich Courier
Norwich Packet
People's Advocate (New London)
Pennsylvania Gazette

Pennsylvania Journal
Pennsylvania Packet
Providence Evening Press
Providence Gazette
Royal Gazette (New York)
Salem Gazette (Massachusetts)
The Day (New London)

Periodicals

American Monthly Magazine. Volume VII, July–December 1895.

The Bulletin of the Fort Ticonderoga Museum. Volume 27, No. 1, 2016.

Collections of the Connecticut Historical Society. Volume VII, February 1899.

The Connecticut Magazine, An Illustrated Monthly. Volume 11, Autumn 1907.

Journal of the American Revolution. February 17, 2014; December 10, 2014.

Journal of the Early Republic. Winter 1990.

Journal of the Johannes Schwalm Historical Association. Volume 5, Number 3, 1995.

Magazine of American History. Volume 7, No. 3, September 1881.

Military Collector & Historian: Journal of the Company of Military Historians, Washington D.C. Volume XXI, No. 3, Fall 1969.

The Naval Chronicle, for 1805: Containing a General and Biographical History of The Royal Navy of the United Kingdom; With a Variety of Original Papers on Nautical Subjects: Under the Guidance of Several Literary and Professional Men. Volume 14, July–December 1805.

New England Magazine and Bay State Monthly, Volume 5, No. 1, November 1886.

Pennsylvania German Society. Volume VII, 1897.

Transactions of the Royal Society of Edinburgh. Volume I, 1788.

Index

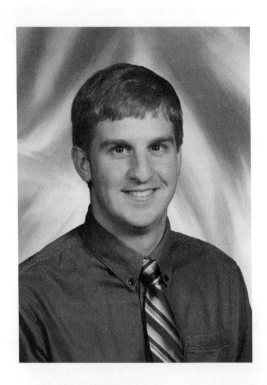

About the Author

Matthew Reardon is a native of northeastern Connecticut. He earned his BA in history and MA in education from Sacred Heart University. His research interests mainly focus on Connecticut during the American Revolution and the Civil War. He served as executive director of the New England Civil War Museum & Research Center for more than 15 years. He currently works as a middle school teacher in Vernon, Connecticut, and serves as a command historian for the Connecticut Military Department. Matthew, his wife Melisa, and son Michael live in Enfield, Connecticut.